History of the Scottish Episcopal Church

HISTORY

OF THE

SCOTTISH EPISCOPAL CHURCH.

HISTORY

OF THE

SCOTTISH EPISCOPAL CHURCH

FROM THE

REVOLUTION TO THE PRESENT TIME.

BY

JOHN PARKER LAWSON, M.A.

AUTHOR OF "THE LIFE AND TIMES OF ARCHBISHOP LAUD," ETC.

EDINBURGH:
GALLIE AND BAYLEY, GEORGE STREET.
LONDON: JAMES BURNS, PORTMAN STREET, PORTMAN SQUARE.
GLASGOW: THOMAS MURRAY.   ABERDEEN: A. BROWN AND CO.
OXFORD: J. H. PARKER.   CAMBRIDGE: J. & J. J. DEIGHTON.
DUBLIN: W. CURRY AND CO.

M.DCCC.XLIII.

EDINBURGH PRINTING COMPANY.

TO THE

RIGHT REVEREND WILLIAM SKINNER, D.D. PRIMUS.
RIGHT REVEREND PATRICK TORRY, D.D.
RIGHT REVEREND DAVID LOW, LL.D. AND F.S.S.A.
RIGHT REVEREND MICHAEL RUSSELL, LL.D. AND D.C.L.
RIGHT REVEREND DAVID MOIR, D.D.
RIGHT REVEREND CHARLES HUGHES TERROT, D.D.

BISHOPS OF THE SCOTTISH EPISCOPAL CHURCH,

THIS VOLUME

IS MOST DUTIFULLY AND RESPECTFULLY

INSCRIBED.

PREFACE.

In submitting this Volume to the Public the Author does so with very great diffidence, and he wishes to be distinctly understood that the Church of which he is a humble member is not to be held responsible for any opinions or inferences he advances. Although it is hoped that nothing herein recorded is at variance with the principles of the Scottish Episcopal Church, the Author wishes this to be candidly kept in view by all, whether friends or foes, into whose hands this volume may fall, on the same principle that it would be illiberal to consider the Presbyterian Establishment at large as identified with such works as the "History of the Church of Scotland," by Mr Hetherington of Torphichen, or that all its members approved of the commemoration of the Glasgow General Assembly of 1638, held in Edinburgh in 1838, when very offensive and insulting remarks were uttered towards the Church of England, the Scottish Episcopal Church, and the Church at large; and a feeble and unsuccessful attempt made on the part of certain Presbyterian leaders to revive the bigotry, the prejudices, and the intolerance of the Covenanting times.

In this historical narrative the Author has as much as possible refrained from controversy, and confined himself solely to facts and to what appeared the legitimate deductions. It is, of course, impossible to avoid strong statements respecting the events immediately succeeding the Revolution, when a fierce theological warfare was for years carried on between the supporters of the Presbyterian Establishment and the members of the ejected Church, and much personal bitterness and acrimony were evinced by both parties. Some quotations are given from the writings of the Episcopal clergy of the time, which sufficiently indicate the state of public feeling; while those passages from Wodrow in particular show at once the insecurity in which the Presbyterian Establishment was long considered to be placed even by its own zealous adherents, and the very slight hold which it possessed in many districts of Scotland on the affection of the people. These are matters of history which may be viewed differently, but which cannot be denied or controverted. In narrating the events of more recent times the Author studiously avoided any reference to, or collision with, the Presbyterian Establishment, except when such was forced upon his notice, as showing the enmity cherished towards the Scottish Episcopal Church. In the present state of religious feeling in Scotland such a work as this will not probably be considered out of place. The Church is continually assailed in the most rancorous bitterness, although its members exhibit no proselytizing spirit. Every act is misrepresented or perverted, to prejudice the unthinking and the wrong-thinking. The names of individual Divines in England are applied in the most sectarian spirit; their alleged theological opinions are maintained as openly avowed by the Scottish Episcopal clergy; and the old charge of an inclination to Romanism is repeatedly brought forward. It is most extraordinary that in Scotland any person who chooses to hold different opinions from the Presbyterians is sure to be assailed by them as a Papist, or as having imbibed the principles of Romanism. Under these circumstances a regular History of the Scottish Episcopal Church since the Revolution, narrating its persecutions, depressions, vicissitudes, and present state, appeared to be necessary, more especially as much misconception exists on the subject. The Author takes this opportunity of reminding the reader of the valuable " Annals of Scottish Episcopacy," by the late Very Rev. John Skinner, M.A. of Forfar, for a detail of all the correspondence connected with the repeal of the Penal Laws in 1792, and for various matters to the year 1816. That Work resumes, as it were, the "Ecclesiastical History of Scotland," from the earliest times to 1788, by Mr Skinner's venerable grandfather, the Rev. John Skinner of Longside, in two volumes, now extremely scarce, and only to be found in libraries. Bishop Russell's "History of the Church in Scotland," in two small volumes, is on the plan of Mr Skinner's Ecclesiastical History, commencing from the introduction of Christianity, and the space devoted to the history of the Church after the Revolution is exceedingly limited.

It may be here stated that in this narrative the adherence of the Church for a century after the Revolution to the Stuart Family is prominently brought forward. At this time, when such political feelings are completely forgotten, it would be folly to deny the attachment of the clergy and laity to that unfortunate Dynasty, for their adherence to which they had suffered the loss of all things. The Presbyterians may, if they please, raise their old clamour of the long continued disaffection of the Scottish Episcopal Church to the House of Hanover, and the fact is readily admitted. But it must be remembered that a great principle of legitimate right was considered to be involved—that the Jacobites, as they were called, whether members of the Church, Roman Catholics, or even Presbyterians, were neither Jacobins nor Revolutionists—and that they contended for what appeared to them to involve the very existence of the monarchy. Time has shown that they were mistaken, and a succeeding generation views the matter in its proper light. Yet the attachment to the Stuart Dynasty was as sincere as it was romantic; and amid all the taunts of disloyalty occasionally levelled against the Scottish Episcopal Church by its sectarian opponents, its members have no reason to be ashamed of the political principles of their forefathers. When, in 1788, the Bishops, clergy, and laity, willingly tendered their allegiance to the reigning Sovereign, they did so with the same sincerity which had marked their conduct for a century previous, and the principle was well understood and even commended by the public men of the day. It is needless to observe, that since the period alluded to the Sovereigns of Great Britain, and the Monarchy and Constitution, have not more devoted subjects, or zealous supporters, than the Scottish Bishops, clergy, and laity.

It may probably appear to some readers, who are well informed in the History of the Scottish Episcopal Church, that sundry matters are omitted of which they expected to find details. It is hoped that these are few, and comparatively unimportant, and can little affect the general scope of the narrative. Some transactions have been purposely excluded, because it appeared, after careful deliberation, that they never could have led to beneficial or practical results. Such, for example, was the correspondence with a branch of the orthodox Greek Church, any statement of which is from its very nature altogether superfluous, and would only have placed in the hands of the sectarian enemies of the Scottish Episcopal Church an additional weapon for calumny and misrepresentation. Many of the prosecutions of the clergy and other events are also so similar, that a few cases are quite sufficient to explain the whole, a minute investigation of which would have made the volume tedious and too large. The successions in the Episcopate are carefully narrated as of the utmost importance, for while the ordinations of Deacons and Presbyters are merely local and personal, the Church at large has a vital interest in the consecration of every Bishop. The APPENDIX could have been extended, but it was considered in the meanwhile unnecessary. The CANONS are inserted, by permission, at the request of several distinguished individuals.

In conclusion, it may be stated to those Presbyterian Journalists who may honour the Author by their vituperation, that it is expected they will confine themselves to the facts recorded, and refrain from the vulgarities and personalities which they are too apt to indulge in the prints and periodicals with which they are connected. Abusive epithets, distorted statements, unfounded insinuations, and imputations of motives which have been repeatedly disclaimed, are mean and ungenerous, and do no injury to those who are so assailed. That much in this volume will be offensive to a particular section of the Established Presbyterians, who seem to be animated by a fierce jealousy and bitter hatred to the Scottish Episcopal Church, is to be expected, nor is it possible that such could altogether be avoided; but they ought to recollect that the productions of such persons as Mr Hetherington of Torphichen, Mr Gray of Perth, and Dr Brown of Langton, and the numerous speeches and anonymous writings of their friends, are not particularly scrupulous as to Christian charity and common politeness, and contain much which is scurrilous, malignant, and vindictive. These Presbyterian journalists may be farther assured that they will yet have much to do in their contest with the Scottish Episcopal Church—an aggressive contest, let it be remembered, for that Church wages no warfare except with " false doctrine, heresy, and schism," from which its members daily pray to be delivered, as they also pray to be preserved from " hardness of heart, and contempt of God's holy will and commandments." The present Author is only a gleaner in this field of the ecclesiastical history of his country; and he is well aware that not a few in Scotland are now girding on the armour, ready to defend to the uttermost those doctrines, principles, and polity, which have stood the test of ages, and are embodied in the time-hallowed Liturgy of the Church.

EDINBURGH, *November* 1842.

CONTENTS.

	PAGE
INTRODUCTORY REMARKS,	xxxiii

CHAPTER I.

The two Periods of the History of the Scottish Episcopal Church,	1
First Consecration of Scottish Bishops in 1610,	2
Extinction of that Succession,	ib.
Bishop Sydserff of Galloway,	ib.
Archbishop Tillotson's ordination,	3
Second Consecration of Scottish Bishops in 1661,	4
Archbishop Sharp of St Andrews,	5
Hatred cherished towards him by the Presbyterians,	6
Kirkton's character of him,	7
His conduct as Primate,	ib.
Story told of him by Wodrow,	8
Falsehoods propagated against him and his family,	9
Kirkton's character of Archbishop Fairfoull,	ib.
His character of Archbishop Leighton,	10
Anecdote of Leighton and Sir James Steuart of Goodtrees,	11, 12
Kirkton's character of Bishop Wishart,	13
Of the other Bishops,	14, 15
Proceedings at the Consecration of Archbishop Sharp and his brethren,	15

xiv CONTENTS.

	PAGE
Singular notions of some Presbyterian writers on Baptism,	16, 17
Perversion of Bishop Jolly's opinions by Mr Andrew Gray of Perth,	18
First Consecration held in Scotland after 1661, in the Chapel-Royal of Holyrood,	19
Contemporary Account of that Consecration,	20
Account of the mode of conducting Divine Service in the Episcopal Church of Scotland after the Restoration,	21
The Results of the Glasgow General Assembly of 1638 stated,	22
Religious condition of the Highlands in the seventeenth century,	23
State and Ritual of the Church after 1662,	24
Fanaticism in Scotland,	24, 25
Moderation of the Bishops to the Presbyterian Ministers,	25
Revenues of the Scottish Bishoprics previous to the Revolution,	26, 27
Erection of the Court of Teinds,	28
Gross dilapidation of the Episcopal revenues,	28, 29
Ecclesiastical Divisions of Scotland,	29, 30
Notices of Archbishop Ross of St Andrews,	30
⸺ Bishop Rose of Edinburgh,	30, 31
Bishop Hamilton of Dunkeld,	31
Bishop Hallyburton of Brechin and Aberdeen,	ib.
Bishop Hay of Moray,	32
Bishop Drummond of Brechin,	32, 33
Bishop Douglas of Dunblane,	33
Bishop Ramsay of Ross,	ib.
Bishop Wood of Caithness,	33, 34
Bishop Bruce of Orkney,	34
Archbishop Paterson of Glasgow,	34, 35
Bishop Gordon of Galloway,	35
Dr Monro, Bishop-elect of Argyll,	ib.
Bishop Graham of the Isles,	36
Observations on the state of the Government,	36, 37

CHAPTER II.

The Revolution of 1688,	38
Proceedings of the Scottish Bishops,	38, 39

CONTENTS. XV

	PAGE
Bishop Rose of Edinburgh's journey to London,	39, 40
His interview with the Archbishop of Canterbury,	40
And with the English Bishops,	40, 41, 42
Conversation between the Bishop of Edinburgh and the Bishop of London,	42, 43, 44
Interview of the Bishop of Edinburgh with the Prince of Orange,	44, 45
Conduct of the Scottish Bishops at that period,	46
Reflections,	47, 48

CHAPTER III.

Vindication of the Established Episcopal Church of Scotland,	49, 50
Bishop Burnet in Scotland,	50, 51
Mode of performing Divine Service,	51, 52
The Old Confession of Faith,	52
Character of the Compilers of the Westminster Confession of Faith by Clarendon and Neal,	53
Government of the Episcopal Church,	54, 55, 56
Misrepresentations of the Presbyterians,	57, 58
Their calumnies against the Parochial Clergy,	58, 59
Eccentric account of the state of a parish in Dumfries-shire,	59, 60

CHAPTER IV.

Riots at the Revolution,	61
The real prosecutors of the Covenanters,	61, 62
Sufferings of the Episcopal Clergy after the Revolution,	63, 64
Description of the state of the Church by Mr Morer,	65, 66
The Cameronians,	ib.
Bishop Sage's account of the Sufferings of the Clergy,	66, 67, 68
Violent conduct of the Cameronian Presbyterians,	69
They are defended by Presbyterian writers,	69, 70
The Episcopal Church of Scotland never persecuting,	71
Principal Monro's description of the Presbyterians,	72–79
His Replies to some libels against himself,	80

CHAPTER V.

	PAGE
State of Parties in Scotland at the Revolution,	79
Ker of Kersland's account	ib.
Proceedings of the Presbyterians,	80
Meeting of the Scottish Estates in 1689,	81
Archbishops, Bishops, and Nobility present,	ib.
Declaration signed by the Archbishops and Bishops,	82
They withdraw from the Meeting,	ib.
Oath of Allegiance exacted by the Estates,	83
Proclamation against Papists,	ib.
Congratulatory Letter to the Prince of Orange,	84
The Scottish Throne declared vacant,	ib.
Claim of Right,	ib.
Crown offered to William and Mary,	ib.
Allusion to the Episcopal Church,	ib.
Oath of Allegiance to William and Mary,	ib.
Oath of Allegiance before the Revolution,	85
Speech of the Earl of Arran,	ib.
Bishop Short on the Oath of Allegiance,	86
Acts of the Scottish Estates against the Episcopal Church,	87
Acceptance of the Crown by William and Mary,	87, 88
Deprivation of some of the Edinburgh Clergy,	88
Conduct of Bishop Burnet of Salisbury,	ib.
Dr Scott, Dean of Glasgow, delegated to London by the suffering Clergy,	ib.
Violence of a mob in Glasgow,	89
Disorderly conduct of the mob at Edinburgh,	ib.
The Estates issue a Proclamation ordering the Clergy to pray for William and Mary,	90
The Committee of the Estates eject numbers of the Parochial Clergy,	90, 91
The Duke of Hamilton and Archbishop Ross of St Andrews,	91
The Duke of Gordon and the Viscount of Dundee,	92
Seige of the Castle of Edinburgh,	92, 93
The Viscount of Dundee withdraws from the Estates,	93
The Cameronian plot to murder him and Sir George Mackenzie,	93, 94

CONTENTS. xvii

	PAGE
The Viscount's romantic conference with the Duke of Gordon,	94
Excitement of the inhabitants of Edinburgh,	95
The Viscount leaves Edinburgh for the Highlands to raise the Clans,	ib
A warrant issued against him by the Estates,	ib
Advance of General Mackay against the Viscount of Dundee,	ib.

CHAPTER VI.

First Parliament of William and Mary,	96
Dr George Cook's vindication of the Scottish Bishops and Clergy,	97, 98
Act passed " abolishing Prelacie,"	98, 99
Battle of Killiecrankie and death of the Viscount of Dundee,	99
Proceedings of the Parliament against the Episcopal Clergy,	99, 100
The Scottish Episcopalians styled Jacobites by their opponents,	101
First Session of the Parliament,	102
The Duke of Hamilton's conduct,	ib.
Bigotry of the Presbyterians,	103
Second Session of the Parliament,	ib.
Character of the Earl of Melville,	ib.
Acts passed in favour of the Presbyterians,	103, 104, 105
Defence of the Scottish Bishops and Clergy by the Duke of Hamilton,	106
His Grace retires in disgust from the Parliament,	107
Act passed for visiting the Universities and Schools,	ib.
Deprivation of all who refused to comply with Presbyterianism,	108
University of St Andrews visited,	ib.
The Principals, Professors, and Masters, ejected,	109
Insolent conduct of the Earl of Crawfurd,	ib.
The University of Glasgow visited,	ib.
The Principal and three Professors ejected,	ib.
The University of Aberdeen visited,	ib.
The Committee unable to eject the Episcopal Professors there,	110
University of Edinburgh visited,	ib.
Insolent conduct of the Commission,	110, 111
Causes the publication of the " Presbyterian Inquisition" by Dr Monro,	ib

xviii   CONTENTS.

	PAGE
Notices of Principal Monro,	111, 112
Charges exhibited against him,	113, 114
His Replies to these Articles,	114–119
He is deprived of the office of Principal,	119
Professors Strachan, Drummond, Douglas, and Burnet, deprived,	ib.
Professor Gregory allowed to remain,	ib.
Dr Monro's opinion of the proceedings of the Commissioners,	120, 121

CHAPTER VII.

Proceedings against the Episcopal Parochial Clergy,	122
Retirement of the Bishops from public affairs,	123
Bishop Short on the religious state of Scotland,	123, 124
Notices of the ejected Bishops,	124, 125
George Ridpath's attacks against the Church,	126, 127
Parochial Clergy deposed,	128–134
Religious destitution in Scotland by ejecting the Clergy,	134, 135, 136

CHAPTER VIII.

Attachment of the people to their Episcopal pastors in various towns and districts,	138—149

CHAPTER IX.

he first Presbyterian General Assembly after the Revolution,	150
Proceedings at the commencement,	150, 151
Letter from King William,	152
Conduct of several of the members,	153, 154
A Fast enjoined,	154, 155
Publication of the " Scotch Presbyterian Eloquence,"	156, 157
Its supposed compilers,	157
Account of this production,	157, 158
The " Answer" by George Ridpath,	158, 159
Principal Monro's " Reply,"	159, 160
Opinions of the Scottish Episcopalians on the " Scotch Presbyterian Eloquence,"	160—163
Account of some of the ecclesiastical proceedings by a Presbyterian,	164, 165, 166

CHAPTER X.

	PAGE
State of the Episcopal Church after its non-establishment,	167
Extracts from the "Culloden Papers," . .	168—172
Deaths of some of the Scottish Bishops, . .	172, 173
Depressed state of the Episcopal Church during the reign of William III.	173
The King personally not an enemy of the Scottish Episcopal Church, ...	174
Death of King James II. . . .	175

CHAPTER XI.

Accession of Queen Anne, ...	176
State of Parties, ...	176, 177
The Queen is petitioned by the Scottish Episcopal Clergy,	177
Gracious reception of the Deputation, . . .	178
Unnecessary alarm of the Presbyterians, . .	ib.
Letter of the Estates to Queen Anne, . .	178, 179
The Faculty of Advocates prosecuted, . .	179
Favourable sentiments of the Queen towards the Scottish Episcopal Church, ...	ib.
An Act of Toleration suggested, . . .	ib.
Fiercely opposed by the Presbyterians, . .	180
Episcopal places of worship in Edinburgh and Glasgow at that period, ...	180, 181
Peaceful State of the Church, . . .	181
Death of Archbishop Ross of St Andrews, . .	ib.
Consecration of Bishops Fullarton and Sage, .	ib.
Biographical Account of Bishop Sage, . .	182—185
Notices of his Works, . . .	185, 186
A Toleration again suggested, . . .	186, 187
Character of the Duke of Queensberry, . .	187
The three Political Parties in Scotland, . .	187, 188
The Union between England and Scotland, .	188
Death of Archbishop Paterson of Glasgow and Bishop Hay,	ib.
Consecration of Bishops Falconer and Christie, .	189

CHAPTER XII.

	PAGE
Adoption of the English Liturgy in the Scottish Episcopal Church,	190
Favourable reception by the people,	ib.
Alarm of the Presbyterians,	190, 191
Principal Carstairs,	191
The Differences between the Scottish and English Liturgies stated,	192
The Presbyterian General Assembly denounce the English Liturgy,	193
Prosecution of several of the Episcopal Clergy,	ib.
Imprisonment of the Rev. George Graham,	ib.
Erroneous statements of De Foe,	194, 195
Case of the Rev. Mr Greenshields,	196—200
Character of Lord Grange,	200
Tyrannical conduct of the Presbyterians,	201
Proceedings of the Lord Advocate against the Episcopal Chapels,	203
Act of Toleration passed,	205
Particulars respecting it,	206—209
Despondency of the Presbyterians,	209, 210

CHAPTER XIII.

Consecration of the Hon. and Rev. Archibald Campbell,	211
Notices of him,	ib.
Dr Johnson's anecdote of Bishop Campbell,	212
Pecuniary distress of the Episcopal Clergy,	ib.
Controversy between the Rev. Robert Calder and Mr John Anderson,	213, 214, 215
Mr Thomas Rhind, a Presbyterian minister, conforms to the Church,	215
Death of Queen Anne,	216
Accession of George I.	ib.
Enterprise of 1715,	ib.
Its suppression,	ib.
Proceedings of the Government against the Episcopal Clergy,	217, 218

CONTENTS. xxi

	PAGE
Act of Parliament of 1719,	219
Consecration of Bishop Gadderar,	220
Consecration of Bishops Millar and Irvine,	ib.
Death of Bishop Rose of Edinburgh,	ib.
His character,	221

CHAPTER XIV.

Meeting of the Episcopal Clergy of Edinburgh after the interment of Bishop Rose,	222
Extraordinary proposal to govern the Church by a College of Bishops,	223
Their acknowledgment of the Bishops,	ib
Advice of Bishop Falconer,	ib.
Bishop Fullarton chosen Primus,	224
Erroneous account by Mr Lockhart of Carnwath,	ib
Hostility to Bishop Campbell,	225
Lockhart's correspondence with the Chevalier St George,	225, 226
The Scottish Bishops address the Chevalier,	226
The consecration of Bishop Freebairn opposed by the Bishops,	227
The College Party,	228
Bishop Falconer elected Diocesan of Forfar and Kincardine shires,	ib
Bishop Campbell elected Diocesan of Aberdeen,	ib.
The "Usages"—account of the controversy,	229—231
Consecration of Bishops Cant and Freebairn,	233
Consecration of Bishops Duncan and Norrie,	ib.
Opposition of those Bishops to the College Party,	ib.
Mr Lockhart complains of Bishop Gadderar to the Chevalier,	ib.
Dislike of the Chevalier's adherents to Bishops Campbell and Gadderar,	234, 235
Subserviency of the College Party to the Chevalier,	236
Mr Lockhart's reasons for the consecration of Bishop Norrie,	237, 238
The Chevalier writes to the College Party recommending certain Presbyters to be consecrated Bishops,	238, 239
Interview of Bishop Gadderar with the College Bishops at Edinburgh,	239

xxii   CONTENTS.

	PAGE
The " Usages" again discussed,	239, 240
Correspondence of Mr Lockhart with the Chevalier,	240—244
Consecration of Bishops Rose and Ouchterlonie,	ib.
Death of Bishop Fullarton,	ib.
Bishop Gadderar the only Diocesan then in Scotland,	ib.

CHAPTER XV.

Proceedings of the Scottish Bishops at the death of Bishop Fullarton,	246, 247
Bishop Gadderar's opposition to the College Party,	247
Bishop Millar attacked by Mr Lockhart of Carnwath,	ib.
Remonstrance against the consecration of the Rev. John Gillan,	ib.
Wodrow's account of Bishop Gadderar's proceedings in the Diocese of Aberdeen,	249
Disputes in the Church,	250—253
Bishop Millar elected Diocesan of Edinburgh,	253
First decisive blow to the College Party and influence of the Chevalier,	ib.
The College Party refuse to confirm the election of Bishop Millar,	ib.
They appoint Bishop Freebairn to superintend the Diocese,	ib.
They consecrate the Rev. John Gillan and the Rev. David Rankine,	ib.
The Diocesan Bishops follow up the advantages they gained,	254
They encourage the Presbyters of the Dioceses to elect their own Bishops,	255
They consecrate Dr Rattray of Craighall, the Rev. William Dunbar, and the Rev. Robert Keith,	ib.
Mr Lockhart's account of the proceedings of the College Party,	255, 256
Death and character of Bishop Millar,	256
Death of Bishop Norrie,	ib.
Extraordinary conduct of the Presbyters,	ib.
Election and consecration of Bishop Lumsden,	257
The dispute between the Diocesan and College Bishops adjusted by the Concordate in 1732,	ib.
The Articles of agreement,	257, 258.

CONTENTS. xxiii

	PAGE
Feuds and Dissensions in the Presbyterian Establishment,	258, 259
Peace restored to the Scottish Episcopal Church,	259
Unfair account of the dispute between the College and Diocesan Bishops by Dr Brown of Langton,	259, 260
Zeal of the influential laity of the Episcopal Church,	261
Wodrow's account,	ib.
His dread of the English Liturgy,	262

CHAPTER XVI.

Death of Bishop Lumsden,	263
Death of Bishops Duncan, Rose, and Gadderar,	ib.
Character of Bishop Gadderar,	ib.
He is succeeded by Bishop Dunbar,	ib.
Bishop Keith elected Diocesan of Fife,	ib.
Consecration of Bishop White,	264
Consecration of Bishop William Falconer,	ib.
Death of Bishops Gillan and Freebairn,	ib.
Peaceful state of the Church,	265
Death of Bishop Ouchterlonie,	266
Consecration of Bishop Rait,	ib.
Death of Bishop Rattray, the Primus,	267
His character and Works,	267, 268
Bishop Keith elected Primus,	268
Consecration of Bishop Alexander,	ib.
Episcopal Synod of 1743,	ib.
Canons enacted therein,	268, 269
These Canons offend the Presbyters of Edinburgh,	269
Controversies which ensued,	269—276
Bishop Keith remonstrates with Bishop Smith,	276, 277, 278
Bishop Keith's declaration against Bishop Smith's interference in the affairs of the Scottish Episcopal Church,	278, 279
Bishop Alexander's declaration,	279, 280
Third Address of the Presbyters of Edinburgh to the Scottish Bishops,	280, 281, 282
Bishop Keith's letter in reply,	282—284
Unpopularity of Bishop Keith,	285

CHAPTER XVII.

	PAGE
The Enterprise of 1745,	287
Imprisonment of the Rev. Robert Forbes and others,	288
Zeal of an Episcopal clergyman after the Battle of Prestonpans,	ib.
Suppression of the Enterprise,	ib.
Cruelties of the Duke of Cumberland,	289
Grief of the adherents of the exiled Dynasty,	290
Episcopal Chapels destroyed,	291
Severe Act of Parliament against the Scottish Episcopal Church in 1746	ib.
Penalties inflicted,	292
Political privileges forfeited by the Act,	293
Consecration of Bishop Gerard,	294
Prosecutions of the Episcopal Clergy,	294, 295
Act of 1748 against the Church,	295
Opposition to it in Parliament,	ib.
Speech of Bishop Maddox of Worcester,	296
Speech of Bishop Sherlock of London,	297
Speech of Bishop Secker of Oxford,	ib.
Speech of Lord Sandys,	298
Objects of the Act of 1748,	299
The erection of "qualified" Chapels,	300
Distresses of the Clergy and their people,	301, 302, 303
Imprisonment of the Rev. John Skinner,	303
Prosecution of the Rev. James Connachar,	305—308
Prosecution of the Rev. Walter Stewart,	308, 309
Death of Bishop Keith,	309
His literary Works,	310
Consecration of Bishop Edgar,	ib.
Death of George II.	311

CHAPTER XVIII.

Accession of George III.	312
Prosecutions of the Episcopal Clergy discouraged,	313
State of the Scottish Episcopal Church,	313, 314, 315

CONTENTS.   XXV

	PAGE
Religious State of Scotland at the Accession of George III.	315, 316, 317
Prevalence of Sectaries in Scotland,	317, 318
Prosperous state of the Scottish Episcopal Church,	318
Account of the consecration of a Presbyterian burying-ground in Edinburgh by Bishop Falconar,	318, 319, 320
Revisal of the Office for the Administration of the Holy Communion,	320
Consecration of Bishops Forbes, Kilgour, Rose, and Petrie,	321
Death of Bishop Falconar,	ib.
Death of Bishop Rait,	ib.
Consecration of Bishop Innes,	ib.
Consecration of Bishop John Skinner,	322
Death of the Chevalier St George,	323
Feelings of his adherents,	324

CHAPTER XIX.

State of the Church,	325
Consecration of Dr Seabury as the first Bishop in the United States of America,	326, 327, 328
Controversy on that event in the "Gentleman's Magazine,"	328, 329, 330
Reception of Bishop Seabury in America,	330, 331, 332
Alleged application of the Rev. John Wesley to the Scottish Bishops to consecrate the Rev. Dr Coke for America,	333
Consecration of Bishops Macfarlane, Abernethy Drummond, and Strachan,	334
The repeal of the Penal Laws projected,	ib.
Sentiments of the Archbishop of Canterbury,	ib.
Death of Prince Charles Edward,	335
Meeting of the Scottish Bishops and Clergy at Aberdeen,	ib.
They resolve to pray for George III. and the Royal Family by name,	336
Loyalty of the Scottish Episcopal Church,	ib.
Bishop Skinner elected Primus,	ib.
Death of Bishop Kilgour,	ib.
Memorial transmitted to Lord Sydney,	ib.

xxvi CONTENTS.

	PAGE
Addresses sent to the Archbishops of Canterbury and York,	336
Reply of Lord Sydney,	ib.
First draught of the Bill to repeal the Penal Laws,	337
Proceedings of the friends of the Church in that matter,	338
Opposition of Lord Chancellor Thurlow,	ib.
The first Bill refused in the House of Lords,	ib.
The Bill again brought forward in 1791,	ib.
The counties, cities, and royal burghs, petition in its favour,	.ib.
Proceedings in the House of Lords,	339
Subscription to the Thirty-Nine Articles recommended by Bishop Horsley and others,	ib.
The Thirty-Nine Articles at once adopted,	340
Repeal of the Penal Laws,	ib.
Abstract of the Act,	340, 341
Testimonials presented by Bishop Skinner to the Rev. Dr Gaskin, Mr Justice Park, and William Steven, Esq.	ib.

CHAPTER XX.

Synod of Laurencekirk,	342
Projected institution of the Widows' Fund,	ib.
Consecration of Bishop Watson,	343
Diocesan Synod of Aberdeen,	ib.
Loyalty of the Scottish Episcopal Church at the time of the French Revolution,	344
Exertions of Bishop Skinner to effect the union of the Clergy of English and Irish ordination with the Scottish Episcopal Church,	344, 345, 346
Proposed Consecration of the Rev. Jonathan Boucher as a Scottish Bishop,	346
Bishop Skinner's correspondence on the subject,	346, 347
Mr Boucher declines to be consecrated,	348
Bishop Skinner's Letter to Sir William Forbes, Bart.	347, 348
Institution of the Scottish Episcopal Friendly Society,	348, 349
Consecration of Bishop Jolly,	349
Sentiments of Bishop Skinner respecting the consecration of Bishop Jolly,	350

CONTENTS. xxvii

CHAPTER XXI.

	PAGE
Bishop Skinner's Publications,	351
His successful exertions in promoting the union of the English Clergy officiating in Scotland with the Church,	352
He publishes his "Primitive Truth and Order Vindicated,"	353
Cause of the publication of that Work,	ib.
Convention of the Church held at Laurencekirk,	356
The Rev. Dr Sandford of Edinburgh acknowledges Bishop Skinner as his Diocesan,	ib.
His reasons for uniting with the Scottish Episcopal Church,	356—360
Other Clergy imitate his example,	360, 361
Exertions of Sir William Forbes, Bart.	361
His character,	ib.
His munificence to the Scottish Episcopal Church,	362
St John's Chapel, Edinburgh, erected chiefly by the exertions of Sir William's eldest son, Sir William Forbes, Bart.	ib.
St Paul's Chapel, Edinburgh, erected chiefly by the exertions of Sir William's second son, the Hon. Lord Medwyn,	ib.
Conduct of the Rev. Dr Grant of Dundee,	ib.
He is reproved by Bishop Horsley,	ib.
Law action raised in the Court of Session against the congregation in Banff,	364
Munificent subscription obtained by Bishop Horsley to defray the legal expenses,	364, 365
Consecration of Dr Sandford as Bishop of Edinburgh,	365
His first Confirmation,	366
Letter of Sir William Forbes, Bart. to Bishop Skinner,	ib.
Sir William Forbes, Bart. and Colin Mackenzie, Esq. project the Scottish Episcopal Fund,	366, 367
The Committee of that Fund in London,	367
Death of Sir William Forbes, Bart., William Steven, Esq., and Bishop Horsley,	ib.
Death of the Rev. John Skinner,	ib.
His character, learning, and acquirements,	368
Death of Bishop Watson,	369
His character,	370

	PAGE
Consecration of Bishops Torry and Gleig,	370
Death of Bishops Abernethy Drummond and Strachan,	ib.
Character of the former,	371

CHAPTER XXII.

Loyal Address of the Scottish Bishops and Clergy to George III.	372
First order issued by the Privy Council to the Bishops and Clergy,	ib.
Synod of Aberdeen,	373
Business of that Synod,	374
Services of Bishop Skinner,	375
Letter of Bishop Walker to the Rev. John Skinner,	ib
The Rev. Martin J. Routh, D.D. President of Magdalen College, Oxford, dedicates his " Reliquiæ Sacræ" to the Scottish Bishops and Clergy,	376
Death of Bishop Skinner,	377
Sketch of his life and character,	378
State of the Church in the city of Aberdeen about that period,	379, 380

CHAPTER XXIII.

Consecration of the Rev. William Skinner,	381
Bishop Gleig elected Primus,	ib.
Death of Bishop Macfarlane,	ib.
Consecration of Bishop Low,	ib.
The Bishops and Clergy address George IV. at his visit to Edinburgh in 1822,	382
Consecration of Bishop Luscombe,	383
Synod of Laurencekirk,	384
Synod of Edinburgh,	ib.
Death of Bishop Sandford,	ib.
His character,	384, 385
Consecration of Bishop Walker,	385
State of the Church,	386, 387, 388

CHAPTER XXIV

Bishop Gleig's statement of the constitution of the Scottish Episcopal Church,	390 391

CONTENTS. xxix

	PAGE
Institution of the Gaelic Episcopal Society chiefly by Bishop Low,	392
Sympathizing Address to the Clergy of the Irish Church,	ib.
Consecration of Bishops Russell and Moir,	393
Bishop Gleig resigns the office of Primus,	ib.
Bishop Walker elected Primus,	ib.
Sermon by the Very Rev. E. B. Ramsay, M.A. at the consecration of Bishops Russell and Moir,	393
Extracts from it,	394, 395, 396
Death of Bishop Jolly,	396
His character,	397
The Diocese of Moray annexed to Ross and Argyll under Bishop Low,	398
Synod of Edinburgh,	399
Canon for founding the Scottish Episcopal Church Society,	399, 400
Objects of the Society,	400, 401, 402
First Patron and Vice-Patrons,	402, 403
First Public Meeting of the Society,	403
First stated Annual Meeting of the General Committee,	ib.
First stated Annual Meeting of the Society,	404
Bishop Low presides and addresses the Meeting,	ib.
Report read by the Very Rev. E. B. Ramsay,	404—414
Speech of Adam Urquhart, Esq., Advocate,	414, 415
Pastoral Letter of 1839,	415
Act of Parliament in favour of the Scottish Episcopal Church in 1840,	416
Speech of the Archbishop of Canterbury in the House of Lords,	417
Death of Bishop Gleig,	418
His character,	ib.
Death of Bishop Walker,	419
His character,	ib.
Consecration of the Very Rev. Dr Terrot,	421
Bishop Skinner elected Primus,	ib.
Members of the Episcopal College in 1842,	422
Visit of Queen Victoria and Prince Albert to Scotland,	ib.
The Very Rev. E. B. Ramsay officiates before her Majesty in Dalkeith Palace,	ib.

CONTENTS.

	PAGE
Misrepresentations of the Presbyterians and others,	422, 423, 424

CHAPTER XXV.

State of the Scottish Episcopal Church,	426
Diocese of Edinburgh,	ib.
Speech of the Right Hon. W. E. Gladstone, M.P.	427
Diocese of Glasgow,	428
Diocese of Brechin,	ib.
Speech of Erskine Douglas Sandford, Esq., Advocate,	429
Diocese of Aberdeen,	430
United Diocese of Dunkeld, Dunblane, and Fife,	ib.
United Diocese of Moray, Ross, and Argyll,	ib.
Speech of the Rev. Robert Montgomery,	431
Episcopal Nobility of Scotland,	432
State of Presbyterianism in England,	433, 434
Annual Meeting of the Scottish Episcopal Church Society,	436
Speech of the Right Hon. W. E. Gladstone, M.P.	436, 437, 438
Speech of Sir John M'Niel,	439
Institutions connected with the Scottish Episcopal Church,	ib.
Anderson's Mortification,	ib.
Pantonian Fund,	440
Episcopal Free School,	441
Scottish Episcopal Friendly Society,	441, 442
Scottish Episcopal Fund,	442, 443, 444
Scottish Episcopal Church Society,	444
Third Annual Meeting,	445
Speech of Bishop Terrot,	446, 447, 448
Speech of the Rev. Henry Mackenzie of St James', Bermondsey, Surrey,	449, 450
The SNELL EXHIBITIONS at Oxford,	450
Extracts from Mr Snell's Will,	451–455
Extracts from Parliamentary Reports,	455, 456
The conditions for qualification,	456
Gross misapplication of the Founder's intentions,	457
Instances of these misapplications,	458, 459

CONTENTS. xxxi

	PAGE
Answers from the University of Glasgow to the University Commissioners,	460
Injustice of presenting Presbyterians and Sectarians to the Snell Exhibitions,	461
TRINITY COLLEGE,	ib.
Violent opposition to its erection,	462
Folly of this display of bigotry by the Presbyterians,	462, 463
Necessity of such an Academical Institution in the Scottish Episcopal Church,	463, 464
Failure of the clamour against it,	465
Address of the Committee,	466
The Synodal Letter of the Scottish Bishops,	467, 468
Proposals for establishing Trinity College,	468, 469, 470
List of some of the first S	470, 471
Overture of the Presbytery of Perth to the General Assembly against the erection of Trinity College in that city,	472, 473
Speech of Mr Andrew Gray,	473
His quotations from the writings of Episcopal authors,	473, 474, 475
The Citizens and Town Council of Perth disregard the Overture and Mr Gray's Speech,	476
Proposal of Sir William Drysdale in the Town Council of Edinburgh,	477
General Observations on the Scottish Episcopal Church,	477, 478
Means of promoting its prosperity,	478, 479
Concluding extract from Bishop Russell's Charge to the Episcopal Clergy of the City and District of Glasgow in 1842,	479—482

APPENDIX.

I. Statistics of the Scottish Episcopal Church from the Reports of the Commissioners to inquire into the State of Religious Instruction in Scotland,	485
1. Diocese of ABERDEEN,	ib.
2. United Diocese of DUNKELD, DUNBLANE, and FIFE,	492
3. United Diocese of MORAY, ROSS, and ARGYLL,	495

xxxii   CONTENTS.

	PAGE
4. Diocese of BRECHIN,	498
5. Diocese of GLASGOW,	501
6. Diocese of EDINBURGH,	506
Religious State of Edinburgh,	513
Religious State of Glasgow,	514
II. State of the Episcopal Church in 1708,	515
III. Contemporary Sketch of the State of the Scottish Episcopal Church from 1715 to 1745, from a MS. in the Advocates' Library, Edinburgh,	517
Prosecutions of the Clergy,	518, 519
Results to the Church on the death of Bishop Rose,	521
Proceedings of the College Party,	522
The "Usages,"	523
Complaints against Bishop Gadderar,	525
Address of the College Bishops to the Clergy and Laity,	527, 528, 529
Terms proposed for an adjustment of the dispute between the College Party and the Diocesan Bishops,	531
Death of several of the Bishops,	533
State of the Church,	533—538
The Enterprise of 1745,	538, 539
Bishop Rankine's condemnation of the Usages,	539—545
IV. Code of Canons of the Scottish Episcopal Church, as revised, amended, and enacted, in the Synod of Edinburgh, 1838,	546—575
V. Succession of the Scottish Episcopal Church,	576

INTRODUCTORY.

THE reader will perceive from this volume that a regular succession of Bishops has been carefully preserved in Scotland since the Revolution—that a branch of the Church Catholic has since that period existed to the present time, notwithstanding the vicissitudes, depressions, and severities to which it was long subjected—and that in these days the Scottish Episcopal Church well deserves the attention, respect, and sympathy of the Church of England. The following facts are also deducible, if any reliance is to be placed on historical documents—1. That at the Revolution the Scottish people were not generally, except in a few districts, so much inclined to Presbyterianism as is generally supposed: 2. That it was much more difficult to overthrow the Established Episcopal Church than is admitted by its opponents: 3. That if that Church was at the present time the Establishment of Scotland, it would be supported in its temporalities precisely in the same manner as the one by which it was supplanted, so that its ejection was no pecuniary relief to the people.

These are the principles elicited in the following narrative, in addition to the more important point—the Apostolical and Primitive constitution of the Church. Two statements, repeatedly brought forward with extraordinary pertinacity by certain of the Presbyterian Establishment, require to be noticed in these introductory remarks—the one, that the Scottish Episcopal Church was "founded" by Archbishop Laud; the other, that the Scottish Liturgy and Book of Canons were drawn up by that Primate.

It is indeed a novelty to be informed that Archbishop Laud "founded" any Church whatever, and indicates an extraordinary hallucination, ignorance, or perversion of history, and especially of the Archbishop's life and principles. The English Primate had no more to do with the present Scottish Episcopal Church than he had with "founding" the Church of Jerusalem, the Church of England, or the Church of Rome. This will appear by a simple statement of the facts. If by this " founding" of a church, our Presbyterian opponents maintain that Archbishop Laud assisted at the first consecration of Bishops, and was thereby one of the parties associated in extending the Episcopal succession into a country where it became extinct at the Reformation, though this is a very novel notion of the origin of any National Church, history completely sets at rest that statement. In 1610 Archbishop Spottiswoode, then of Glasgow, and the Bishops of Galloway and Brechin, were consecrated in the chapel of London House, and this was the first consecration held in England to impart the succession to the Scottish Church. Now, Archbishop Laud was not advanced to the episcopate till 1620, when he was nominated Bishop of St David's, and he therefore could have no possible connection with the consecration of the Scottish Bishops ten years previous, when he was simply Rector of West Tilbury in Essex, and of Cuckstone in Kent. Laud accompanied James in his visit to Scotland in 1617, but he is accused of no more than urging the King to introduce a liturgical form of prayer in the public worship of the Scottish Church. When Bishop of London, he was a second time in Scotland, at the coronation of Charles I. in 1633, and on the 30th of June preached before the King in the Chapel-Royal of Holyrood Palace. Before the departure of Charles, a Committee of the Scottish Bishops was appointed to prepare a Liturgy, and to correspond with Laud; and this is all the intercourse he appears to have had with ecclesiastical affairs in the North. On the 10th of January 1644-5, he was brought to the scaffold by his enemies. At the Restoration only one of the Bishops of the Spottiswoode line was alive, yet though they had all, or a majority of them, been in life, and though the succession of the present Scottish Bishops were derived from that line, Archbishop Laud could have no connection with the consecration of Spottiswoode and his brethren, because he was not a Bishop till ten years afterwards. The very circumstance of old Bishop Sydserff being the only surviving Prelate at the restoration of the first succession, rendered the second consecration in Westminster Abbey in 1661 indispensable, upwards of seventeen years after Archbishop Laud was in his grave. Surely we will now hear no more of the Archbishop as the "founder" of the Scottish Episcopal Church—a Church which was almost extinct at the Restoration, otherwise an ignorance will be exhibited truly contemptible. If there was any "founder" at all, in the Presbyterian sense of the term, it must be applied to those English Bishops who consecrated Archbishop Sharp and his brethren.

As to the other charge, that Archbishop Laud prepared the Scottish Liturgy and Book of Canons, this also is altogether unfounded, and he had as much to do with either as with the compiling of the Liturgy and Canons of the Church of England. These were the work of the Scottish Bishops themselves in the reign of Charles I. previous to 1637, for there is the most undoubted evidence that what are often called Laud's Canons and Prayer-Book were of home compilation. This is admitted by Dr George Cook, in his "History of the Church of Scotland."* The allegation against the Archbishop was aggravated by additional falsehoods in the "Charge of the Scottish Commissioners against Canterburie," printed in 1641, and is inserted in the Archbishop's History of his own Troubles and Trials, where it is answered in every paragraph by himself in the most conclusive manner. Kirkton, indeed, declares—" I have seen the principal book corrected with Bishop Laud's own hand, where, in every place which he corrected, he brings the word as near the Missal as English can be to Latin." Now this Presbyterian writer was utterly ignorant of the matter. If the King *sent down* the Liturgy to Scotland, it was first *sent up* to England, and as to the assertion that it was

* Vol. ii. p. 356, 366.

corrected with the Archbishop's own hand to bring it as near as possible to the Roman Missal, an examination of the book, which is a most admirable " form of sound words," is a complete refutation. The composition, or rather compilation, was exclusively Scottish, and the Archbishop, with Bishops Juxon and Wren, merely revised it—the last named Prelate, according to Clarendon—" very learned, and particularly versed in the old Liturgies of the Greek and Latin Churches." The Scottish Bishops who framed the Liturgy and the Book of Canons were Archbishop Spottiswoode of St Andrews, Archbishop Lindsay of Glasgow, Dr James Wedderburn of Dunblane, Dr John Guthrie of Moray, Dr John Maxwell of Ross, and Dr Walter Whiteford of Brechin. Though urged to adopt the English Liturgy, they evinced repugnance to it on account of the supposed prejudices of the people, who might have thought it a sacrifice of the ancient independence of the Scottish Church, as would doubtless have been successfully urged by the Presbyterians and Covenanters. And yet, though all the odium fell upon Archbishop Laud, and his moderation in the matter was alleged against him at his trial as a most heinous crime, he was so anxious that nothing should be done in opposition to the laws and statutes of the kingdom, that he had repeatedly stated, in his correspondence with the Scottish Bishops, that " it was their part to be certain that they should propose nothing to the King in the business contrary to the laws of the land, which he could not be thought to understand, and that they should never put any thing in execution without the consent of the Privy Council."

In connection with the preceding statements, to a certain extent, an article was printed in the CHRISTIAN OBSERVER for October 1842 (No. 58 of the New Series), under the title of " View of Public Affairs," and ostensibly written by the Editor. As this periodical is supported by a section of the Church of England, some observations are not inapplicable. The article now mentioned is grounded on the Queen's Visit to Scotland, and its author views the Sovereign's non-attendance at Presbyterian religious worship in the edifice in Edinburgh called the High Church in a very proper and judicious manner; but he thereafter rambles into a variety of subjects connected with the Scottish Episcopal Church, is evidently impregnated with extraordinary fears and peculiar opinions, assails the Scottish Bishops for designating themselves—" We, the Bishops of the Reformed Catholic Church in Scotland"—in their Synodal Letter respecting Trinity College; and attacks Bishop Russell of Glasgow, and Bishop Terrot of Edinburgh, for sundry opinions alleged to be maintained in the Charges of these Prelates to their Clergy, published in 1842. All these admonitions, remonstrances, and denunciations, are expressed in the most friendly mode of fraternizing with the Presbyterian Establishment, and are very ingeniously connected with " Oxford Tractarianism," with which, according to the Editor of the CHRISTIAN OBSERVER, the Scottish Episcopal Church is deeply imbued. He then proceeds—

" But we have one word more in reply to those of the Episcopal Church in Scotland who are ruining her cause by making her the ally and Coryphæus of Tractarianism, and that is, that their own ecclesiastical descent is not so free from genealogical difficulty that they should be the first to unchurch other churches. We will quote a passage from the pen of Dr Bernard in 1658, in illustration of Archbishop Usher's judgment of the ordinations in the Reformed Churches. ' If the ordinations of Presbyters in such places where Bishops cannot be had were not valid, the late Bishops of Scotland [those of the Spottiswoode line] had a hard task to maintain themselves to be Bishops, who were not (even) priests, for their ordination was no other. And for this passage in the History of Scotland, wrote by the Archbishop of St Andrews [Spottiswoode], it is observable, that when the Scots Bishops were to be consecrated by the Bishops of London, Ely, and Bath, here at London House, anno 1609, he saith a question was moved by Dr Andrews, Bishop of Ely, touching the consecration of the Scottish Bishops, who, as he said, must first be ordained Presbyters, *as having received no ordination from a Bishop.* The Archbishop of Canterbury, Dr Bancroft, who was by, maintained ' that thereof there was no necessity, seeing, where Bishops could not be had, the ordination given by Presbyters must be esteemed lawful, otherwise that it might be doubted if there were any lawful vocation in most of the Reformed churches.' This was applauded to by the other Bishops. Ely acquiesced, and at the day, and in the place appointed, the three Scottish Bishops were consecrated.' "—" Our Northern Brethren," adds the Editor of the CHRISTIAN OBSERVER, " must not be surprised that we remind them of these things, when they are so loudly boasting of their superiority over the Anglican Church, in that they have from the first escaped the 'malign influence'[*] to which we were exposed, and have ever held those opinions respecting apostolical succession, sacramental justification, and so forth, which have recently ' revived in the South.'"

Now, without reference to the opinion of Archbishop Bancroft respecting the consecration of Archbishop Spottiswoode and his brethren, that "where Bishops could not be had, the ordination given by presbyters must be esteemed lawful"—the validity of which cannot be admitted for a moment, even though it hazards the "lawful vocation in most of the Reformed Churches"—surely the Editor of the CHRISTIAN OBSERVER ought to have made himself better acquainted with historical facts before he alleged of the Scottish Episcopal Church, that " their own ecclesiastical descent is not so free from genealogical difficulty that they should be the first to unchurch other churches." He is evidently altogether ignorant of the consecration of the Scottish Bishops in Westminster Abbey in 1661, from whom the Scottish Episcopal Church derive "their ecclesiastical descent," and about which there cannot be the least "genealogical difficulty" in the mind of any man of the most ordinary comprehension. The ignorance of the Editor of the CHRISTIAN OBSERVER of the consecrations of 1661, of which it appears he never heard, is proved by his passage from the "pen of Dr Bernard," who, let it be noted, wrote in 1658, *two years before* the Restoration of Charles II., and *four years before* Archbishop Sharp and his brethren were consecrated in Westminster Abbey. So far, therefore, as Dr Bernard is concerned, the extract from his "pen" is intelligible, but it is different when adopted *one hundred and eighty years* after the consecration of 1661, in reference to the "ecclesiastical descent" of the Scottish Episcopal Church. There is no more "genealogical difficulty" in the matter, than in tracing the "ecclesiastical descent" of every Archbishop and Bishop of the Church of England since the Restoration. With the Spottiswoode line of the succession of Bishops the present Scottish Episcopal Church never

---

[*] These words are quoted from the Charge delivered to the Episcopal Clergy of the District of Glasgow by Bishop Russell, in 1842

had the slightest connection; the last representative of that succession was, as repeatedly stated, the old Bishop of Galloway, who died in the See of Orkney in 1633; and it is therefore hoped that the Editor of the CHRISTIAN OBSERVER will accept of this information, apparently unknown to him, on Scottish Episcopal matters, before he again lectures his "Northern brethren" about "ecclesiastical descent" and "genealogical difficulty." This journalist should, moreover, remember that the Scottish Episcopal Church does not "unchurch other churches." Those "churches," if they are entitled to be so called, "unchurch" themselves, who refuse to acknowledge the uninterrupted succession of Bishops, and the three orders of Bishops, Priests, and Deacons. He must also be informed that the Scottish Episcopal Church is not "the ally and Coryphæus of Tractarianism," as he interprets what he calls "Tractarianism;" and her cause is, humanly speaking, more likely to be "ruined" by the laxity or latitudinarianism of persons, both clerical and lay, who look upon schism with indifference, and whose opinions and practices are utterly subversive of Apostolical truth, order, and discipline. The Editor of the CHRISTIAN OBSERVER concludes by stating that "the Church of England desires to aid its beloved sister in Scotland, so long 'scattered and peeled'"—a fact which may be said to be daily corroborated by experience, and is duly appreciated in the most grateful manner.

In concluding these introductory observations, the following passages from a work by John Gibson Lockhart, Esq., published in 1819, contain the reflections of that distinguished writer on the Scottish Episcopal Church:—" Presbytery was not established in this country [Scotland] without a long and violent struggle, or series of struggles, in which it is too true that the mere tyrannical aversion of the Stuart Kings was the main and most effectual enemy the Presbyterians had to contend with, but in which, notwithstanding, there was enlisted against the cause of that sect no inconsiderable nor weak array of fellow citizens, conscientiously and devoutly adhering to an opposite system. It was a pity that the Scottish Episcopalians were almost universally Jacobites, for their adoption of that most hated of all [political] heresies made it a comparatively easy matter for their doctrinal enemies to scatter them entirely from the field before them. Nevertheless, in spite of all the disfavour and disgrace with which for a length of years they had to contend, the spirit of the Episcopal Church did not evaporate or expire, and she has of late lifted up her head again in a style of splendour that seems to awaken considerable feelings of jealousy and wrath in the bosoms of the more bigoted Presbyterians who contemplated it. The more liberal adherents of the Scottish Kirk, however, seem to entertain no such feelings, or rather they take a pleasure in doing full justice to the noble stedfastness which has been displayed through so long a period of neglect by their fellow Christians of this persuasion. To the clergy of the Episcopal Church in particular they have no difficulty in conceding a full measure of that praise which, from adherence to principle, has at all times the power of commanding, and the adherence of these men has indeed been of the highest and most meritorious kind. With a self-denial and humility worthy of the Primitive ages of the Church, they have submitted to all manner of penury and privation rather than depart from their inherited faith, or leave the people of their sect without the support of that spiritual instruction for which it was out of their power to offer any thing more than a very trivial and inadequate kind of remuneration. Nay, in the midst of all their difficulties and distresses, they have endeavoured with persevering zeal to sustain the character of their own body with regard to learning, and they have succeeded in doing so in a way that reflects the highest honour not only on their zeal, but their talents. Not a few names of very considerable celebrity are to be found among the scattered and impoverished members of this Apostolical Church; and even in our own time the talents of many men have been devoted to its service, who might easily have commanded what less heroic spirits would have thought a far more precious kind of reward, had they chosen to seek, in other pursuits and professions, what they well knew this could never afford them."*

* Peter's Letters to his Kinsfolk, vol iii. p. 88, 89, 90.

HISTORY

OF THE

SCOTTISH EPISCOPAL CHURCH.

CHAPTER I.

GENERAL VIEW OF THE ESTABLISHED EPISCOPAL CHURCH OF SCOTLAND PREVIOUS TO THE REVOLUTION.

THE history of the Episcopal Church of Scotland may be said to comprise two periods—the one commencing from the Reformation in the sixteenth century, or at least from 1572, and terminating at the Revolution of 1688, during which, excepting various casual changes and occurrences, that Church was the legal Establishment. The second period dates from the Revolution, when the Church, from political principles on the part of its Bishops and Clergy, which, whether mistaken or not, deserve the highest veneration, because they suffered their deprivation from conscientious motives, ceased to be vested with the rights and privileges of a legal Establishment, and was superseded by Presbyterianism. This period is the subject of the present volume.

The Church in Scotland twice received the Episcopal Succession from the Church of England, first in 1610, and again in 1661. After the tumultuous reformation of religion the Roman Catholic Hierarchy became extinct, and consequently those persons nominated by James VI. to the Archbishoprics and Bishoprics, from 1572 to 1610, were merely nominal, though they were in possession of such of the revenues of their Sees as had escaped the general plunder of the temporalities at the dissolution of the Roman Catholic Hierarchy. It may be doubted

A

whether it was possible that those persons, who, though undoubtedly laymen, were styled Bishops, could have been otherwise situated at the time. The succession had become extinct in a country which was still a separate independent kingdom under its own monarch, and Queen Elizabeth might have chosen, from various motives, to prevent the Archbishops and Bishops of the Church of England from holding any consecrations of Scottish Prelates during her reign. But the union of the two crowns, by the accession of James VI. to the English throne, removed every obstacle, and accordingly, in 1610, Archbishop Spottiswoode of St Andrews, Bishop Hamilton of Galloway, and Bishop Lamb of Brechin, were summoned to London by order of the King, and consecrated in the Chapel of London House on the 21st of October that year, by Dr George Abbot, Bishop of London, Dr Lancelot Andrewes, Bishop of Ely, Dr Richard Neale, Bishop of Rochester, and Dr Henry Parry, Bishop of Worcester. Dr James Montague, Bishop of Bath and Wells, was nominated as one of the consecrating Prelates in the royal commission with the Bishops of London and Ely, but his Lordship could not attend, and his place was supplied by the Bishops of Rochester and Worcester.

The newly consecrated Bishops returned to Scotland, and canonically conferred the episcopal function on their brethren who filled the other Sees. This succession is generally designated the Spottiswoode Line, which became all but extinct after the troubles which terminated in the murder of Charles I, and the domination of Cromwell. Only one of the Bishops of that succession was alive at the restoration of Charles II., when the Church was re-established as it had been previous to the noted General Assembly of Glasgow in 1638. This Prelate was Dr Thomas Sydserff, Bishop of Galloway. It is worthy of notice, that Bishop Sydserff admitted into Deacon's Orders Dr John Tillotson, Archbishop of Canterbury. In the Life of Archbishop Tillotson, by the Rev. Thomas Birch, it is stated—" The time of Mr Tillotson's entering into holy orders, and by whom he was ordained, are facts which I have not been able to determine."* But we owe the fact of the ordination of Archbishop Tillotson by Bishop Sydserff to the Rev. John Beardmore, M.A., who was admitted sizar, and tutor to him at Clare Hall, Cambridge, in April, 1651, and whose " Memorials" of that celebrated Primate were " written upon the news of his death for his own satisfaction, and out

* Life of Dr John Tillotson, p 17. London edit. 1752

of honour to his Grace's memory."* The information was communicated to Mr Beardmore by the Archbishop himself. Tillotson's father was a rigid Puritan and Calvinist, who carefully educated his son in his own principles, and sent him to Cambridge in 1647, when the Presbyterians had the control of that University. "He did not appear as a preacher," says Mr Beardmore, "till after the Restoration in 1660, taking orders (*as he hath told me*) from the old Scottish Bishop of Galloway, who at that time had great recourse made to him on that account. King Charles II. was then so favourable to the Presbyterian party, that he offered Bishoprics to some of that persuasion, as to old Mr Calamy for one; and Mr Tillotson told me, in the year 1661, that the good old man deliberated about it some considerable time, professing to see the great inconvenience of Presbyterian parity." Bishop Burnet, who designates Bishop Sydserff as a "very learned and good man," informs us that he went to London at the Restoration expecting to be advanced to the Archbishopric of St Andrews, but that he gave great offence to the English Bishops by the promiscuous ordinations he held when he first came to England: "For," says Burnet, "when the act of uniformity required all men who held any benefices there to be episcopally ordained, he (Sydserff) who, by observing the ill effects of the former violence of the Scots Bishops, was become very moderate, with others of the Scots Clergy who gathered about him, ordained all those of the English clergy who came to him, without demanding either oaths or subscriptions of them. This was supposed to be done by him merely for a subsistence from the fees for the letters of orders granted by him, for he was poor. However, he was translated to the Bishopric of Orkney, one of the best revenues of the Sees in Scotland, in which he lived little more than a year."† The circumstance of Bishop Sydserff dispensing with "oaths or subscriptions" was probably the principal reason that induced Tillotson, whose Presbyterian principles then warped him, to procure ordination from his hands. Bishop Sydserff died in the See of Orkney in 1663, at a very advanced age. He is mentioned in a ratification of the Scottish Parliament, "in favour of Thomas Bishop of Galloway," in September, 1662, confirming the rights to sundry teinds or tithes in various parishes to be enjoyed by "James, now Bishop of Galloway."‡

* This sketch is printed Number I. in the Appendix to the Life of Archbishop Tillotson by Birch.   † Burnet's History of His Own Times, vol. ii p. 132, 133.
‡ Acta Parliamentorum Scotorum, edited by Thomas Thomson, Esq. vol. vii. p. 436, 437.

The succession of the Bishops of the first consecration having become extinct before the Restoration, with the exception of Dr Sydserff, the re-establishment of the Scottish Church rendered the investment of the episcopal functions again necessary in England. As this is the line from which the Scottish Bishops and Clergy derive their consecration and ordination, some attention to this important event is indispensable, more especially as every outrageous and ignorant calumny regarding the consecrations after the Revolution is often industriously and indiscriminately paraded. Although these attacks are, in the most instances, founded on assumptions so flagrant and notorious, and so unfairly and uncandidly brought forward, as to carry with them their own refutation, yet it is imperative that the whole matter should be laid before the reader in a clear and unhesitating manner. Four parish ministers were summoned to London by the King's Letter, dated Whitehall, 14th August 1661. These were Mr James Sharp, of a respectable family in the county of Banff, who had officiated as minister of Crail in the county of Fife, and as Professor of Divinity in the neighbouring University of St Andrews; Mr James Hamilton, minister of Cambusnethan, a son of Sir James Hamilton, and brother of the first Lord Belhaven; Mr Robert Leighton, minister of Newbattle near Dalkeith, the son of Dr Alexander Leighton, who had thought proper to publish a violent tirade against the Church of England in the reign of Charles I., for which he was severely punished; and Mr Andrew Fairfoul, a native of Anstruther in Fife, who had been successively minister of North Leith and of Dunse. Mr Sharp was nominated to the Archbishopric of St Andrews, Mr Fairfoul to the Archbishopric of Glasgow, Mr Hamilton to the Bishopric of Galloway, the aged Sydserff having been transferred to Orkney, and Mr Leighton to the Bishopric of Dunblane. They were all consecrated in Westminster Abbey on the 15th day of December 1661, having been previously ordained deacons and priests, by Dr Gilbert Sheldon, Bishop of London (afterwards Archbishop of Canterbury), Dr George Morley, Bishop of Worcester (afterwards of Winchester), Dr Richard Sterne (afterwards Archbishop of York), and Dr Hugh Lloyd, Bishop of Llandaff Archbishop Juxon of Canterbury was unable, on account of his great age and infirmities, to be present, and Archbishop Frewen of York was prevented by some cause or other from attending.

Of the parties who were consecrated in Westminster Abbey on this occasion, none has been assailed with greater malignity than Archbishop Sharp. The high office he was selected to fill as Primate and Metropolitan of the Church of Scotland, and his former connection with the Presbyterians, caused him to be maligned by the latter with a ferocity almost unexampled, and even at this distance of time, when different circumstances should have assuaged party resentment, the most extraordinary odium is still heaped on his memory. It is unnecessary here to enter into any minute investigation of the Archbishop's conduct, and his inhuman murder by a band of armed fanatics might surely in some degree excite respect for his alleged conduct after his elevation to the Primacy, as well as for the means by which he is very erroneously supposed to have attained the Metropolitan See. The Episcopal Church of Scotland, however, is not responsible for any acts of Archbishop Sharp, and it would be as unreasonable to connect her constitution with his private or public life as it would be to charge all the Presbyterians with being implicated in his murder, or to hold them responsible for the dangerous extravagances, intolerant principles, and violent proceedings, of the Covenanters, in an age when forbearance was little understood or practised by either party who were in possession of power. It is certain that the Church would have been re-established in Scotland without the aid of the Archbishop, and in defiance of his opposition. This is directly admitted even by the Presbyterian writer Wodrow, who alleges that William, ninth Earl of Glencairn, Lord Chancellor of Scotland after the Restoration, was " the chief statesman that has brought in Prelacy."* Nothing can be more evident to an unprejudiced mind than that the Archbishop has been more blamed than he deserved for promoting Episcopacy, and the serious charge that he previously deceived and betrayed his constituents, when sent from Scotland to the Court, remains still to be proved. The Presbyterians maintained that he was guilty of this treachery, and bestowed on him such epithets as Judas, an apostate, a wretch, and other raving soubriquets, and we accordingly find one of the most noted preachers, Mr Alexander Shields, in his extraordinary performance, entitled " A Hind Let Loose," exulting with savage delight at his barbarous murder, and daringly connecting this crime with the name of the Deity, applauding the perpetrators as " *worthy gentlemen.*"—" That truculent traitor," says Mr Shields,

---

* Wodrow's Analecta, MS., Advocates' Library.

"James Sharp, Archprelate, &c., received the just demerit of his perfidie, perjury, apostacy, sorceries, villanies, and murders, sharp arrowes and coals of juniper. For, upon the 3d of May 1679, *several worthy gentlemen, with some other men of courage and zeal for the cause of God, and the good of the country,* executed righteous judgement upon him in Magus Muir near St Andrews." Language such as this, expressing as it does the feelings of the heart, only shows that Shields would have been a tyrant of the most implacable kind if it had been in his power. The Archbishop's own party always asserted that he acted fairly, and that in reality he did not represent them, or bear any commission from them, when he conformed to the Church, and accepted the Primacy—an elevation by no means enviable in that turbulent and fanatical age. It was impossible for the Archbishop's Presbyterian contemporaries, excited as they were by the most malignant and frantic hatred towards him, writing and speaking of him in the most intolerable manner, and alluding to him in the most offensive language in their field-preachings, to be competent judges of his conduct, and it is not surprising, when all things are taken into account, that this revengeful spirit should be cherished at the present day.

These observations are here introduced, because the Presbyterian writers obstinately persist in identifying the name of Archbishop Sharp with the Scottish Episcopal Church, of which he was no more than Primate at its re-establishment by the second consecration in England. That Church, as a branch of the Holy Catholic, and Apostolic Church, acknowledges the name of no man, or set of men, however pious, learned, and distinguished, for with that universal communion, whether established by law as in England, or existing as in other countries, the Scottish Episcopal Church asserts her apostolicity, as derived from the Church of England by the consecrations of 1661, and claims a similar foundation on the Prophets, Apostles, and Primitive Fathers, Jesus Christ himself being the chief-corner stone. She acknowledges only her great Head, and she depends for the success of the ministrations of her Bishops and Clergy to His gracious promise, that by the guidance of the Third Person of the glorious Trinity He will be with his Church and people always to the end of the world. But to revert to Archbishop Sharp, it would be an easy matter to show that most of the calumnies heaped upon him are utterly unfounded, and the scandals circulated against him so false, as to be utterly unworthy of notice. Mr James Kirkton, a well known Presbyterian contemporary, describes him as " a man of parts and a schollar, as he shewed himself when a regent in St Andrews, but a schollar rather cautious than able; rarely would he ever engadge in a dispute, lest he might fall under disadvantage, and never would be the opponent, which he knew was the most difficult part."* These latter qualifications, however, such as they are, must be received as mere matters of opinion. This same Kirkton, who was one of the Archbishop's bitter enemies, proceeds to describe him as held by all who knew him, " to be no better than a flat atheist," recording a story affecting his moral character so utterly false, that it is astonishing it was believed for a moment even in that credulous age, and gravely assuring us that many considered him to be a " demoniack and a witch."' As Mr Kirkpatrick Sharpe observes, the story alluded to " seems to have been founded on the ravings of a mad woman, who disturbed the congregation while at sermon in St Andrews, and bestowed many scurrilous epithets on the Archbishop;" and who declared that she once saw him and two gentlemen, one of whom was the Rev. Robert Rait, minister of Dundee, *all dancing in the air!* It is satisfactorily known that as Primate of the Church, Archbishop Sharp's deportment was regular; and during the twelve years he was previously minister of Crail, in the Kirk-Session records of which his handwriting is still to be seen, he was a rigid disciplinarian, discharging his duties with the utmost strictness, punctuality, and diligence. The writer of the " True and Impartial Account of the Life of the most Reverend Father in God, Dr James Sharpe, Archbishop of St Andrews," &c. who is at least as much entitled to credit as the Primate's bigoted enemies, assures us that his " methods were Christian and prudent, and attended with very great success," and that " he entertained his clergy with much brotherly love and respect, and was a great judge and encourager of learning, wisdom, and piety." Bishop Burnet, indeed, is pleased to say that he " had a very small proportion of learning, and was but an indifferent preacher;" but it must be remembered that this is the opinion of an avowed and inveterate enemy.

The gossiping and garrulous Mr Robert Wodrow, a well known

* The Secret and True History of the Church of Scotland, from the Restoration to the year 1678, edited by Charles Kirkpatrick Sharpe, Esq 4to. 1817, p. 83.

Presbyterian minister, who had the dishonesty to garble the Archbishop's letters to Douglas, tells the following story, in his own peculiar manner, respecting the wife of a Mr John Baird, Presbyterian minister at Innerwick, in the Presbytery of Dunbar—which Wodrow designates a "woeful Presbitry," for "one Mr Wood, a minister among them, turned a Bishop, and all the other eight turned curates."* The story may be considered a fair specimen of the ridiculous scandal in which the Archbishop's enemies delighted to indulge against him. The said Mr John Baird married Margaret Bruce, daughter of Mr James Bruce, minister of Kingsbarns, the parish adjoining that of Crail, of which the Archbishop was, as already mentioned, twelve years the incumbent. "It was by a very strange providence that she escaped being Mr James Sharp's wife, who became Primate, and was then minister of Crail in Fife. He was very earnestly wooing her. She on a Saobath day, in a disguise, went to Crail to hear Mr Sharp preach, and he preached extraordinarily well, as she thought, so that she really had some design to embrace his offer, if he came again to renew and urge his proposal. She was always a very curious and inquisitive person. When her father went out, she used to try if he had left his chamber door open. Accordingly, after she had heard Mr Sharp preach his sermon, she goes to her father's chamber, and finds his study door open; she goes in, and presently falls upon a new English sermon, which her father, Mr Bruce, had gotten out of England, and it was upon the very same text that Mr Sharp had preached. She reads the sermon, and she finds that Mr Sharp had stollen the whole sermon, and had most faithfully repeated the most part of what was in that printed English sermon, which opened her eyes so clearly, that when he came again to renew his proposall, she utterly rejected his offer, and it was indeed a happy providence to her, for if she had fallen in *that wretch's* company she had been miserable in time."† Wodrow says of this silly woman, in whose story there is probably not a word of truth, that "she declared that God took

---

* The "Mr Wood" here mentioned as one of this "woeful Presbitry," was Andrew Wood, a nephew by his mother of the worthy Bishop Guthrie of Moray. He was successively minister of the parishes of Spott and Dunbar, consecrated Bishop of the Isles in 1678, and translated to the See of Caithness in 1680. His death is noticed elsewhere

† Wodrow's Analecta, MS., Advocates' Library.

her by the heart when she was but six years old." The Archbishop married Miss Moncrieff of Randerston in Fife, a lady described by his libellers as " an ordinary swearer, tippler, scold, and prophaner of the Sabbath-day," while his defenders, and those who knew her intimately, speak of her as a most worthy, excellent, and pious person. But this lady was not a Presbyterian, and the abuse so ungallantly and uncharitably awarded to her is easily understood. If Archbishop Sharp was the man he is represented to have been by his traducers, it is not likely that his son and daughters would have occupied the position in society which they subsequently maintained. His son, Sir William Sharp, Bart. married Margaret Erskine, daughter of Sir Charles Erskine, Bart. of Cambo, near Crail, Lord Lyon King of-Arms, the third son of the first Earl of Kellie, and brother of the second and third Earls. Isabel, who was in the coach with her father when he was inhumanly murdered, married Cunningham of Barns, a gentleman of ancient family in Fife; and Margaret, the only other daughter, married William, eleventh Lord Saltoun, from whom the Barons of that branch of the Noble Family of Frazer are lineally descended. Lady Saltoun died at Edinburgh in 1734.

The Presbyterian writer Kirkton gives us his opinion of the other prelates consecrated in 1661. "Mr Andrew Fairfoull for Glasgow, a man of good learning and neat expression, but was never taken for a man either serious or sincere, and was moreover judged a man both profane and scandalous. Mr James Hamilton, minister at Camnethan, was appointed for Galloway, a man only noticed for his wary time-serving, otherwise a man of contemptible parts." But if those and the other Bishops were really such as he represents them, imputing to some of them the grossest immoralities and the most scandalous vices, it is little to the credit of his beloved Presbyterianism, or its discipline, that they were allowed to continue so long ministers of their respective parishes, before they conformed to the Church, and were invested with episcopal authority. They officiated as incumbents of their parishes during years when Presbyterianism was rampant in its most stringent form—years to which the supporters of that system usually refer with exultation, as the *purest* and *best years* of their existence. Those were the years of the Solemn League and Covenant; and the parties who in the General Assembly of 1638 had the audacity to excommunicate all the then Bishops of Scotland, and libel them as guilty of every atrocious crime possible to be committed, might have easily silenced a few obscure parish ministers, if they were really the characters delineated by Kirkton and his associates. But the truth is, that nothing was ever charged against them, either publicly or privately, until they conformed to the Church, and were invested with episcopal functions, when they were instantly discovered by the Presbyterians to be addicted to the grossest vices, and to be actuated by the basest motives Even Archbishop Sharp, who is justly described as "for sobriety next to a miracle," is falsely represented by his unscrupulous maligners as a sensualist. The Presbyterians may be assured that a new generation views these charges in a very different manner.

Leighton, Bishop of Dunblane, and subsequently Archbishop of Glasgow, is specially noticed by Kirkton His well-known theological works are still admired even by Presbyterians, and by his reputation for mildness of disposition, piety, and learning, he is the only one of the Scottish Bishops of that age whose character has not been wilfully and maliciously traduced. Previous to his consecration in London he had been, as already observed minister of Newbattle near Dalkeith, and Principal of the University of Edinburgh "Burnet," it is observed, "says that Leighton, who had been trained up to entertain the strongest antipathy to the whole frame of the Church of England, quickly broke through the prejudices of his education. The Presbyterians offered few attractive qualities to his notice. He found them bitter and persecuting in their political sentiments, sour in their temper, and narrow-minded in spiritual things. Having gone over to the Episcopalians, he accepted the bishopric of Dunblane, a small diocese with a little revenue. He administered his pastoral care with a watchful eye and a liberal hand. 'He went round,' we are told by Burnet, 'continually every year, preaching and catechising from parish to parish.' His elevation in the Church did not change the humble tenor of his life; he pursued the same path of humility and peace, bestowing abundant alms upon the poor, and enforcing by his own practice the doctrines which he taught."*

Kirkton thus notices Leighton:—he "was made Bishop of Dunblane; thus he choose to demonstrate to the world avarice was not his principle, it being the smallest revenue—a man of good learning, excellent utter-

* Pictures of Christian Life, by Robert Aris Wilmott, B A· of Trinity College, Cambridge London, 1841, p 251

ance, and very grave abstract conversation; but almost altogether destitute of a doctrinal principle, being almost indifferent among all the professions that are called by the name of Christ." In other words, Leighton's mildness and pious deportment were viewed with contempt by his Presbyterian contemporaries, who considered him a latitudinarian, because he refused to go the whole length of Presbyterianism and the Solemn League and Covenant. That Leighton was supposed to be a person of no fixed opinion on ecclesiastical matters, which is the evident meaning of the very charitable Mr Kirkton's accusation that he was "destitute of a doctrinal principle," is evident from the following anecdote, which gives a tolerable idea of the feeling of those times. The anecdote refers to a visit by Leighton after his consecration to the mansion of Goodtrees, now called Moredun, near the village of Gilmerton, upwards of three miles from Edinburgh, on one of the post roads to Dalkeith—a stately chateau, at that time the property and residence of Sir James Stewart of Goodtrees, who had been an eminent merchant in Edinburgh, and was nephew of Lord Carmichael, Lord Treasurer-Depute of Scotland. Sir James was a noted Presbyterian leader, and was Lord Provost of Edinburgh in 1649 and in 1659, but he was dismissed from his civic dignity at the Restoration, for being a Covenanter, and committed to Edinburgh Castle, from which he was released by the interest of Sir Archibald Primrose, Lord Register, father of the first Earl of Rosebery. The name *Gutters* is merely a local corruption of Goodtrees.

It seems that in one of Sir James Stewart's visits of business to London he became acquainted with the elder Leighton, who entrusted his son, the future Bishop of Dunblane and Archbishop of Glasgow, to Sir James' care to be educated at the University of Edinburgh.—" The father entreated (and the son was present) to train him up in the true Presbiterian forme, and Robert was strictly enjoined, with his father's blessing, to be steady in that way. While attending the University he was expelled for writing a satirical stanza 'on the Lord Provost of Edinburgh's name, Aikenhead, and the many pimples on his face.' "—" When Episcopacy became fashionable after the year 1660," says the writer, Sir Archibald Stewart Denham, Bart., " he forgot his father's injunction, and was Bishop and Archbishop, amicable compositor of parties, and what not, in Scotland; and in the end, disgusted with all, he threw himself flee, and ended his days in a kind of monastick life in England." In a note at this passage it is stated—" Mr Leighton was a learned divine, and a man of value in many ways, but had a good deal of whine and pedantry. As to his pulpit performance, Bishop Burnett runs him up too high, and by aggrandizing his pulpit gift makes one esteme the published sermons really less than they truly deserve; and I judge the Bishop has overdone in the whole character."—"After Mr Leighton came from London, consecrate Bishop of Dunblan, he went to dine at Gutters (Goodtrees, now Moredun) near Edinburgh, and, as he said, with his old friend, or his best friend, Sir James Stewart. The first salute from this best friend was—'Welcome, Robin! you loved gauding abroad too much; you have the fate of Dinah, Jacob's daughter, for now I may say the Shechamites have catched and defloured you.'" This passed easy, and Sir James turned to other subjects of discourse, and there was no more talk of his having deserted Zion's plea for presbytery at that time. Only, because Burnet, in his History of his Own Times, says that Leighton had no angry passions, we shall add this. Though his Lordship of Dunblane took easy what Sir James Stewart said, he did not so easy digest what his eldest son Thomas put closer home in private with him. He said to one who saw him in some confusion, instantly upon his return from Gutters—"I have dined at Goodtrees; I wish I had stayed at home, and chawed gravel. That young man, Sir James Stewart's son, Thomas, is as hott as peper; he was never off this turff of Scotland, has gott a Presbyterian crotchet in his perecranium, and will never get it out again." When the Bishop went from Gutters, all Sir James Stewart said was—"Mr Leighton is a man of many oddities or irregularities, and it does not surprize me what he has done; still I shall think him a pious good man. The Court have called up three little better than Judas, and seduced one Nathaniell." In Sir James Stewart's Diary is this notice—"Robin Lighton, much in Mr Forbes' way, who was the first Bishop of Edinburgh, and was of the same whimsical stamp, a prey to novelties."* The substance of the conversation is given more minutely in another part of the volume,† from

* Coltness Collections, printed in 1842 for the Maitland Club, in one volume 4to, p 22, 23, 24

† Coltness Collections, p. 68, 69. The state of party feeling, as cherished by the loyalists towards their opponents, and there was no love lost between them, is indi-

which it appears that Leighton had at one time approved of the National Covenant, but that he had always opposed the Solemn League. Leighton's defence of himself is also inserted.—" Mr Stewart," he said, " man is a mutable changing essence, both in body and mind, and frequently is misinformed, yet acts according to his light at the time, and acts safe ; but if years, and experience, and inquiry, give further light, so he is still to act an ingenious part, as God, his word, and his confidence direct ;" and the Bishop cited that text—" When I was a child, &c. but now have I put away childish things." A passage in the " Memorialls" by Mr Robert Law, shows that Leighton was not inattentive to the affairs of his Diocese when Archbishop of Glasgow, under date 1673. " Bishop Leighton, at the last meeting of the Synod of Glasgow, appoints some of the brethren, viz. Mr Ross, Parson of Glasgow (afterwards Archbishop), Mr Stewart at Bonhill, Mr Whyte at Air, and some others with him, to go to Edinburgh and present some grievances, viz. against the Indulged (Presbyterian) brethren, that they baptized children of other parishes, and did not keep the 29th of May, the King's birth and restoration day ; and that they did not keep the injunctions of the Council ; 2dly, against conventicles ; against some of them they alledged treasonable speeches, and charge some with adultery and fornication ; 3dly, against some young men that preach, as they alledge, without appoyntment of the Church officers."*

It is amusing to peruse Kirkton's characters of the Bishops who were consecrated by the Archbishop and his colleagues after their return from London. " Mr George Wishart," he observes, " he was for Edinburgh, a *man of learning*, who had been censured by the old Covenanters at Dunse Law ;" but he adds some malicious scandal as usual—" He was a daily drunkard, and ane infamous swearer, even upon the streets." The very name of Bishop Wishart, to all who know his history, is a refutation of this falsehood, and the wonder is that he is not accused of murder, or some other revolting crime. Bishop Wishart had been chaplain

cated by the manner in which Sir John Lauder, Lord Fountainhall, mentions Sir James Stewart and his son :—"James Stewart, that *arrant rogue* (after Advocate to Queen Anne), son of that *nefarceous villain*, Sir James Stewart, some tyme Provost of Edinburgh, a bitter enemy." Chronological Notes of Scottish Affairs from 1680 till 1701, chiefly taken from the Diary of Lord Fountainhall, with Notes, edited by Sir Walter Scott, 4to, p. 57.

* Law's Memorialls, p. 56.

to the great Marquis of Montrose, and was *guilty* of writing in elegant Latin the well-known history of that illustrious nobleman's exploits in behalf of his sovereign, a copy of which was suspended, by the contemptible spite of his Covenanting enemies, from the neck of the Marquis when he was executed, or rather judicially murdered. That Bishop of Edinburgh well knew the tender mercies of the Covenanters. They had immured him during their domination seven months in a dark and loathsome dungeon, in which he was only once allowed to change his linen, and was so seriously assailed by rats, that he bore the marks of their voracity on his face to the day of his death. Yet, knowing well the horrors of incarceration, this worthy Bishop liberally supplied with food the Presbyterian insurgents taken at the battle of Rullion Green near the Pentland hills, and imprisoned in that part of St Giles' Cathedral in Edinburgh, long known as Haddo's Hole, so denominated from Sir John Gordon of Haddo, ancestor of the Earls of Aberdeen, who was confined in this part of the edifice, now removed, previous to his execution at the Cross of Edinburgh for loyalty to Charles I , by order of the Scottish Parliament in 1644. Burnet mentions that the insurgents confined in this and other places in the city were so plentifully provided by Bishop Wishart and several persons, that they almost became martyrs, having no exercise, to unwonted repletion. Bishop Halyburton, formerly minister of Perth, consecrated to Dunkeld, escapes tolerably easy from Kirkton's aspersions. He is admitted to have been a " *man of utterance,*" but " who had made more changes than old infamous Eccebolius, and was never thought sincere in any." We are simply told that " Mr David Mitchell, once minister at Edinburgh, but deposed for heresy, was for Aberdeen ;" " Mr David Fletcher, minister at Melrose," who is acknowledged to have been " a man of many pious prefaces," yet, " who never missed ane occasion of embracing this present world, was made Bishop of Argyll ;" and Bishop Forbes of Caithness is designated " the degenerate son of ane excellent father, Mr John Forbes." He seems to have had nothing to record against Bishop Wallace of the Isles, Bishop Strachan of Brechin, Bishop Paterson of Ross, and Bishop Mackenzie of Moray, except that the first was a relation of the Lord Chancellor Glencairn, the second was also a near relative of the Earl of Middleton, and his Lordship's parish minister at Fettercairn, and the two last were in his opinion " very inconsiderable, and therefore obscure." Yet they were not at least more "obscure or inconsiderable" than the ordinary Presbyterians ministers of the time. Bishop Paterson was the father of John Paterson, successively Bishop of Galloway and Edinburgh, and Archbishop of Glasgow. The former before his elevation was minister of the parish of Foveran in the county of Aberdeen, and his son was Dean of Edinburgh. Another son of Bishop Paterson of Ross was created a Baronet of Nova Scotia in 1687, and was Clerk of the Privy Council when he purchased the estate of Granton on the shore of the Frith of Forth, near Edinburgh, now the property of the Duke of Buccleuch. As to Bishop Mackenzie of Moray, he was so "obscure" as to be a younger son of Mackenzie of Gairloch, the elder branch of the Noble Family of Mackenzie, Earls of Seaforth, had been ordained by Bishop Maxwell of Ross, and after serving as a military chaplain in the wars of the great Gustavus Adolphus, was successively minister of Contin in the county of Ross, next of Inverness, and latterly of Elgin, his own episcopal seat. The truth is, that conformity to the Church was the great source of offence of those Bishops to the Presbyterians, who in consequence on every occasion vilified their public conduct and private life.

It is already stated that Archbishop Sharp and his colleagues were ordained deacons and priests before they were consecrated—a procedure which had indeed been discussed and overruled in the case of Archbishop Spottiswoode and his brethren at their consecration in 1610. It was then held that the episcopal function involved the orders of deacon and priest, but Bishop Sheldon took a different view of the matter, and held that Presbyterian ordination was invalid. However much this may be explained or modified, it is maintained by the Church of England and the Church universal at the present day, and no man can officiate within her pale unless he has been episcopally ordained. A remarkable illustration of this occurred towards the end of 1841. The Rev. James Marshall, one of the Established Presbyterian ministers of Edinburgh, after officiating twenty-two years in that city and Glasgow, conformed to the Church, and was admitted into deacon's orders by Bishop Maltby of Durham. As it respects Archbishop Sharp, it is stated on the authority of Bishop Burnet that he was averse to be ordained before his consecration, but the English Prelates were resolute in their determination to proceed in what they considered the canonical manner enjoined by the practice of the Church. The only difficulty in the consecration of

1661 is connected with Bishop Hamilton of Galloway According to Bishop Keith, he had been ordained incumbent of Cambusnethan by Archbishop Lindsay of Glasgow in 1634, in which parish he continued till his consecration Whether that ordination was admitted to be valid is nowhere stated.

An extraordinary notion has been set forth by the Presbyterians, in some of their attacks upon the Church, that the consecration of the four Scottish Bishops in 1661 was invalid, because at least two of them, Archbishop Sharp and Bishop Leighton, were not episcopally baptized. This notion is merely based on the doctrine of the Church respecting the validity of baptism administered by a person who is not in holy orders, or episcopally ordained, and is conspicuously introduced in an eccentric pamphlet, entitled " Oxford Tractarianism, the Scottish Episcopal College, and the Scottish Episcopal Church, the substance of a Speech delivered before the Presbytery of Perth, on the 30th of March 1842, by the Rev. Andrew Gray, A.M., Minister of the West Church of Perth." This very superfluous production, which is a lugubrious complaint against the Scottish Episcopal Church, for its alleged exclusiveness respecting the validity of ordination, with numerous extracts, culled from the works of Episcopal authors, is concluded by an Appendix, in which is the following passage, in reference to the Bishops consecrated in 1661. " But with that fatality which has hitherto characterized every attempt to introduce Prelacy into our land, not one of these men was prelatically baptized. The two first, it is acknowledged on all hands, received only Presbyterian baptism. But the baptism of the other two was just as invalid, for it was received only from those who, as we have shown, had never been baptized themselves, and were not accordingly in order at all. These four, being thus incapable of orders, received no grace from the imposition of hands by the Anglican Prelates. But what they did not receive they could not communicate. The orders of our present Prelates, Priests, and Deacons, are utterly invalid The sum of the whole matter is, that the orders of our present Scottish Prelatists are derived from persons whom, as Bishop Jolly says, ' pretendedly ordained persons had pretended to baptize.' "

The singular hallucination which seems to possess Mr Andrew Gray, Presbyterian teacher in Perth, would be unworthy of the least notice, were it not for his most unwarrantable and wilful perversion of the sentiments of the venerable Bishop Jolly. That truly good and learned

Prelate is now gathered to his fathers, but there are those who may safely be presumed to know more of his opinions than can be ascertained through the distorted notions of any Presbyterian preacher, particularly such a man as Mr Andrew Gray of Perth. This is not the place to discuss the important principles to which he alludes respecting " pretendedly ordained persons," the sacraments administered by whom are undoubtedly "perfectly null and invalid ;" and if Mr Gray chooses to continue in such a position, to his own Master he stands or falls. Baptism has ever been considered by the whole Church, from the days of the Apostles, though their baptism is not mentioned, to be solely confined to the recipients as it respects the spiritual advantages derived, and the benefits conferred. Three things are generally held to be indispensable in the case of valid baptism—the *authority* of the administrator, the *element used,* and the *words pronounced ;* but baptism in its effects is strictly limited to those who by its regenerating influence are duly entered within the communion of the Church, and cannot be transmitted in the same ecclesiastical manner as in the case of ordination, or if Mr Gray has no objection to the stronger term, the apostolical succession. Though the four Prelates from whom the Church in Scotland derives her episcopate and authority had no other than Presbyterian baptism, that could not in the very nature of things invalidate their consecration, or affect in the least degree their ecclesiastical power. It is true that doubts were raised in the primitive times about the validity of baptism as administered by heretics, and it is denied to be valid by Tertullian in one of his treatises, on the ground that those heretics had not the same God and the same Christ as the orthodox. St Cyprian summoned a Synod of sixty-six Bishops at Carthage, in which it was determined that no baptism was valid out of the pale of the Catholic Church, and that therefore it was necessary to rebaptize those who had been heretics. But Pope Stephen III. disapproved of this decision, and even the Romanists, who pretend that their system is unchanged and unchangeable since the days of the Apostles, do not rebaptize Presbyterian converts, or those whom they are pleased to consider heretics, but admit their baptism, if done with water in the name of the Trinity. The Scottish Bishops were not summoned to England to be baptized. They were to be invested with the episcopal functions, which they were to transmit and perpetuate to their successors in the usual canonical manner. It was a power conferred, and at the same time derivative. If they were not themselves validly baptized, they were affected solely as individuals, but it could not possibly have any influence on their acts as regularly consecrated Bishops of the Church, the ordinations they held, and the sacraments they administered, even though, as in the case of Quakers, they had never been baptized at all. The hallucination under which Mr Andrew Gray labours completely proves that he is utterly ignorant of the real nature of the sacrament of baptism, as well as of the perpetuation of the Christian ministry in uninterrupted succession as a purely spiritual descent, in conformity to the declaration of the great Head of the Church Catholic, that his kingdom is not of this world. Mr Gray's perversion of Bishop Jolly's sentiments can only excite feelings of pity at such an utter want of candour, or at such an obtusity of comprehension. He asks—" What now, then, becomes of the pretended apostolical succession among our Scottish Prelatists ?" We answer, that it is just where it was before he meddled with the matter, and where it will ever be, as an indispensable element in the constitution of the true Church. He asks—" Will they (the Scottish Prelatists) claim it (the apostolical succession) still ? " We answer, that we *will claim* it, in defiance of all that he or his friends, such as " John Brown, D.D., Minister of Langton, Berwickshire," can write to the contrary ; because to relinquish it would be to put ourselves on the same level with the Presbyterians and modern sectaries. Mr Gray finally asks—" What inducement now can they hold out to us to join them ? Have they purer doctrines—more faithful discipline—more efficacious sacraments—a more valid ministry—or even a better title to the apostolical succession than ourselves ?" We answer, that in all these particulars we conscientiously believe WE HAVE, and hence the grand and fundamental reason why we are, what he calls us, *Prelatists*.

In the " Diary of Public Transactions and other Occurrences, chiefly in Scotland, from 1650 to 1667, by John Nicoll,"* who resided a considerable portion of his life in Edinburgh, in his professional character of Writer to the Signet and Notary-Public, and who is supposed to be the John Nicoll put in nomination as Clerk to the noted Glasgow General Assembly of 1638, when Sir Archibald Johnstone of Warriston was

---

* Published in 1836, in one vol. 4to, by the Bannatyne Club.

elected, we have an account of the first consecration held in Scotland, after the return of Archbishop Sharp and his colleagues from London This was in the Chapel-Royal of Holyrood, now in ruins, then called the Abbey Church, and used as the parish church of the Canongate, on Wednesday the 7th of May 1662. Nicoll, who writes as if he had been present, and he probably was, informs us that the consecrating Prelates were Archbishop Sharp of St Andrews, Archbishop Fairfoull of Glasgow, and Bishop Hamilton of Galloway, and that they consecrated seven of their brethren on this occasion, viz. George Halyburton, Bishop of Dunkeld;* Murdoch Mackenzie, Bishop of Moray; David Strachan, Bishop of Brechin; John Paterson, Bishop of Ross; Patrick Forbes, Bishop of Caithness; David Fletcher, Bishop of Argyll; and Robert Wallace, Bishop of the Isles. According to Keith, however, this last mentioned Bishop was consecrated at St Andrews in January 1661–2. Nicoll says, that " eftir this consecratioun of seven Bischops, thair being three absent (and twa of thame af [out of] the kingdome), viz. the Bischop of Orknay, the Bischop of Edinburgh, and the Bischop of Abirdeene, they came not to Edinburgh till the 24th of May, and so thair consecratioun did continue till the first day of June thaireftir."† As to Bishop Sydserff of Orkney, there was no necessity for his attendance, and the two absent Bishops elect were Dr George Wishart, already mentioned as the Marquis of Montrose's chaplain, nominated to Edinburgh, and Dr David Mitchell, nominated to Aberdeen. There is no doubt that those two Prelates were consecrated on the 1st of June 1662, and it appears from Bishop Keith that it was done at St Andrews Both of them were in episcopal orders, for Bishop Mitchell, who had retired into England after the General Assembly of 1638, got a benefice, and was one of the Prebendaries of Westminster when he was created Doctor of Divinity at Oxford in 1661; and Bishop Wishart, who had been minister of North Leith before the Assembly of 1638, was presented to the rectory of Newcastle-upon-Tyne.

Nicoll's Account of the consecration in the Chapel-Royal of Holyrood

* This Bishop is prominently mentioned in some of the " Letters and Journals" of Principal Baillie of Glasgow, edited by David Laing, Esq., Librarian to the Writers to the Signet, Edinburgh, published in 1841, in two volumes large octavo, particularly vol. ii p. 47, 50.

† Nicoll's Diary, p. 336.

is interesting. "All the nobles, gentrie, and utheris that wer heir for the tyme, and the toun of Edinburgh, with thair Counsell and officeris in thair best apparell, wer reddie to contribute thair best endeavours for his Majestie's honor and respect to the Bischops. The church of Halyrudhous being prepared and maid redy for thair consecratioun, numbers of pepill wer convenit, bot nane enterit the church except such as had passportis. The two Archbischops went to the church in throw the Abbay, clothed in thair white surplices under thair black gownes, except thair sleves, which were of thin white of delicate cambric or lawn. All the inferior Bischops wer consecrat, nane absent except thrie, quha are to be heir with diligence. These that were consecratouris were the two Archbischops, and Mr James Hamilton, now Bishop of Galloway, quha ordered that business very handsumlie and decentlie. Befoir the consecratione thair wes a sermon maid be ane Mr James Gordoun, minister at Drumblade, in the North (Aberdeenshire), whose text wes the fourt chaptour of the Second Epistle to the Corinthianes, fyft vers; quhairin he actit his pairt very learnedlie, and held out the faltis of thair predecessouris that made thame to fall, desyring thame not to encroach upon the nobilitie, bot to keip thameselffis sober, and not to exceed the boundis of thair functioun—and much more to this purpois. The Archbischop of St Androis sat thair covered with his episcopall cap, or four-nukit bonnat. All that wes said by the Bischop at the consecratioun wes read of ane buik, and thair prayeris wer lykwyse read. The first prayer wes the Lordis Prayer, and sum schort prayer or exhortatioun eftir it; next wes the Belief, and sum lytill exhortatioun eftir it; thridlie, the Ten Commandis red, and eftir it sum few wordis of exhortatioun; much more to this purpose not necessar to be written." The Parliament met on the following day, when Bishop Hallyburton of Dunkeld preached a sermon, " quhilk," says Nicoll, " indured the space of two hours and moir." All the Bishops attended in their gowns as Peers, and " wer resavit with much honour, and placed according to thair severall degrees."

At the re-establishment of the Church no Liturgy was adopted, but our local chronicler supplies us with some information respecting the mode of conducting divine service, as authorised by Dr Wishart, Lord Bishop of Edinburgh, in that city and diocese. On the 10th of September 1662, the Privy Council, then sitting in the Palace of Holyroodhouse, passed an act "for halding of Diocesian Assemblies," which is printed by Wodrow.* It was proclaimed on the 13th, and with great state at Glasgow on the 1st of October by the Earl of Middleton, Lord High Commissioner to the Parliament, the Earl of Glencairn, Lord Chancellor, the Earl of Newburgh, Captain of the Life Guards, attended by numbers of the nobility and persons of distinction. "Eftir the publcatione of the foirsaid act of Councill," says Nicoll, "maid at Glasgow the 1st day of October 1662, thair wes a diocesiane meeting or assemblie haldin at Edinburgh by the Bischop of Edinburgh, and by his Dean and Chapter, upon the 14th day of the same moneth, quhairin these particulars following were actit: viz. first, thair wer appoynted by the Bischop two of every Presbyterie to prepare business for the Sinod, quhome he termed the bretherene of the Conference; nixt, it was enactit that thair sould be morning and evenyng prayeris in every burgh, and in everie uthir place quhair thair is ony confluence of pepill; item, that the Lordis Prayer sould be repeited once by the minister at every preaching, or twyse, as the minister pleased; item, that the Doxologie, or 'Glorie to the Father,' being a song composed and universallie sung in the Church when the Arianes and other sectis denyed the deitie of our Saviour, that the same be agane revived and sung, this being a tyme quhairin many sectareis deny the godhead of Christ; item, that the Belieff, or Apostles' Creed, be repeited at the sacrament of baptism by the father of the chyld, or by the minister at his discretione; item, that all the ministers of the diocese who did not conforme to the act of Councill above mentionat, haldin at Glasgow, repair to the same, and be indulged to cum in and accept of collatione from the Bischop betuix and the 25th day of November nixt to cum, utherwayis the Bishop is to proceid againis thame, and fill thair kirkis with other ministeris. To countenance this meeting, which consisted of fifty-eight ministeris, the King's Advocat, and my Lord Tarbet, ane of the Lordis of his Majestie's Counsell and Session, with the Provost and Bailleis of Edinburgh, were present. This meeting endit the morne thairoftir, and wes appoyntit to meet eftir Pascho (Easter) next. The Bischop of Edinburgh tacht that day. His text wes the fyft verse of the 4th chaptour to the Philippianes, in these wordis:—' Lat your moderation be knawn to all men; the Lord is at

* Vol. i. App p 69, 8vo edit. vol. i. p. 280.

hand.' But all this did not pleis the pepill, for thair wes much hatred of the Bischops among thame, favouring still thair awin ministeris and thair doctrine, and haiting Episcopacy."*

This hatred to the Church, which Nicoll and other contemporary writers, both Episcopal and Presbyterian, record, was only peculiarly violent in some districts, and was studiously fomented by the Covenanting preachers. Nor could it be otherwise, considering the dreadful convulsion which the country had so recently encountered, and which had been latterly kept in check only by the vigorous government of Cromwell, who during his domination never allowed the Presbyterian General Assemblies to meet, and his strong military forces were the best preservers of the public peace. The internal state of Scotland at the time is admirably delineated in a letter addressed to Mr William Cunningham, one of the Presbyterian ministers of Edinburgh, which appeared in one of the newspapers published in that city, in October 1839, from which the following is an extract. The letter, let it be observed, is written by a Presbyterian. "If, again, we turn to the golden age of the Kirk," from 1638 to 1649, and subsequently, "what do we find in the page of history? Under the banner of the Solemn League and Covenant, which you and your allies so often hail in strains of grandiloquence almost poetical, we find a barefaced and open usurpation of civil and political as well as spiritual authority—civil wars of the bloodiest description—intolerance unmitigated—persecution by *the Kirk* in its most aggravated forms, and the calamitous drama wound up by the entire subversion of the constitution, by the murder of the sovereign, the destruction of the peerage in England, and the national liberties and independence of Scotland trodden under foot by an usurper, brought into the bosom of their native land by the traitorous co-operation of the dominant *Kirk party* in Scotland. These were the undeniable results of a power in the Kirk, with revivals of which you and your compatriots would once more favour us." Such were some of the fruits of that dreadful convulsion fomented by the well-known Glasgow General Assembly of 1638, and the results of it were too recent to be eradicated in 1662 from the minds of an ignorant, opinionative, and obstinate peasantry, whose brains were constantly inflamed and agitated against the

* Nicoll's Diary, p 380, 381.

Episcopal Established Church by the falsest misrepresentations, the most unscrupulous assertions, and the most malignant hatred, of her preaching enemies.

As to the public feeling respecting the Church in the Highland counties, the following extract from a valuable work printed in 1842 will best elucidate the state of matters as operating among the Chiefs and their Clans. The Argyll here mentioned was Archibald eighth Earl and first Marquis of Argyll, the political rival of the Marquis of Montrose, who was beheaded for high treason at Edinburgh on the 27th of May 1661. What is said of the Clan Cameron is equally applicable to many other Clans in reference to their religious opinions. "That which engaged the Clan Cameron to Argyle was not any antipathy that they had to the Bishops or Service-Book, &c. more than their neighbours the Ardgylemen, being that most of the people in these places are barbarouse, or if they incline to anie profession it is mostlie to Poperie. But the Clan Cameron joyned with the Covenanters in opposition to Huntlye's familye, to whom most of them are vassalls in Lochaber, and had been several times before crubbed by the Earles of Huntly by force of arms, which made them now glad for to lay hòlde upon anye occasion of revenge. Besyde, this Argyle had ane eye to these places, either to weaken Huntly, as seeing much of his greatnesse did consist in his Highland following, or if he could get a pretext for to giipp to Huntly's Highland laundes himself, as afterward he did. But all such at that tyme were welcome to the Covenant; albeit afterward, about the time of Charles II. his incoming, anno 1650, they changed their principles, and Argylle was accessory to the purging as knowing and civill men out of the King's army as either the Argylle men or the Lochaber men were. Yet lett it be remembered that a part of the Clan Cameron at this tyme and long afterward owned the King's quarrell, for most of the Highlanders are inclyned, being left to themselves, to be Royalists, happy, at least, though they have little learning, that they have not learned to distinguish themselves out of their loyalty by notions unknown till the latter ages."*

Our local diarist Nicoll supplies us with several curious information respecting the state of the Church in 1662. "The indulgency given

---

* Memoirs of Lochiell, Notes and Illustrations, 4to, p. 313, printed in 1842 for the Maitland, and other Clubs.

by the Bischop of Edinburgh to the ministrie of his diocese did move many of thame to cum in, and to accept collatioun from him before the day appoynted, and to submit thameselffis to the prelaticall ordouris. The instabilitie of the church government for many yeiris bygane hes bene observit in severall of my paperis, and among utheris how that the reiding of Scriptures by reidars and singing of Psalms did ceis, and in place thairof the examining brocht into the Church by two boyes, and thaireftir lectures by ministers, which did not satisfy the pepill; quhairfoir the singing of Psalms wes brought in agane in the kirkis of Edinburgh in the beginning of October 1653; and now this yeir, 1662, the reiding of Scriptures wes of new brocht in agane, and the Psalmes sung, with this additioun, 'Glorie to the Father, to the Son, and to the Holy Ghost.' This now brocht in by autoritie of the bischops with greater devotioun than ever befoir, for all the pepill rais at the singing, 'Glorie to the Father,' &c."* These decent and becoming observances in public worship were bitterly assailed by the Presbyterian preachers as superstitious and unscriptural, and it is not a little remarkable that in many parts of Scotland the people, especially those of them who are Presbyterian Dissenters, dislike and object to the reading of the Scriptures by their teachers in the public congregation. "While fanaticism prevailed in Scotland," says Mr Charles Kirkpatrick Sharpe, "it was customary to give free vent to all the pious feelings, and to practise every grimace of hypocrisy, during the celebration of divine service:— '12th October, 1650. In Edinburgh and other places the Scots came to hear our ministers, and they made such a groaning noyse in the time of prayers as I never saw, as if they were extraordinarly affected therewith, but it seems it is the custom of the people here to do soe, by a form and custom that they have used.'"† Yet the reflecting classes were rapidly beginning to subside in their opposition to the Church, as may be inferred from the following flaming expostulation by the noted Alexander Peden, in a sermon preached by him at Glenluce:—" Ye were all perjured in the beginning in complying with Prelacy, and hearing these cursed curates, after ye had covenanted and sworn to God,

---

* Nicoll's Diary, p. 381, 382. † Letter from an Englishman at Edinburgh printed in the Diurnal Note, *apud* Mr Charles Kirkpatrick Sharpe's edition of Kirkton's History of the Church of Scotland, p 150, 151.

and engaged yourselves in that covenanted work of Reformation; and as long as ye mourn not for *that sin* as much as for *whoredom, adulterie, murder, or stealing,* the gospel will never do you good." This man Peden was held in great repute among his party as a kind of prophet. Even Kirkton, when recording that of the 900 ministers in Scotland, by the Act of Uniformity 300 were turned out and became field preachers, *hill men,* or *wild men,* as they were called, states, after praising their conduct—" Yet such was the weakness of the people that many of them began to censure what they had formerly approven, and the ministers' bitter suffering turned with some rather into offence than ane edifying example. Such was the cloud upon us at that time, ignorance, scrupulosity, and censure, being frequently conjoyned in our sad experience."*
He refers in this passage to the year 1662.

Nicoll farther records—" The Bischops became indulgent to the ministeris that refuised to take thair ordouris, and gave mony of thame libertie to preache openlie till the [first] day of Februar nixt 1663. But this licenso and libertie were refuised to such as wer panellit [under legal or criminal prosecution], and to such quhais kirkis were provydit to uther ministeris during their disobedience.''

It may probably be supposed, that the Bishops immediately consecrated by Archbishop Sharp and his colleagues were induced to conform to the Church on account of the temporalities they would derive from their respective Sees. The very reverse was the case. Those revenues were greatly inferior to the incomes of the Roman Catholic Bishops before the Reformation. It is appropriately observed by a well known local writer, that " the episcopal dignitaries in 1572, down to the Revolution, hardly enjoyed that rank or influence which their brethren in England possessed; for on the one hand they were narrowly watched, and their conduct strictly scrutinized, by the Covenanting Presbyterians, while the ambitious nobility made an undue use of them, by stripping the Church of its revenues, that they might apply the greater part to their own use, under the colour of law." † But statistical facts are of more importance on this subject than mere opinions, and some idea may be formed of the episcopal revenues of the Scottish Church, from the Restoration to the Revolution, by the following table, as accounted

* Kirkton's History of the Church of Scotland, p. 152. † Dr Cleland's Annals of Glasgow, vol. i. p 121.

for by the Receiver-General of Bishops' rents in the Scottish Exchequer. The reader will observe that the gross sums are those of 1831, and include the revenues in money Scots, and what was paid to the Archbishops and Bishops in produce, such as wheat, barley, oats, pease, &c. The sums are in money sterling.

Archbishopric of St Andrews,	L.1544 6 1
Bishopric of Edinburgh,	93 6 10
Bishopric of Moray,	198 8 1
Bishopric of Brechin,	76 6 11
Bishopric of Aberdeen,	288 10 11
Bishopric of Dunkeld,	152 8 8
Bishopric of Dunblane,	43 19 1
Bishopric of Caithness,	547 4 10
Bishopric of Ross,	452 0 7
Bishopric of Orkney,	1366 2 8
Archbishopric of Glasgow,	1294 5 7
Bishopric of Galloway,	228 12 0
Bishopric of Argyll, Bishopric of the Isles,	140 0 0

It thus appears that the love of money could not be the inducement of the Bishops of Scotland after the Restoration to conform to the Church, the greater part of the immense property of which had been seized by the rapacious nobility at the Reformation. Even Kirkton notices Bishop Leighton favourably when he accepted the nomination to Dunblane:—"Thus," he says, "he choised to demonstrate to the world avarice was not his principle, it being the *smallest revenue ;*" and certainly a bishopric, the income of which was only L.43, 19s. 1d., was as limited a revenue as the fiercest Covenanter could have wished to be awarded. He farther observes—" Mr David Strachan was made *poor* Bishop of Brechin," and poor it was with its income of L 76, 6s 11d. So poor was this See that Bishop Laurie, one of his successors, retained his incumbency, or, as Keith expresses it, he " continued to exercise a particular ministry," of Trinity College Church in Edinburgh, with the Deanery of that Diocese. Bishop Fletcher of Argyll retained his parish of Melrose for the same reason, the revenues both of that See and of the Isles having been appropriated by the Earls of Argyll to their own use at the Reformation. It is admitted by a Presbyterian writer, that " the remnant of the Popish Church estates which descended to the

Reformed Episcopal Church appears to have been *very inconsiderable indeed;* and if we take the present computed estimate of their annual value, the whole Episcopal Hierarchy of Scotland seem to have subsisted on what is now reckoned insufficient for a single Prelate in England or Ireland. But we strongly suspect that this limited patrimony, independently of avowed appropriations to secular as well as sacred purposes, has been much dilapidated by modern encroachments." It is certainly almost incredible that the Bishops of Edinburgh, from the Restoration to the Revolution, should have had no greater revenue from the See than L.93, and those of Brechin and Dunblane respectively L.76 and L.43; yet these are the total amounts of the several revenues of the Sees now mentioned as having passed to the Crown at the Revolution, and as they are now set down in the reports of the Scottish Exchequer, when the management was transferred to the Board of Woods and Forests in 1832. It is also surprising that the revenues of the Bishops of Dunkeld, Argyll, and the Isles, should have dwindled to the paltry sums, in the case of Dunkeld, of L.152, 8s. 8d., and in the case of the two others to about L.120 conjointly. The same remark applies to the two Archbishoprics and the other Sees, for it is at present inexplicable that benefices of such dignity and importance, the revenues of which were for the most part paid in produce, and not much liable to permanent depreciation, should have sunk so low. It is officially admitted, that " upon the abolition of Episcopacy, when the Bishops' rents came into the possession of the Crown, the rentals thereof delivered over to the officers of the Crown were very inaccurate and defective, and it was found impossible to discover the persons or lands liable in payment of many of the duties contained in them."* It is therefore clear that no serious attempt has ever been made by the competent authorities to investigate the condition of the Church estates in Scotland, since they passed from the possession of the Bishops in 1689, and that considerable dilapidations have taken place in consequence of careless superintendence. Of this latter fact there are several strong proofs. The clear rental of the Bishopric of Galloway at the Revolution amounted to L.5634, 15s. Scots, a sum only exceeded by the revenues of the two Archbishops; and the rental of the Bishopric of Moray is L.2307, 9s. 4d. Scots, as it

* Report of the General Collector of Bishops' Rents in Scotland, in Eleventh Report of the Board of Woods and Forests, dated 29th July 1834.

now stands in the Collector's books, but at the Revolution it was about L.6000 Scots, or L 500 sterling. In this latter diocese, as was probably the case in the others, the temporalities were granted by King William's Government to noblemen and gentlemen of the district, and the superiorities are still paid to the crown.

The ancient Court of Exchequer in Scotland, the officers of which collected the royal revenues, passed crown gifts, and discharged other important duties, and the judges of which decided in all cases connected with those revenues, was remodelled, or rather refounded, after the Union. Those judges might be either English or Scottish lawyers, but they were enjoined to decide according to the English forms.. In this Court was the officer called the *Receiver-General of Bishops' Rents,* who was discontinued in 1834, though the rents are still collected by authority of the Court. The *Court of Teinds,* or of *Tithes,* originated in episcopal times, namely, in 1617, 1633, and 1661, when commissions were appointed for "planting" churches and "modifying" stipends to the parochial clergy. The members of those commissions, with which the Bishops were always connected, could erect new churches, regulate stipends, unite small churches, divide parishes, remove churches to more convenient parts of the parishes, and value and sell tithes. After the establishment of Presbyterianism a commission was named in 1693; but in 1707 all the powers of those commissions were transferred to the Judges of the Supreme Court in Scotland, whose proceedings are subject to the review of the House of Lords.

With whomsoever the fault may be respecting the dilapidation of the Church revenues in Scotland, nothing dishonourable or selfish can be charged, or has ever been insinuated, against the Archbishops and Bishops at the Revolution It is subsequently narrated that those upright and conscientious Prelates were summarily compelled to quit their Sees, and their revenues were held to have devolved to the Crown *jure coronæ,* though those revenues were never annexed to the Crown by any special parliamentary statute, with the exception, probably, of the act passed in 1690, "anent the superiority of lands and others which formerly held of Prelates or Bishops and their Chapters, to be now held of the King and Queen."* Small pensions were allowed by the new sovereign and

* Acta Parliamentorum Scotorum, vol. ix. p. 199.

government to the ejected Bishops during their lives, which is another proof that they were not parties to any act of dilapidation or private appropriation. The disestablishment of the Episcopal Church, therefore, was of no pecuniary advantage to the Scottish people; and those who think proper to compliment the Presbyterians for overthrowing what they ignorantly call an expensive Hierarchy have evidently never studied the matter, or inquired into the facts, which are proved by official and parliamentary documents of undoubted authenticity. The most active and bitter opponents of the Church never clamoured about the Bishops possessing wealthy revenues. The Crown assumed them when the Church was disestablished, and continues to the present time to levy the episcopal revenues in the same manner as if there was a Bishop recognized by law in every See in Scotland. The only exceptions to this actual state of affairs are the Bishoprics of Argyle and of the Isles. It appears that by gift from Queen Anne, dated July 14, 1705, the rents and revenues of these Bishoprics, amounting conjointly to about L.140, are granted during pleasure, or until the same shall be recalled by any of her Majesty's royal successors, to the Moderator and Provincial Synod of Argyll in the Presbyterian Establishment, in trust, to be by them applied for instituting schools, repairing churches, educating and training ministers, and other ends and uses. These rents are collected by a person appointed by the Synod, and are appropriated to the purposes mentioned in the grant.

If Scotland has gained nothing in a pecuniary point of view by the deposition of the Bishops at the Revolution, no alteration has been made by the Presbyterian parochial ministers. The present incumbents are paid their stipends in the same manner as were their canonically ordained predecessors of the Episcopal Church, from the tithes, or teinds, as they are called, and the landed proprietors and heritors are legally-obliged to defray all the public burdens of their respective parishes.

It is not within the scope of the present volume to glance at the troubles and contentions in Scotland from the Restoration to the Revolution. It is sufficient to state that during the establishment of the Church the kingdom was ecclesiastically divided into two Archiepiscopal Provinces. In the Metropolitan Province of ST ANDREWS were the suffragan Bishoprics of Edinburgh, Aberdeen, Brechin, Caithness,

Dunkeld, Dunblane, Moray, Orkney, and Ross. In the Province of GLASGOW were the suffragan Bishoprics of Galloway, Argyll, and the Isles.

The industry of Bishop Keith has preserved a few notices of the Bishops who occupied the Sees of the Scottish Church at the Revolution. His mode of classification is followed in the subsequent "catalogue." A few additional particulars are collected from various sources

The Archbishop of ST ANDREWS at the Revolution was the Most Reverend Arthur Ross, the son of a clergyman in the Diocese of Aberdeen. When "Parson" of Glasgow he was promoted to the See of Argyll, at the death of Bishop William Scroggie in 1675, to which he was consecrated at Edinburgh in the month of May, with Bishop Paterson for Galloway, by Archbishop Leighton of Glasgow, Bishop Young of Edinburgh, and another Bishop whose name is not mentioned,[*] from which he was translated to the Archbishopric of Glasgow in 1679, and to the Primacy of St Andrews, by royal letters patent, in October 1684. He died in 1704, and was probably interred in the church-yard of Restalrig, near Leith, for a monumental inscription in the Canongate burying-ground, Edinburgh, records that his tomb or family vault is in that cemetery His daughter Anne married, in 1687, John fourth Lord Balmerino, and was the mother of Arthur sixth Lord, beheaded on Tower-Hill in 1746 with the Earl of Kilmarnock, for being concerned in the Enterprise of Prince Charles Edward.

The Right Rev. Alexander Rose, Bishop of Moray in 1687, was translated that year to Edinburgh. This Prelate, whose name is invested with a peculiar interest in the Church, as the longest survivor of the ejected Bishops, was of an ancient family in the North of Scotland. He took his degree of Master of Arts at King's College, Aberdeen, and studied theology at Glasgow under Dr Gilbert Burnet, afterwards Bishop of Salisbury. His first preferment was to be minister of Perth, and he was afterwards appointed Professor of Divinity in the University of Glasgow. In 1684 he was nominated by the Crown to be Principal of St Mary's College, St Andrews, and the royal warrant for his consecration to the See of Moray was dated the 8th of March 1687, from

---

[*] Law's Memorialls, 4to, 1818, p. 77.

which he was translated to Edinburgh "before," says Bishop Keith, "he had taken personal possession of this See of Moray." In 1684 Bishop Rose published a very eloquent and learned discourse, entitled, "A Sermon preached before the Right Honourable the Lords Commissioners of His Majesty's Most Honourable Privy Council at Glasgow,"* and is dedicated to the Duke of Hamilton, Lord Lundin, Secretary of State, and Lord Collinton, Lord Justice-Clerk. The discourse is founded on Acts xxvi. 28 —"Almost thou persuadest me to be a Christian." It comprises four heads :— " 1. The different parties of our divided Zion. 2. The malignancy of the national sin of schism. 3. The necessity of Episcopacy for supporting the prime concernments of Christianity 4. A brief application." This sermon proves Bishop Rose to have been a man of profound learning.

The Right Reverend John Hamilton, Bishop of Dunkeld, was a son of John Hamilton of Blair, and of his wife, the Honourable Barbara Elphinstone (called Mary in the Peerage Lists), second daughter of James first Lord Balmerino. The father of this Prelate, according to Bishop Keith, was a descendant of John Hamilton, last Roman Catholic Archbishop of St Andrews, who obtained an act of legitimation from the Scottish Parliament in favour of his children, from which it appears that, like his predecessor Cardinal Beaton, he did not practise a life of continency. Bishop Hamilton was either nominated or consecrated to the See of Dunkeld on the 19th of October 1686.

The See of Aberdeen was filled by Dr George Hallyburton, descended from a collateral branch of the ancient family of Hallyburton of Pitcur in Forfarshire. His first preferment was the parish of Cupar-Angus in that county, and he was consecrated Bishop of Brechin in 1678. In this See he continued till his translation to Aberdeen in 1682. While Bishop of Brechin he was Provost of that city in 1678, and is often subsequently mentioned in the burgh records as sitting in the Town Council when any public business of importance was to be transacted. "Bishop Hallyburton's attention to civil matters," says a local writer, "does not appear to have interrupted the proper discharge of his ecclesiastical duties, for he often presided at meetings of session, frequently preached

* This very scarce production is in a volume of pamphlets in the Advocates' Library, Edinburgh, marked FF. 7. 10, in small 4to

during week days, and was always present at Christmas, although, as we believe, he did not generally reside in Brechin."*

The Bishop of Moray at the Revolution was Dr William Hay, who was born in 1647, educated at King's College, Aberdeen, in which city he was admitted into holy orders by Patrick Scougall, Bishop of the Diocese from 1664 to 1682, and whose character is finely delineated in the Preface to the Life of Bishop Bedell. Bishop Hay was at first incumbent of Kilconquhar in Fife, from which he was removed to Perth, where he was at the time of the warrant for his consecration, which Bishop Keith says was dated the 4th of February 1688, the very year of the Revolution. He was consecrated at St Andrews on the 11th of March. In the old church-yard of Inverness a monument was erected to his memory, with an inscription in elegant Latin to the following effect —" Sacred to the Memory of the Right Reverend Father in God, William Hay, Professor of Theology, a most deserving Bishop of Moray—a Prelate of primitive holiness and great eloquence, at all times a constant maintainer of the Church and regal dignity, as well in their afflicted as in their flourishing condition. He adorned the episcopal mitre by his piety, and honoured the same by the integrity of his life and affable behaviour Exhausted by study and a twenty years' palsy, a most blessed end followed his upright life. John Cuthbert, his son-in-law, erected this homely monument."

The Bishop of Brechin was the Right Rev. James Drummond, son of the Rev. James Drummond, minister of Foulis in Perthshire. This Bishop was successively incumbent of Auchterarder and Muthill in the same county. He was consecrated on Christmas Day 1684, in the Chapel-Royal of Holyroodhouse He was a near relative of the Earl of Perth, who was a zealous Roman Catholic nobleman, but " the Bishop is reported to have been a man of strict Protestant principles, and a decided opponent of King James' interference with the Church, although he, like most of his brethren, was a keen supporter of hereditary monarchy, and took a decided part with King James when most of his courtiers deserted him. Bishop Drummond preached in Brechin for the last time on Sunday, 18th April 1689, on the occasion of the administration of the holy sacrament of the Lord's Supper. His text was taken from the 12th chapter, first verse, of St Paul's Epistle to the Ro-

* History of Brechin, by David D. Black, Town Clerk, 1839, p 86.

mans, a text which does not imply that he thought this sermon was the last which would be delivered by a Bishop in the Cathedral Church of Brechin."* He was Provost of Brechin in 1685, when he was present in the Town Council on the 25th of September, and preached in the Cathedral on the 1st of October. He succeeded Dr Alexander Cairncross, translated to the Archbishopric of Glasgow, who, after the Revolution, became Bishop of Raphoe in Ireland.

Dr Robert Douglas filled the ancient and venerable See of Dunblane. He was the grandson of Sir Archibald Douglas of Glenbervie. His first promotion was the benefice of Laurencekirk in Kincardineshire, to which he was appointed during the existence of the so called Commonwealth. After the Restoration he was presented by Charles II. to the parish of Bothwell in Lanarkshire, and thence he was removed to the small royal burgh of Renfrew, in the county of that name. He was next translated, on the presentation of his near relative the Duke of Hamilton, to the parsonage of Hamilton, which included the Deanery of Glasgow; and he was soon afterwards nominated and consecrated Bishop of Dunblane. A son of this prelate, the Rev. Robert Douglas, minister of Bothwell, was also deprived of his benefice at the Revolution.

The See of Ross was filled by the Right Rev. James Ramsay, son of the Rev. Robert Ramsay, minister of Dundonald in Ayrshire, and afterwards Principal of the University of Glasgow. His first preferment was the parish of Kirkintilloch in the county of Dunbarton, from which he was removed to Linlithgow. He next received the Deanery of Glasgow, to which the parsonage of Hamilton was annexed, and in this preferment he was consequently the predecessor of Bishop Douglas. When Bishop Leighton was translated to the Archbishopric of Glasgow, Mr Ramsay was consecrated his successor, and in May 1684 he was removed from that See to the Diocese of Ross.

The Bishop of Caithness was the Right Rev. Andrew Wood, son of the Rev. Andrew Wood. His mother was a sister of the celebrated John Guthrie of Guthrie, Bishop of Moray in the reign of Charles I., who had the courage to defy the excommunication issued against him by the Presbyterian General Assembly held at Glasgow in 1638, for

---

* History of Brechin, by David D. Black, p. 97, 98.

having "in the year 1633 preached in a surplice before His Majesty King Charles I. in the High Church of Edinburgh, to the great scandal of the *zealous* people there." Bishop Wood's first change was the parish of Spott, from which he was removed to Dunbar, both in the county of Haddington, and while incumbent of the latter he was consecrated Bishop of the Isles in 1678, from which he was translated to the See of Caithness in 1680. In this See he was at the Revolution.

The See of Orkney was filled by the Right Rev. Andrew Bruce, whose father held the honourable office of Commissary of St Andrews, and who had previously been Archdeacon of that metropolitan diocese. He was consecrated Bishop of Dunkeld in 1679, and he sat in this See till the year 1681. Bishop Keith makes the following observations respecting this prelate, which are particularly worthy of notice, because they disclose the principles by which the Scottish Bishops were guided at this memorable era. "He was deprived by the Court for showing his dislike to the design of repealing the laws against Popery; yet the King [James II.] perceiving the disagreeableness of such proceedings, did recommend him to the See of Orkney upon the death of the preceding Bishop.* The King's *conge d'elire* and recommendation both bear date the 4th of May 1688; but the Revolution coming quickly to take place, he was deprived with the rest of his order."†

We now come to the Archiepiscopal See of Glasgow, which was filled by the Most Rev. John Paterson, formerly Dean of Edinburgh, and successively Bishop of Galloway and of Edinburgh. He was consecrated to the former See in May 1675, at Edinburgh, along with Archbishop Ross, by Archbishop Leighton of Glasgow, Bishop Young of Edinburgh, and another Bishop whose name is not given. He succeeded Archbishop Cairncross, who, in 1686, having "incurred the displeasure of the Lord Chancellor, the Earl of Perth (and deservedly, too, if all be true

---

* The Right Rev. Murdoch Mackenzie, descended from the Mackenzies of Gairloch, and a cadet of the Noble Family of Seaforth. This venerable prelate died in about the hundredth year of his age, yet "in the perfect use of all his faculties until the very last," in the month of February 1688. He was spared the grief of seeing the Church of which he was once a governor overthrown by political intrigue and noisy fanaticism.

† Keith's Catalogue.

which Dr James Canaries, minister at Selkirk, relates*), the King sent a letter to the Privy Council, removing him from the Archbishopric of Glasgow, of the date January 13, 1687—a very irregular step surely. The King should have taken a more canonical course.'' The Bishop might have added that this was one of the many proceedings of James II. which alienated the English nation from him, and brought about the Revolution. Archbishop Paterson was translated to the See of Glasgow in January 1687.

Dr John Gordon, called by the King in the charter of nomination under the Great Seal, dated February 4, and sealed September 4, 1688, " Doctorem Theologiæ Joannem Gordon, nostrum capellanum apud New York, in America," was consecrated Bishop of Galloway at Glasgow. He had done little more than taken possession of the See when the Revolution happened, and he followed King James first into Ireland, during the attempt to recover that kingdom, and then into France. He resided at St Germains, with the unfortunate sovereign's little court, and performed divine service to such of the exiles as were members of the Church, though one account alleges that he became a Roman Catholic. Bishop Gordon does not appear to have returned to Scotland.

The See of Argyle was vacant in consequence of the death of Bishop Hector Maclean, in 1687. A conge d'elire was issued in favour of Dr Alexander Monro, Principal of the University of Edinburgh, directed to the Dean and Chapter of the Diocese, dated 24th October 1688. It does not appear that this learned clergyman, who was one of the most distinguished men of his time, was consecrated. He was deprived of his office in the University for not conforming to King William's government, and was succeeded by the famous Dr William Carstairs, a great leader of the Presbyterian party. Dr Monro is more particularly noticed in the sequel.

---

* This parenthetical statement of Bishop Keith must be received with great caution. Archbishop Cairncross accepted the Bishopric of Raphoe in Ireland from King William, which gave great offence to the Scottish Bishops and clergy. Keith says, that " he lived privately until the Revolution in 1688, after which period he was taken notice of by the new powers, who, finding him not altogether averse to make compliance with them, he was made Bishop of Raphoe the 16th May 1693, and in that See he continued till his death, anno 1701."

The remote See of the Isles was filled at the period of the Revolution by the Right Rev. Archibald Graham, of the family of Graham of Kilbride, who had been minister at Rothsay in Bute. He was promoted to the See in 1680. This prelate had sufficient interest with King William's Government, or probably his claim was irresistible, to obtain an act of Parliament in 1695, ordaining that "military assistance shall be given to the said Archibald, *late* Bishop of the Isles, and John Graham of Dougalston, or their factors," to recover certain rents indebted to him by the tenants.*

It will thus be seen from the preceding narrative that the Scottish Bishops at the time of the Revolution were men of the highest respectability, and some of them connected with ancient and distinguished families. Among the inferior clergy were many persons of great talent and erudition, some of whom subsequently became prominent in the defence of the Church, when it was left to the voluntary support of its members, and encountered the ordeal of persecution. Those clergy were the parochial ministers, commonly termed *curates* by the Presbyterians, by way of reproach, though there is neither sarcasm nor wit apparent in such an application of the word. In every field harangue delivered by the Covenanting preachers, the Bishops and clergy were often assailed in the most scurrilous language, their conduct studiously misrepresented, and unscrupulously accused of every species of crime To such an extent was the ignorant credulity and superstition of the peasantry influenced by the Covenanting preachers in the rural and remote districts, that the Bishops were actually believed to be cloven-footed, and had no shadows, and many of the *curates*, if we are to credit Kirkton and others of his enthusiastic persuasion, were little better than wizards—an accusation, however, which the clergy occasionally retorted on their maligners. It is appropriately stated that "at this period the Royalists were believed by the adverse party to be as much devoted to Satan as to King Charles II.; that the military officers who were employed to pursue the Whigs (Covenanters) into their lurking places wore coats of proof, and bestrode horses that could clamber among rocks like foxes; and that the justices of peace commissioned to try the fugitives were seen familiarly conversing with the foul fiend."†

* Acta Parl. Scot vol. ix. p. 448.
† Prefatory Notice to Law's Memorialls, p. lxxix.

These absurdities were religiously propagated by the field preachers, and readily credited as undoubted facts.

Nevertheless, after the accession of James II. indications of repose were apparent even in the Western counties, and if the rude peasantry had not been kept in an incessant state of religious excitement by noisy enthusiasts, who continually appealed to their passions by perverted applications of passages and events in the Old Testament, the Church would not have been the object of their dislike. "The system pursued at the time," says one of the distinguished ornaments of the Church, "in the disaffected districts of Scotland, for putting down the rebellious fanatics who broke the peace and set the Government at defiance, has afforded much occasion for sincere regret, as well as for party invective and theological recrimination; and it is readily admitted that there could be little Christian charity, and still less political wisdom, in the kingdom, when it became necessary, or was thought expedient, to dragoon fanatical peasants into sound opinion or ecclesiastical subordination. But this admission, it is clear, amounts to nothing more than the acknowledgment that men do not act upon principles which they refuse to receive, while, to form a correct estimate of the line of policy actually adopted, it would be necessary to weigh well the probable effects of any other that might have been recommended in its place. The men who fought at the Pentland Hills and Bothwell Bridge were not only open rebels, banded against the civil government of the country, and against a Church not only established by law, but preferred by a large majority of the kingdom; they were, moreover, in arms against religious toleration and liberty of conscience, determined not to accept these privileges in their own case, and far less to grant them to others."

CHAPTER II

GENERAL VIEW OF THE STATE OF SCOTLAND AND OF THE CHURCH AT THE REVOLUTION.

The Revolution of 1688 had been planned by the Prince of Orange a considerable time previous to its actual occurrence. A powerful party considered him as the protector of their liberties, many of the highest persons in the kingdom corresponded with him, and he only waited for a favourable opportunity to invade England. He sent Dykvelt as envoy to look after his interests, and to assure the people, that though he refused to be a party to the Indulgence granted by the King his father-in-law, he was himself quite willing to be the author of one which would satisfy all denominations except the Roman Catholics. All this was well known in England except to the unfortunate monarch whom it most concerned; but it was different in Scotland, where the people heard of the landing of the Prince of Orange, his assumption of the government, and the flight of the King, with surprise and not a little consternation.

The Scottish Bishops appear to have been aware of the meditated invasion of the Prince of Orange only in October 1688, and as a number of them were in Edinburgh at that time they drew up a loyal address, which they transmitted to the King. This we learn from a letter of Dr Rose, Bishop of Edinburgh, to the Hon. and Right Rev. Archibald Campbell, written on the 22d of October 1713, the "original holograph" of which Bishop Keith says he possessed. An answer was returned, dated Whitehall, 15th November, after the Prince of Orange had been ten days in England. When the Scottish Bishops knew that the Prince had landed, they resolved to send two of their number to

London, with a renewal of their allegiance to James, and to wait on the English Bishops "for advice and assistance," says Bishop Rose, "in case that any unlucky thing might possibly happen to occur with respect to the Church." This was communicated to the Privy Council, and the Earl of Perth, Lord Chancellor, officially announced that it met with the approbation of their Lordships. At the next meeting of the Bishops, Dr Rose of Edinburgh and Dr Bruce of Orkney were delegated to proceed to London. It was thought that these two Bishops would be more acceptable to their Anglican brethren, as they were unconnected with the sanction given by the Bishops of the Scottish Church to the toleration granted by the King to the Roman Catholics, which had given great offence at the time in England generally, whereas Bishop Bruce had so strongly opposed it as to draw upon himself the severe displeasure of James, "and I," says Dr Rose, "not concerned, as not being a bishop at that time."

In conformity to this resolution, sanctioned and approved by the Privy Council, a commission was signed by the Archbishops and Bishops on the 3d of December 1688, authorising the Bishops of Edinburgh and Orkney to proceed to London. Some business called the latter prelate to the country, but he promised to return in a few days, that he and Bishop Rose might travel together. It happened, however, that when the Bishop of Orkney was to join the Bishop of Edinburgh in that city he was suddenly taken ill, and he was therefore under the necessity of intimating to Dr Rose that the state of his health would not permit him to join him, and urged him to set out by himself, promising to join him as soon as he was able.

The Bishop of Edinburgh proceeded to London, and a journey to the British metropolis from Edinburgh in those days was a very different affair from what it is at the present time. His Lordship was some days on the road before he came to Northallerton, and there he first heard of the important political movements, the assumption of the government by the Prince of Orange amid the acclamations of the great majority of the English nation, and the flight of James from Rochester. This induced Bishop Rose to hesitate whether he ought to go forward or return: "But," he says, "considering the various and contradictory accounts I had got all along the road, and that, in case of the King's retirement, matters would be so much more dark and perplexed, I resolved to go on, that I might be able to give just accounts of things to my brethren here [in Scotland] from time to time, and have the advice of the English Bishops, *whom I never doubted to find unalterably firm to their master's interest.*"

In this expectation Bishop Rose was disappointed. Seven, including the Primate—the illustrious and celebrated Seven Bishops—remained "unalterably firm" to the interests of the unfortunate and infatuated sovereign, but the Church of England conformed to the Revolution, acknowledged William and Mary as the lawful sovereigns, and the refractory Bishops were deprived. Bishop Rose arrived in London, and found a very different order of government from what he expected. On the day after his arrival his Lordship waited on Archbishop Sancroft, with whom, he says, he had been personally acquainted a few years before. He presented his commission to the Primate, and explained the circumstances which had prevented the Bishop of Orkney from accompanying him. The Archbishop, having read the document, told his Lordship, in the most desponding manner, that "matters were very dark, and the cloud so thick or gross that they could not see through it; and that they [the English Bishops] knew not well what to do for themselves, far less what advice to give to others." His Grace farther informed Bishop Rose that there was to be a meeting of the Bishops with him that very day, and the interview terminated by his Grace desiring his Lordship to see him during the following week.

Bishop Rose next waited on the celebrated Dr Stillingfleet, Bishop of St Asaph, with whom he was also personally acquainted. His Lordship does not narrate the conversation, but from what he states the nature of it may be easily inferred. "I could not," says his Lordship, "but see through his inclinations, wherefore I resolved to visit him no more, nor to address myself to any others of that order [or party], till I should have occasion to learn something about them." At the time appointed the Bishop of Edinburgh again waited on the Primate at Lambeth Palace, and told his Grace what had passed between him and the Bishop of St Asaph. "The Archbishop," says his Lordship, "smiling, told me that St Asaph was a good man, but an angry man; and withal told me that matters still continued very dark, and that it behoved me to wait the issue of their convention, which he expected was only that which would give light to the scene; and withal desired me to come to him from time to time, and if any thing occurred he would signify it unto me."

At this critical season, "wearisome to me," says Bishop Rose, "because acquainted with few, save those of our own countrymen, and of those I knew not whom to trust," his Lordship waited on Dr Compton, Bishop of London, and requested that Prelate to use his influence with the Prince of Orange to protect the Episcopal clergy in Scotland. The Bishop of London refused to interfere, as did also Dr Burnet, afterwards Bishop of Salisbury, who, though at one time an incumbent of the Church in his native country, coolly told Bishop Rose that he "did not meddle in Scots affairs." The Bishop of London, although he either would not or could not render the Bishop of Edinburgh any assistance, advised his Lordship to wait upon the Prince, and present his Royal Highness with an address respecting the treatment of the clergy in Scotland. This suggestion was eagerly recommended by several Scottish peers. "I asked," says the Bishop, "whether I or my address would readily meet with acceptance or success, if it did not compliment the Prince upon his descent to deliver us from Popery and slavery? They said that it was absolutely necessary. I told them that I neither was instructed by my constituents to do so, neither had I myself clearness to do it, and that in these terms I neither could nor would visit or address his Highness."

The Bishop during his stay in London had repeated interviews with the Archbishop of Canterbury, and Dr Turner, Bishop of Ely, who received him kindly, and as they were about to be sufferers in the same cause with himself and his Scottish brethren, the friendship would be peculiarly intimate. At length the vote of abdication in reference to James II. was passed, and on that day Bishop Rose, who saw at once the probable fate of the Scottish Church as the national establishment, went to Lambeth. His Lordship tells Bishop Campbell that, as his interview with the Primate was strictly private, he does not feel himself at liberty to narrate the conversation. He intimated to his Grace that he was preparing to return to Scotland, and that he would wait upon him once more before he left London.

The Prince of Orange had already accepted the crown conjunctly with his consort, and proclamations were issued enjoining obedience to King William and Queen Mary, releasing the people from their allegiance to King James, and threatening all who resisted the authority of the new sovereigns. But these are matters on which we shall not dwell at present. While making his farewell visits to his countrymen and friends in London, the Bishop of Edinburgh was informed that some Scottish noblemen and gentlemen who had set out to their own country had been stopped at the first stage, and that no one could procure a pass until he waited on the King. His Lordship immediately repaired to the Archbishop at Lambeth Palace, and his Grace agreed that it would be proper to wait on the King, or the *Prince*, as he studiously calls William III. He applied to the Bishop of London to introduce him. Dr Compton asked his Lordship if he had any thing to say to the *King*. " I replied," says the Bishop, " that I had nothing to say, save that I was going to Scotland, being a member of the Convention; for I understood that without waiting on the *Prince* (that being the most common Scots style), I could not have a pass, and that without that I must needs be stopped upon the road, as several of my countrymen had been. His Lordship asked me again, saying, ' Seeing your clergy have been so routed and barbarously treated by the Presbyterians, will you not speak to the King to put a stop to that, and in favour of your own clergy ?' My reply was, that the Prince had been often applied to in that matter by several of our nobility, and addressed also by the sufferers themselves, and yet all to no purpose ; wherefore, I could have no hopes that my intercessions would be of any avail ; but that if his Lordship thought otherwise, I would not decline to make them His Lordship asked me farther, whether any of our countrymen would go along with me, and he spoke particularly of Sir George Mackenzie. I replied, that I doubted nothing of that ; whereupon his Lordship bid me find him out, and that both he and I should be at Court that day against three in the afternoon, and he should surely be there to introduce us."

The Bishop easily found Sir George Mackenzie, who liked the proposed audience with the King, but suggested to his Lordship the expediency of having some of the Scottish nobility present on the occasion. To this the Bishop replied, that he much doubted whether they would be admitted if they came in a body, and that they would be greatly offended if they were denied access, when they came upon his and Sir George's invitation merely. But his Lordship strenuously recommended to meet the Bishop of London punctually at the time appointed, and take that prelate's advice on these and other matters, to which Sir George readily agreed.

At the time specified the Bishop of London met the Bishop of Edinburgh and Sir George Mackenzie at Whitehall. The latter mentioned to the Bishop of London his suggestion of having some of the Scottish Episcopal noblemen and gentlemen present, and his Lordship heartily conceded with the proposal, He said that he would go in to the King, and inquire if his Majesty would appoint a time for the Scottish Episcopal noblemen and gentlemen to wait upon him, in favour of their persecuted clergy in Scotland. Leaving the Bishop and Sir George Mackenzie in a room near the apartment in which the King was, his Lordship was absent a full half hour, when he returned, and informed them that the King would not agree to the proposal, lest it might offend the Presbyterians, that at the same time he would not allow the latter to approach him in a body, because it would give offence to the other party, and that he would not allow more than two of either party at a time to speak to him of Scottish ecclesiastical affairs.

The Bishop of London now addressed himself in an almost official manner to the Bishop of Edinburgh.—" My Lord," he said, " you see that the King, having thrown himself upon the water, must keep himself a-swimming with one hand. The Presbyterians have joined him closely, and offer to support him; and therefore he cannot cast them off unless he could see how otherways he can be served. And the King bids me tell you that he now knows the state of Scotland much better than he did when he was in Holland; for while there he was made to believe that Scotland, generally all over, was Presbyterian, *but now he sees that the great body of the nobility and gentry are for Episcopacy*, and it is the *trading and inferior sort that are for Presbytery*. Wherefore he bids me tell you, that if you will undertake to serve him to the purpose that he is *served here in England* he will take you by the hand, *support the Church and order*, and throw off the Presbyterians."—" My Lord," replied the Bishop of Edinburgh, " I cannot but humbly thank the Prince for this frankness and offer; but withal I must tell your Lordship, that when I came from Scotland, neither my brethren nor I apprehended any such revolution as I have now seen in England; and therefore I neither was nor could be instructed by them what answer to make to the Prince's offer And, therefore, what I say is not in their name, but only my own private opinion, which is, that I truly think they will not serve the Prince so as he is served in England : that is, as I take it, to make him their king, or give their suffrage for his being king. And though as to this matter I can say nothing in their name, and as from them, yet for myself I must say, that rather than do so I will abandon all the interest that either I have, or may expect to have, in Britain." The Bishop of London commended the candour of this reply, and said that he believed the Bishop of Edinburgh spoke the sentiments of all the Scottish Prelates "All this time," said his Lordship to Bishop Rose, " you have been here, neither have you waited on the King, nor have any of your brethren, the Scottish Bishops, made any address to him ; so the King must be excused for standing by the Presbyterians."

This conversation had scarcely terminated when the Prince of Orange passed through the apartment in which were the two Bishops and Sir George Mackenzie The latter took leave of his Majesty, who immediately left the room without noticing the Bishops. The Bishop of Edinburgh was not a little chagrined that this opportunity of taking leave had been lost, but the Bishop promised to present him on the forenoon of the following day Considering what depended on this interview and the results, it is extremely interesting ; and it either does not appear that William had been informed of what had passed between the two Bishops on the previous day, or, as the Bishop of Edinburgh also conjectures, the " Prince purposed to try what might be made of him by a personal appeal." When his Lordship was announced, William came a few steps forward from his company, and said—" My Lord, are you going for Scotland ? "—" Yes, Sir," replied the Bishop, " if you have any commands for me."—" I hope," said the King, " you will be kind to me, and follow the example of England."—" Sir," replied his Lordship, " I will serve you so far as law, reason, or conscience, shall allow me." William instantly turned from the Bishop in silence, and mingled with his friends, and the Bishop immediately retired

Such was the memorable interview of the Bishop of Edinburgh with King William III., at which the fate of Scottish Episcopacy as the national establishment was sealed. It is given almost in the Bishop's own language, and is therefore entitled to the utmost confidence. One fact is clearly deduced from it—that if the Scottish Prelates and clergy had followed the example of the Church of England, and recognized William as the sovereign, the Episcopal Church would have been at this moment established in Scotland. The Bishop of London explicitly stated this to Bishop Rose, when he told his Lordship that the King knew the state of Scotland much better than when he was in Holland—that instead of the Scotch being nearly unanimous for Presbyterianism, there was a numerous, a powerful, and a most influential party who were its determined opponents—that he had discovered " the nobility and gentry were for Episcopacy," and only the " trading and inferior sort were for Presbytery." Bishop Rose farther says, respecting his conversation with Bishop Compton—" Whether what the Bishop of London delivered as from the Prince was so or not I cannot certainly say, but I think his Lordship's word was good enough for that; or whether the Prince would have stood by his promise of casting off the Presbyterians, and protecting us, in case we had come into his interest, I will not determine, though this seems the most probable unto me, and that for these reasons :—He had the Presbyterians now on his side both from inclination and interest, many of them having come over with him, and the rest of them having appeared so warmly that with no good grace imaginable could they return to King James' interest;—next, by gaining, as he might presume to gain, the Episcopal nobility and gentry, which he saw was a great party, and, consequently, that King James would be deprived of his principal support I am the more confirmed in this, that after my downcoming here [Edinburgh], my Lord St Andrews [the Primate] and I taking occasion to wait upon the Duke of Hamilton, his Grace told us a day or two before the sitting down of the Convention, that he had it in *special charge from King William that nothing should be done to the prejudice of Episcopacy in Scotland*, in case the Bishops could *by any means* be brought to befriend his interest, and he *prayed us most pathetically, for our own sakes, to follow the example of the Church of England.* To which my Lord St Andrews replied, ' That both by natural allegiance, the laws, and the most solemn oaths, we were engaged in the King's [James II.] interest; and that we were by God's grace to stand by it, in the face of all dangers, and to the greatest losses.'" The Archbishop farther volunteered an advice to the Duke of Hamilton respecting what he considered to be his Grace's duty at this crisis; but the Duke nevertheless followed his own inclinations, and was a zealous promoter of the Revolution.

Whatever may have been the reasons which induced King William after his arrival in England to alter his opinions respecting the ecclesiastical state of Scotland, as intimated by the Bishop of London, it is now admitted that the establishment of Presbyterianism was arranged in Holland, and of course confirmed in London after the Scottish Bishops had declared their resolution to remain in the interests of King James. It is also stated that Bishop Burnet had then no inconsiderable share in the matter when in Holland, and if this charge is true it is a disgraceful stain on his character, when we consider that he had at one time been a parochial incumbent in the Scottish Church. The conduct of the Scottish Bishops is the more remarkable, and must have resulted from the most upright principle, when it is recollected that the *indulgence* or *toleration* granted by King James in 1687, in virtue of the dispensing power assumed by him, had not only secured full liberty to all classes of Presbyterians, but even encouraged dissent from the Episcopal Church, which he evidently intended to weaken, on account of the powerful barrier it presented against the Roman Catholics. This indulgence had been received with the utmost gratitude by the Presbyterians. Loyal addresses were transmitted to the King from various quarters, and more particularly from the Presbyterians of Edinburgh, thanking his Majesty for this boon, declaring that they would stand by his sacred person on all occasions, and praying the continuance of his princely goodness and care; and yet those very persons were amongst the first to offer their services to the Prince of Orange, complaining of the "hellish attempts of Romish incendiaries, and of the just grievances to all men relating to conscience, liberty, and property." King James knew, as every Romanist knows, that Popery had nothing to fear from Presbyterianism, about which the Papists even at the present day give themselves little concern.

As to the conduct of the Scottish Bishops, who have been often represented as men of narrow minds and bigoted principles, it resulted from what they considered to be their solemn religious duty. It is easy to sit in judgment on them at this distance of time, and reasoning from our own consciousness to assail them for their want of prudence, their now obsolete and exploded notions, and their obstinacy in clinging to the fortunes of an illustrious and unfortunate Royal House. But it must be recollected that the times were widely different from our own; it was a period of strong political excitement; and it was never contemplated even by many of those who were concerned in the Revolution, that the House of Stuart was to be finally excluded. There can be little doubt that if James II. had acceded to the proposition of King William, and sent his infant son to be educated in England, the succession would have been secured to that prince. And if we take into account that Scotland was at that time an independent kingdom, that it had its own legislature, and was unconnected with England except by the union of the crowns, we may form some kind of estimate of the principles by which the Scottish Bishops and Clergy were guided in their solemn determination not to acknowledge King William as their sovereign, believing, as they conscientiously did, that nothing could absolve them from their oath of allegiance to King James.

And what an extraordinary train of reflections must occur, if we suppose for a moment that the Scottish Bishops and Clergy had conformed to the Revolution settlement of the crown. Here, indeed, much is speculation and uncertainty; we know the history of the past, but we cannot calculate even the probabilities of the future. For the wisest of purposes, doubtless, the great Head of the Church permitted the Scottish branch of his Catholic communion and fellowship to be affected in its temporal condition by political changes, and, it may be, by human passions, prejudices, and errors. To suppose that the angry feelings of the disappointed would soon have subsided, or that any thing like a general recognition of, or conformity to, apostolical truth and order would have been exhibited on the part of the more violent Presbyterians, and especially those sects of them called the Covenanters and Cameronians, would be to suppose what is utterly visionary, fanciful, and contradicted by experience. We know well that schisms, heresies, and dissents, have existed from the earliest times, and that these still exist in countries where apostolical episcopacy is maintained and supported as the national ecclesiastical establishment. In Scotland the leaven of schism was introduced with the Reformation, and we need not wonder at such being the fact, when we consider the tumultuous and disgraceful manner in which that Reformation was conducted. To the celebrated Andrew Melville, however, must be ascribed the introduction of the

Genevan polity, which fermented and increased in violence during the latter end of the sixteenth and the whole of the seventeenth centuries. If the Scottish Bishops and Clergy had conformed to the principles of the Revolution, as did the Church of England, and thus preserved the Church as the national establishment, the Presbyterians would have formed a considerable party of Dissenters, though it is believed not more numerous than the sect called Seceders, who have departed from the present Establishment. If the Episcopal Church had continued the establishment of Scotland, the Presbyterians, we say, would have formed a large body of Dissenters, who for many years probably would have respected neither the views, the principles, nor the polity of the Church, until time softened their resentments, or a new and better educated generation would consider the subject unprejudiced by ignorance and fanaticism. In that case where would have been the various sects of Presbyterian Dissenters—the Secession, the Relief, and others, both numerous and powerful, who left the present legal Establishment long after the Revolution of 1688 ? Would they have had an existence at all, when the causes of the separation from the Kirk could not have excited their dissatisfaction? The answers to such questions as these must be matters of opinion, and it would be rash to decide imperatively or confidently on either side.

CHAPTER III.

GENERAL VIEW OF THE ESTABLISHED EPISCOPAL CHURCH OF SCOTLAND AT THE REVOLUTION—CONTINUED.

It is stated in the outset of the present work, that, in a temporal sense, the substitution of Presbyterianism for the Church in Scotland was of no pecuniary benefit to the country. This is an important fact, which must be kept in view, as illustrating in a remarkable manner the history of that age. We have seen that the Crown seized the whole of the Episcopal revenues, and that these are levied at the present day as if every See in Scotland was filled by its legitimate Bishop. Let us now attend to more important matters than mere temporalities, and take a short view of the doctrine, discipline, and form of worship of the Episcopal Church of Scotland, previous to and at the period of the Revolution.

That Church has been often represented as an intolerable burden on the people, and as compelling them to submit to rites and ceremonies which they inveterately disliked. We hear much, too, of the persecuted Covenanters, as if the Church had been the great cause of persecuting those persons. The very reverse, however, is the case. Whatever the Presbyterian writers may say to the contrary, it is well known that at the Restoration the re-establishment of the ancient form of Church Government was agreeable to a large proportion of the people, and many well informed Presbyterians attended public worship in their parish churches. It is a remarkable fact, which shows the conduct of the Covenanters and their leaders in its true light, that from the Restoration to the Revolution there was *scarcely an outward distinction*

50   HISTORY OF THE

between the Episcopalians and the Presbyterians in faith, worship, or discipline.

Every reader knows the failure of the attempt to introduce the Scottish Liturgy in the year 1637, and the serious riot which occurred in the cathedral church of St Giles at Edinburgh on that occasion. The General Assembly at Glasgow was held on the following year, when the Scottish Archbishops and Bishops were accused of every possible crime, however odious or fanciful, and excommunicated. The great Civil War commenced, and the murder of King Charles I. consummated the national turmoil. The Scottish agents in that tragedy seem to have been conscience-stricken at the result, which they had chiefly assisted in accelerating, and they accordingly attempted to oppose Cromwell's career, by espousing in their own way the cause of Charles II. Cromwell, however, who knew them well, baffled all their projects, and he conquered Scotland, which was quiet during his domination by the strong arm of military power. The man who had braved and dismissed, as a pack of traitors, the Parliament of England, was not likely to be alarmed at, or tolerate the meetings of, a General Assembly of Presbyterian ministers.*

At the Restoration of Charles II., when the Church was re-established, no liturgy or public form of prayer was introduced, and no Presbyterian could plead a violation of his conscience by acknowledging that to which he might entertain conscientious objections. The Liturgy of the Church of England, which does not differ much from the Scottish Liturgy, was indeed used in some places, but it was with the entire consent and approbation of the people. In the North of Scotland, and particularly in the city and county of Aberdeen, where the Episcopalians have always been numerous since the Reformation, the Liturgy was probably used in some churches. We know that it was used in the Chapel-Royal of Holyroodhouse, and in the parish church of Salton in Haddingtonshire by Dr Gilbert Burnet, during the four years of his incumbency, before he was invited to the chair of Theology in the Uni-

* During the troubles in the latter end of the reign of Charles I. the communion was seldom administered in the city of Glasgow, and it was not celebrated in the years 1646, 1647, 1651, 1652, 1653, 1658, and 1659.—New Statistical Account of Scotland—Lanarkshire, p 118.

versity of Glasgow, from 1665 to 1669.* Some of the parochial incumbents compiled forms of prayer for the use of their respective congregations, with some petitions and collects taken from the English Liturgy; but this was merely optional, and the prayers were generally extempore, or said in the same manner as those who reject a liturgy or set forms of prayer. All the clergy, however, concluded their prayers, whether previously arranged or not, with the Lord's Prayer, which was followed by singing the Doxology, or *Gloria Patri*, both of which observances the Presbyterian enthusiasts denounced as formal and superstitious; and it is curious, that in many parts of Scotland the people to this day have a very great objection to hear the Lord's Prayer said, or the Scriptures read in public, alleging that they can do so at home themselves. We need not be surprised at this folly, to say the least, on the part of an illiterate peasantry, when we find a Presbyterian minister of great repute gravely maintaining that the Lord's Prayer is a *Jewish*, and not a *Christian prayer*, and cannot with propriety be introduced into *Christian worship* !†

But it appears that even the offensive Doxology was sometimes omitted to please the tender consciences of the objectors. This occurred at least in the Presbytery of Paisley, and may have happened in other quarters. Some of the clergy were brought before the Archbishop of Glasgow, in whose diocese they were, on this account It was urged, in defence, that none of the people would join in the psalmody, and that the minister and clerk (called in Scotland the *precentor*) being the only performers, and sometimes both of them alike destitute of a musical

* While noticing Salton in connection with Bishop Burnet, it may be mentioned, that when he was placed in his more elevated station he was not unmindful of this scene of his early labours. He bequeathed in trust the sum of 20,000 merks, the present value of which is L.2000, producing the annual sum of L 80, being invested on heritable security at 4 per cent, for the education and clothing of thirty children of the "poorer sort," for the erection of a new schoolhouse, and affording an augmentation of the schoolmaster's salary; for the increase of a library begun to be formed " for the minister's house and use;" and the remainder for relieving the necessitous poor. The children connected with this fund are familiarly termed *bishops* in the parish, and the gallery appropriated for their use in the church is likely always to retain its appellation of *the Bishop's Laft*.

† Sermons by Andrew Thomson, D.D, Minister of St George's Church, Edinburgh.

ear, the effect was bad, and the discord intolerable. Nevertheless, these pleadings were of no avail, and the Archbishop ordered them to obey the injunction of singing the Doxology every Sunday, to explain it to the people, and exhort them to compliance.*

It is farther to be observed, that there were no organs in the parish churches, for the cathedrals, with three exceptions, Glasgow, Edinburgh, and Kirkwall in Orkney, had been almost demolished by the leaders of the Reformation and their destructive followers in the previous century. Perhaps the only exception, at least one of the very few with respect to organs, was the Abbey church of Holyroodhouse. There were no fixed communion tables, neither the Bishops nor the clergy wore their episcopal robes and surplices during the ordinary performance of divine service, and it is not even certain whether the latter wore black gowns, though it appears from various contemporary portraits that the Bishops did so on ordinary occasions. As there was no Liturgy, no responses were made, or expected to be made, by the congregation. The two sacraments of Baptism and the Eucharist were administered by both Episcopalians and Presbyterians nearly in the same manner, without signing with the sign of the cross in the one, or kneeling at the other. Only, when administering baptism, the Episcopal clergy required an assent to the Apostles' Creed, as the ground of the infant's religious education, a condition to which no Presbyterian could reasonably object, since they demanded an acknowledgment of all the dogmas of the Westminster Confession, and the more violent of them even an assent to that precious document, the *Solemn League and Covenant.*

As it respects the doctrines of the Church, although these were avowedly the same as the Thirty-Nine Articles, yet these Articles were seldom or never even mentioned. The old Confession of Faith, drawn up by the early Scottish Reformers, and ratified in 1567, had been all along the received and common standard of both parties; but the Presbyterians had introduced that lengthy compilation, which is now their favourite standard, the Westminster Confession, in many points different from, and in some directly opposed to, the old Scottish Confession. It is well known that the Westminster Assembly, which met by an ordinance of the Parliament in 1643, and sat till February 22, 1648-9,

* New Statistical Account of Scotland—Renfrewshire, p. 131.

about three weeks after the murder of the King, had for their object the *modest design* of establishing an uniformity of doctrine, discipline, and worship, throughout England, Scotland, and Ireland, which they designed to do in the most compulsory manner; and the English, Irish, and Scottish Churches, and the Irish Roman Catholics, were to be compelled to recognise Calvinistic Presbyterianism. The prospect of establishing Presbyterianism in England was held out by Cromwell as a snare to the leaders of the party, and this was one of their inducements to sell the King—fanaticism thus uniting with avarice in the most odious transaction which stains the annals of the Scottish nation. Of the compilers of the Westminster Confession, as also of the Larger and Shorter Catechism, now recognised by the Presbyterian Establishment of Scotland, Lord Clarendon allows that " about twenty of them* were reverend and worthy persons, and episcopal in their judgments, but as to the remainder they were mere pretenders to divinity; some were infamous in their lives and conversations, and most of them of very mean parts and learning, if not of scandalous ignorance, and of no other reputation than of malice to the Church of England." It is possible, as Eachard intimates, that these statements of the Noble historian are too severe, especially that of some of them being " infamous in their lives." Neal, the historian of the Puritans, says of them, that " though their sentiments in divinity were in many instances too narrow and contracted, yet, with all their faults, *among which their persecuting zeal for religion was not the least,* they were certainly men of real piety and virtue, who meant well, and had the interest of religion at heart;" and, " if they had not grasped at coercive power or jurisdiction over the consciences of men, their characters would have been unblemished.—The *divine right* of the Presbyterian government first threw them into heats, and then divided them, engaging them with the Parliament, and then with the Independents and Erastians. Their opposing a toleration raised them a great many enemies, and caused a secession in their own body."

Such are the sources from which the Presbyterians of Scotland de-

---

* The names of Bishop Reynolds, Wallis, Twisse, Arrowsmith, Greenhill, Gataker, Selden, Lightfoot, and others, will always be mentioned with respect. Those sent from Scotland were men of poor abilities, little learning, and of no reputation, except as agitators, and restless leaders of an enthusiastic peasantry.

rived their theological standards, and at the period of the Revolution they cherished all the intolerance of which even the prejudiced historian of the Puritans complains. Yet will it be believed that those very men, who adopted a religious code the most exclusive and the most tyrannical, if all it contains was practised, and who wanted to deny to others what they claimed for themselves, accused the Scottish Episcopal Church of cruelty and oppression? Those very men, who in their Solemn League and Covenant bound themselves by an oath to extirpate, *with the sword*, Popery, Prelacy, by which latter they meant the Church, Erastianism, Independency, Anabaptism, and all the mushroom modern sects then in existence, which had departed from the communion of the Church catholic, complained that their consciences were violated by an ecclesiastical establishment, the fundamental doctrines and principles of which they either would not or could not understand, or which they either ignorantly or wilfully perverted and misrepresented. It is distinctly denied that the Episcopal Church of Scotland was viewed as a grievance by the great mass of the nation, the deluded peasantry of the western counties excepted. With regard to discipline, the dioceses were composed of Presbyteries, as the Synods are at the present time. Every parish had its kirk-session, at the head of which was the incumbent. In the parish of Salton, for example, already mentioned, where Dr Patrick Scougall was incumbent five years before he was elevated to the Bishopric of Aberdeen,* it is admitted, on the authority of its Presbyterian minister, that " during the period of his incumbency the eldership appears to have been much more numerous, in proportion to the amount of population, than in modern times. From the Kirk-Session records it appears that in 1633-35, when the number of the inhabitants of the parish was probably under six hundred, there were no fewer than nineteen elders in office."† Does this appear as if the Episcopal Church of Scotland had been obnoxious to the mass of the people? Other instances are adduced in the proper place in the sequel.

* Bishop Scougall was the immediate predecessor of Bishop Burnet He was the father of the eminent and pious Henry Scougall, author of the " Life of God in the Soul of Man," who died while Professor of Theology in King's College, in the twenty-eighth year of his age. To Henry Scougall may be applied the favourite adage of Archbishop Leighton—*Diu vixit qui bene vixit*

† New Stat. Account of Scotland—Haddingtonshire, p. 110.

The Presbyteries of the several dioceses were constituted in much the same manner as they are at present under the Presbyterian system, and in these Presbyteries the moderator or chairman was always nominated by the Bishop of the diocese. In the Provincial Diocesan Synods the Bishop always presided, or in his absence the Dean, or some one by his appointment, and in the General Assemblies, whenever the Government deemed it expedient that such convocations should be held, the Archbishop of St Andrews, as Primate of all Scotland and Metropolitan, would have presided as Moderator, especially if the meeting had been held in any town in his own or in his suffragan dioceses.

Many further illustrations could be adduced, but the town and Presbytery of Paisley, as given on the authority of the Established Presbyterians themselves, will furnish an example.*

When the Church was re-established at the Restoration the *Presbyterian Presbytery* was dissolved; but it was re-constructed in 1663 by an act of Dr Fairfoull, Archbishop of Glasgow, and the Synod of Glasgow and Ayr. The first meeting was held on the 29th of October that year, and consisted of only five members, with two correspondents from the Presbyteries of Glasgow and Dunbarton. If the reader is surprised at the limited number of members of the Episcopal Presbytery of Paisley, it must be recollected that Renfrewshire was one of the most fanatical counties in the West of Scotland, and even at the present day the leaven of Covenanting prejudices is not a little prevalent. In 1684, Dr Arthur Ross, then Archbishop of Glasgow, ordered the meetings of the Presbytery of Paisley always to take place in that town, instead of the neighbouring royal burgh of Renfrew, where some meetings had been held. In 1670, a meeting was held at Paisley between Archbishop Leighton and Dr Gilbert Burnet on the part of the Church, and certain " brethren " of Paisley, Glasgow, and neighbourhood, on the side of the Presbyterians; but the demands of the latter were so extravagant, that no accommodation could be made between the parties. In 1679, a meeting of Presbyterian ministers was held at Paisley, when a warning against Popery was drawn up by them, together with a short vindication of Presbyterian principles, but the paper was never printed. "After this," says Wodrow, their champion and historian, " till the

* New Statistical Account of Scotland—Renfrewshire, p. 221, *et seq.*

Revolution, Presbyterian ministers had few meetings; and I shall have little more to say of them but that they remained in retirement, few venturing to preach in the fields, and some now and then in private houses: and through the following years I shall have little more to relate but a continued scene of persecution of ministers and people, and heavy oppression of the whole country." What Wodrow considers *persecution* and *oppression* is simply because the Government would not allow the wild preachers to say and do anything they pleased, and because, when they excited the peasantry to open rebellion and bloodshed, such of them as were taken prisoners were punished as rebels. No one knew better than Wodrow that those Presbyterian ministers who chose to live peaceably were protected by the Government, and against those preachers the Covenanters and other dangerous zealots were as furious as against the Episcopal Clergy. Many Presbyterian teachers complied with the indulgence, against which the Covenanters and Cameronians testified as vehemently as against the Church; and they were ironically designated the *King's Curates*, in common with the regular parochial clergy, who were styled the *Bishop's Curates*. What the Duke of Lauderdale said, when he refused to relieve the field preachers confined on the Bass Rock, in the mouth of the Firth of Forth, was applicable to too many of the Presbyterians in Scotland:—" The party," he declared, " were unworthy of any favour." In Paisley, some of their preachers procured the *indulgence*, and were allowed to retain their benefices. In the parish registers of that town, which contain some curious notices of manners, and of passing events in civil and ecclesiastical history, we find the following entries connected with what Wodrow designates the " Prelatical Synods and Presbyteries," and what the Presbyterian writers of an Account of the Town and Parish of Paisley politely call the " *leaven of Episcopacy*"—a Church viewed by these two persons with great honour:*—" January 12, 1681.—The said day the acts of Synod were read; and the brethren interrogat as to their attending thereof, all of them report that they say the Lord's Prayer, and either sing or say the Doxologie: and they promise that, so soon as the country shall in any measure settle cheerfully, to go about obedi-

---

* Dr Robert Burns and Mr Robert Macnair, two of the present Kirk ministers of Paisley, in the New Statistical Account of Scotland—Renfrewshire, p 224, 242

ence to the act of the administration of the Lord's Supper. December 21, 1681.—The Moderator produces ane order particularlie directed to him from the Archbishop (Dr Arthur Ross), requiring him, in presence of the remanent brethren, to administer the oath called the Test to all schoolmasters, doctors, and chaplains, within the bounds of the Presbytrie; and to report his diligence hereanent betwixt and first of January 1682."

A careful inquiry into the state of the Scottish Episcopal Church will more and more convince us that the Covenanters and Presbyterians of every description had no *real grievances* of which they could complain; and, with the exception of the title and functions of Archbishop and Bishop, and the canonical succession thereof, there is scarcely anything to be perceived analogous to the present state of the Scottish Episcopal Church. There was no Liturgy, no ritual of any kind, no ceremonies: and, although the Church was essentially episcopal in her constitution, and her clergy apostolically ordained Priests and Deacons, the outward services of religion were conducted precisely as the Presbyterian preachers did themselves. Every Episcopalian knows that a Liturgy or set form of prayer for public worship, and the administration of the sacraments and offices of religion, is no part of Episcopacy, any more than the want of it is any peculiar feature of Presbyterianism; and he supports the Church from very different principles, and by other arguments, than those which are successfully urged respecting the expediency and necessity of a liturgical form of prayer, in which all can join and be edified, in opposition to the often irreverent phraseology of extemporary praying. When Calamy, a well-known and celebrated English Presbyterian, was informed of the procedure of the Episcopal Church of Scotland and its services, he exclaimed, in reference to the conduct of the Presbyterians and Covenanters—" What would our brethren in Scotland be at, or what would they have? Would to God we had these offers."* And yet, in defiance of all this incontrovertible evidence, the Presbyterian writers persist in accusing the Episcopal Church of *forcing upon the people a mode of faith and worship which they conscientiously deemed to be unscriptural.* Is it candid, fair, or honest,

* Appendix to Keith's Catalogue of Scottish Bishops, edited by Bishop Russell, p. 403.

to bring forward such statements, when they can be all proved to be false, and utterly opposed to facts?

It does not appear in what peculiar way the Scottish Bishops exercised their authority; and it probably varied according to the state of the diocese. In the South and West of Scotland, where the Covenanters particularly abounded, a vigilant eye was kept on their conduct; and the Government deemed it necessary to deal severely with those intolerant persons. It appears from the following statement, that in some parishes there was a regular calling of the names of the parishioners before divine service was commenced. Mr Robert Aird in 1666, and Mr William Cunninghame in 1683, were the Episcopal incumbents of the parish of Lochwinnoch, in Renfrewshire. "One of them," we are told, "was very strict in requiring the parishioners to conform to Episcopacy, and in reporting those who were irregular and refractory; but the other was easy and indulgent, and if they appeared to *answer to their names at the commencement of public worship*, he connived at their retiring, without requiring them to remain and join in the service; and, therefore, he has left a favourable impression behind him in the parish"* In the town and parish of Haddington every parent was obliged, under a penalty, to have his child baptized by the incumbent.

It is curious to observe the manner in which the Presbyterian ministers speak of the Episcopal Clergy of Scotland before the Revolution, when they happen to notice them. Of course, according to them, the partizans of their party were all pious, virtuous, liberal, and amiable; while the Clergy are often described as the reverse. Two incumbents successively held the parish of Langton, in Berwickshire, before the Revolution—Mr Robert Hooper from 1677 to 1683, and Mr Patrick Walker from 1683 to 1688. We are told that "the first seems to have been a peaceable man; the second was a bigoted Prelatist."† The period between the Restoration and the Revolution is, by another person, called the "period of Episcopal domination." The Presbytery of Haddington were "*beginning* to adopt *Episcopalian views and practices* at the Revolution;" and Mr Laurence Charteris, their Moderator, who had been so from 1671 to 1676, was appointed by the Lord Bishop of

* New Statistical Account of Scotland—Renfrewshire, p 94
† Ibid. 1836—Berwickshire, p. 242

Edinburgh (Dr Alexander Young), in January 1676, to be Professor of Divinity in the University of that city. After the Revolution he died minister of Dirleton. In December 1682, Mr Robert Meldrum, minister of Garvald, was appointed by the Bishop of Edinburgh (Dr John Paterson) to be minister of Yester, in the county of Haddington. "In this situation," we are told, "he remained till December 1699, notwithstanding the political and ecclesiastical changes which during his incumbency had taken place in the nation. The change from Prelacy to Presbytery at the Revolution does not seem to have changed his determination to continue minister of Yester; and though this circumstance might make some regard him as a second *Vicar of Bray*, yet he appears to have been a faithful minister. The following entry in reference to him is made in the Session Records:—' December 17, 1699—No sermon, our minister being dead, having faithfullie, in the office of the ministery, served at this church exactly seventeen years, from the serving of his edict here to the next day after his funeral.'"*

In the account of the parish of Errol, in Perthshire, there is the following extract from the Kirk-Session Records:—" Sabbath, September 8, 1689—No sermon, because the troopers came into the town with sound of trumpet, and dissipat the people; and the minister was informed that they would offer violence to him." The minister here referred to was John Nicolson, D.D., incumbent from 1666 to 1691-92, when he was deprived for not submitting to the new Government. His faithfulness in the discharge of his duties is honourably recorded:—" November 1, 1689.—The Session this day, with ane voice, declared that the Doctor had been very painful and faithful in the exercise of all the points and parts of the ministerial function among them."

But as these matters are more copiously treated in succeeding chapters, the reader's attention is directed to the following exquisite specimen of Presbyterian writing, illustrative of the parish of St Mungo in Dumfries-shire, from a work to which reference is often made in these pages. In 1795, "the church was a ruin—without bell, pews, Bibles, or utensils for administering the sacraments, and the *minister occasionally officiated in a shepherd's plaid.* There was no schoolhouse, schoolmaster, or provision for one: *now* every thing necessary is provided for the

* New Statistical Account of Scotland—Haddingtonshire, 1835, p 169 church; there is an endowed school and well educated schoolmaster; and the minister is attired in that *Popish rag* a *gown*. Formerly the Seceders would not be present when any Established minister was celebrating any divine ordinance, and the *Episcopal Clergy, in terror of the people, performed the rites of burial in private.* The present incumbent has been sent for to attend the sick and dying Seceders, and the *funeral rites of the Episcopal Church are performed openly in our churches and burial grounds.*"*

* New Statistical Account of Scotland—Dumfries-shire, 1834, p 217.

CHAPTER IV.

PERSECUTION OF THE SCOTTISH EPISCOPAL CLERGY AFTER THE REVOLUTION.

THE Revolution was commenced at Edinburgh by a riot in the city, an attack on the Palace of Holyrood, the Chapel-Royal of which was dilapidated by the mob, and the houses of those who were considered Roman Catholics were pillaged. Similar excesses occurred in other towns, and in too many instances they were indirectly encouraged by the authorities. The parochial Episcopal clergy, however, were the principal sufferers.

The Church of England has been repeatedly assailed on account of the Act of Uniformity of 1662, and a certain class of sectarian writers continually recur to what they term the *Black Day of St Bartholomew*, in their endeavours to stigmatize the Church of England as the enemy of liberty of conscience. It would be easy to show that these charges are unfounded, and that they can be satisfactorily retorted on the sects to which those belong who advance them. In like manner, the Episcopal Church of Scotland is accused of persecuting the Presbyterians and Covenanters, who are invariably represented by their supporters as patriots and martyrs. If the Covenanters were persecuted at all, they were persecuted by the State, and not by the Church, on charges of murder, rebellion, and treason, inasmuch as they denounced the royal authority, and took arms against the legal Government of the time. The measures which that Government thought it necessary to follow against the Covenanters may be denounced, deplored, or defended, according to the views entertained of the principles and opinions of the age, but any candid person who peruses with impartiality the writings, speeches, and other memorials of the Presbyterians of the seventeenth century, especially the Covenanters, will at once perceive they would have far exceeded the Episcopal Church in the work of persecution if they had possessed the power. "A man's writings," it is well observed, "may always be taken as evidence of his opinions, and the writings of the Episcopalians will not appear to their disadvantage when arranged on the same page with those of the Presbyterians.—What is the language of the public documents of the Presbyterians? The divine right of Presbyterial Government is positively asserted in the Confession of Faith and the Book of Discipline. The Articles of the Church of England breathe the spirit of liberality, but the Covenant bound every Presbyterian to endeavour to extirpate Episcopacy. The Episcopalians were never bound by their creed to destroy their opponents The Presbyterians fought not for liberty of conscience, but to impose the uniformity of the Covenant."* As it respects Scotland, the Episcopalians had as much right to the temporal benefits of a national establishment as the Presbyterians. The supporters of the Episcopal Church were numerous, certainly as respectable, many of them superior in rank, and of great family and local influence; while it will not be denied that the clergy as a body were *at least* as pious, learned, and upright as their opponents.

Smollett, who cannot be accused of an undue partiality towards the Church, represents the Presbyterians, when they became triumphant after the Revolution, as "proceeding with ungovernable violence to persecute the Episcopal party, exercising the very same tyranny against which they had themselves so loudly exclaimed." Guthrie, noticing the vote in the Convention that "prelacy and superiority of any office in the Church above Presbyters is and has been a great and insupportable grievance to this nation," says—"Though this vote was absurd, and founded upon *more falsehoods than one*, yet it was expedient, if not necessary. The friends of prelacy," in his opinion, "had slavish notions of prerogative, and it was found necessary not to represent Episcopacy as a grievance, but to make its abolition one of the *pacta conventa* of the new settlement."—"The re-establishment of Presbytery," continues this writer, "was attended with the most dreadful consequences. About

* History of the English Episcopacy, by the Rev. Thomas Lathbury, M A. Oxon p. 337, 350, 351.

threescore ministers were alive of those who had been turned out in the year 1662, and they were replaced in their former livings, with orders to fill up the vacancies in the best manner they could. This opened a door for terrible abuses. The young men who had been privately ordained in the Presbyterian way, and were called to the vacancies, were many of them enthusiasts, and had been heated almost into frenzy by zeal and persecution. They drove the Episcopal ministers, their wives and families, from their livings into the fields, with a barbarity that would have disgraced the worst of infidels, and some of them perished with cold, hunger, and blows."*

In the western and south-western counties of Scotland the persecution of the Episcopal clergy was most severe after the outbreaking of the Revolution, even before it was known what kind of ecclesiastical government was to be continued or established in Scotland. The counties of Ayr, Renfrew, Lanark, and Dumfries, were peculiarly turbulent. In these districts the Covenanters abounded, and those who were chiefly prosecuted by the Government had been connected with them, or kept them in a continual ferment and agitation. In particular, that party of the Presbyterians known by the name of *Cameronians* or *hill men*, from the well-known preacher Richard Cameron, who was killed in an action with the royal troops, were numerous, composed of the misled and ignorant peasantry, under the guidance of field preachers. The Cameronians were peculiarly sullen and dangerous, and asserted to the letter the principles of the Solemn League and Covenant. Taking advantage of the excitement of the period, and of the unsettled state of the Government, on Christmas-day 1688 a body of ninety of them attacked the Episcopal incumbents of Cumnock and of Auchinleck, and perambulated the whole county insulting the parochial clergy. On the same day similar riotous proceedings commenced in the county of Dunbarton, and gross outrages were committed in the counties already mentioned. "Their method in general," says a venerable writer, "was to assemble in the night-time in armed bodies, here and there, and to force themselves in any man's house against whom they had any private quarrel; but particularly those of the clergy, whom they plundered and abused as they pleased. They then carried the minister to the

---

* Guthrie, vol. x. p. 303, 304.

churchyard, or to some other public place of the town or village, and there, with all the personal abuse they could think of, exposed him as a condemned malefactor, giving him a strict charge, under the severest penalties, never to preach any more, but to remove himself and family immediately; and, for a conclusion of their wanton malice, they never omitted to tear their gowns over their heads, and rend them in pieces, or throw them into the flames. When they had done with the poor men themselves, they locked the kirk doors, and carried the keys with them. And when any minister was so hardy as to expostulate with them, or ask them by what rule, either of religion or of morality, they could justify such excesses, they answered, *By the rule and law of the Solemn League and Covenant, by which they were bound to extirpate prelacy, and bring malignants to condign punishment.*"* Dr Cook, in referring to this desolating progress of the Cameronians, volunteers the following singular explanation of their conduct, in which he persists in the face of all evidence, and of his own recorded opinions, in insinuating that the Presbyterians had been persecuted by the Church. " Improper as were these excesses, how light were they when put in the balance against the enormities which under Prelacy had been perpetuated? For no *personal violence*, no tortures, no murders, disgraced a sect which had been borne down with every species of outrage. These incidental ebullitions of popular sentiment had no connection with the general arrangements of the Presbyterians, who prudently considered what steps should be taken to regain their influence, and to conjoin with the accession of the new sovereign the settlement of their church."† It thus appears, according to Dr Cook's view of the matter, that because sundry *enormities* were inflicted on men in open rebellion "*under Prelacy,*" namely, when the Episcopal Church was the legal and authorized ecclesiastical establishment of Scotland, the said Church is responsible for these alleged acts of cruelty—an inference or conclusion completely at variance with historical facts. What had the Church to do with the acts and the proceedings of the Duke of Lauderdale, and the other noblemen and gentlemen connected with the Scottish executive Government? Did Graham of Claverhouse perambulate the disaffected districts with a

* Skinner's Ecclesiastical History of Scotland, vol ii. p. 217.
† Cook's History of the Church of Scotland from the Reformation to the Revolution, vol. iii. p. 438, 439

commission in his pocket, signed by a Scottish prelate as his authoritative missive?

Among the various pamphlets illustrative of the history of this memorable era, there is one entitled " An Account of the Persecution of the Church in Scotland, in several Letters."* On the back of the titlepage is the following note in MS.—" The author of the Life of the reverend and learned Mr John Sage, printed at London in 1714, says that Mr Sage was the author of the second and third letters, that the first was written by an English clergyman, Mr Thomas Morer, Chaplain to an English Regiment lying at Glasgow, and that the fourth letter was written by the great and learned Dr Monro," who is already mentioned as Principal of the University of Edinburgh, and Bishop elect of Argyle when the Revolution took place. Of Sage much remains to be said in the sequel. He was one of the two first post-Revolution Bishops of the present Scottish Episcopal Church, and was one of the ministers of Glasgow before 1688. His statements, therefore, respecting the sufferings of the clergy in the district in which he resided are valuable and conclusive.

But we shall first glance generally at the letter ascribed to Mr Morer, who was an eye-witness of those tumults and disorders.—" The Church of Scotland," says he, " is at this time under the claw of an enraged lion; Episcopacy abolished, and its revenues alienated; the clergy routed,—some by a form of sentence, and others by violence and popular fury; their persons and families abused, their houses ransacked, with many other injuries and indignities done them which I forbear naming, that I may not martyr your Lordship's patience by the bare recital of them. My post in the Army has carried me into many places of this kingdom, and has given me many opportunities to see and lament their condition. The occasion of all these disasters is the prevailing strength of the Cameronian party, a faction here taking its name from one Cameron, formerly their leader, who was slain in his rebellion.†

* London, printed for S. Cook, 1790. Advocates' Library, Edinburgh. A Series of Letters Addressed to a Nobleman.

† Bishop Sage observes of this man—" One Mr Richard Cameron, who, being sometime schoolmaster of Falkland [in Fife], and turned out of that employment for insufficiency, betook himself to the trade of field preaching, became wonderfully admired of the giddy multitude, was killed at last in open rebellion at Aird's Moss, and so commenced martyr, *anno* 1680."—Letter II. p. 8.

They are a sort of rigid Presbyterians, or rather Fifth Monarchy Men, valuing neither King William nor King James any further than as these princes happen to please them. Some designing heads in the Council and Parliament have made use of these men's hands to bring their ends about, whose weakness always was too discernible. The Church party, both for number and quality, were predominant in this nation, the nobles and gentry are generally episcopal, and so the people, especially northward, where to my own knowledge they are so well affected, that it would be no hard task to bring them *cultui et ritibus cum Anglis communibus subscribere*, as Buchanan saith the ancient Scots did when they stood in fear of the French, and desired England's assistance against them. My frequent reading of our Service and preaching in their churches to the audience's satisfaction, the caresses of the gentry, and respect of the ordinary people whenever I met them, infer so much, and plainly discover that they neither abhorred me nor my way of religion. At Perth I was readily admitted into the church and pulpit, though the magistrates refused the same favour to the Lord Cardross, a Privy Councillor, and the Lord Argyll, in behalf of two Cameronian preachers Even at Edinburgh the faction were so weak that they were forced to send privately to the West for assistance, before they durst attempt any violence against the regular clergy; but the College of Justice being informed of their coming, armed themselves and their friends, and so were secured, both they and their ministers, until an order was obtained for laying down their arms again. Indeed, at Glasgow the faction is stronger, and this town may be said to be the warmest nest of the Cameronians; and yet to my knowledge the most considerable, and persons of the best quality, are very well affected, and would prevail, were it not for the assistance of the mountaineers, which the malignants have sometimes brought privately into the town to assault and overawe the others."

" It was on Christmas-day" (1688), says Sage " that day which once brought good tidings of great joy to all people—that day which once was celebrated by the court of Heaven itself, and whereon they sang glory to God in the highest, on earth peace and good will towards men—that day which the whole Christian Church has since solemnized for the greatest mercy that ever was shown to sinful mortals—that day, I say, it was on which they began the tragedy." About six in the evening, Mr Russell, minister of Govan near Glasgow, was assaulted by a number of men in his own house, who cruelly beat his wife and daughter, carried off the poor's box, and threatened him with more severe treatment if he ever preached in the parish church again. A party of enthusiasts entered the house of Mr Finnie, minister of Cathcart. This gentleman was from home, but they thrust his wife and four or five young children out of the house, threw out all the furniture, and were with difficulty persuaded to allow her to shelter herself and her children from the inclemencies of the weather in one of the outhouses. Mr Boyd, minister of Carmunnock, and his family were treated in a similar manner. Mr Bell, minister of Kilmarnock, was kept some hours exposed to the cold without covering, and his sexton was compelled to tear his gown in pieces from his shoulders. This gentleman had a copy of the Book of Common Prayer, which they burnt in the market-place of the town, declaring that, " in pursuance of the Solemn League and Covenant, they were now to burn publicly this Book of Common Prayer, which is full of superstition and idolatry." Mr Milne, minister of Cadder, was attacked in the same way by another party of Presbyterians. Mr White, minister of Ballintrae in the Bishopric of Galloway, was struck on the face by an enthusiast with the butt of a musquet in his own house; another made a thrust at him with a sword, and it was almost providential that he was not murdered; while some others assaulted his wife, then far advanced in pregnancy. Mr Brown, minister of Kells, in the same diocese, then residing at Newton, was carried to the market-place at four in the morning, and tied almost naked to a cart, in which position he would have certainly died if he had not received some kindness from a poor woman.

The wife of Mr Ross, minister of Renfrew, was turned out of her house with a helpless infant only three days old. The family of Mr Guthrie, minister of Keir, were all expelled from his house, and the furniture thrown out after them, though three of his children were dangerously ill of fever and the small-pox, and two of them died in consequence of this treatment. A party of them assaulted Mr Skinner, minister of Dailly, and so alarmed his daughter that she was thrown into a fever. About six days afterwards they returned to ransack the house, under the pretence of looking for arms; and their appearance so greatly excited this young lady, only twenty years of age, that she died, frequently repeating among her last words, " O these wicked men will murder my father." Numbers of other clergymen were similarly treated in the western counties, or *rabbled out*, as it was elegantly termed in the phraseology of the Cameronians.

Monro of Foulis, Bart., a gentleman of an ancient family, and a great leader among the Presbyterians, seeing a clergyman walking in his gown in the Parliament Square, Edinburgh, pointed towards him, and exclaimed, " Behold, Antichrist! Will no one tear the gown from him?" The clergyman replied, " Sir, you are the Beast,"—a retort which was applicable to his personal appearance, and caused a laugh from the spectators. The incumbent of Lasswade, about five miles from Edinburgh, was assaulted half way between his house and that city, received ten or twelve wounds in his body, and was otherwise injured in the most shameful manner. The incumbents of the parishes of Cumnock, Auchinleck, Mauchline, Galston, Riccarton, and Tarbolton, were all insulted in most ferocious language, and threatened with death if they continued to officiate.

A party of armed Cameronians surrounded the house of Mr Stirling, minister of Baldernock, and alarmed his wife and servants, her husband being from home, telling the former that they would cut off her *Popish nose*, and using the most indecent language. Another party assaulted Mr Duncan, minister of Kilpatrick Easter, struck and abused him, broke his furniture, and thrust him and his family out of doors.* The incumbents of Evandale, Rutherglen, Cumbernauld, Barony Parish of Glasgow, and numerous other parishes, were treated in a similar manner, and in the city of Glasgow the clergy were in hazard of their lives.† It is attested by Fullarton, afterwards one of the Scottish Bishops, then minister of Paisley, that all the clergy of that Presbytery were "forced for the safety of their lives to flee from their several habitations," and to leave their wives and children exposed to the fury of the fanatical assailants. The incumbents of the Presbytery of Irvine declare that "all their houses have been invaded by armed men, not only in the day-time, but for the most part under silence of night, and so many mi-

* "The Case of the present Afflicted Clergy in Scotland truly represented, to which is added for probation the Attestation of many unexceptionable Witnesses to every particular." London, 4to. 1690, p. 4

† Case, *ut supra*, p 43.

nisters as did not secretly escape were most disgracefully taken to the market crosses and other public places, and their gowns torn in pieces. They have also turned many of their wives and children out of doors, and are still proceeding to do so to others, exposing them to the extremity of the winter cold, and to perish for want of bread, when the ministers themselves durst not come near them for relief." This is attested by Charles Littlejohn, minister of Largs, and Alexander Laing, minister of Stewarton.

In a well-known and valuable work is the following notice, the writer of which is a Presbyterian :—" Of Æneas Morison, the last Episcopal minister of Contin in Ross-shire, many anecdotes are related, illustrative of his wit and benevolence. This excellent man suffered very harsh treatment for refusing to conform to Presbytery. He was rudely ejected from his own (parish) church, to which he had fled as a sanctuary, and he closed a long, honourable, and useful life in great indigence."*

It was the usual procedure of the armed Cameronians and others, besides the personal injuries they inflicted on the clergy, and the gross insults they heaped upon them, to rifle their houses, break their furniture, and in many cases to carry off what money they found. Their stipends were refused to be paid to them, and the parish churches were in many instances occupied by the Presbyterian preachers before it was known whether that system was the form of polity to be established by law. These were the persecutions mentioned by Bishop Rose in London, when the clergy in vain requested protection, though they were still the legal incumbents. Their common saying, when any of the clergy fell into their hands, was—" *Strip the curate,*" an appellation which they considered a peculiar disgrace, and they consequently applied it to all the episcopal incumbents. The tearing and destroying of the gowns they called their *testimony against Episcopacy.* Nearly three hundred clergymen were turned out of their benefices by these Cameronians and others in the west and south-west of Scotland.† In a sermon before the first Presbyterian General Assembly held after the Revolution, a preacher named Meldrum offered to " justify the barbarities of the rabble, and the ill usage which the episcopal clergy

---

* New Statistical Account of Scotland—Ross and Cromarty, p 237.
† Perth MSS. Hospital Registers, Advocates' Library, Edinburgh.

met with, alleging that their errors, vices, and scandals, deserve no better at the people's hands." This statement is made in a pamphlet of the time,* and consequently it nullifies Dr Cook's assertion that the Presbyterians in general had no concern in these atrocities. "There was a formed design," says the author of this valuable pamphlet, "of disgracing the episcopal clergy, and of rendering them infamous for immorality, but it will be much for their advantage, that after earnest desires and endeavours to blacken them, there was little or nothing made out against them. When any real scandals were found they were loudly talked of, publicly proclaimed, and laid to the charge of the whole party, as if it were a matter extraordinary to find some unworthy persons among nine hundred or a thousand."

It would be easy to multiply the instances of persecution endured by the episcopal clergy of Scotland immediately after the Revolution, during the winter of 1688-9, but to insert more would far exceed the limits of the present volume. Those excesses were the fruits of the opinions inculcated on the peasantry by the more violent of the Presbyterian preachers, of which we have numerous specimens in their printed books. In the "Hind let Loose," Mr Shields thus syllogistically delivers himself.—" A prelate's depute is no minister; a curate is a prelate's depute; *ergo*, that a prelate's depute is no minister of Christ, I prove not only from that, that a prelate, *qua talis*, is not a servant of Christ, but an enemy, and therefore cannot confer upon another that dignity to be Christ's servant." We are told that "never can it be instanced these twenty seven years [from 1660 to 1687], that the curates have brought one soul to Christ, but many instances may be given of their murdering souls; hence those who cannot but be soul-murderers may not be heard or entertained as soul-physicians, and the curates cannot but be soul-murderers " We are accordingly informed that " the meetings of the curates for administration of ordinances in their way *the Lord hates*, and hath signally forsaken ; therefore we should *hate and forsake them."* And to give only one more quotation from this precious record of hatred, fanaticism, and intolerance, the " hearing of curates reductively involves us under the guilt of idolatry and breach of the second commandment, therefore we ought *not to let them*

* An Historical Relation of the late Presbyterian General Assembly held at Edinburgh, 1691, 4to London, p. 61.

dwell in the land, lest they make us sin; we should *destroy their very names out of the place.*" Another of them, Frazer of Brae, in a performance entitled "Prelacy an Idol," declares—"I fear all bairns that are baptized by the curates are the children of whoredom."

These passages show the spirit fostered and encouraged by the Presbyterian ministers against the Episcopal clergy of Scotland at the Revolution, and the treatment they encountered from a people stirred up by their perverted interpretations of Scripture and infamous assertions. As of all hatreds a religious hatred is the most implacable, so of all persecutions that dictated by fanaticism is the most dangerous and relentless. The Episcopal Church of Scotland was never guilty of persecution. It is again repeated that the prosecutions of the Covenanters and others in the reign of Charles II. were state or government prosecutions, occasioned by their own sullen conduct, and their *sufferings,* as they are called, were considered as punishments for the crimes which the Government and the law declared they had committed It is no part of the design of the present work either to explain, defend, or censure the Government of that period, or to discuss the wisdom of the measures which were deemed expedient to be adopted against the thousands of armed zealots, who contrived to keep the country in a ferment for some years. A defence of it was written by Sir George Mackenzie, the Lord Advocate, one of the ablest lawyers of his time in Scotland. It may be simply observed, that the statement that the cause of what is called civil and religious liberty was maintained by the Presbyterians of Scotland, is altogether fallacious, contrary to fact and to historical evidence, and is refuted by the sentiments, both political and ecclesiastical, which they maintained, and the conduct they exhibited.

As might have been expected, many pamphlets and other productions appeared at the time from both parties, denouncing the clergy, and explaining or defending on the part of the triumphant Presbyterians. The persecution endured by the Episcopal clergy was so undeniable, that we find some of the leading Presbyterian ministers of that day attempting to throw the whole blame upon the Cameronians, who, it is said by Mr Gilbert Rule, "stood at a distance from the sober Presbyterians," although even he insinuates that the "zealous party," as he calls them, made it "their work *only to deprive,* and not to murder, the Episcopal ministers," while he inconsistently, in his defence of the Presbyterians written by order of the General Assembly, states that the Cameronians were a people rendered *mad*. The general topic of a work written by this same Mr Gilbert Rule, who became one of the Presbyterian ministers of Edinburgh at the Revolution, is to prove that the Cameronians are not Presbyterians. This work is entitled " A Vindication of the Church of Scotland," and is an answer to five productions on the side of the Episcopal clergy. It was answered by the learned Dr Alexander Monro, of the University of Edinburgh, in a valuable essay, entitled " An Apology for the Clergy of Scotland, chiefly opposed to Censures, Calumnies, and Accusations of a late Presbyterian Vindicator, in a Letter to a Friend." Some passages of this reply are worthy of the reader's perusal.

" All along he [Rule] seems to disown the Cameronians as Presbyterians, or as men not of their communion. At other times he acknowledges that they are *zealous godly men*, and if he proves that the barbarities committed upon the clergy were not committed by *sober* and *intelligent* Presbyterians, he thinks the Presbyterians are sufficiently vindicated from all imputations of cruelty and violence ; and, therefore, unless we prove them sober and intelligent he thinks all our complaints of the outrage and tumults of the Presbyterians are vain and impertinent. But are not the Cameronians Presbyterians ? To what communion, then, do they belong ? Have they any principles, discipline, or worship, different from the Presbyterians ? Were not their leading men lately owned and received by the pretended General Assembly, without retracting any articles of doctrine, or disowning any of their practices that they so zealously recommended to their followers in the West? This is a very pleasant fancy, that the author should endeavour to hide the tumults and insurrections of that party by changing the name of Presbyterian into Cameronian.—We know no opinions that Mr Cameron* propagated or entertained which were peculiar to himself. He

---

* Richard Cameron, the field preacher, killed in rebellion already noticed. It is proper to notice, that there is a sect of Presbyterian Dissenters in Scotland, whose founders would not conform to the Presbyterian Establishment at the Revolution, popularly called *Cameronians*, though the title they themselves adopt is the *Reformed Presbyterian Church* or Synod I am not aware of any peculiarity which distinguishes them from the Establishment in point of doctrine or mode of worship. It is said that they contend for the Solemn League and Covenant, for the abolition of lay patronage,

followed most closely and ingeniously the hypothesis of the old and zealous Presbyterians, and the plain truth is, Mr Cameron was not a man very proper to be the founder of a new sect. He built upon the notions he was taught by his brethren, and the Presbyterians are obliged for this word *Cameronian* to the Episcopal clergy, who mean no more by this word than a *Presbyterian whose zeal for his faction* (after the example of Mr Cameron) *over drives him violently beyond all bounds of discretion.* The word *Presbyterian* is known in England, but the word *Cameronian* is not, and therefore this distinction is a very plausible defence in England to disprove all the complaints made by the Episcopal clergy, as if the Cameronians were a new species of schismatics different from the Presbyterians, and that we had three considerable divisions of Christians in Scotland—the Episcopal party, the Presbyterians, and the Cameronians, whereas indeed we know of none but two, and the Cameronians are those Presbyterians who have studied their own principles most accurately, and drawn from them those principles and practical conclusions which they naturally and necessarily yield. The whole nation knows that those Presbyterians whom he nick-names Covenanters did assert their Presbyterian principles when others were very silent, and upon this they value themselves as the most active, pious, and ingenious of the whole party, who differ not from others in their principles, but do exceed some of their brethren in higher degrees of zeal and sincerity to promote the interest of their combination. What is it that Cameronians have done that they might not have done upon Presbyterian principles? What is there in the most barbarous rabbling of the clergy inconsistent with the Presbyterian principles? What is there in their tumultuous rabblings that the Presbyterians can disown?

" I think the author is to blame for saying that the Cameronians are not *intelligent,* for certainly they took their measures by the best directions that could be had, and their agents gave them exact intelligence

and some other matters which the mass of the Presbyterians in Scotland do not acknowledge They were furious opponents of the Union, and one of their great objections to it was that the English Bishops were acknowledged in the Treaty as *Lords Spiritual* They are now a quiet and inoffensive sect, bigoted enough in their own way, and obstinately wedded to their own opinions. Their numbers are very limited, and in 1842 consisted of what they call six Presbyteries, with between thirty and forty congregations.

of what they might venture upon, and when, accordingly, a company of wicked incendiaries, who had declared war against King Charles the Second, when he governed the nation by those laws that were made in times of peace by the most unanimous and solemn Parliaments that ever the nation had, and who declared in their seditious pamphlets and papers that he had forfeited all right to the crown, because, forsooth, he had broken their Covenant—I say, they were the men who at the beginning of this Revolution (as they were directed) fell violently upon the clergy, and drove them from their houses and residences, to the scandal of Christianity, and reproach of our nation; and this is not at all to be imputed to the casual efforts of passion or revenge, but to an uniform combination of the whole society · and this appears, because the clergy were not generally rabbled by their own parishioners, but by those firebrands who concerted their measures with their own societies, and did nothing of that nature without advice and directions. The cruelties the clergy met with proceed from a *League* and *Covenant* amongst their enemies, since those mischiefs did not light upon a few of the clergy, who might possibly have provoked their parishioners by some indiscretions, but upon the *whole order*, even upon such (who, mistaking the true objects of pity and compassion) as had frequently interposed with their superiors to mitigate the legal penalties against the Nonconformists. Add to this, that several of the gentry in the West, who were better natured, and had better principles than their Presbyterian neighbours, were very forward to resent the affronts and indignities done to the clergy, until they understood that the tide had risen too high to be resisted, and that such of the Presbyterians as were then out of the nation, and directed the methods that the rabblers were to take, would rigorously resent the least stop put to their career. Does this author [Gilbert Rule] think that the present generation knows nothing of the history of Presbyterians? That all the British tragedies from the year 1638 are buried in eternal silence? That all the monuments of their daring insolence are extinct? That the Acts of the General Assembly are lost? That the villanies of the Presbyterians are recorded nowhere? Why, then, does he think to impose upon the world by telling us that, indeed, they are very sorry for the tumults that happened in the West, but that the Presbyterians were no actors in these disorders?"

The following passages are so applicable to the present times that no apology is necessary for transferring them to these pages. "The Presbyterians in Scotland," says Dr Monro, " plead for their national, classical, spiritual power, *independent upon kings.* They are generally blinded with this fatal prejudice, an evidence of their incurable enthusiasm, that they think no man can act against them but he immediately acts against the light of his own conscience. They take it for granted that *their way* is the only true religion,—that it is *plainly* revealed,— and that *they* give greater evidences of piety and religion than any other society of Christians on earth ; and if you do not believe this presently, without examination, you are *far from the kingdom of God*, nay, you are *alienated from the life of God.* Hence it is that the Presbyterians conclude that whatever is done against their party is done rather against the light and conviction of their opponents, than the petulance and vanity of their own fraternity, and therefore they insinuate upon all occasions, that all reasonings against them proceed from profanity and atheism, or from men void of all principles and religion. You may as easily reason a bedlamite out of his fancied honours and principalities, as persuade any of their disciples that they are in error ; and this they owe to their teachers, who tyrannise over their belief as imperiously as the cruel Brahmins do among the Indians "

There are other matters discussed in this rare and valuable production which must not be omitted in the present chapter. It cannot be denied that, in addition to the personal injuries and persecutions suffered by the Episcopal clergy of Scotland at the Revolution, their characters were most wantonly aspersed, and all manner of crimes were imputed to them. It was not only falsely alleged that the people were injured by the clergy—that they rigorously and peevishly pressed conformity—that they were heterodox, and were intruders, because they had obtained their benefices by presentation from the legal patron and collation from the diocesan, instead of being popularly elected, but they were charged with ignorance and gross immorality.* " I am acquaint-

* This was an old practice of the Presbyterians in Scotland, who, whenever they wanted to excite an odium against the Episcopal clergy, accused them of all manner of crimes, such as murder, incest, atheism, profane swearing, theft, &c. The General Assembly of Glasgow in 1638 accused all the Bishops of these crimes, and, will it be believed in the nineteenth century, the great, the learned, the virtuous Archbishop Spottiswoode of St Andrews was specially singled out among their infamous charges? The recollection of these and other facts makes the blood boil at the

ed," says Dr Monro, " with few of the clergy of the western shires, but I am informed by judicious and intelligent men that generally the clergy in those shires were grave, sober, and assiduous in the work of the ministry. As for the scandalous aspersions cast upon the clergy by the Western Presbyterians, it is certain that by one of the Vindicator's own *Rules** we ought not to believe them, because they are all of them of a party, and indeed of such a party who, from their first appearance in the world, placed much of their strength in reproaching the clergy. If some of the ministers in the West did not live according to the dignity of their characters, we ought rather all of us, *who have not renounced our baptism,* to lament rather than insult and upbraid them with it. Indeed, a minister whose employment is to fit other men for eternal life, and yet lives in open and scandalous opposition to his *rule*, is the most monstrous thing in nature. If any of the clergy be guilty of such things as are clamorously alleged by Presbyterians, it is no argument against the common cause of the Catholic Church, and the apostolical succession of the hierarchy of Bishop, Priest, and Deacon, continued from the days of the Apostles until now. We have had late instances of the Presbyterian activity against the reputation of the clergy, and no man could escape a libel that enjoyed a comfortable benefice. Nothing could have made the Presbyterians more contemptible than this treacherous and sneaking method of libelling, when it is visible to all men that those scurrilous papers were intended for no more than to ruin and disgrace the most innocent and deserving men. And it is very odd that they could venture to blindfold the nation by this baffled and hypocritical sham. How comes it that the clergy in the West are represented as criminals, when they dare not attack the clergy in the North? The reason is obvious. The people in the West date their conversion from the time they forbear to bear the *curates,* and they think themselves bound by all those ties and solemn covenants to ruin and disparage those limbs of Antichrist. But the people in the North can discover no such beauty in their Presbyterian discipline; they love and honour their own ministers, they hear them preach the articles of Christ-

villanies, as the Bishop elect [Dr Monro] of Argyll properly calls them, of the Presbyterians of the seventeenth century. The same infamous conduct was pursued at the Revolution

* A witty allusion to his name—*Gilbert Rule.*

ian faith and true and solid morals, and they cannot be persuaded but that the oracles of God may be preached without affectation, and yet with all requisite gravity and recollection."*

"But it is necessary," says Principal Monro, "to put those proud and supercilious men in mind that they are but ordinary mortals, encompassed about with the same infirmities as other men, and that they should consult the Scriptures and the Fathers for arguments, rather than the Cameronian zealots in the western shires. I know not a more unblameable company of men upon earth than the Episcopal clergy of Scotland; nor do I know any five of them in the whole nation who could not undergo the severest examination used in the Christian Church preparatory to ordination. God will clear our innocence as the sun in his meridian elevation, and I hope to the conviction of our enemies, that in the simplicity of our souls we designed the reformation of sinners, and that we look upon ourselves as dedicated to the immediate service of God; and the sooner we retire into our consciences, and discover the secret springs of our present calamity, the sooner will our heavenly Father remove the marks of his indignation. There is no argument so proper to convince the ignorance of foolish men as by *well-doing*, and though we should not be so successful in gaining proselytes in the midst of a crooked and perverse generation, yet we fortify the peace and tranquillity of our consciences, we strengthen ourselves against those things that are most terrible to flesh and blood, we 'rejoice with joy unspeakable and full of glory,' in the midst of all calamities and reproaches that are cast upon us. And let not them that are untouched think that their brethren, upon whom the tower in Siloam fell, are greater sinners than their neighbours."

* Principal Monro says, in another place, that the Presbyterians "always accused the Episcopalians that their sermons were cold, and dry, and moral discourses, and were not calculated to the capacities and affections of the people as *theirs* were; and, therefore, they complied so much with the *genius* of the people that they forgot the majesty of religion, and the distinction between things sacred and profane. There may be so many stories added of their abusive distortions of the Scriptures with authentic attestations, that it were their wisdom to let this debate fall. For preaching after their way is become of late so trifling an exercise, that no man could perform it to the satisfaction of their thorough-paced disciples but he that was either an extraordinary hypocrite or well advanced in madness; and whatever men pretend who have considered that affair superficially, it is necessary to expose that absurd, sensual, and ludicrous sect, who metamorphose religion and its solemn exercises into theatrical scenes."

This is a noble and eloquent declaration, coming as it does from one of the most learned men of his time in Scotland, the Principal of a University, whose respectability of character, honour, and veracity, were well known throughout the kingdom, and never called in question. The only attack on Principal Monro is found in the Answer to the Scotch Presbyterian Eloquence, written by George Redpath, alias *William Laick*, in which it is stated—" It is well-known that Mr Monro, commonly called Dr Monro, a mighty agent for the [Episcopal] party, and one of their present pamphleteers, rode several years in the Pope's Guards—which methinks looks somewhat strange that such kind of men should be the greatest sticklers for the party." This charge was probably made against the Principal, because he was thought to have some concern in the publication of the famous exposure of the Presbyterians, entitled " The Scotch Presbyterian Eloquence." Principal Monro, in a postscript, containing remarks on some of Redpath's falsehoods against the clergy in his Answer to the Scotch Presbyterian Eloquence, thus speaks of himself in the third person :—" I am sufficiently acquainted with the Doctor, and he says so little of him, that I may be allowed to examine it particularly. First, he is *commonly called Dr Monro,* and the meaning of this is one of two, either a fanatic squeamishness that will not allow the title of *Doctor* to any clergyman, or an insinuation that he has not graduated Doctor at an University. If the first be intended, it is but a piece of Quakerism; if the second be meant, he was not called *Doctor* till the month of February 1682, when he received his degree in the Theological School of the New College at St Andrews, from the learned Dr Comrie, then Vice-Chancellor of the University. Our libeller adds, that he is *a mighty agent for the party* If he has any good qualities to recommend him, that of a good agent is none of them And, again, he is represented to be one of the *Episcopal pamphleteers.* I do not know what he means by this, unless he charges him with being the author of the *Presbyterian Inquisition.* But the saddest blow against the Doctor is this, that it is *well known he rode several years in the Pope's Guards.* But I ask, to whom is this known ? To the *Presbyterians only,* who know *all secrets,* and discover plots in the world of the moon ! For the time the Doctor was abroad he was never out of France and the confines of it, nor nearer to Rome than about four hundred and eighty Italian miles."

CHAPTER V.

STATE OF PARTIES IN SCOTLAND AT THE REVOLUTION, AND ITS CONSEQUENCES AS AFFECTING THE ESTABLISHED EPISCOPAL CHURCH.

THE Presbyterians, in their attacks against the Episcopal Church, continually assert that the great mass of the people were in favour of their system. This may be admitted to a certain extent in some districts, but there is abundant evidence to prove that even the peasantry were not so inimical to the Church as an establishment as is commonly supposed. In the " Memoirs of John Ker of Kersland, Esq.," a prominent Presbyterian leader of the time, published in 1726, we have an analysis of the three parties existing in Scotland at the period of the Union, whom he designates the " Presbyterian, Cameronian, and Episcopal:"—and of the last he says—" The Episcopal party, whose principles I shall not describe, farther than that they are generally in the Pretender's interest, and are *near one half of the nation*, among whom are to be reckoned the most part of the Highland Clans, whose numbers, notwithstanding their late misfortunes, are rather increased than diminished, for the commiseration of such, who with their families have suffered lately, hath brought over several converts to that side."*

During the reign of James II. indulgences or tolerations were granted to all Presbyterians, the Covenanters and Cameronians excepted, who denounced those licences in the most furious manner. This same Mr Ker of Kersland, whose brother was a noted leader of the Cameronians, and in arms against the Government, thus notices the proceedings of the King :—" After the Duke of Monmouth's and Argyll's death,

* Memoirs, p 16.

King James, supposing he was firmly established on the throne, endeavoured to restrain the penal laws against Papists and Protestant Dissenters, no doubt to promote the Popish interest; but missing his aim in Parliament, for the Scots strenuously opposed it, he in 1687 granted a toleration to all Papists and Dissenters in general, whereupon the Presbyterians built meeting-houses, and in their General Assembly addressed the King with abundance of pretended loyalty and allegiance, promising inviolable adherence to his interest to the last drop of their blood, which how well they performed will appear in the following history."*

Many of the Presbyterians took advantage of the indulgence, as it was called, and not only preached publicly, but formed themselves in their own way into judicatories, as they designate their several associated meetings, in which they enacted such regulations as were considered obligatory on themselves as a religious community of Dissenters. After the landing of the Prince of Orange they met in a kind of general convention at Edinburgh in January 1689, and sent a congratulatory address to the future King. This must have been during the absence of the Bishop of Edinburgh in London. About this time they also revived their Kirk-Sessions, Presbyteries, and Provincial Synods, according to their own notions, but so low had they fallen as a party that a Presbyterian authority explicitly states—" The scarcity of ministers was great, and in many places of the kingdom a sufficient number could not be found to constitute a synod, far less to constitute particular presbyteries."†

It is already stated that the interview between King William and the Bishop of Edinburgh decided the fate of the Scottish Episcopal Church with respect to its legal establishment. Nevertheless, the Revolution Government had not interfered in Scottish affairs. On the 22d of January 1688-9, the English Parliament declared their throne vacant by the abdication of King James, who had " violated the fundamental laws, and withdrawn himself out of the kingdom." On the 13th of February a deputation from both Houses of Parliament waited on William and Mary, with a resolution for their public proclamation

* Memoirs, p. 10.
† Perth MSS. Advocates' Library, Edinburgh, entitled *Hospital Registers*, in the handwriting of Mr James Scott, one of the Presbyterian ministers of Perth.

as " King and Queen of England, France, and Ireland, to hold to them during their joint lives, and the life of the survivor of them :" the succession confined to the heirs of the body of Princess Mary, with remainder to her sister the Princess Anne of Denmark and her descendants, and to the descendants of William. The meeting of the Scott'sh Estates, first called together under extraordinary circumstances on the 14th of March 1689, was " turned into a Parliament" on the 5th day of the following June, and as that meeting has uniformly been held and recognised as a legitimate assembly of the legislature, its acts have obtained a place in the chronological series of the records of the Parliaments of Scotland. During the interval between the meeting of the Estates in March and April, and the Session of Parliament in June thereafter, the regulation of public affairs devolved on a Committee of Noblemen, Barons, and Burgesses, nominated for that purpose by the Estates, whose sittings commenced on the 29th day of April, and were continued to the 23d of May.

The meeting of the Estates on the 14th of March was convened by circular letters from the Prince of Orange to " the Lords of the Clergie and Nobility, and to the Sheriffe Clerks for the severall Shyres, and to the Toune Clerks for the Royall Burghs." The Archbishops of St Andrews and Glasgow, and the Bishops of Edinburgh, Dunkeld, Moray, Ross, Dunblane, Orkney, and the Isles, were present.* In the letter addressed to the Estates by the Prince of Orange, signed William R., nothing is stated respecting the establishment of Presbyterianism. The first act of importance adopted by the meeting was one declaring it to be a free and lawful convention of the Estates. The macer having intimated that a person was in attendance with a letter from King

* The Nobility were the Duke of Hamilton, who was constituted President, the Duke of Queensberry, the Marquises of Douglas and Atholl, the Earls of Argyll, Crawford, Erroll, Marischal, Sutherland, Mar, Morton, Glencairn, Eglinton, Cassillis, Linlithgow, Home, Dunfermline, Lauderdale, Lothian, Airlie, Callendar, Leven, Annandale, Panmure, Selkirk, Tweeddale, Kincardine, Balcarras, Forfar, Tarras, Dundonald, Kintore, Viscounts Kenmure, Arbuthnot, Oxenford, Tarbet, Dundee (Grahame of Claverhouse); Lords Sinclair, Elphinstone, Lovat, Ross, Torphichen, Lindores, Balmerino, Blantyre, Cardross, Melville, Forrester, Bargany, Dunkeld, Belhaven, Carmichael, Duffus, Rollo, Ruthven, Rutherford, Bellenden, Newark. A curious biography could be written of some of those personages. It is unnecessary to enumerate the Commissioners for the counties and burghs.

James, he was called in, and allowed to present it, but the letter of the Prince of Orange, by whom they were assembled, was first read and recorded. They then passed the act, which is thus expressed :—" For as much as there is a letter from King James the Seventh presented to the meeting of the Estates, they, before opening thereof, declare and enact, that notwithstanding any thing that may be contained in that letter for dissolving them, or impeding their procedure, yet that they are a free and lawful meeting of the Estates, and will continue undissolved until they settle and secure the Protestant religion, the government, laws, and liberties of the kingdom "* The Prelates who subscribed this important declaration along with the Nobility, Barons, and Burgesses, were the Archbishop of Glasgow, the Bishops of Dunkeld, Moray, Ross, Dunblane, the Isles, and Orkney.† The letter of King James, dated on board the St Michael, 1st March 1689, was then read, but it contained no order for dissolving the meeting of the Estates, and earnestly enjoined them to be loyal, at the same time threatening punishment to all who continued disaffected in their allegiance after the last day of that month—a denouncement which, as the event proved in his case, was utterly harmless. This letter is not recorded in the Books of the Convention, but it is still preserved,‡ and the manner of its reception by the Estates was significant of their future proceedings. King James was at that moment their rightful and undoubted sovereign ; with what had taken place in England, respecting the acknowledgment of the Prince of Orange as King, the Scottish people as an independent nation, and as possessing their own legislature, had no concern ; and yet the letter of the King was thrown aside with cool indifference.

The Archbishops and Bishops withdrew from the Estates after their first meeting, and they are never subsequently mentioned as having

* Act. Parl. Scot. fol. vol. ix. p 9, in which is inserted a fac-simile of the original document, with the signatures of the Bishops, Nobility, Barons, and Burgesses.

† The signatures are in the following order :—" Jo. Glasgow, Jo. Dunkelden. Will. Moravien J. Rossien Ro Dunblanen. Arch Sodoren. And. Orcaden." The declaration was signed by the Duke of Hamilton and forty-three noblemen, among whom was the Viscount of Dundee, better known as Graham of Claverhouse, who, in this stage of the proceedings, approved of the meeting of the Estates adopting measures for securing the " Protestant religion, laws, and liberties of the Kingdom," but who never imagined that they were about to renounce their allegiance to James II.

‡ Printed in Act. Parl. Scot vol. ix. p. 10.

been present On the 19th of March the Estates passed an " act for putting the kingdom in a posture of defence ;" in which, after declaring that they would " continue their meeting undissolved until they should settle and secure the Protestant religion, the government, laws, and liberties of the kingdom," the said Estates " doe advertise and require the whole Protestants of the kingdom, between sixtein and sixty, to be in readiness with their best horses and armes upon advertisement from the meeting of Estates; and likewayes to have their militia in readiness, to receive such orders as shall be direct to them from the said Estates, for securing the Protestant religion, the lawes, and liberties of the kingdom."* They next resorted to the extraordinary expedient of requiring a kind of oath of allegiance to themselves, " to be taken by all persons in military employments,"† and passed an act approving of the " good services done by the noblemen and gentlemen of this nation, who lately at London did make and signe a tymeous and dutyfull address to his Highness the Prince of Orange, containing just and thankfull acknowledgments of the great benefits done to the nation, in delyvering them from the eminent incroatchments on our lawes and fundamentall constitutions, and from the near dangers which threatened ane overturning of the Protestant religion, and the humble proffer of their lives and fortunes to his Highness for sustaining him in prosecution of so good a cause; as also, desyring his Highness to accept on him the administration of the government of this kingdom ; while a meeting of the Estates thereof were called to consult on a farther settlement, they do ratifie, approve, and homologate the said address in all its tenor and contents ; and declair the same to have been ane act of duety, tending to the good of the Protestant religion in general, and of this nation in particular, in all its concernes."‡

On the 20th of March the Estates issued a fierce " proclamation against Papists ;" and on the 23d an act was passed for " securing suspect persons." On the latter day a congratulatory letter to the Prince

* Acta Parl. Scot. vol. ix. p. 13.

† " Whereas I have accepted of a commission from the Estates of Scotland, or am continued in command by them, I faithfully promitt, in presence of the Almighty God, and swear that I shall demean myselfe faithfully to the Estates now presently mett, so long as I continue in that statione."—Acta Parl. Scot. vol. ix. p. 14.

‡ Acta Parl. Scot. vol. ix. p. 14.

of Orange, as King of England, was read, approved, and signed by the Duke of Hamilton as President, and a number of the nobility, barons, and burgesses. The reasons for declaring the Scottish throne vacant were produced on the 4th of April; and these are exclusively founded on the unhappy conduct of King James in favour of the Roman Catholics, and his avowed religious principles; but no allusion is made to the Episcopal Church either directly or indirectly. It was at the same time ordered that the Committee for settling the Crown on William and Mary " bring in ane act" to that effect, and " to consider the termes of the destinatione of the aires (heirs) of the Crown." On the 11th of April this declaration of the Estates, containing what they called the " Claim of Right," and the offer of the Crown to " William and Mary, King and Queen of England," was read, and after several amendments finally approved This document recapitulates at great length the reasons assigned on the 4th of April for declaring the throne vacant; and the only allusion to the Episcopal Church is in one of the articles, the twenty-second in the order of arrangement. It is to the effect that " Prelacy and the superiority of any office in the Church above Presbyters is, and hath been, a great and insupportable grievance and trouble to this nation, and contrary to the inclinations of the generality of the people ever since the Reformation, they having reformed from Popery by Presbyters, and therefore ought to be abolished." The succession of the Scottish Crown was regulated similarly to that of England. It was also ordered that the following oath " be taken by all Protestants of whom the oath of allegiance and any other oaths and declarationes might be required by law in stead of them, and that the said oath of allegiance, and other oaths and declarationes, may be abrogated:—I do sincerly promise and swear that I will be faithfull and bear true allegiance to their Majesties King William and Queen Mary. So help me God." On that day William and Mary were ordered to be proclaimed at the Cross of Edinburgh by the Lord Lyon King-at-Arms, and throughout the kingdom; and the Estates also passed an act " declaring that they are to continue in the Government until the King and Queen of England accept the Crown."*

It is to be here observed that the oath of allegiance before the Revolu-

---

* Acta Parl. Scot. vol. ix. pp. 37—41.

tion was very different from the above enacted by the Scottish Estates, and this was the great stumbling-block in the way of the bishops, clergy, several of the nobility, numerous gentlemen, and even of many Presbyterians, who refused to acknowledge King William and Queen Mary on conscientious principles. The oath before the Revolution was as follows :—" I do promise to be true and faithful to the King and *his heirs*, and truth and faith to bear, of life and limb and terrene honour, and not to *know or hear of any ill or damage intended him*, without defending him therefrom." No oath of abjuration was then required from any order of men. The opinions expressed by James Earl of Arran, afterwards fourth Duke of Hamilton, eldest son of William and Anne Duke and Duchess of Hamilton, were those of the Scottish Bishops and clergy, and of a powerful body of influential laity. His Lordship stated his opinions at one of the conferences held by the Scottish nobility in London after the arrival of William. " I have all the honour and deference imaginable," said his Lordship, " for the Prince of Orange. I think him a brave Prince, and that we owe him great obligations for contributing so much to our deliverance from Popery, but while I pay him these praises I cannot violate my duty to my master. I must distinguish between his Popery and his person ; I dislike the one, but I have sworn and do owe allegiance to the other, which makes it impossible for me to sign away that which I cannot forbear believing is the King my master's right ; for his present absence from us in France can no more affect my duty than his longer absence from us (in Scotland) has done all this while ; and, therefore, as the Prince has desired our advices, mine is, that we should move his Majesty (James II.) to return and call a free Parliament for securing our religion and property, which, in my humble opinion, will at last be found the best way to heal all our breaches "* This nobleman, who adopted different views of the Revolution from his father, and whose life, from the Revolution to his death in the fatal duel with Lord Mohun in Hyde Park in 1712, evinced a continual struggle between his sense of duty and his inclination to support the interest of the exiled Family. It is now unnecessary to express any opinion regarding the policy or justice of the Earl of Arran's sentiments, which may now be considered as exploded, and it is only sufficient to state, that they

* Douglas' Peerage of Scotland (Wood's edition), vol. i. p 711

prevailed to a very great extent throughout Scotland. It is now admitted that protection and allegiance are to a certain extent reciprocal. Dr Paley understands the present oath as not requiring us to continue our allegiance to the sovereign if actually deposed, or driven into exile. Whatever notion may be formed of the soundness of this interpretation of the present oath, the former one was considered in a different light by men of the highest rank in Scotland. All persons in office had sworn to be faithful to King James and *his heirs*, and, as Bishop Russell observes, " though the Scottish Convention had voted that King James, by his mal-administration and his abuse of power, had forfeited all title to the crown, the Bishops might, without absurdity or narrow-mindedness, consider themselves as still bound by their oaths to be faithful to his infant son, who could have done nothing to forfeit *his* titles."*

On the subject of oaths of allegiance, as administered at this period, the following observations, though applicable rather to the English Nonjurors than to the Scottish Bishops and Clergy, are worthy of notice. " No oaths of whatever description," says Bishop Short, in his admirable remarks on the English Nonjurors and the Revolution of 1688, " will bind bad men, when the sentiments of the mass of the people are contrary to the tenor of the oath ; and there is no more frightful particular presented to us by history than the frequency with which oaths are imposed and broken. In this case many upright men, whose bold and temperate opposition to James had been chiefly instrumental in fixing the opinions of the nation, and who, under God, had contributed more than any others to effect the change which had taken place, were the first to suffer for their uprightness. No one can fail to admire their conduct, and to pity them, if indeed any one who suffers in the performance of his duty can be an object of pity ; but surely the Government which imposes the oath by which such persons were ejected, has no reason to expect that it will be served by honest men."† In addition, the circumstances of the times must be taken into account. It is observed by a very competent judge, that while the Revolution was conducted *constitutionally* by the English Parliament, it was conducted *unconstitutionally* by the Scottish Convention, the members of which were,

* Keith's Catalogue of Scottish Bishops, Appendix, p. 497.
† Sketch of the History of the Church of England to the Revolution of 1688. By Thomas Vowler Short, D.D , in 1841 Bishop of Man, vol. ii p. 371, 372.

with hardly any exceptions, all of one party.* If this is the deliberate opinion of recent times, it must have been intensely felt at the Revolution, when no one could have predicted its advantages, and when a powerful party never believed that the new Government would be permanent.

On the 13th of April the Scottish Estates issued a stringent proclamation "against owning of the late King James, and appointing public prayers for William and Mary, King and Queen of Scotland." The only allusion to ecclesiastical matters is one of the "grievances" voted and approved—" That the first act of Parliament 1669 is inconsistent with the establishment of the Church government now desyred, and ought to be abrogated."† This act, which is properly the second of that Parliament, is entitled an " Act asserting his Majestie's Supremacie over all persons and in all causes ecclesiastical."‡ On the 16th of April the form of the oath to be taken by William and Mary at their acceptance of the Crown was read, voted, and approved in the usual manner, yet it has no reference either to the Episcopal Church or to Presbyterianism, and it is generally expressed that the new sovereigns were to " maintain the true religion of Christ Jesus, the preaching of his holy Word, and the due and right ministration of the sacraments, *now* received and preached within the realm of Scotland."§

The Earl of Argyll, Sir James Montgomery of Skelmorlie, and Sir John Dalrymple, were deputed by the Estates to proceed with a letter to William and Mary, announcing that they had been duly proclaimed with so "much unanimity, that of the whole House there was not one contrary vote." This unanimity is explained by the fact that all the nobility and members who adhered to the exiled Family had retired from the Convention. The Estates add—" We beseech your Majesties, in presence of these sent by us, to swear and signe the oath herewith presented, which our law hath appoynted to be taken by our Kings and Queens at the entry to their government, till such tyme as your great affairs allow this kingdome the happines of your presence, in order to the coronation of your Majesties."‖ On the 24th of May a letter was

---

* Ward's Inquiry into the Law of Nations, vol. ii. p. 513. Chalmers' Caledonia, vol. i. p. 864. † Acta Parl Scot. vol iv. p. 45.
‡ Acta Parl. Scot vol. vii. p. 554. § Acta Parl. Scot. vol. ix. p. 48, 49.
‖ Acta Parl. Scot. vol. ix. p. 60

received, signed William R , announcing that he and his consort had taken and signed the oath, and adjourning the Estates to the 5th of June, when they were to meet as a Parliament.* The only hostile act previous to this adjournment against the Established clergy was the deprivation, on the 26th of April, of Dr John Strachan, Professor of Divinity in the University of Edinburgh, Mr Andrew Cant, and Mr John Macqueen, both ministers of the city, for not " making publick prayers for King William and Queen Mary," and confessing that " they had not freedome to give obedience thereto in tyme comiiig."†

It is now proper to recur to the Church during the period of the preceding political sketch We have already seen that no sooner was the landing of the Prince of Orange known in several districts of Scotland, than the legal Episcopal incumbents of the parishes, ignorantly and insolently termed *curates*, as a title of opprobrium, were subjected to the most wanton maltreatment by the excited peasantry Of all this the Bishop of Edinburgh was well aware, and he has recorded the answer of Bishop Burnet, who, when earnestly requested to exert himself in behalf of his distressed countrymen, coolly told him that he "did not meddle in Scottish affairs." The suffering clergy, when they perceived that there was no prospect of a termination of the miseries they were enduring from the dangerous rabble, delegated Dr Scott, Dean of Glasgow, on the 22d of January 1688-9, to proceed to London, and " represent to the Prince of Orange, and to the Lords Spiritual and Temporal, the grievances, oppressions, and injuries they were labouring under in Scotland for their firm adherence to Episcopacy ," and they offered to prove the truth of all their allegations if they could obtain a fair and impartial hearing.‡

On the 6th of the following February a proclamation appeared in consequence, " prohibiting and discharging," as it is expressed in the Scottish legal phraseology, " all disturbance and violence upon account of religion, or the exercise thereof, or any such like pretence, and that no interruption be made, or, if any hath been made, that it cease, in the free and peaceable exercise of religion, whether in churches or in public or private meeting-houses, of those of a different persuasion." All persons in arms were also ordered peremptorily to " separate, dis-

* Acta Parl Scot vol ix. p 93, 94   † Acta Parl Scot. vol ix. p 68.
‡ Skinner's Ecclesiastical History of Scotland, vol. ii. p 520

miss, and disband themselves, and retire to their respective dwellings." But instead of this proclamation being obeyed by the tumultuous Presbyterians they became more violent, and in the city of Glasgow, on the Sunday after it had been read at the market cross, a mob of those misguided zealots assaulted the magistrates and congregation when assembled in the cathedral church for divine service, wounding a number of persons. It happened that Dr Fall, the Principal of the University, was then in London, and an account of this outrage was transmitted to him to be presented to the Prince of Orange. Dr Fall had an audience of the Prince, and laid the statement before his Highness, who told him that at the approaching meeting of the Estates all such complaints would be submitted for redress

The violence of the mob at Edinburgh, towards all whom they considered in the interest of King James, must not be overlooked during the sitting of the Convention. Crowds of the Cameronians beset the entrance of the Parliament House, studiously insulting those noblemen and gentlemen who were attached to the Church, and especially threatening and abusing the Bishops, who were still legally entitled to a seat in the Convention. In addition to this riotous conduct, several thousands of the most violent peasantry from the western counties appeared in Edinburgh, and were ordered by the Convention to be formed into a regiment under the command of the Earl of Leven, a noted supporter of the new polity. This was on the 18th of March, and the presence of this illegal body of armed men deterred many members, from a fear of their personal safety, from attending the meeting of the Estates in the Parliament House, while the Bishops no longer appeared. The Convention was now composed of persons of the same political principles. The arrival of a body of regular troops under General Mackay rendered the services of the West country Cameronians unnecessary, although Leven obtained an act empowering him to march this regiment where he pleased in Fife, and they were dismissed as " well affected to the Protestant interest," with a vote of thanks for their " reasonable assistance." The West country invasion is thus noticed by a contemporary:—" This day [18th of March 1689] the Cameronians, to the number of 7000, lately come to Edinburgh, to take the guarding of the Convention, drew up in the publick great streets of the city. These Cameronians, so called from one Cameron, a preacher, or famous ringleader among them, are the worst kind of Presbyterians, who confyne the

. Church to a few of the Western shyres of the kingdome of Scotland; disclaime all kings who will not worship God after their own way; think it their duty to murder all who are out of the state of grace, that is, not of their communion; in a word, who take away the second table of the Decalogue upon pretence of keeping the first; and who are only for sacrifice, but for no mercy at all."*

The proclamation issued by the Meeting of Estates, prohibiting the acknowledgment of King James, ordered " all ministers of the gospel within the kingdom to publicly pray for King William and Queen Mary, as King and Queen of this realm; requiring likewise the ministers within the city of Edinburgh, under pain of being deprived and losing their benefices, to read this proclamation from their pulpits on Sunday next, the 14th instant, at the end of the forenoon sermon, and the ministers to the south of the Tay to read it on the 21st, and those to the north of the Tay on the 28th, under the above penalty; and prohibiting any injury to be offered, by any person whatever, to any minister of the gospel, either in kirks or meeting-houses, who are presently in possession and exercise of their ministry therein, they behaving themselves as becometh under the present Government."

It will be subsequently seen in what manner this proclamation was obeyed by the Episcopal parochial clergy, who, it is obvious, could not act according to its injunctions without the consent of their Diocesans. The Estates, as already mentioned, deprived Dr Strachan and Messrs Cant and Macqueen before their adjournment; and the Commitee on whom devolved the regulation of public affairs between the adjournment and the meeting of the Parliament " took orders" with a few more. On the 2d of May they deprived Mr James Wauch, minister of Leith, and Mr John Somerville, minister of Cramond. On the following day, Mr Arthur Millar, minister of Inveresk, was similarly treated, and proper intimations were enjoined to be made to the patrons of the respective parishes. On the 6th of May Mr George Barclay, minister of Mordington in Berwickshire, was deprived, and two days afterwards, Mr Alexander Irvine, minister of Inverkeithing in Fife, Mr Andrew Auchinleck, minister of Newbattle, and Mr David Laurence, minister of Carrington. On the 10th were deprived Mr George Henry, minister of Cor-

* Siege of the Castle of Edinburgh, 1669, 4to, printed for the Bannatyne Club in 1828, p. 37.

storphine, and Mr Robert Ramsay, minister of Prestonpans. Mr Robert Wright and Mr Alexander Young, ministers of Culross, were deprived, and the noted preacher named Frazer of Brae appointed to officiate. On the 14th, Mr Alexander Hamilton, minister of Stenton, and Mr Alexander Cumming, minister of Libberton, were deprived; and on the following day Mr John Mather, minister of Ceres. Two days afterwards, Mr James Scrimgeour, minister of Currie, and Mr John Taylor, minister of Dron, were deprived. Some others, however, who had complied with the proclamation, but who had nevertheless been assaulted by the rabble, were ordered to continue as the incumbents of their parishes.

One great objection which influenced many of the Episcopal incumbents of the parishes to decline complying with the proclamation of the Estates, was the language of the oath which William and Mary subscribed. According to its phraseology, we are almost apt to infer that no true religion had been known or professed in Scotland, previous to the Revolution, except by the Presbyterian Cameronians and Covenanters. The new sovereigns were required to swear that they would " serve the eternal God to the utmost of their power, according as He has commanded in his most Holy Word, revealed and contained in the Old and New Testaments, and according to the same Word shall maintain the true religion of Jesus Christ, the preaching of his Holy Word, and the due and right ministration of the Sacraments now received and preached within the realm of Scotland." In this nothing is objectionable, and it strictly applied, though the framers of the oath probably meant differently, to the Episcopal Church, which was still the legal national establishment of the kingdom, though the clergy'had been visited by persecution in several districts. Previous to the meeting of the Estates, the Duke of Hamilton had earnestly entreated Archbishop Ross of St Andrews and Bishop Rose of Edinburgh, "*for their own sakes to follow the example of the Church of England,*" assuring the Primate that "nothing would be done to the prejudice of Episcopacy, if the Bishops could by any means be brought to befriend" the interests of William. The reply of the Archbishop to the Duke is previously noticed, by which it sufficiently appears that the Bishops had unanimously resolved to adhere to the exiled dynasty in " the face of all dangers, and to the greatest losses." So far, then, as the oath was expressed no possible objection could be offered, but the intolerant and persecuting clause followed, that the new Sovereigns were to swear that they would be "careful to root out all heretics and enemies to the true worship of God, that shall be convict by the *true Kirk of God of the said crimes, out of their lands and empire of Scotland.*" But William refused to subscribe this clause to the letter, as it literally bound him to sanction the *rooting out* and *extirpation* of all those whom the Presbyterians chose to malign as "heretics and enemies to the true worship of God," by which they meant exclusively their own system. This, it is admitted by Dr George Cook, the distinguished ornament of the Presbyterian Establishment, appeared to William " to imply that he was to persecute those who dissented from the ancient faith, and shrinking from the idea, he requested it to be understood that he did not by the oath bind himself to persecute any of his subjects for following the dictates of conscience "*

During the sitting of the Estates and the interval before the meeting of Parliament, the Duke of Gordon and the Viscount of Dundee caused an infinitude of alarm and trouble to the predominant party. The former nobleman was George, fourth Marquis of Huntly, advanced to the dignity of Duke of Gordon in 1684. At the Revolution he was Governor of Edinburgh Castle, and held that important fortress for King James in defiance of the Estates. His Grace was a Roman Catholic, yet he evinced his dislike of the measures of King James for encouraging the Papal system in Scotland by removing the penal laws and tests, and was in consequence much vilified by the Romish priests and their adherents. He was summoned to surrender, and on his refusal was proclaimed a traitor. This gave the Duke of Gordon little concern, and though a siege of the fortress was commenced, his Grace, notwithstanding the limited number and weakness of the garrison, and the want of provisions, held out till the 14th of June, when he surrendered on honourable conditions, and marched out unmolested. During the siege he behaved with great humanity in not allowing sallies, and abstaining from firing on the city. A contemporary account of this siege was printed for the Bannatyne Club by Robert Bell, Esq., Advocate, in

---

* Dr George Cook's History of the Church of Scotland from the Reformation to the Revolution, vol. iii. p 447.

1828. It is stated that the greater part of the garrison were Protestants, who were at first inclined to revolt, suspecting that the Duke of Gordon would oblige them by oath to maintain the Roman Catholic religion, but his Grace " assured them that he had no such intention, and that he required no other oath of them than to maintain *the religion established by the laws,* and to be obedient to the King (James II.) and their superior officers. The most part of the garrison renewed this oath, and those who refused it were disbanded, and turned out of the Castle."* The besiegers lost several men during the attack, but did little injury to the fortress. Several curious notices occur of the operations at the siege. A parley was beat on the 3d of April for a cessation of hostilities during the interment of Sir George Lockhart, Lord President of the Court of Session, in the Greyfriars' churchyard, who was assassinated by Chiesley of Dalry on Easter Sunday, when returning from the High Church to his residence in the Lawnmarket. " I cannot say whose work the besiegers were about," observes the contemporary writer, " but they never failed to ply it hard on the Lord's day, upon which one of our Highlanders observed, that though he was apt to forget the days of the week, yet he well knew Sunday, by some mischief or other begun, or hotly carried on by our Reformers."†

The other nobleman was the celebrated John Graham, created Viscount of Dundee on the 12th of November 1688 by patent, better known as Graham of Claverhouse, and the terror of the Presbyterians, who designated him *Bloody Claverhouse,* while he was the very idol of the Highland Clans, with whom his chief, the great Marquis of Montrose, had also been most enthusiastically popular. The Viscount of Dundee was a zealous supporter of the Episcopal Church, and it was his repeated declaration that the more that Church was assailed by the Presbyterians and Covenanters the more he loved it. The Viscount withdrew from the meeting of the Estates, alleging that a plot was concocted to murder him, which is not unlikely, considering the detestation in which he was held by the West country Presbyterians, several thousands of whom were then in Edinburgh. There was in reality some project to this effect concocted, and it is expressly stated by a contemporary that six or seven Cameronians intended to murder him and Sir George Mac-

---

* Siege of the Castle of Edinburgh in 1686, 4to, p. 20.   † Ibid p. 54.

kenzie * This nobleman departed from the city at the head of sixty troopers, and marched in the direction of Linlithgow and Stirling to summon the Highland Clans to the standard of King James. He left Edinburgh by the old steep alley called Leith Wynd, and slowly rode with his troopers over the ground, then called the Lang Raw, now occupied by the magnificent line of Prince's Street. When he reached the west end of that street, he halted his troopers near where St John's Episcopal Chapel now stands, and ascended the west side of the rock on which the Castle is built to hold a conference with the Duke of Gordon. He reached with no small difficulty the bottom of the walls, and met the Duke at what was called the *Postern Gate*. This was on the 19th of March, and the substance of the interview between the Duke and the Viscount is thus recorded by the contemporary writer already quoted :—
" The day following, the Governor, with a telescope, perceived some horsemen appearing on the north side of the town, and drawing towards the Castle. It was the Viscount of Dundee, who seeing the Convention had resolved to renounce all alledgiance to their lawfull soveraigne, and laid asyde all kind of respect for him, he abandoned their assemblie, and coming to the foot of the rock, the Governor spoke to him from the top of the wall, and then went out and discoursed with him. He told what had passed in the Convention at the receiving of the King's letter, and the small impression it made upon the members of that assembly. The Governor asked a sight of the letter, but Dundee had no copy, and the Governor never saw it. Then Dundee parted from the Governor, and returned to his own party of about thirty or forty horse, and went away with them towards his own dwelling beside Dundee After that time the Governor never received any letters from him "† It appears that Dundee exhorted the Duke to hold out the Castle, which he promised to relieve within twenty days.‡ Another account states that the Viscount urged the Duke to resign the fortress to the command of a faithful lieutenant, and accompany him to the Highlands to raise the Gordon clan in favour of James; but that the Duke declined, alleging that a soldier could not in honour quit the post assigned to him. He, however, assured the Viscount that he would hold out the fortress

* Locheill's Memoirs, 4to, 1842, p. 235.
† Siege of the Castle of Edinburgh, 4to, 1828, p 38.   ‡ Ibid. p. 70.

as long as possible, and the latter descending from the rock, rejoined his men, and resumed his march.

This singular conference caused great excitement in Edinburgh, and rumour was not idle. The Estates were then sitting, and it was stated that the result of the interview between the two Cavalier noblemen would be that the Duke would fire upon the Parliament House, but their fears were groundless and imaginary. Some thousands ran to witness the conference, and the Viscount's enemies alleged that they were all his adherents, and that he had collected two thousand of the disbanded troops of King James to surprise the meeting of the Estates. An order was issued to the Earl of Leven to secure the peace of the city, but Dundee, with his forty, or, as it was said in the Convention, sixty troopers, was allowed to depart unmolested. A warrant was sent to his seat near Dundee, citing him to appear before the Estates on the 22d of March, to which he paid no attention. Having been informed that the Viscount had halted at Linlithgow, the militia were commanded to dislodge him, and the Viscount and Lord Livingstone were ordered to lay down their arms within twenty-four hours, under pain of high treason. On the 30th of March the Viscount was denounced a rebel at the Cross of Edinburgh, but these proceedings were set at defiance, and he set out for the Highlands to raise the Clans, for the cause, as he expressed it, of " King James and the Church of Scotland." The Earl of Balcarras, another nobleman supposed to be in league with the Viscount, was apprehended at his seat of Balcarras in Fife, and was committed a close prisoner to the Tolbooth, and to the Castle of Edinburgh after its surrender by the Duke of Gordon.

General Mackay advanced against the Viscount of Dundee, whose extraordinary career among the Clans it would be out of place to narrate in the present work. Among his exploits may be mentioned his rout of Colonel Ramsay, which caused the retreat of General Mackay, who was pursued by the Viscount in the direction of Glenlivet. He was joined by Sir Donald Macdonald of Slate, ancestor of the Lords Macdonald, with seven hundred men, and by the Captain of Clanranald with six hundred men, in addition to the large reinforcements he had received from the Camerons of Locheill and other Clans.

CHAPTER VI

THE DISESTABLISHMENT OF THE SCOTTISH EPISCOPAL CHURCH.

The first Parliament of " our high and dread Soveraigne Lord and Lady William and Mary" met at Edinburgh, according to the order for adjourning the meeting of the Estates, on the 5th of June 1689, the Duke of Hamilton Lord High Commissioner. His Grace announced that "his Majesty having been pleased to comply with their desire, in turning this meeting of the Estates into a Parliament," produced William's letter, which was duly recorded, and an act passed, and publicly proclaimed at the Cross of Edinburgh, that " none pretend ignorance," declaring that this was a lawful Parliament. Upwards of a month was occupied in routine business, and by the members taking the oath of allegiance. On the 9th of July a letter was received from King William, in which he states that " we have likewayes instructed our Commissiouner to hasten our people's satisfaction in settling the church government, and for enacting restitution to all who have been lately injured by fines, forfeitures, or compositions on their accounts."*

It is evident from the preceding narrative that the opposition of the Presbyterians to the Church was apparently confined solely to its episcopal constitution. They had no conscientious grievances to urge in the matters of doctrine and ceremonies, and many of them never pretended to allege any, with the exception of their objections to the Doxology, the Lord's Prayer, and the reading of the Scriptures at public divine service. The charge brought against the Archbishops and

* Acta Parl. Scot. vol. ix. p 102

Bishops of slavish servility to King James, and of favouring his projects for encouraging Romanism, has been long abandoned as utterly groundless. The following observations by a distinguished member of the Presbyterian Establishment are of importance on this subject :—" Of the Episcopal clergy," says Dr George Cook, " many were so warped with notions of the obligation of non-resistance to the supreme magistrate, and were so convinced that the stability of the Hierarchy could be secured only by supporting the sovereign, that they felt the utmost reluctance to oppose his schemes; and allowing themselves to believe that he would never so far violate the solemn pledge he had given as to attack the Protestant religion, they were not averse that concessions should be made to those of the same faith with himself. But there were others of this [the Episcopal] body who saw the danger which threatened in all its magnitude—who were convinced that if, while the throne was filled by a bigoted monarch, the penal statutes against the Roman Catholics should be repealed, and every office of trust and authority laid open to them, the superstition of Rome, with all its intolerance and all its slavish maxims, would soon be restored Laying aside, therefore, their enmity to the Presbyterians, they cheerfully joined with them in warning the people; and the Synod of Aberdeen, in particular, addressed their Diocesan, imploring him to stand firm in defence of the principles which the piety and the zeal of the Reformers had after many struggles introduced." Again, when speaking of the Scottish Parliament of 1686, in which the unhappy subject of the Popish penal statutes was introduced— " Ross and Paterson, two of the Bishops, argued in favour of the repeal, but some of their brethren acted a very different part. The Archbishop of Glasgow with some timidity opposed the measure : but the Bishop of Galloway, though an old man, and the Bishops of Dunkeld and Ross, made a *determined stand*, and resisted all the methods which were employed to seduce them from their duty. Of the rest of the prelates, most, although they were silent, resolved to vote against compliance with the Court, and a few did not attend; but it was apparent that there was the utmost aversion to repeal the statutes, and that this aversion was founded on conscience." And after King James, to further his fatal projects, had granted a toleration in Scotland, Dr Cook says:—" The Established [Episcopal] clergy, notwithstanding the acquiescence of some of the Bishops, looked with uneasiness upon the liberty which all sects now enjoyed [in 1687 and 1688]. Many of them dreaded the restoration of Popery, and perhaps more apprehended that the unrestrained efforts of the Presbyterians would render the torrent of popular opinion against the Hierarchy difficult to be resisted. They in consequence became discontented, and they did not conceal what they felt. Even the Council were irritated at several of the King's measures, and though they used the most submissive language, antipathy to Government was daily gaining ground, and only waited for a favourable opportunity to display its strength."*

It is farther admitted by Dr Cook, that it was the avowed inclination of King William to continue the Episcopal Church as the national Establishment:—" Although he wished that all should be permitted, without molestation, to worship God according to conscience, yet he thought it desirable that the same form of church government should be established through the whole of Britain; and if the Episcopal party had now cordially joined him, if they had acknowledged him as their lawful sovereign, and consented to those modifications of Episcopacy which he contemplated, for including within the pale of the Establishment those who otherwise would not have entered it, there can be little doubt that he would earnestly have contended for the continuance of the Hierarchy, and it is probable that by his influence this continuance would have been accomplished."† The truth is, that William knew nothing of the actual state of Scotland at the time. He admitted that he had been grossly misinformed on the subject when in Holland, and he was sufficiently sagacious to perceive the advantages which would result from the same ecclesiastical establishment being preserved in the three kingdoms.

On the 19th of July the act was passed " abolishing Prelacie." It sets forth that " wheras the Estates of this Kingdome, in their Claime of Right of the eleventh of Aprile last, declared that Prelacie, and the superiority of any office in the Church above Presbyters, is, and hath been, a great and unsupportable grievance to this nation, and contrair to the inclinationes of the generalitie of the people ever since the Reformation, they having reformed from Poperie by Presbyters, and therefore ought to be abolished, our Sovereigne Lord and Lady, the King and Queen's

---

* Dr Cook's History of the Church of Scotland from the Reformation to the Revolution, vol. iii p. 419, 420, 422, 432. † Ibid. p. 440.

Majesties, with advice and consent of the Estates of Parliament, do hereby abolish Prelacie, and all superioritie of any office in the Church in this Kingdome above Presbyters." The act concludes—" And the King and Queen's Majesties doe declare that they, with advice and consent of the Estates of this Parliament, will settle by law that church government in this kingdome which is most agreeable to the inclinationes of the people."*

In the meantime, the apprehensions of the Presbyterian party, and not unlikely the hopes of the Episcopal clergy and laity, were not a little excited by the movements of the Viscount of Dundee. He had been favoured with a passing notice in a warrant granted on the 9th of July, in which the Parliament actually authorised *torture* to be used in the case of those who were found in correspondence with him. On the 1st of August the Viscount was ordered to be personally cited, along with the Earl of Dunfermline, before the Parliament, but by that time he was beyond the reach of political strife and resentment. On the evening of the 29th of July he encountered General Mackay and King William's troops at the head of the Pass of Killiecrankie. The result of that extraordinary conflict is well known. The Viscount gained a decisive victory, but received a mortal wound, and expired the following day. He is truly described as the life of a cause which was annihilated by his death.

The Parliament which deposed the Episcopal Church continued its session on the 2d of August. On the 22d of that month the Privy Council, at the head of whom was William sixteenth Earl of Crawford, a zealous Presbyterian, renewed an order issued on the 6th, " allowing and inviting the parishioners and hearers of such ministers as have neglected and slighted the reading of the proclamation, and have not prayed for King William and Queen Mary, to cite such ministers before the Privy Council." This was a direct encouragement to the discontended and malicious to become inquisitors, and informers against the clergy. Citations were soon prepared; they were summoned to appear within a specified day; and those who refused were to be deprived for contumacy. Those who obeyed, and came prepared with defences, were treated in the most summary manner, unless they could prove that

* Acta Parl. Scot. vol. ix. p 104.

they had literally complied with all the terms of the proclamation ;.so this, says our venerable historian, "drove out most of the parochial clergy in the counties of Berwick, Haddington, Edinburgh, Linlithgow, Stirling, and Perth, besides some in Aberdeen and Moray, who had been particularly informed against."*

A series of petty and contemptible annoyances were now inflicted against the Episcopal clergy, which show the weakness of the Government, and the despicable means adopted to eject the incumbents. On the 14th of August the Privy Council appointed a day of solemn fasting and humiliation to be observed on *Sunday*, the 15th of September, in the Southern, and on *Sunday*, the 22d, in the Northern counties. The Privy Council, as the writer just quoted observes, "enforced their appointment with a canting proclamation, squinting at Episcopacy among the sins of the late times, and reflecting on it as the great hindrance of the gospel work of reformation. This proclamation they ordered the ministers to read, by way of intimation of the fast, on the Sunday before, and on the Sunday of observance; and if any neglected to obey this injunction, *as few who had any regard for Episcopacy*, or understood the *primitive design of the Lord's Day*, could with any good grace obey it, they were sure to be deprived upon that score, without any other charge or accusation."†

On the 19th of September an order was published, "signifying his Majesty's royal pleasure that warrant be given to Alexander Hamilton of Kinkell," one of the leaders in the battle of Bothwell Bridge, to "draw and uplift the tithes and other rents of the Archbishopric of St Andrews, and that fit persons be appointed for drawing and uplifting the tithes and rents of the other bishoprics for this present crop and year of God 1689" By this proclamation, more oppressive than any measure recorded in the ecclesiastical annals of Scotland—for even the Popish Bishops at the Reformation were allowed to retain two-thirds of their revenues at their own valuation, payment of "any rent or duty to Archbishops, Bishops, Deans, or any others of superior order and dignity in the Church above presbyters," was prohibited, and "fit persons" were appointed to receive the "teinds, rental bolls, feus, blanch, or tack-duties, formerly paid to the Bishops and others foresaid." This seizure

* Skinner's Ecclesiastical History of Scotland, vol. ii p. 534.
† Ibid vol. ii. p. 535.

of all the episcopal and other revenues by the Exchequer, without allowing their legal possessors the smallest portion for their subsistence, was followed by an act of the 29th of December, which deprived the parochial incumbents of " any chance of recovering their current stipends, or bygone arrears, which were most unjustly detained from them, to the utter starving of many a poor family," who, if they had no private resources, were left to be supported by the charity of their friends.*

About this time the Scottish Episcopalians, among their other soubriquets, had the title of *Jacobites* conferred upon them by their opponents—a name by which they were very generally known in the subsequent century. It was not, however, exclusively confined to them, for many Presbyterians were adherents of the exiled sovereign It is a curious fact, that even in the summer of 1689, before the battle of Killiecrankie, when the courage of their friends began to rally, and their hopes were sanguine, numbers, who at the outset of the Revolution approved of its principles, were annoyed at what was very generally considered a violation of all natural feeling on the part of King William to his father-in-law. An alliance was at one time meditated between those Presbyterians who held very extreme religious tenets and the Episcopalians—a most unnatural union if it had been accomplished—for the furtherance of their political purposes Both in England and Scotland were many persons of all ranks, who, though they decidedly approved King William's invasion, never contemplated that he would assume the Crown, and were in consequence by no means satisfied with the new Government Among the Scottish Jacobites, as a political party, must also be included the Roman Catholics, many of whom were influential chiefs and gentlemen of ancient descent in the Highlands and other districts, who considered themselves identified with the interest of King James. They had felt little alarm at that monarch's arbitrary proceedings, and not the less that he was, as they thought, a sufferer for their religion.

Some occurrences previously took place, however, during this session which must not be omitted. While the Parliament was sitting, a most extraordinary document was presented to the House, in the form of " An Humble Address from the Presbyterian Ministers and Professors

* Skinner's Ecclesiastical History of Scotland, vol. ii p. 536, 539.

of the Church in Scotland " The Duke of Hamilton thought the demands in this paper so unreasonable that he would not allow it to be laid on the table, and its rejection from such a quarter caused considerable mortification. After this, when the " Draught of an Act for establishing the Church Government" was presented to the House by order of the Court, Presbyterianism was proposed generally, but it contained a clause which gave great offence to the party, as it reflected on the conduct of several of their leaders in preceding reigns. The clause was :—" In regard that much trouble hath ensued unto the State, and many sad confusions have fallen out in the Church, by churchmen meddling in matters of state; therefore their Majesties, with advice and consent aforesaid, do hereby discharge all ministers of the gospel within this kingdom to meddle with any state affairs, either in their sermons or judicatories, publicly or privately, under the pain of being disaffected to the Government, and proceeded against accordingly;" and " it is declared, that their Majesties, if they think fit, may have always one present in all the Provincial Synods and Presbyterial Assemblies, as they have in the General Assemblies, that in case any affair that concerns the state or civil matters, and that does not belong to the jurisdiction of the Church, shall come in before the said Assemblies, the said persons appointed by their Majesties shall inhibit and discharge every such Assembly to proceed in any such affair till their Majesties and the Privy Council be acquainted with the same, that they may declare their pleasure thereanent." This necessary restriction excited the utmost indignation of the preachers, one of whom publicly said, that " rather than admit such a mangled mongrel Presbytery, they would have the Bishops back again." By the influence of their leaders and supporters among the Nobility, such as the Earls of Crawford and Sutherland, Lords Cardross and Ross, and others, this clause was withdrawn with considerable difficulty and opposition.*

The first session of the Parliament passed in this manner, and during the interval of the next many upon examination were beginning to think that Episcopacy was not such an insupportable grievance as it had been represented by the Convention. It was considered necessary, therefore, to commence a crusade, by denouncing it from the pulpits,

---

* Skinner's Ecclesiastical History of Scotland, vol. ii. p 541, 542.

and to excite the prejudices of the people by misrepresentations and odious statements. Some went so far as to designate the Episcopal clergy *priests of Baal*; they were accused of being tyrannical, obtruding, heretical, ignorant, and immoral; of wilfully perverting the gospel, and of banishing it from the land; of keeping the country in a state of spiritual darkness many years; and of being Papists, Jesuits, or Jesuits in disguise. The Scriptures were interpreted to suit the views of those preachers, and continued allusions were made to the examples in the Old Testament history, which were all applied to the Episcopal clergy. On the other hand, they set forth the praises of Presbyterianism in the highest strains of panegyric; they declared that it was the only true and scriptural system; that they alone were the Lord's people; and that Presbyterian ministers were the *only true* ministers. They went among the people in private, endeavouring to imbitter their feelings against the clergy, and the press was busily employed in publishing attacks against the Church. While the preachers were thus employed, their zealous supporters among the Nobility and others were equally active, and employing all their influence in the same direction. But the " Episcopal writers," says a venerable author, " who were equally able and willing to enter the lists on the other side, might have as soon attempted to pull a star out of the firmament as get one sheet published in defence of that cause, under the iniquitous pretext of reflecting on the civil government, which, indeed, in that infant and unsettled state of it could hardly be avoided."

The second session of the Parliament met on the 15th of April 1690, and as the Duke of Hamilton had given some offence to the now dominant party, by refusing to countenance their extreme demands, he was superseded by George first Earl of Melville, a zealous Presbyterian nobleman, who had been so peculiarly obnoxious to King James, that he was one of a number of persons intended to be exempted from his Act of Indemnity. This nobleman is described by Smollett as " weak and vacillating," who had " taken refuge in Holland from the violence of the late reigns; but the King chiefly depended for advice upon Dalrymple, Lord Stair, President of the College of Justice, an old crafty fanatic, who for fifty years had complied in all things with all governments." On the 24th of April an act was again passed, rescinding the first act of the second Parliament of 1669, which asserted the King's supremacy in ecclesiastical causes, and also another act was passed, "restoring the Presbyterian ministers who were thrust from their churches since the 1st of January 1661" By this act they were to have "forthwith free access to their churches, that they may presently exercise the ministry in these parishes without any new call thereto; and allows them to bruike and enjoy the benefices and stipends thereunto belonging, and that for the haill crop 1689; and immediately to enter to the churches and manses, where the churches are vacant; and where they are not vacant, then their entry thereto is declared to be to the half of the benefice and stipend due and payable at Martinmas last, for the half year immediatelie preceding, betuixt Whitsunday and Michailmas, declaring that the present [Episcopal] incumbent shall have right to the other half of the stipend and benefice, payable for the Whitsunday last bypast: And to the effect that these ministers may meet with no stop or hinderance in entering immediately to their charges, the present [Episcopal] incumbents in such churches are hereby appointed, upon intimation, to desist from their ministry in these parishes, and to remove themselves from the manses and glebes thereunto belonging, betwixt and Whitsunday next to come, that the Presbyterian ministers formerly put out may enter peaceably thereto."* This act was ordered to be proclaimed at the Cross of Edinburgh on the 12th of May.†

A Committee was appointed to seal the doom of the Episcopal Establishment, and prepare a bill for the settlement of the Presbyterian polity, which was presented on the 23d of May, on which day the Westminster Confession of Faith was ordered to be brought in by the Clerk-Register. On the 26th that Confession, notwithstanding its length, was "read and considered word by word;" and on the 7th of June the act was passed "ratifying the Confession of Faith, and settling Presbyterian Church Government" This act ratified the act of the former session abolishing Episcopacy, confirmed all acts made against Popery and Papists, sanctioned and established the Westminster Confession of Faith as the "public and allowed Confession of this Church, containing the sum and substance of the doctrine of the Reformed Churches," established, ratified, and confirmed the "Presbyterian Church Government and Discipline by Kirk Sessions, Presbyteries, Provincial Synods,

* Acta Parl. Scot vol ix. p 111   † Ibid vol. ix. p. 115.

and General Assemblies ;"—" rescinding, annulling, and making void, four acts of James VI. and five of Charles II., with all other acts, laws, statutes, ordinances, and proclamations, in as far as they are contrary or prejudicial to, or inconsistent with, or derogatory from, the Protestant religion and Presbyterian Government now established ;" appointing the " first meeting of the General Assembly of this Church, as above established, to be at Edinburgh on the third Thursday of October, in this present year 1690 ;" and, " that the disorders which have happened in this Church may be redressed, they allow the general meeting and representatives of the foresaid Presbyterian ministers and elders, either by themselves, or by visitors authorised by them, to try and purge out all insufficient, negligent, scandalous, and erroneous ministers, by due course of ecclesiastical process and censures; ordaining, that whatever minister, being summoned before those visitors, shall refuse to appear, or on appearing shall be found guilty by them, every such minister shall by their sentence be *ipso facto* suspended from or deprived of their kirks, stipends, and benefices."

The reader is already aware that the "ministers" here designated " insufficient, negligent, scandalous, and erroneous," or whom the inquisitorial visitors were authorised to consider as such, were the Episcopal clergy; and as the Committee who prepared the act were assisted by the most conspicuous and noted of the Presbyterian preachers, the suggesters of these very charitable epithets may be easily inferred. The act, parts of which are inserted above, was twice read to the Parliament, and several of its articles keenly discussed. The petition had desired the establishment of the Westminster Directory and Catechisms, as well as the Confession of Faith, but the reading of the latter had occupied so much time that the Duke of Hamilton protested against hearing any more of such mystical, tiresome, and incomprehensible compositions; and as the Presbyterians had by this time discovered that the Directory recommended the regular reading of the Scriptures and the use of the Lord's Prayer in the public congregation, both of which practices they condemned as *superstitious*, the objection of his Grace was sustained. That clause in the act which placed the entire ecclesiastical government in the hands of the preachers expelled in 1661 from benefices of which, during Cromwell's domination, they had possessed themselves in violation of the law, and in defiance of the rights of private property,* was the subject of much debate. A petition was presented from those of the Episcopal clergy who were disposed to transfer their allegiance to King William, but it was unceremoniously rejected, chiefly because they offered to defend Episcopacy against the Presbyterians—a challenge which the Earl of Melville considered in the highest degree presumptuous, and which was on no account to be permitted.

A member proposed that at least those ministers then alive, who had been deposed by their own "judicatories" before the re-establishment of Episcopacy at the Revolution, should not be included among the number of those who were become judges by this act. This amendment was also rejected, though strenuously supported by the Duke of Hamilton. "For what was this," his Grace said, "but instead of fourteen prelatical Bishops, to give unlimited authority to fifty or sixty Presbyterian ones, from whom the Episcopal clergy could expect little justice and less mercy?" The debate upon the hardships inflicted on those of the clergy who had been expelled from their benefices by the mob was particularly strong. The incumbents had been most maliciously and falsely represented as having *deserted* their parishes, that the violence of the mob might be mitigated, and the atrocity of their conduct concealed, softened, or justified. In supporting a supplication from those unfortunate clergymen presented by Sir Patrick Scott of Ancrum, the Duke of Hamilton thus expressed himself:—" It was wonderful to call these men *deserters*, when it was notorious all the kingdom over that they were driven away by the most barbarous violence; and it was no less wonderful to declare their churches vacant, because of their being removed from them. For what could be the sense of the word *removed*, in this case, but neither more nor less than *rabbled*; and what might the world think of the justice of the Parliament, if it should sustain that as a sufficient ground for declaring their churches vacant?" But notwithstanding all the arguments and remonstrances of the Duke, the claim in the act was carried by a considerable majority. The Duke indignantly told the House that he was " sorry he should have ever sat in

---

* " For which illegal intrusion it was," says Mr Skinner, whose excellent digest I chiefly follow in the text of this part of the present work, " and not on the score of non-conformity or non-compliance, that they lost what they never had a just title to, so could not be restored to such possession without homologating the injustice by which they first obtained them."—Ecclesiastical History of Scotland, vol. ii p 545

a Scottish Parliament where such naked iniquity was to be established into a law—that it was impossible Presbyterian government could stand, being built upon such a foundation; and it grieved him to the heart to consider what a reflection this act would bring upon the Government, and justice of the House." His Grace immediately retired, followed by several members; and when it was proposed to vote the whole act entire, the Duke of Queensberry, the Earls of Linlithgow and Balcarras, and many gentlemen, also withdrew, and would not vote. Only a few remained to vote against the act—one part of them to prevent the boast that Presbyterianism had been established without opposition; and another, who advocated the Cameronian or extreme principles, because it was not established in what they considered its full power and independency—in other words, an *imperium in imperio*, above all law, responsibility, and control. The act was prepared on the 28th of May for the royal assent, which it received on the 7th of June 1690, and "so obtained," observes Mr Skinner, "that force and authority which it has retained ever since."

If it be a matter of surprise that such an important act did not encounter greater opposition, it must be remembered that almost the whole Episcopal nobility and gentry had retired to their country seats, in discontent and disaffection to the new Government, both political and ecclesiastical; the Bishops were in concealment, or, as the Viscount of Dundee observed in a letter some time before the battle of Killiecrankie, *the Church was invisible*. On the 29th of May, indeed, the Earl of Linlithgow proposed to the House a draught of an act "for giving toleration to those of the Episcopal persuasion to worship God after their own manner, and particularly that whoso were inclined to use the English Liturgy might do it safely."* This was allowed to be read, but no farther notice of it was taken.

On the 4th of July an act was passed for visiting the Universities and schools, prohibiting all persons from being eligible to any professorship or school within the kingdom who did not subscribe the Confession of Faith, comply with the Presbyterian form of government, and take the oath of

* "Which shows," says Mr Skinner, "that though our clergy had no authorised form imposed upon them, they had no aversion to set forms, but were acquainted with, and willing to make use of, the English Book."—Ecclesiastical History of Scotland, vol. ii. p 550.

allegiance, excluding all persons then in office who did not so "acknowledge and confess." Fifteen noblemen; twenty-eight gentlemen, and twenty of the newly established Presbyterian ministers, were appointed to be visitors, " with full power and commission to them, or a quorum of them, to meet, visit, take trial, *purge out*, and remove, according to the foresaid qualifications." They were ordered to meet on the 23d of July, and to continue or adjourn, according to their convenience, during the royal pleasure. On the 19th of July, however, an act was passed which gave great dissatisfaction to some of the Presbyterian preachers, because it deprived them of the capricious power of annoying and persecuting the deposed clergy. After rescinding, in general, all former acts, and parts and provisions in any act, since 1661 inclusive, against nonconformity, or for conformity to the Church, as established under and governed by Archbishops and Bishops, the Parliament "rescind, cass, and annul, all acts for denouncing excommunicate persons, and anent sentences of excommunication, with all other sentences of the same import, and without prejudice of this generality, all acts enjoining civil pains upon sentences of excommunication whatever." On the same day two acts were also passed—one vesting the superiorities and other casualties which formerly belonged to the Episcopal Church in the Crown; the other is quaintly entitled " An Act or Commission for *Plantation of Kirks* and Valuation of Teinds," purporting to be founded on sundry laws passed in 1633 by Charles I., all of which, engrossed together, are called a *good work*, which their Majesties " are resolved to prosecute for the universal good of their subjects, and especially for the encouragement of the ministers of the gospel." Having finally deposed the ancient Church, and completely established Presbyterianism, the Parliament concluded its *labours*, and rose on the 22d day of July.

The manner in which these acts were put in operation and enforced must now be noticed. Beginning with the Commissioners for visiting the Universities, which were the first objects to which they directed their attention, they met at Edinburgh on the 23d of July, and divided themselves into four committees, one for each of the four Universities, *to make purgation*, who proceeded to the several seats of these institutions, St Andrews, Glasgow, Aberdeen, and Edinburgh The commission for St Andrews consisted of sixteen persons, among whom were the Earls of Crawford, Morton, Cassillis, and Kintore, several country gentlemen, and a few Presbyterian ministers The visitation was conducted by the zealous Earl of Crawford as President. This University then consisted of three Colleges, St Salvador's, St Leonard's (now united to the former), and St Mary's. The Principals, Professors, and Masters, having positively refused to conform to Presbyterianism and sign the Confession of Faith, were all ejected on the 25th of September, and their places in course of time filled by persons of the new Presbyterian principles. We are told thát the Earl of Crawfurd " acted with remarkable harshness and severity, and was much blamed even by his friends for his rough uncivil behaviour to the Masters, particularly the reverend Dean, Dr Wemyss, Principal of St Leonard's College, who had been a regent forty-five years, and taught Crawfurd his philosophy; yet my Lord would not allow him the favour of a seat, and when the old man's infirmities obliged him to rest on the step of a stair, he sent an officer of court, and made him stand."*

The Commission to *purge* the University of Glasgow was composed of sixteen persons, among whom were the Duke of Hamilton, the Marquis of Argyll, the Viscount Stair, and Lord Carmichael, the others being country gentlemen, and an adjunct of Presbyterian preachers. The visitation of the University of Glasgow was superintended by Lord Carmichael, who, though a zealous Presbyterian, is characterized as a " man of temper and good breeding." Dr James Fall, Principal, and three of the Professors, were ejected, among the latter of whom was Dr James Wemyss, Professor of Divinity. It ought to have been mentioned, that on the last day of November 1688, the Earl of Loudon and several others, then students in the University, thought proper to burn in effigy the Pope and the Archbishops of St Andrews and Glasgow without any opposition.†

At Aberdeen, however, the Presbyterian commission was by no means so active as those in the southern and western Universities. This was probably on account of the known attachment of the citizens, and indeed of the great mass of the population of the counties north of the Tay, to Episcopacy. Probably the members of the commission were not over-zealous in the discharge of the duty they had undertaken; for

* Skinner's Ecclesiastical History of Scotland, vol. ii. p. 555.
† Cleland's Annals of Glasgow, vol. ii. p 56.

although some of them, Lord Cardross, and probably Lord Elphinstone, were, with the five Presbyterian ministers associated with them, most zealous for the new system of church government, there were others who were avowed members of the Episcopal Church, among whom were the Earl Marischal, the Viscount of Arbuthnot, the Master of Forbes, Brodie of Brodie, and Grant of Grant. We find Dr George Middleton, who was appointed Principal of King's College in 1684, retaining his office till 1717, when he was ejected for being disaffected to the House of Hanover. The northern University was, in short, permitted to remain in the possession of the Episcopal Professors, either from inability on the part of the commission to procure their ejection, or from some other cause which is not recorded.

It is mentioned by Arnot, respecting those Presbyterian commissions to *purge*, as they called it, the Scottish Universities of all Episcopal Professors—" From such specimens of their conduct in a visitorial capacity as we have been able to discover, we are entitled to say that those parliamentary visitors proceeded with great violence and injustice."* In no University city was this more conspicuous than in Edinburgh. Proclamation was made, and printed edicts posted, at the Cross and on the College gates; as also in Stirling, Haddington, and other provincial towns, charging the Principal and Professors of the University, and the schoolmasters of the city, county, and neighbouring counties, to appear before the committee of visitors on the 20th of August 1690, to answer upon the points contained in the act of Parliament; also summoning and warning *all the lieges who have anything to object against the said Principal and Professors, and others,* to appear before them on the said day and place to give in *objections.* " After an edict," observes Arnot, " which bespoke that the country, although it had been subjected to a revolution, had not acquired a system of liberty, nor the rudiments of justice—after an invitation so publicly thrown out by the commissioners of Parliament in a nation distracted by religious and political factions, it is not to be supposed that informers would be wanting."†

Sir John Hall, Bart. of Dunglass, Lord Provost of the city, sat as President of the Commission,‡ which consisted altogether of sixteen

* History of Edinburgh, 4to, p. 393.
† Ibid. p. 394.
‡ This gentleman had been created a Baronet in 1687 by King James II.

persons, among whom we find the Earl of Lothian, Lord Ruthven, several Judges of the Supreme Court, and some well known Presbyterian ministers—James Kirkton, Gilbert Rule, and others. The whole proceedings of this remarkably tyrannical and unjust commission were published in the following year (1691), in a pamphlet which is now rare, entitled " The Presbyterian Inquisition, as it was lately practised against the Professors of the College of Edinburgh, August and September 1690 "* The motto affixed is most appropriate, being the 23d verse of the 19th Psalm:—" For the mouth of the wicked and the mouth of the deceitful are opened against me; they have spoken against me with a lying tongue; they compassed me about also with words of hatred, and fought against me without a cause."

The Commission assembled in what was then called the Upper Hall of the old College, every part of which is now supplanted by the present University Buildings, and the Principal and Professors met in the Library. After waiting some time, the latter were at last informed that the investigation would be delayed for a week, as it was intended to *make purgation* of the schoolmasters, many of whom resided a considerable distance from the city; but in reality the libels against the Principal and Professors were not then sufficiently prepared. On the day appointed the Commission of visitors met, and the first object of attack was the reverend Principal, Dr Alexander Monro, repeatedly mentioned in a previous part of this narrative.

The reader will naturally wish to know some particulars of the life of this excellent and learned clergyman, before perusing the extraordinary articles drawn up against him by the " Inquisition." These few particulars may be briefly stated. Dr Monro was educated at St Andrews, or at least, as he states himself, he received his degree there in 1682: he had spent much of his time abroad, and was known to be a good scholar, and a man of talent.† He was appointed Principal of the University on the 9th of December 1685, which he held with the incumbency of the High Church of Edinburgh. It is remarkable that the

---

* " In which," continues the title-page, " the spirit of Presbytery, and their Present Method of Procedure, are plainly discovered, Matter of Fact by undeniable instances cleared, and Libels against particular Persons discussed."—Licensed November 12, 1691. London, 4to, pp. 106.

† Bower's History of the University of Edinburgh, vol. i p 309.

declaration of the Prince of Orange was presented to the magistrates of the city by Dr Monro on the 13th of February 1689,* instead of being sent directly to them by the Government. The history of this curious transaction is now lost, but Dr Monro performed his part of the duty, and resigned the incumbency of the High Church in the month of May. After his deprivation of the office of Principal, Dr Monro officiated as an Episcopal clergyman in Edinburgh, and died much respected in 1715. "It has been frequently alleged," says Bower, "but I think without sufficient evidence, that Dr Monro, upon his expulsion from the College, carried away with him several of the records. Party spirit at that time ran so high, that it was quite common for recriminations of this kind to be exchanged upon a very slight foundation."

Principal Monro was more obnoxious to the Presbyterians than any of his colleagues. He was their ablest polemical opponent in the capital, or perhaps south of the Forth. Respecting the articles exhibited against him, some, it will be seen. are of a very trifling nature; others, if they had been proved, involved his moral character; but the great charge was his disaffection to the Revolution, and his undisguised attachment to the exiled family. It appears that a Professor named Andrew Massie became remarkably officious on this occasion to ingratiate himself with the prevailing Government. This gentleman had been a regent in the University of Aberdeen before he came to Edinburgh. "His compliance with the politics of the times," says Bower, "was very accommodating. He was also accused of want of discipline, great carelessness in the discharge of his public duty, and his general conduct so notorious that it was even the subject of common conversation among the students. Representations against him were given in to the Visitors, upon which they pronounced no judgment, because, according to the Episcopal party, he had taken the oaths to the new Government; yet two gentlemen, the one a Doctor of Medicine, and the other a Master of Arts, had given this information."† We are told that tradition ascribes this interference on the part of the " Doctor of Medicine" to the celebrated Dr Archibald Pitcairne, or to Dr Sibbald, afterwards known as Sir Robert Sibbald, both eminent men in their day.

* Records of the Town Council of Edinburgh, MSS vol. xxxii. p. 297.
† Bower's History of the University of Edinburgh, vol. i. p 315.

The articles exhibited against the Principal were ten in number, and to the following effect—the first of which shows that the visitors acted as if they had been anxious to associate the Episcopal Church with Popery, and therefore, in the libels put into the hands of Dr Monro and others they are directly charged with both. The First article is—" That he renounced the Protestant religion in a church beyond seas, and subscribed himself a Papist." The Second contains some alleged instances in proof of this which occurred respecting the students in the College. Third—" That he set up the English Liturgy within the gates of the College—a form of worship never allowed in this nation; and though it were tolerated, yet no toleration allows any of different form of worship from the State to enjoy legal benefices in the church, or charge in the University. Fourth, The act for visitation of Colleges requires that none carry charge in them but such as be well affected to the Government in Church and State: but so it is, that it is well known by all who know Dr Monro, that he is *highly disaffected to both*, as appears by a missive letter written by him to the late Archbishop of St Andrews, dated the 5th day of January 1689, and which may also appear by his leaving the charge of the ministry [resigning the incumbency of the High Church] to them, not praying for King William and Queen Mary, and his rejoicing the day that the news of Claverhouse* his victory came to town; and how much he dislikes the present government of the Church may appear by the bitter persecuting of all that persuasion to the utmost of his power." Here several alleged instances were produced. Fifth—" At the late public laureation [graduation] he sat and publicly heard the Confession of Faith, after it had been approved in Parliament, ridiculed by Dr Pitcairne; yea, the existence of God impugned, without any answer or vindication. Sixth, He caused take down out of the Library all the pictures of the Protestant Reformers; and when quarrelled by some of the magistrates, gave this answer— ' That the sight of them might not be offensive to the Chancellor, when he came to visit the College.' Seventh, When Mr Cunninghame had composed his *eucharistic*† verses on the Prince of Wales, he not only approved of them, but presented them to the Chancellor with his own

* The Viscount of Dundee's victory over General Mackay at Killiecrankie.

† This word must mean *eulogistic* verses in praise of the son of James II., father of Prince Charles Edward Stuart.

hand. Eighth, That the said Doctor is given sometimes to cursing and swearing. Ninth, That the Doctor is an ordinary neglecter of the worship of God in his family." The Tenth accused him of baptizing a child in a neighbouring parish without intimating it to the parish minister.

Such were the articles exhibited against the excellent, pious, and learned Principal Monro. He answered readily the two first charges, but when he heard them reading the remainder, which appeared to him to be a long list of accusations which he was conscious were false and malicious, he complained of such an unjust and illegal procedure, desired to know his accusers, and time to prepare his defences. Dr Monro was accordingly presented with a copy of the information against him, which he found *not subscribed* or *authenticated* by any individual, and a few days were allowed him to give in answers to the charges. The answers are printed in the " Presbyterian Inquisition."

To the first charge Principal Monro replied, that it was a " spiteful and malicious calumny" that he had turned Papist beyond seas, appealed to all who had known him for the previous twenty years of his public life, reminding the inquisitors that it was " impossible to be ordained a presbyter of our Church without renouncing Popery ; and our ecclesiastical superiors, who ordained priests and deacons according to the forms of the Church of England always since the Restitution [Restoration], took care, I hope, to distinguish Papists and Protestants by the most solemn oath and national tests." He moreover asks— " What good evidence for my being inclined to Popery ? Had I not a fair opportunity to take off the mask some years before the Revolution ? Was it any of the sermons I preached against Popery in the High Church of Edinburgh, and in the Abbey of Holyroodhouse, *when our zealous reformers were very quiet,* to all which some hundreds of the best quality of the nation were witnesses ? But as I have been in France, *I must therefore behove to be a Papist,* and this is enough for this libeller. I am very sure none of the Papists ever thought me one."*

---

* We are told that " this article was let fall, for after all their industry they could say nothing upon that head, and no report of it was made to the commission of the General Visitation."—Presbyterian Inquisition, p. 30. It was a common trick of the Presbyterians of those times to accuse the Episcopal clergy of Popery, and this was

The second charge was connected with the first, and entered into particulars, all of which the reverend Principal explained in a satisfactory manner. The third accusation—the formidable one of reading the Liturgy of the Church of England in his own family—he admitted, and on this subject a few of his observations are interesting. "The libeller," whom Dr Monro suspected to be Gilbert Rule, one of the visitors, and his Presbyterian successor as Principal, " forgets that this quite frustrates his first attempt. They must be odd kind of Papists who read the service of the Church of England on the 5th of November. But the libeller adds that the Book of Common Prayer was never allowed here [in Scotland] since the Reformation. Does he mean that the service of the Church of England was used here *before* the Reformation? The Book of Common Prayer was read in many families in Scotland even since the restitution of King Charles II., and publicly read in the Abbey of Holyroodhouse in the reign of Charles I. But upon inquiry it will be found that they were the *first prayers read in Scotland after the Reformation*, for Buchanan tells us so expressly, and his testimony is the more remarkable that the Confession of Faith was ratified in Parliament that very year.* But the plain matter of fact is this. When I left off preaching in the High Church, I advised with some of my brethren, and the result was, that we should read the Book of Common Prayer, and preach within our families, *per vices*, since most of them were acquainted with the Liturgy of the Church of England; neither did we think, when Quakers and all other sects were tolerated, that we should be blamed for reading those prayers within our private families which we prefer to all other forms now used in the Christian Church. Nor had we any design to proselytize the people to any thing they had no mind to, else I might have read the Liturgy in one of the public schools within the College, and it must not be said that we were afraid to venture upon the public exercise of it because of

one of their successful attempts in the western counties of Scotland to excite the people against the Church.

* The year 1567, and the Old Confession is here meant. This fact, quoted by Principal Monro, is thus stated by Buchanan, who, whatever he was in religion, was not an Episcopalian :—" Scoti ante aliquot annos Anglorum auxiliis e servitute Gallica liberati religionis cultui et ritibus cum Anglis communibus scripserunt."—Hist. Scot. Lib. xix.

the rabble, for during the session of the College it is very well known in the city that the mobile durst not presume to give us the least disturbance. But the matter succeeded beyond what we proposed or looked for. We preached to the people upon the Sundays They came by hundreds more than we had room for,* and very many became acquainted with the Liturgy of the Church of England, and perceived by their own experience that there was neither Popery nor superstition in it. I look upon the Church of England as the true pillar and centre of the Reformation, and if her enemies should lay her in the dust, which God forbid, there is no other bulwark in Britain to stop or retard the progress of either Popery or enthusiasm. And I wonder men should retain so much bitterness against the Church of England, valued and admired by all foreign Churches, and whose Liturgy, as it is the most serious and comprehensive, so it is most agreeable to the primitive forms. But if there was no law for it, there was none against it; there was no national church government then [part of 1689 and 1690], and why might we not read the prayers of that Church from which we derive our ordination to the priesthood since the Restoration of Charles II ?"†

The fourth charge, that of disaffection to the Government, Principal Monro admitted in a modified and explanatory manner, and this was in reality the grand accusation against him. As to the accusation of resigning the High Church, because he would not pray for King William and Queen Mary, he says—" Let the libeller consider the paper by which I demitted my office in that church, and see if there be any such reason for my demission inserted in that paper. I could name

* Principal Monro here refers to the period, nearly twelve months, in 1689 and 1690, between the abolition of Episcopacy as the national establishment and the ratification of the Presbyterian polity The Principal and his brethren appear to have officiated in halls, and other large apartments in Edinburgh, and in private houses.

† Presbyterian Inquisition, p 33. It is stated in a note—" This answer to the third article of the Doctor's libel did exasperate the Presbyterians to the highest degree, and those to whom it was recommended to view and examine his answers thought they discovered strange consequences in this. But some of the nobility who were present when this was tossed would not suffer such fooleries as were then objected to be inserted in their report, partly that the Presbyterians might not be exposed, partly that they might not be witnesses to such palpable impertinences, and partly that none might say the ministers, to whom the government was committed, were such fools as to fly in the face of the Church of England at this juncture. This article was let fall, and no report made of it to the General Commission."

other reasons for my demission, and I do not believe that the Presbyterians were angry with me on that head, that I left off preaching in a church which they were to have in their own possession. —The libeller does not think I rejoiced at the fall of my Lord Dundee. I assure him of the contrary, for no gentleman, soldier, scholar, or civilized citizen, will find fault with me for this. I had an extraordinary value for him, and such of his enemies as retain any generosity will acknowledge that he deserved it; and the libeller should consider that the victories obtained in a civil war are no true causes of joy, for our brethren, friends, acquaintances, and fellow Christians, must fall." Dr Monro denied that he had prosecuted the Presbyterian party to the utmost of his power. "I thank God," he says, "I have no such Presbyterian temper, for I never hated any man for his opinions, unless by it he thinks himself obliged to destroy me and mine, and such truly I consider as the tyrannical enemies of human society; but the libeller would have acted his part more skilfully, if he could have named some dissenters in the parishes of Dunfermline, Kinglassie, or Wemyss, where I was once minister, whom I had prosecuted before the secular judge for non-conformity, which I might have easily done, had I been so very fierce as the libeller represents me, having easy access to the greatest men of the State at that time."

As to the fifth accusation of hearing Dr Pitcairne* ridicule the Westminster Confession of Faith, and impugn the existence of a Deity, without answering him, Principal Monro says:—" I was not in the desk, nor bound to preside at those exercises, and so not concerned to answer; but my good friend Dr Pitcairne is more able to answer for both himself and me than I am; only the sneaking libeller is grossly ignorant and malicious, for the Doctor did not impugn the existence of a Deity. He endeavoured fairly, like a true philosopher, to load some propositions in the thesis with this absurdity (*hoc posito sequeretur illud*). The most sacred fundamentals in religion are thus disputed in the schools, not with a design to overthrow them, as the libeller ignorantly fancies,

* This was the celebrated Dr Archibald Pitcairne, often mentioned in this part of the narrative, one of the most illustrious ornaments of the medical profession whom Scotland ever produced. The Doctor was a staunch Churchman, and, being a man of wit, often burlesqued and ridiculed the Presbyterian ministers, who were all afraid of his satire, and heartily hated him.

but to establish and set them in their true light, that they may appear in their evidence. Yet I foresaw that some ignorant or malicious people would misrepresent this argument, and therefore I desired the Doctor to let it fall, and without any more he did so."

The charge of removing the pictures of the Reformers from the Library of the College, or rather the motive for removing, was, like the others of which then Dr Monro was accused, altogether malicious and false. It came out in explanation that Sir Thomas Kennedy, then Lord Provost of the city, expected that certain Visitors intended to be appointed by King James, would sit in the College Library, and his Lordship gave orders that the paintings of the Reformers should be removed, lest the sight of them might cause some unpleasant altercations between the Popish and Protestant members of the visitation; and we are told that though Dr Monro did so, yet he required no order for it, as it was " in his power to remove and set up pictures, or any other furniture he pleased." This was proved by a written declaration from Sir Thomas Kennedy, when he was made acquainted with this accusation against the Principal, dated 7th October 1690, in which he takes the whole responsibility upon himself, and considers himself bound in duty and honour to declare that what Dr Monro did " in this particular was done at my desire and appointment, I being Lord Provost of Edinburgh at that time, which was intended and done by me upon no other motive, and for no other end, but that there being a visitation of the College immediately to ensue, when I had reason to suspect several Romish priests and Jesuits would be present, I thought it a prudent caution to be used for saving these pictures of our worthy Reformers from being abused or ridiculed: This made me think it convenient that for some few days these should be removed, as they accordingly were, and as soon as this occasion was over they were immediately hung up in their former places again. At the same time I took care to have kept out of the view of such priests whatsoever might prove tempting or inviting about the College, to kindle their endeavours for getting it a seat or seminary for them or their religion, and I gave the necessary orders accordingly, which is well known to several masters of the College."

The other charges are answered by the Principal in a similar satisfactory manner, and having lodged his defence, it was read to the Visitors on the 23d of September. He was now asked if he was willing to take all the tests, religious and political, lately imposed by law, and answering in the negative, sentence of deprivation was pronounced against him on the 25th, by the Earl of Crawfurd, and Gilbert Rule was soon afterwards appointed his successor.

Dr John Strachan, minister of the Tron Church, and Professor of Divinity in the College, was the next object of the "Presbyterian Inquisition." He was accused of having, in a sermon before the Diocesan Synod of Edinburgh, advocated a reconciliation with the Church of Rome—of being an Arminian, and maintaining "Arminian and Pelagian principles and tenets"—of "innovating the worship of God in setting up the English service"—of neglecting his duty in the College, or at least of not discharging it in a satisfactory manner—of celebrating marriages and baptisms irregularly—of dissatisfaction to the Government—and "that the said Doctor does ordinarily neglect the worship of God in his family." Dr Strachan defended himself against these calumnies, but it was of no avail, and he was deprived on the same day with Principal Monro.

Three others of the Professors of the University were expelled at the same time—Mr John Drummond, Professor of Philology, Mr Alexander Douglas, Professor of Oriental Languages, and Mr Thomas Burnet, Professor of Moral Philosophy. The celebrated Dr David Gregory also refused to take the test, and conform to Presbyterianism, but his great reputation made the Visitors unwilling to injure the University by too rigid an enquiry into his political principles. He soon, however, left their establishment, for in 1691 he was admitted Savilian Professor in a University more congenial to his religious principles—that of Oxford.

The preceding narrative will enable the reader to obtain a tolerably correct knowledge of the proceedings of those times, and of the summary manner in which the supporters of the deposed Church were treated. The Presbyterians, now that their system was the law of the land, and had received the Royal Assent, are not to be blamed for supplanting the ejected incumbents with men of their own principles, but the manner in which they did so was often disgraceful, malicious, and contemptible. Instead of openly and manfully asking if the incumbents would take the religious and political tests, they had the meanness to resort to their old wretched subterfuge of stringing together a number of charges of a personal nature, affecting the moral character of individuals, such as false accusations of profane swearing, holding what they chose to designate Popish or Arminian sentiments, and of neglecting family worship. "It is not usual," says Principal Monro, in reply to one of those charges against him, "for the Presbyterians to load men of a different opinion from them with ordinary escapes. They must represent them as abóminable, and as sinners of the first-rate, for all that are not of their way can have no fairer quarter." And again, when noticing the charge of neglecting family worship, the learned Principal observed—" Sometimes I am accused of having too many prayers in my family, and now that I ordinarily neglect prayers. But this is a common-place, and all of the Episcopal persuasion must be represented as atheists and scandalous, void of all devotion and piety." In reference to the proceedings of the Visitors of the Universities, it is well observed by one of the ejected sufferers—" The Visitors might have been well assured that no Master or Professor of any conscience who had been *episcopally ordained*, or acquainted with the primitive constitution of the Church, could in any way comply with conditions so severe and rigid as taking the test. It had been soon enough then for the Presbyterians to have fled to their old experimented way of *libelling*, when the Masters had stood their ground against that new test, which originally had no end but to make vacant places. The Presbyterian preachers, who earnestly wished to be employed in the toil and drudgery of this affair, made it their business to search into all the actions of the Professors' lives, especially such as were capable of being transformed into a libel, and having the assistance and zeal of some of the new magistrates of Edinburgh to second their endeavours, it is easy to foresee what quarter those might expect who differed from them Because they pretended to be most *accurate reformers*, they would therefore do their work thoroughly, and strip their opponents as bare of their good name and reputation as of their livelihoods and preferments; and having got the jurisdiction and revenues of the Church into their hands, it was not safe for them to want the government and possession of the seminaries of learning; and therefore the Presbyterians who preached before the Parliament never forgot to exhort such as were in power *speedily to reform the Universities*, which is no less, in their language, than to plant them with Presbyterians. To accomplish this, it was necessary to represent the Masters of Universities under the episcopal constitution as *very ill men, enemies to the godly, Socinians, Papists.* The people could not discern when they spoke contradictions, for though Socinianism and Popery be two opposite points of the compass, yet some of their emissaries scrupled not to accuse one and the same person of both "*

When the pretensions set forth by the Presbyterians respecting the scriptural authority of their system are considered, these remarks will appear just and moderate. It was better, they presumed, to libel the Professors and Clergy, than to eject them for scruples of conscience, because in the latter case they might have procured public sympathy. Men who held, as one of them maintained, that " it was not possible the power of godliness could prevail but under Presbytery," were not likely to be scrupulous in their calumnious attacks of the Episcopalians. Moreover, the test, as it was intended to be understood and applied, meant that " every master should thereby declare the Presbyterian church government to be preferable to any other whatsoever, and the only government left by Christ and his Apostles in the Church, and warranted by Scripture"—a statement denied by the whole Christian Church throughout the world in all ages. As to the Westminster Confession of Faith, it was altogether impossible for a clergyman to recognize it in any way whatsoever; yet some of the leading Presbyterians in those commissions maintained that by " the acknowledging and subscribing it is not only meant an owning of it so far as it is a system of theology conform to the Holy Scriptures, and one of the best designed for distinguishing the Reformed Church from the heretics and schismatics who now disturb it, but that it also imports an absolute owning of every particular article thereof, as the *only* and *most perfect* Confession that hath been or can yet be composed, and that therefore it was to be acknowledged, professed, and subscribed without any limitation, restriction, or reservation whatsoever."

* Presbyterian Inquisition, p. 4, 5.

CHAPTER VII.

PROCEEDINGS AGAINST THE EPISCOPAL PAROCHIAL CLERGY.

The act which established the Presbyterian form of Church Government in Scotland authorized its supporters to "try and purge out all *insufficient, negligent, scandalous,* and *erroneous ministers,* by due course of ecclesiastical process and censures ; and it was ordained that whatever minister, being summoned before them, or before visitors appointed by them, should refuse to appear, or, appearing, should be found guilty by them, was to be by their sentence *ipso facto* suspended from or deprived of his church, stipend, and benefice." Every incumbent who had obtained possession of his parish by ordination and institution from the Bishop of the Diocese was included under the epithets *insufficient, negligent, scandalous,* and *erroneous ;* and whoever refused to appear before this new tribunal, and declare that the constitution and doctrines of the Church were "contrary to the Word of God," was to be deprived of his benefice by a judicial sentence. The clergy were also expected to recognize the "Acts of Assembly" and the "solemn engagements of the land," by which latter were meant the National Covenant and the Solemn League and Covenant concocted at the rebellion against Charles I.

The manner in which those measures were carried into operation will be immediately seen, as also the results in many districts. Meanwhile the Bishops were no longer permitted to occupy their episcopal residences, or publicly to discharge the functions of their office. The act of 1690, "anent the superiority of lands and others which formerly held of Prelates" was sufficiently stringent After reciting the old and usual assertion, that "Prelacie and the superiority of any office in the church above presbyters is and hath been an unsupportable grievance and trouble to this nation," and that their Majesties have "abolished the office of

Bishops or Prelates out of this kirk and kingdom," the act thus proceeds—
" Therefore, for removing of all doubts and questions that may arise anent the superiorities of these lands, mills, fishings, heritable offices, and others, which formerly held of the Prelates or Bishops, or of their Chapters, or of Deans, Sub-Deans, and Arch-Deans, or any other beneficed person, by reason of the abolishing of the said offices and Chapters foresaid furth of this kirk and kingdom ; and to the effect the subjects and vassals of those holdings may be put in assurance hereanent : Have statute, ordained, and declared, and by these presents statute, ordain, and declare, that all these superiorities which formerly pertained to the said Bishops and their Chapters, or Deans and others foresaid, do now pertain and belong, and shall hereafter pertain, immediately to their Majesties and their successors in all time coming."

The ejected Bishops quietly betook themselves to honourable and patient retirement, satisfied of the conscientious integrity of their principles, and contented to abide the result of the new arrangements of the Government. In the language of Bishop Short—" The authority by which every bishop or priest acts is derived by succession from the Apostles, each succeeding generation communicating to the next the authority under which they themselves have been acting. The division of the country into dioceses and parishes is a civil arrangement, which regulates the place where the individual shall exercise his ministry, *but the civil power neither confers the ministerial authority nor can alter it.* When, therefore, the civil authority deprived those nonjuring Bishops of their temporal jurisdictions, it could not divest them of the sacred office to which they had been called, and they conceived that as this was still continued to them, they were bound still to exercise it.* The same thing is actually taking place at this moment in Scotland. The legal church government there is Presbyterian, yet is there a regular succession of Protestant Bishops, who fill certain Sees without any authoritative power derived from the State, and constitute perhaps the purest form of Episcopacy in the world. As far as Scotland is concerned, her Bishops are, in the opinion of an Episcopalian, fully borne out in this apparent schism, because the rest of the church there, though

---

* In the above remarks Bishop Short refers to the English Nonjuring Bishops, but they equally apply to those of Scotland.

legally established, has discarded the apostolical order of Bishops, and the division must be charged by us on those who have introduced the anomaly of a Christian church without Bishops."*

Most of the Scottish Bishops spent their lives in retirement after the Revolution, and only a few of them, as far as can be ascertained, officiated in places of worship fitted up for them, called *meeting-houses*. Archbishop Ross of St Andrews is already mentioned as having died in 1704. It is not known where he resided during his latter years. In the Canongate burying-ground, near the north-west corner of the parish church, is the tombstone, previously noticed, erected, as the inscription bears, to the memory of " George Stuart Forbes, Esq., representative of the ancient family of Brux, and his spouse, Margaret Stewart, only daughter of Captain John Stewart, R N., a cadet of the honourable family of Ballechin." On the back of this tombstone it is stated— " The proper burying-place of this family is in Restalrig, in the tomb of his Grace Arthur Ross, last Archbishop and Primate in Scotland, whose great-great-grandson, George Stuart Forbes, here interred was, but he, having died suddenly in Edinburgh, was privately interred here, formerly the burying-place of the Eglinton Family."

Archbishop Paterson of Glasgow retired to Edinburgh, where he died in 1708, in the 76th year of his age. His death is here noticed by anticipation, for he is subsequently introduced as sustaining a prominent part in the welfare and continuance of the Episcopal Church. The Archbishop was interred on the 23d of December in the Chapel-Royal of Holyrood Palace, and " lies on the north side in the east end against the third window of the said north side. His feet lie at the foot of Bishop Wishart's monument."†

Bishop Rose of Edinburgh continued to reside in the city, and it appears that his house was in the Canongate. Two sons of Bishop Rose are mentioned as born at Perth—Alexander in 1679, and Arthur in 1681.‡ He married Euphemia, one of six daughters of Patrick Threipland, Esq. of Fingask Castle, Perthshire, who was created a Baronet of Nova Scotia in 1687.

* Sketch of the History of the Church of England to the Revolution of 1688, vol. ii p. 373, 374
† MS. Funeral Records of the Abbey and Chapel-Royal of Holyroodhouse.
‡ Perth Registers, MSS., in Advocates' Library, Edinburgh

Of the other ejected Prelates we find Bishop Hamilton of Dunkeld continuing to officiate as an Episcopal clergyman in Edinburgh, and he retained his appointment of Sub-Dean of the Chapel-Royal. Bishop Hallyburton of Aberdeen lived in complete seclusion after the Revolution, and died in his own mansion of Denhead near Cupar-Angus in 1715, in the 77th year of his age. The death of Bishop Hay of Moray is already mentioned in his son-in-law's house at Castlehill, Inverness, in 1707. Bishop Drummond of Brechin resided chiefly with the Earl of Erroll, till his death in 1695. This nobleman was Sir John Hay of Killour, who succeeded as eleventh Earl of Erroll in 1674. His son Charles, who became twelfth Earl, is noticed as " Lord Hay, one of the hopefulest young gentlemen in the kingdom, *and an enemy to Presbytery* "* Bishop Drummond resided with the Earl of Erroll at Slaines Castle in Aberdeenshire as his Lordship's private friend. Bishop Wood of Caithness died at Dunbar in 1695, in the 76th year of his age. He also appears to have lived in strict retirement after the Revolution. Bishop Douglas of Dunblane died at Dundee in 1716, at the venerable age of ninety-two, and, as it is said of him, " full of piety as well as of years." Bishop Ramsay of Ross died at Edinburgh in 1696, and was interred in the Canongate churchyard Of Bishop Bruce of Orkney it is merely recorded that he died in March 1700. It is already observed that Bishop Gordon of Galloway followed the fortunes of King James, and resided at the exiled Court of St Germains. Nothing is known of Bishop Graham of the Isles. The Bishopric of Argyll was vacant at the Revolution. Principal Monro received a *conge d'elire* to the See on the 24th of October 1688, but the fate of the Church at the Revolution prevented his consecration.

The ejected Bishops were held in the greatest respect and veneration during their lives by the members of the Church. Even the descendants of some of their predecessors in the episcopate were highly esteemed by many in their localities. An illustration of this occurs in the case of the family of Dr William Lindsay, who had been one of the incumbents of Perth, and died Bishop of Dunkeld in 1679, in the second year of his consecration. His lady died a short time before him, and his surviving children were placed under the care of a relative in Perth. The old

* General Mackay's Memoirs, p. 247.

women of that town "used to stroke the heads of his little grandchildren, and bless them for their grandfather's sake, who they were sure was a good man."*

The ejected Archbishops and Bishops gave the new Government no trouble, for they quietly relinquished their Sees, and were consequently unmolested, but it was different with the parochial clergy. Committees were appointed to perambulate the kingdom, and *purge* the parishes of the Episcopal incumbents. This was carried on by serving them with libels to appear before the newly constituted Presbyteries, and as these libels were of course found proven, sentence of deprivation was recorded. In a pamphlet written by an enemy, the noted George Ridpath already mentioned, under the title of *William Laick*, some curious particulars are given of the proceedings against the clergy. Of this individual, who was of considerable and not very creditable notoriety in his day, little is now known, and his pamphleteering enmity to the Episcopal Church has sunk like himself into oblivion. He was a native of Berwickshire, and appears to have been connected with a respectable family, notwithstanding the epithets of *varlet* and other degrading names bestowed upon him by Sir William Paterson, Bart., the son of Archbishop Paterson of Glasgow. He was considered of such importance to the Presbyterians as a writer that his antagonists designated him the "head of their party in Scotland," in the preface to a pamphlet written in reply to some of his falsehoods, entitled, "The Spirit of Calumny and Slander examin'd, chastis'd, and exposed, in a Letter to a Malicious Libeller, more particularly addressed to Mr George Ridpath, Newsmonger, near St Martin's-in-the-Fields, containing some Observations on his Scurrilous Pamphlets published by him against the Kings, Parliaments, Laws, Nobility, and Clergy of Scotland ; together with a Short Account of Presbyterian Principles and Consequential Practics." The motto is—*Tenue est mendacium, perlucet si diligenter inspexeris.*†

The title of Ridpath's production is, "The Scots Episcopal Innocence, or the juggling of that party with the late King, his present Majesty, the Church of England, and the Church of Scotland, demonstrat-

---

* Perth Registers, MSS , Advocates' Library, Edinburgh.

† London, printed for Joseph Hindmarsh, at the Golden Ball, over against the Royal Exchange, 4to. 1693.

ed; together with a Catalogue of the Scots Episcopal Clergy turn'd out for their Disloyalty and other Enormities since the Revolution. And a Postscript, with Reflections on a late malicious Pamphlet, entitled *The Spirit of Calumny and Slander*, particularly addressed to Dr Monro and his journeymen, Mr Simon Wild, Mr Andrew Johnstone, &c. near *Thieving Lane*, Westminster." It is addressed to the " Right Honourable and Right Reverend the General Assembly of the Church of Scotland," and it appears from Ridpath's own admissions that the Presbyterians were severely annoyed by the satires of their opponents, for he hopes that the *Right Reverend Assembly* will " take such measures as their wisdom shall suggest to provide antidotes for those poisonous libels, which fly abroad here against them in such numbers by the united endeavours of their enemies." But the most extraordinary assertion he makes in the very outset of his pamphlet is—" I am well assured that the far greater part of the Scots Episcopal clergy did always pretend to believe that *no particular species of church government was of Divine Institution*, but that it was alterable, according to the pleasure and conveniency of the State, and this I have heard asserted by some of the most learned of their communion." Who those "most learned" were William Laick, or Ridpath, does not inform us, yet in the face of this statement he gives us a list "of the Episcopal ministers deprived by the Committee of Estates in May 1689," amounting to eighteen, and he then enumerates *one hundred and eighty-four*, most of whom were afterwards ejected from their benefices for maintaining the divine institution of Episcopacy, amongst whom are many whose names are well known in the subsequent history of the Scottish Episcopal Church. The *disloyalty and other enormities* of which the deprived clergy were *guilty* were of course attachment to the exiled sovereign, refusing to read the "proclamation enjoined by the States," and "not praying for King William and Queen Mary." It also appears that in many cases the clergy were present when they were deprived, and admitted the charges, thus choosing rather to relinquish their temporalities than to violate their consciences by swerving from what they considered to be the principles of loyalty. Is it likely that some hundreds of men would have acted in this manner, if they had been of the opinion that "no particular species of church government was of divine institution, but that it was alterable according to the pleasure and conveniency of the State?"

Mr Patrick Trant, minister of Linlithgow, was deposed for "praying for the late King, and that God would restore the banished." Mr John Barclay, minister of Falkland in Fifeshire, acknowledged that "he had not prayed for their Majesties," and he was consequently "deprived, and discharged from preaching in the parish." Mr David Murray, minister of Blackford, Perthshire, accused of "not reading, and not praying, and not obeying the thanksgiving, and for hindering the reading of the proclamation for a collection for the French and Irish Protestants," was present, and as he "acknowledged that he did not read, nor pray (for King William and Queen Mary), nor keep the thanksgiving, nor read the proclamation," he was deprived. One of the ministers of St Cuthbert's, Edinburgh, was accused of being "imposed on the parish by the Bishop, and for his acting as a spy, and otherwise as an intelligencer to the Castle of Edinburgh then besieged." Mr Robert Graham, minister of Abercorn, did not deny the charges brought against him, but insisted that "the libel might be proven" according to law, for which "disingenuity," as it is called, this gentleman was deprived, and "committed to prison during pleasure."

Mr John Barclay, minister of Kettle in Fifeshire, was deprived "for not reading and not praying, and not only praying for the late King, but also that God would confound all his enemies, and that he hoped to see the late King on his throne." This gentleman was farther accused of "always running out of the church when his reader read the public papers contained in the libel." Mr Paul Gelly, minister of Avoth, was accused of exhorting his hearers to pray for King James in private, and of saying that "he expected a blessed reformation, but that they had only gotten wretched tyrants and ungodly rulers to govern them, and that the people had no security for life or property." Mr John Cameron, minister of Kincardine, in addition to the general charge, was accused of "bringing down the rebels," the Viscount of Dundee's troops, "to rob his parishioners." Messrs Graham and Cowper, ministers of Dunfermline, were charged with declaring, when they heard of the defeat of General Mackay's troops at Killiecrankie, that "no less could come of them for rebelling against their lawful King." Mr George Chalmers, minister of Kennoway, was accused of saying that "there were three papers lying in the Parliament House at Edinburgh, which were like to cause the members to sheathe their swords in one another's sides." Mr

John Falconer, minister of Carnbee [afterwards a Bishop], was deprived on the general charge. Mr John Liddell, minister of Hopkirk, was deprived for "not praying for their Majesties," and for 'saying that he "never would pray for them as long as his blood was warm." Mr Henry Knox, minister of Bowden, was accused of saying that "he had rather the Papists should gain the day than the Presbyterians." He was "present, acknowledged the same, and was deprived." Mr John Park, minister of Carriden, was accused of praying " that the walls of the Castle of Edinburgh might be as brass about the Duke of Gordon." Mr David Spence, minister of Kirkurd, was libelled for saying that "it was as lawful to go and hear mass as to hear a sermon in a Presbyterian meeting-house." Mr William Cairns, minister of the Tolbooth Church, Edinburgh, was deprived for praying in this modified manner—"God have mercy upon King William and Queen Mary, *and the Royal Family.*" Mr William Maclethny, minister at Bonhill, was accused of saying that as he had "taken an oath to King James, he would not obey King William's authority." Mr John Blair, minister of Fintry, was deprived for declaring—" Let the Whigs pray for King William and Queen Mary, he would not, for he never got good by them ;" and farther, that "he would not pray for them till Queen Mary had got her father's blessing."

Some hundreds of instances might be quoted similar to the above in all parts of Scotland. Many of the clergy, it is to be observed, repudiated the expressions imputed to them, but their denial was not received. Many, it is alleged by Ridpath, were deprived for "praying for the late King's happy restoration to the throne, and the confusion of his enemies." Others were ejected for opposing the Westminster Confession of Faith and the Larger and Shorter Catechisms. In addition to all this, libels were often served against the clergy, accusing them of what were considered crimes and scandals. It was intended to libel a clergyman for "plucking a few pease on Sunday," but " that being so parallel to the case of the disciples, which our Saviour defended, it was not permitted to be made use of." One was accused " because he sometimes *whistled*; and another because, one time playing at bowls, he broke an innocent jest, which none could have construed profane but they who were impure."*

* Introduction to Historical Relation of the late Presbyterian General Assembly, 1690, 4to, 1691, p. 10.

But even *taking the test*, as it was called in common phraseology, did not always save the incumbents who complied. Mr Cooper, previously mentioned, one of the ministers of Dunfermline, was libelled as a "great persecutor of the godly—supinely negligent, contrary to 1 Tim· iii. 2"—as having "horribly profaned the ordinance of the Lord's Supper by admitting unclean persons to that holy ordinance"—as allowing and keeping "on his *session* ungodly scandalous elders, some of whom are drunkards, others swearers, and the most part ignorant, and neglecters of the worship of God in their families, profaners of the Sabbath." He was also accused of having "sacrilegiously robbed the poor of the charitable offerings of the people, which is aggravated by this, that he hath bestowed the same to carry on persecution against poor well-meaning godly people"—that "he entered, and hath been admitted, to the charge of the parish of Dunfermline by presentation of the patron, collation, and institution of the prelate, and that against the consent of the generality of the *godly and serious persons* within the said parish—that he hath in all things joined and complied with and assisted Prelacy, *contrary to the word of God*, established law of the Church, and the Land's solemn engagements thereto, and, *by taking the oath of the test*, has manifested his incorrigibleness: for which, and the forenamed scandals, the generality of the godly in this place never accepted him or received him as minister, but have been groaning under his persecutions upon that account."

A great part of this libel relating to persecution, robbing the poor, and other matters, was denied as "utterly false." It was declared that "every family in the town was visited ordinarily once a-year and twice examined"—that "the sick, upon notice given, are carefully attended, and the Scriptures explained, sometimes in larger, sometimes in lesser portions"—that "all due endeavours are used to debar scandalous and notarly vicious persons from the Lord's Supper"—that "the elders are men of as unquestionable integrity as any of their quality in the parish, at least nothing to the contrary of either communicants or elders was ever publicly or privately signified"—and that "his entrance to the charge was by presentation of the heritors and magistrates, the then undoubted patrons; his admission was legal and approved by the favourable reception of the parish; his ministry countenanced by all, a few excepted."

A similar libel was prepared against this gentleman's colleague, Mr

Graham, with the additions that "he takes no notice of Quakers in his parish, who exercise all the duties of their religion without controul"—that he profaned the Lord's day by allowing people to "bring in kail and fan barley for the pot that day," and "by allowing his children to play with others"—it being "of verity that the said Mr James Graham is guilty of these scandals, enormities, and transgressions." Mr Johnstone, minister in Burntisland in Fife, was libelled as a "man of bad principles and jesuitically inclined," and they had no evidence of his having done any thing to signify his satisfaction with the "change in Church and State *except his praying for King William and Queen Mary,* which is not doubted was done by advice to keep off a present stroke." Mr Crawford, minister of Ladykirk, was libelled for terming the Solemn League and Covenant a *bond of rebellion,* and Mr Heriot of Dalkeith was prosecuted for having called the Duke of Monmouth and the Earl of Argyle traitors, though he had simply read the proclamation issued against those noblemen, which was appointed by the King and Council to be read in churches. Mr Wood, minister of Dunbar, was libelled for saying to an individual who expressed his fears about the introduction of the Book of Common Prayer—"God send us no worse ;" and because he had never expressed his thankfulness for the deliverance of the kingdom from Popery and Prelacy. He replied, that he "thanked God heartily for any deliverance of the land from Popery, but he could not do so for the overthrow of Prelacy unless he either acted the hypocrite, or was convinced that Presbytery was the greater blessing, and the more ancient and apostolical government, which he had never seen made out."* He objected to the word *Prelacy,* because he was "sensible it was too mean for so great and so glorious a Church as that of England." Mr Johnstone, minister of Saline, was accused of "being too much affected to the episcopal government, and for recommending superstitious and erroneous books to the people, as they were pleased to call the *Whole Duty of Man,* which was expressly mentioned." The minister of Abbotshall was libelled for opposing the Westminster Catechism, and using the one published by the authority of the Diocesan Synod of Edinburgh, afterwards enlarged by Bishop Scougall of Aberdeen, one of the most pious men of his time. When Mr Purves, minister of

---

* An Historical Relation of the late Presbyterian General Assembly, p. 11.

Glencorse, objected to some of the witnesses as bearing malice against him, he was told that "if these men had done so out of malice and personal prejudice, they ought not to be received as witnesses, *but if they had done it for the glory of God, there was no reason why they ought not to be admitted.*"

It would be easy to multiply these examples, but enough has been adduced to show the extraordinary proceedings of the now triumphant Presbyterian party. The facts are admitted by the Presbyterian ministers themselves, in their statistical accounts of the parishes of Scotland,* and their Presbytery records are cited in evidence. We may take as an example the Presbytery of Perth, certainly one of the most important in the kingdom. It appears from the Perth MSS.† that " before the 30th July 1690, the ministers of the following parishes had been deprived—Perth, Kinnoull, Aberdalgie, Dumbarney, Abernethy, Forgandenny, Errol The only ministers in the Presbytery of Perth who conformed to Presbyterian government were Mr Alexander Pitcairn, minister of Dron, who never could properly be said to be a supporter of the Church, and Mr James Inglis, minister of St Martin's, who, though he had complied, appears from the Presbytery Register to have been in some degree a malecontent. Several of the incumbents, particularly Mr John Gall, minister of Kinfauns, seem in the beginning to have imitated the clergy in England, who, from the apprehensions they entertained of Popery and arbitrary power, approved of the Revolution. But when the Church was disestablished by the Parliament, and Presbyterian government restored in its full exercise, it would seem that those ministers left off mentioning the names of King William and Queen Mary in their prayers, and thereby laid themselves open to civil as well as ecclesiastical censures.

"It appears," continues this MS document, "that the Episcopal ministers of Perth continued to preach for some time after their deprivation, but after the battle of Killiecrankie they thought it advisable to desist. It is reported of Mr David Anderson, that he was first told of this battle by James Robertson, residenter in Balhousie, whom he had accosted on the street of Perth with some threatening expressions. James laid hold

---

* Both in Sir John Sinclair's Statistical Account of Scotland, and in the New Statistical Account.

† Entitled Hospital Registers, from 1665 to 1712.

of his gown when he was going to pass from him, told him what had happened, and that the King's troops were on their way to Perth. Mr Anderson thereupon saw it necessary, it is said, to provide for his own safety, and very soon after fled from the town."

A field preacher named Melville succeeded the incumbent of the parish of Arngask, who, nevertheless, it is said, still continued to reside there unmolested by the civil power, and to keep possession of a great part of the stipend. The incumbent of Collace was not deprived till 1692, and he is described as a " most respectable man, neither did he occasion any trouble in the parish after his deprivation." Mr Alexander Balneavis, minister of Tibbermuir, was libelled in the usual manner for disobeying the Government and not reading the proclamations. He was also accused of not residing in his parish, but constantly on his own estate of Carnbadie, about eight miles distant; and, " though he came pretty regularly to preach, yet it was frequently the Sabbath morning before he came, and he often returned to Carnbadie the same evening." He was charged with being " guilty of unnecessary travelling on the Sabbath betwixt Carnbadie and Tibbermuir, and crossing the river Tay twice in boats." Mr Balneavis did not appear, and he sent no defence. He was deprived, but " he did not altogether acquiesce in the sentence, for the Presbytery sometimes heard both of his preaching in private houses, and of his baptizing children."*

In the city of Edinburgh, which then contained six incumbents, the clergy were all superseded by Presbyterian ministers in July 1690.† There is nothing particularly recorded respecting the proceedings, and the registers of that period are not extant, having been accidentally consumed by fire, and the present reach no farther back than about the beginning of the eighteenth century.‡ But from the instances already given throughout the various districts of the country, it is sufficiently

---

* Perth MSS., Advocates' Library, Edinburgh.

† Town Council Records.

‡ Information communicated by Dr Gilchrist, one of the ministers of the Canongate, and Clerk of the Presbytery of Edinburgh. In the Town Council Records the following entry occurs :—" The said Council remove Mr William Halkhead from his office of chaplain to the Trinity Hospital, because he has not given obedience to authority, by praying for King William and Queen Mary, but allow him his stipend till Lammas next." They appear to have acted with considerable generosity towards the Dean of Edinburgh, the Rev. John Annand.

apparent in what manner the proceedings were conducted to eject the incumbents. " Nothing," says an authority of the time, " came before the Presbyteries except citations and libels against Episcopal ministers, and to make the greater despatch they sat every week."

The compiler of the Perth MS. Register mentions, that "many of the incumbents or deprived Episcopal ministers went into England, where, it is said, some of them acquired a great reputation by their learning, piety, and devotional writings." This corroborates Principal Monro's declaration already quoted—" I must tell you that I know not a more unblameable company of men upon earth than the Episcopal clergy of Scotland; nor do I know any five of them in the whole nation who could not undergo the severest examinations used in the Christian Church preparatory to ordination." From the manner in which the intimation of the future proceedings of the Episcopal clergy is mentioned in the Perth Register, it appears as if intended to be general, and not confined to the members of the Episcopal Presbytery of Perth. It is farther stated—" King William settled pensions on the deprived Bishops, which pensions were continued by Queen Anne A large collection in England was made in Queen Anne's time for the ejected Episcopal clergy in Scotland; also many of the Presbyterians are said to have given liberally to their relief."*

The consequence of the *rabbling* by the mobs, and ejecting of the clergy by the newly constituted Presbyterian authorities, may be anticipated. A great part of the country was left destitute of religious instruction, and of the rites and services of the Church, for a considerable time, until the Presbyterians found persons of their own principles to fill the vacant benefices. In the two important diocesan Presbyteries of Haddington and Dunbar were only five Presbyterian ministers, although these Presbyteries contained at that time nearly thirty parishes within their bounds. The Presbyteries of Dunse and Chirnside, in Berwickshire and Roxburghshire, consisting of between twenty and thirty parishes, mustered the like number. There was only one Presbyterian minister in the Presbytery of Auchterarder, which contained nearly twenty parishes, and when the adjoining Presbytery was added three persons were the whole Presbyterian strength. Sir Colin Campbell de-

* Hospital Registers, Advocates' Library, MS. p. 283.

clared, in the first Presbyterian General Assembly after the Revolution, that " for twenty miles westward of Perth there were but two or three ministers, meaning those of the Presbyterian persuasion, which shows how little agreeable either their persons or government are to the people." This fact is corroborated by the Perth MS. so often quoted. " In order," says the compiler, himself a Presbyterian minister, " that a *sufficient number* of qualified ministers and ruling elders might meet, there were *added* to the Presbytery of Perth the *whole Presbytery of Dunkeld* and *one half of the Presbytery of Auchterarder*. The country, therefore, over which they had legal jurisdiction was very extensive ; but there were only *six ministers* qualified to meet, and two or three ruling elders, who occasionally gave their assistance, and who were *men of mean station* in life." We are farther told by the same authority, that the discontent of the generality of the people at the deprivation and ejection of the Episcopal clergy was great; and he mentions a preacher called " Mr John Anderson, appointed by the Presbyterian judicatories to officiate at Perth, who was obliged to be taken under the protection of the King's troops, and was accompanied every day to and from the pulpit by a *military guard!*"*

Much might be said on this important subject, which could be con_firmed by the reluctant or unwitting testimony of the Presbyterians themselves, but the following extract from a contemporary writer at the time gives a complete and happy illustration of the state of Scotland, and the proceedings of the Presbyterian ministers at the ejection of the Episcopal parochial clergy:—" More than a third part of the churches in the kingdom wanted ministers, and the most of them for more than a year; but, as if that was only a small matter, it was overlooked, and all pains and care laid out in emptying those churches where the Episcopal ministers continued to preach. Their [the Presbyterian] beloved *West* was destitute of ministers, the churches there and in Galloway were almost all shut up; so that when the Assembly met, two ministers declared before them that where they lived there was not so much as the face of a church, there being no ministers but themselves and one other. Yet none were sent thither, but they showed greater inclination to seat themselves in the Lothians and the South of Scotland, which is

* Hospital Registers, MS. pp. 175, 177.

indeed a better country, but where there was less room for them, and where they were not so acceptable to the people It was sad and lamentable to see so many desolate congregations in all parts of the land, such multitudes of persons without the gospel, and without the direction of pastors; and yet they [the Presbyterians] would endeavour to deprive those of this blessing who, by the good providence of God, had it still continued with them. However, they did this either to force the people to join with them when none other could be had, or, being conscious of their own ignorance and inability, they thought it neither fit nor their interest to tolerate those who were more judicious, and who could accustom the people to sensible and solid discourses, which held forth the true nature and design of the gospel, and which armed people against fanatical delusions When some were asked why they studied to cast out all the Episcopal clergy, seeing they could not yet supply their churches, and why they would preach in a meeting-house, where there was an Episcopal minister unblameable in his life and doctrine, and draw the people from him rather than go to another parish which wanted a pastor altogether, it was answered—*That there was less prejudice both to church and people by the want of preaching, than by the preaching of men of Episcopal principles and persuasions;* and Mr Frazer of Brae, in a sermon before the Parliament, declared—*That it was better that the temple of the Lord did lie sometime unbuilt and unrepaired, than be reared up by Gibeonites and Samaritans.*"

CHAPTER VIII.

OPPOSITION OF THE PEOPLE IN VARIOUS DISTRICTS TO THE SETTLEMENT OF PRESBYTERIAN MINISTERS.

THE facts already given completely refute the idea long entertained and asserted, that the whole Scottish nation welcomed the establishment of Presbyterianism, and felt Episcopacy to be an " intolerable grievance." The attention of the reader is now requested to the following details, many of them the admissions of Presbyterian writers, which show the determined resistance of the people in various dioceses to the ejection of their pastors, and the intrusion of Presbyterian ministers. Some of the Episcopal clergy were indeed enabled to retain their benefices by the influence of the nobility and gentry, but in the great majority of cases the people were bitterly opposed to the new system of church government.

The act, it has been repeatedly stated, which established Presbyterianism, gave the new judicatories authority " to try and purge out all *insufficient, negligent, scandalous, and erroneous ministers,*" and we have seen that sentences of deprivation were accordingly passed, but it was not easy to put these sentences every where in force. In the counties north of the Tay, the nobility and gentry, and the great majority of the people, were decidedly in favour of Episcopacy, and it was well known that William III. had declared his desire in very strong terms, that those of the clergy who took the oaths of allegiance to his Government should be allowed to retain their benefices during life, without being subjected to the jurisdiction of presbyteries. This wish of the King gave great offence to the Presbyterians, who were nevertheless compelled to submit to it from various causes, though they took effectual care that those clergy should have no successors of the same principles, and no share in the administration of their system. Some submitted to all the conditions, and were gladly enrolled as members of the new ecclesiastical government On the other hand, " those who had taken the oaths required by law, and prayed publicly for the King and Queen's Majesties, but who would not abjure Episcopacy, were indeed suffered to keep possession of their churches and their stipends, but were perpetually teazed and harassed by answering questions concerning their *sufficiency and orthodoxy*, whilst the vengeance of the Government, both civil and ecclesiastical, fell chiefly on those who, refusing to take the oaths of allegiance to King William and Queen Mary, were henceforth distinguished by the denomination of *Nonjurors*. Among the Nonjurors are to be classed all the Bishops, and almost all the inferior clergy who had been driven from their parishes by a lawless rabble, before Episcopacy was legally abolished To these must be added a very great number of the most learned and respectable of the parochial clergy, who, disdaining to conceal their sentiments and retain their livings by such contrivances as those, by which many who were as really attached to the exiled prince as they were suffered to retain their livings, voluntarily retired from their parishes."*

The compiler of the Perth MS. says—" In the West of Scotland the ejection of the Episcopal ministers by numbers of tumultuous people began December 25, 1688 In a few months, about three hundred ministers were in that manner forcibly excluded from their parishes. But in the North of Scotland the situation of affairs was *quite different*, not only the nobility and gentry, but also *the bulk of the people, were fondly attached to the Episcopal incumbents*. In the Presbytery of Perth, such ministers as had given greatest offence by their disaffection to the new Government were deprived very early, *not with the minds of the people, but contrary thereto* " In enumerating the parishes from which the clergy were ejected he observes—" *But it was no easy matter to prevail afterwards with most of these parishes to accept of Presbyterian ministers.*"

We are informed respecting the county and Diocese of Moray, and the North of Scotland, that "the Episcopal ministers conformed generally

* Scottish Episcopal Magazine, 1821, vol ii p. 180.

to the civil government, and were indulged to keep their churches and benefices during life. By this means the number of Presbyterian ministers *was so small* that they made but *one Presbytery*, called the Presbytery of Moray, till the year 1702."* Upwards of forty of the Episcopal clergy in the Diocese of Moray retained their benefices, though it was well known that they joined the laity in endeavouring to restore King James, and re-establish the Church. Some were continued in their parishes by the influence of the patrons and heritors, and others by the inclination of the people, who threatened the Presbyterian ministers with the most summary punishment if they attempted to supplant their pastors. In the town of Elgin, the magistrates, influenced it is said by Lord Duffus, resisted the settlement of a Presbyterian minister, and kept the benefice vacant eight years. In the important town of Inverness, at the death of one of the Episcopal clergy in 1691, the magistrates and citizens would not allow a Presbyterian minister to succeed to the vacancy, and for ten years no one could effect a peaceable settlement in that town. They even surrounded the parish church on one occasion with armed men, and placed double sentries at the doors, that no Presbyterian minister might enter; and in August 1691, the Earl of Leven's regiment was actually ordered thither to preserve the peace of the town and district, and to protect the few Presbyterians from the violence of the excited Episcopalians.†

In the Diocese of Aberdeen the people were most inveterately opposed to Presbyterianism, and in the city of Aberdeen the episcopal form of worship was generally observed by the citizens after the Restoration, although a number of them continued to favour the Roman Catholic religion. We are told that " although the Episcopal form of government had been abolished at the epoch of the Revolution, yet it appears that the ministers and session of Aberdeen paid little regard to the law by which it was annulled. They persevered in the exercise of their several functions under the authority of the Bishop for several years afterwards, without interruption."‡ It was not till 1694 that the Presbyterians formed the new church establishment in Aberdeen, about which time the three ministers of St Nicolas, Dr William Blair, Dr George

---

* History of the Province of Moray, by Mr Lachlan Shaw, new edition, 4to, 1826, p. 341.

† Shaw's History of Moray, p. 418, 419.

‡ Kennedy's Annals of Aberdeen, 4to, vol. ii. p. 49, 50

Garden, and Dr Andrew Burnett, were ejected from their benefices by a Committee of the General Assembly. The deprivations in the county and Diocese excited the greatest opposition, and in many cases were successfully resisted

In the Diocese of Ross the same feeling prevailed. Inverness is already mentioned, and in the united parishes of Moy and Dalarossie, in that county, the Episcopal incumbent continued till about 1727, when the first Presbyterian minister was settled. Mr George Campbell, minister of Alvah in Banffshire, kept possession of his parish till 1718, when he was ejected. The same remark applies to other parishes, and in many instances there was no possibility of getting rid of the clergy till their death. In the Diocese of Brechin, Presbyterianism was decidedly unpopular, and its introduction into the parishes often threatened to excite serious commotions. An Episcopal minister officiated in the parish of Tannadyce till the year 1716, when he was ejected for being favourable to the enterprise of 1715. The parishioners got a Presbyterian minister, but in the course of six years he became so unpopular, and was so grossly slandered, as to be deposed.*

It would be easy to lay before the reader numerous illustrations of the opposition of the people in various dioceses to the establishment of Presbyterianism, and of strong attachment to the Episcopal clergy, but the limits of the present work admit only of the most prominent being noticed. Mr Peddie, incumbent of the parish of Lunan in the diocese of Brechin, died minister of that parish in 1713. He bequeathed some plate for the communion service in the church of Lunan, on this singular condition, that any Episcopal congregation within seven miles of the parish should have the use of it when required. "It is said that he was among the last surviving clergymen of the Episcopal persuasion in this part of the country who refused to take the oaths to the new Government, nevertheless, along with others he was allowed to remain in his charge without molestation He was much respected by the Jacobite families in the neighbourhood, who came from various quarters to attend his ministry, and it is handed down by tradition, that on the Sabbath day a long line of carriages would have been seen approaching the humble church of Lunan. It is at least certain that for several years, as appears from the Presbytery records, the people, countenanced

---

* New Statistical Account of Scotland—Forfarshire, p. 203.

by the heritors, unanimously resisted the introduction of a Presbyterian clergyman, till strong measures were taken to effect the settlement of a Mr Irvine, afterwards minister of Maryton."*

The Presbytery of Perth lies in the archiepiscopal diocese of St Andrews, and in it there was the most vigorous opposition. The incumbent of the parish of Methven was enabled to retain his benefice till his death in 1693. The Laird of Methven, the patron of the parish, refused to deliver the keys of the church to the new Presbytery, and prevented a Mr Dunning, who was appointed to declare the parish vacant, from entering it. He reported to the Presbytery, that "on Sabbath, January 28, 1694, he went to the parish kirk of Methven, where he found a great rabble of people stopping his access, and that Mr David Young, late incumbent of Strowan and Monievaird, who had been deprived by their Majesties' Privy Council, was within the said kirk at the same time." He preached to those who were disposed to listen to him in the churchyard, and declared the parish vacant according to the Presbyterian form. The Laird subsequently offered terms of agreement on the condition of a preacher named Moncrieff being admitted, which were accepted; but, says the Register, "there were uncommon circumstances attending his ordination. When the Presbytery, with their Moderator, Mr Robert Anderson, at their head, went to Methven, and were proceeding to the kirk, they found the Laird of Balgowan, Busbie, David Smythe, brother of the Laird of Methven, and several parishioners, standing as a guard before the kirk door. Mr Robert, in name of the Presbytery, desired he might have access to perform the intention on which he and his brethren had come there, but he was answered with a positive refusal. He and his brethren thereupon protested, and then met together in a house near the kirk to consider what they were to do next. There they determined that Mr Robert should preach in the kirkyard, and, as they could not get access to the kirk, should perform in the kirkyard the solemnities of the ordination, which was accordingly done."†

The parish of Forgandenny did not receive a Presbyterian minister till 1695, and that of Forteviot till 1696. These parishes had been

---

* New Statistical Account of Scotland—Forfarshire, p. 323.
† Perth MS. Advocates' Library, Edinburgh.

vacant from the year 1690, but the opposition of the people to Presbyterianism was such that the new judicatories were afraid to venture among them. Mr Liddell, Episcopal minister of Scone, in which parish is the palatial residence of the Noble family of Mansfield, " was a man of extraordinary good character. He is yet spoken of with much respect by the people, who heard from their parents many good things concerning him. Though he did not conform at the Revolution, yet his noble parishioner David fifth Viscount of Stormont, father of William (first) Earl of Mansfield, long protected him in the possession of the parish, and in the exercise of his ministry."* The first Presbyterian minister of Scone was not able to officiate till 1698, and Mr Liddell "afterwards gave *offence* to the Presbytery by administering divine ordinances," and by preaching in what the Presbyterians were pleased to designate *conventicles*.

The incumbent of Kilspindy continued for more than seven years after the Revolution in possession of his parish The Presbyterians prosecuted him in every possible manner, but he set them at defiance, and treated their sentence of deposition with contempt. We are told that " ministers sent from time to time by the Presbytery sometimes were allowed to preach at the *kirk-door*, and sometimes *were not allowed by the people to come near the kirk at all* "† At length the Presbyterian minister obtained possession in 1698.

Mr Hall, incumbent of St Madoes, was "vigorously supported a long time by his heritors in the possession of his parish. He was in the beginning attached to the Revolution, and mentioned King William and Queen Mary in his prayers, but when he found that the Episcopal Church was wholly overturned under the new administration, and that Acts of Parliament and of Privy Council, which appeared to him too severe, were made from time to time, not only ejecting the former ministers, but forbidding all Episcopal ministers in Scotland, however well affected to the civil constitution, to execute any part of the ministerial office, *he seems to have become less loyal.*"‡ Mr Hall was deposed by the Presbytery, after various petty proceedings against him, in 1697, for not praying for King William, and "for that he had baptized a child in his own kirk brought from the parish of Kilspindy."—" Mr William Dick, who

---

* Perth MS. † Ibid. ‡ Ibid

was appointed to preach at St Madoes, and intimate the Presbytery's sentence, reported, September 1, 1697, that he went for that purpose, but *met with such opposition* from the Lairds of Pitfour, elder and younger, and their associates, that he could get *no access* to preach in the kirk, nor on the ground of the parish, being all Pitfour's land [property]. Yet, notwithstanding, he intimated the sentence, and declared the kirk vacant, and required old Pitfour, and another man and a woman, to be witnesses, all others being kept at a considerable distance from him."*
The first Presbyterian minister did not obtain possession till 1699, but " he felt himself in such an uneasy situation" that he left it about the end of three months

Mr William Popley, incumbent of the parish of Rhynd, " was long kept in possession of his parish and exercise of his ministry by his noble parishioner, who resided at Elcho Castle, viz. Margaret Countess of Wemyss in her own right, and dowager of James Wemyss, Lord Burntisland."† After various processes against him, the Presbyterians obtained possession of the parish in 1699. It appears that Mr Popley " came to the Presbytery, July 15, 1696, and delivered up the keys of the kirk doors The utensils of the kirk he also afterwards delivered to commissioners sent by the Presbytery. But notwithstanding his resignation he continued to preach, though not in the church of Rhynd, but *in the fields or private houses*, till he was ordered by a particular act. of Privy Council totally to remove at Whitsunday 1700."‡

The incumbent of Redgorton was deposed in 1691, but he " still continued to officiate in his parish, and, together with the Laird of Balgowan, refused to deliver up to the Presbytery the keys of the kirk. At last the Privy Council, by their act, June 1698, deprived him of the benefice of Redgorton, and ordered that he and his family should depart out of the bounds of the parish before the next Martinmas at farthest." It was not, however, till April 1700 that the parishioners were reconciled to the reception of a Presbyterian minister.

. Mr John Gall, incumbent of Kinfauns, " was, according to many traditionary accounts, a man of the most respectable and amiable character. . He was well affected to the revolution of civil government, and thankful that the three kingdoms were happily delivered from the apprehen-

---

* Perth MS. † Ibid. ‡ Ibid.

sions justly entertained of the intended introduction of Popery. But the utter ruin of the Episcopal Church, and the prosecutions against its ministers, alienated his affections from the new Government, so that he left off mentioning King William by name in his public prayers. He was deposed by the Presbytery, July 28, 1697, and Mr David Shaw was appointed to declare the kirk vacant, *but met with such opposition*, that he could only be allowed to preach in the kirkyard, where he intimated the Presbytery's sentence. In the year 1698, Council letters were procured and executed against Mr Gall, who then left the parish wholly, and gave no more trouble to the Presbytery."* His Presbyterian successor was not admitted till 1700

The incumbent of Monedie "kept possession of the parish a long time after the Revolution. At last, after the usual processes, the doors of the kirk were made patent to the Presbytery, and Mr James Fleming, preacher of the gospel, was ordained and admitted minister at Monedie, June 26, 1701."

In the Diocese of Dunkeld the same opposition was offered to the settlement of Presbyterian ministers in the parishes. The parish of Muthill may be here instanced. A preacher named William Hally was appointed to succeed the ejected incumbent, but he had the greatest opposition to encounter. Almost the whole population of the parish were Episcopalians; they held out against Mr Hally's ordination, and the incumbent kept possession of the parish church. "The opposition," according to the Presbytery record, "proceeded to the extent of a riot, several individuals of the parish kept the doors of the kirk and kirkyard, armed with swords and staves, which they made use of in beating and wounding several that had come there to hear the *word*." Hally was obliged to officiate a long time in the churchyard, and was often annoyed by the parishioners, who viewed him as an intruder; and it was only by the interference of the Duke of Atholl that he obtained possession of the parish church in March 1705.

The following remarkable circumstance occurred in the united parishes of Glenorchy and Inishail in the Diocese of Argyll, and is related by Dr Macintyre, the Presbyterian incumbent when Sir John Sinclair published the Statistical Account of Scotland in 1793. "At the Re-

* Perth MS.

volution, when Presbytery was last re-established in North Britain, a Mr Dugald Lindsay was the Episcopal minister of Glenorchy. Mr Lindsay would not conform. Pressed by the Synod of Argyll, the Noble proprietor [the Earl of Breadalbane] of the country reluctantly wrote a letter of invitation to a Presbyterian probationer in the shire of Fife, to be minister of Glenorchy. He accepted, came on the close of a week to the parish, but could find no room to receive him, or person to make him welcome. In his distress he was drove to the house of the man whom he came to supplant, and was received with a cordiality and kindness becoming a minister of the gospel. Over the whole parish there was a strong ferment. People of all ages and conditions assembled from all quarters in the churchyard on Sabbath, long before the usual hour of worship. At the appearance of the stranger, accompanied by their own pastor, there was a general murmur of indignation. Twelve armed men with drawn swords surrounded the astonished intruder. Two bagpipes sounded the *March of Death*. Unmoved by the tears and remonstrances of Mr Lindsay, in this hostile and awful form, they proceeded with their prisoner to the boundary of the parish and of the county. There, on his bended knees, he solemnly engaged never more to enter the parish, or trouble any person for the occurrences of that day. He was allowed to depart in peace, and he kept his promise. The Synod of Argyll were incensed; time cooled their ardour; the proprietor was indulgent, Mr Lindsay was deserving, and the people loved him. He continued in the undisturbed possession of his charge till his death, more than thirty years after the foresaid event."*

Innumerable other instances might be given of the strongest manifestations of attachment to the Episcopal Church of Scotland, and respect for the parochial clergy on the part of the people in the various Dioceses. It is stated by contemporary writers, that even when King James granted his famous indulgence in 1687, "not fifty gentlemen," even in the West of Scotland, took advantage of it to attend the Presbyterian meeting-houses, and scarcely " a fifth or sixth part of the nation did so." We are farther assured that "the clergy stood all for Episcopacy, there being, of about a *thousand*, scarcely *twenty trimmers* betwixt

* Sir John Sinclair's Statistical Account of Scotland, vol. viii. p. 354, 355.

the Bishop and the Presbyterian Moderator," and that the members of the College of Justice, as the several legal institutions in Edinburgh are collectively called, and those of the College of Physicians at Edinburgh, were so averse to the establishment of Presbyterianism, that " the generality of them were ready last summer (1689) to take arms in defence of the Episcopal ministers."

The inhabitants, for example, of the parish of Coldingham in Berwickshire were stanch Episcopalians at the time of the Revolution, and zealously opposed the induction of the Presbyterian minister, a person named John Dysart, who had been removed from Langton to Coldingham in 1694 by sanction of the Privy Council They were so strongly opposed to the introduction of Presbyterianism, that it was deemed necessary to employ a body of military to prevent a riot Dysart obtained possession of the parish church, but few of the parishioners would listen to his sermons, and they engaged an Episcopal clergyman, who for several years officiated in a barn, situated a short distance from the parish church, and whom they supported by voluntary contributions.* The following extract from the records of the parish shows the little respect in which the Presbyterian authorities were held by the people years after the Revolution : " June 28, 1696—Joseph Minto was found in time of divine service idling away his time, lying upon a heather stack or turf, and being interrogated by the elders what he was doing there, and why he was out of the church, answered— *What was that to them?* The elders told him that it was not the first time they had found him breaking the Lord's Day He answered, that it shall not be the last time neither. Being further reproved for the sin, and exhorted to repentance and reformation, he answered, that it was *an ill world since the like of them were reproving folks for sin.* The Session, considering the perverseness of the youth, and that his parents were frequenters of the schismatical meeting-house [were Episcopalians], did recommend to the minister to deal privately with him."†

The ancient episcopal city of Brechin in Forfarshire is already mentioned. Its ecclesiastical state at the Revolution, as evincing the dislike of the citizens to the Presbyterian Establishment, may be inferred

* Carr's History of Coldingham, p. 213. † Ibid p 213, 214.

from the following particulars preserved by an intelligent local writer, The incumbent specified, Mr Lawrence Skinner, is designated by Wodrow a "*cousin of ours :*—he is pretending to be an intruding curate at Brechin."* He had been inducted in 1650, and was probably not episcopally ordained till after the Revolution. We are told that he was "heartily received by the magistrates and others of the parish as their minister."—"The officiating clergymen of Brechin at this date" [the Revolution], says Mr Black, "were Mr Lawrence Skinner and Mr John Skinner his son, and in continuing to officiate as clergymen after the removal of the Bishop, they laid themselves open to no charge of change of doctrine. Mr Lawrence Skinner continued to labour till his death in 1691. Looking at the texts recorded in the Session Minutes, as those from which he preached on the 29th of May, the birth-day and anniversary of the restoration of Charles II, we should say he was a determined loyalist. Mr John Skinner, refusing to sign the test required when Presbyterianism became predominant, was deposed in 1695, but he remained about Brechin, and appears to have had no little influence among his flock, notwithstanding his deposition."† At the death of his father he discharged the whole parochial duty till 1695, when Mr Abercrombie, Presbyterian minister at Lauder, "took possession of the forenoon's diet of preaching in the church of Brechin, and declared vacant that charge, formerly supplied by the Bishop." Mr Skinner nevertheless continued to officiate in the afternoon till the 1st of August 1697, when another Presbyterian minister declared that charge also vacant. Mr Skinner, however, resumed his clerical duties in March 1703, when he "at his own hand invaded the pulpit, took possession of the afternoon's diet of preaching, and dispossessed the Presbytery thereof." In this state matters continued till the 3d of December that year, when Mr John Willison, well known as the author of several devotional treatises, was inducted as Presbyterian minister.

Public opinion was strongly in favour of Mr Skinner, and even the Town Council speak unceremoniously of "Mr Willison and his *pretended Session.*"—"Mr Willison's Presbyterian principles," says Mr Black, "were not in accordance with the feelings of the people of Brechin, and

---

* Wodrow Correspondence —Letter to Mrs Wodrow, vol i p 13.
† History of Brechin, by David D Black, Town Clerk, p. 99.

we are informed that he was persecuted in every way by the inhabitants, especially by those of the higher ranks, most of whom were violent Jacobites and Episcopalians. When he removed to Dundee he found it impossible to command the services of a Brechin carter to convey his furniture to his new charge, so violent was the prejudice against him." In 1705 Mr Skinner again repossessed himself of the afternoon service, and Mr Willison reported that he durst not encounter the people, who were resolved to support the Episcopal clergyman, "to which they were not a little encouraged by the magistrates, who refused all concurrence or assistance to him [Mr Willison] in this matter." The deposition of Mr Skinner was only enforced by warrant of the High Court of Justiciary in 1709. He officiated as minister of the parish again during the continuance of the Earl of Mar's enterprise in 1715, and he subsequently in 1722 attempted to form a congregation in the town, which he soon left, and went to Edinburgh, where he died about 1725.

The proceedings of the Presbyterian Establishment for years after the Revolution excited much odium against it in several districts. It appears that the English Presbyterian leaders had no particular regard for the high pretensions of their Scottish brethren, if the celebrated Dr Calamy is admitted as representing their sentiments. " I know," says Wodrow, " the Doctor has no great regard for our judicatories, and is a great enemy to church power."*

If it is asked, then, how it happened that the descendants of those who so zealously stood out for the Church in several districts should have merged into the Presbyterian Establishment, various reasons might be assigned. One has always appeared of importance to the present writer, and this was the want of a Liturgy in the public service of the Church. The mode of divine worship followed by the parochial Episcopal clergy was nearly the same as that practised by the Presbyterians, and in many cases the people did not understand the difference in fundamental principle and constitution. There can be little doubt that the want of a Liturgy in the Episcopal Church of Scotland at that period was a great misfortune. The Presbyterian Establishment had the advantage of being supported by political power and the law; its incumbents were now entitled to all the temporalities of the ejected clergy;

* Wodrow's Analecta, vol. iii. p. 144.

and not a few of them took advantage of the credulity of the people, by representing that there was no essential difference between their system and the Church. To these and other reasons may be added the prosecutions to which the clergy were frequently subjected in the legal courts, and the various discouragements which the Church encountered when it was repeatedly smitten to the ground by the ruling powers, and discountenanced in every possible manner. Yet Divine Providence has preserved this Church, which has risen superior to adversity and misfortune, exhibiting the light of gospel truth, and strong in the affections of its members, who are now neither few nor unimportant, although supplanted by an Establishment, from whose bosom has emanated a variety of sects, who acknowledge themselves to be as much its decided enemies as they appear to be of the Church of England.

150   HISTORY OF THE

CHAPTER IX.

THE FIRST PRESBYTERIAN GENERAL ASSEMBLY AFTER THE REVOLUTION—THE " SCOTS PRESBYTERIAN ELOQUENCE" AND THE " ANSWER"—CONTROVERSIES OF THE TIMES—PROCEEDINGS OF THE GOVERNMENT AND OF THE ESTABLISHMENT IN REFERENCE TO THE EPISCOPAL CHURCH

The first General Assembly of the Presbyterian Establishment was allowed to meet at Edinburgh on the 16th of October 1690, John second Lord Carmichael, created Earl of Hyndford in 1701, Lord High Commissioner. The appointment of this nobleman as the royal representative was, says Mr Skinner, " to the grievous mortification of the fiercer sort, who wished their good friend Lord Crawfurd to have been cloathed with that important trust." The proceedings commenced in the forenoon by a sermon preached by a certain Mr Gabriel Cunninghame, who is described as " moderator of the last general meeting," from the passage (St John ii. 17)—" And his disciples remembered that it was written, The zeal of thine house hath eaten me up." Mr Cunninghame is accused of borrowing this sermon *verbatim* from a Mr Oliver Bowles, who preached it before the English Parliament in 1643 * " I assure you," says a contemporary writer, who published an account of this Assembly, " that Mr Gabriel made an exact repetition, and followed his author *verbatim*, only he left out some things in the close of Mr Bowles' sermon, and added some bitter reflections on the Episcopal

* The celebrated Mr David Williamson, who died minister of St Cuthbert's, or the West Kirk, Edinburgh, the " Dainty Davie" of the well known Scottish ballad, composed on a noted amorous adventure of his related in the Memoirs of Captain John Creighton, written by Dean Swift, is also accused of borrowing the greater part of a sermon which he preached before the Parliament from Bishop Brownrig. See " The Spirit of Calumny and Slander Examined," &c. 1693.

party. There was a parallel carried on between Presbytery and that miracle of our Saviour, in whipping the buyers and sellers out of the Temple; the setting up of Presbytery at this time was compared to the work of Reformation, and was made a more wonderful and signal act of Providence; the Episcopal party were called *formal and nominal Protestants,* who, professing the fundamentals, did pervert and corrupt the very doctrine, and all the ordinances, of Jesus Christ." In the afternoon Mr Patrick Simson, described as " moderator of the preceding general meeting," preached from Zach. iii. 7 ; and, says the writer above quoted, " when his matter and expression were considered, no one thought his sermon was borrowed, as that in the forenoon had been. He ascribed to their meeting a supremacy absolute and immediate, next under Christ himself." Nevertheless, Mr Gabriel Cunninghame " did, in the Assembly's name, represent to his Grace [the Lord High Commissioner] how great a mercy it was to this Church and Kingdom, that their Majesties had countenanced this Assembly with their authority, and honoured it with a representative of their royal persons."*

The contemporary writer informs us that this General Assembly was composed of only one hundred and eighty persons. " There were no commissioners from the shires of Angus [Forfar], Mearns [Kincardine], Aberdeen, or any of the more northern parts of the kingdom, and even several places on the south side of the Tay had none; only here and there, in a corner, where the Presbyterians had seated themselves, and assumed the name of a Presbytery, were one or two chosen and commissioned to represent them in the Assembly None of the Universities or Colleges had any representatives save that of Edinburgh, so that this was no more a General Assembly of the Church of Scotland than that of Trent can be called a General Council of the Catholic Church; nor did any other spirit rule in the one than what prevailed in the other —a spirit of faction, prejudice, and interest, though there were prayers enough put up for another spirit, if they had been disposed for it."

King William, in his letter to this Assembly, informed them that " having been informed that differences as to the government of this Church have caused greatest confusions in the nation, we did willingly concur with our Parliament in enacting such a frame of it as was judged

---

* Acts of the General Assembly, folio, vol. 1. p. 21.

to be most agreeable to the inclinations of our good subjects; to which, as we had a particular regard in countenancing this Assembly with our authority and a representative of our royal person, so we expect that your management shall be such as we shall have no reason to repent of what we have done. A calm and peaceable procedure will be no less pleasing to us than it becometh you. We never could be of the mind that violence was suited to the advancing of true religion, nor do we intend that our authority shall ever be a tool to the irregular passions of any party. Moderation is what religion enjoins; neighbouring churches expect from you, and we recommend to you."* This letter, abounding as it does with significant advices and admonitions, gave considerable offence, but the answer to it was on the whole respectful: —" After so many and so great favours received from God and your Majesty, we hope we may with confidence assure you that our management shall be such as your Majesty hath so just reason to expect, and shall never give you cause to repent of what you have done for us. The God of love, the Prince of peace, with all the providences that have gone over us, and circumstances that we are under, as well as your Majesty's most obliging pleasure, require of us a calm and peaceable procedure; and if, after the violence for conscience sake that we have suffered and so much detested, and those grievous abuses of authority in the late reigns, whereby through some men's irregular passions we have so sadly smarted, we ourselves should lapse into the same errors, we should certainly prove the most unjust towards God, foolish towards ourselves, and ungrate towards your Majesty, of all men on earth."

To such sentiments no objections could possibly be offered; and the General Assembly, now that Presbyterianism was legally established, were naturally right in adopting every measure for their own security. But the spirit and principles which pervaded them on this occasion were very different from their declaration to the King. Mr Gabriel Cunninghame, in one of his extemporaneous prayers at the opening of the meeting, began with an acknowledgment of our Saviour as Supreme Head and Governor of the Church, and added—" Thou knowest, O Lord, that when we own any other it is only for *decency's sake*." At one of their devotional exercises a preacher, after indulging in some

* Letter *apud* Acts of General Assembly, folio, vol. i. p. 4.

petitions for the spirit of moderation and brotherly kindness, thus concluded—" But, O Lord, to be free, it would be better to make a clean house," viz. to turn out all the Episcopal clergy from the parishes. The case of one Mr Gabriel Semple was discussed at length. He had received a " call " from the parishes of Jedburgh in Roxburghshire, and Kilpatrick on the Clyde in Dunbartonshire, and the people of each petitioned the Assembly to station Mr Semple among them, on account of " spiritual *sibness* and pastoral relation which they had to him." He had exercised his vocation as a preacher in the county of Northumberland, and his followers there sent an address to the Assembly requesting that " Mr Gabriel might not be taken from them, he having taken compassion on them while they lay weltering in their blood, and no eye to pity them ; and showing that England was overgrown with briers and thorns, which would overrun Scotland also if Mr Gabriel did not weed them out." Mr Gilbert Rule supported this address, and maintained that " it was charity to *plant the gospel in England!*" He alleged that between Berwick and Newcastle there was less practice of piety than among Papists or heathens, and therefore it was fit to send ministers among them. Mr James Kirkton mentioned a rumour that Mr Gabriel Semple " durst not return to England, there being an order from several Justices to apprehend him." Mr Gabriel confessed this to be true, and he was located at Jedburgh at his own desire, declining Kilpatrick because there was no manse for him, and he could not maintain a horse in that parish.

A well known Mr Veitch was objected to because he had a " popular call" to the parish of Peebles. He replied—" This ought not to militate against me, for if by such a *call* be meant an *unanimous call* of all or the greatest part of the parishioners, it can be expected in very few places to a Presbyterian minister, and never at all to be hoped for in the parish of Peebles." The Lord High Commissioner requested them to "deal tenderly" with a certain Episcopal clergyman, to which the Moderator, or chairman, replied—" Your Grace will find that we shall use great tenderness towards the young man, and we shall be very discreet, for we shall only take his kirk from him." The inhabitants of Dundee had evinced the utmost reluctance to the settlement of Presbyterianism in their town, and when their refractory conduct was brought before the Assembly, the Moderator declared that " they could and would plant ministers and elders therein whether the Town Council would or not."

An act was passed prohibiting the administration of baptism in private, and of the eucharist to the sick, the reason assigned being " the superstitious notion nourished that they are necessary to salvation, not only as commanded duties, but as means without which salvation cannot be attained "* Mr Gilbert Rule, in support of the act, which was evidently levelled at the Episcopal clergy, contended that baptism should be administered *only in public and after sermon*, designating the private administration of baptism " not only as superstitious," but as " sorcery and witchcraft," and as " contrary to Scripture and antiquity." Mr James Kirkton replied with some warmth, that Mr Rule's opinions were " disputable," and that he could " buckle him or any man upon that point, though he would not debate it now." He added, that " by their rigorous imposition of things indifferent, he had lost five men of considerable note the last week ;" and " though there were a thousand acts against baptism in houses, he would rather baptize in private than suffer children to be taken to the curates." Mr Hugh Kennedy, the Moderator, expressed himself on this subject in the following eccentric manner:—" There was a distinction both of times and places, for in times of persecution I think an honest minister riding on the road may go into a man's house, baptize a bairn, and come out, and take his horse again!"

A Fast Day was ordered to be observed on the second Thursday of January 1690-1, and when the report stating the object was read, the Moderator exclaimed—" Brethren, this is a savoury paper ; indeed, it is a most savoury paper, and worthy to be heard over again " The only direct reference to the Episcopal Church in this act is expressed in few words—" It is undeniable that there hath been under the late Prelacy a great decay of piety, so that it was enough to make a man be nicknamed a fanatic if he did not run to the same excess of riot with others." A long detail of enormities is given, and if the Scottish people were really in the religious and moral condition set forth in this act of the General Assembly, they must have been the most wicked and depraved in Europe. There is little doubt that this Fast was partly intended to annoy the Episco-

* Acts of General Assembly, vol. 1 p 12

pal clergy. None, as our contemporary writer observes, could sanction or observe it, unless " they could be persuaded that Episcopacy is not only unlawful, but the cause and the occasion of much wickedness and impiety, and that the setting it up is to apostatize from God, and to make defection from the truth. None could observe this Fast for the reasons enjoined, but at the same time they must condemn the Church of England and other Churches, nay, the Catholic Church of Christ from the Apostles' time down to Calvin." He adds in the language of indignation at the whole proceedings—" The Assembly understood well enough how contrary the design of reasons of this Fast were to the sentiments of those who were commanded to observe it, and that they could not keep it without being guilty of the greatest hypocrisy and mocking of God ; and, therefore, for them, for their own particular ends, to require men thus to mock God and play the hypocrite, was a most horrid and unjustifiable piece of villany. This shows that they fast for strife and envy, and not to please God, but to ensnare men—not to avert the divine judgments, but that they may have occasion of executing their wrath and malice under the colour and shadow of zeal against sin."

Much might be said respecting this Fast enjoined by this General Assembly of 1690. Even Archbishop Leighton has recorded his opinion of the Presbyterians of his own time, describing them as persons who " made themselves the standards of opinions and practices, and never looked either abroad into the world to see what others were doing, nor yet back into the former times, to observe what might be warranted or recommended by antiquity." It is not surprising, therefore, if men of more decided principles than Archbishop Leighton are found expressing themselves in a peculiarly indignant strain. Whatever the clergy of Scotland suffered at and after the Revolution was chiefly on account of their adherence to the Episcopal Church, whereas in the previous reigns no Presbyterian was prosecuted simply because he was a Presbyterian. This is most satisfactorily proved by Sir George Mackenzie, who, as Lord Advocate in the reign of Charles II., and consequently the conductor of all the prosecutions in Scotland.* A contemporary writer of that time observes—" There never was any severity showed towards them

---

* Sir George Mackenzie's Defence of the Reign of Charles II. 4to.

[the Presbyterians] till they were found plotting, and then indeed the security of the Government did oblige our rulers to have a strict eye over them, and to curb them by all means. And what government would not be severe to men of their principles, who held it lawful to dethrone and kill kings, and to murder those employed by them, if they do not act agreeably to their minds, and who put these principles in practice as often as they had occasion?"

The instances of insult practised by the Presbyterian ministers of that period to the supporters of the fallen Church are numerous. It was commonly declared in their sermons that during the time of Episcopacy the people had been " without a ministry and without sacraments." We are told that "one Mr Cassine in Fife, when he was admitting elders in the kirk of Flisk, caused them before the congregation to renounce their baptism, and all the sacraments and ordinances which they had received from *curates*, as he called Episcopal ministers by way of contempt. This is so true that the heritors and parishioners of Abdie did upon this very head protest against Mr Cassine coming among them, but notwithstanding the Presbytery of Cupar admitted him."

Numerous instances of a similar description might be quoted, and it was probably a representation of this conduct to the Government which induced King William, in the month of June 1691, to transmit a letter to his " right reverend and well beloved ministers and elders, commissioners to the General Assembly," wherein his Majesty signified his wish that " neither they nor any church-meeting do meddle in any process or business that may concern the purging out of the Episcopal ministers." It is unnecessary to narrate the proceedings which followed in the Establishment, as it is with the affairs of the ejected Episcopal Church that we are chiefly concerned.

While the Presbyterians were exerting every effort to strengthen their Establishment, a work was published which excited their consternation and dismay. This was the celebrated volume entitled, " The Scotch Presbyterian Eloquence, or the Foolishness of their Teaching discovered, from their Books, Sermons, and Prayers," and was ironically dedicated to the peculiarly zealous Presbyterian nobleman the Earl of Crawfurd, by *Jacob Curate*. The mottos on the title-page are significant of its contents. The one is from Baxter's Cure of Church Divisions, and is to this effect—" It grieveth my soul to think what pitiful, raw, and ignorant preaching it crowded most after, merely for the loudness of the preacher's voice, how often I have known the ablest preacher undervalued, and an ignorant man by crowds applauded, when I, who have been acquainted with the preacher, *ab incunabilis*, have known him to be unable to answer questions in the common Catechism." The other is from that eminent " Flower of the Kirk," as he was designated, Mr Samuel Rutherford, whose writings are characterized by Swift as a compound of blasphemy, obscenity, and nonsense. It is found in an epistle addressed to his parishioners, and his advice respecting the Episcopal clergy is turned against himself and his party—" Follow not the pastors of this land, for the sun is gone down upon them ; as the Lord liveth, they lead you from Christ, and the good old way."—" This remarkable work is divided into four parts." I. The True Character of the Presbyterian Pastors and People of Scotland. II. Containing some Expressions out of their printed Books. III. Containing Notes of the Presbyterian Sermons taken in writing from their mouths. IV. Containing some few Expressions of the Presbyterian Prayers.

The following account of the origin of this celebrated work is transcribed from a biographical memoir of George Ridpath already mentioned, prefixed to his " Correspondence with the Rev. Robert Wodrow,' written by James Maidment, Esq. Advocate, and printed in the First Volume of the Abbotsford Miscellany. " In the year 1692 a work appeared which naturally created a great sensation, especially in Scotland After the Revolution the Presbyterians obtained the upper hand, and, as usually happens, the successful party was not inclined to be tolerant to its opponents ; and, in some instances, it can hardly be disguised that several of those who adhered to Episcopacy were somewhat rigorously dealt with. Among other individuals who had smarted for their religious opinions were Dr Monro, Principal of the University of Edinburgh, Dr John Strachan, Professor of Divinity, and Mr Massie,* regent in the College, all of whom had been deprived of their respective situations. Incensed by the treatment they had received, it was rumoured that, in conjunction with the Reverend Mr Canaries, and, as some assert, Mr Robert Calder, or Cadder, who was celebrated for his satirical powers,

* Mr Massie, however, was not ejected, he having complied with the new Government, as previously stated on the authority of Bower in his " History of the University of Edinburgh."

they resolved to act upon the offensive, by producing a work the object of which was to hold up the Presbyterian divines to the ridicule of the world. Whether there was any real foundation for this alleged combination cannot be satisfactorily ascertained, but it is sufficient to say that Ridpath and the other Presbyterian writers firmly believed that at least some of the before named persons were the veritable authors of 'The Scots Presbyterian Eloquence, or the Foolishness of their Teaching discovered, from their Books, Sermons, and Prayers, and some Remarks on Mr Rule's late Vindication of the Kirk Session. Printed for Randal Taylor, near Stationers' Hall, 1692.'

"This celebrated work, of which a second edition, with additions, appeared the ensuing year, and has since been frequently reprinted, was calculated, if not contradicted, to inflict a serious injury on Presbytery. Ridpath was thereupon selected as the party best qualified to answer it. The task thus devolved upon him was difficult, inasmuch as many passages of the offensive work were merely extracts from the printed works of Presbyterian divines, the authorship of which could not be denied. But, on the other hand, the greater portion of the volume consisted of specimens of the style of oratory of many of the clergymen then living, intermixed with various ridiculous anecdotes of their life and conduct. Ridpath, therefore, thought it best, after denying generally the statements founded on oral testimony, to resort to the plea of recrimination, and he set about, with great good will, to rake up all the scandal that could be collected against the unfortunate Episcopalians, in which attempt he was so far successful, that if the third part of what he states is true, his opponents acted very rashly in provoking him to the combat. In 1693 appeared his 'Answer to the Scots Presbyterian Eloquence, in Three Parts. I. Being a Catalogue of the Cruel and Bloody Laws made by the Scots Prelatists against the Presbyterians, with instances of their numerous murders and other barbarities, beyond the extent of those laws; with Reflections throughout, *demonstrating the lenity of their Majesties' Government* against the Scots Prelatists and Clergy. II. Laying open the Self-Contradictions, Impudent Lies, Horrible Blasphemies, and Disloyalty of the obscene scurrilous Pamphlet called Scots Presbyterian Eloquence. III. Being a collection of their ridiculous expressions in Sermons, and instances of the vitious Lives of their Bishops and Clergy. London, printed for Thomas Anderson, near Charing

Cross.' This was followed by 'A Continuation of the Answer to the Scots Presbyterian Eloquence, dedicated to the Parliament of Scotland: being a Vindication of the Acts of that august Assembly, from the Clamours and Aspersions of the Scots Prelatical Clergy, in their Libels printed in England, with a Confutation of Dr M[onro]'s Postscript in answer to the former, proving that it's not the Church of England's interest to countenance the Scots outed Clergy. As also, Reflections on Sir George Mackenzie's Defence of Charles the Second's Government in Scotland, &c. By William Laick. London, printed in the year 1693'

" If Ridpath supposed that his two pamphlets would silence his opponents he was very much mistaken, for they lost no time in producing a rejoinder, in the shape of a tract, entitled, 'The Spirit of Calumny and Slander Examined, Chastised, and Exposed,' written with much more temper and calmness than was to have been expected. Ridpath, however, returned to the charge, and gave to the world his 'Scots Episcopal Innocence,' which is principally valuable as containing some information relative to the life of the author "

To attempt anything like an analysis of the " Scotch Presbyterian Eloquence" is impossible in these limits, and the truth is, that it must be perused by itself to be appreciated. It has been always admitted that the " Answer" to it by Ridpath, or WILL. LAICK, as he calls himself, is a failure. It is ironically dedicated to Archbishop Paterson of Glasgow, against whom Ridpath and others circulated a number of ridiculous and scandalous stories. Principal Monro, in his remarks on Ridpath's Answer, which conclude his eloquent and admirable little work, entitled " An Apology for the Clergy of Scotland," thus speaks of the attack on the Archbishop :—" The first that he [Ridpath] endeavours to abuse is Dr Paterson, Archbishop of Glasgow, and that in a style becoming the true race of the Gnostics, I mean Scotch Presbyterians, who have no other precedents in history than these impure sectaries, whose lives were a disgrace to human nature as well as a reproach to religion. The world is not so besotted as to think that the Archbishop of Glasgow needs particular answers. Indeed, I must acknowledge that the author has pretty well secured himself against such apologies. His accusations are so obscene, that no Christian must name them, and therefore he has hid himself in a cloud of forgeries that none can repeat but a devil, and none could invent but the author. The

Archbishop's character, merit, and parts, cannot but draw upon him the odium of the whole party, and I wish with all my heart that they had not tried his patience by more terrible methods than those of pasquils and calumnies."

The opinion of the Scottish Episcopalians respecting the "Presbyterian Eloquence" is contained in a curious pamphlet published in 1692, entitled "A Letter to a Friend, giving an account of all the Treatises that have been published with relation to the Present Persecution against the Church of Scotland," which was not unlikely written by Principal Monro. "The occasion of publishing this tract" [the Scotch Presbyterian Eloquence], "as I am informed, was this. You may observe that the Presbyterians of Scotland in all their vindications endeavour to justify their proceedings against the orthodox clergy with this topic, by pretending that a great many of them were turned out merely for their *ignorance* and *insufficiency*. This was the great test by which the Presbyterian teachers pretended to proceed, in judging and depriving such of the Episcopal clergy as condescended to appear before their Assemblies. Upon this account, therefore, it seems, the publisher of this treatise thought it convenient to inform the world a little of the qualifications and learning of our Presbyterian doctors, and, if it were possible, to make them sensible of their own infirmities, and for the future ashamed of their insolence, that they should deprive men for ignorance who are so many degrees above the reach of their low capacities—that they who in their preachings and writings appear to be not only void of all manner of learning, but likewise destitute of common sense and reason, should be so arrogant as to think themselves fit judges of any man's qualifications for the office of the holy ministry. They might have acted perhaps more prudently if they had set this topic aside, and made choice of another test for depriving the Episcopal clergy, and that is, as they are pleased to call it, *the want of grace*. Then in all appearance they had not given our author this occasion of proclaiming to the world their scandalous ignorance, and they would have acted more consonantly to their own principles and doctrines, when they run down all kind of human learning as a thing truly antichristian "

After accusing the triumphant party as the enemies of literature, and of having compelled " some of the most conspicuous of our lawyers, physicians, and mathematicians, to desert their native country"—a charge the justice of which it is unnecessary to inquire, the writer proceeds to give an account of the Scotch Presbyterian Eloquence. "This discourse," he says, "is a collection of several remarkable passages taken out of the writings and sermons of the Presbyterian pastors, in which their gross ignorance in matters of learning, and their ridiculous way of worship, are sufficiently described. The author has collected a great many instances of the madness and delusions of the Presbyterian vulgar, how they are passionately moved with a sermon of the greatest nonsense, if it be pronounced but with a loud voice and a whining tone— how they contemn the Creed, the Lord's Prayer, and the Ten Commandments, as childish ordinances, and far below their care or concern— and how upon their deathbeds they take it as a certain sign of salvation that in their lifetime they never heard a *curate* preach. In the next place, he describes the peevish and unconversible temper of their pastors, how they have enslaved themselves so wholly to the humours of their people, that to gratify them they must divest themselves of common civility as well as of Christian charity. He shows that their pretences to learning go no farther than to understand the doctrines of election and reprobation, and how by their indiscreet sermons upon these subjects they often drive many of the ignorant multitude into such a high despair of God's mercy, as to make them lay violent hands upon themselves, and this they call *the saving of souls*. They infuse into the minds of their hearers sordid and low notions of the high and eternal God. They represent Him as a severe and unmerciful Being, and have not the prudence to intermix God's offers of mercy with his threatenings. They not only force their followers into despair, but likewise sometimes encourage them in direct impieties, by telling them that if they be among the number of the *elect*, they may be guilty of the greatest sins without hazarding their salvation. They talk of the mysteries of religion in such homely, coarse, and ridiculous expressions, as are very unsuitable to the gravity and solemnity with which these sacred mysteries ought to be treated. All these particulars the author of this treatise proves against them by such undeniable instances, that I believe they will hardly be so bold as to offer to confute them, lest thereby they expose themselves to the greater scorn and derision."

This severe explanation of the "Scotch Presbyterian Eloquence" is followed by a passage too curious and important to be omitted. "I think

I need not caution you to read this Discourse I here speak of, with a due regard and veneration to those sacred things you see thus polluted and profaned, and not to improve it to such a bad use as I too much fear some of our open profaners of all religion will be inclined to do.—I must therefore entreat you to improve the reading of this treatise to the true design for which it was published, viz. that all good men, being rightly informed of the present misery and desolation of the Church of Scotland, and being sensible of the great detriment that accrues thereby to religion in general, may contribute their assistance, by their prayers and other lawful means, for restoring that national Church to its primitive and apostolical institution.—Is it a matter of no moment to see a whole national Church, with its apostolical government, quite overturned and destroyed—to see many hundreds of the ministers of God's word, together with their families, exposed to the extreme necessities of poverty and want, and by that means to the contempt of the laity? Is it nothing to see religion in this manner abused and polluted by sordid and stupid men, who assume to themselves the name of pastors—to see them profane the sacred mysteries of our holy religion by their drollery and ridicule? These are matters not of mere jest and diversion, but of great concern and importance."

Principal Monro's observations on the " Scotch Presbyterian Eloquence" are printed in the postscript to his tract, entitled "An Apology for the Clergy of Scotland," in which he attacks Ridpath, the author of the " Answer."—" I have heard," says the reverend Principal, " that the *Scotch Presbyterian Eloquence* has been much talked of, and, therefore, I take the liberty to acquaint you with the reasons that induce me to believe that there was no injury done to the Scotch Presbyterians by the publication of that book. *First*, Because the printed accounts cited from their books are equal to the unprinted relations of their sermons and prayers. Mr Rutherford's Letters alone have in them many coarse and abusive metaphors, and applications which are mean and loathsome. *Secondly*, The most blasphemous stories in the book called *The Scotch Presbyterian Eloquence* can be proved by the best and most undeniable evidence, viz. that of Mr Urquhart concerning the Lord's Prayer, that of Mr Kirkton concerning the Holy Ghost, and that he believed *Abraham ran out of the land of Chaldea for debt*. Now, we fairly offer to prove these three, the first against Mr Urquhart, the other two against Mr Kirkton. *Thirdly*, Suppose that one had a mind to make stories to the disadvantage of the Scotch Presbyterians, yet their jargon is so extravagant, that it is not possible for any man to speak their language unless he has been educated therein ; and the harmony between their printed books and their unprinted sermons is so exact, that none can doubt of the last who read the first "

Principal Monro gives other reasons in his reply to Ridpath's " Answer," and then proceeds to defend those of the Bishops and clergy, with whom he was personally acquainted, who had been prominently aspersed by Ridpath. Dr James Canaries, formerly incumbent of Selkirk, who was peculiarly hated by the Presbyterians, is made the subject of some ridiculous anecdotes in Ridpath's " Answer." Principal Monro says—" The Doctor told me that these were not the first essays of their civility towards him, for he being employed by some of the Episcopal clergy to state their grievances at Court, the Presbyterians from that very moment fixed their eyes upon him, and prosecuted him with all the calumnies that their fury and common practices in such cases could suggest; but still they found the Doctor too hard for them, and the wise men among them have frequently owned to him that as they hated such methods, they highly disapproved the particular injustice that was done to the Doctor."

From these extracts it is sufficiently clear, that, whoever was the author or compiler of the " Scotch Presbyterian Eloquence," the leading Episcopal clergy of Scotland at that time maintained the authenticity of the facts recorded in that extraordinary work, and that, though themselves personally attacked in retaliation, Ridpath's " Answer" gave them very little concern. Various pamphlets were published for a series of years by both parties against each other, the most zealous on the Presbyterian side being Mr Gilbert Rule, who met with an able opponent in Dr Monro. Some of these are already quoted, and as they are all of a controversial nature, intermingled with various personal and local accusations, their contents may be readily inferred. It must not, however, be forgotten that the Presbyterians evidently indicated that they were the defeated party, by resorting to their old accusations against their opponents of Popery and Atheism. Dr Pitcairne, already mentioned as one of the most celebrated physicians of Scotland, was branded with the latter epithet, because he wrote a satirical poem on the General Assembly, which annoyed and incensed the members in no ordinary manner. It has even been stated in various recent Presbyterian publications that Dr Pitcairne entertained infidel principles, while it is well known, for the evidence is undeniable, that this distinguished man, like thousands of others in Scotland, was in religion a decided and determined member of the Episcopal Church, and in politics a Jacobite, or adherent of the exiled sovereign.

A Presbyterian writer* favours us with *his* version of some of the ecclesiastical proceedings of those times. After noticing that those incumbents, who, having qualified to the Government, nevertheless joined the Jacobite laity in their endeavours to restore " their King and Episcopacy," he says—" In order to this last, it was contrived that a body of Episcopal ministers, more numerous than the Presbyterians, should apply to the next General Assembly to be received into a coalition, upon such terms as they thought could not be refused. If received, they hoped soon to overturn Presbytery: if rejected, they would represent the Presbyterians to the King and Parliament as of an unpeaceable, seditious, and persecuting spirit, and hoped in this way to succeed; and if Prelacy was once restored, they would work up the nation to a new revolution. This scheme seems to have been formed by the Viscount of Tarbet, a nobleman of some learning, but of less integrity, who insinuated himself into King William's favour, and yet lived and died a keen Jacobite. The Scottish Bishops communicated a part of this design to the English Bishops. They, together with Lord Tarbet, prevailed with the King, who was a stranger, to defer calling an Assembly in 1691, for the sake of peace, as they pretended, but in fact that their scheme might be ripened. All things being now ready, an Assembly was called to meet in January 1692, and the King in his letter recommended to receive into a share of the government all who should desire to be thus comprehended. Then Dr Canaries, at the head of one hundred and eighty Episcopal ministers, and in the name of many more, appeared and desired to be received, and they would subscribe the following formula—' I, A. B., do sincerely promise and declare, that I will submit to the Presbyterian government of the Church, and that I will

* Mr Lachlan Shaw, in his History of the Province of Moray.

subscribe the Confession of Faith, and the Larger and Shorter Catechisms, ratified by Act of Parliament in the year 1690, as containing the doctrine of the Protestant religion professed in this kingdom.'"

We are farther told by the same authority, that " the Assembly knew Dr Canaries' character; they saw the design of these men was no more than what a Jesuit or a Mahometan might offer. These men did not promise to believe the doctrine, and not to overturn the government of the Church. In short, such equivocation was condemned, and their offer rejected. Upon this Dr Canaries appealed to the King for redress, and the Earl of Lothian, Commissioner, dissolved the meeting *sine die*; but the Assembly asserted unanimously the right of the Church, and appointed the time of their next meeting. The Jacobites now hoped to triumph, but were disappointed. Their designs were seen into, the King was undeceived, and the Parliament having met in April 1693 ordained, ' That no one be admitted or continued a minister or preacher, till he first subscribe the allegiance and assurance; also subscribe the Confession of Faith, and own the doctrine therein contained to be the true doctrine, to which he will constantly adhere; and likewise our Presbyterian church government, submit thereto, and never endeavour, either directly or indirectly, the prejudice or subversion thereof, and observe the worship as at present performed; and that they apply, in an orderly way, each man for himself to be admitted.' The Parliament likewise addressed his Majesty to call an Assembly, which he did, and they met in March 1694, and drew up a formula, agreeable to the act of Parliament, offering to receive all who would subscribe it. Few complied with the Act of Parliament. Many qualified to the civil Government, and kept their churches without molestation, but the zealous Jacobites would not conform to Church and State."

Without entering into the details of the statements here given, which are partly correct and partly erroneous, it is obvious that the Presbyterians, as established by law, were entitled to take every step consistent with their own security. Whatever were the motives, religious or political, of the numerous body of Episcopal clergymen, headed by Dr Canaries, who made this application, and who had been publicly recognized by the King, those ascribed to them by the writer now quoted are not set forth in a pamphlet explanatory of the whole matter which the clergy considered necessary to be published in 1704. This pamphlet is entitled, a "Vindication of the Address made by the Episcopal Clergy to the General Assembly of the Presbyterians, anno 1692, from the sinister and false constructions put upon it by the enemies of that Order, but more especially of that particular Address given in by Mr Robert Irving, minister of Towie, and Mr John Forbes, minister of Kincardine, in name of, and by commission from, their brethren the ministers of the Synod of Aberdeen, they being expressly reflected upon, and named by the author of the Remarks upon the Case of the Episcopal Clergy." It appears from this production that the clergy were chiefly accused of being Arminians, which is repelled by the author, who asserts that "howbeit the Episcopal clergy are generally clamoured upon as Arminians, yet the first of that sect and his proselytes were all Presbyterians, for James Hereman, minister in Amsterdam, and afterwards Professor of Divinity in the University of Leyden, under the name of *Jacobus Arminius*, by which he is best known, was the first that brought in those opinions, which now bear so ill, into the Reformed Church, so that they owe their rise not to Prelacy but to Presbytery. He was the first who did disseminate and propagate them among Protestants, and, consequently, Presbytery and not Prelacy must bear the first blame."

Some of these statements about Arminius and his *errors*, as they were called by the Presbyterians, might be questioned, but they are offered in this pamphlet rather as a reply to a direct charge than in a controversial manner. It is unnecessary, however, to enter into all the minute details of this particular transaction, which has been long forgotten. It was unsuccessful, and such a coalition is not likely to be ever attempted between the Scottish Episcopal clergy and the Presbyterian ministers, unless the latter admit and recognize the doctrine of the Apostolical Succession, and the divine institution of Bishops, Priests, and Deacons.

CHAPTER X.

POLITICAL CHARACTER OF THE SCOTTISH EPISCOPALIANS BY THEIR OPPONENTS.—RELIGIOUS STATE OF PARTIES DURING THE REIGN OF WILLIAM III.

LITTLE is recorded of the measures adopted by the Bishops and clergy at this period to perpetuate the Church. The ejected pastors officiated in the cities, towns, and villages, to congregations large or small, according to the circumstances and religious principles of the inhabitants, and the accommodation they were able to obtain. In the year 1696 most of the Bishops were alive, and continued to receive, as their successors still receive, that canonical obedience to which those were entitled who derived their authority, through the Church of England, from the Divine Head of the Catholic Church. Kings and Parliaments could deprive them of their temporalities, and confer these on other parties, but no executive government could deprive the clergy of the ejected Church of that spiritual authority with which they had been invested, or render their ministrations void and nugatory. It had been repeatedly represented not only by the Presbyterian ministers, but by their leaders in the Scottish Parliament and elsewhere, that *Prelacy*, as they chose to designate the Episcopal Church, was not only identified with arbitrary power, but that it was near akin to Popery, as if the fundamentals of religion are to be rejected simply because the Romanists maintain them, though adulterated and obscured by their errors and fanciful traditions.

Among these writers it is curious to find the respectable name of Duncan Forbes of Culloden, the father of the distinguished Lord President of the Court of Session in Scotland. In the "Memoir of a Plan for preserving the Peace of the Highlands, written a short time after the

Revolution," by Mr Forbes, and published by his family,* the following passages occur :—

" It is to be minded that there is a party in Scotland whose affections can never be gained to the King [William III.], *and those are they who call themselves Episcopal,* but really are indifferent of that and all other matters of that nature, and are addicted to nothing but King James, under whose protection they formerly oppressed others, and, in spite of all the kindness and forbearance can be showed them, will only comply to gain him back if they can. This appears as clear as the sun, from three or four following evidences."

One of these "three or four evidences" adduced by Mr Forbes is— ." From the testimony of the best officers in the army, who declare that after all their converse and endeavours with these men, they find not one in Scotland *who favours Episcopacy* but to the best of their conjectures he hates the King and the Government, and would have back King James ; nor do they find one Presbyterian, let him have never so many faults, but would venture all for His Majesty, both against King James and all his other enemies."

Mr Forbes then deduces certain "positions" from his "evidences," which he says are " undeniably true," among which are specified :—" 1. That the things now done [the establishment of Presbyterianism] are of *infinite value* to the nation, and without which the people could *never be easy*, and therefore behoved to be done. 2. That the nation, having received so great obligations from the King, will never be ungrateful to him, but will make returns to him of all they are worth, ask it when he will. 3. *That no Jacobite, or hardly any in Scotland who calls himself Episcopal, can be trusted by his Majesty.*" This gentleman then says— " I know that evil designing men suggest two inconveniences in what is done, and they are both groundless. The first is, that the Presbyterian *churchmen* will employ the freedom the King and Parliament have given them too rigorously against those of the *Episcopal persuasion*, which may irritate the Church of *England.* Verily, such as suggest this know very

* Culloden Papers, comprising an extensive and interesting correspondence from the year 1625 to 1748, 4to, London, 1815, p. 14, 15, &c. It is stated—" The original is in the handwriting of Duncan Forbes of Culloden, the President's father, and every part of his plan seems to have been closely followed, in every point of any consequence "

little of the Presbyterian ministers' concern for the King's satisfaction, and prosperity of his affairs."

In the "Addenda" to the "Culloden Papers," purporting to be a "State of Things in 1696," there is a curious document, of which this explanation is given—" This Statement is by Mr Duncan Forbes of Culloden, who was a member of the Scottish Parliament at the period of which he treats, and was alleged to have contributed to the Protestant succession, and to have supported it as ably as any person of his time." The whole argument in this document is an attempt to prove that Scottish Episcopacy was altogether a political affair, and that its supporters contended for it *solely on political principles*. Never was there any opinion given on more fallacious assumptions or views of human action. That the Episcopalians, in common with the Roman Catholics, and with many Presbyterians, were favourable to the exiled sovereign, and inimical to the Revolution, or rather to the assumption of the throne by King William and Queen Mary, is admitted; but they were actuated by nobler motives, because they were influenced by religion. They loved the Episcopal Church—a Church which they considered pure, apostolical, and national—a Church which presented the scriptural system of Christianity, and was opposed to the fanaticism of the age. They loved this Church because her bishops were *true bishops*, and her priests and deacons truly and apostolically ordained—and they identified her politically with the exiled sovereign, solely on account of the Royal House of Stuart being linked or connected with her as an ecclesiastical establishment. It is monstrous to state that the Scottish Church was merely *politically* Episcopalian. The sacrifice her Bishops and clergy made at the Revolution is an unanswerable argument to the contrary. The wisdom and prudence of their conduct at that memorable period are fair matters of opinion, but, although deprived of their temporalities, and supplanted by a different religious party, they preserved the Church as she is to this day, primitive and orthodox in her ritual, standards, canons, and ordinances.

It is, however, a remarkable fact, that the Scottish people, who are proverbially cautious and calculating, or supposed to be so, are liable to run in to extremes both in politics and religion. No nation in Europe abounds more with sectaries, and the wildest enthusiasts are sure to gain adherents. The Presbyterians of the Revolution thought that their establishment would carry all before it—that the Episcopal Church, and even Romanism, would be speedily exterminated; but their successors now see their error, with the unenviable fact well-known to them, that there are numerous and powerful sects, of their own polity and principles, who are their deadliest opponents. But to revert to the " State of Things in 1696."—" It can hardly," says Mr Forbes, " be found that ever Scotland was in a worse taking than it was in before this last Revolution, or that any people had a better occasion of redressing their wrongs and settling their liberties, to the honour of God and good of posterity, than they had by this Revolution." The admissions which follow this statement are not a little remarkable " And yet, hardly shall it be found that one occasion of this nature was ever more mismanaged than this has lately been, when there was little more arisen to us yet, than *the unhappy debate amongst ourselves of who is to be most blamed*, and that is pursued so closely with calumnies against some, and artifice in vindication of others, that without a true information of matter of fact from some who perfectly know it, *it is hard for honest men to distinguish who have been in the right or who in the wrong.* Therefore it is thought fit to make a memorandum of what passed since the meeting of the Estates in a few articles. The Estates having met, it was soon found that the stronger party there was of such who wished the freedom of their Church from *Prelacy*, and the freedom of their State from *arbitrary government*. Any who were led by both or either of these principles, cemented so closely together in favour of the Revolution, and to set up this present King [William III.], that every point seeming to retard or delay was by them thrown out of doors. *On the other hand*, the adverse party, being solely made up of Prelatists, and such as, under the notion of serving them in the last Government, had *persecuted*, and advanced *tyranny*, believing, from a guilt of conscience, no salvation to be for them but in the standing of King James, used all their endeavours, by force or artifice, to hinder, or at least retard, all proposals in favour of King William."

After a variety of details respecting King William and the Revolution Government in Scotland, Mr Forbes writes—" There was only one matter of import which seemed to take its rise from them, viz. some of the English Officers of State and Bishops had been with the King, desiring him to put a stop to Presbytery in Scotland, assuring him that the Parliament of that kingdom was not so much inclined to Presbytery as was imagined; that they were informed Episcopacy had not been abolished had it not been to gratify him, and if his Majesty pleased to call that Parliament together presently, and give them freedom to settle the civil rights of the nation, they would stop any farther advancement of Presbytery; and that this might be very confidently asserted, for these very men, to wit, *the Club*, who were the abolishers of Episcopacy to pleasure the King, would be hinderers of the advance of Presbytery to obtain their civil rights, &c. My Lord Melville spoke of this to Sir Patrick Home with a great deal of regret, by whom he is not believed, but in a manner laughed at. However, within some few days there is a second onset made upon the King by the same persons to the same purpose, without receiving any positive answer from him, who, within an hour after they were gone, called for Sir Patrick Home, upon whom he looked but very shyly since the presenting of the address."

We are next informed that the King "inclined to call for Sir Patrick Home, but Sir Patrick happening not to be about the Court, Culloden [Forbes] was brought for him, who happened to be there." What follows presents a curious and instructive view of the opinions of the nation with respect to Presbyterianism. King William, during his interview with Forbes of Culloden, "had several questions anent the condition of Scotland and the Parliament, *particularly if the Presbyterian party were the stronger*, and if the peace of the country could be secured without *settling the government of the Church;* and if Skelmorlie's [Sir James Montgomery] interest with his adherents was such in the Parliament as could oblige the nation to lay aside their Church government? To all which there were plain and positive answers given, with reasons to enforce what was said, wherewith the King appeared satisfied; after which he broke out into an expostulation of the notorious injuries he had received from Sir James Montgomery and some others, in creating him all the troubles and mischiefs imaginable, reckoning that as one among the rest—that they had put the Church of England upon [against] him, either to break with them, or break with the Presbyterian interest in Scotland. This was no small occasion of admiration to Culloden, who could do no other than call the verity of the matter in question; whereupon the King gave him liberty to inquire for his own satisfaction, which within a day he did, and *he found Sir James Montgomery own that the Presbyterian party were the least, and least considerable in the Parliament of Scotland,*—that the interest of the nation ought not to be lost for our Presbytery, and that Queensberry, Atholl, &c , were very honest men. This passed at the Blue Posts in the Haymarket, in presence of Annandale, Ross, Riccarton, and Sir William Scott, after a full account had been given by Culloden of what the King had said the night before."*

Much might be said respecting these important disclosures, but it is unnecessary. It is at once apparent that for some years after the Revolution the Presbyterian Establishment was exceedingly frail and tottering, and that the leading men of rank and talent in Scotland were often inclining to the restoration of the ejected Church in all her temporal rights and privileges Meanwhile the surviving Bishops and clergy lived in patient retirement, officiating unostentatiously to all who resorted to their ministrations, and maintaining the religious and political principles for which they had suffered. Previous to the year 1696 two of the Bishops died—Bishop Drummond of Brechin, and Bishop Wood of Caithness; and Bishop Ramsay of Ross died in 1696 " in very low circumstances." †

Dr Ross, Archbishop of St Andrews, Dr Paterson, Archbishop of Glasgow, Bishop Hamilton of Dunkeld, Bishop Graham of the Isles, and Bishop Rose of Edinburgh, resided in the Scottish metropolis, where they died. Of Archbishop Paterson, who was an object of peculiar hatred to the Presbyterians, it is said, that " he seems to have had a good deal of influence even with some who were at the helm of affairs." ‡ The Archbishop was nearly related to several ancient families, and the esteem in which his Grace was held by many of the most distinguished persons in Scotland to the day of his death in 1708, is a sufficient refutation of the contemptible scurrilities which were propagated against him. It is known that in private life, after he was ejected from his dignified situation in the Church, the Archbishop exhibited all the hospitality and kindness of a Scottish gentleman; and his body was honoured by being interred, as already mentioned, in the Chapel-Royal of the Palace of Holyrood. It is proper to observe, however, that a

* Culloden Papers, p. 328.
† Bishop Russell's Appendix to Keith's Catalogue of the Scottish Bishops, p. 517.
‡ Bishop Russell, *ut supra.*

severe character is given of this prelate even by a friendly hand. He is represented as " a man of extraordinary parts and great learning, but extremely proud and haughty to all the inferior clergy of his diocese, and very much destitute of those virtues that should adorn the life and conversation of one so highly exalted in the Church. He had a great management of the government of both Church and State before the Revolution. After the abolishing of Episcopacy he lived privately, indulging that avaricious worldly temper which had sullied his other qualifications in all the capacities and stations of his life."* It is clear that this is the language of political animosity and resentment, accusing Archbishop Paterson of faults which are merely matters of opinion. The chief charge against his Grace is *avarice;* but avarice is a word which has various definitions, according to the feelings and views of individuals. It is well known that the leading adherents of the exiled Family in Scotland were continually quarrelling amongst themselves, and that they often said bitter things of each other, of which they repented in their moments of serious reflection.

As to the state of the Episcopal Church during the reign of King William, it may be generally and comprehensively said that the laity were greatly discountenanced by the Government, and the clergy subjected to many hardships. These hardships were inflicted for political reasons by the ruling powers, and for what were considered religious grounds by the Presbyterians. An act passed in 1695 may be instanced as a proof of the conduct of the latter. This act *prohibited* and *discharged* every *outed minister,* as an Episcopal clergyman was called, " from *baptizing any children,* or solemnizing marriage betwixt *any parties,* in all time coming, under pain of imprisonment, ay and until he find caution to *go out of the kingdom, and never to return thereto.*" This act was evidently aimed at the *religion* of the ejected clergy, but it appears to have been the only one passed by the Scottish Parliament against them during the reign of William III., while those against the " growth of Popery " are frequent. Some of them ventured to celebrate divine service in their own hired houses on Sundays, and other holidays sanctioned by the Church, and the doors of those houses were left open to enable all who were inclined to enjoy the benefits of reli-

* Lockhart Papers, vol. i. pp. 84, 85.

gion. This was considered a heinous offence ; and a list of the principal parties was transmitted to the Privy Council, who prosecuted two of them, but the sentence pronounced is not recorded. Nevertheless, as Bishop Russell observes, " the greater part of the nobility and landholders of ancient families continued strongly attached" to the Episcopal Church, and " the time was now approaching when they expected and obtained gentler and more equitable treatment."

It is only justice to the memory of William III. to say that personally he was not the enemy of the Scottish Episcopal Church. This is undeniable from various historical documents, and he even seems to have respected the Bishops and clergy for their conscientious adherence to his father-in-law. Smollett, moreover, says, that " the Presbyterians in Scotland acted with such folly, violence, and tyranny, as rendered them equally odious and contemptible The transactions in their General Assembly were carried on with such peevishness, partiality, and injustice, that the King dissolved it by an act of state, and convoked another for the month of November in the following year. The Episcopal party promised to enter heartily into the interests of the new Government, to keep the Highlanders quiet, and to induce the clergy to acknowledge and serve King William, provided he would balance the power of Melville and his partizans in such a manner as would secure them from violence and oppression—provided the Episcopal ministers should be permitted to perform their functions among those people by whom they were beloved, and that such of them as were willing to mix with the Presbyterians in their judicatories should be admitted without any severe imposition in point of opinion. The King, *who was extremely disgusted at the Presbyterians*, relished the proposal, and young Dalrymple, son of Lord Stair, was appointed joint secretary of state with Melville.* Again, it is stated by the same historian:—" The King had suffered so much in his reputation by his compliance to the Presbyterians of Scotland, *and was so displeased with that stubborn sect of religionists*, that he thought proper to admit some prelatists into the administration. The Episcopalians triumphed in the King's favour, and began to treat their antagonists with insolence and scorn, the Presbyterians were incensed to see their friends disgraced, and their enemies distin-

---

* Smollett's History of England, 4to, edit. 1758, vol. iv. p. 64.

guished by the royal indulgence. They insisted upon the authority of the law, which happened to be on their side ; they became, *more than ever, sour, surly, and implacable ;* they refused to concur with the Prelatists, or abate in the least circumstance of discipline ; and their Assembly was dissolved without any time or place assigned for the next meeting. The Presbyterians *pretended an independent right of assembling annually, even without a call from His Majesty ;* they therefore adjourned themselves, after having protested against the dissolution. The King resented this measure as an insolent invasion of the prerogative, and conceived an aversion to the whole sect, who in their turn began to lose all respect for his person and government."*

Similar passages might be quoted from various historians to show that King William's support of Presbyterianism in Scotland was altogether political, and that he was often irritated at the conduct of the party on whom the temporalities of the ejected Church had been conferred. The truth, however, is, that the government of Scotland during the whole of King William's reign was in the most wretched condition, and the spirit of partizanship was carried even into private life. Attachment to the exiled or to the reigning dynasty was the grand topic of public and private discussion, and influenced even the religious principles of the people. The settlement of the succession in 1700 in favour of the House of Hanover increased the irritation of the adherents of the fallen monarch, but the death of King James made no alteration in their principles and prospects ; for they considered his son, who had been recognised and proclaimed his successor by the King of France, the Duke of Savoy, and the Pope, as their legitimate sovereign, to whom their allegiance was indisputably due, and in all their correspondence with this unfortunate heir of the House of Stuart they recognised him as such. It was, therefore, a sincere principle of what they deemed loyalty which animated the Protestant Jacobite party, for they well knew, as has been justly stated, that King James, " in his last illness, conjured his son to prefer his religion to every worldly advantage, and even to renounce all thoughts of a crown if he could not enjoy it without offering violence to his faith."

* Smollett, vol. iv. p. 77.

CHAPTER XI.

ACCESSION OF QUEEN ANNE—FIRST CONSECRATION IN SCOTLAND AFTER THE REVOLUTION.

The accession of Queen Anne in 1702 was hailed with peculiar satisfaction by the adherents of the exiled dynasty. The Jacobites, as they were called, persuaded themselves that, as her Majesty could now leave no heirs, natural affection and inclination would secure her exertions in behalf of her brother, whom the French monarch, the Pope, and others, had already recognised as King of Great Britain. They in consequence submitted to the Queen's authority, viewing her as a kind of regent for the Chevalier St George, whose restoration they firmly believed the sovereign intended to secure.

At the accession of Queen Anne the Government of Scotland was in a most unsettled condition. While the Cavalier party rejoiced at their fancied prospects under the new reign, the Presbyterians felt themselves in a very hazardous position According to the author of the "Lockhart Papers," first published in 1817, they "looked upon themselves as undone; despair appeared upon their countenances, which were more upon the melancholic and dejected air than usual, and most of their exhortations from the pulpit were to stand by and support *Christ's cause*, the epithet they gave their own. They knew the Queen was a strenuous asserter of the doctrines of the Church of England; they were conscious how little respect the great men of their faction had paid her during the late reign; they saw the Church party were preferred to places and power in England; they knew that the Scots nation, especially the nobility and gentry, were much disgusted at them, because of their promoting the *Court Interest* in the last reign against that of the

Country ;* and upon these and such like accounts they dreaded a storm impending over their heads." This writer gives the following severe character of the Presbyterians of that time, which is merely inserted here to show the estimation in which they were held by the zealous Jacobite nobility and gentry. The Cavaliers, "being, I say it impartially, of generous spirits, and designing good and just things, believe every man is so too, and are not at such pains as is necessary to cement a party's councils and measures together ; whereas the Presbyterians, acting from a selfish principle, and conscious of their ill actions and designs, are, like the devil himself, never idle, but always projecting, and so closely linked together, that all go the same way, and all stand or fall together."

Queen Anne was a devoted member of the Church of England, the orthodox clergy of which she always considered the real friends of monarchy and religion. Her accession caused a change of the Ministry in Scotland, which was favourable to the depressed Episcopal Church—a Church held in the utmost respect by the sovereign, who well knew the sufferings endured by its adherents for their attachment to her Family. A letter was procured by James Duke of Hamilton† to the Scottish Privy Council, in which the Queen expressed her desire that the Presbyterian incumbents should live in peace and friendly intercourse with such of the Episcopal clergy who were still in possession of the parishes, and who submitted to the Government. Encouraged by such favourable manifestations, the clergy presented an address to the Queen, imploring her royal protection, and beseeching her to allow those parishes in which the Episcopalians were the majority to be held by episcopally ordained ministers. This address or petition was laid before the Queen by Dr Skene and Dr Scott, who were introduced to her Majesty for

---

* The *Court Interest* and the *Country Interest*, the Whigs and Tories of those times, were then the common designation of the two great political parties.

† This Nobleman, styled Earl of Arran, was the eldest son of William and Anne, Duke and Duchess of Hamilton. He delivered his sentiments, previously quoted, respecting the invasion of the Prince of Orange, in presence of his father at the meeting of the Scottish Nobility in London in January 1689. According to the Marquis of Annandale's confession to King William, he was deeply implicated in the plot of Sir James Montgomery of Skelmorlie for the restoration of the exiled dynasty, for which he was twice committed to the Tower of London

that purpose by the Duke of Queensberry. . The Queen received them favourably, assured them that she would do all in her power to relieve their necessities, and exhorted them to be mildly disposed towards the Presbyterian ministers who were then in legal possession of the parishes. This was followed by a proclamation for a general indemnity, of which many Scottish gentlemen in France and on the Continent took advantage. They qualified themselves to sit in Parliament, and thus the members of the ejected Church increased in numbers and influence even as a political party in Scotland.

Notwithstanding the alarm of the Presbyterians at the prospect of their affairs, their influence preponderated in the first Parliament of Queen Anne, held at Edinburgh on the 9th of June 1702, the Duke of Queensberry Lord High Commissioner. It is said that Sir William Bruce of Kinross, sheriff of that county, was expelled from the House for maintaining, in reply to a motion for an act to secure the Presbyterian Church government, that Presbytery was inconsistent with monarchy. It is proper to state, however, that the name of Sir William Bruce is not on the parliamentary roll as present on that occasion.

Whatever may have been the inclinations of the Queen, there was evidently no intention to disturb the Presbyterian Establishment In her Majesty's letter presented by the Lord High Commissioner it is stated—" We give you full assurance that we are firmly resolved to maintain and protect them [the people] in the full possession of their religion, laws, and liberties, and of the Presbyterian government of the Church as at present established."* It was moved that " an act be brought in next sederunt of Parliament for securing the Protestant religion and Presbyterian Church government " This act was produced on the 11th, and passed, on which occasion a national fast was ordered. In this Parliament an act was also passed " enabling her Majesty to appoint Commissioners to treat for an union betwixt the two kingdoms of England and Scotland." In the letter addressed to the Queen on this important subject by the Estates of Parliament they declare—" It fell under our consideration, that when the meeting of the Estates did, at the late King's accession to the throne, nominate commissioners for the like treaty, they expressly reserved our Church government as it

* Acta Parl. Scot. vol. xi p 12

should be established at the time of the Union. But the Presbyterian religion being founded on the Claim of Right, with our entire confidence in the full assurance your Majesty has been pleased to give us, that you are firmly resolved to protect and maintain us in the full possession of the Presbyterian government of the Church as at present established, are our satisfying security. And, therefore, hoping that your Majesty, both in the naming of the commissioners and in the whole procedure of the treaty, will have a gracious and careful regard to the maintaining of the Presbyterian government of the Church as now, established by act of Parliament; and, satisfied by your Majesty in this session of Parliament, and which in the experience of all is found to be the true interest and solid foundation of the peace and quiet of this kingdom, we heartily wish for such an accomplishment of this great work as may be to your Majesty's perpetual honour, and the lasting welfare and happiness of both kingdoms."*

This letter to Queen Anne is moderately expressed, and no one can object to the Presbyterians using every exertion to secure the stability of their Establishment, and possession of the temporalities. This was to be expected from any religious party in their situation, and already sanctioned by several acts of Parliament. In some of the proceedings of this Session the Estates evinced their sincerity in the matter. The learned body of Scottish barristers, called the *Faculty of Advocates*, were prosecuted for having voted at one of their meetings in accordance with the sentiments alleged to have been urged by Sir William Bruce. They were " charged and pursued by my Lord Advocate before the Parliament, where, after several long debates, they were severely reprimanded." This, however, must have been done by the Privy Council, to whom the whole case was ultimately referred.†

The favourable sentiments expressed by Queen Anne to the clergy and laity of the Scottish Episcopal Church sufficiently indicated that her Majesty would discourage any attempts at legal prosecution against them. In 1703, the Rev. Robert Calder published a small work which excited the fierce resentment and opposition of the Presbyterians, entitled, " Reasons for a Toleration of Episcopacy." This caused a regular

---

* Acta Parl. Scot. vol. xi. pp. 26, 27.
† Acta Parl. Scot. vol. xi. pp. 27, 38. Lockhart Papers, vol. i. pp. 47, 48.

pamphlet war. Although, however, no toleration was issued by the Government, numbers of the clergy now collected congregations in chapels, and regularly celebrated divine service, praying for the Queen by name. In the city of Edinburgh, in the alley on the north side of the High Street called Carrubber's Close, is St Paul's Episcopal Chapel, externally a plain oblong building. An inscription over the door intimates that it was erected in 1689, and the tradition is, that it was the scene of the ministrations of Bishop Rose after his ejection from his own cathedral church of St Giles farther up the street. If this could be substantiated this little chapel would be deeply interesting to every churchman; but it appears, after a careful investigation, that Bishop Rose did not statedly officiate to any particular congregation as pastor after the Revolution. Several chapels were fitted up in other alleys of the Old Town of Edinburgh, the New Town not being in existence for upwards of eighty years afterwards. At a recent visit by the present writer to one of those former scenes of pastoral duty, where Bishop Abernethy Drummond officiated, called Skinners' Hall, in Skinners' Close, on the south side of the High Street, he found it occupied by a disreputable set of *strolling players*. This "Hall" is the upper storey of an antique tenement at the bottom of the alley, which was long respectable, and attended by persons of the first rank. In the Mint Close, below Skinners' Close, were several temporarily fitted up chapels, or *meeting-houses*, as they were called, to which access was obtained by the common stairs leading to the several storeys. Todrick's Wynd and Blackfriars' Wynd could also boast of their Episcopal "meeting-houses." As it respects Glasgow, we are told that "the Scottish Episcopalians were the first religious body, not connected with the [Presbyterian] Church of Scotland, who regularly met for worship after the Revolution."* Glasgow was then a small city, the population at the Union being scarcely 14,000. The kind of accommodation which the members of the Church provided for themselves is not mentioned, but it must have been very indifferent, for in 1715, when Bishop Alexander Duncan, formerly minister of New Kilpatrick on the Clyde, became the first stated officiating pastor, the congregation assembled in a dwelling-house in the now uninviting Bell

* Cleland's Annals of Glasgow, vol i p 139.

Street, and in subsequent years we find them removing to Candleriggs Street and Stockwell Street.

The example of those clergy who collected congregations in the cities and towns, and acknowledged the Government, was followed by those who refused to pray for the Queen by name, among whom were the surviving Bishops; yet their conscientious political scruples gave no offence to her Majesty, and they were permitted to go on in their own way Bishop Rose, of Edinburgh, was even allowed a pension out of the Episcopal revenues, or Bishops' Rents, which he enjoyed till after the accession of George I. in 1716.

The death of Archbishop Ross of St Andrews, in 1704, seems to have drawn the attention of the surviving Bishops to the immediate and imperative necessity of preserving and perpetuating the Church. After the death of the aged Primate, Bishop Rose appears to have exercised the metropolitan authority over the Presbyters during his life, under the ancient Scottish title of the Bishops of St Andrews—that of *Primus Scotiæ Episcopus*, before the See was constituted archiepiscopal.

Two Presbyters were selected for the episcopate,—the Rev. John Fullarton, formerly one of the ministers of Paisley, and the Rev. John Sage, formerly one of the ministers of Glasgow. It was expressly stipulated with the new Bishops that the government of the Church was to remain exclusively with the ejected Prelates during their lifetime, and that they were to exercise no diocesan power, or be appointed to the superintendence of any particular district. The sole object in the meantime was to preserve the episcopal succession. It appears that the consecration was performed at the residence of Archbishop Paterson in Edinburgh, on the 25th of January 1705. The Archbishop, Bishop Rose, and Bishop Douglas, performed the consecration, the " letters " of which were first published by Bishop Russell,[*] and must not be omitted in this narrative, because the document explains the motives which induced the venerable Bishops to advance the two Presbyters to the episcopate.—

" Apud Edinburgum, die vicesimo quinto mensis Januarii, anno ab incarnato Domino et Servatore nostri millesimo septingentisimo quinto.

" Nos—Joannes, providentia divina Archiepiscopus Glascuensis, Alexander miseratione divina Episcopus Edinburgensis, et Robertus miseratione divina Episcopus

[*] Appendix to Keith's Catalogue of the Scottish Bishops, p 518.

Dunblanensis, in timore Domini ponderantes plerosque fratrum nostrorum carissimorum, et in collegio Episcopale collegarum (hoc nupere elapso, et ecclesiæ nostræ luctuoso curriculo) in Domino abdormiisse, nosque perpaucos qui divina miseracordia superstites sumus, multiplicitus curis, morbis, atque ingravescente senio tantum non confectos esse; Quapropter ex eo quod Deo Supremo, Servatori nostri, sacrosanctæ ejus ecclesiæ, et posteris debemus, in animum induximus, officium, caracterem, et facultatem Episcopalem, aliis probis, fidelibus, ad docendum et regendum idoneis hominibus committere; inter quos quum nobis ex propria scientia constet, reverendum nostrum fratrem Joannem Sage, artium magistrem, et Presbyterum Glascuensem, tanto muneri aptum et idoneum esse; nos igitur divini muneris presidio freti, secundum gratiam nobis concessam, die, mense, anno suprascriptis, in sacrario domus Archiepiscopi Glascuensis, supradictum Joannem Sage, ordinavimus, consecravimus, et in nostrum Episcopale Collegium co-optavimus. In cujus rei testimonium sigilla Joannis Archiepiscopi Glascuensis, et Alexandri Episcopi Edinburgensis (Sedis Sancti Andreæ nunc vacantis) huic instrumento (chirographis nostris pius munito), appendi mandavimus. Sic subscrib

"Jo Glascuen. Alex. Edinburgen. Ro. Dumblane."

Of Bishop Fullarton, who was ejected from Paisley at the Revolution, little is personally known, or rather no particular events of his clerical life appear to be of marked importance. He was a man of considerable learning, great piety and respectability, and held in the utmost esteem by his brethren. Like Bishop Sage, he was invested with an office at all times of great responsibility, and at that crisis an office of very peculiar personal danger, when no temporal motives could induce any man to accept it. The talent, the industry, and the sufferings of Bishop Sage, entitle him to a particular notice in this narrative, as one of the distinguished ornaments of the Scottish Episcopal Church.

Bishop Sage was born in the parish of Criech in Fife, in 1652. His parents, though of limited resources, were of good station, and his ancestors had resided in the parish for seven generations. His father was a captain in the regiment commanded by Alexander first Lord Duffus, engaged in the defence of Dundee, when that town was stormed by General Monk in 1651, and as his property was considerably affected by his loyalty, a liberal education was all he could bestow on his son, who was educated at the University of St Andrews, where he took the degree of Master of Arts in 1672. Bishop Sage soon afterwards became parochial schoolmaster successively of Ballingry in Fife, and of Tippermuir near Perth. The incidents of his life are expressively narrated in the "Biographical Dictionary of Eminent Scotsmen" by Mr Robert Chambers "Though in these humble situations [as schoolmaster] he wanted many of the necessaries, and all the comforts of life, he prosecuted his studies with unwearied diligence. Unfortunately, however, in increasing his stock of learning, he imbibed the seeds of several diseases which afflicted him through the whole of his life, and, notwithstanding the vigour of his constitution, tended ultimately to shorten his days. To the cultivated mind of such a man as Sage, the drudgery of a parish school must have been an almost intolerable slavery, and he, therefore, readily accepted the offer of Mr Drummond of Cultmalundie of a situation in his family, to superintend the education of his sons He accompanied those young persons to the grammar school of Perth, and afterwards attended them in the capacity of tutor to the University of St Andrews. At Perth he acquired the esteem of Dr Rose, subsequently Bishop of Edinburgh, one of the most distinguished men of his age, and at St Andrews he obtained the friendship and countenance of all the great literary characters of the period." Having superintended the education of his pupils, Sage was recommended by his friend Dr Rose, who then filled the theological chair in the University of Glasgow, to Archbishop Ross, who admitted him into holy orders, and presented him to one of the parish churches of that city. " At the period of his advancement in the Church he was about thirty-four years of age; his knowledge of the Scriptures was very great; he was thorough master of school divinity, and had entered deeply into the modern controversies, especially those between the Romish and Protestant Churches, and also into the disputes among the rival churches of the Reformation. He was in consequence very highly esteemed by his brethren, and was soon after appointed clerk of the Diocesan Synod of Glasgow, an office of great responsibility." In his Life by Bishop Gillan, published in 1714, we are told that during the few years he was in Glasgow anterior to the Revolution, his " wise and prudent conduct, his exemplary life and conversation, and the faithful discharge of his ministerial office, made him to be honoured and beloved by all good men, as one of the greatest lights of the Church, and esteemed and applauded even by the Dissenters. About the end of 1688, when the barbarous rabbling of the Episcopal ministers was set on foot in the West country, though he did not escape the common fate, yet he was more civilly treated by those impious despisers of all human and divine laws than some of his brethren. The *saints* contented themselves with giving Mr Sage a warning to depart from Glasgow, and threatenings if he ever returned." He was told to "shake off the dust from his feet, and withdraw from Glasgow, and never venture to appear there again."

Sage retired to Edinburgh, carrying with him the Diocesan Books which he delivered to Bishop Rose, as they were found in that venerable Prelate's possession after his decease, and delivered by his nephew to the Presbytery of Glasgow. Those books had been repeatedly demanded by the Presbyterians, and decidedly refused, from a hope which Sage continued to cherish that a second restoration of the Church would take place To forward that great object, though occasionally officiating in the episcopal congregations of the Scottish metropolis, he chiefly occupied himself in those polemical works which are monuments of his learning and zeal, and infinitely annoyed his adversaries. He resolutely refused to acknowledge the Revolution Government, and was in consequence expelled from the city by order of the Privy Council. He found refuge with Sir William Bruce, in that gentleman's country seat of Kinross, where the Rev. Mr Christie, the ejected incumbent of Kinross, afterwards a Bishop, also occasionally resided. Sage was peculiarly obnoxious to the Government, as was also his friend Sir William Bruce, who admired his virtues and approved his principles. About 1694 or 1695, he ventured on one occasion to Edinburgh to transact some private business, when he was recognised in the streets, and carried before the magistrates, who compelled him to find security that he would leave the city, and never return, though he *did* return in the succeeding reign. In 1696, when Sir William Bruce was committed a prisoner to the Castle of Edinburgh on a charge of corresponding with the exiled Family, a warrant was issued to search the houses which Sage was known to visit for his apprehension. He escaped to the Grampian Mountains in Forfarshire, where he lived destitute and friendless under the assumed name of Jackson, eluding his persecutors some months under the pretence to the natives that he required goat's milk and a change of air. The liberation of Sir William Bruce was attended with a relaxation of the severity of his enemies, and he afterwards became chaplain to the Countess of Callendar, a grand-daughter of the great Marquis of Montrose, and preceptor to her son, who succeeded his father as fourth Earl of Callendar in 1692, and his uncle as fifth Earl of Linlithgow in 1695. When his services were no longer required in that capacity he was received into the ancient family of Stewart of Grandtully. In 1706, about a year after his consecration, he was confined by a dangerous illness nine months in the house of Mr Christie near Kinross. " After patiently lingering in Scotland without improvement, the persecutions to which he was subject increasing his malady, he was induced to try the efficacy of the waters at Bath in 1709. But this also failed him; the seat of his disease lay deeper than medical skill could reach. He remained a year at Bath and London, when the great recognised and the learned caressed and courted him, and where it was the wish of many distinguished persons that he should spend the remainder of his life. The love of his country and of his native Church overcame all entreaties, and he returned to Scotland in 1710 with a debilitated body, but a mind as vigorous as ever. Worn out with disease and mental anguish, Bishop Sage died at Edinburgh on the 7th of June 1711, lamented by his friends, and feared by his adversaries."

Such was the man on whom, along with Bishop Fullarton, the first episcopate was conferred in Scotland after the Revolution. The works of Bishop Sage are now very scarce, and are chiefly found in the libraries of the collectors of polemical literature. One of them is entitled the " Principles of the Cyprianic Age with regard to Episcopal Power and Jurisdiction," published in London in 1695. Gilbert Rule, the Presbyterian successor of Principal Monro in the University of Edinburgh, and one of the chief pamphleteering writers in defence of his party, asserted in one of his controversial productions that if Episcopacy could be traced to the time of St Cyprian in the third century, he [Rule] would renounce Presbyterianism and conform to the Church. The challenge was accepted by Sage, and he wrote the valuable and learned work above mentioned, one of the most conclusive demonstrations of the apostolical and primitive authority of Episcopacy. But Rule would not or could not be convinced, and published a reply in 1696, entitled, " The Cyprianic Bishop examined, and found not to be Diocesan, nor to have Superior Power to a Parish Minister, or Presbyterian Moderator, being an Answer to John Sage his Principles of the Cyprianic Age; together with an Appendix, in Answer to a railing Preface to a Book entituled, The Fundamental Charter of Presbytery." This produced a reply from Sage in 1701, in the form of " A Vindication of the Principles of the Cyprianic Age." The " Fundamental Charter of Presbytery" appeared in 1695, and was written by Sage in the house of his friend Bishop Christie near Kinross. His other works are, " An Account of the late Establishment of Presbytery by the Parliament of Scotland in 1690 ;" " Some Remarks on a Letter from a Gentleman in the City to a Minister in the Country, on Mr David Williamson's Sermon before the General Assembly," Edinburgh, 1703 ; " A Brief Examination of some things in Mr Meldrum's Sermon preached on the 6th of May 1703, against a Toleration to those of the Episcopal Persuasion ;" " The Reasonableness of a Toleration of those of the Episcopal Persuasion inquired into purely on Church Principles," 1704 ; the " Life of Gawin Douglas," 1710 ; and an Introduction to the Works of Drummond of Hawthornden, to which publication his friend the learned Ruddiman lent his assistance. Bishop Sage also wrote the second and third Letters concerning the persecution of the Episcopal Clergy in Scotland, and left many manuscripts on various subjects mentioned in his Life by Bishop Gillan, which were published in 1714.

At the time of the consecration of Bishops Sage and Fullarton a legal " Toleration" was greatly desired by the Episcopal clergy, and the Duke of Queensberry, to preserve the interest he had obtained with sundry English Churchmen of influence, induced the Earl of Balcarras and Archbishop Paterson to proceed to London, to assure them of his Grace's inclination to serve and protect their Episcopal brethren in Scotland. This expedition appears to have dissatisfied sundry parties, for Lockhart of Carnwath, a zealous adherent of the exiled dynasty, makes some severe reflections on the Earl and the Archbishop, whom he designates "two renagadoes." Of the latter, to whom he cherished a private dislike, he says that he was moved " to embark in this design, which, when he left Scotland, and even after he came to London, he kept as a mighty secret, pretending to the Cavaliers, he undertook that long journey in the middle of winter, so dangerous to his grey hairs (his own expressions), only to supplicate Queen Anne to bestow the vacant Bishops' rents on the poor starving Episcopal clergy. Yet when this matter was under the consideration of Queen Anne and her servants, his charitable zeal did allow him to accept of four hundred pounds sterling per annum out of them, though there remained but twelve hundred pounds after his four hundred were deducted (to be divided among his needy brethren), that were not appropriated to other uses ; and his

Lordship was worth twenty thousand pounds of his own. This Noble Lord and reverend Prelate served the design they came for most religiously, and the latter had the impudence to assure Queen Anne that the Duke of Queensberry was the best friend the Episcopal clergy had in Scotland, and would have procured them a toleration (which it seems they desired), had he not found they were so disaffected to her interest, that to show them favour would be to encourage and enable her enemies; adding, with tears in his eyes, 'She might depend upon the truth of this information, since it came from him, who could be no gainer, but on the contrary was a great loser by their being kept under.' This last part I had in half an hour after it was performed from one who had it from Prince George, who declared he and Queen Anne were confounded at the account." This is a severe charge against Archbishop Paterson, but it is altogether involved with the Duke of Queensberry, whom Lockhart in his character of him describes as " to outward appearance, and in his ordinary conversation, of a gentle and good disposition, but inwardly a very devil, standing at nothing to advance his own interest and designs. To sum up all, he was altogether void of honour, loyalty, justice, religion, and generosity, an ungrateful deserter of and rebel to his prince, the ruin and bane of his country, and the aversion of all loyal and true Scotsmen!"*

It would be out of place in the present work to enter into an examination of this severe character of the Duke of Queensberry. There were then three great political parties in Scotland. The first were the Revolution party, to whom the Duke of Queensberry belonged, but though their proceedings were firm and consistent, it is admitted that none of their leaders were much of principle except the Earl of Marchmont. This party were supporters of the well known Union—a measure then in contemplation, and bitterly opposed by the Scottish nation at the time. But the Duke of Queensberry was thought to be sometimes under the influence of the Court, and the wrath of the Cavaliers against him, as expressed by Lockhart of Carnwath, was generally excited by the duplicity of his Grace. The second party were called the *Country Party*, who opposed the Union chiefly on the romantic plea of maintaining the independence of the Scottish crown, and who also insisted that

* Lockhart Papers, vol. i. p 45.

ample satisfaction should be given for the injuries which Scotland had suffered during the reign of William III., especially for the failure of the celebrated Darien scheme, and for the atrocious massacre of the Macdonalds of Glencoe The third party, then headed by the Earl of Home, consisted of the avowed Jacobites, and formed a numerous and powerful body in the Northern and Highland counties. They often coalesced with the *Country Party*, many of whom would have gone over to the Cavaliers at once, but abstained from openly declaring themselves from prudential considerations The Union with England was also opposed by other parties or sections from various motives. The more zealous Presbyterians denounced it, because they would be compelled to acknowledge the English Bishops in the Acts of the British Parliament.

By an act of the Scottish Parliament in June 1702, Queen Anne was enabled to appoint commissioners to treat for the union of the kingdoms of England and Scotland, and in September 1705 another similar act was passed. In 1707, the Union was carried into effect amid the most riotous opposition of the Scottish people, who imagined that their country was betrayed, sold, and prostrated by this important measure, and whose constant theme of complaint for two succeeding generations was the "sorrowful Union," to which they ascribed every calamity which visited the kingdom. The old Scottish Parliament was for ever annihilated, and the Lord High Commissioner transferred solely to the annual General Assembly of the Kirk, completely divested of his state importance. The Union gave a security to the Presbyterian Establishment which it did not previously possess; but it gave no toleration to the Episcopal clergy, though the Government was now of milder mood, and seldom offered any disturbance. The very proposal of a toleration to the Episcopal Church would have excited the fierce opposition of the Presbyterian ministers to the Union itself, and no great exercise of their angry passions was necessary to agitate an already irritated populace.

The death of Bishop Hay in 1707, and of Archbishop Paterson in 1708, reduced the number of Bishops to five, viz. Bishop Hallyburton, formerly of Aberdeen, Bishop Rose of Edinburgh, Bishop Douglas, formerly of Dunblane, and the two recently consecrated Bishops Sage and Fullarton. Mr Skinner says of Bishop Hallyburton, that he had become " so weak in his intellectuals, beyond what his more aged brother of Dunblane was, that though he was still able to perform the office of ordination for such vacancies in his diocese as applied to him, it was not judged convenient, as it was not necessary, to employ him in any business of importance that required a certain degree of secrecy and caution."* There were thus only four on whom the care of the Church devolved. After the death of Archbishop Paterson it was found necessary to hold another consecration. The Rev. John Falconer, ejected minister of Carnbee in Fife, and the Rev. Henry Christie, already mentioned as the friend of Bishop Sage, were selected for the episcopate. They were consecrated at Dundee, the usual residence of Bishop Douglas, by Bishops Rose, Douglas, and Sage, on the 28th of April 1709.

Nothing is known of Bishop Christie, farther than that he lived respected and beloved by his brethren till his death in 1718. Of Bishop Falconer it is stated by an undoubted authority, that he " was an intimate acquaintance and great favourite of good Bishop Rose, who pressed him most warmly, for the good of the Church, to take the burden of the episcopate upon him in those times of trial and difficulty. And indeed no man could have been fitter for it in any condition of the Church, as, from the many letters which remain of him, he appears to have been not only a man of great piety and prudence, but likewise a consummate divine, and deeply versed in the doctrines and rites of the Primitive Church, which, both by example and argument, he studied to revive and bring again into practice in the softest and most inoffensive manner possible." Bishop Russell observes—" As a proof that this eulogy is not unfounded, we are informed that he was likewise very highly esteemed by the eminently learned Henry Dodwell, with whom he corresponded relative to a book which he had intended to publish against Deists, and other such enemies of Christianity. Dodwell's opinion of Falconer may be farther collected from a wish which he expressed that the latter would execute a work projected by himself on the Law of Nature and Nations. I know not, however, that the Bishop did not actually become an author. There is preserved in manuscript a little tract written by him for the use of the Viscountess Kingston, which may be described as a popular exposition of the various covenants of God, and especially of the privileges, the sanctions, and the conditions of the Christian covenant."

* Skinner's Ecclesiastical History of Scotland, vol ii. p. 607.

CHAPTER XII.

INTRODUCTION OF THE LITURGY OF THE CHURCH OF ENGLAND INTO THE SCOTTISH EPISCOPAL CHURCH—ALARM OF THE PRESBYTERIANS—PROSECUTIONS OF THE EPISCOPAL CLERGY—ACT OF TOLERATION OF 1712.

WHILE the important measure of the Union was in dependence, an order was issued by the Government to shut up all the Episcopal chapels in Scotland. This was probably to pacify the Presbyterians, whose General Assembly opposed the Union in a remarkable document published by De Foe. The order, however, was soon revoked, the Union was effected in defiance of the most tumultuous opposition, and the Episcopalians were again for a short time unmolested.

Immediately after the Union the English Liturgy was adopted in the service of the Scottish Episcopal Church, and has ever since been the ritual for public worship. It is singular that the introduction of the English Liturgy should have been favourably received even by many Presbyterians. For this fact we have the admission of their own gossipping writer Wodrow :—" What may be the design of Providence," he says, " in suffering innovations and *inclinations to the English Service* to increase in several parts of this [Presbyterian] Church now, more than they were even when Prelacy was established by law? I desire to be sober in putting meanings upon Providence, but this may perhaps be one design among others. *I find a woefull disrespect to the ministry, and a disrelishing of Presbyterian Government.* I believe Episcopacy without ceremonies would be fallen in with totally by too many."* This

---

* Wodrow's Analecta, vol. iii p 218

important admission is under date 1709, and is peculiarly valuable as the recorded opinion of a zealous Presbyterian. In a letter to one of his friends the same year he says—" Let me have a full account of the business of the building of the chapel at Holyroodhouse for the English Service:" and again, in a letter to Mr Alexander M'Cracken, Presbyterian minister at Lisburn in Ireland, in which he laments the decay of religious feeling among the people, Wodrow says—" The English Service is setting up very busily in the North, at Inverness, Elgin, Aberdeen, Montrose, and many other places, to the great grief of our brethren there, and the weakening, or rather ruining, our discipline."*

Some curious reaction must have taken place in favour of the Episcopal Church at this period, which is farther intimated by Wodrow. Principal Carstairs, a man of great ability and worldly wisdom, preached the sermon at the opening of the General Assembly in April 1709. Wodrow heard this sermon, and says—" He recommended charity and ingenuity in dealing with those of the Episcopal communion who did not think it fit to join with us, and avoiding harshness and bitterness of spirit towards them; and told us that morosity and disingenuity will no way recommend us in dealing with them: which expressions some looked upon as what contained a tacit reflection upon ourselves. He had certainly a very neat and well-worded discourse."† Dr Carstairs, or *Cardinal Carstairs*, as he was popularly designated, was a very distinguished man, and much superior to the ordinary mass of his party. Although perhaps the most efficient enemy the Episcopal Church of Scotland ever had, it is related of him that he continually exercised deeds of charity towards her unfortunate clergy. When his body was laid in the grave, in the Greyfriars' Churchyard, Edinburgh, in 1715, two persons were observed to turn aside from the rest of the company, burst into tears, and lament their mutual loss. They were ascertained to be Episcopal clergymen, whose families had been supported a considerable time by his benefactions.

In 1706 the Rev. Robert Calder published a short treatise " On the Lawfulness and Expediency of Set Forms of Prayer," and as it was levelled against the Presbyterians, it gave them considerable annoyance.

* Wodrow Correspondence, printed for the Wodrow Society in 1842, vol i. p. 30.
† Wodrow Correspondence—Letters to Mrs Wodrow, vol. 1. p. 2.

This very excellent little work, however, is merely general, though its author strongly defends the Liturgy of the Church of England It may surprise some that the Church did not adopt the Scottish Liturgy prepared in the reign of Charles I., the introduction of which in 1637 caused the well-known outrage in St Giles' church, Edinburgh. To this it may be answered that there is in reality little difference between that Liturgy and the Book of Common Prayer of the Church of England ;* and it was wisely considered expedient that the ritual which was universally known should be adopted in the public service of the Church. The members of the Anglican Church when in Scotland would thus enjoy the spiritual benefits of their own Liturgy, and connect themselves with a communion of the Church Catholic, which, though deprived of its temporalities, is pure in doctrine and apostolical in constitution and practice. It tended, moreover, to promote that connection with the Church of England which the Scottish Episcopal Church has always preserved, and which will be perpetual.

The enmity of the Presbyterians to the Anglican Liturgy is well known, though it must be admitted that many of them, by the influence of education, and by a candid investigation of the matter, have relinquished their prejudices, and admire its offices. The use of a Liturgy is no essential part of the Episcopal Church, as many ignorantly suppose, for a religious society may adopt a set form of prayer, and still be schismatical. The Dutch Presbyterians have such set forms, and the Wesleyan and Calvinistic Methodists in England use the Morning and

* As the Presbyterians persist in designating the Scottish Liturgy by the term *Popish*, and most absurdly maintain that it was the compilation of Archbishop Laud, the perusal of L'Estrange's " Alliance of Divine Offices," folio, 1659, will at once show wherein the Scottish Liturgy agrees, and wherein it differs, from the Liturgy of the Church of England, particularly pages 65, 66, 68, 70, 85, 86, 89, 92, 93, 107, 109, 110, 162, 164—169, 195, 201—209, 303. Collier, in his Ecclesiastical History, enumerates all the differences between the Scottish and English Liturgies, and gives an account of the manner in which the former was framed; vol ii. p 767—769, compared with Neal's History of the Puritans, vol. ii. p. 208, 209. We have the recorded opinion of Bishop Horsley respecting the Scottish or King Charles' Liturgy that it is an admirable compendium, in his opinion even superior to the English; and he declares that if it was in his power he would give it the preference. See also " The late Scottish Service-Book, with all the Variations, and upon them all Annotations, vindicating the Book of Common Prayer from the main Objections of its Enemies," published at London in 1669.

Evening Service of the Book of Common Prayer, in whole or in part, at their public devotions, but that does not alter the position in which they choose to place themselves as schismatics. An extemporaneous prayer must of necessity be a form, as much as is the Liturgy of the Church. The person who utters it has either composed it, or he has acquired the habit of indulging a certain common-place phraseology. The psalms and hymns which the Presbyterians and sectaries sing in their public worship are forms of prayer, especially the Psalms of David; but, to be consistent, instead of adopting always the *same psalms*, as they object to the *same prayers* in the Church, they should have new psalms and hymns for every act of public worship. The apostolical benediction, which they also use, is a *form*, and sitting at the communion is as much a form as kneeling. The Presbyterian mode of worship is as much a form as is the liturgical, and no argument can be urged against the one which cannot be as effectually brought against the other.

At the period referred to after the Union, many copies of the Book of Common Prayer were gratuitously sent into Scotland by pious persons in England. But it must not be inferred that the English Liturgy was previously unknown. It was in the possession of hundreds of the parochial incumbents before the Revolution was even anticipated, and had been publicly adopted in divine service at various places with the cordial approbation of the people. The almost general adoption of the National Anglican Liturgy by the Scottish Episcopal Church excited the fiercest opposition of the Presbyterian Establishment. It was denounced in their General Assembly, and the Government was peremptorily called upon to interfere. In 1708 seventeen Episcopal clergymen in the city of Edinburgh were prosecuted by the magistrates for officiating in " meeting-houses," and expressly prohibited from " keeping" any such " within the city of Edinburgh, Canongate, Leith, and the suburbs and liberties thereof, and from preaching, or exercising any part of the ministerial function within the same in all time coming, under the pain of imprisonment, and to find caution to that effect." Among those clergymen we find the names of the Rev. Andrew Cant, the Rev. David Freebairn, and the Rev. David Rankine, afterwards Bishops. One of them, the Rev. George Graham, was ordered to be imprisoned in the common jail, until " the Lords of her Majesty's Privy Council should inflict on him such farther punishment as they should think meet," simply because in the Liturgy he " passed over and omitted" the Queen's name. The Episcopal clergy throughout Scotland were at this period greatly annoyed by a regular system of espionage encouraged by their enemies. An account of this prosecution, or rather persecution, was published by those clergymen in " A Narrative of the late Treatment of the Episcopal Ministers within the City of Edinburgh since March 1708, until their Imprisonment in July thereafter, with their Circumstances and Defences, together with some Reflections upon the same."* A Reply appeared, in the form of " The Scots Narrative examined, or the Case of the Episcopal Ministers in Scotland stated," which, from the style, and its publication in London, was probably written by Ridpath. Its object is to defend the magistrates of Edinburgh, whose conduct is described " in all the parts of it to be *merciful and charitable.*"

De Foe gives his distorted account of the matter, which is too important to be overlooked.† It appears that five of the Episcopal clergy of Edinburgh were sent to the jail by the magistrates, when the order was issued for shutting up the " meeting-houses" in that city, during the excitement occasioned by the Union. They were soon released, but instead of their imprisonment having the desired effect, it only tended to render them more determined in what they considered their religious and political duty. De Foe has the boldness to assert that the Episcopal clergy courted persecution, and finding their " refusing the oaths, and to pray for the Queen, nay, actually praying for the Pretender, would not provoke the Government and the magistrates in Scotland to persecute, they find out another expedient which they are assured will not fail, being what they know the Scots will not bear, whatever it cost them, and this was erecting the Common Prayer, or English Liturgy, in Scotland." He then proceeds to state the manner in which the introduction of the Liturgy was managed, and discovers that those concerned in it " had other aims than merely the liberty of their consciences and the worshipping of God."—" But the design being con-

---

* London, printed and sold by John Morphew, near Stationers' Hall, 1708. This pamphlet, which is eloquently written, extends to forty quarto pages, closely printed, and charges the Presbyterian authorities as the originators of the prosecution.

† Preface to the History of the Union, by Daniel De Foe, 4to. 1776, p. 19, *et seq.*

certed, they found a tool. A poor curate of L.15 a year in Ireland, but born in Scotland, comes over to Edinburgh to mend his commons, and having taken the oath he falls in with this party, who, finding him a person of *prostituted morals, a large stock in the face,* and ready, if well paid, to do their work, they promise him fourscore pounds a-year, and accordingly begin a subscription for it. Some English gentlemen had, it seems, promised him encouragement towards that sum to be raised, and this they make a handle of presently, and reported that this was set up to accommodate the English strangers who could not conform to the Presbyterian Church. But the English gentlemen seeing into the design, and that they were likely to be made a property to embroil the Government, and foment a division between the two lately united nations, soon abandoned him and his design. However, he resolved to put his project into execution, and accordingly takes a house just at the Cross of Edinburgh, and begins to read the English Service. The people, as every body knew they would, immediately took fire at the thing, but not doing him the honour to rabble him, which seemed to be what his party expected, they complain to the magistrates. The person that had let him the house, finding what use he was putting it to, began with him, and, on pretence of his having made some spoil in pulling down partitions, &c. not authorised by his contract, gets him turned out of the house, and so he betakes himself to a place less public, but still goes on with his Service-Book worship. It gave less offence there, the other seeming to be a defiance of the laws. It happened at this time, or in a few days after, that the Commission of the General Assembly was to meet, and as soon as they sat down a representation is made to them by the inhabitants of Edinburgh and other places against this thing. The paper mentions other complaints indeed, but this was the main thing aimed at."

From this most erroneous statement the reader will easily form an idea of the annoyances to which the Episcopalians were subjected by the Presbyterian Establishment. But to show how De Foe has completely perverted the circumstances he relates, the following is an account of this transaction from a Presbyterian writer,[*] who has candour to acknowledge the bigotry of his party.

[*] The History of Great Britain during the Reign of Queen Anne, by Thomas Sommerville, D D. Minister of Jedburgh, 4to, London, 1798.

The case of the " poor curate of L.15 a year," which De Foe notices, is that of the Rev. Mr Greenshields. He had been ordained by the Bishop of Ross, and afterwards held a curacy in Ireland in the Archiepiscopal diocese of Armagh. He came to Edinburgh, officiated in the manner stated, and he was in consequence cited by the Presbytery of Edinburgh to appear before them, and give an account of his licence and authority to exercise ministerial functions. Mr Greenshields very properly declined their jurisdiction, and they prohibited him from performing any clerical duty within their bounds, with what is called, in Scottish legal phraseology, *certification* that if he transgressed, he should be imprisoned, and suffer such other punishment as they might think proper to inflict. The magistrates of Edinburgh were ordered to enforce this sentence. It was founded, says Dr Sommerville, " upon these two arguments: 1. That he exercised the ministry within the bounds of the Presbytery without their allowance, and was an intruder. 2. That he introduced a form of worship contrary to the purity and uniformity of the church established by law."*

Mr Greenshields was summoned by the magistrates of Edinburgh to appear before them, and as he still persisted in refusing to submit to the sentence of the Presbytery, he was sent to prison, where he lay several months. He applied to the Court of Session for liberation, but was refused on the ground of the first argument, namely, that no minister ordained by an *exauctorate*, namely, by a bishop deprived of authority, has ordination according to the law which established Presbyterianism. At length, on the 15th of September 1709, this persecuted clergyman was released by order of the House of Lords. " Though this," says Dr Sommerville, " was agreeable to every principle of liberality and justice, yet it *gave great offence to the clergy and members of the Establishment,* who complained of it as injurious to the purity of religion, and contrary to the existing laws "

As early as 1703, on the 30th of January, a riot took place at Glasgow, in consequence of the Rev. Mr Burgess, who had taken the oaths to Government, performing divine service according to the form of the Church of England. The mob, according to the statement in the letter of the Lord Chancellor of Scotland dated 8th March, forced open the

* History of the Reign of Queen Anne, p. 469.

doors, broke the windows, and if the magistrates had not interposed, would have committed personal violence on the principal members of the congregation. In opposition to the arguments and statements of De Foe, Dr Sommerville represents the conduct of the Scottish Episcopal Church in a manner honourable to his candour. "About the beginning," he says, "of the present reign [Queen Anne], a great change of sentiment began to operate upon the Scottish Episcopalians. It was natural for them, in their depressed condition, to cherish the idea of a relation to that religious community in the neighbouring nation which, under the sanction of law, enjoyed a constitution and polity consonant to their own principles, and this propensity paved the way for a nearer conformity, by adopting the English modes of worship. It was also reasonable to conclude, that as the sovereign was herself a member of that Church, and zealous for its interest, so, by accepting and using the Liturgy, they were likely to stand on fairer ground for obtaining her protection, when she had a safe opportunity of bestowing it. The same idea of the importance of a general uniformity in worship and government was fondly cherished by some dignitaries of the English Church, who recommended contributions to purchase copies of the Common Prayer Book for the use of the Scottish Episcopalians. A few of the clergy of that description, who had been ordained by the English bishops, and who officiated in the episcopal congregations in Scotland, read the prayers of the English Church, though only in more private meetings, and *occasionally*, because it was disliked by the generality of their adherents, and exposed the worshippers to the double danger of legal penalties and the fury of a bigoted mob." The latter are the true reasons. The Liturgy of the Church of England was not *disliked* by the Scottish Episcopalians, with the exception, probably, of a few opinionative individuals, and the fact is proved by its general adoption by the congregations of the Church. Dr Sommerville proceeds to account for the change in his own way :—" A variety of circumstances contributed to forward the proselytism of the Scottish Episcopalians to the English forms of worship, and to encourage them to make a more open avowal of it. The Queen had often expressed her solicitude to obtain indulgence from the ecclesiastical courts in behalf of such of the superseded clergy as were well affected to the Government, and esteemed for their moderation and prudence.* The enthusiasm kindled in England by the affair of Dr Sachaverell was conveyed beyond the Tweed, and raised a congenial spirit in those of similar principles in Scotland. The disgrace of the Whig ministers who had patronised the Presbyterians, and the exemplary zeal of their successors, allured the attachment of the Scottish Episcopalians, in whose behalf it was exercised, and of whose rising prosperity they themselves participated."

But as the case of Mr Greenshields illustrates, in a remarkable manner, the state of the times in reference to the *animus* evinced by the Presbyterian Establishment towards the Episcopal Church, the following cavalier account of it is worthy of notice as expressing the sentiments of the other party :

"This gentleman was the son of a Scots Episcopal minister, who, being rabbled out of his church at the Revolution, and being afterwards in Ireland, educated this his son in the study of divinity; and he being admitted into holy orders by one of the Scots Bishops, after he had served a cure some years in Ireland, at Edinburgh set up a meeting-house, where he used the Liturgy of the Church of England, which at that time was not practised in the other Episcopal meeting-houses there. The godly, having their friends then at the helm of affairs, resolved to crush this enterprise in the bud, and for that end prevailed with the magistrates of Edinburgh to shut up the door of the meeting-house, and imprison Mr Greenshields. He having applied for the benefits of the *habeas corpus* law, and being refused the same, unless he found bail never to exercise any part of his ministerial office in that city, his next recourse was to the Lords of Session, before whom he brought an action of wrongous imprisonment against the magistrates, but their sentence being affirmed by that Court, he then appealed to the Queen and Parliament; and being released when the magistrates were weary of keeping him so long in prison, he made haste to London to prosecute his ap-

* " You are to prevent, as much as possible, the turning out of their churches such of the Episcopal ministry as are qualified conform to act of Parliament. You are to encourage any inclinations you find in the Assembly to assume such of the ministry who preach under Bishops, and are qualified by law," &c. Instructions to the Earl of Glasgow, Commissioner to the General Assembly of the Church of Scotland, Kensington, 22d March 1708, MSS. State Paper Office, cited by Dr Sommerville, in his Reign of Queen Anne, p. 468.

peal; but the House of Lords being then wholly taken up with Dr Sachaverell's impeachment, did this session only receive his petition and lodge his appeal. Next year, when the old Ministry was discarded, and the face of affairs changed, the Tories thought it a reasonable opportunity to push Mr Greenshields' affair, and have his appeal discussed. The Ministry at the time did all that in them lay to have this affair put off, on the old pretence of waiting till a more proper season, and most of the Scots Peers, except the Earl of Eglinton, and Lord Balmerino, joined with them. But those two Lords, seconded by the Commons, buoyed up Mr Greenshields, and prevailed with him to stand his ground, and not yield in an affair which might be of so much use to those of his profession.

"Some little time after this Mr Harley, not being then advanced to the Peerage, took me one day aside out of the House of Commons into the Speaker's chamber, and calling upon Mr Secretary St John, Sir Thomas Hamner, and two or three more to come alongst, he addressed himself to me in words to this purpose—that he was much surprised and very sorry to hear that I and others of my country were so violent in pushing Mr Greenshields' appeal, which could not fail to be attended with bad consequences, as the Church party in England would take it ill if he was not protected, and the Scots Presbyterians would highly resent any favour he met with, and therefore he had called these gentlemen to be present, that they might join with him in desiring it might be dropt till a more proper season. I answered, that I could assure him we were much mistaken if any bad consequences happened from supporting Mr Greenshields in his just plea, for the contrary was designed by those who pushed it:—that the Scots Presbyterians were as much exasperated already as they could be, and had neither ability nor courage to give any disturbance, for their interest in the country was very small, as sufficiently appeared from the great majority of Tories in this Parliament, which he knew was not owing to any assistance they got from the Court, but arose wholly from the inclinations of the people:—that as for himself, he had no reason to show them any favour, for they preached and prayed against him *nominatim*, giving him over to the gallows and the devil from their pulpits, and I was confident, at least hopeful, he would never give them reason to have a better opinion of him:—that there was no time to be lost, for we were rather worse than better since the change of the Ministry, as the Lord Grange,* brother to the Earl of Mar, who was lately made Justice-Clerk, seemed more violent than his predecessor against the Episcopal clergy :—that the Ministry never had nor could have so fair an opportunity to relieve the Episcopal party, without any apparent danger or inconvenience, if they thought it worth their pains to truckle under and would be amused with imaginary fears of the Presbyterians, for Mr Greenshields had lodged his petition, and expected justice even during the late Administration, and the discussing of this appeal could not properly be an act and deed of the Ministry, seeing they could not hinder any man from demanding justice in a legal way ; and if this did not satisfy him, he was at liberty from me to let the Presbyterians know we insisted much against his will. As for the season, I was no politician, but I always believed no season improper for doing good, and whatever others might do I would regulate my measures accordingly; and I did not make the least question but the clergy and laity of the Church of England would think themselves bound to assist their Scots brethren, who were persecuted for no other reason than being of their communion. Having thus spoke my mind very freely, the other gentlemen who were present instead of condemning approved my resolution, and promised to contribute all they could to bring this affair to a right issue ; whereupon Mr Harley slipt off not very well pleased, and much disappointed.

" In the mean time, the Scots Commons exerted themselves with the utmost rigour, supplied Mr Greenshields with money to defray the charge

* This unprincipled zealot, for such he was, was a son of Charles tenth Earl of Mar by his Countess, the eldest daughter of George second Earl of Panmure, and was next brother of John eleventh Earl of Mar, who led the Enterprise of 1715. He was elevated to the Bench in the Supreme Court of Scotland in 1706, and took his seat in March 1707 by the title of Lord Grange In 1710 he was appointed Lord Justice Clerk, and subsequently entered keenly into the politics of the times. He married Rachel, sister of Major Chiesley of Dalry, whom he treated with the utmost cruelty, while he preserved his reputation in the " Kirk" of being a godly "professor" of religion. He caused her to be kidnapped and confined in the Island of St Kilda, among the remote Hebrides, and a curious account of this infamous transaction is inserted in the Edinburgh Magazine for 1817. Lord Grange subsequently became intimate with Wodrow, and his letters to him are preserved in the Advocates' Library, Edinburgh. His Lordship is severely assailed in some satirical verses, in which the notorious Colonel Charteris is said to be "in villany outshined by hypocrite Lord Grange.'—Argyll Papers, 4to, 1836, p 166

of his process, and encouraged him not to submit or yield on account of the money that was offered, and the promises of more money and preferment in case he would drop his appeal. And when the day prefixed for discussing the appeal drew near, they divided themselves into several classes, to each of which was assigned a certain number of English Lords, on whom they waited, and gave a true and clear representation of the case, which had so much weight, and produced such good effects, that the underhand dealings of the Ministry were entirely baffled; for the appeal was heard, the sentence of the Lords of Session reversed, and the city of Edinburgh ordered to pay swinging costs to Mr Greenshields, to which the Ministry themselves were obliged to give their approbation, not daring to expose their reputations by appearing openly against an affair of this nature and consequence."*

It is admitted by Presbyterian writers that the conduct of their party, as the legal establishment, to their ejected opponents was malevolent and annoying. Their sermons abounded with tirades against what they called Prelacy, and the lower orders were seriously taught to believe that there was no difference between the Church and the Romanists. That they were bitter enemies to toleration is evident from an address of certain persons in the city of Edinburgh to the Commission of the General Assembly, the statements in which form a striking contrast to present circumstances. "To our very great surprise," they allege, "several of the Episcopal clergy, prompted and instigated by the Jacobite party, who are equally disaffected to the civil as to the ecclesiastical constitution, have of late not only erected meeting-houses in this city after the Scots Episcopal way, but also in several places here have *set up the English Service*, which, as it is contrary to our Establishment, and very grievous and offensive to us, and all others who are well affected to her Majesty and the present Establishment, so it will prove of fatal and dangerous consequence to the church if not speedily remedied." De Foe publishes this address, and says that it was signed "in less than three hours by between two and three hundred people." The wonder is that it did not receive as many thousands of signatures, and is a proof of the feelings of the intelligent portion of the community.

It is curious to observe that the Presbyterians seriously believed the

* The Lockhart Papers, published from the original MSS. in the possession of Anthony Aufrere, Esq of Hoveton, Norfolk, 4to, 1817, vol. i. p. 345, 349.

introduction, or "setting up," of the Anglican Liturgy in Scotland would destroy their Establishment. In 1711 was published "The Scots Representations to Her Majesty against setting up the Book of Common Prayer in Scotland;" and, according to a manuscript note on the copy in the Library of the Faculty of Advocates at Edinburgh, it was the production of Ridpath "and his associates, Mr William Carstairs, mentioned in the History of the Rye-House Plot, and Daniel De Foe." As to De Foe, who wrote much about Scottish ecclesiastical and political affairs, his principles are completely ascertained from a question which he proposes in his work on the Union—" Whether Episcopal deposed clergy have a right to ordain ministers?" He answers thus:— "Indeed, the question seems rather to be here, whether such preachers as shall be licensed or ordained by the exauctorate Bishops ought to be esteemed as ministers, especially in that Church which has deposed them" The malignity or ignorance of De Foe is here perceptible. The "exauctorate Bishops" of Scotland were never deposed by the Presbyterians; they were ejected from their temporalities by the Revolution Government, and supplanted by the present Establishment, which certainly succeeded in expelling many of the clergy from their parishes, but instead of any attempt at deposition, numbers of the Episcopal incumbents kept possession of their benefices during life, and those who conformed by taking the oaths to Government, and acknowledging the Presbyterian polity, were received with open arms.

In a pamphlet entitled, "A Short Account of the Grievances of the Episcopal Clergy in Scotland," published at London in 1712, the author, after narrating a number of cases of severe oppressions inflicted on the Episcopal clergy, thus proceeds:—" Another instance is in the case of the inhabitants of Old Aberdeen. These people, being desirous to worship God according to the form of the Church of England, called for that end an Episcopal minister who had given early proofs of his affection to the Government, and the better to secure themselves sent up a loyal address to the Queen, craving her protection in the peaceable exercise of their religion, which she was graciously pleased to assure them of in a letter written by the Earl of Cromarty, then Secretary of State. But my Lord S. [Sunderland], late Secretary of State to Her Majesty, *to show his zeal against the spreading of the English Service*, wrote to Sir David Dalrymple, her Majesty's Advocate in Scotland, to suppress their meeting-house; and accordingly an order was sent by the said Advocate to suppress it; and having given an account of his diligence to the said Earl, had in return a very obliging letter, the tenor whereof follows:—' I have laid before the Queen the order you have given for shutting up the chapel at Aberdeen, with which her Majesty is very well pleased, and orders me to tell you that you cannot do her more acceptable service than to discourage such innovations *every where.*' Thus the word *innovation* had its rise, and is still in use in all our Presbyterian judicatories to *express the Liturgy of the Church of England.*"

The Lord Advocate's exploit in shutting up the chapel at Aberdeen, and endeavouring to prohibit the use of the Liturgy, was not allowed to pass unnoticed. A petition from the "gentlemen and other inhabitants of Old Aberdeen" was transmitted to the Queen, requesting her Majesty to put a stop to the prosecutions to which they had been subjected. They stated that—"Notwithstanding the repeated assurances we have got of your Majesty's protection in the exercise of our religion, yet to our great surprise an order is lately come from your Majesty's Advocate in North Britain to shut up our chapel, for no other reason, whatever may be pretended, but because we make use of the Liturgy of the Church of England. Were we guilty of any invasion upon the rights of the Established Church, or were there any standing law in North Britain against the Liturgy of the Church of England, we would not claim your Majesty's protection, but seeing neither of these can be justly alleged, we are assured your Majesty will not suffer us to be oppressed, merely for serving God after your own way. We never doubted but, seeing we could not in conscience join with the [Presbyterian] Church which, by the Treaty of Union, is established in North Britain, it would give least offence to use that form of worship which by the same treaty is established in South Britain. But we find it far otherwise, for though the French Liturgy has been these many years publicly read in the College Hall at Edinburgh, and though the Quakers have a meeting-house near by us, and all sectaries are undisturbed in their way throughout this and your other dominions, yet no sooner does any one own himself a son of the Church of England but forthwith the cry is raised against him, and he is charged with the most horrid innovations that ever crept into the Church of God."

The author of this interesting pamphlet observes—" I could by many other instances besides this convince the true sons of the Church of England, that the prosecutions of the Episcopal clergy in Scotland were not founded upon the account of their disaffection to the civil government, as is falsely given out by their enemies, and too easily believed by their friends in England, but for their *steady adherence to Episcopacy, and their affection to the Liturgy of the Church of England.*"

It was the constant recurrence of those prosecutions which induced the Government, in 1712, to pass the well known Toleration Act, respecting the Scottish Episcopal Church. Soon after the Queen's accession, the Earl of Strathmore had proposed in the Scottish Parliament an act for the toleration of all " Protestants" in the exercise of their religious worship, with the evident purpose of obtaining relief to the Episcopal Church, of which his Lordship was a member ; but the General Assembly remonstrated against it in such a violent manner, that it was deemed prudent to abandon it for a time. By the United Parliament that relief was given to the Scottish Episcopalians which was denied to them by their own Parliament before the Union. On the 3d of March 1712, the famous Toleration Act was passed, to " prevent the disturbing those of the Episcopal communion in that part of Great Britain called Scotland, in the exercise of their religious worship, and in the use of the Liturgy of the Church of England, and for repealing the act passed in the Parliament of Scotland, entitled, An Act against irregular Baptisms and Marriages." This act declared it lawful for all of the Episcopal communion in Scotland to assemble for divine service in any town or place, except the parish churches, to be performed by clergymen ordained by a Protestant Bishop, and, if they shall think fit, to use the Liturgy of the Church of England. It is declared free and lawful for such Episcopal ministers not only to pray and preach in those congregations, but likewise to administer baptism and to celebrate marriages, without incurring any pains or penalties, notwithstanding any law or statute to the contrary. All sheriffs and magistrates were strictly enjoined to give all manner of protection to such Episcopal ministers and their congregations, and not to disturb or hinder them, under a penalty of L 100 sterling for each offence ; but every such Episcopal minister was required, before he could enjoy the benefits of this act, to produce his letters of orders before the justices of the peace at their general or quarter sessions, to be entered on record by the clerk, and to take and subscribe the Oaths of Allegiance, Assurance, and Abjuration ; and that every time he officiates in his place of worship so protected he shall pray in express words for her " most sacred Majesty Queen Anne, the most excellent Princess Sophia, and the rest of the Royal Family, under the penalty of L 20 sterling for the first offence, and for the second of forfeiting the benefit of this act, and being declared incapable of officiating as pastor of any Episcopal congregation during the space of three years ; provided always that no minister offending herein shall suffer such penalties, or either of them, unless he be prosecuted for the same within two months after the offence is committed."

In the House of Commons only seventeen opposed the passing of this act, of whom fourteen were Scottish members ; in the House of Lords it was opposed by some of the Bishops on certain points, but it was carried with a few amendments, which, however, were rejected by the Commons. The Presbyterians were then in the utmost alarm at the " setting up " of the English Liturgy in Scotland, and the Commission of the General Assembly transmitted a strong representation of what they called their " *case*" to the Queen, at the same time petitioning the House of Lords for permission to state their objections to the bill. " The stress of the argument," says Dr Sommerville, " in this representation was laid upon the several acts establishing the Presbyterian government, doctrine, and discipline,* and the confirmation given to these by the Act of Security, which was incorporated with the Treaty of Union. It complained also of the injury that would arise to the Establishment by exempting Dissenters from the censure and penalties of the ecclesiastical judicatories. It was farther urged by the counsel for the Commission, that this act would be productive of the most dangerous consequences to the ' Protestant' interest in general, because, under colour of the toleration granted to Episcopal ministers, Popish priests might perform the Romish service with impunity."†

The present state of Scotland proves the fallacy of these objections. The Toleration Act of Queen Anne, essentially an important boon to the Church at the time, is now a dead letter. It has been even stated in

---

* The acts passed in 1690, 1693, 1695, and 1702.
† History of the Reign of Queen Anne, p. 470.

the Presbyterian General Assembly that the towers of Episcopacy are rising in all directions in the large cities and towns of Scotland, and Romish priests not only perform their " service with impunity," but they publicly advertise their pontifical masses and other ceremonials undisturbed ; nay, celebrating funereal rites at the demise of the Popes. The allusion to " Popery" in the remonstrance of the Presbyterian Commission was entirely unnecessary, because the toleration was expressly limited to such persons as had received ordination from a " Protestant Bishop," and who would subscribe the Oaths of Allegiance and Abjuration. The real origin of their opposition was the fact, that by the Toleration their " judicatories" would no longer be able to harass the laity by their censures. This seems to be admitted by Wodrow, who in a letter to one of his friends thus writes :—" There are lamentable representations of the effects of Toleration in the North. The Episcopal party meet in Session and Presbytery, and license young men, and mar all discipline, by taking off persons from their appearance before [Presbyterian] ministers, and passing them at their meetings very overly."* The Presbyterian historian of the Reign of Queen Anne candidly acknowledges the unfair conduct of his party. " The legal toleration of Episcopacy in Scotland," says Dr Sommerville, " though it restrained acts of violence, rather tended to inflame than to extinguish that spirit of rancour and persecution which the Presbyterians had too long indulged against the Protestants who differed from them. The [Presbyterian] clergy, dreading the progress of Episcopacy, from the patronage of the Court, and the openness with which it was now professed in every part of the country, nourished the deluded zeal of their hearers by declaiming against the heresies of that sect, and recommending the peculiarities of their own Establishment, rather than the simple and practical truths of the gospel." If Dr Sommerville had been a member of the Episcopal Church, he could scarcely have expressed himself in stronger language.

Some curious particulars respecting the Toleration are recorded by Mr Lockhart of Carnwath, to whom the reader is referred.† The leaders of the Presbyterian Establishment were farther annoyed by a rumour

* Wodrow Correspondence, vol. i. p. 455.   † Lockhart Papers, vol. i. p. 375, 385.

that the Queen intended to bestow the deprived Bishops' rents to support such of the Episcopal clergy as conformed to the new act.* Although this was never done, it appears that in 1714 such a measure was in contemplation, which was probably frustrated by the death of the Queen. Mr Lockhart informs us, that he and his friends were assured by several influential persons connected with the House of Commons, that " the Queen was sincere and hearty in the measure, looking upon the application of these revenues to other uses, as nothing less than sacrilege." This gentleman, who had long prepared such a bill, but who had not pressed it on account of political quarrels and discussions, was with great difficulty persuaded to take it under his charge, having received a pledge that all former differences should be forgotten, and he actually moved and got leave to bring in the bill; but the Ministry were either insincere, or the former political animosities were revived, in which the Earl of Mar acted with great duplicity. "What moved his Lordship, the Lord Bolingbroke, and other gentlemen, to act after such a manner, is not easy to account for." After assigning various reasons, Mr Lockhart observes—" And as some or rather most of the Ministry were so much afraid of doing any act and deed, by which they might demonstrate their being what they at other times affected to be thought, and I believe really were, friends to the Episcopal and Jacobite interest, they had not courage and resolution to undertake, at least persevere, in prosecuting such measures; being so desirous and accustomed to keep on the mask, it was become habitual to them, and as part of their natural bodies; and thence I presume it was that some alarmed the Queen with dismal stories concerning the consequences of this bill, and others, whose office it was and interest, did not undeceive her by setting matters in a true light before her." It appears, however, that a few weeks after this affair, the Ministry, of their own accord, " moved for, brought in, and carried through the House of Commons a bill to appoint commis-

---

* " It's talked our Jurant tolerated curates at Glasgow and Edinburgh are to have some of the Bishops' stipends given them You know the Principal of Glasgow College is gone to Court, to get the College tack of the Bishop of Glasgow renewed, and expects to get his request, but I yet can scarcely believe he will succeed. Our divisions and flames in this country are no way decreasing."—Wodrow Correspondence, Letter to Mr John M'Bride, Minister at Belfast, December 4, 1713, vol. i. p. 526.

sioners to inquire into, and report to the next Session, the state of the Scots Bishops' revenues ; but when it was carried up to the House of Lords it stuck so long, that the Parliament was prorogued before it made any advance in that House, and so came to nothing."*

Mr Lockhart has preserved the short speech he delivered in the House of Commons, on the motion which he introduced of conferring all the Bishops' revenues in Scotland seized by the Crown at the Revolution :—" I stand up on behalf of a very learned and unfortunate set of men, the Episcopal clergy of Scotland. I will not take up your time by enumerating the many hardships these gentlemen have been exposed to for the sake of conscience, but I must take notice that many of them were turned out of their livings by no better authority than that of the mob, and that when the Parliament of Scotland came afterwards to abolish Episcopacy and settle Presbytery, so short a time was allowed for performing the terms on which the remaining Episcopal clergy were permitted to continue in their livings, that many were not apprised thereof till the time was elapsed, by which means, and the subsequent rigorous proceedings of the Kirk judicatories, both the laity and clergy of the Episcopal Communion were reduced to very hard circumstances. The laity had not an opportunity to worship God, and receive the holy sacraments after the manner and from the hands they approved of. The clergymen in holy orders, and dedicated to the service of God, could not approach and have access to the altar ; and, to the perpetual scandal of the reformed religion, were sent in a starving condition to beg their bread throughout the world, being destitute of all means to support their indigent numerous families, and were frequently rabbled, imprisoned, fined, or banished, for no other reason than performing divine service in a few private meeting-houses. And though I may venture to affirm that no clergymen were ever treated after so barbarous a manner, in this deplorable condition did the Scots Episcopal clergy continue, from the time that King William came over to secure our religion and liberties, till they got some relief from the Act of Toleration which passed about two years ago. This Act has been attended with none of the dreadful consequences we were threatened with by those who opposed it ; but its good effects have so well answered gentlemen's hopes and designs,

* Lockhart Papers, vol. i. p 452.

that it has given general satisfaction, and great numbers of all ranks and qualities have complied with and declared for the Liturgy of the Church of England. So that nothing seems wanting to fix and establish the same, but a fund for giving a reasonable allowance to such of the Episcopal clergy as comply with the terms and claim the benefit of the Toleration Act; and there being now no [Established] Bishops in Scotland, their revenues seem a proper fund, and much better bestowed after this manner, than in grants to the laity and Presbyterian clergy, both of which, being diametrically opposed to the intention of these pious foundations, I take both, at least without all controversy the first, to be nothing less than a sacrilegious misapplication; and the Presbyterian clergy, being still allowed to enjoy the benefices appointed by law for their predecessors of the Episcopal Communion, may be well satisfied therewith, and have no ground to repine at what is done for the other."*

The members of the Presbyterian Establishment were compelled to submit to acts passed in the Session of 1712, which more immediately affected themselves. A clause in the Act of Toleration rendered it necessary that they also should take the Oaths of Allegiance and Abjuration, which gave great offence. The famous act was passed rescinding that of 1690, and "restoring the patrons to their ancient rights of presenting ministers to the churches vacant in that part of Great Britain called Scotland." This levelled at their claims of spiritual independence, which they had often asserted in the strongest manner.

The despondency and the mutual quarrels of the Presbyterians at this period are fully doled forth in a letter from Wodrow to the well known Dr Cotton Mather in America:—" Upon the late change of Ministry we had a very unfavourable change in our Parliament men from Scotland, many of whom, with the Highflyers in England, are catching at every thing whereby they may encroach upon this [Presbyterian] church. We have a boundless toleration put upon us, to the great strengthening of the French and Jacobite interest here; and the English Service is setting up in all corners of the church; Pelagian and Popish doctrines are vented by the protected party, and shipwreck made of the faith of many. The Magistrate's concurrence in obliging obsti-

* Lockhart Papers, vol. i. p. 559, 560, 561.

nate offenders to compear before our judicatories is removed, and the most vicious persons, when prosecuted for scandals, have no more to do but tell us they are not of our communion. The truth has fallen in our streets, and lewdness abounds. The sinful and church-ruining power of patrons, in presenting pastors to vacant congregations, is restored, the consequences of which I tremble to think upon; and the people's charter Christ hath given them, to elect their own ministers, is given up. For these things (and our great guilt hath procured them), our eyes run down with tears, and the Comforter is far away—a sensible restraint upon the Holy Spirit; and no wonder; we have vexed him, and much of the spirit of the world, of fear, of wrath, and bitterness, in his room. The staff of bonds is sadly broken, and if mercy prevent not, we are like to bite and devour one another, till we are destroyed one of another. The imposing of the Oath of Abjuration upon the ministry of this Church is like to have fatal consequences. We have different views of it, and many think it looks at the sinful conditions of Government, bound as a burden upon the Protestant succession in the English Acts, referred to in the oath. And others take it to be a homologation of something this church testified against as sinful in the Union with England, such as the civil places of churchmen, and the approbation of the fixing of the English Hierarchy there. Other good and knowing persons see none of these in the oath, and have gone into it. The anger of the Lord has divided us. About a third part, or more, of us have refused the oath, and so lie at the mercy of the Government."*

As to the Toleration Act of 1712, though many of the Episcopal clergy could not conscientiously, with their political principles, enjoy its full benefits, it protected them from State prosecutions. The Government permitted them, as long as they were peaceable, to act as they pleased; the Liturgy was no longer the cause of Presbyterian agitation; and, on the whole, it may be said that the Church enjoyed peace and prosperity during the brief remainder of the reign of Queen Anne.

* Wodrow's Correspondence, vol. i. p. 390, 391, dated Jan. 23, 1713. The Presbyterians were divided by the Abjuration Oath, or rather by their views of it, into *Jurants* and *Non-Jurants*, or, as the latter are called, *Nons*, and in many cases they would not hold ministerial communion with each other. Wodrow, *ut supra*, p. 399, 400.

CHAPTER XIII.

INTERNAL AFFAIRS OF THE CHURCH—DEATH OF QUEEN ANNE—ACCESSION OF GEORGE I.—PROCEEDINGS OF THE GOVERNMENT AGAINST THE SCOTTISH EPISCOPALIANS—CONSECRATIONS OF BISHOPS—DEATH OF BISHOP ROSE.

HAVING delineated the history of the Scottish Episcopal Church to the Act of Toleration in 1712, it is necessary to glance at some internal matters. The due succession of the Bishops had been preserved, and the adoption of the English Liturgy was of the utmost advantage in promoting the " unity of spirit and bond of peace " in the celebration of divine service. After the death of Bishop Sage in 1711, the Hon. and Rev. Archibald Campbell was consecrated at Dundee, on the 25th of August 1711, by Bishop Rose, Bishop Douglas, and Bishop Falconer. This gentleman was the second son of Lord Neil Campbell by his first wife, Lady Vere Ker, third daughter of William third Earl of Lothian. Lord Neil was the second son of Archibald eighth Earl and first Marquis of Argyll, beheaded at the Cross of Edinburgh for high treason on the 27th of May 1661, and of his Countess, Lady Margaret Douglas, second daughter of William second Earl of Morton, whose elder son was Archibald ninth Earl of Argyll, the uncle of Bishop Campbell. Some notices are preserved of the Bishop's early life. He engaged in the rebellion attempted by his uncle and the Duke of Monmouth in 1685, so fatal to both of them, and he escaped to Surinam to elude the vengeance of the Government. His elder brother, the Hon. Charles Campbell, who was also implicated in that invasion, surrendered himself to the Earl of Dunbarton, was tried before the High Court of Justiciary at Edinburgh, and condemned on his own confession, but his sentence of death was commuted into banishment, which was rescinded at the Revolution. We are told that Bishop Campbell "had been brought up a violent Whig," of which there is no doubt when his near relationship to the Noble Family of Argyll is taken into account; but, says Dr Samuel Johnson, "he afterwards kept better company, and became a Tory." When he returned from Surinam, where he resided a considerable time, he became zealous for Episcopacy and for monarchy; and at the Revolution not only adhered to the ejected Church, but refused to communicate in the Church of England, or to be present in any place of divine worship in which King William's name was mentioned. "He was, I believe," continues Dr Johnson, "more than once apprehended in the reign of King William, and once at the accession of George I. He was the familiar friend of Hickes and Nelson. He was released from prison on application to Lord Townshend, and he always spoke with respect of his Lordship, saying—'Though a Whig, he had humanity.'"

In 1712 the Episcopal College consisted of Bishops Rose, Douglas, Fullarton, Falconer, Christie, and Campbell, Bishop Rose acting as Primus Bishop Campbell after his consecration continued to reside chiefly in London, where he was of great service to the Church in her state of depression and poverty. At this period the Scottish Episcopal clergy were in the utmost pecuniary distress, and public collections were made for them, the distribution of which was entrusted to a Committee in Edinburgh under Bishop Rose. As it is usually impossible in such cases to satisfy every individual, the Rev. George Barclay, minister of a congregation in Skinners' Close, Edinburgh, publicly accused the Committee of partiality in the distribution of the money in a journal called the *Flying Post*. This elicited a printed declaration, signed by Bishop Rose, four of the clergy, and eight of the most influential citizens, among whom is Sir Robert Sibbald, M.D, denying the charge in the strongest manner. A pamphlet also appeared on the subject, entitled, " A Full Vindication of the Lord Bishop of Edinburgh, and the other Administrators of the Charities, from the Calumnious and False Aspersions of Mr George Barclay, in his Defamatory Libel published in the *Flying Post*, No. 3181, with an inhuman as well as unchristian Design to hinder the Charity of good Christians towards the Relief of the suffering Episcopal Clergy in Scotland." *

In 1713, the Rev. Robert Calder, one of the reputed compilers of the " Scotch Presbyterian Eloquence," published a learned and curious periodical work at Edinburgh, in folio, by the title of " Miscellany Numbers relating to the Controversies about the Book of Common Prayer, Episcopal Government, the Power of the Church in ordaining Rites and Ceremonies, &c., defended by Scripture, Reason, Antiquity, and the Sentiments of the most learned Reformers, particularly Mr John Calvin." Thirty of those " Miscellany Numbers" successively appeared. Mr Calder, who officiated to a congregation in Toddrick's Wynd, High Street, Edinburgh, had involved himself in a polemical controversy with Mr John Anderson, minister of Dunbarton, afterwards of Glasgow, whom he sarcastically designates " Presbyterian holder-forth" there. Mr Anderson had been preceptor to the celebrated John Duke of Argyll and Greenwich, and was grandfather of John Anderson, F.R.S, Professor of Natural Philosophy in the University of Glasgow, the founder of the Andersonian Institution, sometimes dignified with the title of *University*, in that city. In 1710, some time after his settlement as incumbent of Dunbarton, Mr Anderson published a " Dialogue between a Curate and a Countryman concerning the English Service, or Common Prayer Book of England;" and in the following year appeared a " Second Letter." Mr Calder, who lost no opportunity of replying to the adversaries of his own Church, answered these productions in his " Number Miscellanies," and was assailed by Mr Anderson in a pamphlet, entitled, " Curate Calder Whipt." Much angry and irritating language passed between them. The last of Mr Calder's " Miscellany Numbers" is designated " The Nail struck to the Head, or an Indictment drawn up against Mr John Anderson, the Presbyterian Incumbent of Dunbarton, before all the Colleges in Britain and Ireland, or any other inferior Literary Courts in city or country, and that before persons of knowledge, conscience, and candour, of whatsoever principle or party they are, by Mr Robert Calder, Minister of the Gospel, who is acting and suffering for the Book of Common Prayer in Scotland."

* London, printed and sold by G. Strachan, at the Golden Ball, over against the Royal Exchange in Cornhill. This pamphlet is preserved in a curious folio volume, marked M. 4, 4, in the Advocates' Library, Edinburgh.

So bitter was the acrimony between Mr Calder and Mr Anderson, and so irritating and personal their language, that the following eccentric advertisement appeared from the former, which is a curious specimen of the *odium theologicum* :—" These are to give notice, to all men of candour and knowledge, of any party or persuasion, who love the truth, and hate impudent liars, and who allow that all public impostors and impudent cheats should be exposed to the world, and be chastised with all the severities that fraudulent villains deserve, that Mr Robert Calder, minister of the gospel, for the present at Edinburgh, has printed a sheet of paper against Mr John Anderson, the Presbyterian incumbent at Dunbarton, who makes it his business, by lying, slandering, and writing pamphlets, to discredit the Church of England, its clergy, and Book of Common Prayer, and also the Liturgical clergy of Scotland—that the said Mr Calder demonstrates, from the pamphlets written by him and Mr Anderson, that the said Mr Anderson is one of the grossest liars that ever put pen to paper. And, for the probation thereof, Mr Calder invites any who please in the city of Edinburgh to his meeting-house in Toddrick's Wynd, on Wednesdays and Fridays, for three weeks after the date hereof, betwixt eleven and twelve in the morning, and two and three in the afternoon, that they may see with their eyes, and hear with their ears, Mr Calder's indictment against Mr Anderson proven from the books cited in the libel, which, when proved, is to be sent to all the Universities in the three kingdoms, whence we are to expect the censure that such a deceiver deserves."

The violence of the above language is certainly inexcusable, and Mr Calder thought it necessary to apologize in the Preface to his " Miscellany Numbers" in the following manner :—" I am blamed by some of my own friends for using invectives against my adversary, but when they read his answers, and found that there were not six lines in nine sheets of paper without either railing, scolding, lying, or pedantry, they told me he deserved ten times more ; but that satire, personal reflection, or uncharitable truths should not proceed to drop from the pen of an Episcopal minister, because that was like the party we condemn ourselves. I took very well with the reproof, and therefore in my last Number I used not one harsh expression, but an advertisement to all parties to come to my meeting-house, that I might let men see with their eyes, from the books which we both mentioned, how palpably my adversary falsified in the chief points debated between us. I am ready to renew the same challenge in any place within the city of Edinburgh. I did this to the conviction of all that came to hear me, but none of my antagonist's party came to the place. I refer it to the Universities, and if they do not find him an impudent liar, I shall undergo what penance they please to impose upon me."

About this time the incumbent of Dunbarton involved himself in a controversy with another individual. A certain Mr Thomas Rhind, who, it appears, had been a Presbyterian minister, conscientiously perceived it his duty to separate " from the Presbyterian party, and to embrace the communion of the Church." This gentleman's conduct is the more remarkable, because at that period no earthly inducements could tempt any man to come over to the "suffering Church," as Mr Rhind most truly calls it, but conviction and conscience. He published a work explanatory of his conduct, entitled, "An Apology for Mr Thomas Rhind, or an Account of the Manner how, and the Reasons for which, he separated from the Presbyterian Party, and embraced the Communion of the Church."* This work was, as it really is, considered so learned, so conclusive, and so admirably written, that the Presbyterians saw that it would materially injure them if left unanswered. Accordingly, Mr Anderson appeared as the champion of his party in a volume entitled, "A Defence of the Church Government, Faith, Worship, and Spirit of the Presbyterians," the work by which he is best known, in answer to a book entitled, "An Apology for Mr Thomas Rhind," Glasgow, 1714, in 4to, dedicated to Archibald Earl of Islay. This work has been occasionally reprinted. The reply is completely on the defensive, and though it displays some learning, it merely brings forward various propositions and assertions which have been repeatedly overturned and refuted. Mr Rhind's work, on the other hand, extorted this opinion of it even from his opponent :—" I hate to grudge," says Mr Anderson in his Preface, " even an adversary his due. I frankly own Mr Rhind has done as well as the subject was capable of. I own his book is, of its bulk, the most comprehensive in its subject I have seen. Some authors have attacked us upon the head of *government*, some upon our *doctrine*, some upon our *worship*, and some, too, though those not always excessively

---

* Printed at Edinburgh, 8vo. 1712.

qualified either morally or intellectually for such an undertaking, upon our *spirit* and *practice*. But Mr Rhind has widened the compass, and taken all four within his circle, hinting at every thing of a general nature that has been wont to be objected to us; and all this in so very pointed a style, that, had his probation been equal, there had been an end of the matter, and the world had heard its last of Presbytery for ever." Mr Anderson, like his party in general, was determined not to be convinced, and Mr Rhind's admirable work remains at the present time unanswered.

But other matters more important than private controversies demand consideration. Queen Anne died on the 1st of August 1714, and on the same day the Elector of Hanover was proclaimed as George I. in the order of succession as the nearest Protestant heir to the throne of Great Britain. A change of Ministry was the consequence, and a proclamation was issued for putting the laws in force against all reputedly disaffected persons. The hopes of the Jacobites, and among these of the great body of the Scottish Episcopalians, were grievously disappointed at the sudden death of the Queen, and the accession of a prince whom they considered an usurper The precautionary measures which the new Government deemed it necessary to adopt excited very general disgust, and in 1715 the well known Enterprise was attempted by the Earl of Mar in favour of the Chevalier St George, as the son of James II. was called, though he was usually styled James VIII. of Scotland by his numerous adherents

The established Presbyterians hailed the accession of George I., and transmitted a congratulatory address to the new sovereign, but the Episcopal clergy and laity viewed the accession of the House of Hanover in silence and sorrow, though not in despair. The battle of Sheriffmuir, near Dunblane, and the affair of Preston in England, completely decided the fate of the Enterprise. The suppression of the Enterprise was followed by several confiscations, attainders, and executions, and the Chevalier, who had arrived in Scotland when it was too late, was compelled to betake himself to his exile, without having in the slightest degree done any service to his cause.

It is well known that the Scottish Episcopal clergy were all in favour of a prince, for attachment to whose family the Church had severely suffered, and some of them were in the army of the Adventurers. On

Sunday the 22d of October, the Rev. Mr Irvine, afterwards one of the Scottish Bishops, as narrated in the sequel, who acted as chaplain to the Earl of Carnwath, officiated in the parish church of Kelso to the division of the Adventurers under the Viscount of Kenmure, who were advancing into England to effect a junction with the English Jacobites. The discourse abounded with serious exhortations to the hearers, who were composed of Episcopalians, Roman Catholics, and even Presbyterians, to be resolute in the cause of their legitimate sovereign ; and it is said that the reverend gentleman, according to his own statement, had preached the same sermon nearly thirty years before to the Viscount of Dundee and his army in the Highlands. "It was remarked by a person present," says Mr Chambers, "that the Highlanders on this occasion behaved with the utmost decency while in church, making the responses according to the rubric with a degree of readiness, and also of solemn feeling, which might have ashamed many who pretended to higher intelligence and breeding." But the Nonjuring clergy who chose to interest themselves personally in the Enterprise attended the chief division of the Adventurers under the Earl of Mar, who, it is said, usually selected the texts of Scripture from which they preached to their hearers.*

The proceedings of the Government against the Episcopal clergy were vigorous, though these can hardly be called severe. On the 12th of May 1716, King George I. wrote a letter to the Lords of Justiciary in Scotland, which is countersigned by Mr Secretary Stanhope, stating that His Majesty understood there were meeting-houses in Edinburgh, and other places in Scotland, in which divine service was performed without praying for the King and Royal Family, and requiring their Lordships " to give strict orders for shutting up all such meeting-houses,' and to proceed against offenders in time coming. Their Lordships returned an answer to Mr Secretary Stanhope, stating that they would willingly proceed against such offenders, but as to shutting up the meeting-houses, they said—"We are humbly of opinion that our forms do not allow such summary procedure till after trial and conviction by the due course of law." It is said that those judges suspected they were only authorized to exact the penalties prescribed by law, but not to shut up

* History of the Rebellion in 1715, p. 233, 248, 249.

the meeting-houses. At the same time their Lordships enjoined the Crown lawyers to prepare indictments against all Episcopal ministers guilty of this alleged offence.

In consequence of this the Rev. Daniel Taylor and twenty-four other Episcopal clergymen in Edinburgh, the Rev. Arthur Millar, presbyter in Leith, the Rev. Robert Colt, and the Rev. James Hunter, Musselburgh, were indicted for preaching to Episcopal congregations without letters of orders from a Protestant Bishop, according to the statute of the 10th of Queen Anne in 1712, and for not praying for King George by name. Defences were prepared, which were overruled, and most of the accused clergymen, to save trouble to the Court, confessed both charges. The whole of them, except one, who had produced letters of orders from an *exauctorated* Scottish Bishop, were prohibited from officiating until they exhibited their letters of orders in terms of the act. Twenty-one of the accused clergymen were fined L.20 sterling each, one half to the informer, and the other half to the poor of the parish; but as no informer applied, the Lord Advocate about six months after prayed the Court for warrant of L.10 against each of them, *to be paid to his Lordship as informer.* Their Lordships had by their sentence commanded all sheriffs and magistrates of burghs to prevent those clergymen from officiating within their jurisdictions, but it appears that the defenders soon produced letters of orders, which were registered in terms of the act. The magistrates of Edinburgh were now at a loss as to the manner in which they ought to proceed, more especially as it had been intimated to them by the Lord Advocate from a very high quarter, that they were considered remiss in executing the sentence of the Justiciary judges, and they now requested the directions of the Court. "Their Lordships," says Arnot, "returned an answer to the petition of the magistrates, dark and mysterious as the Sybilline oracles, importing that the process was ended, and that they could not alter their own sentence.— I apprehend that the Lords of Justiciary and magistrates of Edinburgh had reciprocally endeavoured to devolve on each other the *odium of the people* for executing the sentence, or the *indignation of the prince* for not executing it. It appears that the shutting up of the meeting-houses was by no means rigorously enforced, for I find several of those very clergymen within a few months again convicted for the same offence.

Indeed, the criminal records for some years after this are in a manner engrossed with prosecutions against Episcopal Nonjurors."*

After the suppression of the Enterprise of 1715, a strict inquiry was instituted respecting the religious condition of several districts by the Presbyterian Establishment. This was altogether uncalled for on their part, and their reports were drawn up with the evident intention of throwing odium on the Scottish Episcopalians, and exciting the Government against them. In the " Report from the Commissioners appointed to inquire of the Estates of certain Traitors, &c. in that part of Great Britain called Scotland," printed at Edinburgh in 1717, there are various instances of this officiousness. One may be cited as a sample of the whole. The Moderator of the Presbytery of Brechin is pleased to say, that " the people of this corner" have been " hitherto diverted from the principles of loyalty by Jacobite factors, *curates*, and others."

No alteration appears to have been made in the law against the Scottish Episcopal Church till 1719, when the Government became alarmed at the rumour of, or attempt at, another insurrection in behalf of the Chevalier. In April 1719, an act was passed in the United Parliament " for making more effectual the laws appointing the oaths for the security of the Government to be taken by ministers of churches and meeting-houses in Scotland " This act rendered every Episcopal clergyman liable to six months' imprisonment, during which period his meeting-house was to be shut up, if he performed divine service without having taken the oaths required by the Toleration Act of Queen Anne ; and every house in which nine or more persons were assembled, exclusive of the family, at divine service, was declared to be a meeting-house within the meaning of the Act.

This was a severe law, and there can be as little doubt of the intention as of the quarter in which it originated. Several prosecutions followed, but the act does not appear to have been rigorously enforced. Nor could the previous government proceedings against the Clergy make the Bishops regardless of the continuance of their own order, and consequently of the existence of the Church. The consecration of the Hon. and Rev. Archibald Campbell, in 1711, is already mentioned, and in 1712 the Rev. James Gadderar, who had been ejected from his

* A collection of Celebrated Criminal Trials in Scotland, by Hugo Arnot, Esq. Advocate, 4to, p. 343-346.

parish of Kilmaurs, in Ayrshire, in 1688, was consecrated at London by Bishops Campbell, Falconer, and Hickes, the last named Bishop having been the celebrated and learned Dean of Worcester. We are told "that this step, apparently somewhat out of the usual course, was taken not only with the consent of Bishop Rose, but even at his express desire, and was consequently approved by all his brethren in Scotland "* Bishop Gadderar, however, like his friend Bishop Campbell, resided chiefly in London till the year 1724, and we must therefore direct our attention to the actual state of the Episcopate in Scotland. At the death of Bishop Christie, in 1718, there were only three Prelates in Scotland—Bishop Rose, and Bishops Fullarton and Falconer. The Bishop of Edinburgh saw the necessity of immediately strengthening the succession, while there was a sufficient number of Bishops to constitute the consecrations regular and canonical. On the 22d of October 1718, the Rev. Arthur Millar, formerly minister of Inveresk in the county of Edinburgh, mentioned among those prosecuted in 1716 for not praying for the King, and the Rev. William Irvine, formerly minister of Kirkmichael in Ayrshire, were consecrated at Edinburgh by Bishop Rose and the two Bishops.

This was the last important service rendered to the Church by the venerable Bishop Rose of Edinburgh. This sole survivor of his brethren ejected at the Revolution—this primitive and upright Prelate, who had lived in strange, exciting, and eventful times, and had presided over the Church with all dignity, was soon afterwards gathered to his fathers. He died, beloved and lamented, at the residence of his sister in the Canongate, Edinburgh, in the 74th year of his age, on the 20th of March 1720. Bishop Rose's own house was also in the Canongate, at that time inhabited by many families of rank. The house in which he died is still pointed out. He was interred within the little church of Restalrig, near the city, but no stone intimates the hallowed spot where he was deposited. The edifice was then roofless, having been dilapidated by order of the General Assembly, after the Reformation, as a "monument of idolatry," but restored as a Presbyterian place of worship since 1836. In the cemetery surrounding the church of Restalrig many members of the Scottish Episcopal Church were interred at their own dying re-

* Bishop Russell's edition of Keith's Catalogue, p. 531.

quest during the eighteenth century. Here the last solemnities of religion were performed without molestation, threats of persecution, or the indecent interruptions of idle and ignorant persons attracted by curiosity as spectators.

Bishop Keith says of Bishop Rose—" He was a sweet-natured man, and of venerable aspect." His death was severely felt by the Church, although it was a great consolation that he was spared to a good old age. Mr Lockhart of Carnwath mentions his loss as irreparable. In a letter to the Chevalier, or the " King," as he terms him, he says—" You are not a stranger to the great honour and reputation the Scots Episcopal clergy have justly gained by their unshaken constancy and uninterrupted unity, from the commencement of their misfortunes to this time, and that the same may be in a great measure imputed to the prudent conduct of the late Bishop of Edinburgh." Mr Skinner describes him as "a man of whom it was acknowledged by all who knew him, that ' for all the virtues which adorn the gentleman or the scholar, the Christian or the Bishop, he was scarcely equalled, and could not be excelled.' What a valuable pilot he was, while he steered the helm of our tossed vessel, was but too sensibly known by some unhappy divisions which followed soon after his decease."

CHAPTER XIV.

DISSENSIONS IN THE SCOTTISH EPISCOPAL CHURCH—THE USAGES—BISHOP GADDERAR OF ABERDEEN—LETTERS TO AND FROM THE CHEVALIER—THE COLLEGE PARTY—NEW CONSECRATIONS—DEATH OF BISHOP FULLARTON.

The presbyters elevated to the Episcopate during the life of Bishop Rose were consecrated solely for the purpose of preserving the succession. No *portio gregis* was assigned to them, and we have seen that it was expressly stipulated at the consecration of Bishops Sage and Fullarton, that they were to exercise no diocesan jurisdiction while the ejected Bishops were alive. The authority of Dr Rose, who as Bishop of Edinburgh was vicar-general of the Archbishop of St Andrews during the establishment of the Church, was acknowledged by the clergy of that metropolitan province after the death of the Primate Ross; but, as the hope of the restoration of the exiled royal family was still fondly indulged, the Bishop was probably unwilling to interfere with what he might consider unwarrantable in his peculiar circumstances. The same principles seem to have actuated the deprived Bishops in England commonly called the Nonjurors, who refrained from nominating those whom they consecrated to any of the regular Sees, but contented themselves with their own ecclesiastical arrangements.

On the 22d of March 1720, after the remains of Bishop Rose had been deposited in the little church of Restalrig, a meeting of all the Episcopal clergy of Edinburgh and the vicinity was held in the afternoon, to deliberate on the peculiar circumstances of the Church. On this occasion one of the clergy proposed that they should immediately acknowledge Bishops Fullarton, Falconer, Millar, and Irvine, as the Episcopal

College, to whom as such canonical obedience was due. In this suggestion evident injustice was done to Bishops Campbell and Gadderar, who, though then residing in London, had an equal right to be considered members of that College, yet they were not even mentioned. The proposal was to the effect that instead of diocesan jurisdiction—the practice of the Church Catholic in the primitive ages—the Scottish Episcopal Church should be governed by a College of Bishops in common, much in the same manner as the Presbyterians manage their affairs on a more extensive scale in their Presbyteries, Synods, and General Assemblies.

This extraordinary proposal found adherents, but before the matter was discussed, it was urged by some of the clergy present, that though they knew that the four right reverend persons named were duly invested with episcopal authority, it was necessary that their letters of consecration should be exhibited before they could be acknowledged as Bishops. This was readily conceded by those who were in favour of the College scheme, and they promised that when Bishop Fullarton, who happened to be then in the country, returned to Edinburgh, the instruments of the respective consecrations would be produced to the clergy. Bishop Fullarton came to Edinburgh on the 28th of March, and the clergy, having obtained the satisfaction they required, immediately "honoured Mr John Fullarton, Mr John Falconer, Mr Arthur Millar, and Mr William Irvine, as Bishops of this Church." The four Bishops were present, and Bishop Falconer intimated that "though he and his brethren were Bishops intended for preserving the episcopal succession in this Church, yet they did not pretend to have jurisdiction over any particular place or district." He advised the presbyters to elect a proper diocesan to exercise jurisdiction over them, and withdrew from the meeting with the other Bishops.

The presbyters adjourned to the following day, when, after electing a chairman, the question was immediately discussed—"Whether they had any right or authority to elect a Bishop to reside and exercise episcopal functions in Edinburgh?" It was unanimously agreed that they had this right, and they expressed themselves gratified with the acknowledgment of the Bishops to that effect on the previous day. A keen debate next ensued, whether the nomination of the Diocesan should be referred to the Bishops. No allusion, however, was made to Bishops Campbell and Gadderar, who were alleged to be zealous advovocates of certain "Usages," to which the majority of the presbyters in Edinburgh were supposed to be hostile. It appears that the omission of those two Bishops was intentional, and that the hostile opinions held on the subject of these *Usages*, which are subsequently noticed, originated the proposal to refer the nomination of the Diocesan to the four Bishops; but it was negatived by a *single vote*, or *two votes*. The presbyters then proceeded with the election, and Bishop Fullarton was chosen to succeed Bishop Rose, and to act as *Primus*, or presiding Bishop, in ecclesiastical Synods, with the limitation that he should not lay claim to those vicarious powers which his predecessor had exercised as vicar-general in the Province of St Andrews.

The account given by Mr Lockhart of Carnwath of this transaction is worthy of notice. " It being absolutely necessary that some one of the Bishops should be appointed to reside at Edinburgh, and take the chief government of the Church upon him, there was some appearance of factions and divisions amongst the Episcopal clergy on this head, but Mr Paterson and I kept close in town with them, and were at much pains to prevail with them to take no resolutions till the College of Bishops was convened. And as it was of great importance that one of a good character was made choice of for this charge, we earnestly recommended Bishop Fullarton, as he was qualified for the trust, and in some respects entitled to it, being the senior Bishop of those now alive. In a short time the Bishops met, and, with the concurrence of the presbyters of that diocese, made choice of him to be Bishop of Edinburgh; and to encourage him the more cheerfully to undertake it, I engaged to get a hundred pounds sterling per annum settled upon him by a certain number of well-disposed persons, to enable him to bear the charge of living at Edinburgh, which was accordingly performed."

Mr Lockhart errs in stating that the Bishops elected Bishop Fullarton with the "concurrence of the presbyters." The procedure was the very reverse, for the presbyters elected, and the Bishops concurred. It appears that the Chevalier St George was duly informed of the proceedings of the Episcopal clergy by his "Trustees," and his concurrence was considered necessary. Our cavalier statesman always terms him *King* in his narrative, and farther writes :—" Though the King should have been acquainted with this choice, *and his approbation obtained*, yet, because it was not advisable to delay it, lest the clergy had split and divided, it was thought sufficient that his Trustees here did approve of it. However, it was proper to communicate this step to the King, and to desire he would write a letter to the clergy, recommending unity among themselves and obedience to their superiors, particularly to Bishop Fullarton, who was appointed Primus of the College of Bishops, as well as Bishop of Edinburgh."

Such a letter was written to the Chevalier, dated 25th April 1720, and is printed in the " Lockhart Papers." It is of considerable length, and is chiefly remarkable for a severe attack on Bishop Campbell. After requesting the Chevalier to write the proposed letter in favour of Bishop Fullarton to the clergy, Mr Lockhart says—" If it is approved by you, you will be pleased to transmit such a letter to me as soon as possible, lest difficulties arise and inconveniences happen, especially seeing we hear that Mr Archibald Campbell (who, though adorned with *none* of the qualifications requisite in a Bishop, and remarkable for some things inconsistent with the character of a gentleman, was most imprudently consecrated some years ago) is coming here from London, with a view of forming a party, and propagating those doctrines which were most unreasonably broached some few years ago in England."—He farther informs the Chevalier—" Bishop Fullarton is come to town [Edinburgh], and we think it will be necessary that henceforwards he reside constantly there, but as it is unreasonable he should be at so great a charge in serving the public, though he has a handsome little estate of his own, a certain number of people have resolved to contribute annually such a sum as will sufficiently enable him to support his character, and make up the odds of his living retiredly at home and publicly in Edinburgh."

The cause of the hostility to Bishop Campbell is subsequently noticed. The Chevalier wrote the desired letter to Bishop Fullarton, dated Albano, June 12, 1720, and he concludes by informing the Bishop—" You will sufficiently find by this the confidence and esteem I have for you. I do not fear being disappointed, and all I have in particular to recommend to you is the preaching of union and charity both to clergy and laity, since it is that alone which can, with God's blessing, make us see an end of our misfortunes; both while these last, and after it may please God to put a period to them, the welfare of the Scots clergy I shall ever have at heart, as I shall at all times be desirous of showing you the deep sense

I have of your personal merit, and attachment to me and my just cause."*

It is not stated what effect this letter had upon the clergy, but we find the Bishops, a short time after the election of Bishop Fullarton as Primus, transmitting an address to the Chevalier, giving him an account of their whole proceedings. The Chevalier returned a complimentary answer, dated Rome, July 2, 1720, in which he says—"It is a satisfaction to us to know that the Bishops who survived the unhappy Revolution in our kingdoms have promoted persons of your character to their order; and since the circumstances of past times have not permitted certain forms to be observed, we think it proper hereby to approve of your promotion, in so far as our authority is necessary to it by the laws and constitution of that our ancient kingdom; but as to such future promotions, as may be thought necessary for the preservation of your order, we think it equally for our service and that of your Church, that, notwithstanding our present distance from you, you should propose to us such persons as you may think most worthy to be raised to that dignity. We shall, you may be assured, have all possible regard for your opinion in such cases, and ever be willing to give you marks of our favour and protection, and of our particular esteem for your persons."†

It appears from these transactions that the Scottish Episcopalians, like the English Nonjurors, and the Roman Catholic Jacobites, seriously indulged the vain hope of the restoration of the exiled prince, and his possession of the throne of his ancestors. Nor was this at all so improbable an event as at this distance of time the reader may imagine. George I. was very unpopular with the nation at large; his undue and imprudent partiality for his German dominions, and his predilection for his German followers, irritated and disgusted many of his subjects who were keen supporters of the House of Hanover; the parties who adhered to the exiled dynasty were numerous, powerful, and men of high rank; a host of the peasantry, and especially the Highland clans, were attached to the House of Stuart from ancient associations; and the claims of the Chevalier were maintained by some of the most powerful continental sovereigns. "I have it farther to remark," says Wodrow, under date 1727, "that the Jacobites reckon upon the bulk of our nobility and

* Lockhart Papers, vol. ii. p. 35, 39. † Ibid p. 42

gentry as gained to their interest, and the truth is, the generality of our nobility and gentry give too much occasion to them to reckon upon them; and even in the West of Scotland how very few have we that in any choak can be trusted to?"* The Chevalier's policy, therefore, in preserving his influence in the Scottish Episcopal Church was obvious. By maintaining this connection he could always command the influence of a numerous body of clergy and laity, whom persecution had attached more strongly to his interest.

But although the Chevalier had intimated his desire that the names of all persons proposed to be consecrated should be submitted to him for his consent and approval, he found that the Bishops and clergy were not disposed to render implicit obedience to his will. Some time during this year, 1720, he had named the Rev. David Freebairn to be consecrated, and this nomination they were disposed to resist. " I found," says Mr Lockhart, " this step was not agreeable to and approved by the clergy, both on account of the person named and the manner of doing it—that though he (Mr Freebairn) was not under any bad character, they did not think him adorned with those qualifications of learning, good sense, and the like, so necessary in one of that station, and that he was in no reputation among his brethren or the laity of his communion— that as the King at the distance he was, and from the little knowledge and experience he had of private men's character and circumstances, could not judge thoroughly, so as to be sure of making a right choice, it was hoped that before he proceeded to a nomination he would have consulted the Bishops—that as this method would prevent his making a bad choice, it would endear him much to the clergy, and be attended with this further benefit, that it would prevent his being solicited, and obliged, perhaps, to give denials; for were it known that he made no such promotions but by the advice and approbation of the Bishops, people would apply to them before they presumed to teaze him with solicitations."† It is surprising, when we consider the times, and the peculiar circumstances of the Church, what could be the objects which those Presbyters had in view who longed so earnestly for the episcopate, as this important passage intimates. Nothing short of a positive belief of the

* Wodrow's Analecta, MS., Advocates' Library.
† Lockhart Paper's, vol ii. p 49, 50.

restoration of the exiled dynasty could have induced men to solicit the unfortunate Chevalier for the only influence he had it in his power to exercise.

But although Bishop Fullarton was elected to the diocesan jurisdiction of Edinburgh, the idea of the government of the Church by the College of Bishops, instead of Diocesans, was not abandoned. On the contrary, it was attempted by a party, and it was sanctioned by the Chevalier and some of his advisers, which at once discloses to us Mr Lockhart's severe attacks on Bishop Campbell, and afterwards on Bishop Gadderar, both of whom were supporters of diocesan government as the only true and primitive practice, according to the eighth canon of the first Council of Nice. There can be little doubt that the Bishops who were in favour of diocesan government were as strongly attached to the cause of the Chevalier as the College party, but they considered that in their then circumstances, as entirely unconnected with the State, it was the inherent right of the clergy to elect their diocesans to whom they were to render canonical obedience; and also that the idea of a Church governed by such a College, the members of which might be increased by intrigues or dissensions, was not only preposterous, but might be attended with the most disastrous consequences.

Before narrating the proceedings of the *College Party*, it is necessary to attend to the affairs of the Church after the election of Bishop Fullarton. About the same time, in 1720, Bishop Falconer received a letter from a great body of the Episcopal clergy in the counties of Forfar and Kincardine, and also from the Presbyters of St Andrews in the county of Fife, requesting him to become their diocesan, and promising "to acknowledge him as their proper Bishop, and to pay all due and canonical obedience to him as such." This invitation he willingly accepted, with the approbation of the other Bishops, though Bishop Irvine is thought to have dissented; and he continued to exercise diocesan jurisdiction over them till his death, which took place on the 6th of July 1723, to the regret of all who knew him, and to the great loss of the Church.

The clergy of Aberdeen, in imitation of their brethren in other districts, elected Bishop Campbell, on the 10th of May 1721, to be their diocesan. As this Bishop does not appear to have resided at Aberdeen, but continued in London, and as he soon resigned in consequence of his views respecting the "*Usages*" not being in accordance with those of the clergy, it is necessary to take a brief glance at the cause of the differences of opinion on points comparatively unimportant.

At the death of the celebrated Dr Hickes, already mentioned as one of the Bishops of the English Nonjuring Church, a controversy arose about the nature of the Eucharist, and the manner in which it ought to be administered, which found its way into Scotland. The most eminent and learned divines of the Church of England since the Reformation considered the Holy Communion as a commemorative sacrifice; others maintained that it was a feast on the one sacrifice of Christ once offered by himself for the sins of the whole world; others adopted that view set forth by Bishop Hoadley, which is the opinion of the Presbyterians in Scotland, and of the Dissenters generally both in that country and in England, that the Lord's Supper is a mere commemoration of our Saviour's death—or simply a rite, without any particular benefits resulting from it to the devout participator.

It would be out of place in the present work to enter into any discussion on these three different views of this important subject, and as the controversy has been long forgotten, it would be perhaps imprudent to revive it, or to attempt any analysis of the arguments urged by the several disputants. Suffice it to say, that the *Usages* appear to have been limited to four—1. Mixing water with the wine. 2. Commemorating the faithful departed in the Communion Office. 3. Consecrating the elements by an express invocation. 4. Using the oblatory prayer before administering, as in the Office of the Holy Communion in the Scottish Liturgy. These were the *Usages* for which many of the ejected clergy of the Church of England, who became connected with the Nonjuring Church, resolutely contended as ancient and primitive, and as having been acknowledged at the commencement of the Reformation. They farther argued that they were now at liberty to observe these "Usages," because they were no longer connected with the Church of England as by law established, and therefore not trammelled by parliamentary enactments in the discharge of their ministerial functions. The controversy was carried on among the English Nonjurors with considerable heat of argument, and at the death of Bishop Hickes in 1715, the *Usagers* were headed by the celebrated and learned Bishop Collier, supported by Dr Brett; while their opponents, who contended for the Office as it is in the Book of Common Prayer, were led by Bishop Spincks, formerly one of the Prebendaries of Sarum, and Rector of St Martin's in that diocese. It was agreed on both sides to consult the Scottish Bishops, and to refer the controversy solely to their decision. Accordingly, a clergyman named Peck was sent by the *Usagers* into Scotland in 1718, and applied to Bishops Rose and Falconer for a synodical declaration, which those Bishops refused. At the same time they received letters from Bishop Spincks, urging them to decide in favour of his party—a request which they also declined, stating, however, that they were willing to act as friendly mediators, recommending peace and forbearance until the people were satisfied and their minds prepared for the reception of the Usages, whatever these might be, of the Primitive Church. Bishops Rose and Falconer requested Dr Rattray of Craighall to draw up proposals of accommodation for reconciling these differences, which he did in a paper characterized by Bishop Rose of Edinburgh as "written with much judgment, full of Christian temper, and making much for peace;" but although it offended neither party, it met with the common fate of all such attempts to reconcile conflicting opponents.

In a letter to Bishop Rose, written on the occasion of Mr Peck's arrival on his mission, Bishop Falconer thus gives his deliberate opinion on the matter. It is dated May 15, 1718 :—"I have reason to believe that these primitive usages, the restoring of which is so much laboured by these pious and learned persons, were indeed apostolical, they being delivered to us by men who contended for the faith once delivered to the saints, some of whom sealed that faith with their blood, who lived near the fountain head, who under God were the conveyancers of the Holy Scriptures to posterity, and who themselves also were endued with *charismata*. These qualifications state them most veracious and unexceptionable witnesses; and to think otherwise is in my opinion to sap the foundations, even to shake the credulity of the blissful Scriptures, and of the Church, the ground and pillar of the truth. Hence it will follow that the restoration of them is most desirable, the rather that Catholic Unity, which to preserve when subsisting, and to restore when broken, is the indispensable duty of every Christian, chiefly of the governors of the Church, cannot be established but on this primitive footing." On the 22d of May, Bishop Rose writes to Bishop Falconer, probably in answer to the above letter—" As for my own part, seeing so much stress is laid upon these Usages, I am very desirous of farther information, being resolved, God willing, if I find them strictly necessary, to embrace them with all the disadvantages that may attend them. If only lawful, some way useful or desirable, prudence in such case, and in such cases only, ought to be consulted."

It was not till after the death of Bishop Rose that the controversy about the Usages divided the Scottish Episcopal Church. Bishop Falconer, it is evident, was in their favour, as were also Bishops Campbell and Gadderar, whose residence in England had enabled them to form an intimacy with Bishops Hickes and Collier, and who had been induced from conviction to declare for the adoption of the Usages; Bishops Fullarton and Millar were neutral, and Bishop Irvine openly and determinedly opposed them. It seems, when in London in 1715, he had become acquainted with Bishop Spincks. Having been satisfied on the subject, he somewhat rashly undertook to secure the Scottish clergy on the side of those who opposed the Usages, and when he returned to Scotland he laboured to induce Bishop Rose to declare against them; and "though," says Mr Skinner, "he failed in his attempts upon that wise and judicious prelate, yet his assiduity and arguments among the other clergy laid the foundation of all the disturbance that appeared about the Usages after Bishop Rose died."

Such is a condensed account of this controversy, and the reader will now perceive that two questions agitated the Scottish Episcopal Church after the death of the Bishop of Edinburgh—whether the Usages should be observed, and whether the Church should be governed by district Diocesans, or by a common College of Bishops. On the latter subject, Bishop Fullarton wrote to Bishops Campbell and Gadderar at London, dated 15th September 1720—" I freely own that the project of dividing the kingdom into districts, and having a Bishop to superintend in every district, is a most desirable thing, if the practice were as easy as the theory. But, alas! there is none of us able to maintain ourselves in these districts, and the people will give little or nothing to subsist them; nay, the very presbytery that officiate among them are in great straits.*

* This statement of Bishop Fullarton was too true. The Episcopal clergy at this period were in the greatest pecuniary distress, and suffered most severe privations. In the account of the parish of Morham in Haddingtonshire, for example, I find the following among other extracts from the records of the Kirk-Session.—" Sept. 30, 1722, given by the minister's order to an Episcopal minister, L.1, 10s. Scots.

Dr Falconer will be very acceptable to the most part of our clergy and laity too of our communion on the north side of the Forth, and perhaps there might be a way fallen on to settle him in some part of that country; but we have no view of getting any to settle elsewhere, unless you two would come down and take two districts."

This letter discloses at least one fact, that Bishop Fullarton's great object, exclusive of his endeavours to effect an accommodation of the difference existing among the clergy occasioned by the *Usages*, was the establishment of a regular diocesan superintendence on the part of the Bishops, and he appears to have viewed the difficulties as great simply on account of the poverty of the Church, and the apparent impossibility of getting Bishops to reside in and superintend those districts. It is true some of his brethren were in favour of the College scheme, but Bishop Fullarton evidently did not view their opposition as formidable. Nor does he allude to the request of the Chevalier to have the approval of those who were to be consecrated. Bishops Campbell and Gadderar entertained similar views with the Primus as to diocesan jurisdiction. This accounts for the bitterness with which both these Bishops are assailed in the Lockhart Papers, more especially the former, who nevertheless laid himself open to attack, when, notwithstanding his acceptance of the diocesan jurisdiction, he wished Bishop Gadderar to act as his representative while he continued to reside in London—a proposal which the clergy very properly resisted. "The election," says Mr Skinner, "of a man of Bishop Campbell's known principles in the present controversy shows how his electors stood affected to the *Usages*, and upon that account was not so very agreeable to the other Bishops, who gave but a conditional and limited approbation of it For which reason, and to avoid giving any unnecessary cause of offence to his brethren, Bishop Campbell yielded his right to Bishop Gadderar, who had been proposed a candidate along with himself, and whom, on his coming down, the clergy of Aberdeen gladly received, with professions of canonical obe_ dience, and entire satisfaction in all that they knew of his principles."

There were now two parties in the Scottish Episcopal Church—those who were either favourable to or neutral respecting the *Usages*, and who were the supporters of diocesan jurisdiction, and those who were against

Aug. 18, 1723, to an old distressed Episcopal minister, 10s. Scots." New Statistical Account of Scotland, Haddingtonshire, p. 266.

the Usages, and in favour of the College of Bishops ; the latter, who were the *College Party*, entirely under the influence of those of the laity in correspondence with the Chevalier To prevent a decided majority of the Bishops favouring the Usages, the Rev Andrew Cant, formerly one of the ministers of Edinburgh, and the Rev. David Freebairn, already mentioned, were consecrated at Edinburgh on the 17th of October 1722, by Bishops Fullarton, Millar, and Irvine ; and to retain the majority they had now gained the same three prelates consecrated other two opponents of the *Usages* in the year 1724—the Rev. Alexander Duncan, formerly minister of Kilpatrick Easter, and the Rev. Robert Norrie, presbyter in Dundee.

In the meantime the conduct of Bishop Gadderar, who was a decided and zealous supporter of the *Usages*, irritated the adherents of the Chevalier, and especially those Bishops of the College Party who opposed the Usages as innovations. That Bishop would not submit to the College, and it was thought necessary to represent him to the Chevalier. On the 21st of May 1723, Mr Lockhart writes to the exiled prince— "Since my last, Gadderar having gone to the North, and boldly contemned both the advices and orders of the College and *your Trustees*, by openly advancing his opinions, and practising his *Usages*, and having gained several of both clergy and laity over to his way of thinking, is in a fair way of creating a terrible schism, which cannot fail in having dismal effects, by dividing those that have hitherto lived cordially, and been ready to join hand in hand for the service of the Church and State." It farther appears from this letter to the Chevalier, that the College *actually intended to suspend* Bishop Gadderar and those of the clergy who supported him, but they delayed, "because they would gladly shun proclaiming this unhappy division to the world, having at the same time too much reason to apprehend their authority, as matters stand, will not meet with the regard that is due to it." Mr Lockhart then entreats the Chevalier to write a letter to the *College*, approving of their conduct, and "recommending to each of them singly, and to all the inferior clergy, to show a regard and give due obedience to the authority and direction of the College."*

The following passage, written with much bitterness, discloses the real secret of the dislike of the "Trustees" of the Chevalier to Bishops

* Lockhart Papers, vol. ii. p. 99, 100.

Campbell and Gadderar They saw that by supporting the College Party they could always exercise any influence they pleased over the Bishops and clergy—that they could at any time make the former subservient by increasing the number of consecrations indefinitely at the recommendation of the Chevalier; and this they actually did at their convenience, for Bishops Freebairn, Cant, Duncan, and Norrie, were actually consecrated under the sanction of the exiled prince; whereas diocesan jurisdiction struck at the root of such influence, for by dividing the country into certain districts or dioceses, as in the time of the Establishment of the Church, order would be preserved, unnecessary' consecrations prevented, and discipline maintained among the clergy " Here it will be expedient," says Mr Lockhart, " to show Gadderar a little more plainly in his proper colours, by exposing the title on which he claimed to act as Bishop of Aberdeen. Some two or three years ago the presbyters in that diocese applied to the College that they would appoint a Bishop to preside over them, and reside with them. The Bishops, fearing they would choose Dr Gairns, who, having publicly advanced Madame Borignon's wild doctrines, was by no means fit to be promoted, answered, that there was no need of consecrating a new Bishop for that end, but if they, the presbyters, would name any of the College that was agreeable to them, he should be appointed to reside with them, if they, the Bishops, approved of him. The presbyters accordingly met, and to the surprise of everybody elected Mr Archibald Campbell. The College, upon notice hereof, wrote to Campbell, signifying their being willing to approve of what was done, provided he would promise under his hand to maintain and propagate no new doctrine or *usage* not preached and warranted by the Canons of this Church To this Campbell wrote a most impertinent answer, positively refusing to give that satisfaction, and styling Bishop Fullarton as pope, and Millar and Irvine his cardinals, of the Church of Scotland. This letter confirmed the College in their resolution not to approve of Campbell repairing to Aberdeen, and thereof acquainted the presbyters. However, Campbell, slighting the authority of the College, reckoned himself canonically elected by the presbyters; and though he came not from London to reside among them personally, he sent Gadderar with a commission to act as his vicar. Now, as this was all the right and title that Gadderar could claim, the world may judge of him for accepting what is so illegal; and the truth of it is, from his own and his associates in Scotland and England, their conduct first and last in this matter, as they manifested a base contempt of the *authority of the College of Bishops and of the King's friends*, there is too much reason to apprehend they had some secret views and motives which they did not think fit to own, or that they were stirred up by some who at the bottom had designs prejudicial to the *King and Church.*"

This most unwarranted and prejudiced statement is followed by a letter to the Chevalier, dated September 10, 1723. It was written after the death of Bishop Falconer, who died that year, and this loss to the Church is noticed in the most respectful manner. It seems that although Bishop Falconer had some time previous submitted to the *College*, yet, according to Mr Lockhart's suspicions, he was by no means zealous to maintain that novel scheme of governing the Church; and, says our cavalier statesman to the Chevalier, " there was too much reason to apprehend that he and Gadderar designed very soon, *without asking your or the other Bishops' approbation*, to have consecrated several other Bishops, with a view of strengthening and increasing their party." After accusing them of privately circulating a paper in which they remonstrated against, and declined the authority of, the College, and declaring that they " owed no subjection to any other, or even to them all acting in a collegiate body," Mr Lockhart proceeds to inform the Chevalier—" As Falconer was much respected, or rather reverenced, on account of his learning and piety, his opinion in these matters moved many to have a favourable opinion of them; but now that he is dead, we hope there will be less difficulty to keep them within due bounds. If Campbell come down I believe the College will quickly suspend him, having sufficient grounds to warrant such a step, besides his promoting this schism. As his character is no ways suited to the station he was advanced to in the Church, since Falconer's death the College think it expedient to make a further promotion of Bishops, to be settled in those counties, such as Fife, Angus, and the Mearns, over which he presided, and in such other places, as Aberdeenshire, &c., where Gadderar applies himself to propagate his schism; at least, seeing most of the present Bishops are men of a great age, they think it very necessary to have your allowance and direction to consecrate, at such times as they shall see cause and think it expedient, a certain number of other persons."

The whole of this letter shows the subserviency of the College Party to the Chevalier, which was studiously promoted for certain purposes by such politicians as Mr Lockhart who acted as the " King's Trustees," and managed his affairs in Scotland. Nothing annoyed them so much as diocesan superintendence, and every one who did not adopt their College scheme was most unscrupulously abused. Bishop Gadderar was a truly excellent and pious man ; and as for Bishop Campbell, he is described by Mr Skinner as " highly commendable for his learning and other valuable accomplishments, which his various writings, though out of the common line, testify."* He is farther said to have been " among the first projectors, and, by his activity and connections, a constant promoter of that charitable fund which was a great support to the poorer clergy in their straitened circumstances." Bishop Campbell bequeathed to Sion College, London, the records of the General Assembly of 1638, of which the Presbyterians alleged he obtained possession in a very questionable manner. Not being acquainted with the circumstances, the present writer cannot give any opinion on the truth or falsehood of this charge. The records have been repeatedly demanded by the General Assembly, but it seems that Bishop Campbell expressly declared that on no account were the members of Sion College to give them up until the Episcopal Church was again re-established. Bishop Campbell held some peculiar theological opinions, but these did not affect his principles as a Churchman. In his old age he performed an action most extraordinary in its nature, but with which the Scottish Episcopal Church had no concern, as it was done in England, where he chiefly lived and died. " He carried his singularities to such a length," says Mr Skinner,

* The works of Bishop Campbell here alluded to by Mr Skinner are the following:—Queries to the Presbyterians of Scotland, 8vo, 1702. A Query turned into an Argument in favour of Episcopacy, 8vo, 1703. The Doctrine of a Middle State between Death and the Resurrection, folio, 1731 A Discourse proving that the Apostles were no Enthusiasts, 8vo, 1730 Inquiry into the Orgin of Moral Virtue, Edinburgh, 1733, 8vo Oratio de Vanitate Luminis Naturæ, Edinburgh, 1733, 8vo. Remarks on some Books published by him, with his Explications, &c , Edinburgh, 1736. Remarks on the Report of the Committee for Purity of Doctrine, Edinburgh, 8vo, 1736. The Necessity of Revolution, or an Inquiry into the Extent of Human Powers with respect to Matters of Religion, especially the Being of God and the Immortality of the Soul, London, 8vo, 1739. Bishop Campbell is also stated in the Bibliotheca Britannica to have written and published a Life of Bishop Sage in 1714.

"as to form a separate Nonjuring communion in England distinct from the Sancroft line; and even ventured, in contradiction to the advice and opinion of his brethren, upon the extraordinary step of a single consecration by himself, without any assistance." This "separation," which Mr Skinner mentions as existing " in some of the western parts of England to this day," is now extinct, like the Nonjuring Church.

It appears from Mr Lockhart's letter to the Chevalier, that the chief design of consecrating Bishop Norrie was to send him to " counteract Gadderar, and inspect the affairs of the Church in the northern counties." It was to have been done without the knowledge of the Chevalier, and his correspondent enters into a long explanation, in which the alleged urgency of the case is the chief argument, " being hopeful you will not disapprove of it, seeing it was really," he says, " a case of necessity, *and the application made to your Trustees preserves your prerogative unviolated.*" He then advises the Chevalier in the following language of sophistry—" It will, I believe, be expedient that you write two letters to the College, one authorising them to make the promotions in the manner desired, the other approving of what they had done with respect to Norrie, *therein taking notice of the applications made to your Trustees*, and of his consecration being hastened without waiting for your previous direction, because of the inconveniences attending a delay, and that therefore you approved of what was done, and of his taking upon him the government of the Church in the diocese of Aberdeen, *and such other places as the College think fit to appoint.* This authority from you will raise his credit, and make him more regarded in those counties, where every thing that comes from you hath its due weight. I took a proper occasion also to acquaint Bishop Fullarton, that though I did not question his own and his brethren's regard for the royal authority, yet the step they were to make with respect to Norrie might perhaps be adduced many years after this as a precedent against it, seeing nothing would appear to show the method that was taken, and the true cause of it; for which reason I proposed the College should write a letter to me, disclaiming any design of encroaching upon your prerogative, and showing the reason of their proceeding so hastily in that matter. He desired me to draw such a letter, which having done, he laid it before his brethren, and returned it to me signed with some few additions of their zeal and loyalty to you. This letter I shall keep for your service, lest in any time coming men of unruly tempers make a bad use of what was truly done with no bad views, and merely from necessity."*

All this, however, was prospective, for we find that Mr Norrie was not consecrated at that time. Bishop Gadderar and the " Usages" seem to have given as much annoyance to the Chevalier and his " *Trustees*" in Scotland, at least the latter, as if the cause of the exiled dynasty had solely depended on silencing the former. The clamour against the *Usages* that they were Popish was altogether unfounded, and on the part of the " Trustees" was never intended to be serious. They were opposed to diocesan episcopacy for obvious political purposes; they wanted the Chevalier to nominate the Bishops as if he had been the reigning sovereign, instead of the clergy of the dioceses electing their own Bishops, and presenting those so elected to the Primus and the other Bishops for consecration. It appears from a postscript to the letter from which the preceding extracts are taken, that Bishop Fullarton had either persuaded Bishop Gadderar to offer a compromise, or that the latter did not wish to excite any divisions in the diocese of Aberdeen by the appearance of Bishop Norrie. " The day before I was to send this off," says Mr Lockhart to the Chevalier, " I received a letter from Bishop Fullarton, acquainting me that Gadderar having made some show of submission, the College did resolve to delay the consecration of Mr Norrie until they knew your pleasure therein, and desired that, instead of Mr Gordon [minister at Elgin] I should insert Mr Ochterlonie, minister at Aberlemno, in the list of the persons they recommend. I have not time to subscribe this, and leave out what relates to Norrie being immediately consecrated, so I beg you would forgive this being written by way of postscript."

On the 18th of March 1724, the Chevalier addressed a letter to the Bishops of the College Party, in which he laments the want of union and harmony between them and their brethren, expresses his deepest sense of gratitude and regard for their constant loyalty, submission, and attachment, and authorizes them to add to their number the four persons they proposed to him—Mr John Ochterlonie, Mr Robert Norrie, Mr Alexander Duncan, and Mr James Rose. " But," says the Che-

* Lockhart Papers, vol ii. p. 106, 107

valier, " as I am most tender of any thing that might in the least disturb your peace, or give our adversaries any handle to exercise new cruelty towards you, and considering my present distance from you, I leave to your determination to delay the adding to your number the four above named persons as long as you shall think fit, to the end that by taking a proper time to make that step it may be void of all inconvenience, and only tend to your advantage, as I intend and wish it may prove." In virtue of this authority, Messrs Norrie and Duncan were consecrated that year as already mentioned; but that of the other two was delayed.

It is to be observed that Bishops Fullarton and Gadderar were the only Diocesan Bishops at that time in Scotland, and that to none of the other Bishops was any district or diocese assigned; consequently Bishops Millar, Irvine, Cant, Duncan, and Norrie, had no spiritual authority whatever, though invested with the Episcopal office. It was impossible that this irregular and uncanonical practice could long continue, because it was not only the occasion of confusions and divisions in the Church, but it greatly tended to retard its prosperity. Those Bishops were in the exact position of Mr Henry Doughty, an English Nonjuring clergyman, of the parish of St Anne, Westminster, whom Bishops Fullarton, Millar, Irvine, and Freebairn, consecrated at Edinburgh on the 30th of March 1725, but for what purpose does not appear.

Bishop Gadderar, when he perceived that the College of Bishops were determined to proceed against him, came to Edinburgh, and met his brethren. An interview took place, at which, besides the Bishops, the Earls of Wigton, Panmure, and Kincardine, and Mr Lockhart, all of whom it may be presumed were the Chevalier's " Trustees," were present. The Bishop contended that the " Usages" were practised by the Primitive Fathers, and though he did not consider them essential, he nevertheless thought them integrals in the worship of God, and in particular he esteemed it his indispensable duty to mix water with the wine in the administration of the holy communion; yet, for the sake of peace, he would willingly co-operate with those who did not hold this opinion. The Bishops replied, that they viewed the " Usages" as matters of indifference in themselves, but that as their enemies misrepresented them, they felt it their duty to oppose the introduction of such observances, and they maintained that Bishop Gadderar, as a son of the Church, ought to submit to the authority of the College in every thing which had a reference merely to the rites and ceremonies, and to the external government, of the Church. An agreement was eventually made, and Bishop Gadderar bound himself not to insist on the observance of the Usages within his diocese, and to conform to the canons of the Church of Scotland, excepting the mixture of the cup in the communion, to which the Bishops had no objections, if Bishop Gadderar " performed it only to those that demanded it, and with privacy and prudence, as not to give offence to others who startled at such innovations."—" I cannot," says Mr Lockhart, " express the disorder that was at this meeting, for there was little reasoning on the matter, most of the discourses being invectives and unmannerly reflections against Gadderar, who, being on the other hand as obstinate as a mule, nothing to purpose would have attended this conference had not the noblemen above mentioned interposed, and by their solid reason and authority adjusted matters in the manner I have briefly related."

A long account is given by Mr Lockhart of some subsequent proceedings respecting the consecration of Bishop Norrie, at which our cavalier statesman and the Earl of Panmure were present, and a stormy discussion ensued.* A letter was dispatched to the Chevalier on this subject by Lockhart, dated December 8, 1724, representing that Bishops Norrie and Duncan had been consecrated Bishops at large—that some time afterwards the former had been appointed to the superintendence of Angus and Mearns, and the latter to the diocese of Glasgow—that this arrangement respecting Bishop Norrie was carried by the majority of the Bishops, seconded by the Earl of Strathmore and other persons of distinction, in opposition to Bishops Fullarton and Gadderar, who protested against it, and were supported by a great number of influential gentlemen—and that " not only are the Bishops broken in pieces among themselves, but the divisions and heats among the laity are also very great, and have occasioned such a breach and misunderstanding as will not, I fear, be easily or soon accommodated, to the prejudice of the common interest in these loyal shires." Mr Lockhart then tenders the following advice to the Chevalier, as likely to prevent in future " such divisions and discord as have arisen on this late occasion, and will at

* Lockhart Papers, vol ii p. 124, 128.

the same time support and maintain the power *lodged in and practised by the Crown* in the nomination and appointment of Bishops."—" Your Trustees humbly offer as their advice, that you would be pleased to write to the Bishop of Edinburgh, signifying that, though you allowed them to consecrate a certain number of Bishops that the order may be continued, yet you desired the College should not for the future proceed to settle any to the charge and inspection of any particular diocese or province, until they have acquainted your Trustees of the person's name, that they may inquire how far he will be acceptable to your faithful subjects, and may be in other respects fit for that part of the country; and after making a report thereof to you, you signify your pleasure therein."

These passages clearly show the importance attached to the Scottish Episcopal Church by the Chevalier's " Trustees." This is farther proved by a letter from Mr Lockhart to the Chevalier, dated August 18, 1724, in which he notices the great age of the Primus, Bishop Fullarton, and urges him, in the event of that prelate's death, to nominate Bishop Irvine as his successor. " He is a gentleman," he says, " of good sense and experience in business, and by his joining my Lord Dundee and Lord Kenmure, on which first account he was obliged to retire several years to France, and lay long in prison after the unhappy action at Preston, his loyalty and zeal for your service are unexceptionable. The Viscount of Kilsyth and most of those now with you know him well, and will confirm what I say of him. Though this person is certainly the fittest to succeed Mr Fullarton, it would not be proper that you should nominate him or any other till the event happen. But it is the humble opinion of many of your Trustees that it would tend much for preserving the peace and unity which you so much and on such good grounds do recommend, if you would send a letter directed to the Bishops, signifying that whereas you are at a great distance at present, and cannot give such speedy directions on several matters as the importance often requires, and being sensible that many inconveniences may arise to the Church of Scotland if Mr Fullarton, the present Primus, should happen to die, for want of one of the College duly authorised to supply the vacancy, until you have time and opportunity to name one to succeed him—that therefore you have sent previously this letter to be ready and delivered to the College of Bishops, on the event foresaid, and that you do thereby direct Bishop Irvine to reside at Edinburgh, and preside in the College of Bishops, until you name another to act and officiate as Primus. It is proposed that this letter should be kept so very secret, that none of the clergy, nor any other but those by whose directions I write this, should know of it till the time of its being delivered; and it is thought an expedient, nay, the only one that will prevent the heats and divisions which will otherwise infallibly happen, to the no small prejudice of your interest here; for as the episcopal party, which daily becomes more numerous, are all entirely devoted to you, and that in some measure you are in the actual exercise of your regal power, in so far as they willingly follow your directions in what you require of them, it is certainly for your service to keep them entire and at one in all matters civil or ecclesiastical; and while they are in this good temper, I am fond of every occasion that casts up for you to exercise your royal authority over so great a number of loyal subjects, willing to receive your commands."*

Thus advised and flattered, the Chevalier addressed the required letter to the College of Bishops, dated October 27, 1724, but this intrigue was unsuccessful, for Bishop Irvine died in 1725, and his death is thus noticed by Lockhart in the postscript to a letter to a certain person whom he styles "Lord Inverness," dated 18th December 1725:—"The King has the other day lost a faithful useful servant by the death of Bishop Irvine, and it will be no easy matter to supply his place, as he was the only one of all the present Bishops fit to succeed Fullarton, who is quite dosed, and cannot last long Some purpose Mr Rattray of Craighall, and if he would lay his whims aside till a more proper juncture he is a very fit person, as he is a man of good sense and learning, and has an estate to support his rank Others propose your and my old friend, John Gillan, who has been in orders for some years, and is in as great esteem as any of the Episcopal clergy in Edinburgh You know him to be an excellent man in all respects."

In a letter to the Chevalier, dated January 31, 1726, the same subject is discussed at large; Bishop Irvine's death is noticed in language of deep regret; the increasing infirmities of Bishop Fullarton are mentioned; and the Chevalier is informed by his confidential correspondent,

* Lockhart Papers, vol ii. p. 119, 120.

that as there is not "among the present number of Bishops one fit to be placed at the head of the Church," it is necessary that he should take this matter into his serious consideration. "If Bishop Cant," says Mr Lockhart, "was not, by reason of his old age, become very infirm, he is a person in all respects qualified to be at the head of any Church in Christendom, being a man of great learning and integrity; however, he may be able to officiate for some time till you come to a final resolution. There is another, Bishop Duncan, though not a man of such parts and learning as the other, yet eminently distinguished and esteemed for his great probity and zeal for you and the Church's interest." The Chevalier is then advised to write to the College, suggesting either Bishop Cant or Bishop Duncan, "as shall appear most convenient, to preside in the College of Bishops, and take care of the affairs of the Church in your capital of Edinburgh and diocese thereof, until you determine yourself in the choice of a person duly qualified and agreeable to your people, to be settled in a post of such consequence with respect to the interest of both Church and State."

The same subject is discussed in a letter, dated April 30, 1726, in which Mr Gillan is strongly recommended by Mr Lockhart on account of his "excellent sense and learning," and his "zeal and firmness to go through with what he thinks for the good of the cause;" but, because the several Bishops aimed at the office of Primus themselves, the "best way to prevent envy would be to advance a presbyter, or one such as Gillan, if he is previously consecrated, that is not dipt in their cabals." This confidant is therefore earnestly required to lay this matter before the Chevalier, or the "King," as Mr Lockhart calls him, with all possible alacrity. Meanwhile, in compliance with his correspondent's advice, the Chevalier sent a letter to the College of Bishops, dated May 1, 1726, nominating Bishop Cant to officiate temporarily as Primus in the event of Bishop Fullarton's death, and, failing him, Bishop Duncan.

On the 7th of July that year Mr Lockhart informs the Chevalier that his "Trustees" had recommended to the College, under his authority, the Rev. James Rose, a brother of Dr Rose, Bishop of Edinburgh, and formerly minister of Monimail in Fife, to be consecrated, and that the College had some thoughts of consecrating Mr Ochterlonie also, and "of applying to have your liberty of setting him over the shires of Ross and Moray, where the party increases, and a Bishop is much wanted."

As it respects Mr Gillan, who was entirely devoted to the College Party, an order was transmitted by the Chevalier, dated July 20, 1726, for his consecration, and this was accompanied by another document enjoining the College of Bishops, when there were any vacancies, and when they think it necessary to add to their number, to lay before his Trustees a list of such persons, whom the said Trustees were to send to him, with their opinions upon it: "And further," says the Chevalier, "it is my will and pleasure that no Bishop amongst you shall be appointed to have the care and inspection of any particular district without my previous authority, and that, when you think an appointment necessary, you give your opinion in writing to my Trustees, to be transmitted as above." These letters were delivered to Bishops Norrie, Millar, Freebairn, and Cant, the others being in the country, who, we are told, "heartily approved of the scheme the *King* had laid down, and promised to consecrate Mr Gillan with all due expedition, and to give exact conformity to all the several particulars the *King* required of them!" The results of this will immediately appear. The consecration of Mr Gillan was delayed, but on the 29th of November 1726, Mr Rose and Mr Ochterlonie were consecrated at Edinburgh by Bishops Freebairn, Duncan, and Cant. Bishops Fullarton, Gadderar, and Millar, refused to have any concern in the consecration of Mr Ochterlonie, and Bishop Gadderar even protested against the act.

The venerable Primus, Bishop Fullarton, died at an advanced age on the first or second day of May 1727, and at his death Bishop Gadderar became the only Diocesan Bishop in Scotland—all the others, whatever may have been their principles, having no more spiritual authority by toleration than they had in England, or in any other country where the Church existed or was established. "St Cyprian's maxim, *Episcopatus unus est, cujus a singulis in solidum pars tenetur*, is," says Bishop Russell,[*] "so obviously the maxim of common sense, that we believe no clergyman out of Scotland ever supposed that a number of men admitted to the *order* of Bishops, but to whom as individuals the government of *no part* of the Church was committed, had, as a *body* or *college*, a right to claim the government of *the whole*. The reader will observe that we are writing of the Church as a purely ecclesiastical

---

[*] Scottish Episcopal Magazine, 1821, p. 197.

society, totally unconnected *as a society* with the State. Such was the whole Church of Christ for the three first centuries, and such was the Episcopal Church in Scotland after the Revolution, though at the death of Bishop Rose she had no particular constitution formed for herself on Primitive principles. All her members, both clergymen and laymen, knew perfectly that as an Episcopal Church she must be governed by Bishops, but they differed among themselves whether she should be governed by a College of Bishops in common, or be divided into districts or dioceses, to be governed each by its proper Diocesan."

CHAPTER XV.

PROCEEDINGS OF THE SCOTTISH BISHOPS AT THE DEATH OF BISHOP FULLARTON—SUCCESSFUL OPPOSITION TO THE COLLEGE PARTY—ADJUSTMENT OF THE CONTEST BY THE CONCORDATE IN 1732.

THE Chevalier's two letters to the Bishops, dated July 20, 1726, respecting the consecration of Mr Gillan, and the prohibition of diocesan superintendence without his own sanction, had been received by Bishops Norrie, Freebairn, Millar, and Cant, in the absence of the others, with "all the dutiful respect imaginable," and the Trustees thought that all contention and opposition were allayed. But in this they were grievously mistaken. The dispute about the Usages had been adjusted, but Bishop Gadderar still asserted the right, in the then peculiar circumstances of the Church, of the presbyters to elect their own Bishops without any dependance on the Chevalier, though he was called the "King," or on the College of Bishops The latter, he rightly maintained, was altogether a novelty, unknown and never practised in any era of the history of the Catholic Church of Christ; and as to the former, although his *rights* were undoubted, it was plain that he could not exercise any acts of regal power, inasmuch as he was not *de facto* sovereign, and the Church had ceased to be the National Establishment. If the exiled Family were restored, and the Episcopal Church once more established by law, it was right that the sovereign should exercise his prerogative; but even then he could only issue his *conge d'elire* according to law when a diocese became vacant, and he could not multiply the consecrations as he pleased, which was evidently the principle on which the College was constituted. It was on these grounds that Bishop Gadderar evidently rested his opposition to the College scheme, although it was supported by his brethren and by not a few of the influential laity.

Bishop Gadderar was supported in his views by the Rev. Dr Rattray of Craighall, and by various noblemen and gentlemen among the laity; and the question was again agitated in connection with the consecration of Mr Gillan, whose devotion to the College Party was well known. Bishop Millar, one of the four who had received and answered the Chevalier's letters of the 20th of July, now opposed Mr Gillan's consecration, and urged Bishop Freebairn to unite with him; but that prelate, whose notions on the subject of ecclesiastical patronage were also well known, and who often allowed his political principles to interfere with or regulate his episcopal functions, positively declined. The conduct of Bishop Millar is, as may be expected, bitterly assailed by Mr Lockhart. He is accused of being of a " hot turbulent temper, ambitious, proud, and positive, and withal was but meanly endowed with learning, prudence, or discretion;" but as this is the language of political invective, it must be received with the necessary limitations. It appears that he had been wavering in his views of the College scheme, and had attempted to obtain the episcopal jurisdiction of the county of Fife; but being unsuccessful, he at last " turned his thoughts on succeeding Fullarton in the See of Edinburgh, who, being mightily decayed both in body and mind, could not long hold out."*

The angry Cavalier statesman proceeds to accuse Bishop Millar of employing a series of unwarrantable means to secure his own election as successor to the Primus, in opposition to Mr Gillan, who was the person nominated by the Chevalier, and supported by his Scottish Trustees; and it appears that a remonstrance against Mr Gillan's consecration was signed by twenty of the presbyters of Edinburgh, " though some of them," says Mr Lockhart, " afterwards deleted their names, or signed a recantation." Among those who signed this remonstrance was the celebrated Robert Keith, afterwards Bishop Keith, " who," says Mr Lockhart, " secretly grudged that Gillan, though a person of good age, that is, above sixty, yet but lately admitted into holy orders, should step over them his seniors."

The remonstrance was presented to the College Bishops, and is de-

* Lockhart Papers, vol. ii. p. 324, 325.

scribed as representing the encroachments made on the rights of the Church since the Reformation, earnestly requiring and exhorting the College to embrace this favourable opportunity of regaining what was lost, since it was evident that the "*Crown*" was not in a condition to maintain them. The Chevalier was accused of violating the promise he had given, that he would recommend no person to the Episcopal office without previously consulting the College, and it concluded with expressions of dissatisfaction respecting Mr Gillan's character and qualifications, the proofs of which they reserved for a future occasion. When this paper was presented to Bishop Duncan, who firmly believed that the Stuart dynasty would be restored and the Church re-established, he told the presbyters that out of regard to them he would throw it into the fire when they submitted it to the College, lest it should appear afterwards *in condemnation against them*—that he considered their conduct seditious, unwarrantable, and disrespectful to their civil and ecclesiastical superiors—that as Mr Gillan was to be consecrated a Bishop at large, and not to any particular diocese, the presbyters of Edinburgh had no more concern with it than those of any other diocese; and that their conduct was "a precedent for destroying all order and government in the Church, and directly inconsistent with that loyalty which had hitherto been the glory of the Scottish Church."

Although Mr Lockhart characterizes the remonstrance as "full of treason, falsehoods, and ill manners," it is evident to every impartial mind that its language was just and its demands reasonable. The besetting infirmity of the College Bishops, who had been all nominated by the Chevalier, was a slavish servility to that unfortunate representative of the ancient dynasty, and in all their correspondence with him not only bestowing upon him the empty title of *King*, but actually addressing him and receiving his commands as if he was the *de facto* reigning sovereign. According to Bishop Duncan, Mr Gillan "was to be a consecrated Bishop *at large*, and not to any particular diocese," yet this was the very grievance set forth in the remonstrance. The presbyters were now becoming sensible of the evils of the College scheme, and of the advantages of Diocesan superintendence. They had themselves experienced the benefits of it under Bishop Fullarton in the diocese of Edinburgh; they had seen its salutary operations in the counties of Forfar and Kincardine, which comprehended the ancient diocese of

Brechin, under Bishop Falconer; and they saw religion prospering and the Church flourishing in the diocese of Aberdeen under Bishop Gadderar, the chosen diocesan of the presbyters. So much was this the case in the latter diocese, that it attracted the notice and excited the alarm of the Established Presbyterians. We find Wodrow thus expressing himself in his own way, under date 1727, which shows how efficiently and fearlessly Bishop Gadderar discharged his important duties. " There was a most pointed representation of grievances from the irregularities of Bishop Gadderar brought in by the Synod of Aberdeen. That pretended Bishop was consecrated by Dr Hickes, and is on the very border of Popery. He goes through the diocese of Aberdeen as their proper Bishop, and confirms and ordains, and by his Episcopal power he takes all causes before him, without any advising with presbyters; by his sole authority deposes prelatick ministers, and that because they join in communion with, and hear, and subject to discipline with schismatical persons, that is, such of the prelatick way as have taken the oaths, or pray for King George, or at least pray not in direct terms for the Pretender, or in words that are applicable to him and the King. One he has deposed for this; and he is going on This pretended Bishop travels up and down, and gathers small sums from those of his own persuasion, and yet is not rich. He stirs up divisions in parishes who adhere to their Presbyterian ministers, which is *no difficult matter in that country*. I think there are upwards of twenty meeting-houses set up in the shire of Aberdeen since last year, and mostly filled with persons fugitate for their being in the Rebellion. In short, the [Presbyterian] ministers in some places there are speaking of leaving their charges."*
Bishop Millar had left the College Party, and Bishop Cant had become extremely lukewarm in their cause; and it was daily becoming obvious that a prince, whatever were his claims, living in exile, ought not in an unestablished Church to exercise that control to which he may have been entitled if he had been the reigning sovereign. The position which they assumed, therefore, and on which they took their stand, was to revert to the primitive ecclesiastical constitution—to contend for diocesan instead of collegiate Episcopacy—and to maintain the inherent right of the presbyters to elect their own Bishops in the circumstances of the Church.

* Wodrow's Analecta, MS, Advocates' Library.

Such principles as these greatly irritated laymen like Mr Lockhart of Carnwath and the other political leaders of the Jacobite party. But the presbyters were not to be diverted from their purpose, notwithstanding the unqualified vituperations they received. They openly and everywhere lamented the state of the Church, and though they were zealous friends to the cause of the Chevalier, they could not refrain from asking, if he could thus act when it was notorious to all the world that he was not in a condition to maintain the Church, what was to be expected if he were on the throne? Mr Lockhart, who was mortally offended at their conduct, had a conference with the Rev. Robert Keith on the subject, telling him that he was surprised to find his name at a paper " so seditious, false, and unmannerly," and expostulated with him in the most earnest manner to withdraw from the party, assuring him that, in the case of Mr Gillan, " *his Majesty* would by no means think of advancing him or any man but with the previous advice and approbation of the College and the presbyters of the diocese." Mr Keith calmly answered, that it was undeniable the State had made great encroachments on the Church, and though he was not altogether certain if the then juncture was the most seasonable time to remove these encroachments, yet they could not conscientiously sit altogether idle, and he had authority to make two propositions for peace—either that the whole affair should be referred to the decision of persons whom he mentioned, or that a clergyman of unquestionable character whom his friends would name should be consecrated with Mr Gillan: " I replied with indignation," says Mr Lockhart, " that the *King* was not reduced quite so low as to make a reference or composition with a parcel of little factious priests in the diocese of Edinburgh, who, as if they were serving the Covenanted cause, should change their black gowns into brown cloaks, and I doubt not they would be received into the godly party, unless ecclesiastic had the same fate with the State traitors, in being despised by those they served "

This altercation between the Collegiate Bishops on the one side, and the Presbyters on the other, headed by Bishops Gadderar and Millar, was so violent that the correspondence between the Chevalier and his " Trustees" became known to the Government, who immediately adopted measures for intercepting all future letters, in the hope of discovering more important matters and intrigues. One of the presbyters of Edinburgh named Middleton, and some of his friends, were accused of conveying this information to the existing authorities, but they took no notice of the disputes of the Scottish Episcopal clergy, or of the influence exercised in the consecration of the Bishops. Some of the more zealous Presbyterians applied to the Earl of Islay, requesting his Lordship to bring those " bold barefaced exercises" of the Episcopal office before the notice of the Government, but that nobleman declined, telling them that " they judged quite wrong, for that the Episcopal party were in the high way of undoing themselves, if let alone, and suffered to go on."

These disputes caused some conversation among the Presbyterians, and we accordingly find Wodrow making them the subject of his gossiping remarks :—" I hear that in the letters lately seized at Leith, come from the Pretender or his friends, were several of the Pretender's *congés d'élire* for our Scots Bishops, which were taken and sent to London. Whether there was one to Mr John Gillan, who is designed by Carnwath [Lockhart] and a party among the Prelatists to be Primate or Bishop of Edinburgh in room of Mr John Fullarton, who is turned eighty, and hath very much lost his judgment, and can be of no farther use to them, I cannot tell. But I am told there is a very great heat among them at Edinburgh. Mr Freebairn, and several others of the old persons of the Episcopal clergy now made Bishops, take it very ill that so young a man as Mr Gillan,* who some years ago was but a tutor and schoolmaster, I think with Mr Forrest, and was made but a preaching deacon within these four or five years, should be advanced to be Bishop of Edinburgh, and the Primacy, as they call it, of the clergy, *sede vacante*, and they be overlooked. Mr Lockhart of Carnwath hath been very active in this matter, and brought in a party to be for Mr Gillan, who is thought to be indeed the author of that book which generally goes under the name of ' Carnwath's Memoires.' Mr Gillan is certainly a man of cleverness and sufficiency, and though he be younger than Mr Freebairn and others, it may be Carnwath thinks him the fitter and the more probable to continue some time in that post."— Wodrow narrates the following proceedings, which were told him by one of his friends, who in turn details them from the above-mentioned Mr Middleton, who " saw all the papers that passed of late this winter and

* Wodrow here means *young* as it respects *status* in the Church, as he notices that Bishop Gillan was considerably advanced in life before he was ordained.

spring [1727] at Edinburgh," but which, in reality, is one of the many proofs that Wodrow, like many of his Presbyterian friends, could not let the Episcopalians alone, but was continually dabbling in their affairs. "There is a terrible heat at Edinburgh among the Episcopal people about Mr John Gillan, of whom somewhat has been noticed formerly. Mr Gillan was Mr Lockhart of Carnwath's governor [preceptor] and chaplain, and Carnwath, by his interest at the Pretender's Court, got a *mandamus*, or *congé d'élire* from the Pretender, to choose Mr Gillan one of the College of Bishops at Edinburgh, and he is designed to be Bishop of Edinburgh after Fullarton's death. The elder Bishops took this very ill, and a long remonstrance, which my informer saw, was given in to the College of Bishops against Mr Gillan's admission It run upon several things, as his not being long enough in orders to be admitted to the College of Bishops They offered to prove several acts of unrighteousness against him in his business as a bookseller, which he hath followed for many years ; and they offered to prove that he had said in conversation, that when he had thoroughly considered the Reformation, and secession from the Church of Rome, there were so many things wrong in it, that had he been alive and known these things, he could not have had freedom to join with any Protestant society at the Reformation. Mr Gillan laboured hard to have liberty to take off these objections, but complained that he was not heard, and the remonstrance and the opinion of many of the Bishops and clergy, of the inconvenience of urging Mr Gillan, being received, were laid before the Court of Boulogne, as they now call the Pretender's Court. However, Carnwath's interest there is so great that a new *mandamus*, in very positive terms, is sent over, ordering Mr Gillan to be received into the Bishops. This, they say, with the letters anent it, was seized at Leith and sent to London, on which Carnwath is absconded, or, as some say, gone to London. However, the Episcopal clergy are still divided in their sentiments, and a second remonstrance is given in to the College of Bishops against receiving Mr Gillan, at which the Jacobite laity are much exasperated, and say it ill becomes the clergy to stand upon their punctilios against the express orders of their King, and the Bishops are so divided, that, though those for Mr Gillan called in Mr A. Duncan from Glasgow, and have made a new Bishop one Rose, Bishop Rose's brother ; yet old Mr Cant and some others are so keen in the Episcopal College against Gillan, that Bishops

Freebairn, Ochterlonie, and some others who are for Mr Gillan, cannot get a sufficient number to consecrate him, and there the matter stands at present."*

In this excited state was the Scottish Episcopal Church at the death of its venerable Primus, Bishop Fullarton, in May 1727. On the 5th of that month, probably the day of the Bishop's funeral, the presbyters of Edinburgh met at the summons of their Archdeacon, the Rev. Andrew Lumsden, formerly minister of Duddingstone, for the purpose of electing a successor to their deceased diocesan. As the Archdeacon had been appointed by Bishop Fullarton, he considered himself as *functus officio*, for he immediately left the chair, and a preses was chosen. It was proposed to proceed immediately to the election, without any reference to the Chevalier and his "Trustees," when one Presbyter left the meeting, because in his opinion it was called by no authority. All the rest remained, and some of them argued against the election, requesting time for deliberation. The vote was then taken to *proceed* or *delay*, when the former was carried by *twenty-one* to *ten*, and the minority immediately rose, protested against the meeting, as not convened by canonical authority, and withdrew. The majority of twenty one then proceeded with the election, when the "Right Rev. Arthur Millar, formerly minister of Inveresk, and one of the Bishops of the Scottish Episcopal Church," was unanimously declared duly elected, and acknowledged as diocesan of Edinburgh.

This was the first decisive blow struck at the schemes of the College Party, and at that undue influence which the Chevalier had exercised in the Scottish Episcopal Church. A violent controversy ensued between the College and the Diocesan Parties, which with respect to Bishop Millar was unnecessary, as Bishop Gadderar, by whom the election was approved, was the only diocesan Bishop in Scotland. The College Party, as was to be expected, refused to confirm Bishop Millar's election, and appointed Bishop Freebairn to superintend the diocese in the interim. Thus there were two parties—one who rendered canonical obedience to Bishop Millar, and the other to Bishop Freebairn. On the 11th of June 1727 the College Bishops added two to their numbers. On that day Mr Gillan and the Rev. David Rankine, formerly minister of Bennathie,

* Wodrow's Analecta, MS., Advocates' Library.

were consecrated at Edinburgh by Bishops Freebairn, Duncan, Rose, and Ochterlonie.

The Diocesan Bishops, on the other hand, were resolved to pursue the advantages they had gained. Encouraged by Bishops Millar, Gadderar, and Cant, and also by Bishop Campbell, the clergy of the different dioceses proceeded to elect proper Bishops for themselves. The presbyters within the ancient diocese of Dunkeld, who had been under no particular episcopal jurisdiction since the death of Bishop Falconer, met and elected the Rev. Dr Thomas Rattray of Craighall, one of their own number, to be their Bishop, and he was consecrated at Edinburgh on the 4th of June 1727, by Bishops Millar, Gadderar, and Cant The Diocesan Bishops being now determined to adhere to the model of the Primitive Church, independent of the influence of the Chevalier and his "Trustees," resolved to increase their number to preserve the succession, in opposition to the College Party. The clergy of the diocese of Moray elected the Rev. William Dunbar, formerly minister of Cruden in Aberdeenshire, to be their Bishop, and as the old age and infirmities of Bishop Millar rendered a coadjutor necessary, the Rev. Robert Keith, presbyter in Edinburgh, was nominated, and those two clergymen were consecrated at Edinburgh on the 18th of June 1727.

The three newly consecrated Bishops were men of the greatest respectability, of most upright principles, and two of them at least of sound learning. Bishop Rattray was proprietor of the fine estate of Craighall in Perthshire, and was the representative of an ancient family. His principles were thoroughly orthodox, and his zeal for the Episcopal Church of Scotland, as a branch of the Church Catholic, was regulated by the most ardent piety. Bishop Keith was connected with the Noble Family of Keith, Earls Marischal of Scotland, and he is well known and justly celebrated as the author of the History of the Church and State in Scotland during the period of the Reformation and the reign of Queen Mary, from which, as Mr Fraser Tytler observes, Dr Robertson drew all his stores Mr Lockhart sneeringly speaks of Bishop Dunbar, as " one Mr Dunbar, a disciple of Gadderar in the North." Bishop Dunbar, there is every evidence to show, was a pious, judicious, and worthy man. He had suffered severely at the Revolution, but the fact of his having been an intimate friend of Bishop Gadderar seems to have been a crime in the eyes of the College Party.

The Collegiate Bishops were mortified at the proceedings of their Diocesan brethren. They saw the succession now secure, independent of their assistance or sanction, and some of them began to be secretly dissatisfied at their scheme and their party. The sentiments of the lay advocates of the Collegiate Bishops may be inferred from what Mr Lockhart himself records. Alluding to the Diocesan Bishops—those who had been consecrated without the Chevalier's sanction or nomination—he says—" The independence of the Church was now in all their mouths, and indeed they showed no regard for any powers, civil or ecclesiastic, but in so far as these were on their side of the question. This was highly displeasing to a great many, nay, the far greater part of the laity, many of whom told plainly that as they had ventured their lives for the *King*, they could not countenance a set of men who advanced maxims and formed measures tending directly to lop off several valuable branches of the royal prerogative ; and so offended were the managers of the most considerable Episcopal meeting-house in Edinburgh, that they dismissed Bishop Cant and Mr Patrick Middleton from being pastors thereof "

The College Party, completely warped by Erastian principles, fomented their notions among the laity, but certainly not with the success which Mr Lockhart intimates. They alleged that the new Bishops were uncanonically consecrated, as if no person could have been a true Bishop unless he had the sanction or recommendation of the " *King*," as they designated the Chevalier, and yet it is not a little remarkable that they acted in a similar manner themselves. It is already stated that they consecrated Bishop Rankine along with Bishop Gillan, but the former was actually consecrated without the Chevalier's knowledge. Let us hear Mr Lockhart, their devoted partizan, on this subject. " The College of Bishops now judged it proper to proceed to the consecration of Gillan, *and it were much to be wished they had stopt there, and not at the same time promoted another Presbyter of Edinburgh*, Mr Rankine ; for as one of their objections against Rattray and the others was that it was done *without the King's knowledge*, it was a firm foundation to stand on, but this step of theirs did quite take it off, though for their justification they offered that it was done by the particular express direction of Messrs Graham and Hay, two of the *King's Trustees*, who, believing it for the service of the Church, advised the measure ; and the *opposite set* alleged the authority and approbation of Lord Panmure, *another of the*

Trustees, and that the service of the Church required also what they had done; which, like many texts of Scripture, is often produced to justify contradictions and serve party views."*

Bishop Millar died at a very advanced age a few months after his election to preside over the clergy in the Scottish metropolis. This prelate, who is bitterly assailed in the Lockhart Papers for deserting the College Party, had been deprived of his benefice of Invcresk, six miles from Edinburgh, at the Revolution, and from that time he had devoted all his energies to serve his native Church After the Revolution, when the Episcopal clergy were subjected, by expulsion from their parishes, to the greatest privations, and their families were overwhelmed in poverty, subscriptions were collected in various parts of the country to supply their pressing wants, and Bishop Millar, then a Presbyter, went repeatedly to Ireland to promote this benevolent object, where he was kindly received by the dignitaries of the Church, and honoured with their advice as well as their generous contributions. "The Duke of Ormond, who was at that time Lord Lieutenant," says Bishop Russell, "granted to him a brief (an official warrant, which I believe corresponds to His Majesty's letter in England), and this countenance and authority on the part of the Government, it need hardly be observed, contributed very essentially to promote the purpose of his mission. He met with opposition, it is true, in other quarters, but the friendship and zeal of the Archbishop of Dublin, the celebrated Dr King, author of the well known work on the *Origin of Evil*, supported him against his bitterest enemies, and proved to him a full requital for all the bigoted hostility with which he had repeatedly to contend, and to which on one occasion he had nearly fallen a victim."†

Of the College Party, Bishop Norrie died in the month of March 1727, and of the Diocesan Party Bishop Millar in the month of October that year. At the death of the latter the Presbyters met to elect a successor, and on this occasion they were joined by those of their brethren who had refused to co-operate with the majority who elected Bishop Millar. They had the boldness to bring with them two of their Bishops, who, contrary to their practice on former occasions, and without considering the dignity of their own order, actually claimed a right to sit and vote with the Presbyters of Edinburgh. Whether they had resolved

* Lockhart Papers, vol ii p. 334.   † Edition of Keith's Catalogue of Scottish Bishops, p. 526

to make a last effort in favour of the College, or whether they were anxious that one of those Bishops should be elected, is not known ; but the other party were anxious that Bishop Keith, who had acted as coadjutor to Bishop Millar, should be chosen his successor. Both parties, however, were disappointed, for the election of the presbyters fell upon the Rev. Andrew Lumsden, their Archdeacon under Bishop Fullarton, and he was consecrated at Edinburgh, on the 2d of November, by Bishops Cant, Rattray, and Keith.

The adherents of the College Party, and even their Bishops, now perceived that all their efforts and influence could not resist the progress of their Diocesan opponents, and in 1731 they intimated an inclination to enter into terms of agreement, by which the dispute would be satisfactorily adjusted for the future peace of the Church. Conferences were held between the junior Bishops of each party, Bishop Keith in behalf of the Diocesans, and Bishop Gillan on the side of the College adherents. A meeting was held towards the end of December 1731, and a deed was accordingly prepared, called a *Concordate*, which was subscribed by all the Bishops on the 13th of May 1732, which completely ended the novel scheme of governing the Church by a College of Bishops, and gave that internal peace to the Scottish Episcopal Church which has been ever since enjoyed.

The contents of this important document are given by Mr Skinner. They are entitled " Articles of Agreement amongst the Bishops of the Church of Scotland," to the following effect :—" I. That we shall only make use of the Scottish or English Liturgy in the public divine service, nor shall we disturb the peace of the Church by introducing into the public worship any of the ancient Usages, concerning which there has been lately a difference amongst us ; and that we shall censure any of our clergy who shall act otherwise. II. That hereafter no man shall be consecrated a Bishop of this Church without the consent and approbation of the majority of the other Bishops. III. That upon the demise or removal elsewhere of a Bishop of any district, the presbyters thereof shall neither elect, nor entrust to, another Bishop, without a mandate from the Primus, by consent of the other Bishops. IV. That the Bishops of this Church shall, by a majority of voices, choose their Primus, for convocating and presiding only, and that no Bishop shall claim jurisdiction without the bounds of his own district. V. We, the

Bishops of the Church of Scotland, have chosen and appointed Bishop Freebairn to be our Primus, for convocating and presiding only, according to the foregoing article." The sixth article allots the diocese of Glasgow to the inspection and superintendence of Bishop Duncan, " excepting only Annandale, Nithsdale, and Tweeddale, together with the diocese of Galloway, which shall be under the inspection of Bishop Freebairn." To Bishop Gillan was allotted the diocese of Dunblane ; the counties of Fife, Clackmannan and Kinross, to Bishop Rose ; the diocese of Dunkeld to Bishop Rattray ; the diocese of Brechin to Bishop Ochterlonie ; the diocese of Aberdeen to Bishop Gadderar ; the dioceses of Moray and Ross to Bishop Dunbar ; the diocese of Edinburgh to Bishop Lumsden ; and Caithness, the Orkneys, and the Isles, were placed under the superintendence of Bishop Keith. To this arrangement, by which the boundaries of the ancient dioceses are preserved, is added— *" By the foresaid divisions of districts we do not pretend to claim any legal title to dioceses."* This paper was signed by the Bishops Freebairn, Ochterlonie, Rattray, Gillan, and Keith, and subsequently by all the others.

Such was the Concordate of the Scottish Bishops, which put an end to the College Contest During its agitation it excited considerable interest even among the opponents of the Church, but as Mr Skinner appropriately observes, it " need not afford any matter of triumph to our Presbyterian neighbours, when they look to the great breach among themselves, which was beginning about this time, and is still widening, instead of being closed, as ours at last was, and still continues to be." Mr Skinner here alludes to the rise and progress of that numerous sect in Scotland called Seceders, which began under the auspices of the two brothers, ministers of the Presbyterian Establishment, named Ralph and Ebenezer Erskine, and some others, which was followed by another hive from the Established party, who gave themselves the title of the *Relief*. The seeds of dissent from the Presbyterian Kirk were now sown throughout Scotland, and soon grew up in rank luxuriance. The chief alleged grievance was the exercise of lay patronage in presentations to. the parishes, which interfered with the assumed right of the people to elect their own ministers. Other grievances were also urged, which, however, it is not within the province of the present work to state, as the Scottish Episcopal Church never had any connection with the Presbyterian Establishment, and still less with the sects which emanated from their parent, such as the Relief Presbyterians, the Seceders, who soon split among themselves, and were long known by the soubriquets of *Burghers* and *Antiburghers, Old Light Burghers* and *New Light Burghers, Cameronians, Glasites,* and others. Respecting the *Seceders,* an opinion may be formed of their principles, shortly after they constituted themselves into a separate body, and also of the extent of their learning and information, from the fact, that in one of their printed *Testimonies,* as they designate their official effusions, amongst the sins of the times which they enumerate, and which they considered likely to provoke the Divine vengeance, they specify as *grievances* the *repeal of the laws against witchcraft, and the open toleration of Episcopacy !* It is a singular coincidence that the Presbyterian Establishment began to be agitated by its own peculiar schisms, discords, and divisions, at the very time when the contest, for it never was more serious in the Scottish Episcopal Church, was concluded by the Concordate. " From this time," observes Mr Skinner, " the Collegiate system fell to pieces every day, and the Primitive Diocesan Episcopacy revived, though not to the former legal extent, yet as far as the circumstances of the Church required or allowed."

As it respects the Concordate of the Scottish Bishops in 1732, which restored peace to the Church, and was probably [one of the most important events in her internal history since the Revolution, an instance of either gross ignorance or wilful misrepresentation is paraded with the utmost ostentation by a Presbyterian minister, and eagerly seized as a precious discovery by the public prints belonging to his party. This occurs in " Letters on Puseyite Episcopacy, by John Brown, D.D., Minister of Langton, Berwickshire," published in 1842, in a series of Letters addressed to the Rev. Dr Pusey of Oxford. What notice Dr Pusey may think proper to take of this production, if indeed he may think it worth his notice at all, it is of course impossible for the present writer to conjecture ; but as Dr Brown must needs travel out of his way to attack the Scottish Episcopal Church, a few remarks are necessary. It surely ought to have occurred to a gentleman who is a Doctor of Divinity, that if there is no valid ordination in the Scottish Episcopal Church, there can be none in the Church of England, for the consecrations of 1661 are the sources from which the Episcopate in

Scotland is derived. Dr Brown must either have been aware of the Concordate of 1732, or he must not ; and if he was not, it shows how utterly incompetent was the task he undertook in his " Letters on Puseyite Episcopacy." The passage in question was thus ostentatiously designated —" the Scottish Episcopalians not a Church of Christ according to their own principles ;" and he quotes a document signed by the College Bishops, in which they " suspend" the Bishops consecrated by the Diocesan Party. His great authority for this " discovery" is a certain Mr Norman Sievewright, who was a number of years minister of an " English" congregation in Brechin, a man who never acknowledged the authority of his proper Bishop, and who lived and died a schismatic. Mr Sievewright was one of that anomalous set of men episcopally ordained in England, who became "qualified" minister at Brechin, in other words, was in Scotland an *Independent*, though he used the English Liturgy, and made a pretence of belonging to the Church of England. It surely might have also occurred to Dr Brown, that if an Episcopal Church without a Bishop is an absurdity, surely an Episcopal congregation, the pastor of whom is not under diocesan superintendence, of necessity ceases to be episcopal. Mr Norman Sievewright chose to assail what he called the "pretensions of the Scottish Bishops," in other words, their claims to jurisdiction and authority over the presbyters, yet who or where was his Bishop? He affected to be in communion with the Church of England, yet what Bishop of that Church could recognize him, or in whose diocese did he consider himself? This "discovery" will not add to the reputation of Dr Brown and his party. If he was ignorant of the Concordate of 1732, he ought, as a " learned" Doctor of Divinity, to have made some inquiries into the history of the Church which he feebly endeavours to assail ; but if, on the other hand, he was well aware of this document, and purposely suppressed it, he displayed a dishonesty and malignity so marked as to make all his opinions and statements utterly valueless and contemptible And, after all, what is the whole affair ? Simply a dispute on one particular point, certainly of importance to the peace of the Church, but not in the least invalidating the proceedings of either party. Are there no wranglings, contentions, and mutual vituperations in the Presbyterian Establishment ? Are not some of its " depositions" of its parish ministers declared by a large party within its pale to be altogether illegal, and in reality not considered to be "depositions" at all? Let the cases of Strathbogie and other quarters answer these questions

The dispute between the Diocesan and College Parties, though carried on with acrimony, did not retard the zeal of the influential members of the Church. Wodrow himself gives us a very graphic delineation of those times under the date 1727 :—" I am told that Lady Ann Callendar, as she styles herself, the Earl of Linlithgow's daughter,* married to the Earl of Kilmarnock, hath set up a meeting-house for the English Service at the Brigend of Linlithgow, but it is not much frequented— that by her means a fine large meeting-house is setting up at Falkirk, and a great many of the country thereabout are contributing to it— that the Lady Kilmarnock usually goes to a meeting-house of Mr James Grahame,† who is married to her aunt, the late Earl of Linlithgow's sister, but it [the Episcopal meeting-house] is so distant, and she was in such hazard going to it when last with child, that she is very active to get one near her. I believe in all these, though the people who attend are Jacobites, yet the King is prayed for, and the Act of Toleration is the foot upon which they go. At this rate we shall very soon have a *general setting up of meeting-houses for the English Service*, and our gentry and nobility, who are *tinctured with that way by their being in England*, and the Jacobites, who countenance them from their *regard to Prelacy*, and to bring over young gentlemen to Jacobitism, and weaken the Established Church ; and, I fear, I may add too many of our young *bright images*,‡ as they are called, who are at least ambulatory

---

* This lady's father was James fourth Earl of Callendar, and fifth Earl of Linlithgow, attainted for his connection with the Enterprise of 1715, hence Wodrow's sneer—*as she calls herself*. She married William fourth Earl of Kilmarnock, and it is said that she was so zealous in favour of Prince Charles in 1745, that she never gave his Lordship rest till he joined the Adventurers, for which he was beheaded with Lord Balmerino in 1746. Her Ladyship and all her connections were zealous Episcopalians, but the Earl of Kilmarnock appears to have been a Presbyterian. The mansion of Callendar House, near Falkirk, was then the Family residence.

† This gentleman was James Graham, Esq of Airth, in the county of Stirling, a few miles beyond Falkirk, and not far from the Earl's seat of Callendar House. He filled the office of Judge-Admiral of Scotland till his death in 1734 Wodrow mentions him as if he had been clergyman of the "meeting-house"

‡ This is a hit at certain parties in the Presbyterian Establishment, who entertained enlightened views on church matters, and were much disliked by such old gentlemen as Wodrow, who gave them the ridiculous soubriquet of *Bright Images*

in the matter of church government and outward modes and circumstances. Laying all these together, I fear a very few years will bring about a terrible and fearful change in this church, and the inclinations of the most part will be for *bringing in the English Services among us;* and some think, were it not for the listlessness of the English as to any worship, and their apprehensions that it's not safe at present to break in upon this reserved article of the Union, we had had Prelacy and ceremonies among us by this time. The Lord pity us!"*

These admissions on the part of Wodrow are additional proofs that the Presbyterians by no means considered their Establishment secure, and they undeniably indicate that in many districts they were not certain of the attachment of the people. The "meeting-houses," or congregations of the Scottish Episcopal Church, were then numerous throughout the kingdom, and were supported by persons of the highest rank and influence. We shall see that the Enterprise of 1745 was the cause of a heavy "discouragement" to the Church, from which it did not recover for upwards of half a century.

* Wodrow's Analecta, MS, Advocates' Library.

CHAPTER XVI.

INTERNAL AFFAIRS OF THE SCOTTISH EPISCOPAL CHURCH—DEATHS OF BISHOP GADDERAR, BISHOP RATTRAY, AND OTHERS—PEACEFUL AND PROSPEROUS STATE OF THE CHURCH PREVIOUS TO 1745—EPISCOPAL SYNOD OF EDINBURGH IN 1743—DISPUTES ON THE CANONS OF THAT SYNOD.

At the signing of the Concordate in 1732, nine diocesan Bishops formed an Episcopal Synod, of whom Bishop Freebairn was Primus or presiding Bishop. We have seen that this Prelate, at the death of Bishop Lumsden of Edinburgh in the month of July 1733, was elected by the presbyters of that diocese as their ordinary. Bishops Duncan and Rose also died in 1733; but the greatest loss which the Church sustained was the death of Bishop Gadderar of Aberdeen, in the month of February that same year. This highly respected and distinguished man conferred by his strenuous efforts and his undaunted perseverance the most important benefits on the Scottish Episcopal Church, and he had the satisfaction before his death of seeing that Church a well organized and efficient communion, its clergy numerous and respectable, and its laity attached to its interests by the most zealous bonds of principle and affection.

Bishop Dunbar, to whom had been assigned the superintendence of the Church in the ancient dioceses of Moray and Ross, was elected the successor of Bishop Gadderar by the presbyters of Aberdeen in June 1733. He accepted the election, and resigned Moray. The Clergy of that diocese elected the Rev. George Hay to be their ordinary, but he died before his consecration, and the district remained vacant till 1741. In the year 1733, Bishop Keith was elected diocesan by the presbyters in the county of Fife, all of which lies within the archiepiscopal diocese of St Andrews, and he was connected with them till 1743, when he resigned the district, and was succeeded by the Rev. Robert White, presbyter at Cupar-Fife, who was consecrated at Carsebank near Forfar by Bishops Rattray, Dunbar, and Keith, in 1735. The districts of Caithness and Orkney were vacant till 1741, when, on the 10th of September, the Rev. William Falconer, presbyter at Forres, who had been duly elected by the clergy, was consecrated by Bishops Rattray, Keith, and White. Bishop Falconer was, however, elected by the presbyters of Moray to be their diocesan in the following year.

Bishop Gillan died in 1735, and Bishop White now mentioned was elected by the presbyters of Dunblane to be their diocesan. Bishop White was elected on the 18th of March, and was consecrated on the 14th of June. The Primus, Bishop Freebairn, had issued his summons to consecrate Bishop White at Edinburgh, but the other Bishops disobeyed, and elevated the new Bishop to the episcopate at Carsebank. The reason for thus setting at nought the will of the Primus is thus narrated by Mr Skinner:—" This gentleman [Bishop Freebairn] still retained a tincture of the old political leaven, and attachment to established forms; and having, by means of his son, who was in great favour abroad, got hold of some papers he was fond of, he called a meeting of the Bishops in 1734; but they,-suspecting the design, and not choosing to be longer entangled with any thing of that nature, declined the meeting, and would not so much as look at his papers." Shortly after this Bishop Gillan died, and Mr White having been elected by the presbyters of Dunblane, the Primus was requested by Bishops Rattray, Dunbar, and Keith, to name the day for the consecration of the new Bishop. His conduct, however, excited their suspicions, and those three Bishops held the consecration at Carsebank. " This produced a warm remonstrance from Bishop Freebairn, which was properly answered from the other side; and some other little differences ensued at the instigation of Bishop Ochterlonie, who still sought to keep up the division, but they were not of long duration, for Freebairn died in 1739, and Ochterlonie in 1742."

No event of any consequence occurs in the history of the Scottish Episcopal Church from this period for some time. After the death of Bishop Freebairn in 1739, no diocesan was elected for Edinburgh till 1776, and the reasons assigned for this long vacancy are as contradictory as they are doubtful. Externally the Church enjoyed peace and security George II had succeeded his father without any hostile appearance of opposition from the old quarter, and as no new provocation had been given by the adherents of the exiled dynasty, the laws were not rigorously enforced against them. The Presbyterians had too much business of their own on hand to bestow any attention on the affairs of Scottish Episcopacy. The contumacious Seceders were now giving them year after year an infinitude of trouble, and dissent was making rapid progress among them. Complaints were daily made of the oppression of the people by patronage; the Established "judicatories" were declared to be "corrupt;" and a controversy was again revived respecting the doctrines and principles maintained in a work which excited their enthusiastic minds, bearing the extraordinary title of the *Marrow of Modern Divinity*. Those Presbyterian ministers who took an interest in the opinions set forth in that production were known by the ludicrous distinction of *Marrow-Men*—a title which they assumed themselves. An event also occurred, which was likely to be attended with serious consequences to some of them. In 1737 the celebrated riot took place in Edinburgh, commonly called the *Porteous Mob*, the history of which is well known. The fate of the unhappy Captain Porteous, and the daring conduct of the mob, irritated the Government, more especially as every attempt to discover the ringleaders was unsuccessful; and a proclamation was issued to bring the rioters to justice, which all the Established ministers in Scotland were enjoined to read publicly from their pulpits on the first Sunday of every month throughout a whole year. This excited the greatest clamour, as an extraordinary and flagrant encroachment on the liberties and independence of their polity. These and other subjects completely occupied the attention of the Establishment, while the Scottish Episcopal Church was not only enjoying internal peace, but a very considerable degree of worldly prosperity from the signing of the Concordate to the year 1746. " During that period," says Bishop Russell, " her clergy were numerous, and many of them learned, whilst her chapels were frequented by all orders of the people, from the highest peer to the lowest peasant, even judges and magistrates joining in her worship. Although the King was not prayed for by *name*, and although by far the greater number of the clergy were attached to the exiled prince, political opinions respecting the rights of the sovereign were at no period, at least after the extinction of the College Party, made terms of communion. Some even of the clergy, and indeed one of the most learned of them, disclaimed the very idea of *indefeasible hereditary right*, and declared that they thought the sovereign who afforded protection to the people was in return entitled to their allegiance and prayers; but such clergymen were restrained from deviating from the general practice of their fathers and brethren by the *Oath of Abjuration*, which, supposing a kind of right that, if possessed by any one, they could not but think was possessed by him whom they were called on to abjure, they could not take; and without taking the Oath of *Abjuration* as well as that of *Allegiance*, the praying for King George by name would have been of no advantage to them whatever. Of all this the magistrates, to whom was entrusted the execution of the laws, were fully sensible, and therefore they seldom if ever enforced the penal part of the act of Queen Anne."*

Bishop Ochterlonie, who presided over the clergy in the diocese of Brechin, died in 1742, and the presbyters lost no time in electing a successor. The Rev. James Rait, presbyter in Dundee, was chosen, and he was consecrated on the 4th of October that year, by Bishops Rattray, Keith, and White. This pious and worthy prelate was ordained deacon by Dr Rose of Edinburgh in 1712, and was admitted into priest's orders in the following year. He was personally known to others of the deprived Bishops. The following memoranda of Bishop Rait is worthy of notice. He got immediate possession of a *parish church* after his ordination, " we think the church of Kirriemuir, and, though an inflexible Nonjuror, he kept possession of it through the influence of the patron,† and the attachment of the parishioners at large, until the year 1716, but, as we have repeatedly heard him say, he never received the stipend. He was consecrated a Bishop on the 4th of October 1742, and with that good sense which was the distinguishing trait of his character,

* Scottish Episcopal Magazine (1821), vol. ii p. 207.
† The patron of the parish of Kirriemuir, in the county of Forfar and diocese of Brechin, was at that period Archibald third Marquis of Douglas, born 1694, and created Duke of Douglas, Marquis of Angus and Abernethy, &c. by patent, dated 18th April 1703 His Grace at the period noticed in the text was only twenty years of age. Though a zealous member of the Scottish Episcopal Church throughout his valuable life, his Grace was a determined supporter of the royal succession as secured to the House of Hanover, and was in arms as a volunteer at the battle of Sheriffmuir in 1715.

he never failed to declare, in the letters of orders which he granted, that the Scottish Episcopal Church, in the ordination of his clergy, always, at least since the Restoration, made use of the English forms:—
'Omnibus ubique Catholicis per presentes pateat, Nos, Jacobum Rait, miseratione divina Episcopum, &c. in capella nostra publica quæ Taoduni (Dundee) est—X. Y. sacro diaconatus ordine jam condecoratum—ad sacrum presbyteratus ordinem promovisse, et secundum morem et ritum *Ecclesiæ Anglicanæ in Scotia hucusque usitatum* ordinasse, &c.'"*

In the year 1743 the Church sustained a severe loss by the death of Bishop Rattray of Craighall, diocesan of Dunkeld. He succeeded Bishop Freebairn as Primus in 1739. He was a man whom, as Mr Skinner most justly observes, "the Episcopal Church of Scotland will long look back to with pleasure, in the grateful remembrance of having had such a Bishop, and with a deep regret for having been so soon deprived of him." The venerable writer commemorated the death of this worthy Bishop in some Latin verses published in the third volume of his posthumous works, and Dr Drummond of Logie-Almond rendered his tribute of respect and affection in an English poem which appeared at the time. The literary works of Bishop Rattray evince his orthodox principles and his scholastic attainments In the year 1728 he published an " Essay on the Nature of the Church, and a Review of the Election of Bishops in the Primitive Church, together with some annexed Dissertations " In 1744 his family published his most esteemed work, entitled, " The Ancient Liturgy of the Church of Jerusalem, being the Liturgy of St James, freed from all latter Additions and Interpolations of whatever kind, and so restored to its original purity, by comparing it with the account of that Liturgy by St Cyril in his fifth mystagogical Catechism, and with the Clementine Liturgy, &c., with an English translation and notes; as also an Appendix, containing some other ancient Prayers, of all which an account is given in the Preface." In 1748 there appeared " Some Particular Instructions concerning the Christian Covenant, and the Mysteries by which it is transacted and maintained, collected from the Sacred Scriptures, and earliest Writers of the Christian Church, and from approved Divines of the Church of England." We are told by one of his distinguished successors in the

* Scottish Episcopal Magazine (1821), vol. ii. p. 185.

episcopate—" Bishop Rattray's printed works sufficiently show his learning, which in theology was held in the highest estimation by his ecclesiastical contemporaries both in England and in Scotland, with whom his epistolary correspondence was very extensive. Many of his letters, sermons, and dissertations, yet remain in manuscript, most of which display much reading and sound judgment."[*]

Bishop Rattray was succeeded as Primus by Bishop Keith, who about the same time resigned the diocesan superintendence of Fife, and Bishop White was transferred from the diocese of Dunblane to this charge. Meanwhile the clergy of Dunkeld, having obtained a mandate for that purpose, met and elected the Rev. John Alexander, presbyter at Alloa, to be their diocesan in the room of Bishop Rattray, and he was consecrated at Edinburgh, on the 9th of August 1743, by Bishops Keith, White, Falconer, and Rait. As five Bishops were present at this consecration, a meeting was subsequently held of the Episcopal College; and, on the motion of Bishop Dunbar, they resolved to constitute themselves a regular synod—Bishop Keith being Primus, and Bishop Alexander acting as clerk. Certain canons, drawn up by Bishop Rattray, and suitable to the peculiar circumstances of the Church, were taken into consideration, and ratified, with the addition of six others, in all amounting to sixteen.

These canons embodied all the articles of the Concordate respecting the internal government of the Church, regulating the election and official duties of the Primus, and the mode of electing Bishops to vacant dioceses by the Presbyters. The fourth canon declares—" That upon the demise or translation of any Bishop, the presbyters of the district thereby become vacant shall not be at freedom either to elect, or entrust themselves to another Bishop without a mandate from the Primus, with the majority of the Bishops; but if the Primus shall refuse to grant a mandate, the majority may do it without him." The fifth canon requires the person elected to be sanctioned by a majority of the Bishops, who are entitled to reject him on sufficient grounds, and to require the presbyters to proceed to another election. The sixth relates to the office of Dean, defining the duties and communication with the Primus

---

[*] Edition of Keith's Catalogue of Scottish Bishops, by Bishop Russell, p. 537, 538, 539.

at the death or translation of the Bishop; and the seventh declares that the episcopal duties of a vacant diocese shall devolve upon the Bishop whose place of residence is nearest to the diocese until an election take place, and that in those temporary circumstances, if cases of discipline occur, these shall be referred to the decision of the Primus and a majority of his colleagues. The eighth enjoins letters testimonial when any of the clergy remove from one diocese to another, and prohibits the ordination of any one as a presbyter who has no designation to a particular charge. The ninth enacts—" That seeing, in the present distressed state of this Church, it may happen that a Bishop may have his dwelling and place of worship within the district of another Bishop, in that case those who belong to this his congregation, together with the presbyters or deacons joined with him as his assistants in officiating therein, shall be as much under his jurisdiction as if they were within the bounds of his own district, and shall be exempt from the jurisdiction of that Bishop within the bounds of whose district they are ; and the Bishop in whose district they are shall, by a subscribed deed, agree to this regulation." The other canons, which are all excellent, judicious, and embodying the principles of Primitive Episcopacy, refer to various matters connected with the internal government, discipline, and practice of the Church.

It appears that when these canons were promulgated by the Episcopal Synod to the clergy, some of those in Edinburgh, who had one of their own number in view to be elected their diocesan, and who they knew would not be acceptable to the Bishops, objected to the canon which regulated the election of Bishops as infringing on their rights of election. They also complained that several of the other canons curtailed the powers of their Ordinary as Bishop of Edinburgh. A regular controversy, or rather a series of remonstrances from the presbyters of Edinburgh, ensued, which, though without the acrimony exhibited when the *College Party* agitated the Church, is not without interest, especially as connected with a project for bringing Bishop Smith, a Nonjuror from England, into Scotland, in opposition to the warnings of the Scottish Bishops. These documents are in a MS. volume, entitled, " Disputes of the Episcopalians," preserved in the Library of the Faculty of Advocates at Edinburgh.

The exposition of the views of the Presbyters is dated Edinburgh,

January 17, 1744, and is thus addressed:—" To the Right Reverend the Bishops of the Churches in Scotland, the Presbyters of the Diocese of Edinburgh send greeting:—

" Being convened here in virtue of a letter from our reverend and much respected brother, Mr Thomas Auchinleck, now the senior presbyter in Edinburgh, there was read to us a letter of the 5th of December, directed to him by the Right Reverend Bishop Keith, importing that your Reverences had lately held a Synod, wherein you had established several canons relating to the several dioceses, or, as you are pleased to call them, districts of this Church, whether full or vacant, and particularly one relating to this diocese or district of Edinburgh, whereby your Primus is appointed to write to the senior Presbyter, to convocate us for choosing a Dean who is to represent us in all synodical meetings, by sitting with your Reverences, to propose and reason in all matters of discipline and grievances of presbyters, but not to give any decisive voice; and, last of all, we are allowed to call for a copy of the minutes of your said Synod either from your Primus or clerk, and accordingly a copy was laid before us, transcribed by one of our brethren from an authentic duplicate in the hands of Bishop Keith.

" We shall not at present trouble your Reverences with remarks upon your canons any further than they concern ourselves, and even that would not have been our choice, but that the necessity you have put us under would make our silence sinful; for it is with grief of heart we find ourselves obliged to complain of the proceedings of those whom by principle and inclination we are much disposed to love and obey. But while we honour your sacred office, and do not at all envy you the dignity to which you have attained, we cannot be quite unconcerned for the rights of our own lower order, when we see designs forming to invade those rights, or threaten them with danger. This concern, we humbly conceive, cannot be displeasing to your Reverences, if it is considered only as an imitation of that zeal to preserve those rights which some of your venerable number showed when ye were with us; nor can we think it less incumbent upon us to watch over this sacred depositum, that we have now, by what means we shall not say, been long kept in a state of orphancy without the guidance and protection of a proper head, when, like the clergy of Rome (during the vacancy of that see)—*incumbat nobis qui videmur propositi esse vice pastoris custodire gregem.*

As we humbly apprehend the constitution of a Christian Church is a thing so sacred and so determined, that it cannot be new modelled or altered in essentials upon every revisal made of it by any one of its constituent parts, so it is no more competent to your high order to abolish the presbyterate than it is in our power to renounce or withhold that canonical obedience we owe to our Bishops, so it appears to us (from our histories, from our records, from our laws of the kingdom, establishing episcopacy, from the writings of some of our most judicious divines, and from the testimony of some of our brethren yet living, who saw the Church in vigour, and were eye-witnesses of her good order and government), that by the constitution of the Episcopal Church of Scotland, the presbyters did sit in Synods and Church Assemblies with their Bishops, not barely to hear and propose, but to reason and represent, that they had authoritative voices, and voted decisively in whatsoever question came before them:—that not only the Deans and other dignitaries of each diocese came to those assemblies in their own right, but the rural clergy were duly represented there by some of their own number, chosen by themselves, and sent thither on that purpose, whose votes were numbered with the rest:—and, in short, that the powers of legislation and discipline were not then thought to have been lodged in the Bishops alone, without the advice and concurrence of their clergy.

" As this privilege of the second order has been long struggled for in other Churches, even where papal encroachments went high, and as it is still preserved by our sister Church of England, where nothing can have the force of a canon, or regularly pass into ecclesiastical law, without the consent of presbyters, and where each house of convocation has a negative upon the other, so we humbly think it would be rather superfluous than difficult to show, that all this is copied from the primitive pattern, and is well consistent with the Holy Scriptures, and with the constitution and practice of the Church of Christ in her purest and best ages. To make this appear would be no hard task; but we do not imagine your Reverences need any such ecclaircissement, or that you will ever set us to prove that the Church whereof you are chief officers, and from which you derive your orders, was a Christian Church, sound and well constituted, or, in other words, that she was not blemished with any such gross fundamental error or defect as affected her essentials—the very vitals of religion, which, we humbly apprehend, is the only care can warrant a reform of her model in our present circumstances, when so much dangers must attend every material alteration of her polity as well as doctrine or worship. The constitution of our Church thus appearing to us to be regular and right, and well founded, we humbly conceive that we are obliged in conscience, in virtue of the duty we owe to God and his Church, to your Reverences, to ourselves, and to all them who may succeed us in the second order, earnestly to beg you would stop all further innovation of any sort, and particularly all encroachments upon the rights and privileges of our second order, or whatever may tend to subverting that good and wholesome constitution; for we humbly conceive the case is the same in bodies mystical and politic as in the natural body, that when the constitution is once broken, if it is not soon repaired by immediate care and proper application, nothing but languishing and death is like to ensue. This being our constitution, and considering that you have proceeded single and alone to hold a Synod, wherein you have made or ratified several canons, and treated and concluded in matters of legislation and discipline relating to the whole Church, notwithstanding the presbyters of Scotland were not represented there, nor were called to take that place which belongs to them in Synods and Assemblies of the Church. This being the hard case, we do earnestly beg your Reverences will consider seriously what must be the fatal consequence; whether laws and constitutions can be submitted to where the legislature was uncomplete, or if they should be submitted to, whether the constitution of the Church would not thereby receive a deep wound.

"Having thus declared in general our humble opinion that the canons of the late Synod cannot be obligatory upon the members, either clergy or laity, of this Church, as being destitute of a proper sanction, while they are without the advice and approbation of the majority of the integral parts of our constitution, it is with reluctancy we must now descend to an examination, which we find no less liable to exception than they are in gross, and on account of the stinted authority of which they stand enacted: but in this particular we shall but gently touch a few instances by which we think ourselves most injured, and the peace or being of our Church most endangered. Your ninth canon is—' That, seeing in the present distressed state of this Church, it may happen that a Bishop shall have his dwelling and place for public worship within the district of another Bishop; in that case those who belong to this his congregation, together with the presbyters or deacons joined with him as his assistants officiating therein, shall be as much under his jurisdiction as if they were within the bounds of his own district, and shall be exempt from the jurisdiction of that Bishop within the bounds of whose district they are.' As this Canon seems chiefly intended for serving a particular purpose in the city of Edinburgh, where, if it should take effect, our Bishop, when God shall bless us with one, would be robbed of a part of his flock and a considerable number of his clergy, and all the refugees from his discipline would take shelter under the patronage of the exempt Bishop, as on all those accounts we find it incumbent upon us, in our present circumstances, to guard against it, so we humbly conceive it is directly repugnant to the plan of Primitive Episcopacy, to the polity and canons of the ancient Church, which, instead of encouraging one Bishop to have his place of residence and public worship within the diocese of another, forbade and condemned non-residence, declared there would be but one Bishop in one city, and piously believed that as there is but one God, one Christ the Lord, and one Holy Ghost, so there ought to be one Bishop in a Catholic Church. When your Reverences have thus altered the shape of Episcopal government, and struck at the rights of your own order, we need not be surprised at the little regard showed for those of ours We are assured some years ago that the presbyters of a vacant diocese had inherent rights and privileges, as those of Rome had during the long vacancy of that See after the martyrdom of Fabian—that it belonged to them to elect their own Bishop—that they might of themselves meet for that purpose as well as any other—and that a mandate from the metropolitan, or Bishop of the province, was not necessary unless the presbyters proved backward in the matter; but now we are told the contrary, for your Third Canon decrees—' That if any Bishop shall lay claim to any metropolitan or vicarial power, he shall be suspended from all ecclesiastical jurisdiction, even within his own district, until he renounce that claim, being what may prove of most dangerous consequence to the Church in the present circumstances.' And yet, for what appears to us, excepting these alterations your Reverences have made, the circumstances of our Church are much the same they were about seventeen years ago, when you declared, in like solemn manner, that no good order or unity could be maintained in the

Church without a metropolitan. We would have taken no notice of this if your Third Canon were not intended to give a secret blow to the rights and privileges of the See of Edinburgh, whereof we humbly think ourselves guardians during the vacancy. By your Fourth, Fifth, and Seventh Canons it is decreed—' That upon the demise or translation of any Bishop, the presbyters of the district thereby become vacant shall not be at freedom either to elect or submit themselves to any other Bishop without a mandate from the Primus, with the majority of. the Bishops:—that, if they happen to elect a presbyter, of whose fitness for that office the Bishops shall declare they have sufficient reasons not to be satisfied, in this case the presbyters shall be required by the Bishops to proceed to a new election; and that during the vacancy of any district the presbyters thereof shall apply to the Bishop who shall have his place of residence nearest to them for the performing of episcopal offices amongst them, and no other Bishop shall take upon him to perform any such offices within that district without the consent of the neighbouring Bishop.' By these ordinances, and the one referred to in the beginning of this paper, we humbly conceive the rights of our order are stripped to a shadow, and our privileges greatly shortened of what your Reverences thought once they should be. We might then meet and elect a Bishop without waiting for leave from the metropolitan, but now we must not without a mandate from your temporary Primus. The semblance of power still left us to choose our Bishop is made void and elusory, while your Reverences have reserved for yourselves a faculty of rejecting our elect without giving us a reason, only telling us you have reasons that satisfy yourselves; and thus we must be sent to elect over and over again, till we come to the happy favourite who may be most acceptable to your Reverences, though perhaps least fit for us and for the purposes of his high calling, unless we should happen, like a staunch jury, still to return the same verdict. And as you have thus endeavoured to straiten our access to a proper Ordinary, so have you made our state of orphancy still more comfortless, depending, and perplexed, by your transferring the care of the vacant districts, which in ancient times belonged to the metropolitan, to the neighbouring Bishop, the design whereof is so obvious that we need make no remarks, further than to assure your Reverences that it has but a poor chance to answer the expectation of the contriver. Though, indeed, it looks somewhat odd and designing that, while we seem to be left in possession of the privilege to choose our Ordinary, we should have no power to choose whom of your venerable number we may incline to apply to for Episcopal offices during the vacancy; and, to complete this new scheme of ecclesiastical polity, our second order, which in former times had a right to sit and vote in assemblies of the Church, not only by Deans and other dignified persons, but by the proctors of the inferior clergy, in proportion to their numbers and the extent of each diocese, is henceforth to be represented in your future Synods by one cypher, a mere titular Dean, who may hear and speak, but is by no means to be allowed the privilege of voting. Of this we have already declared our sentiments. Thus we have adventured, as we thought ourselves obliged to give your Reverences our sentiments of the matters before us, and to make a stand for the rights of our order and the peace of the Church, not for ourselves only, but in name of all our fellow presbyters in Scotland, who are equally concerned, and will therefore adhere to us, that you may be acquainted with our judgment on these important subjects, since you have given us no opportunity to declare it in a more proper way. We hope your Reverences will not think us Presbyterians for affirming the just rights of the second order Some of the greatest men our island has produced were of the same sentiments, and the best of our Kings, who died a martyr for the Church, came to find too late that a moderate Episcopacy was the best.

"We solemnly declare, before God and the world, that we have no intention nor desire to restrain the just powers, or to invade the due privileges, of your sacred order, as we dare not surrender those of our own, being sensible that encroachments from either side would be equally fatal to the Church, as equally endangering her constitution.

"Finding ourselves engaged to write to persons of your great learning, we thought it unnecessary to lengthen this paper by bringing the proper vouchers of what we have said; but if your Reverences shall think it needful, we are ready to bring them forth on the shortest warning. As this humble address and memorial is well meant, we hope your Reverences will take it in good part. It is still in your power to restore peace and honour to this distressed Church, by agreeing to let her polity stand upon the old true foundation.

"We shall not cease to pray that God may grant peace and truth in our days, and that all the members of this Church, of whatever order, may be endowed with that wisdom which is from above—which is first pure, then peaceable, gentle, and easy to be entreated, full of mercy and good works, without partiality, and without hypocrisy. As we have just regard for our brother, Mr Thomas Auchinleck, and as your Reverences seem to point at him in your canons, and by Bishop Keith's letter, we have chosen him to preside in our meeting; but that we may copy as nigh as possible your worthy example, we have chosen him our moderator only *pro tempore*, and during pleasure; and, therefore, to assure your Reverences that this present deed contains the sentiments of our hearts, which by the grace of God we are resolved not to depart from, it is subscribed not only by our Preses, but by

"The names of the subscribers are,—Thomas Auchinleck, *Moderator*. Alex. Robertson, *Clerk*. Alex. Hunter. Alex. M'Kenzie. Da. Rae. Henry Fowlis. Ja. M'Kenzie Ja. Windgate. Jo. Addison Jo. M'Kenzie. Jos. Robertson. Tho Drummond Tho. Wilkie. Will. Forbes. Will Harper. Will. Law. Robert Blair."

No observations are necessary respecting the foregoing document. As it respects Bishop Smith, the following letter addressed to him by Bishop Keith, dated May 22, 1744, completely explains the projects he and some of the Edinburgh presbyters had in view:—

"Right Reverend Brother,—At your desire I saw the letter of April 2, which you sent to the Reverend Mr John M'Kenzie of this city. I thank you for the favour, although I can't but acknowledge the contents did surprise me not a little. The suppositions you are pleased to frame to yourself, and the things which you say that you see in our late minutes, my most inward conscience knows to be altogether groundless. I am sorry to find you forming a resolution to set forward an illicit consecration in this country, and thereby to raise a most horrid schism in this free and independent Church, for no cause whatsoever that any indifferent persons even in your own country will be able, I dare presume, to discern. I can assure you there is neither any alteration intended here in the public worship, nor is there any complaint in all this kingdom upon that score, except, perhaps, by the seditious of Edinburgh, who, under that sculk, are fond to palliate their old rancour, envy, and hatred of us Bishops. They will not venture, I suppose, to hold up their hands and take the great omniscient Being to witness, who knows and searches their hearts, that the case of either the English or the Scotch Liturgy is the true cause of their quarrel with us; otherwise, how should it come to pass that all and every one of them have administered the holy eucharist by the Scotch Liturgy only, or by some addition, diminution, or transposition in the English Office, and this of their own accord, without any force or persuasion whatsoever? Must not, then, their application to you proceed from some other secret fountain, and tend towards a different view than what they suffer you to discern? They want to wrest the Episcopate from us, and to obtain this they are willing to purchase your assistance at any rate—an assistance which I humbly think you ought not to send them, as you will be answerable to Almighty God for the many unhappy consequences that must inevitably follow upon it; for, do you think, my dear brother, that your intermeddling in our affairs will create peace amongst us? No, by no means, but rather strife, contention, and every evil work. And will not this prove a melancholy reflection to you at the last, especially since ye have neither just call nor title to mix in our Church? No person could speak more strongly against such a practice than you have done in your letters both to Bishop Gillan and me, excerpts from which (lest ye keep not copies) I here send you, and therefore I would fain hope you will still conform yourself to your former sober and sage declarations. Let not, I beseech you, the fallacious representations of designing men (however varnished over) so far prevail with you as to kindle such a flame in your neighbour's house as may not only consume him but yourself also. Hitherto we have lived in good correspondence with the Church of England. We have declined, when solicited, to act the part which you now threaten us with, as you yourself may very well know. We have always looked upon her as a sister Church, and we desire still to continue in communion and fellowship with her. Her Liturgy was never prohibited in this country, but always allowed; nor, as I wrote you on the 13th December last, shall any clergyman here receive any molestation upon account of his using it, as it is most certain that no person has to this day suffered the smallest frown upon that head. May not I, then, as a brother, as a friend, as a neighbour, obtest you, and even expect, that ye will desist from this unwary enterprise; but if ye needs must proceed in so unjustifiable a step, I believe I may assure you, on very good ground, that the very name of a stranger Bishop coming to meddle in our matters in so extraordinary a manner will ruin the cause you would wish to support more than anything you could devise ; and I am even suspicious that your overdoing at this time by your letters will keep your point at a greater distance than if ye had said less upon the head. People don't like to be imperiously dealt by. Thus, dear Sir, I have discharged the duty I thought incumbent on me, as bearing, though unworthy, the same sacred character with yourself; and God grant that both you and I may so demean ourselves in our office, that when the chief Shepherd shall appear we may receive some approbation from him.

" I had almost forgot to set you at rights in a point of fact. All the ordinations of our Scotch clergymen have not been performed by the English ordinal since the Restoration of King Charles II. ; for I have in my possession just now an original act of ordination, performed at Edinburgh, *anno* 1680, *secundum morem et ritum Ecclesiæ Scoticanæ,* which act I intend to put into the Royal Register of this kingdom, and you may procure an extract of it from thence when you please.

" Together with the excerptions, I send you copies of two or three other papers ;* and I am ready enough to flatter myself that disinterested persons will give attention to such solemn declarations —I am, dear Sir, your affectionate brother and most humble servant,

" ROBERT KEITH."

Bishop Smith's conduct seems to have elicited the following declaration, signed by Bishop Keith, and transmitted to his Right Reverend Brethren for their concurrence, dated July 12, 1744:—

" 1*mo*, Whereas, by the Preface to Bishop Rattray's Ten Canons, passed and ratified in our Synod holden at Edinburgh in the month of August 1744, it is represented, that the Bishops of the Church of Scotland being now by the good providence of God perfectly united in one and the same mind, and that Concordates which were framed while some unhappy differences subsisted among them are thereby vacated, we hereby declare that this expression (which, together with the whole Preface, was

* " These were Bishop Keith's Declaration, April 7 , Bishop Dunbar's letter to Bishop Keith, April 28 ; and Bishop Alexander's letter to Bishop Keith, May 14, 1744 "

the work of Bishop Rattray), as well as the Canons themselves, regards only the Concordates being vacated through the total demise of one party of those Bishops, who contracted and concurred in framing the Concordates ; but that it never was intended (as some persons have suspected) to prohibit or restrict the use of the English Liturgy in this kingdom. So far from this, that we declare the use of this Liturgy has been and shall be as free to any presbyter that chooses to minister by it, as it was and has been at any time by virtue of the Concordates.

"*2do*, We declare that we are in full communion with the Church of England as a sister Church, and are ready to give outward evidence hereof on all occasions, like as we expect the same compliance from the members of that Church when occasion shall offer. May the Church of England long preserve the just esteem and veneration it has gained in the Christian world ; may this esteem be always on the increase ; and may the gates of hell never be able to prevail either against it or this Church ; and may both Churches ever continue to cultivate union and harmony together, to the credit of our holy religion and the promoting of true piety and virtue !

"*3tio*, For ourselves, as we know that in the present situation of this Church we have no external coercive power, so we esteem the concurrence of our presbyters and people the only support, under God, of our episcopal government, and whenever we are made duly sensible of any just grievances, both duty and interest will oblige us speedily to remove them. It is the love and prayers of our clergy and people that must strengthen our hands. Each of us in particular is blessed with most dutiful and obliging presbyters, and we declare that we will do nothing of moment without consulting them ; and this union we trust will stand firm against all opposition. We must stand or fall together. (Signed) Ro. KEITH, *Primus.* WILL. DUNBAR, *Bishop.* Ro. WHITE, *Bishop.* WILL. FALCONER, *Bishop.* JOHN ALEXANDER, *Bishop.*"

Bishop Smith seems to have interfered so unwarrantably in the affairs of the Scottish Episcopal Church, that it was considered necessary to issue the following document, dated Alloa, October 22, 1744 :—
" Whereas the Right Rev. Bishop Smith of England has, by several letters of his to the Right Rev. Bishop Keith, the Rev. Mr John Mackenzie, and others, in Scotland, plainly assumed to himself a superiority, to which he can have no pretension, over the Bishops and Clergy of this

national Church, and has declared that he still owns as a presbyter Mr David Fife [at Dundee], formerly indeed a presbyter of this Church, but canonically deposed by the Bishops thereof, a thing contrary to all order and discipline, and to that principle of unity so carefully preserved in the first and purest ages of the Church :—We, the subscribing Bishop and Presbyters, have thought ourselves in duty bound, for the preservation of our own rights and independency, and in defence and maintenance of the principle as well as forms and constitution of the Catholic Church of Christ, to disclaim, and we do disclaim, and will to the utmost of our power oppose, all usurped authority over, or encroachments upon, the Bishops and clergy of this Church ; and do testify (as we here most sincerely do) our abhorrence of all principles and practice tending to destroy order and discipline, and to defeat that regular exercise of authority without which neither can possibly subsist, and to the producing and fomenting of schisms in the Church, to the great hurt and hinderance of true religion, and with infinite danger to the consciences of men. Declaring always, as we hereby declare, that we are and own ourselves to be of the same communion with the Church of England, and will endeavour on our part to preserve union with her as members of the same mystical body of the Lord Jesus. (*Sic subscribitur*) JOHN ALEXANDER, Bishop of Dunkeld. WILL SEION, Dean, and Presbyter in Forfar, and ten other presbyters."

The " Third Address of the Presbyters of Edinburgh to the Bishops of Scotland" is preserved in the same MS. volume, dated Dec. 22, 1744, and signed " James Mackenzie, Preses " They propose the following articles to adjust the dispute :—" I That you will null and void the Canons of last Synod, as having no proper authority, and redress the grievances consequent upon them ; and that no new Canons be made or binding upon the clergy and laity of this Church without competent authority.— II. That since the first article of the last Concordate has been frequently violated and broke through, viz. that we shall only make use of the Scottish or English Liturgy in the public or divine service, nor shall we disturb the peace of the Church by introducing into the public worship any of the ancient Usages, concerning which there has been lately a difference among us, and that we shall censure any of the clergy who act otherwise ; the present Bishops do each of them subscribe to this as a condition of peace and union, and any who shall be hereafter promoted, immediately before his consecration ; and that they give proper assurance for the due execution of it, without any mutilation, alteration, or transposition, in either of the Offices in the administration of Baptism, Confirmation, and of the Lord's Supper, and in the ordination of deacons and presbyters, and consecrations of Bishops.—III. That the privilege of electing Bishops be ascertained to the presbyters of this Church in their respective districts, and that the Bishops be obliged to consecrate the elect, upon presenting the instruments of election subscribed by a majority of the presbyters of the district, except the local custom impede it, or they make relevant objections against the faith and morals of the elect, and prove them in a regular canonical manner.— IV. That the division of districts made by the Concordate be observed, or reduced by common consent, to six or seven, which will serve all the needful occasions of episcopal administrations in this Church, and that no election be made without calling all the presbyters of that district to it.—V. That in conferring holy orders, and exercising acts of discipline within each district, every thing of moment be managed by common consent of the Bishop and his presbyters ; and in case a majority of the presbyters be against the opinion of their Bishop, he shall have a negative upon them ; for, as Bishop Sage says, by our constitution they can do nothing without him, nor he without them." They thus conclude the address :—" These grievances we humbly conceive we have a right to demand the redress of, but we choose rather to entreat it for love's sake, and for the tenderness of your own paternal bowels, which we still flatter ourselves are not quite shut up against us. If you do but so much as vouchsafe to give us an answer, we shall consider it as a happy interruption of that distance and cold reserve that we have been so long in, and with such a mortifying severity punished withal, and as a blessed presage of having a door opened for our readmission to your good graces, which would once more revive our drooping spirits, not only as it would be the most sensible happiness we could desire for ourselves, but as we think it would be a great step towards restoring peace to the Church, towards relieving the minds of the faithful from distressing jealousies and contentious disputes, and setting them at liberty to exert their whole force in the study and exercise of solid piety and true religion—an aid we are persuaded as desirable to your Reverences as to us.'

This letter, signed by the Rev. James Mackenzie, as " Preses," is written in a very different spirit from one by the same gentleman, dated Aug. 17, 1744, to Bishop Keith, transmitting ten queries on the relative connection of Bishops and presbyters, and very unpolitely thus expressing himself—" I take the freedom to send you the inclosed queries, and I hope you will not treat them as you did my letter about the exemption canon, by smuggling anonymous remarks among your particular admirers, without addressing for me a copy of them, but that you will vouchsafe to send me a direct, proper, and subscribed answer " Such haughty and disrespectful language probably accounts for the " distance and cold reserve," evinced by the Bishops, of which the presbyters of Edinburgh complain as having been for a long time " punished" with a "mortifying severity." What answer Bishop Keith returned to Mr Mackenzie's queries and his angry epistle does not appear, but the " Third Address" of the Presbyters elicited the following letter from the Bishop, dated January 25, 1744–5, addressed to " Mess. James Mackenzie, William Harper, John Mackenzie, Alexander Mackenzie, Alexander Robertson, Patrick Gordon, David Rae,* presbyters in Edinburgh, and William Law, presbyter in Leith "

" MY REVEREND BRETHREN,—There was sent me some time ago a paper that appears to have been signed by your Preses, in your name and by your appointment, and is addressed to the Bishops of this national Church.

" I persuade myself, my brethren, I need but point out to your reflection, without taking any pains to prove, that in the nature of the thing it is impossible that any distinct and decisive answers should be given to the demands or proposals your address contains without a meeting of the Bishops, since no one can take upon him to speak in name of the rest, nor all of us, by single and separate opinions, determine in matters that plainly require the authority of a Synod.

" You will easily understand, too, that such meetings are to some of our number attended with no small difficulty through age, infirmity,

* In another document Mr Rae is called Mr Rait, but he signs his own name David Rae He was probably the Rev. David Rae, formerly of St Andrews, father of Sir David Rae of Eskgrove, elevated to the Scottish Bench in 1782, when he took his seat by the title of Lord Eskgrove, nominated a Lord of Justiciary in 1785, Lord Justice-Clerk in 1800, and created a Baronet in 1804. His Lordship was the father of Sir William Rae, Bart Lord Advocate of Scotland from 1819 to 1830, in 1834 and 1835, and again appointed in 1841 by Sir Robert Peel's Administration.

distance of place, and other circumstances. It is not unreasonable, therefore, that before they submit to all the inconveniences of the thing, they should desire to see that disposition on your part that may encourage them to meet with any agreeable success How shall they be persuaded of this, my dear brethren, whilst you take [no] notice of the paper I lately offered to you, and which contains in it matters of so great moment to our common interests, both yours and ours? How shall they believe that a zeal for the rights of this national Church, under any notion or apprehension of them, really animates your proceedings? If, when her most undoubted rights are openly invaded, her independency struck at, you are careless and unconcerned? But however much this subject may deserve, and certainly it does deserve, your attention, the practices among us that gave occasion for, and receive countenance and encouragement from, the encroachment we complain of, afford matter of more formidable apprehension still, and deeper concern. Order and government, a reverence for the laws, and obedience to those that bear rule, things so valuable and of so great importance to the peace and welfare of all society, are in the Church (from the connection they have with and their subserviency to the great ends of religion) yet more precious and important, and as such have ever been dear to good men. What, then, can more sensibly touch you than the prospect we have now before us? When clergymen so far lose sense of that duty and obedience they owe to their superiors, that, admonished by their Bishops, they disregard it—censured by them, they shake off their authority; when the people come to believe that after a clergyman is canonically deposed his ministrations may be as valid as before, and that with safety to their consciences they may adhere to him as their pastor, though in direct contradiction to the most primitive and truly catholic principles; then, surely, all discipline is dissolved, all government is subverted, and it may seem idle in circumstances of this sort to dispute what is or what ought to be the peculiar constitution of a national Church, since it is evident—demonstratively evident—that when such opinions and such practices prevail, none can be of any signification. These are dangers, my brethren, real and great, and justly alarming. How is it, then, that ye refuse to give attention to them, though called upon to do so? Are the interests of religion, the great ends of true piety, better served? Is the glory of God, is the salvation of men, more advanced by order and discipline, and a due respect for authority, or by licentiousness and revolt, and that confusion which always follows them? Ways there are we know—the Scripture assures us of it—that may seem right to a man in his own eyes, though, in conclusion, they are the ways of death. And never, surely, ought the parties of the Church to watch with more anxious care, or warn with louder cries, than when there is danger of so fatal a mistake.

"You might blame me, perhaps, and I should blame myself, if I passed over in silence those expressions of filial affection this last address from you contains. Nothing could be more agreeable to us—I speak it with confidence for my brethren the other Bishops, as well as for myself—nothing is more the object of our wish, than to be possessed of your love and esteem, and that there should ever subsist between us that indissolvable union which, by the strongest ties of duty, and principle, and common interest, there ought to be. But certainly now is the time when they who have indeed a regard for our order ought to show they have, and when it cannot be doubted that where it appears it really is.

"You see the condition we are reduced to, the difficulties and discouragements that press us on every side You see our authority despised and defeated at home, invaded and insulted from abroad, left destitute of all support but the little it can receive from the principles and conscience of a very few. At a time and in circumstances of so great distress to us, what filial affection can remain insensible? Can it be alive, and not awaken? At such a time, my brethren, do you refuse us that assistance we so much need, and might so justly expect from you? Rather suffer your own rights to be encroached on than join with us in asserting ours. Formally compliment and really arraign us, not considering that when ye do so ye destroy that reverence for our office and character which alone can support it in our present circumstances. Possess the people with fears and jealousies, the never-failing source of discussion and calamity to this nation; give encouragement to opinions and practices of the most dangerous tendency, and extinguish the small remains of Christian principles among us, already as smoking flax in the minds of too many. Judge yourselves, my brethren; I speak as to those that know. Ought these things to be? May the infinite, great, and good God, with whom is counsel, and from whom it comes, direct your consultations, to the glory of his name and the peace of his afflicted Church; and the grace of our Lord Jesus Christ be with your spirits! Amen. (Signed) ROBERT KEITH."

The result of this paternal remonstrance to the presbyters of Edinburgh is indicated in a letter from some of them to Bishop Keith, containing their " Reasons for not subscribing the condemnation of Bishop Smith of England, in answer to a paper of said Bishop Keith urging that subscription." In this letter they acknowledge the Bishop's, above quoted, of the 25th of January, which they allege was not and could not be communicated to them till the 28th. This document is of considerable length, but does not throw much light on the matter, being chiefly an elaborate defence of Bishop Smith from the charge of " usurpation and encroachment" in the affairs of the Church. It is dated February 7, 1745, and is signed by the eight presbyters to whom the Bishop addressed his letter, with an intimation that "other four of the presbyters of this Diocese have already subscribed their adherence to us, and approbation of this paper, viz. Messrs Robert Blair, Henry Foulis at Dalkeith, William Harper at Bothkennar, and William Miln, and it is expected that others will sign." As it respects Bishop Keith and his conduct in this dispute the following extract is probably an explanation:—
" It is," says Bishop Russell, "a trite observation, that the man who most conscientiously does his duty is not always rewarded with the first burst of popular applause; and we find, accordingly, that Bishop Keith was by no means beloved by the presbyters of Edinburgh, among whom he had been so many years resident. He was seldom asked by any of them to perform in their congregations the offices peculiar to his order, and if we were to judge from a variety of addresses, remonstrances, and replies which are still on record, we should say that his intercourse with the inferior clergy was almost entirely confined to disputes about the limits of episcopal jurisdiction and the privileges of the priesthood. The presbyters of Edinburgh, who, at the period in question, used to elect a moderator, and assume considerable powers as a regular and standing *Presbytery*, were extremely jealous of any higher authority in the Church; while the Bishops, on the other hand, regulating their proceedings by a regard to abstract principle and ancient usage, rather than by a due consideration of the circumstances in which late events had placed their Communion, and still less by views of mere expediency, appear on several

occasions to have aimed at the possession of a degree of power which would have inevitably sunk the second order of ministers into absolute insignificance. The enactment of canons in 1743, as laws regulating the practice and defining the obedience of the whole Church, without desiring the advice or concurrence of any of the presbyters, was a stretch of prerogative which could not prove agreeable to the latter description of clergy; and although the Bishops might have no difficulty in proving that they had not on this occasion exceeded the limits of the authority inherent in their order, and which had been frequently exercised by the rulers of the Church in the purest times of Christianity, they would yet have attained their object more effectually by conceding a little to the spirit of the age and the wishes of their Brethren. The share which Bishop Keith had in this rather unseemly controversy will serve as an excuse for the mention which has been made of it in this place. His local situation as being resident in the metropolis, his official station as Primus, and, above all, his personal influence as a man of business as well as of letters, will account for the prominent part he acted as the representative and advocate of the Episcopal Synod."*

The objections to the canons of the Synod of 1743 were overruled by the clergy in general, who anticipated from them the most peaceful and successful results. The Church was now well organized, the congregations were numerous throughout the kingdom; even the leaders of the Presbyterian Establishment had become, as Mr Skinner observes, " more easy and pacific; and the infatuated generation of 1688 being mostly gone, their successors began to adopt more liberal sentiments." The prosperous state of the Church about 1745 was often mentioned by the old members half a century afterwards, when they contrasted their then condition with the severities they experienced after the suppression of the last attempt of the exiled royal family to recover the throne of Great Britain. They saw the blood of some of Scotland's chivalrous noblemen and gentlemen drenching the scaffold, their estates forfeited, their titles and their families attainted, and not a few of them exiled. They saw their religion again proscribed and persecuted, as if none but its ministers and members had been concerned in an enterprise which is one of the most extraordinary and romantic episodes in the history of Scotland since the Revolution.

* Life of Bishop Keith, in Bishop Russell's edition of the " Catalogue of the Scottish Bishops," p xxxi. xxxii. xxxiii.

CHAPTER XVII.

THE ENTERPRISE OF 1745 AND ITS CONSEQUENCES TO THE SCOTTISH EPISCOPAL CHURCH—ACTS OF PARLIAMENT—PROSECUTIONS OF THE CLERGY AND LAITY—ATTACHMENT OF THE PEOPLE TO THEIR PASTORS—DEATH OF GEORGE II.

The Enterprise of 1745 is familiar to every reader. In the month of July that year Prince Charles landed in Scotland and displayed his standard, declaring that his object was a " crown or a coffin." The Highland Clans under their enthusiastic chiefs were summoned, and descended in impetuous thousands to the Lowland counties, where they were joined by various noblemen and gentlemen ; and when they took possession of Edinburgh they mustered a very considerable force, rude indeed, ill-disciplined, and wretchedly armed, but all animated by the most sanguine dreams of success.

The old Chevalier, for whom Prince Charles professed to act as " Regent," had never been personally popular among his adherents in Scotland. His reception at his arrival about the conclusion of the Earl of Mar's adventure in 1715 was a complete proof that, as an individual, he was disliked. " Our men," says the Master of Sinclair, " began to despise him ; some asked if he could speak." But it was different with his son, then young, of most prepossessing appearance, ardent, confiding, full of lofty hopes, and the representative of one of the most ancient royal dynasties in Europe.

The enthusiasm with which the Prince was received by his supporters in some districts evinced the devotion of the Jacobites to his claims. It is not difficult to ascertain the feelings of the great mass of the Episcopal clergy and laity at the appearance of the Adventurers, and although as a Church they had no connection with the Enterprise, and though many of them were not Jacobites, yet it is needless to deny that the majority were attached to the exiled dynasty—that many of the laity and a few of the clergy embarked in the cause—and numbers of them suffered the penalty of their rashness on the scaffold. But it ought also to be remembered, that all the Adventurers did not belong to the Episcopal Church—that many were Roman Catholics, and others were certainly not Episcopalians.

After Prince Charles obtained possession of Edinburgh he held levees in the Palace of Holyrood, which were numerously attended by his followers, and numbers of the Episcopal clergy considered it their duty to pay their respects to him as "Prince of Wales" and "Regent," according to the tenor of his proclamations. The victory gained by the Adventurers over the troops of King George under Sir John Cope, near Prestonpans, excited the most sanguine and exulting hopes. Some of the Episcopal clergy followed the march of the Adventurers, as did several Presbyterian ministers in the Royal army. A few of the former, however, were prevented from connecting themselves with the Enterprise by being committed to prison. This was the case with the Rev. Robert Forbes of Leith, afterwards a Bishop, two other clergymen, and two gentlemen, who were apprehended at St Ninian's, near Stirling, on the 7th of September 1745, at the commencement of the insurrection, and carried first to Stirling Castle, and thence to the Castle of Edinburgh, from which they were not liberated till May 1746. After the battle of Prestonpans one Episcopal clergyman immediately set out on foot on the Saturday for the scene of his ministrations, beyond Doune in Perthshire, a distance of at least seventy miles from the field of action, and was so much stimulated by his zeal that he arrived in time on Sunday to announce to his flock, at the ordinary hour for divine service, the victory at Prestonpans, invoking at the same time blessings on the Chevalier and his cause.

But whatever were the political hopes of the Jacobites in general, as a party, these were completely annihilated by the battle of Culloden. The Adventurers were utterly defeated and dispersed, the Enterprise completely crushed, and its leader, for whom this desperate attempt was made, was necessitated to wander among the mountain fastnesses of the

Highlands and the stormy Hebridean Islands, suffering the greatest hardships, privations, and distress, before he effected his escape to the Continent. The numerous executions which followed the, suppression of the Enterprise sufficiently intimate the alarm of the Government, and exhibit a malignant severity which might have been spared by those at the helm of affairs

The Duke of Cumberland's victory of Culloden over a body of wretchedly armed, dispirited, and fatigued Highlanders, suffering from long marches and other misfortunes, was followed by cruelties seldom exemplified in modern warfare, and which have made his name execrated to this day in Scotland. All writers admit those horrible barbarities practised on the poor, defenceless, and innocent peasantry, in the most wanton and unprovoked manner, by the Duke of Cumberland's authority and sanction. The unhappy and fugitive Highlanders were everywhere cut down, and numbers of persons, who from motives of curiosity were mere spectators of the battle, were sacrificed by the indiscriminating vengeance of the victors. "They had been provoked," says Smollett, "by their former disgraces to the most savage thirst of revenge. Not contented with the blood which was so profusely shed in the heat of action, they traversed the field after the battle, and massacred those miserable wretches who lay maimed and expiring; nay, some officers acted a part in this cruel scene of assassination—the triumph of low, illiberal minds, uninspired by sentiments, untinctured by humanity. In the month of May the Duke of Cumberland advanced with the army into the Highlands as far as Fort-Augustus, where he encamped, and sent off detachments on all hands to hunt down the fugitives, and lay waste the country with fire and sword. The castles of Glengarry and Lochiel were plundered and burned; every house, hut, or habitation, met with the same fate without distinction; all the cattle and provisions were carried off; the men were either shot upon the mountains like wild beasts, or put to death in cold blood without form of trial; the women, after seeing their husbands and fathers murdered, were subject to brutal violation, and then turned out naked with their children to starve on the barren heaths. One whole family was enclosed in a barn, and consumed to ashes. Those ministers of vengeance were so alert in the execution of their office, that in a few days there was neither house, cottage, man nor beast, to be seen in the compass of fifty miles ; all was ruin, silence, and desolation."* While these cruelties were inflicted on the unhappy Highlanders, and on many who had no concern in the Enterprise whatever, the Government was preparing its career of blood for the prisoners with whom the public prisons were filled. Severity to the vanquished Jacobites was not only recommended in various publications, but demanded ; and even the pulpit was occasionally made the place where those inhuman sentiments were delivered. It is said that on the 21st of August 1746, a shocking instance occurred in the magnificent Minster of York. The chaplain of the High Sheriff had the inhumanity to preach before the Judges who were to try the prisoners from a passage of Scripture, and the spirit of his sermon is sufficiently indicated by the text. It was from the Book of Numbers (xxv 5)—" And Moses said unto the judges of Israel, Slay ye every one his man that was joined unto Baal-peor."

" The intelligence of the battle of Culloden," says Mr Chambers, " so important in its nature and results, produced different effects upon the public mind, according to the sentiments of those by whom it was heard. The Jacobites received it as a total overthrow to their fond and long-cherished hopes, while it excited in the partizans of the Government a transport of joy too overpowering to admit of a thought upon the misery in which it involved so many of their countrymen. The news reaching Edinburgh on the night between Saturday and Sunday, and being announced to the ears of the slumbering inhabitants by discharge of cannon, many of the unhappy Jacobites were found stretched next morning upon their couches in a state of insensibility. Some of the ancient gentlewomen, whose daily prayers for fifty years had included the restoration of the Stuarts, and whose wishes had been wound up during the progress of the insurrection to a state bordering upon insanity, never afterwards rose from the beds upon which the afflicting intelligence had found them, but continued as long as they lived shrouded from the light of day, and inaccessible to consolation. The misery of those who had friends, or kinsmen, or lovers, concerned in the dreadful event was far more poignant, distracted as they were betwixt the fear that they were slain, or, what was still more dreadful, that they survived as captives. To add to their grief, the loyal part of the community and the

* Smollett's History, 4to edit vol iv p. 673, 674.

Presbyterians, now triumphant in their turn, took every opportunity of lacerating their feelings. They even dared not to inquire regarding the fate of those most dear to them, from the dread of persecution to themselves, or proscription—perhaps death to the ill-starred objects of their affection."*

The Duke of Cumberland, in his march to the North, visited all the Episcopal chapels in Forfarshire, Kincardineshire, Morayshire, and Banffshire, with military law. They were ordered to be shut up, and in many places the people were incited to destroy the seats and other furniture, and to set fire to the humble edifices. These ravages were carried into some districts of Aberdeenshire; and scarcely a week had elapsed after the battle of Culloden, before his Royal Highness had succeeded in prohibiting any congregation from assembling for divine service in which a Nonjuring clergyman officiated. The most shameful and wanton outrages were committed, and the clergy and laity were often personally maltreated and insulted. In other counties the mob did the work of the military in the North. The chapel in Cupar-Fife, in which Bishop White officiated, was assailed and gutted, and the seats, pulpit, reading desk, and communion-table, burnt in the streets On Sunday the 27th of April there was divine service in very few of the chapels in Edinburgh, and before next Sunday they were all ordered to be shut up by the Sheriff.†

In the summer of 1746 the Government thought proper to take notice of the Scottish Episcopal Church in the most summary manner. An act was passed, enjoining the strict execution of all former laws against " Nonjuring ministers," with such additional regulations as would place them under more severe restraint. It was enacted, that from and after the 1st of September 1746, every person exercising the function of a pastor or minister in any Episcopal meeting in Scotland, without registering his letters of orders, and taking all the oaths required by law, and praying for his Majesty King George and the royal family by name, shall, for the first offence, *suffer six months' imprisonment*; and for the second, or any subsequent offence, being thereof convicted before the

---

* History of the Rebellion of 1745, vol. ii. p. 120, 121.
† Scots Magazine, 1746, vol viii. p 247.

Justiciary or any of the Circuit Courts, shall be *transported to some of his Majesty's plantations in America for life*; and in case of his return to Great Britain shall *suffer imprisonment for life.*

The penalty for the first offence is set forth in the act 5th George I., and it is there declared that if any person performed divine service in any Episcopal "*meeting-house,*" without praying in express words for the King and royal family, and without having taken the Oaths of *Allegiance, Abjuration,* and *Assurance,* he was to suffer six months' imprisonment, and the "meeting-house" was to be shut up during that time. By that act eight persons were allowed to be present at the celebration of divine service besides the family; but in the act of 1746 there was this limiting clause:—" And for ascertaining what shall be deemed an Episcopal *meeting-house* in Scotland, where *five persons* or more shall be met together to hear divine service, over and besides those of the household; or, if it be in a place not inhabited, where any such five or more persons shall be so met together, and where divine service shall be performed by a pastor or minister, being of or professing to be of the Episcopal communion, every such meeting shall be deemed to be an Episcopal *meeting-house* within the meaning of this act." It is farther enacted that the sheriffs of counties and magistrates of burghs, "whenever they shall find that any *meeting-house* within their jurisdiction hath been set up or maintained," without the ministers qualifying according to the terms of the act, are "required to cause such offences to be prosecuted before them, to shut up or otherwise suppress such meeting-houses, and to inflict the legal penalties on the ministers and pastors officiating." By the act 5th George I. the hearers were not subjected to any penalties; but by this act it was enjoined that "if any person, after said 1st of September, shall resort to, or frequent any Episcopal meeting-house in Scotland, whereof the pastor's and minister's letters of orders shall not be registered," and the other terms of the statute observed, "every person so offending, who shall not, within *five days*, give information of such illegal meeting to some proper magistrate, shall, upon being convicted before any two or more justices of peace, or before any other judge competent summarily, for the first offence forfeit *five pounds sterling*, one moiety to the King, and the other to the informer, and suffer *six months' imprisonment,* unless or until the same be paid; and for the second or any subsequent offence, being convicted before the Justiciary or any of the Circuit Courts, shall suffer *imprisonment for two years* from the date of conviction."

The severity and even malignancy of this clause cannot be mistaken. It not only put a restraint on the members of the Church, of whatever rank, by threatening them with fines and imprisonment, but rendered both clergy and laity exposed to all the annoyances of common informers, to whom it actually held out rewards. It was farther declared that all letters of orders would be deemed void in the registration except those granted by a Bishop of the Church of England or the Church of Ireland, and the time for commencing every prosecution was extended to *twelve months* instead of two months. The injury done to the Scottish Episcopal Church by this prosecution, or rather persecution, of the clergy, would not probably have been of great or of long continuance, if it had not extended to the laity as above mentioned and cited. It was declared that no Peer of Scotland should be capable of being elected one of the sixteen Peers of Parliament, or of voting at such election of representative Peers—that no person should be capable of being elected a member of Parliament for any county or burgh in Scotland, or of voting at such election—or of acting as a magistrate or counsellor for burghs, or to any government or municipal situation, who shall have been present twice within one year in any such Episcopal "meeting-house."—And that "if any person, after said 1st of September, either peers or commoners, who shall hold any office, civil or military, in Scotland, shall resort to an illegal meeting-house in Scotland, and where the pastor or minister shall not pray in express words for his Majesty, &c., by name, and all the royal family, as before directed, every person so offending, being thereof convicted before any two or more Justices of Peace, or before any other judge competent, shall be disabled from thenceforth to hold such office, and adjudged incapable to bear any office civil or military in Scotland for one year after such conviction." If the judges or magistrates were to be found guilty of wilful negligence of their duty in putting this act in force, they were to be fined each L.50 sterling, one half to the informer, and the other half to the poor of the parish.

Such is the act of 1746, passed against the Scottish Episcopalians, and which, it will be immediately seen, was amply enforced. Its object was to destroy the Church, or cause the communion to become extinct. This indeed is almost avowed in the clause respecting the Peers of Scotland, in which " the present happy Establishment"—the Presbyterian Kirk, is noticed; and one reason assigned for involving the Scottish Episcopal nobility and gentry in this persecution and proscription, by which they were denied their civil rights, is, that " they should be restrained from hurting that Establishment, to *which they show such disaffection.*" The sole *offence,* or *crime,* as it was considered by the Government, was the omitting the name of King George II. in the Liturgy of the Church of England by about two hundred clergymen, who had not the power to injure the Government in the slightest degree. But if one object of this act was to annihilate the Scottish Episcopal Church by destroying the succession, its framers were disappointed. In the beginning of the year 1746 the venerable Bishop Dunbar of Aberdeen died, and the passing of the act did not so far paralyze the remaining Bishops as to prevent them from considering the present and future condition of their order. The presbyters of Aberdeen elected one of their number, the Rev. Andrew Gerard, to be their diocesan, and he was consecrated, doubtless privately to avoid the prosecution of the Government, on the 17th of July 1747, by Bishops White, Falconer, Rait, and Alexander. Bishop Keith, the Primus, is not mentioned as having been present.

After the passing of the act some of the clergy, who had never been remarkably conspicuous for their political predilections, thought it their duty to render their chapels *legal* places of worship, and they repaired to the proper magistrates, registered their letters of orders, and took the oaths to Government within the time required by law. Among these are recorded Messrs Walker at Old Meldrum, Laing at Poutachy, Livingstone at Old Deer, Skinner at Longside, and Farquhar at Dumfries, " Nonjuring Episcopal ministers, who have qualified in terms of the law act."* But this compliance with the act, in the case of those and other clergymen, was of no avail, nor did it at all preclude them from its operation. In December 1747 four soldiers rushed suddenly into a room in Perth, in which the Rev. George Sempell was performing divine service, and finding his audience more numerous than the law allowed, they secured him; he was carried before the magistrates on the following day, and committed to prison for six months, in terms of the act.

* Scots Magazine (September, 1746), vol viii p 846.

The persons present were also cited to appear, and to pay their fine of L.5 each, but they proved that they had given information within the proper time, and were " assoilzied."* In the month of March 1748, the Rev. Messrs John Petrie at Drumlithie, Alexander Greig at Stonehaven, and John Troop at Muchals, Episcopal ministers, were apprehended for violating the act, and committed prisoners to the jail of Stonehaven for six months.† The act of 1746 left the Episcopal clergy only *four* hearers besides the family, but in May 1748 that act was *revised* and *amended*; and it was enacted—for clearing a doubt, whether by a clause in the act 19th George II. concerning Episcopal meeting-houses, any letters of orders other than those granted by Bishops of the Church of England or of Ireland, were entitled to be registered before the 1st of September 1746—" That no letters of orders not granted by some Bishop of the Church of England or of Ireland shall, from and after the 29th of September 1748, be sufficient to qualify any pastor or minister of any Episcopal meeting in Scotland, whether the same were registered before or after the said 1st of September 1746, and that every such registration, either made before or after the said 1st of September, shall, from and after the said 29th of September 1748, be null and void." There was another clause which prevented any persons from officiating as chaplains in private families, or from preaching or performing any divine service in houses or families of which they were not the masters, except " the ministers, elders, or preachers of the Established Church of Scotland."

When this act was introduced into Parliament it met with some opposition in the House of Commons. It nevertheless passed, chiefly through the management of Mr Grant, Lord Advocate, afterwards a judge in the Supreme Court by the title of Lord Prestongrange. It appears from the list of Scottish members in this Parliament, that with very few exceptions they were in favour of the clause, being determined enemies to the exiled dynasty. But the clause was received in a different manner in the House of Lords. In committee it was unanimously opposed by the Bishops and several Peers, and it was thrown out by a majority of 32 against 28. A new debate ensued, however, upon the report, when, by the influence of the Lord Chancellor Hardwicke, who was supported by all the Scottish Representative Peers except the Earl

---

* Scots Magazine, vol ix p 608   † Ibid vol x. p 150.

of Moray, it was replaced, and carried by a majority of 37 to 32. It is not unlikely that the Scottish Peers were considerably influenced by the Earl of Leven, who held the office at this time of Lord High Commissioner to the General Assembly. There can be little doubt, at least, as was hinted in the House of Lords, that Presbyterian interest suggested the clause which passed into a law. Not one of the English Bishops, not even Dr Hoadley, spoke in favour of it, and some of them, especially the Bishops of London, Lincoln, Oxford, and Worcester, strenuously opposed it, as interfering with the rights of ordination, and as a matter beyond the limits of parliamentary cognizance.

The debate in the House of Lords was of considerable interest. The most extraordinary opinions were stated by several Peers, who denied that it was a hardship to the clergy, *seeing they could take orders in England or Ireland a second time!* Bishop Maddox of Worcester indignantly denounced the proposed new act. "As to these poor clergymen," he said, "who may by this clause be deprived of their only means of subsistence, notwithstanding their having taken the oaths to the Government, I am really sorry to hear it suggested by an honourable gentleman that they might choose some other employment for the support of themselves and families. Alas! a clergyman in holy orders is expressly forbid by the canons to give himself to any base or servile labour; and what other sort of employment can a poor man choose, who has no stock, unless it be a stock of learning, and a few books in his study? To deprive these men, therefore, of the liberty of officiating in any meeting-house in Scotland is really to deprive them of their daily bread This clause is fraught with such dangerous consequences to the public, and such great hardships upon private men, that I can neither as a Christian, a Churchman, an Englishman, a faithful subject of his Majesty, nor as a man of any humanity, give my consent to its being passed into a law."

In this speech there are some admirable remarks, which are worthy of being brought before the notice of the reader. It had been argued by some of the Government party that no man would receive orders from a Nonjuring Bishop in Scotland unless he had been educated from his infancy in Jacobite principles. "This supposition," says his Lordship, "there would, I shall grant, be some ground for if those of the Episcopal persuasion in Scotland had any choice. But we all know they have no choice. A man who is of that religion in Scotland, and designs to be a minister of the gospel of Christ, must necessarily receive orders from a Nonjuring Bishop, because there are none others in the country. I say he must necessarily receive orders from such a Bishop, unless he has money to bear the expense of a journey to England or Ireland, and friends there to give him a title and testimonials, which we cannot suppose any man has who designs to exercise his functions in that country, where he can expect no preferment, nor any maintenance but what depends upon the generosity and good will of his hearers, which they diminish or wholly withdraw whenever they please. For these reasons I must think there is not the least ground for this supposition. On the contrary, as there is nothing in the ceremony of ordination, no oaths to be taken, nor promises made but what may be taken and made by a man perfectly well affected to our present happy Establishment; and as I have been credibly informed that the Nonjuring Bishops in Scotland have added nothing to this ceremony, I think I have good reason to suppose that the Nonjuring Bishops in Scotland have ordained several persons who have been bred up in principles agreeable to our present constitution, and who were ready to take the oaths to the Government as soon as necessary; for no man ought, I think, to take an oath, not even the oaths to the Government, till it becomes necessary for him to do so." The Bishop farther declared, that "if the clause in the former act be explained as intended by that now under our consideration, I shall look upon it as contrived and promoted by the Presbyterians in Scotland, not with a design to secure, but to endanger our present happy Establishment, by leaving the Episcopal party in Scotland still under the influence of Nonjuring clergymen, and bringing upon his Majesty's reign the odium of having passed an act to abolish the remains of Episcopacy in that kingdom."

Dr Sherlock, Bishop of London, concluded a very able speech in the following manner:—" In short, there are so many difficulties, that I must suppose this clause to have been suggested by *some Presbyterian*, or some enemy to the Church of England; and, therefore, I hope that next session something new will be thought of for supplying the Episcopal Church in Scotland with qualified Bishops as well as ministers. In the meantime I shall be against any thing that will deprive the Church there of any of the qualified ministers they now have, and shall therefore be against the clause now under our consideration."

Dr Secker, then Lord Bishop of Oxford, was not less happy and forcible in his illustrations. After reciting a part of the act of 1746, which rendered it necessary that all Episcopal clergymen in Scotland should register their chapels according to law, he proceeded—" Now, by this act you gave an opportunity to, and consequently invited, all ministers of Episcopal congregations who had not before qualified to come in and take the oaths appointed by law without distinction, whether they had received their orders from a Nonjuring Protestant Bishop in Scotland, or from a Bishop of the Church of England or of Ireland ; and upon this invitation I am told that several of the Episcopal ministers who had received orders from the Nonjuring Bishops in Scotland did accordingly take the oaths and register their meetings, in hope that for the future they would be entitled to exercise their functions, and thereby support themselves and families, without let or disturbance. But what are you now to do with this clause ? These poor men have probably disobliged some of their best friends, and rendered themselves obnoxious to their whole party, by accepting your invitation, and now, by a law *ex post facto*, you are to deprive them of the only means of subsistence they have left. After what I have said, I think I need not observe that the clause now under our consideration really seems to be an encroachment upon the Christian religion as professed by the Church of England. It seems, in my opinion, to arrogate to the civil authority a power to determine whether a priest has been duly and regularly ordained, or a Bishop consecrated—a question with which no true member of the Church of England will allow the civil authority to have any thing to do. It is the Church only that can determine this question, and if the Church determines that a priest has been duly and regularly ordained, he ought not by any civil authority to be debarred the exercise of his function, provided he conforms in every other respect to the law."

Lord Sandys observed—" There were certainly Bishops in the Christian Church long before there was any thing like a *congé d'élire*, or any authority from the supreme power in the country to choose a Bishop. Suppose that at the time of the Revolution the clergy of the Church of England had adhered as obstinately to their principle of passive obedience and non-resistance as the clergy of the Church of Scotland did, and that in consequence the Church of England had undergone the same fate with her sister Church of Scotland, could not the Church party in England have fallen upon a method for continuing their succession of Bishops, without having an authority from the King for so doing? Nay, would they not by the tenets of their religion have been bound in conscience to do so, and would it not have been persecution to have punished them solely for doing so?—I do not believe that King William would have subjected them to any punishment, if they had chosen for themselves Bishops in the room of those deceased, after the same manner that Bishops were chosen by the primitive Christians before Christianity came to be the established religion of any kingdom or commonwealth. We can have no reason to exclude from the pastoral office even those who have been ordained by the Protestant Bishops in Scotland; and I must think that this affair should have been a little more inquired into before we agreed to that clause in the former law (1746), which declares all letters of orders insufficient unless given by some Bishops of the Church of England or Ireland. I heartily wish that a great many more of the Episcopal ministers in Scotland had come in and qualified, and I think that we ought not to reject the assistance of those that have; therefore I hope this unnecessary clause will be left out of the bill."

There can be no doubt that the intention of these statutes of 1746 and 1748 was utterly to annihilate the Episcopal succession in Scotland; for it was now impossible for a clergyman of indigenous ordination to obtain a congregation, and the attachment of the laity to their native Church was attempted to be alienated by placing them under political and civil disabilities if they still persisted in adhering to the religion of their fathers. Even in the reign of Charles II., which the Presbyterians designate the time of persecution, their ministers were permitted to retain the parish churches, when the Episcopal Church was the national legal establishment, if they accepted the *Indulgence*, which was simply yielding obedience to the Government. But the Scottish Episcopalians in 1748 were denied the privilege of political repentance, and the conduct they exhibited under their sufferings and heavy depression was that of the meekness of true Christians under calamities which they could not avert. Instead of denouncing the Government in their private assemblies, or betaking themselves to the fields, like the dangerous enthusiasts of the preceding century, they sought to administer the rites of religion in as private and unostentatious a manner as possible, trusting to better times, and to the Providence of their Divine Master, who maketh " all things work together for good to them that love Him."

The encouragement given by the act 1746 to clergymen of English and Irish ordination, brought numbers of those gentlemen into Scotland, who soon obtained qualified chapels and congregations in the large towns. Since the reign of Queen Anne there had always been a few clergymen of such ordination, but they recognised the Scottish Bishops as their Diocesans. After 1748 the number increased, yet their congregations could not be called *Episcopal*, for they were under no Diocesan, and it need hardly be observed that an Episcopal Church without a Bishop is a contradiction in terms. The English or Irish Bishops who ordained them could have no jurisdiction in Scotland, yet it is stated that the celebrated Bishop Pococke, when in Scotland on an antiquarian tour, administered confirmation in some of those congregations; and Bishop Trail, of Down and Connor, who was originally a Presbyterian, actually admitted a person into priest's orders in Scotland, though a Scottish Bishop resided in the very town where his Lordship chose to hold this singular ordination. In Edinburgh and other cities and towns several qualified chapels of this description were soon opened or erected, and the following record is curious as contrasted with the present time:—
" An organ was set up in one of the qualified meeting-houses in Edinburgh, about the beginning of December 1747, and draws several persons thither out of curiosity."*

So vigilantly were the Scottish Episcopal clergy watched after the passing of the clause in 1748, that it was with the utmost difficulty they could celebrate any of the services of religion. There are instances of individual clergymen performing public worship no less than sixteen times in one day, yet the more they were persecuted the more were their people attached to them. The contrivances to which the clergy were put, in order that they might perform the rites of religion without incurring legal vengeance, were at least as singular as those of the clergy of the Church of England after the murder of Charles I. The sacrament of baptism was often administered in woods and sequestered places, and the holy communion with the utmost privacy; confirmations were

* Scots Magazine, vol ix. p. 608.

held with closed doors in private houses, and divine service often performed in the open air in the Northern counties, amid the mountains, or in the recesses of forests. The chapels were all shut up and the doors made fast by iron bars under the authority of the sheriffs, who often had to discharge this obnoxious duty amid the tears, entreaties, execrations, and decided hostility of the people. In the register of the Episcopal Chapel at Muthill in Perthshire, for example, there is an entry, under date March 20, 1750, in the handwriting of the Rev. William Erskine, presbyter there, father of the late William Erskine, Esq. one of the Judges of the Scottish Supreme Court under the title of Lord Kinneder—" N.B.—With such excessive severity were the penal laws executed at this time, that Andrew Moir, having neglected to keep his appointment with me at my own house this morning, and following me to Lord Rollo's house of Duncruib, we could not take the child into a house, but I was obliged to go under the cover of trees in one of Lord Rollo's parks to prevent our being discovered, and baptize the child there."

Numerous examples of a similar kind might be given of the hardships, privations, and sufferings of the Scottish Episcopal clergy after the suppression of the Enterprise of 1745, and especially after the act of 1748. But they persisted in discharging their sacred functions, and no acts of Parliament could alienate the affections of their people, among whom they continued to reside, and by whom they were enthusiastically supported. The expedients adopted to evade the law which *liberally* allowed the clergy *four hearers*, besides the members of the family, in celebrating divine service, were various and ingenious. In some cases in several districts the people were congregated at the mansions of noblemen and gentlemen. The service was performed by the officiating clergymen in a large room on the ground floor; into which were the clergyman, the family, and *four persons*. The window frames, however, were removed, and as many as could look in or hear from the outside listened and responded. If the apartment was so constructed that it communicated by wide folding doors with another room, the doors were removed for the time, and that room was filled with people, who could hear and see with the greatest ease, while in the other apartment were only the clergyman, the family, and four persons. If the apartment was not so constructed, the passages and staircases were crowded with auditors, and every spot in the vicinity of the room where the pastor's voice could be heard. This mode of procedure was very common in the counties of Perth, Forfar, Kincardine, and Aberdeen, and it is said that among others, the Noble Family of Airlie in Forfarshire particularly distinguished themselves, by affording such facilities to evade the enactment by keeping the people together, and regularly celebrating divine worship.

The service was also often performed in farm-houses, or in the outhouses of the farm-house, if these were conveniently constructed. In either case the clergyman, the family, and four persons, were in the apartment, and dozens or hundreds of others, in proportion to the attendance, stationed themselves in as favourable positions as they could, to listen to the prayers of the Church. Sometimes divine service was celebrated under a shed, in which was the number allowed by law, while the people stood at a small distance in the open air. At times, again, when there was no apparent danger, pastor and people met in the recesses of woods, in secluded glens, and on the sides of sequestered mountains, when the vault of heaven was their covering, the moss turfs their humble altar, and perhaps a solitary seat the pulpit, and all would kneel together in one holy bond, beseeching God to have pity on the suffering Church, evermore to preserve them in its unity, and to deliver them from " all false doctrine, heresy, and schism."

In the towns and villages various expedients were adopted to bring the people together, and to edify them by the performance of divine worship. At times parties of them would resort to the residence of the clergyman in succession, when the service of the Church was read, and a short sermon delivered ; at other times the clergyman was invited to private houses, where he found a number of people assembled in various rooms. The outer doors were instantly locked, and stationing himself in the passage or staircase, he in this position, and elevating his voice, performed the whole service. It is said that the delight and edification which the people declared they felt at the conclusion of the morning and evening service, in such circumstances and on such occasions, almost surpassed credibility.

By resorting to such and other expedients the suffering Episcopal clergy and laity of Scotland pursued the "even tenor of their way" some years after 1748. It is hardly necessary to observe, that at such meetings no psalms were sung, as that would have attracted notice from the outside or at a distance. I have not been able to ascertain the numbers of the clergy thrown into prison for six months. Many were apprehended, who after a short confinement were liberated on bail, or on their own recognizances. In 1753 the Government chose to prosecute a clergyman whose name will ever be remembered with veneration in the Scottish Episcopal Church, and is imperishably associated with Scottish poetry and song, but still more with theological learning and ecclesiastical history. This was the Rev. John Skinner of Longside, in the county of Aberdeen, who, it is already mentioned, was one of those who qualified himself in 1746, but which was of no avail to him by the amended act of 1748.

The commitment of Mr Skinner is thus recorded in the Scots Magazine for June 1753:—" Mr John Skinner at Longside, Aberdeenshire, a Nonjurant Episcopal clergyman, was carried to Aberdeen in May last, on an information that he had transgressed the late acts, which forbid every such clergyman to preach or perform divine service in any house or family of which he is not master, or even in his own house, if more than four persons besides his own family be present, and was on his own confession committed to prison for six months by the sheriff."*

It is stated by a near relative of Mr Skinner, that although he "became a conscientious convert from Presbyterianism to Episcopacy, and had no scruple to join with the Scottish Episcopal Church in a warm and generous sympathy for the sufferings of the unfortunate House of Stuart, yet did he never entertain a wish for the restoration of that exiled family with a view to any benefit that might have been expected from it, either to the nation at large, or to that particular religious society of which he was a member."† " When liberated in course of law," says the same relative, "and anxious to resume the care of his destitute flock, he felt the ties of duty as their faithful pastor greatly strengthened by gratitude for their attention during his absence to his wife and helpless family, which then consisted of six young children, all, under God, depending on him for their support. During his residence

* Scots Magazine, vol. xv. p. 309.
† Theological Works of the late Rev. John Skinner, with a Memoir by the Rev. John Skinner, M. A., Forfar, vol. i. p. 204.

in a common prison, and suffering all the hardships of close confinement, next to a humble trust in the Divine goodness his chief resource lay in the conversation of a few worthy friends at the hours when they were allowed to visit him, and in the liberal supply of books which they had the means of procuring for him. These were his constant companions when all others were excluded, and he has been often heard to say that no six months of his life ever passed away with so little interruption to his studies and improvement as the term of his legal imprisonment."

Previous to this affair, however, Mr Skinner had suffered severely from a military *visit*. " On coming home one evening," says his grandson, " from performing an occasional office in the way of his duty, he found his house in the possession of a military party, some of them guarding the door with fixed bayonets, and others searching the several apartments, even the bed-chamber where Mrs Skinner was lying in of her fifth child, and little able to bear such a rude unseasonable visit. No lenity was to be looked for from such unfeeling visitors, who pillaged the house of every thing they could carry with them, hardly leaving a change of linen to father, mother, or child in the family. The chapel, with all its furniture, was destroyed, and for several years the congregation could find no place to meet in for public worship but the clergyman's house, which not being sufficiently large, many of them were obliged to stand in the open air during divine service. As this inconvenience, with other disheartening circumstances, was likely to operate on weak minds, to the discouragement of Episcopal principles, Mr Skinner was induced to write a small tract, which was printed in the year 1746, under the title of a *Preservative against Presbytery*, chiefly designed for the instruction of the people under his immediate charge, and suited to the alarming apprehensions then entertained of the total extirpation of Scottish Episcopacy, as far as human power could accomplish such an object."

With his usual characteristic modesty, Mr Skinner, in his valuable Ecclesiastical History of Scotland, omits any direct allusions to his own sufferings and privations in the cause of the Church. For many years, in consequence of the severity of the laws, he was obliged either to officiate to his own congregation in *fours*, or to take four within, and allow the rest to hear him as they best could through the open doors and windows. Mr Skinner passed sixty-five years in the laborious charge of a numerous congregation, and he answered almost literally to Goldsmith's well known description of a village pastor—

> " A man he was to all the country dear,
> And passing rich with forty pounds a year;
> Remote from towns he ran his godly race,
> Nor e'er had chang'd, nor wish'd to change, his place."

"Those," says a popular writer, "who become acquainted with the Apostolic Church of Scotland through the medium of the handsome fanes which she has reared of late years in the principal towns, know in general little of the humble circumstances in which she exists in the various rural districts where a remnant of her communion has been left. Mr Skinner's parsonage at Linshart, in the neighbourhood of the village of Longside, was simply a thatched cottage of the usual appearance. The fire-places, according to the usage in Buchan, contained no grates —the fires, composed of peats, were kindled on the hearth. So lately as 1826, when the present writer visited the house, and found it occupied by Mr Skinner's grandson and successor, the Rev. Mr Cumming, it remained in this condition—a striking and even affecting memorial not only of the poet, but of the depressed Christian body to which he belonged. The bed and other chief articles of furniture were the same which had served Mr Skinner during his long tenancy of the house, and the walls were still ornamented with a set of family portraits in chalk, the work of some wandering artist."*

Another clergyman who more seriously encountered the vengeance of the Government was the Rev. James Connachar, who was tried before the Circuit Court of Justiciary at Inverary. Of this gentleman it is observed by Arnot—" His residence in a wild district of the Highlands, where there was not within many miles a man of his knowledge and learning, gave him a degree of consequence, to which his irreproachable morals and unaffected piety added singular importance; but his virtues were poisoned by his attachment to an unfortunate Family, and the eminence of his situation and character, which in better times would

* The Land of Burns, 4to, 1838. The Literary Department by Professor Wilson and Robert Chambers, Esq. p. 63, 64.

have commanded felicity, served only to attract the fire of political vengeance He was marked out as a victim, whose ruin was to confound the remains of a vanquished party."*

In 1755, Mr Connachar was apprehended in his own house, upwards of twelve miles north-west of Stirling, by a military party on the 30th of January—a day on which it was expected he and his congregation would be engaged in their proscribed worship. He was carried to Stirling, and committed to the common jail by a warrant of the Lord Justice-Clerk Erskine and the Lords of Justiciary, dated Jan. 21, 1755. This warrant proceeded upon a petition from the Lord Advocate, setting forth that Mr Connachar, "without having letters of orders in terms of law, and without having taken the oaths to the Government, had presumed to officiate as a minister, by praying and preaching to great numbers of people, and administering the sacraments, at divers times and places in the countries of Appin and Lochaber, in the months of September, October, November, and December last:—that Mr Connachar was a stirrer up of sedition, his sermons being calculated to alienate the minds of his hearers from their duty and allegiance:—and that the petitioner intended to bring him to trial for these offences."

Mr Connachar applied to the Lord Justice-Clerk to be admitted to bail, which was granted, but the Lord Advocate was determined not to lose sight of his victim Previous to the bail being admitted, a second petition was presented to the Lord Justice-Clerk, reciting all the charges in the former one, and setting forth that, besides the *offences* for which Mr Connachar was incarcerated, he was also to be tried on the statute of 1 Charles II. 1661, against celebrating clandestine and irregular marriages. By the acts of 1746 and 1748, this clergyman could only, as in the case of Mr Skinner and others, have been imprisoned six months, but by that of Charles II. he might be condemned to perpetual banishment.

The trial took place at Inverary before Lords Strichen and Drummore, two of the Justiciary Judges, and it seems to have been purposely held at that great distance from Stirling, in a district where several important local incidents made it evident that the jury would evince no great inclination to acquit the prisoner. He was charged with two

* Criminal Trials in Scotland, p 339.

offences—the celebration of marriage without being lawfully authorised by the *Established Church of Scotland*, or by any other legal authority, and also for celebrating it in a clandestine and disorderly manner, contrary to 1 Charles II, sess. 1, c 34. "It was pled for the prisoner," to adopt the condensed account of the trial by Arnot, "that the statute libelled on had been established directly with a view to support Episcopacy against sectaries, and therefore to turn it as an engine of destruction against that religion which it was meant to protect was totally to invert its purposes;—that all the acts in favour of Episcopacy had been abolished by William and Mary;—that it behoved Episcopacy either to be the established religion or not If it was the established religion, the priest could not be condemned as unqualified to celebrate marriage. If it was not the established religion, it must be ranked among the sects of Nonconformity, and even in that case the clergyman was equally safe, for all laws against Nonconformists were repealed by act 1690. This construction of the statutes was confirmed by the universal sense of the nation, for although thousands of marriages had been celebrated not only by Episcopal clergymen, but by dissenters of all sorts, no prosecution had ever been brought on this branch of the statute alone. .Nay, so little was our [the Scottish] law scrupulous as to a clergyman, the celebrator of a marriage, being ordained by the Established Church, that a valid marriage might be pronounced by any civil magistrate—indeed, that the ceremony of marriage is totally unnecessary to its validity. As to the second offence charged against him, the celebration of marriage in a clandestine and disorderly way, it was proved on behalf of the prisoner that the parish in which he lived, as well as the next parish, had been some time vacant, so that in the district where he lived there was no clergyman but himself, in a space of twenty miles."*

Other evidence was led to show that Mr Connachar scrupulously celebrated marriages in the most regular manner both as to the legal and ceremonial parts of the contract, and that he had refused to officiate at a marriage in a clandestine manner, although ten guineas had been offered as an inducement. Notwithstanding these statements the Lords of Justiciary found the first as well as the second article of the indictment *relevant*, as it is expressed in Scottish legal phraseology, *to infer the*

* Criminal Trials in Scotland, p. 341, 342.

pains of law. Mr Connachar's counsel reminded the jury, that if they thought proper they were entitled to acquit him of both charges; but, says Arnot, "lest the fountain of justice should purify the stream of political vengeance, it was observed from the Bench that the jury could have no room for doubts, *and that Nonjuring Episcopal clergymen, of the prisoner's activity, were dangerous to the present happy Establishment!* The jury found the prisoner guilty, yet, in respect of certain alleviating circumstances, they recommended him to mercy. *He was condemned to perpetual banishment, never to return under pain of death!*"

In the Scots Magazine, for 1755, the following notice respecting this unfortunate clergyman occurs:—" In the end of August Mr Connachar set out for England in obedience to his sentence. According to a letter sent us by one who was present at his departure, he told his friends that amid those pangs one naturally feels on being for ever expelled from his native country, it gave him great consolation that he was not conscious of having done any thing immoral in celebrating the marriages which occasioned so severe a sentence—that the friends were satisfied and consented to all of them, and there was no private prosecutor—that he had always held the celebrating of a marriage clandestinely, or without the consent of the persons interested, as a crime of a very deep dye, which no bribe would induce him to commit—and that he never imagined it was illegal for Protestant ministers, even those not of the Established Church of Scotland, to celebrate marriages, when the friends gave their consent, and banns were regularly proclaimed, though it was found so in his case, upon a clause of an old act in 1661, which he either never heard of or did not suspect to be in force, as he knew that marriages were openly celebrated almost every day by the ministers of all the different persuasions in this country without challenge. He regretted, most of all, the destitute condition of those poor people to whom he had ministered, and for whom he had spared no labour or fatigue, who, he said, would now have no pastor of their own communion, and, therefore, would be in great hazard of being perverted to Popery by the artifices of Romish missionaries"

In October 1756, the Rev. Walter Stewart of Ochilbeg, in the district of Atholl, was apprehended and brought to Perth by the sheriff-depute, but was liberated on bail. His trial before the sheriff-depute took place on the 28th of December, and he was charged with "having performed divine service in his own house on every Sunday from Christmas 1755 to October last, or at least on one or other of those Sundays, when more than four persons were assembled besides his own family," and craving that the penalties of the act 19 George II. should be inflicted. Mr Stewart confessed the charge, and was sentenced to six months' imprisonment, during which his "meeting-house" was to be shut up. He was accordingly committed to the jail of Perth, and as he was in the *seventieth year of his age*, his friends very naturally dreaded, the consequences of such a punishment. Four of Mr Stewart's hearers were also indicted for being present at divine service, and not giving information. They confessed, and were fined L.5 sterling each, which they paid at the bar; the one half adjudged to the King, and the other to the prosecutor. One of those gentlemen was a notary-public, and he was declared to have forfeited his office, and to be incapable of bearing any office, civil or military, for twelve months.

Such are a few instances of the persecutions which the Scottish Episcopal clergy encountered after the suppression of the Enterprise of 1745, to which many more might be added. Several of the clergy took refuge in England and elsewhere, and it does not appear that they returned. A persecution such as this in a Christian state, by a Government professing the same religious principles, and adhering to the Church of England, of which the Church in Scotland is a branch, has few parallels in history. It is in vain to urge that these severities were inflicted for political considerations and for the internal peace of the country. The clause of 1748 completely refutes that argument, inasmuch as it precluded the Scottish Episcopalians from political repentance, and directly aimed at the extirpation of the Church.

A glance at the internal affairs of the Church will form an appropriate conclusion to this part of the narrative. On the 20th of January 1757 died Bishop Keith, the Primus, at Bonnyhaugh, where he had spent some of the last years of his life, in the seventy-sixth year of his age, and the twenty-seventh of his episcopate. He left a widow and children in straitened circumstances, for although nearly related to the ancient and Noble Family of Keith Earls Marischal, he had no other resources for his support than his professional duties, and that distinguished Family had been attainted and confiscated for their connection with the Enterprise of 1715. "Of the public life of this eminent prelate," says

Bishop Russell, " I cannot discover any notices more recent than the year 1744. The pressure of the penal laws inflicted by the Government in 1746 and 1748 seems to have silenced even the voice of controversy. About the year 1752, he left his usual residence in the Canongate, and fixed his abode in the neighbourhood of Leith, on a small property called Bonnyhaugh, which afterwards descended by inheritance to his daughter and grand-daughter." He was buried in the churchyard of the Canongate, Edinburgh, a few feet from the wall on the western side, and the spot where his remains were deposited is indicated by a plain tombstone in the shape of a square pillar, erected, it is said, by a distant relative from pious respect to the memory of a learned and good man, on which are simply inscribed " BISHOP KEITH," and the date of his decease.

The literary labours of Bishop Keith are well known. His great work—" The History of the Affairs of Church and State of Scotland, from the beginning of the Reformation, in the Reign of King James V., to the retreat of Queen Mary into England," is already mentioned. Only one volume of this stately folio, which is of the greatest value for the collection of documents it contains, was published; at Bishop Keith's death he left a few sheets of his second volume, which it is supposed no longer exist. " Such a book," said Bishop Smith, one of his correspondents and antagonists, " will stand the test of ages, and will always be valued, because no fact is related but upon the best authority." This work appeared in 1734, and in 1755 he published a quarto volume of great value, research, and learning—the well-known " Catalogue of the Bishops of the several Sees within the Kingdom of Scotland, down to the year 1688," of which an edition in octavo was produced by Bishop Russell in 1824, with a Continuation, a Biographical Sketch of the Author, and other important additions. Bishop Keith is also said to have published a translation of Thomas à Kempis.*

Bishop White, diocesan of Dunblane, succeeded Bishop Keith as Primus, and on the 1st of November 1759, the Rev. Henry Edgar, presbyter at Arbroath in Forfarshire, was consecrated at Cupar-Fife, as coadjutor to Bishop White, by that prelate, assisted by Bishops Falconer, Rait, and Alexander. Little is known of Bishop Edgar, and the

---

* Scots Magazine, vol. xix. p. 54

period of his death is nowhere recorded; but it is certain that he succeeded Bishop White in 1761 as the diocesan of Fife, and that he continued to perform the duties of it as long as he lived, several years after his predecessor's death.

Towards the latter end of the reign of George II. the severity of the prosecutions against the Scottish Episcopal clergy was relaxed, and few incidents of importance occur in the history of the Church. The clergy were still prohibited from officiating in public, but they often boldly evaded the law, and performed, as they conveniently could, the rites of religion to their people. On the 25th of October 1760 King George II. died, in the 77th year of his age, and was succeeded by his grandson, George III., at whose accession, by the well known sentiments of the new sovereign, and by the mildness and impartiality of his Government, an auspicious era dawned upon the Church after the ordeals through which the clergy had passed—an era of peace and security.

CHAPTER XVIII.

ACCESSION OF GEORGE III.—RELIGIOUS STATE OF SCOTLAND—INTERNAL AFFAIRS OF THE SCOTTISH EPISCOPAL CHURCH—MILDNESS OF THE NEW REIGN—NEW CONSECRATIONS OF SCOTTISH BISHOPS—DEATH OF THE CHEVALIER ST GEORGE.

The accession of George III. to the throne of the British Empire was followed by the choice of a new Ministry, and the procedure of the sovereign indicated that he wished not to be the king of a party, but of all his people—that he was anxious to extinguish all national prejudices, and by acts of generosity and kindness to allay and overcome that disaffection to his Family which he well knew existed in Scotland. The King had several advantages in his favour. He was the first monarch of the House of Hanover who was an Englishman by birth and by education, and in his youth he had given many indications of that mild, generous, and pious disposition, which made him venerated during his long and momentous reign. His two predecessors had never been personally popular in the nation. Their German predilections often irritated their subjects, and tended greatly to foster that disaffection to the House of Hanover which existed in various parts of the United Kingdom. George III. was divested of all these partialities for his paternal Electorate and for German interests; he was an Englishman in thought, feeling, and in sincerity, and he ascended the throne, to commence one of the most remarkable reigns which occur in British history, amid the acclamations of the people.

It is true the Scottish Bishops and clergy sent no addresses to the throne, but George III. respected their conscientious prejudices, and saw that time would overcome their scruples, and a new generation adopt different sentiments Although the penal laws continued in force, the King would never tolerate the execution of them as in the reign of his grandfather. The nobility and gentry who frequented the ministrations of the indigenous Episcopal clergy submitted to be deprived of several political privileges, but no officious informations were countenanced by the Government, and some of the chapels shut up during the last reign were ordered to be opened. Still, however, it cannot be denied that the recent prosecutions of the clergy and laity, and the various oaths, particularly that of Abjuration, affecting the Scottish Episcopal Church, which continued to be exacted of all who held offices in the State, had a very serious effect on the Church, by reducing the number of congregations, and lessening the zeal of the laity.

In various large towns and villages qualified chapels were continually erecting, and the incumbents were clergymen of English or Irish ordination, who declined the diocesan jurisdiction of the Scottish Bishops. The political privileges of the laity who resorted to the ministrations of those clergymen were in no way affected, and consequently they were respectably attended. We find also the "*qualified Episcopal clergy*" in the counties of Aberdeen, Kincardine, Forfar, Banff, and Moray, transmitting an address of congratulation to George III. at his accession—"signed and subscribed in our name, and by our appointment, at Aberdeen, this 2d of December, in the year of our Lord 1760, by John Gordon, James Riddoch, and George Farquhar, ministers of the chapels in Aberdeen." All these clergy at this period recognised no diocesan, and were rather *Independents* in principle, whatever they may have maintained to the contrary, than *Episcopalians*, in the proper sense and meaning of the word.

In the city of Glasgow the neat edifice near the Green called St Andrew's Chapel was erected in 1751, and the officiating clergyman, being of English ordination, was qualified according to law. It is traditionally said that the builder, who happened to be a Presbyterian, was either excommunicated by his minister, or denied what in their language they call *church privileges*, for no other *fault* than undertaking the erection of this chapel! But the state of the Church in the Scottish metropolis is worthy of a passing notice. In 1716, when Bishop Millar and others were prosecuted for not praying for King George I., there were twenty-five Episcopal clergymen in Edinburgh, and before the Insurrection of 1745 it is said there were twenty-two, but their congregations must of necessity have been small, and probably two would officiate in some of the chapels. In 1722 a qualified chapel was founded by John Smith, Esq., Lord Chief Baron of the Exchequer in Scotland, and he endowed it by vesting a sum of money in the public funds for the purpose of yielding L.40 yearly to the minister, in addition to the stipend arising from the seat-rents, offertories, and other sources. This chapel, however, which stood at the foot of Blackfriars' Wynd in the Old Town,* was not sufficient to accommodate those who resorted to the ministrations of the "qualified" clergy, and others were opened in 1746, in which the officiating clergymen complied with the statute. In the adjoining sea-port town of Leith the Episcopal Chapel was shut up after the suppression of the Insurrection by order of the sheriff of the county; but the Episcopalians there, rather than be deprived of those religious services to which their principles were in unison, engaged the Rev. John Paul, a clergyman in English orders, in 1749.

All those congregations were under no diocesan superintendence, and consequently at that time formed no part of the Scottish Episcopal Church. There were, however, various chapels in Edinburgh in which the indigenous clergy officiated, who recognized the diocesan authority, though they still held Nonjuring political principles. Notwithstanding all the disadvantages to which the Church was liable, and under which she laboured, it is pleasing to record that she "was still cherished, and her clergy respected by many, who, though they did not avow themselves her members, wished to see her in such a state of toleration that they might, without forfeiting any civil privileges, attend her chapels, rather than those chapels so anomalously supplied with ministers from England; and by none was this wish cherished more fervently than by some of those ministers themselves."† Among these is noticed Dr Myles Cooper,

---

* This chapel is now pulled down, and its endowment amalgamated with the large and elegant chapel of St Paul, York Place. The last incumbent of Blackfriars' Wynd Chapel was the Rev. Robert Adam, author of the "Religious World Displayed," in three vols. 8vo, published in 1809.

† Scottish Episcopal Magazine, vol. ii. p. 209.

formerly Fellow of Lincoln College, Oxford, who had been President or Principal of the College of New York, from which he was exiled by revolt of the American Provinces, and who died senior minister of the Episcopal Chapel in the Cowgate, Edinburgh, an edifice subsequently noticed, the foundation stone of which was laid by General Sir Adolphus Oughton in April 1771; and now, after the removal of the congregation to St Paul's, York Place, used as a Presbyterian Dissenting meeting-house. Such, it is farther stated, was also the wish of Dr Patterson, one of the ministers of St Paul's Chapel, Aberdeen, and of many others.

The state of religion in Scotland after the accession of George III. deserves a passing notice. Arnot mentions, in the year 1779, that " in Scotland there are few towns, whether of importance or insignificant, whether populous or otherwise, where there are not congregations of sectaries." If this writer had witnessed the state of Scotland at the present day his observations could not have been more accurate. In another passage he says—" Besides the highflying part of the Established Clergy [the Presbyterian ministers], the Seceders are to a man a set of fanatics. Although they embrace the same Confession of Faith, and observe the same forms of worship with the Established Church, they have separated from it on account of presentations, and that they may enjoy the delightful rhapsodies of their own preachers. The sectaries of different persuasions of late [previous to 1779] have greatly increased." It cannot be denied that the majority of the Scottish people are Presbyterians of some description or other, but the Establishment cannot claim much more than one third of the population as belonging or attached to its communion, while the great mass of the Presbyterian Dissenters, who have emanated from its own bosom, are now its avowed and determined enemies, under the name of *Voluntaries*, or *Voluntary Churchmen*, as they designate themselves. So prone are the Presbyterians of Scotland, even those of the Establishment, to sectarianism, that there is hardly any novelty started in connection with doctrine, church government, and discipline, which will not find adherents; and the Wesleyan Methodists are perhaps the only sect north of the Tweed who never prospered, and have been always in a languishing condition. There are also some sects peculiar to Scotland, not found in any other country, at least I am not aware that there are Glasites, Bereans, or Original Seceders, any where else.* There are sects common in other countries, and in very considerable number, such as Independents, Baptists, Anabaptists (of various kinds), Methodists of different parties, New Jerusalemites, Quakers, Rowites, Unitarians, and others of less note, whose principles are either not known, or whose existence excites no interest; but it may be repeated, that there is not a country in Europe which abounds more with sectaries and dissenters from the Establishment of its own alleged choice than Scotland.

Most of the minor sectaries enumerated above are the offshoots of more recent times than the accession of George III., and it need not be a matter of surprise that the Presbyterian Establishment should be the parent of many schismatical children, who have not scrupled to lift up their hand against their mother and denounce her as full of corruptions. The Presbyterian Establishment of Scotland contains the elements of dissent within itself. The seeds of contention and separation are continually scattered, and falling as they do on ground not previously preserved by the sound and solid fences of ecclesiastical antiquity, they take root in a rank soil, and flourish luxuriantly. Having disregarded and set at defiance the Apostolical constitution of the Church, and having left their people in their celebration of divine service to the extemporizing qualifications of their ministers, not to mention the errors, prejudices, and weaknesses to which, like other men, they are liable, the Presbyterians of Scotland, whether Established or Dissenting, can offer no effectual resistance to the inroads of fanaticism, the inculcation of error, the rhapsodies of ignorance, or the pressure from popular clamour and excitement.

The Scottish Roman Catholics, though numerous in the Highlands, were dispirited by enactments in force against them, and were seldom

---

* Of these the Glasites take their name from a Mr John Glas, established minister of the parish of Tealing, near Dundee, in the last century, who was expelled for preaching against the Solemn League and Covenant, and for maintaining some dogmas concerning what he called the pure spirituality of Christ's kingdom, with some other tenets. They are also called *Sandemanians*, from one Robert Sandeman, who broached some very wild opinions in the most mystical jargon. The founder of the Bereans was also a Presbyterian minister named Barclay, and they profess to follow the example of the ancient Bereans, as they interpret the inspired historian, Acts xvii 11.

heard of in the country. There were as yet few or no Methodists, the Brownist, or Independent system, had not been introduced, and the other sectaries were chiefly Cameronians, Glasites, Bereans, Quakers, and probably Baptists. The entire population, now consisting of nearly 3,000,000, in 1755 amounted to 1,265,380; and of those, after deducting all the Episcopalians and the Roman Catholics—who, inasmuch as they never belónged to the Presbyterian Establishment, cannot be said to be *de facto* dissenters from it, the Seceders, and those calling themselves the *Relief*, daily increasing, soon deprived the Establishment of a vast number of adherents. It has been seen that when Arnot published his History of Edinburgh in 1779, he rates their meeting-houses at three hundred, while the Established party had scarcely added a single chapel-of-ease to their parish churches. In 1842, little more than a century after the commencement of the schism, the Seceders, who have reconciled their *Burgher* and *Antiburgher* animosities, alone numbered upwards of *three hundred and thirty-four* congregations in Scotland, including their preaching stations; the Relief possessed *one hundred and twelve*; the Cameronian Presbyterians, calling themselves the *Reformed Synod*, have thirty-five; those designated the *Associate Synod of Original Seceders*, thirty-one; the *Original Burgher Associate Synod, nine;* and the Independents, or Brownists, one hundred and five congregations, including preaching stations. Add to these formidable lists of deserters the various parties composing the minor dissenting societies, and it will be found, as previously mentioned, that the Presbyterian Establishment has been tolerably prolific in producing dissent. It is proper to add, however, that a most vigorous effort has of late years been made to stop the progress of desertion, and also to provide for the religious instruction of their people, by what is called the "Church Extension Scheme" of the General Assembly. Upwards of a hundred and sixty places of worship, called "*quoad sacra* parish churches," have been erected throughout the country, and numbers of one of the sections of the Seceders have returned to their allegiance, or have been received into the fellowship of the Kirk, though they hold principles inconsistent with those professed by those who are known as the " Moderate Party " in the General Assembly.

. From these facts it is nothing extravagant to assert that the Presbyterian Establishment contains the elements of sectarianism. It may be urged that England abounds with Dissenters, and this is readily admitted; but it must be recollected that of the sixteen millions of population in England and Wales, the Church of England contains from ten to eleven millions. It is the Church of the vast majority of the nation, which is not disputed even by its opponents; and, moreover, Church Extension, in its proper and legitimate sense, has made a progress throughout many of the dioceses altogether without a parallel. But one of the great causes of unity of polity in the Church of England, and in every branch of the Episcopal Church throughout the world, is its constitution. In the Episcopal Church a man who rejects the authority of the Diocesan becomes a schismatic, and must of necessity leave the communion of the Church if he ever belonged to it; while the *ordination* of the Dissenters, in whatever way they conduct it, cannot be and is not recognised, and this principle is well understood by the members of the Church. But in Scotland the ordination of the Presbyterian Dissenters is as valid as that of the Presbyterian Established ministers. The latter cannot charge the former with irregularity, want of authority, or undue assumption of the ministerial office, because it would be instantly retorted against themselves. Such are a few of the results of the rejection of that government and constitution of the Church which was observed from the Apostolical times, and is still observed by every branch of the Church Catholic which adheres to the " old paths," whether established by law as in England, existing as in Scotland, or maintained by the affections of its people, as in the United States of America.

The discouragement given to officious information against the Scottish Episcopal clergy by the Government of George III. was productive of most salutary consequences. Places for public worship were now erected in towns, villages, and country districts; candidates for holy orders appeared, ordinations were held, and vacant congregations willingly received those gentlemen as their pastors. In the month of June 1764, a curious and at one time a hazardous event occurred in Edinburgh, which is not generally known. This was the consecration of a newly-formed Presbyterian burying-ground by Bishop Falconer. On the south side of the city, near the Meadows or Hope Park, is a plain unpretending edifice erected as a chapel-of-ease to the large parish of St Cuthbert's, or the West Kirk, having on each side of it an enclosed cemetery, first opened for funerals in 1763. Arnot, in his History of Edinburgh, thus alludes to this affair, which it appears was alleged at the time to have been sanctioned by the Kirk-Session :—" The neighbourhood of this chapel has, since its erection, been used as a cemetery. But so strong is the prejudice in favour of holy ground, that previous to its being used as a place of interment, a Bishop of the Scottish Episcopal Communion was prevailed upon with all due solemnity to consecrate the ground—this office of consecration, it seems, either being inconsistent with the principles of a Presbyterian clergyman, or that he is not deemed sufficiently sanctified for the function." Without inquiring into the accuracy of these statements of the historian of the Scottish metropolis, and merely noticing that he errs in asserting that the consecration took place *before* there was any interment in the cemetery, an account of the matter by an individual officially connected with the parish may not be uninteresting The consecration was performed privately on the 25th of June in the evening, at the request of a certain person, according to this local writer, and " whose application to the Bishop was at least connived at by five elders and one deacon, who witnessed the ceremony performed." He thus gives an account of the proceedings in his own way :—" The rumour of this secret transaction having reached the Session, a motion was made on the 19th of July following, and unanimously acquiesced in, to make inquiry into an affair which has lately happened at the Chapel-of-Ease, it being publicly reported that the ground surrounding the said chapel has been consecrated by a Nonjuring Bishop, and at which consecration some members of this Session are said to have been present, which consecration has given great offence, as if it had been countenanced by the Session. Finding, however, that of the six members who witnessed the consecration four were not present, the Session delayed farther investigation till the 2d of August. In the meantime the Presbytery interfered, and enjoined the Session to proceed in their inquiry, and without pronouncing any judgment to give a full report to the Presbytery. During the investigation made by the Session, the following detailed account of the ceremony was produced. Having retired to the Chapel on account of the rain, the Bishop proceeded thus :—' Blessed be the Holy and Undivided Trinity. Amen. Then the Lord's prayer. Then was read Genesis xxiii., Psalm xxxi., 1 Corinthians xv., from the 12th verse to the end, and Psalm xxxix. He then read a prayer to the following effect—That Almighty God, who has taught us in his Holy Word that there is a difference between the spirit of a beast that goeth downward to the earth, and the spirit of a man that goeth upward, which ascendeth to God, and likewise hath taught us that the bodies of the saints are committed to the ground in sure and certain hope of the resurrection to eternal life—would accept this charitable work of ours in separating that portion of ground, that the bodies of our faithful brothers and sisters which should be buried here might rest in peace till the last trump shall awaken them, for they shall awake and rise up that sleep in the dust; and that we may all never forget the day of putting off the tabernacle of this flesh, but that in the midst of life, thinking upon death, we may rise from the death of sin unto a life of righteousness. After which he [Bishop Falconer] declared the ground to be separated from all common and profane uses, to be ever afterwards a place of burial for the interment of the bodies of the faithful, saying—I, William Falconer, a servant of the Lord, though unworthy, do set apart this piece of ground within these walls, as a cemetery in all time coming, for burying the dead. Then followed another prayer of a similar import with the above, the reading of the 16th Psalm, and the apostolic benediction.' The six members of Session, who were present at the ceremony, having solemnly declared that they had no hand in the affair, farther than being present at the request of the individual alluded to, for which they expressed their sorrow, and that the majority of them even knew not at first for what purpose they were convened, the Session remitted the whole investigation to the Presbytery. On the 26th of December the Presbytery returned the following sentence to the Session:—' Considering that none of the elders or the deacon had invited Mr Falconer—that they had been led to attend the ceremony of the consecration without reflecting on the nature and consequences of it—and that they had testified their sorrow for being concerned in the matter, the Presbytery go no farther in censure than to express their dissatisfaction at their behaviour, and admonish them to be more circumspect in their conduct for the future; and the Presbytery order that this their sentence be intimated to them by the Moderator of the West Kirk in Session.' "*

The Office for the Administration of the Holy Communion was revised in 1765, to bring it " to as exact a conformity with the ancient standards

---

* History of the Church and Parish of St Cuthbert, or West Kirk of Edinburgh, 1829, p. 139-142.

of eucharistic service as it could bear."* The preservation of the Episcopal order was carefully maintained. In 1762, the Rev. Robert Forbes, presbyter at Leith, had been consecrated at Forfar by Bishop Falconar, Primus, in room of Bishop White, deceased in 1761, assisted by Bishop Alexander and Bishop Gerard. Bishop Forbes was elected to the diocesan superintendence of Caithness and Orkney, which had been long vacant; and on the 21st of September 1768, the Rev. Robert Kilgour, presbyter at Peterhead, was consecrated at Cupar-Fife, by Bishops Falconar, Rait, and Alexander This excellent prelate became the successor of Bishop Gerard in the diocese of Aberdeen. In 1774, the Rev. Charles Rose, presbyter at Doune, was consecrated at Forfar to be diocesan of Ross and Caithness, by Bishops Falconar, Rait, and Forbes; and at the death of Bishop Alexander, in 1776, he was appointed to the superintendence of the ancient diocese of Dunblane.

In 1766, the Rev. Arthur Petrie, presbyter at Meiklefolla, in Aberdeenshire, was elected coadjutor to Bishop Falconar by the presbyters in Moray. He was consecrated at Dundee on the 27th of June by Bishops Falconar, Rait, Kilgour, and Rose, and next year, at the death of Bishop Forbes, he was appointed to the diocesan superintendence of Ross and Caithness; but he soon afterwards had the sole charge of the diocese of Moray assigned to him by the resignation of Bishop Falconar, who was elected to Edinburgh, where he had long resided, and where he died in 1784. Bishop Falconar's death is thus announced in the publications of the time :—" At Edinburgh, in the seventy-seventh year of his age, the Right Rev. Mr William Falconar. He held the highest office in the Episcopal Church of Scotland for forty-three years." †

Bishop Rait died on the 13th of January 1777. His death is thus recorded :—" At Dundee, Dr James Rait, one of the Bishops of the Episcopal Church of Scotland. He was born February 9, 1689, N. S.; was ordained a deacon in October 1712, and a presbyter in June 1713, and was advanced to the highest order in September 1742. From a charge in the country he was called to Dundee in March 1727."‡ The presbyters in the diocese of Brechin elected the Rev. George Innes, presbyter in Aberdeen, who was consecrated at Alloa on the 13th of

---
* Skinner's Ecclesiastical History of Scotland, vol. ii. p. 682.
† Scots Magazine, vol xlvi p 35.   ‡ Ibid. vol. xxxix. p. 54.

August 1778, by Bishops Falconar, Rose, and Petrie, but he died in 1781, and the diocese continued vacant some years.

On the 25th of September 1782, the Rev. John Skinner, presbyter in Aberdeen, was consecrated in the Episcopal chapel of Luthermuir, in the diocese of Brechin, by Bishop Kilgour, who had succeeded Bishop Falconar as Primus, assisted by Bishops Rose and Petrie. Bishop Skinner was appointed coadjutor to Bishop Kilgour. This truly distinguished and learned Bishop, whose virtues, piety, and zeal, will long be remembered in the Scottish Episcopal Church, was the second son of the Rev. John Skinner of Longside, whose sufferings in the cause of the Church ar already noticed His mother was the eldest daughter of the Rev. Mr Hunter, an Episcopal clergyman in the Shetland Islands, since whose death no successor has been appointed. Bishop Skinner was admitted into deacon's orders by Bishop Gerard of Aberdeen, when only in the twentieth year of his age, in 1763, the want of clergymen rendering such an early ordination necessary. He was first settled at Ellon in Aberdeenshire, but in 1775 he was removed to Aberdeen, where he accepted a charge with the greatest reluctance, and almost solely on family considerations. "At the period," we are told, " when he entered on his new charge, it did not consist of three hundred people, yet, such was Mr Skinner's zeal in his holy calling, that he had not served the cure above twelve months when additional accommodation was required. But in 1776, even the idea of erecting an ostensible church-like place of worship dared not be cherished by Scottish Episcopalians. Hence was Mr Skinner obliged to look out for some retired situation, down a close or little alley, and there, at his own individual expense, to erect a large dwelling-house, the two upper floors of which, being fitted up as a chapel, were devoted to the accommodation of his daily increasing flock, and the two under floors to the residence of his family."*

In this structure Mr Skinner continued nineteen years officiating to his numerous and respectable congregation, till a proper ecclesiastical edifice was erected. But as this most active Bishop is more prominently introduced to the notice of the reader in the sequel, it may be here simply stated, in the language of his son, that, after his consecration as coadjutor to Bishop Kilgour, " such in the space of four years was the

---

* Memoir of Bishop Skinner, prefixed to Annals of Scottish Episcopacy, p. xvi. xvii.

confidence with which Bishop Skinner, then only in his forty-second year, inspired the venerable members of the Episcopal College in Scotland, that Bishop Kilgour, having been nominated *Primus Scotiæ Episcopus* on the death of Bishop Falconar of Edinburgh in 1784, did, with the approbation and consent of the College, divest himself of all episcopal relation to the diocese of Aberdeen, retaining the office of Primus only, and was succeeded by his coadjutor, in terms of the ninth Synodical Canon of 1743. From that period the Bishop of Aberdeen is known to have devoted every thought of his heart, and every faculty of his mind, towards rendering the sadly depressed Church in which he served alike respectable, and *worthy of all acceptation*, in the eyes of men, as he trusted, by reason of her resemblance in doctrine and discipline to the Primitive Church of Christ, she would be found acceptable in the sight of God, and conformable to His holy will."

With the political affairs of those times the present work has no connection, and it would be extraneous to digress The Chevalier St George, father of Prince Charles Edward, died at Rome in the beginning of 1776, in the seventy-eighth year of his age, after a residence of nearly fifty years in the metropolis of the Papal dominions. The Jacobites, who invariably designated him "King," heard the intelligence with indifference, for he had never been personally popular, and their attachment was to his alleged hereditary claims rather than to himself as an individual. This unfortunate prince, the representative of a long dynasty of sovereigns, had been confined to his apartment during the last six years of his life by illness; but long before that period he had sunk into obscurity, and held little intercourse with his friends in Great Britain after the suppression of the Enterprise of 1745. The hope of a *Restoration* was now entertained only by a few enthusiastic sentimentalists, who never could persuade themselves that the ancient dynasty would be annihilated. It does not appear that the old Scottish Jacobites ever spoke of Prince Charles as *King*; after the death of his father, and as his only brother had become a dignitary of the Church of Rome, by the title of Cardinal York, he never was an object of interest with those who still cherished a lurking affection for the House of Stuart. The Chevalier St George was interred with all the respect due to his birth at the expense of the Pope; but this terminated the regard for his Family, and the Pontifical Court would not acknowledge Prince Charles as successor to his father's rank. The Prior of the Irish Dominicans, and the Rectors of the English, Irish, and Scottish Colleges of Jesuits established at Rome, were even banished from that city for paying the honour of royalty to the Prince. Mr Sharpe observes, in his " Letters from Italy," written in 1765 and 1766—" The Pope and his Council have come to a resolution, upon the death of the Pretender, to have no more concern in this business, and not only do not acknowledge the title of the present Pretender, but have forbidden all the princes and cardinals to visit him. I have had some conversation with a very sensible ecclesiastic here [Rome], who knows every thing which passes both in the Pope's and the Pretender's palaces. I asked what name the Pretender goes by at present; to which he could hardly give an answer, as he says they so strictly observe the prohibition not to style him King, that he is never mentioned, or, if by chance they are obliged to speak of him, it is under the absurd appellation of *Prince of Wales.*"

CHAPTER XIX.

CONSECRATION OF DR. SEABURY AS BISHOP OF CONNECTICUT BY THE SCOTTISH BISHOPS—ALLEGED APPLICATION OF THE REV. JOHN WESLEY FOR EPISCOPAL CONSECRATION—INTERNAL AFFAIRS OF THE CHURCH—DEATH OF PRINCE CHARLES EDWARD STUART—REPEAL OF THE PENAL LAWS OF 1746 AND 1748.

IT is already stated that after the accession of George III. the persecutions of the Episcopal clergy entirely ceased. Though the Church then enjoyed considerable internal prosperity, nothing of general interest occurred in its history from that period to 1784, and there were many probably in England who had almost forgotten that such a Communion existed. But the Providence of Him who had conducted and preserved the Church through so many vicissitudes, hardships, and depressions—*per varios casus, per tot discrimina rerum*—was now exercised in a remarkable manner. In 1784, an event occurred, or, to quote the language of a venerable writer, in that year, " when our Church had indeed a less number of Bishops than usual, but still such as were sufficient for the time to answer the great end of the office, an unexpected affair of a quite foreign nature was providentially thrown in her way, which contributed to raise her in some measure out of that obscurity into which a run of distress had plunged her, and procured her a particular degree of respect and notice from a quarter where she had not been favoured with much of either for some time before."*

As early as 1713 the consecration of a Bishop for the North American

* Skinner's Ecclesiastical History of Scotland, vol. ii p. 683, 684.

colonies was in contemplation, but it was never carried into effect. Several unsuccessful attempts were made to introduce the episcopate, and Archbishop Secker greatly exerted himself in this important matter, merely requesting from Government the royal permission, without any temporal rank or power. A short time before the American Revolution, when the Stamp Act was the subject of political controversy, the measure was again publicly brought forward by the Rev. East Apthorpe, and by the Rev. Dr Chandler of Elizabeth-Town; but it was unpopular among the Americans themselves, who imagined that it would strengthen the civil government, and it met with the violent opposition of English Dissenters of all sects, who formed a committee in London to prevent its consummation. It was then doubted if the American Republicans would even tolerate the residence of a Bishop exercising episcopal authority within their territories. After the acknowledgment of the independence of the United States, as it was also doubtful if the British Government would permit American clergymen to be consecrated in England, the Danish minister, with the consent of his Sovereign, offered to Mr Adams, the American Envoy at the British Court, to procure their consecration in Denmark

At the termination of the American War the independence of the United States was acknowledged by Great Britain, and all political connection with the mother country was necessarily dissolved. The new democratic government set up in the United States, true to the principles of the peculiar constitution they adopted, declared against the recognition of any religious communion in particular; and the Episcopal clergy, left to themselves, and deprived of diocesan authority, found that they were no longer a regularly constituted ecclesiastical society, for they well knew that no church could be properly so called without a Bishop or several Bishops. Some of the clergy of the State of Connecticut, anxious to remedy this fundamental deficiency, resolved to apply to the Church of England, and they elected the Rev. Samuel Seabury, D.D. Oxon., who had been one of the Missionaries of the Society for Promoting Christian Knowledge, as a clergyman worthy of being invested with the episcopal office. Dr Seabury arrived in England in 1783, bringing with him the most satisfactory testimonials to Archbishop Markham of York, the Primacy being then vacant, with a supplication that his Grace " would espouse the cause of their sinking Church, and afford her that relief on which her very existence depended, by consecrating Dr Seabury to be their Bishop " The objections urged by the Archbishop were both civil and ecclesiastical It was necessary to obtain an Act of Parliament, because at the consecration the oaths of allegiance and supremacy could not be omitted, and these could not be exacted from a citizen of the United States. The consent of the American Government also had not been obtained. As Dr Seabury had been sent by only a few individuals, the Archbishop was doubtful how far this could be considered a proper ecclesiastical election. Other difficulties occurred, which were all carefully considered by Archbishop Moore, after his translation to the Primacy from Bangor in 1783. An Act of Parliament could not be immediately obtained, and as it was most inconvenient for Dr Seabury to remain to the following Session of Parliament, he was advised to apply for consecration to the Scottish Bishops.

But the penal enactments of 1746 and 1748 were still in force, and the circumstances were so peculiar, that the Scottish Bishops considered that it would be imprudent, if not dangerous, to consecrate a clergyman who had first applied to the Archbishop of York, without ascertaining the sentiments of the English Primate. Dr Berkeley, one of the Prebendaries of Canterbury, son of the celebrated Bishop of Cloyne, was then residing at St Andrews for the education of his only son, and he undertook to correspond with Archbishop Moore on the subject. The result was so satisfactory, that Dr Seabury came to Scotland in November 1784, and was consecrated at Aberdeen by Bishop Kilgour, Primus, Bishop Petrie, and Bishop Skinner. When Bishop Seabury returned to America, the utmost gratitude was expressed to the Scottish Bishops They declared that wherever the American Church would be mentioned, this that the Scottish Bishops had done for her would always be remembered. " As under God," says Bishop Seabury, in his Charge at his primary visitation, "the Bishops of the old Episcopal Church of Scotland, which at the Revolution fell a sacrifice to the jealous apprehensions of William III., were solely the instruments of accomplishing this happy work, to them our gratitude is due. And I hope the sense of the benefit we have through their hands received will ever remain fresh in the minds of all members of our communion to the latest posterity. Under the greatest persecutions God has preserved them, and, I trust, will preserve them, that there may yet be some to whom destitute churches may apply in their wants; some faithful shepherds in Christ's flock, who are willing to give *freely* what they have *freely* received from their Lord and Master." It may be here added, that in 1786 the Episcopal clergy of the Southern States, being informed that the obstacles which prevented the consecration of Bishop Seabury in England had been removed, applied to the English Bishops for the consecration of two of their brethren, that thus the canonical number necessary for perpetuating the succession in the United States might be complete. The Rev. Dr White, Bishop-elect of Philadelphia, and the Rev. Dr Prevost, Bishop-elect of New York, were consecrated in the chapel of Lambeth Palace, on the 4th of February 1787, by the Archbishop of Canterbury, assisted by the Archbishop of York, and the Bishops of Bath and Wells and of Peterborough. From Bishops Seabury, White, and Prevost, the succession of the American Episcopal Church is derived. Dr James Maddison was afterwards consecrated in England, and Dr Seabury was duly admitted a member of the House of Bishops in the American Church, or, as it is expressed in the Episcopal Convention, " the Protestant Episcopal Church of America is the Church formerly known by the name of the Church of England in America."

The consecration of Bishop Seabury reminded the Church of England that a depressed branch of the Church Catholic existed in Scotland, having the same orders, and using the same Liturgy. " It first," says Bishop Skinner, " introduced me to the knowledge and acquaintance of some eminent divines of the Church of England. They were the men who thenceforth interested themselves so much in the repeal of the penal statutes, and in the grievously depressed situation of our Church, that for my own part I had only to inform them, and some invaluable and equally zealous lay friends, what my venerable colleagues and I wished to be done, and they did it."*

But Bishop Seabury's consecration was not allowed to pass unnoticed by the enemy, and an anonymous writer in the Gentleman's Magazine for 1785, under the signature of LL, assailed not only the consecration, but the Church, whose governors had presided on the solemn occasion, in the most wanton, ignorant, and contemptible manner. Mr Urban tells us that he submitted the communication to a friend, who desired

* Memoir of Bishop Skinner, p. 32.

to add the notes. The passages of LL.'s letter to which these explanatory notes are prefixed evince the extent of the writer's information on the subject. He asks—"How came the *anonymous* Scottish Bishop who publishes the consecration sermon [Bishop Skinner] by his own title?" The answer properly is—"By the consecration of other Bishops." It is next asked—"Or if he had one, how could he confer it on another without the authority of his sovereign?" The answer is—"Bishops, as such, may consecrate Bishops and convey spiritual jurisdiction, though they can give no temporal powers, or exempt from temporal penalties." It is then doubted with respect to Bishop Seabury, that "the Colonies, who lately shook off the dominion of the mother country, will not be disposed to yield much reverence to the suffragan of those mighty prelates, whom a law enacted in 1748 prohibited from ordaining even a single deacon." It is answered—"The [American] Episcopalians doubtless will revere the superior whom they have recommended and chosen." To this it may be added, that Bishop Seabury never was intended to be the suffragan of those *mighty prelates*, and that so far from the law of 1748 prohibiting them from ordaining a single deacon, the Scottish Bishops not only continued to ordain deacons and priests, but consecrated Bishops as vacancies occurred.

It is next stated that the Presbyterians on the south and the Episcopalians on the north side of the Tweed, "both equally Dissenters, are both equally indebted for many privileges and comforts to the tolerating spirit of the age in which they live." To this assertion it is replied—"This will hardly be allowed by the latter, who are now subjected to more severe pains and penalties than the Papists." The English Presbyterians, it is observed, "strive not to distinguish themselves by any claims to superior rank;" but it is properly asked—"How can they, as *Presbyterians?*" They aspire "to no authority beyond the guidance of a flock which voluntarily elects them for its pastors." Mr Urban's friend here observes—"The Scottish Bishops are also elected by their respective flocks; and so was Bishop Seabury by 30,000 Episcopalians in Connecticut." This, however, is an error. In whatever manner Bishop Seabury was elected, the Scottish Bishops never were nominated by their flocks or congregations. The clergy of the dioceses are the electors. A parallel is then drawn by LL. between the Presbyterian ministers and the Scottish Bishops, in which the latter are accused of "treating the Establishment of that country in which they are tolerated with contempt :"—and that among them, " it seems, there are still to be found Archbishops of St Andrews, though the fabric of its cathedral was not more effectually destroyed by John Knox, *that great deliverer of his country from religious thraldom*, who left behind him a *name superior to all titles*, than the very existence of its pretended metropolitan has since been annihilated by the Act of Union." The gloss mis-statements here quoted sufficiently evince the spirit of the writer. No Scottish Bishop ever assumed the title of Archbishop of St Andrews since the Revolution.

This attack was answered by a writer who signs himself *An Episcopal Clergyman of the Scotch Church*,* and so conclusive is the reply, that Mr Urban adds the following compliment—" We think the correspondence of this learned writer an honour, and shall be happy in the continuance of it. *Sit anima nostra cum suâ* " A keen discussion now commenced between LL. and the Scottish Episcopal clergyman, which brought several antagonists into the field. This controversy attracted the notice of Dr Horsley, then Archdeacon of St Alban's, who was at the time carrying on a warfare with some of Dr Priestley's followers in the same periodical, and he published a letter signed by the initials of his name, in which, though he admits that he was comparatively ignorant of the history and state of the Scottish Episcopal Church previous to the consecration of Dr Seabury, he bestows on it the highest commendations; and if the maxim *laudari a laudato viro* was ever applicable, it was on that occasion.

The reception which Bishop Seabury experienced at his return to America is a triumphant reply to the malignant strictures published against him and the Scottish Bishops. In a long address presented to him by the clergy of Connecticut it is stated—" We, in the presence of Almighty God, declare to the world that we do unanimously and voluntarily accept, receive, and recognize you to be our Bishop, supreme in the government of the Church, and in the administration of all ecclesiastical offices. And we do solemnly engage to render you all that respect, duty, and submission, which we believe do belong and are due to your high office, and which, as we understand, were given by the presbyters to

* Gentleman's Magazine, vol. lv p 437-440, generally said to have been the Right Rev. Bishop Gleig

their Bishops in the Primitive Church, while in her native purity she was unconnected with and uncontrolled by any secular power." After dwelling on the importance of having a resident Bishop among them, and alluding to their first application to their " Parent Church," the clergy of Connecticut observe—" But, blessed be God! another door was opened for you. In the mysterious economy of his Providence he had preserved the remains of the old Episcopal Church of Scotland, under all the malice and persecutions of its enemies. In the school of adversity its pious and venerable Bishops had learned to renounce the pomps and grandeur of the world, and were ready to do the work of their heavenly Father. As outcasts, they pitied us ; as faithful holders of the apostolical commission, what they *freely received* they *freely gave* From them we have received a free, valid, and purely ecclesiastical Episcopacy, are thereby made complete in all our parts, and have a right to be considered as a living, and we hope through God's grace shall be a vigorous, branch of the Catholic Church. To these venerable fathers our thanks are due, and they have them most fervidly May the Almighty be their rewarder, regard them in mercy, support them under the persecutions of their enemies, and turn the hearts of their persecutors, and make their simplicity and godly sincerity known unto all men! And wherever the American Episcopal Church shall be mentioned in the world, may this good deed, which they have done for us, be spoken of for a memorial of them!"

To this affectionate address, which was presented at Middletown, August 3, 1785, Bishop Seabury made a suitable reply. In concluding he observed—" The sentiments you entertain of the venerable Bishops in Scotland are highly pleasing to me. Their conduct throughout the whole business was candid, friendly, and Christian ; appearing to me to arise from a just sense of duty, and to be founded in, and conducted by, the true principles of the Primitive Apostolical Church ; and I hope you will join with me in manifestations of gratitude to them, by always keeping up the most intimate communion between them and their suffering Church."

A letter written from New England at that time contains the following intimations:—" Samuel Seabury, D.D. has arrived, and settled in New London as Bishop of Connecticut, after having been consecrated by the Nonjuring Bishops in Scotland. The Doctor has been recognized by the clergy at Middletown as their Bishop. The general reception that Dr Seabury has met with from all sects and denominations is truly surprising.—The Bishop performs divine service every Sunday in the meeting-house according to the Church of England, as the church was burnt by General Arnold, and all parties attend him there.—We have room for reformation in Church and State. Among the changes daily happening, a coalition between the Episcopalians in the six New England States is approaching. When that event shall take place Episcopacy will do more towards our reformation than all the charities and political manœuvres of Great Britain have done in the century past without a bishop." That coalition soon happened, but whether it was attended by the sanguine results anticipated it would be fruitless now to inquire.

Here it is the proper place to introduce a subject which the present writer well remembers to have heard related, although he has failed in every attempt to recollect or trace his authority. The accuracy, or even authenticity, of the circumstance is not maintained; but as there is nothing improbable in the matter, it may be received with whatever degree of credit the reader pleases. The celebrated John Wesley first came to Scotland in 1761, and brought with him one of his preachers named Christopher Hopper. His first sermon was preached in the town of Musselburgh, six miles from Edinburgh, where a Methodist Society still exists. Wesley was repeatedly afterwards in Scotland, and several preachers were sent thither, who formed congregations; but the people being opposed to Methodism, the Wesleyan Societies never flourished; the alleged Arminianism of their indefatigable founder was a stumbling-block to the resolute Calvinistic Presbyterians; and so bitterly were Wesley and his preachers opposed by the Seceders in particular, that one of the latter maintained the propriety of *hewing the Methodists in pieces before the Lord,* referring to the case of Agag slain by the prophet Samuel. The singular constitution of the Methodist Societies was also an object of dislike to the Presbyterians, who, with all their peculiarities, prefer their ministers to be constantly settled among them to a wandering and ever-changing itinerancy

It does not appear that Wesley had any particular communications with the Scottish Episcopal clergy during his various peregrinations. Their depressed condition precluded them from holding any intercourse with him, if they had been inclined; but his opinions, practices, and itinerating habits, would find little favour with men who could not view him in any other light than as the originator of a serious schism, notwithstanding his repeatedly professed attachment to the Church of England. It is nevertheless said that in the year 1784, or at least after the independence of the United States had been recognized, when Wesley was organizing a plan to extend the Methodist Societies to America, either he, or some one authorized by him, applied to Bishop Kilgour, the Primus, to consecrate the Rev. Dr Coke, one of the few clergymen of the Church of England who joined him. The application was refused, and Wesley, in the year 1784, summoned Dr Coke and a Mr Francis Asbury to Bristol, where, in defiance of all rule, authority, and order, he committed the most extraordinary act of *consecrating* those gentlemen *Bishops* to America, and from them the religious association in the United States, dignified with the title of the *Methodist Episcopal Church*, have their succession of *Bishops*, as they are called, and ministers or preachers. The sentiments of Wesley, with reference to this unprecedented transaction, are contained in his *manifesto* to Dr Coke and Mr Asbury. Although he declares—" I think the Church of England the best constituted Church in the world;" yet " Lord King's account of the Primitive Church convinced me many years ago that Bishops and Presbyters are the same order, and consequently have the same right to ordain." With this, and an abridgment or new arrangement of the Liturgy for his followers, he seems to have satisfied his conscience. Such is the substance of the story respecting Wesley's application in Scotland. He admits that he had himself applied to the Bishop of London to *ordain* " only one " of his preachers, and " could not prevail." It was, perhaps, after this that he caused the application to be made to Bishop Kilgour, but in what way it was done, whether directly from Wesley himself, which is very unlikely, or by another party either orally or by letter, it is impossible to say, as it was never submitted to the Church.*

Returning to the internal affairs of the Church, Bishop Skinner had

---

* It is proper to state, that in mentioning this circumstance to the Right Rev. Bishop Torry, Diocesan of Dunkeld, Dunblane, and Fife, that Right Reverend Prelate, who had every opportunity of knowing much of Bishop Kilgour's correspondence, declared that he had never heard of Wesley's application.

succeeded Bishop Kilgour as sole diocesan of Aberdeen in 1784. In 1787 three consecrations took place. On the 7th of March the Rev. Andrew Macfarlane, presbyter at Inverness, was consecrated at Peterhead by Bishops Kilgour, Petrie, and Skinner, and appointed coadjutor to Bishop Petrie, whom he soon afterwards succeeded as diocesan of the united districts of Ross and Moray. On the 26th of September the Rev. Dr William Abernethy Drummond, of Hawthornden, presbyter in Edinburgh, and the Rev. John Strachan, presbyter in Dundee, were consecrated at Peterhead by Bishops Kilgour, Skinner, and Macfarlane. Bishop Abernethy Drummond was appointed to the diocese of Brechin, that diocese having been vacant since the death of Bishop Innes in 1781, and Bishop Strachan was nominated his coadjutor; but soon afterwards the former was elected by the presbyters of Edinburgh to be their diocesan, and he resigned his connection with the diocese of Brechin to Bishop Strachan.

After the consecration of Bishop Seabury various plans were proposed by the friends of the Scottish Episcopal Church to procure a repeal of the penal laws of 1746 and 1748, but the predilections of some of the older clergy, supported by their laity, proved an obstacle as long as Prince Charles Edward was alive. In the summer of 1786 one of the Scottish clergy resided some time in England, and held many conversations on the subject not only with Dr Horne, then Dean of Canterbury (afterwards Bishop of Norwich), and Dr Berkeley, but with the Primate. It was the unanimous opinion of the Archbishop, and the two dignitaries now named, that no attempt should be made to procure a repeal of those laws during the life of the Count of Albany, as the Prince was styled, which was not then likely to be of long duration. " When you do apply for a repeal," said the Archbishop, " take care not to ask too much, lest you obtain nothing. You were happy and prosperous under Queen Anne's toleration; ask nothing more than to be again placed under its protection. Let him who shall take the lead in your favour in either House of Parliament move for nothing more at first than a simple repeal of the laws of 1746 and 1748. These laws are so severe, and will appear so unjust, that the bare reading of them will carry the motion unanimously; and if you shall find it necessary to ask for more afterwards, more will probably be granted to you."

During this period we are told that " the soundness of this advice was universally admitted at the time by the Episcopal clergy in Edinburgh and its neighbourhood. It so happened before the death of the Count of Albany that a clergyman had been consecrated a Bishop of the Scottish Episcopal Church who had great influence, and deserved on many accounts to have great influence, in that Church, but who was very ill qualified to conduct any measure with address, coolness, and delicacy. When a presbyter he was amongst the loudest in his praises of the plan of proceeding recommended by the Archbishop of Canterbury; but when he became a Bishop he changed his sentiments with respect to Queen Anne's Act of Toleration." This refers to Bishop Abernethy Drummond, who had some scruples respecting the Oath of Abjuration, and who remained inflexible in his opinions " about a new Oath which he had framed for the Scottish Episcopal clergy, to be taken instead of the Oaths of Allegiance, Abjuration, and Supremacy, and founded on that Oath an act for a very ample toleration." But as in all contemplated measures there will ever be differences of opinion, it is unnecessary to enter into details which are now forgotten, and which at the present time would possess little interest.

On the 31st January 1788, Prince Charles Edward expired at Rome, aged sixty-seven years, leaving no issue except an illegitimate daughter, whom he ordered to be designated Duchess of Albany, and to whom he bequeathed all his property, which was very considerable, in the French Funds, while to his brother the Cardinal York he left his claims to the British throne, though that prince had rendered these nugatory by becoming an ecclesiastic. Yet the Cardinal Prince did not hesitate to make a solemn protestation that he did not renounce his pretensions to his hereditary realms—that the sanctity of his ecclesiastical character could be no impediment in the sight of God and man—and that, while thus asserting his own right, he would transmit it to the prince next of kin. All these were empty or at least vain declarations; the race of the Stuarts had run their course, and their claims were at last viewed as utterly hopeless. The Scottish Episcopalians could now offer their allegiance to George III. without derogating from their honour, or abandoning those principles for which they had severely suffered. This duty they performed spontaneously, and without making any stipulations. On the 24th of April 1788, after various preliminary consultations among the clergy, the Bishops met at Aberdeen to deliberate on the affairs of the Church, when, after a conference with the presbyters, it was unanimously resolved that the reigning sovereign and the Royal Family should be prayed for *by name* in all the chapels of the dioceses under their jurisdiction. There were only two who did not cordially approve of this resolution—Bishop Rose of Dunblane, then very far advanced in years and almost in a state of dotage, and the Rev. Mr Browne of Montrose, in the diocese of Brechin. A third is mentioned who entertained some scruples, but as he was " a pious and sensible man," and had " truth for his object," he soon saw it his duty to comply, and " followed the example of his fathers and brethren." The resolution adopted at this meeting was duly notified in all the Edinburgh and Aberdeen newspapers of the time.

It was propitious for the Scottish Episcopal Church at this crisis that Bishop Skinner of Aberdeen succeeded Bishop Kilgour as Primus in 1788, at the resignation of that venerable and pious prelate, who, in March 1790, died at Peterhead in the seventy-sixth year of his age, and fifty-third of his clerical life, twenty-two years of which he had adorned the episcopate. Bishop Skinner not only organized the affairs of his own diocese, but was enabled to promote that harmony throughout the Church which was the harbinger of its present peace and unity.

The Scottish Bishops thought it their duty to lay before the Government a memorial of their proceedings, which was dated April 26, 1788, and transmitted to Lord Sydney, one of the Principal Secretaries of State. Meanwhile his Majesty King George and all the Royal Family were prayed for publicly by name in all the chapels under the jurisdiction of the Bishops, with the exception of the Rev. Mr Browne's, on the 25th day of May 1788. The Archbishops of Canterbury and York were also addressed, and the Scottish Bishops expressed to those Prelates their " humble confidence that upon their Graces' recommending to the Bishops of their respective Provinces the measure of repeal of those penal statutes under which the Episcopal Church in Scotland has so long groaned, they cannot but doubt that, by such powerful assistance, they shall obtain the desirable end they have in view."

The memorial to Lord Sydney was answered by that nobleman on the 28th of June, and in his reply he informed the Scottish Bishops that he had not failed to lay it before his Majesty, who had received " with great satisfaction this proof of their attachment to his person and government" Encouraged by the flattering manner in which this memorial had been received, the Bishops occupied themselves in consulting with various distinguished persons in the State, respecting the most judicious mode in which they might petition Parliament for a repeal of the Acts of 1746 and 1748; but at that time the King's alarming indisposition delayed all business, except that of providing for the exigencies of the Government. His Majesty's recovery, however, in the following year removed the national anxiety, and elicited many loyal addresses, among which was one from the Scottish Episcopal Church. In 1789 the draught of a bill of relief was prepared by Bishop Skinner at the express desire of the Right Hon. Henry Dundas, then Treasurer of the Navy, afterwards Viscount Melville, and forwarded to him at his seat near Edinburgh; but as that gentleman had been unexpectedly summoned to London before he could give his opinion fully on the nature and language of the bill, it was suggested by the active friends of the measure that nothing would likely be done in its favour by either branch of the Legislature unless some of those concerned repaired to London, and watched it in its different stages of progress through the Parliament, by which means any difficulties might be instantly solved, and the measure prevented from being relinquished This was the opinion of George Dempster, Esq. of Dunnichen, member for the county of Forfar, a zealous supporter of the measure, who informed Bishop Skinner that "unless a member of Administration would positively pledge himself to introduce into Parliament the bill for repealing the penal statutes, and to carry it through all its stages, it would be absolutely necessary for some of the Bishops to repair to London, there to appear as loyal subjects, claiming a just and reasonable relief not only for themselves, but for the society to which they belonged." This was, indeed, rendered the more necessary on account of several unfair representations transmitted to influential quarters, not by the leading members of the Presbyterian Establishment, who, to their honour, were all friendly to the repeal, but by more interested parties. "Those English ordained clergymen, who, being Scotsmen by birth and parentage," says the Rev. John Skinner, " had procured orders with no other view but that of opposing Scottish Episcopacy, became very much alarmed at the favourable reception given by all ranks of men in Scotland to the cause and claims of the Church of their forefathers; and Dr Bagot, Bishop of Norwich, had been particularly applied to, to thwart, as far as possible, any measures that might be taken by the Scottish Episcopal clergy for their relief "*

In April 1789, immediately after Easter, Bishops Skinner, Abernethy Drummond, and Strachan, proceeded to London, and acted with the utmost prudence in every respect, except in not paying sufficient deference at first to the Lord Chancellor Thurlow, whose influence they had been earnestly entreated to secure. His Lordship considered their conduct as disrespectful, and as those dissensions had commenced in the Cabinet which eventually separated him from Mr Pitt's Administration, he probably considered their neglect as intentional. The Lord Chancellor's conduct and peculiar opinions are sufficiently delineated in the voluminous correspondence published by the Rev. John Skinner of Forfar, in his " Annals of Scottish Episcopacy." The first bill was lost in the House of Peers on the 6th of July 1789, and it succeeded no better during the two next sessions of Parliament, though the management was entrusted to three gentlemen to whom the Scottish Episcopal Church owes a deep debt of gratitude—the Rev. George Gaskin, D.D., Secretary to the Society for Promoting Christian Knowledge, William Stevens, Esq. Treasurer to Queen Anne's Bounty, and Sir James Allan Park, afterwards the Hon. Justice Park.

Four years elapsed before the Legislature extended the relief to the Scottish Episcopal Church which had been so ardently desired, the chief men in power, as Bishop Russell observes, " having had to combat difficulties which did not in reality belong to the question, and to conciliate parties who at first sight appeared to have no interest in its decision." The Lord Chancellor Thurlow continually harassed the supporters of the Bill and its presenters, by pettish queries and frivolous objections unworthy of his distinguished abilities, and only to be accounted for from his dignity being offended, and the indifference he felt towards the Church in general. It would, however, occupy too much space to give an abstract of the numerous letters written by several Noble and distinguished personages, or a minute account of the various delays and annoyances which were experienced before the measure was successful. A number of the counties, cities, and royal burghs of Scotland, petitioned in favour of the Bill in 1791. On the 2d of April that

* Annals of Scottish Episcopacy, p. 89, 90.

year the Earl of Kellie, one of the Sixteen Representative Peers of Scotland, presented three petitions, and moved for leave to bring in a bill agreeable to their prayer. Two days afterwards the Bill was read a first time without any opposition on the part of Lord Chancellor Thurlow, who merely observed that some alterations would be necessary. On the 2d of May the Earl of Elgin moved the second reading, and on this occasion the Archbishops of Canterbury and York, and the Bishops of London, Durham, Salisbury, St David's, Oxford, Bangor, and Carlisle, were present. After the Earl of Elgin had stated the principle of the Bill to the House, and the situation of those it was intended to relieve, the Lord Chancellor left the Woolsack, and in the course of his speech declared, that though he would not object to the principle of the Bill, he thought it his duty to make some observations on it; and he concluded by remarking, that as the religious principles of the Scottish Episcopalians "were not sufficiently known, or at least no public evidence was given what these were, or how far they deserved that indulgence which was intended by this Bill, he did not think it would be prudent to grant it on such a broad unlimited footing, as it might open a door to many similar applications, and create much unnecessary trouble to the Legislature."

Lord Viscount Stormont replied to the Lord Chancellor, and his Lordship was followed by Dr Horsley, then Bishop of St David's, who, in a speech of considerable length, and characteristic of his distinguished talents, advocated the principle of the Bill. The Earl of Kinnoull made a short speech, in which his Lordship described the members of the Scottish Episcopal Church as a "respectable, quiet, and decent body of people, who in the most trying times had always behaved in a very becoming and exemplary manner, and were therefore well entitled to every indulgence which the Legislature could show them." The question was then put and carried without a division.

In the meantime, it was intimated to Bishop Skinner by Bishop Horsley, and the Earls of Kellie, Elgin, and Fife, that the only condition Lord Chancellor Thurlow now urged was the necessity of the clergy subscribing some public declaration of their religious principles at ordination, to show their approximation to the doctrines of the Church of England; and the subscription of the Thirty-Nine Articles was strongly recommended, " as the best and only means of showing, in a legal manner, what our religious principles were, and that our Church was really such a society as deserved to be tolerated."—" The truth is," says Bishop Russell, " the Church had then no *Articles of Religion* or *Confession of Faith*, which the clergy were required to subscribe previous to ordination. The Protestant clergy in Scotland, as well Episcopal as Presbyterian, had no other Confession of Faith before the overthrow of the Church in the reign of Charles I. than that which was drawn up in twenty-five articles by Knox and his associates, ratified by the Estates of the realm on the 17th of July 1560, and again confirmed by the first Parliament of James VI in 1567.—It was superseded among the Presbyterians during their ascendancy in the seventeenth century by the Westminster Confession of Faith, but, on the restoration of the Episcopal Church by Charles II., the old Confession became again the standard of the national faith till the Revolution. From that period the candidates for orders in the Episcopal Church were not required to subscribe any particular Confession. Being all ordained by the forms of the English Church, they solemnly professed their faith in the Holy Scriptures, declaring that nothing which is not to be found therein, or may not be proved thereby, is be taught as necessary to salvation."*

But the wisdom of the suggestion of Bishop Horsley, who informed Bishop Skinner that he "saw the justice and propriety of the Lord Chancellor's remarks," in reference to the adoption of the Thirty-Nine Articles, is at once obvious and intelligible, and was adopted with little hesitation. The Bill, altered and amended, passed the House of Lords, and on the 1st of June it was regularly introduced into the House of Commons by the Right Hon. Henry Dundas and Sir James St Clair Erskine, afterwards Earl of Rosslyn It went through the usual stages of procedure, and on the 15th of June 1792 received the royal assent.

This act, which repealed all previous statutes, made it imperative that every Episcopal clergyman in Scotland shall at his ordination take the usual oaths in the ordinary manner, and shall subscribe the Thirty-Nine Articles of the Church of England. The penalties for offending are a fine of L.20 for the first offence, and suspension from officiating for three years for the second. It is unnecessary to detail all its provisions minutely. There is one clause, however, which materially affected the Scottish ordained Episcopal clergy. The act provided that " no such pastor or minister of any order shall be capable of taking any benefice,

---

* It is to be observed, however, that there are instances of ordinations by the forms of the Scottish Liturgy.

curacy, or spiritual function, within that part of Great Britain called England, the dominion of Wales, or town of Berwick-upon-Tweed, or of officiating in any church or chapel in either of the same where the Liturgy of the Church of England, as now by law established, is used, unless he shall have been lawfully ordained by some Bishop of the Church of England or of Ireland." How far this clause was expedient or necessary it is now superflous to say; and undoubtedly some exceptions should have been introduced—at least the exclusion from merely officiating in the Church of England was harsh, illiberal, and in some repsects unjust.

Bishop Skinner having now seen his exertions successful, and the Church of which he was the Primus emancipated from the thraldom of the penal statutes, returned to Scotland. Before leaving London he left a token of the gratitude, esteem, and respect of the Scottish Episcopal Communion with the Rev. Dr Gaskin, Sir J. A. Park, and Mr Steven. A polished vase-shaped silver cup and cover was presented to Dr Gaskin, with this inscription:—" THE EPISCOPAL CHURCH IN SCOTLAND, RELIEVED FROM PENAL STATUTES, OFFERS THIS HUMBLE TESTIMONY OF SINCERE GRATITUDE TO THE REV. GEORGE GASKIN, D.D., TO COMMEMORATE HIS KIND AND IMPORTANT SERVICES TOWARDS THE OBTAINING OF THAT RELIEF.—JUNE 11, 1792." A similar cup was presented to Mr Justice Park, with the same inscription. Mr Steven, being unmarried, preferred a literary memorial; and Bishop Skinner presented this excellent man with a copy of " Bruckeri Historia Critica Philosophiæ," &c., with the same inscription as on the cups; and, taking leave of those invaluable friends, arrived at Aberdeen in the beginning of July 1792,

CHAPTER XX.

SYNOD OF LAURENCEKIRK IN 1792—CONSECRATION OF THE REV. JONATHAN WATSON—LOYALTY OF THE SCOTTISH EPISCOPALIANS—CONSECRATION OF THE REV. ALEXANDER JOLLY—ESTABLISHMENT OF THE EPISCOPAL FUND.

THE history of the Scottish Episcopal Church after the repeal of the penal laws in 1792 is of a strictly ecclesiastical nature. A general Convention or Synod of the Bishops and clergy was ordered to be held at Laurencekirk on the 22d of August 1792, for the purposes—" First, Of receiving their Committee's Report of the Proceedings adopted in carrying through the Act of Repeal; Secondly, Of deliberating on an address to his Majesty ; and, lastly, Of devising a plan for establishing a Fund for the Support of the Widows and Children of Episcopal Clergymen in Scotland." Meanwhile letters were transmitted by Bishop Skinner to the Archbishop of Canterbury, the Bishops of Salisbury and St David's, the Earls of Elgin, Kinnoull, Kellie, and Fife, Lords Grenville and Stormont, and to Mr Secretary Dundas, thanking those distinguished persons for their services and exertions in promoting the successful result of the application. Those letters were courteously acknowledged by Bishop Horsley [then of St David's], the Earl of Fife, Stormont and Grenville

The Convention met at Laurencekirk on the day appointed, and, after divine service, was opened by Bishop Skinner with a long address explanatory of his proceedings, after which the thanks of the clergy were unanimously voted " to the Committee in general, and to their Right Reverend Preses, for the rectitude of their conduct in that important trust committed to them, and request that their vote of thanks may be kept in the archives of the Church, as a testimony to after ages." It was then found, that out of the sum of L.305, 0s. 9d., raised by contributions for defraying the expenses of the act of Parliament, a debt of L.213, 12s. had been incurred by Bishop Skinner, which was immediately paid to him, and the balance of £91, 8s. 9d. was also ordered to be deposited in the hands of the Primus, to form the nucleus of a Fund for the Widows and Children of the Clergy; but on the condition that " the congregations, or at least a majority of them, which have not already contributed, shall yet consent to do so, otherwise the foresaid balance shall be returned to the congregations which have contributed, in proportion to the respective sums advanced by each." This concluded the business of the Convention.

On the 20th of September 1792, the Rev. Jonathan Watson, presbyter at Laurencekirk, was consecrated at Stonehaven, in the county of Kincardine, by Bishops Skinner, Macfarlane, Abernethy Drummond, and Strachan. Bishop Rose of Dunblane died at a very advanced age in 1791, and no successor had been appointed, the clergy of that district being attached either to Edinburgh or Dunkeld, as suited their several localities. Bishop Watson having been elected by the clergy of Dunkeld, the district of Dunblane was conjoined, and placed under his jurisdiction. Immediately after the consecration the Bishops formed themselves into an Episcopal Synod, and an address to the King on the proclamation for the prevention of tumultuous meetings and seditious writings, issued in May, was produced by Bishop Skinner, and unanimously approved. The Primus also submitted to the consideration of the Bishops on this occasion the propriety of interesting the clergy in their several dioceses in certain measures sanctioned by the Synod, as matters of the highest importance to the prosperity of the Church. These measures are subsequently noticed. It is sufficient to state here that these proceedings were the preludes to the subscription of the Thirty-Nine Articles in 1804. Some of the measures were submitted to the clergy of the Diocesan Synod of Aberdeen, which met in the city of Aberdeen on the 7th of November following, when Bishop Skinner recommended the clergy to give those important subjects their immediate and serious consideration, and requested them to communicate to him in writing whatever opinions might occur to them concerning " the outward profession of faith in this Church, the celebration of public worship, the exercise of discipline, the catechetical instruction of youth, and the performance of the various occasional offices of religion," that every thing might be done " with as much simplicity of manner and uniformity of practice as possible."

It is almost unnecessary to allude to the political events of that ever memorable period, when the French Revolution, exactly a century after that of Great Britain, burst forth like a volcano in Europe, and its actors exhibited a career of crime, atrocity, and carnage, without a parallel in the history of Europe. The loyalty of the people of Great Britain in those years of extraordinary excitement is well known, and none were more ardent and devoted in their professions of attachment to the reigning sovereign and the monarchy than the Scottish Episcopalians. That Church, the members of which had forfeited all their temporal advantages as an Establishment, and during the greater part of a century had suffered the most severe privations for their conscientious attachment to the House of Stuart, and which had been emancipated from the penal statutes scarcely one year, came prominently forward with expressions of loyalty. The dioceses of Edinburgh, Aberdeen, Fife, Dunkeld and Dunblane, Ross and Moray, severally published declarations. The principles of Jacobitism, or of attachment to the House of Stuart, had become exploded at the death of Prince Charles Edward, or at least were recollected merely as sentimental reminiscences of former times, and as connected with the conscientious scruples, the romantic enterprises, and the personal worth, of a former generation. The formerly suspected *Nonjurors* were found in the ranks of every loyal association; the clergy often addressed their congregations, and exhorted them to resist the contaminating principles which were then busily disseminated by designing and irreligious persons; and to the honour of the laity it can be proudly said, that no Scottish Episcopalian was, " during the arduous and long protracted contest, found in one instance guilty of sedition, or misdemeanour of any sort, or even accused of such malpractices."*

At this period Bishop Skinner and his colleagues were actively employed in effecting the union between all the clergy of English or Irish ordination and the Scottish Episcopal Church, and it was considered of importance to induce those in the city of Edinburgh and their congre-

* Skinner's Annals of Scottish Episcopacy, p 265.

gations to conform to the jurisdiction of the Bishop of that diocese, that an example might thus be afforded to congregations in other cities, towns, and districts throughout Scotland. To understand this in a proper manner, it is necessary to explain the peculiar position of both parties.

Previous to the repeal of the penal laws there were many Episcopalians in Scotland who were not Nonjurors, and who professed to be members of the Church of England. Among these may be classified those English families who resorted to Scotland, and finally fixed their residence in some of the cities and towns; and English mechanics employed in manufactories, potteries, and other pursuits. To those may be added not a few of the Scottish Episcopalians of rank, who resorted to the *qualified* chapels, as they were designated, rather than forfeit the political privileges which the act of 1748 denied them if they persisted in their adherence to the ancient Communion. In the cities and large towns there were congregations of this description, numbering in all about one half of those belonging to the Church. Those congregations easily procured clergymen from England, or, as it sometimes happened, Scotsmen ordained in England or in Ireland, and those clergymen, being duly qualified according to the act of 1748, and having taken the necessary Oaths of Allegiance and Abjuration, were protected by the Government. But as those clergymen had, at their ordination in England or in Ireland, taken the oaths which the Scottish Bishops and clergy refused during the life of Prince Charles Edward, they could not, on account of their political situation, submit to the jurisdiction of the Scottish Bishops. On the other hand, they laboured under all the disadvantages resulting from the want of Episcopal superintendence; and although they professed themselves to be Episcopalians, they were in reality *Independents*, and were under no superior ecclesiastical cognizance. Many of the English ordained clergy were indeed well aware of their peculiar situation, and of the inconveniences resulting from it, but still it appeared to them that so long as the penal laws existed they could not consistently unite with the Church.

The penal laws were repealed, and Bishop Skinner, as his son observes, was " wholly bent towards healing the unseemly schism which political expediency had ceased to render justifiable in the sight of men, and which in God's sight could never be thought be justified." It appeared to the Bishop and others that the most likely means to effect a speedy union would be to invite an eminent clergyman of the Church of England into Scotland, and be there consecrated Bishop of the diocese of Edinburgh. Dr Abernethy Drummond was at that time Bishop of the united dioceses of Edinburgh, Fife, and Glasgow, but he expressed his willingness to relinquish the diocesan jurisdiction of Edinburgh to promote a measure which would tend to strengthen the Scottish Episcopal Church, and make the communion more intimate with the Church of England.

The plan was wise, although it was not on this occasion accomplished. The clergyman proposed was the Rev. Jonathan Boucher, then Vicar of Epsom, who had suffered much for his loyalty in America, and who was respected and revered by all who knew him. So highly was Mr Boucher esteemed, that he was at one time thought of for the Bishopric of Nova Scotia, and the Archbishop of Canterbury was even entreated to obtain him for Canada. In a letter to Bishop Skinner, dated 13th March 1793, Bishop Abernethy Drummond states, that "he most cheerfully adopted the plan which he [Bishop Skinner] and Bishop Watson proposed, and would immediately resign in favour of the worthy Vicar of Epsom, if he should be so good as accept the See of Edinburgh." After some correspondence Mr Boucher visited Edinburgh, and his reception, to use his own words, was highly flattering and favourable. " As for myself," he says to Bishop Skinner, " God is my witness, I have much at heart the furtherance of his glory and the welfare of his Church. If these are promoted, it is very immaterial whether it be by me or not. I can have no worldly interest in view, wherefore do I request and charge you to suffer no undue partiality for me, however flattering and grateful that partiality may, in other respects, be to me, to influence your judgment. The gratifying of such feelings neither is nor ought to be beneath our notice, but in the present instance much higher interests demand our attention. I only add, that if Providence sees fit to send me on this great errand, it shall be the business of my life to pray for the grace of God to enable me to do my duty in so peculiarly arduous a station."

It was arranged that Mr Boucher, after his consecration, should officiate as one of the ministers of the Cowgate Chapel, Edinburgh. The congregation of the Cowgate Chapel, now that of St Paul's, York Place, consisted of upwards of one thousand persons, many of whom were of the first rank and respectability in Edinburgh, and two clergymen, who had the distinction of *senior* and *junior*, always officiated in the Chapel. The gentlemen composing the Vestry, among whom was the late Sir William Forbes, Bart., afterwards prominently noticed, took a deep interest in the success of the measure, but unfortunately the intentions of the Bishops were in this instance frustrated. It was industriously circulated that "the scheme in agitation was to introduce Bishops into Scotland with the sanction of Government, and on such legal footing as would entitle them to some legal jurisdiction." Mr Boucher at once declined proceeding farther in the matter, but he continued throughout his useful life a warm supporter of that Communion which had, by this ignorant or malicious rumour, been deprived of his services. He died suddenly in 1804, regretted by all with whom he was acquainted.

The unfounded allegation is thus discussed by Bishop Skinner in a letter to Sir William Forbes, Bart. :—" That the proposal of bringing Mr Boucher to Edinburgh, as the instrument of uniting the two orders of Episcopalians who have been so long kept asunder, should have given any offence or cause of alarm, can be accounted for in no other way than by supposing that the whole affair must have been grossly misrepresented. The introduction of Bishops into Scotland with any legal claim to temporal jurisdiction, God knows, was as far from the object in view as it is from my view to claim a right to the revenues of the Bishopric of Aberdeen, or to the jurisdiction attached to those revenues; nothing more being intended than to unite the Episcopalians in Edinburgh under one Bishop, who was in all respects to be on the same footing, as you know, with his brethren in Scotland, deriving his spiritual authority from the same source, and exercising it in the same limited manner, as they now do over those who choose to acknowledge it, and over those only. I have perused with great attention your letter to the Archbishop of Canterbury, and cannot but admire the very candid and proper manner in which you stated to his Grace the situation of those of the Episcopal persuasion in this country. The very good and favourable terms in which you have had the goodness to mention the Scottish Bishops deserve my particular notice, and cannot fail to make a deep and lasting impression on our minds. May our heavenly Master pour down his richest blessings on you and yours, and enable us, his unworthy servants, to act up to the character which you have been pleased to give of us! The cause which we have all so much at heart is now in such good hands, and will, we doubt not, on your part be so properly attended to, that we have only to wish and pray for success to your laudable endeavours, whenever the time shall come for exerting them, without incurring any such danger as is now apprehended ; but when that happy period will arrive is best known to Him who knoweth all things, and has not only times and seasons, but the hearts of men in his hands. The spirit of seditious disaffection, which a short time ago threatened to break out into acts of open violence, has received that seasonable and salutary check which was the earnest wish of every friend to social order and good government. Fain would I hope that the laudable end in view, by the proposed union in Edinburgh, would never again be so far misrepresented and mistaken, as to give the least cause of offence or ground of alarm to any person of common sense, whether belonging to the Establishment or to the most zealous sectaries. I shall long to hear of any circumstance that may prove favourable to the cause of that happy union, while I fervently pray that the God of unity and peace may bless and prosper your good designs, and finally crown them with that success which may tend to his glory and the happiness of all concerned "

In 1793, when the Friendly Society Act was passed, Bishop Skinner and the clergy of the Diocese of Aberdeen followed up the sanction of the Convention of 1792, for the formation of a permanent fund for the benefit of the widows and orphans of the clergy, and indigent members, by taking advantage of the provisions of that measure of the legislature encouraging Friendly Societies in general. After defraying all the expenses of the act for the repeal of the penal laws a balance remained, which was applied to the establishment of the fund. The Rev. Roger Aitken, clerk to the Diocese of Aberdeen, was authorized by Bishop Skinner to submit the matter to the other Bishops and clergy, who for the most part readily expressed their approval, and the necessary regulations were prepared for the institution of the Scottish Episcopal Friendly Society. "On the 19th of November 1793, a general meeting of those Bishops and clergy who had intimated their desire to become members was held at Aberdeen, when they formed themselves into a Friendly Society in terms of the Act of Parliament, and the articles finally approved for its government were soon afterwards ratified by the Justices of the Peace for the county of Aberdeen, as the law directed." This Society, which meets annually at Aberdeen, has continued to flourish far beyond the expectations of its most sanguine promoters, and it was liberally supported at the outset by lay contributions. An eloquently written Brief was prepared by Bishop Skinner, sanctioned by the other Bishops, and read by order from the pulpits on the fourth or fifth Sunday of Lent 1794.* The Scottish Episcopal Friendly Society, by the excellent and judicious management of its office-bearers, has ever since its institution continued in a most prosperous condition. Clergymen only are admissible, who must enter within three years after their ordination as presbyters, or induction as incumbents, otherwise they are afterwards precluded from its benefits This Society is more particularly noticed in the sequel.

No farther event of any importance occurred in the history of the Church towards the close of the eighteenth century, except the consecration of the Rev. Alexander Jolly, presbyter at Fraserburgh. That learned and truly esteemed man, now gathered to his fathers, was elected by the presbyters of Ross and Moray as coadjutor to Bishop Macfarlane; but Bishop Skinner, as Primus, dissented from the expediency of the measure, when his sanction was requested. It is only justice to the revered memory of Bishop Jolly, as well as to Bishop Skinner, to state the principles on which the latter at first refused to concur with the election. We are told by the Rev. John Skinner, that " to the learning, the piety, and strictly clerical deportment of the coadjutor elect he bore ample testimony, but as the succession was then sufficiently strong, and as, in his view of things, additional clergymen were more wanted in the Highlands than the aid of an additional and non-resident Bishop, who, though in most respects eminently qualified for the office, was confessedly ignorant of the Gaelic language, the Primus refused to sanction the choice of the clergy of Ross and Moray, or to give his concurrence to the present promotion of a coadjutor to Bishop Macfarlane." The other Bishops, however, took a different view of the matter, and the Bishop-elect was consecrated at Dundee, on the 24th of June 1796, by Bishops Abernethy Drummond, Strachan, and Macfarlane. Bishop Jolly, however, never acted as coadjutor. The dioceses

* This document is published in the "Annals of Scottish Episcopacy," by the Rev. John Skinner of Forfar, p. 273-281.

of Ross and Moray were disjoined after his consecration, and the presbyters in the latter were placed under his jurisdiction. There was no personal feeling in Bishop Skinner's conduct on this occasion, for he was guided by what appeared to him the strongest sense of duty; and during his valuable life he held in the utmost regard, both publicly and privately, the venerated Bishop Jolly. The objection as to the Gaelic language might have been overruled, as it must in all probability be almost impossible to obtain a Bishop so qualified in the present state of the Church. But Bishop Skinner's views were adopted from sincere conviction, as expressed by his son in the preceding extract. The Primus acted on this occasion in his usual upright manner, yielding to the different opinion of his colleagues in the Episcopal College, and cordially acknowledging Bishop Jolly as a brother.

CHAPTER XXI.

INTERNAL AFFAIRS OF THE SCOTTISH EPISCOPAL CHURCH—WORKS BY BISHOP SKINNER—SYNOD OF LAURENCEKIRK—CONSECRATION OF DR SANDFORD—UNION OF THE ENGLISH AND SCOTTISH CLERGY—DEATH OF THE REV. JOHN SKINNER OF LONGSIDE—DEATH OF BISHOP WATSON—CONSECRATION OF DR GLEIG AND DR TORRY.

It was fortunate, under Divine Providence, for the Scottish Episcopal Church that Bishop Skinner was Primus at the close of the eighteenth century. Amid the numerous avocations and extensive correspondence of that distinguished Prelate, he found leisure in 1801 to publish the excellent little work entitled—" A Layman's Account of his Faith and Practice as a Member of the Episcopal Church in Scotland, published with the approbation of the Bishops of that Church; to which are added some Forms of Prayer, &c.; with a Letter from the Rev. Charles Daubeny to a Scottish Nobleman on the subject of Ecclesiastical Unity." The Scottish nobleman addressed then by Archdeacon Daubeny, the learned author of the "Guide to the Church," was the Right Hon. Robert Auriol Hay Drummond, who succeeded in 1787 as ninth Earl of Kinnoull, son of the Hon. and Most Rev. Robert Hay, who assumed the surname and arms of Drummond, as heir of entail of his great-grandfather William Drummond Viscount of Strathallan, and who died Archbishop of York in 1776. The subject discussed in Archdeacon Daubeny's Letter is that of "separate Episcopal chapels," as those independent chapels were called, the incumbents of which were persisting in a state of schism, by refusing to acknowledge the diocesan authority of the Scottish Bishops. A second edition of Bishop Skinner's valuable work was soon demanded by the public, which he personally superintended while in the press, but he omitted Archdeacon Daubeny's Letter, and substituted the Canons of the Church. We are told that " he wished, if possible, to have the schism completely healed, but when out of twenty-two chapels in a state of separation, fifteen had united themselves, he thought it expedient to drop every sort of public appeal, and leave to time to effect, in its silent progress, what had withstood the force of argument drawn from sources human and divine "[*] Subsequent events prove the wisdom and prudence of Bishop Skinner's conduct in reference to a schism which has been completely healed during the episcopate of his son and successor in the diocese of Aberdeen The " Layman's Account of his Faith and Practice," which was at the time of incalculable benefit to the Church, has been often reprinted, and is translated into the Gaelic language

The schism above mentioned has now happily ceased to exist. At the commencement of the century numbers of the clergy acknowledged the jurisdiction and authority of the Scottish Bishops Among the first of those who conformed to proper ecclesiastical order were the Rev. Charles Cordiner of Banff, a gentleman distinguished by his antiquarian researches, and the Rev Dr Stephen of Cruden, father-in-law of Sir James Clarke, Bart, Physician to her Majesty Queen Victoria. So convinced were the clergy of their duty in this respect, that previous to 1805 all those of English ordination in the dioceses of Edinburgh and Glasgow conformed, with the exception of two in the latter diocese—Kelso and Dumfries, both of whom with their congregations subsequently acknowledged the jurisdiction of the diocesan. A few in the northern districts continued several years in a state of separation, and those of Perth and Montrose were the last to conform. St Paul's Chapel, Aberdeen, was united to the Church in 1841, during the incumbency of the Rev. Isaac Harris, A B, who was succeeded in 1842 by the Rev. Sir William Dunbar, of Durn, Bart. There is little doubt that the " Layman's Account of his Faith and Practice" was of essential importance at the commencement of the century in accelerating these unions, and gradually overcoming the schism.

In 1803 Bishop Skinner conferred another benefit upon the Church,

---

[*] Annals of Scottish Episcopacy, p. 293.

and increased his theological reputation, by the publication of another well known work, dedicated to Sir William Forbes of Pitsligo, entitled, "Primitive Truth and Order vindicated from Modern Misrepresentation, with a Defence of Episcopacy, particularly that of Scotland, against an Attack made upon it by the late Dr Campbell of Aberdeen, in his Lectures on Ecclesiastical History; with a Concluding Address to the Episcopalians of Scotland." The work to which Bishop Skinner wrote this most conclusive reply was a posthumous one of the celebrated Dr George Campbell, Principal of Marischal College, who died in 1796, and which contained the substance of his theological prelections to the students as Professor of Divinity in that University, though, in conjunction with Principal Robertson of Edinburgh, he had liberally exerted himself in the repeal of the Penal Laws. Principal Campbell maintained in his Lectures that not only the polity of the Church of England seems to have been devised for the express purpose of rendering the clerical character odious, and the discipline contemptible, but that, as "no axiom in philosophy is more indisputable than that *quod nullibi est non est*, the ordination of our present Scottish Episcopal clergy is solely from presbyters; for it is allowed that those men who came under the hands of Bishop Rose of Edinburgh had been regularly admitted ministers or presbyters in particular congregations before the Revolution; and to that first ordination I maintain that their farcical consecration by Dr Rose and others, when they were solemnly made the depositories of no deposits, commanded to be diligent in doing no work, vigilant in the oversight of no flock, assiduous in teaching and governing no people, and presiding in no church, added nothing at all."

To these and similar bold and preposterous statements, which probably not a Presbyterian at the present time would have the hardihood to defend, Bishop Skinner's volume is a most triumphant reply. This work has been often reprinted, and has had a most extensive circulation. Its author received many congratulatory letters respecting it from some of the most distinguished ornaments of the Church of England. Two years before the publication of "Primitive Truth and Order," in a letter addressed by Archdeacon Daubeny to Bishop Skinner he states —" I do not hesitate to call Dr Campbell's late work the most hostile, the most illiberal, and the most unsupported attack that has been made on the episcopacy of the Church of Christ, while his attack on the episcopacy of the Church in Scotland, added to the notorious falseness of the writer's statement, is, *me judice,* marked with a superlative degree of meanness." There certainly was "meanness" in thus assailing the Church of England, and inculcating on the theological students in Marischal College that the polity of that Church "seems to have been devised for the express purpose of rendering the clerical character odious, and the discipline contemptible," while Principal Campbell was in intimate correspondence with some of the English Bishops and other dignitaries; to say nothing of the attack on the Scottish Episcopal Church, with many of whose clergy and laity he was in habits of familiar private intercourse, and when he was taking an active share in procuring the repeal of the Penal Laws. This is the more obvious when it is considered that the members of the Church had, on the principle of impartiality, as much right to maintain the *jus divinum* of their ecclesiastical constitution, as the Presbyterians had to contend that their system is "agreeable to the Word of God."

Bishop Skinner founds his whole argument, in reply to Principal Campbell's statements, on three positions:—" I. That the Christian religion being, like its Divine Author, 'the same yesterday, to-day, and for ever,' ought to be received and embraced as it is represented and held out in the Scriptures of truth, without adding thereto or diminishing therefrom. II. That the Church of Christ, in which his religion is received and embraced, is that spiritual society in which the ministrations of holy things is committed to the three distinct orders of Bishops, Priests, and Deacons, deriving their authority from the Apostles, as the Apostles derived their commission from Christ. And, lastly, That a part of this holy, catholic, and apostolic Church, though deprived of the support of civil establishment, does still exist in Scotland under the name of the 'Scottish Episcopal Church,' whose doctrine, discipline, and worship, as happily agreeing with the doctrine, discipline, and worship of the first and purest ages of Christianity, ought to be steadily adhered to by all who profess to be of the Episcopal Communion in this part of the United Kingdom." Bishop Skinner's volume elicited the "Presbyterian Letters addressed to Bishop Skinner of Aberdeen, by Patrick Mitchell, D.D., Minister of Kemnay, Aberdeenshire," but this performance excited little attention. It is worthy of remark that the very eminent Presbyterian authority, Principal Hill of St Mary's

College, St Andrews, and Professor of Divinity in that University, confessed that "Primitive Truth and Order" was the best book of the kind in the English language as a defence of Episcopacy, and a complete answer to Principal Campbell.

The extensive perusal of Bishop Skinner's work was attended with the happiest consequences to the Church over which he so worthily presided. It was generally read, and revived the desire on the part of the few "independent" Episcopal clergy and their congregations to acknowledge the diocesan jurisdiction of the Scottish Bishops. To accelerate this desirable measure Bishop Skinner, with the concurrence of his right reverend brethren of the Episcopal College, issued a circular, summoning a general convention of the Church at Laurencekirk, on the 24th of October 1804, the object of which was, as the Bishop stated in the circular, "to exhibit in the most solemn manner a public testimony of our conformity in doctrine and discipline with the Church of England, and thereby to remove every obstacle to the union of Episcopalians in Scotland." This was to obviate one of the great objections urged against the union by the English ordained clergy, that the Church had recognized no standards or articles of faith ; for though the Act of 1792 made it imperative that all the clergy should sign the Articles of the Church of England, such an acknowledgment had either been neglected or delayed, though these Articles were always understood to be received by the Scottish Episcopal Church.

Previous to the meeting of the Convention a correspondence was begun with Bishop Skinner by the Rev. Dr Daniel Sandford, formerly Student of Christ Church, Oxford, who since 1792 had officiated to a respectable congregation then assembling in a temporary hall in West Register Street, Edinburgh, and who appear to have been the first Episcopal congregation in the New Town of Edinburgh, as St George's Chapel, in York Place, was only opened that year. Dr Sandford stated to Bishop Skinner that however much the union was to be desired, subscription to the Thirty-Nine Articles was indispensable ; and that if these Articles were made "the permanent confessional of the Scottish Episcopal Communion, there can be no objection to our union ; nay, on the contrary, that our continuing in separation from you cannot be justified on any grounds which will bear the scrutiny of sound ecclesiastical principles."*

* Annals of Scottish Episcopacy, p. 336; Remains of Bishop Sandford, vol. i. p 46.

As the learning, piety, and worth of Dr Sandford were well known, such representations from him had due influence. The Convocation assembled on the appointed day at Laurencekirk; and Bishops Skinner, Macfarlane, Watson, and Jolly, thirty-eight presbyters, and two deacons, were present. Bishops Abernethy Drummond and Strachan were prevented from attending by old age and infirmity. After divine service was concluded by Bishop Watson, as pastor of the congregation at Laurencekirk, and a discourse from the pulpit by Bishop Skinner, which he was requested to publish, the Convocation was constituted by him, and after due and solemn deliberation the Thirty-Nine Articles were adopted and subscribed, as the permanent standards of the Scottish Episcopal Church, to which assent was to be given by all candidates for holy orders. As many of the indigenous clergy used the Office for the administration of the eucharist as drawn up in the Scottish Liturgy, it was enjoined that the English clergy uniting themselves to the Church should be at liberty to retain the Office as set forth in the Book of Common Prayer. As soon as the Convocation was dissolved, Bishop Skinner addressed letters to the Archbishops and Bishops of the Church of England, the Archbishop of Armagh as Primate of the Irish Church, and subsequently to all the other Irish Archbishops and Bishops, and the Bishop of Sodor and Man, intimating to those Prelates the result Replies were duly received, expressing the most friendly regard for the Scottish Episcopal Church, their approval of the measure, and their hopes that it would promote the interest of religion.

Dr Sandford had now no hesitation in acceding to the union, and he transmitted his acknowledgment of Bishop Skinner as his Diocesan, Edinburgh being then vacant. He announced his resolution to his congregation in a most interesting address, in which he laid before them his reasons for so doing, showing them the benefits of diocesan jurisdiction, and that to continue in a state of separation from the Church was as unnecessary as it was schismatical. Dr Sandford's "Reasons for uniting with the Scottish Episcopal Communion" are still preserved,* dated Edinburgh, Nov. 7, 1804; and though the subject has lost its interest, because the schism, as already mentioned, no longer exists, a

* See " Remains of the late Right Rev Daniel Sandford, D.D., Bishop of Edinburgh, &c. with a Memoir, by the Rev. John Sandford," vol. ii. p 321, 325; Skinner's Annals of Scottish Episcopacy, p 550, 553.

few extracts are of importance, more especially as these are the recorded sentiments of such a truly excellent and pious Bishop. Dr Sandford's third reason is :—" That the Episcopal Church of Scotland is a ' true' Church, ' in the which the pure word of God is preached, and the sacraments are administered, according to Christ's ordinance.'* The doctrines of this Church are the same with those of the United Church of England and Ireland, the Bishops and clergy of the Episcopal Church of Scotland subscribing the same Articles of Religion. The Scottish Bishops are true Bishops of the Church of Christ, and their Apostolical Succession is the same with that of the Bishops of the Church of England, for the present governors of the Scottish Episcopal Church derive their authority in a direct succession from those Scottish Bishops who were consecrated by the Prelates of the Church of England at Westminster, 15th December 1661." The fifth reason is: —" That the continuance of our separation is therefore wholly causeless in every point of view. But *causeless separation from a pure Church* is the sin of *schism*—an offence of which it is impossible that any pious and enlightened Christian can think lightly. ' It is contrary to Christian unity to separate ourselves from a Church which follows the doctrines and ordinances of Christ and his Apostles, and answers every good purpose of Christian worship and Christian fellowship.' " †
" Lastly," says Dr Sandford, " let it be considered that, by the submission of our clergy to the Scottish Bishops, we strengthen instead of weakening our connection with the Church of England ; for the Church of England, as a pure branch of the universal Church of Christ, is in communion with the Episcopal Church of Scotland, also a pure branch of the Universal Church ;‡ and every English clergyman, who would be faithful to the principles which he professed at his ordination, MUST

---

* " See the Twenty-Third Article of Religion "

† " See ' A Short Catechism,' by the Right Reverend Thomas Burgess, Lord Bishop of St David's."

‡ " By calling the Church of Christ Universal, we mean," says the learned Bishop of St David's, in the Catechism above quoted, " that the Church is not limited to any particular nation or people, but comprehends all Christian congregations in which the Word of God is preached, and the sacraments are duly administered by persons rightly ordained ; and that these congregations, however distant or numerous, are ONE, by community of faith and ordinances."

THEREFORE NECESSARILY acknowledge the authority of the Scottish Bishops while he resides within the jurisdiction of their communion."

Dr Sandford had occasion to explain himself more fully in a letter, on the " Spiritual Character and Claims of the Bishops of the Episcopal Church in Scotland," addressed to " a person who solicited information on the subject here considered." It is dated October 27, 1815, but the letter was written some months previous.* After referring to the consecrations of 1661, and quoting an extract from the Register-Book of Archbishop Juxon in the Library of Lambeth Palace on the subject, Dr Sandford says—" From these consecrations, in regular legitimate succession, the present Bishops of the Episcopal Church in Scotland derive their spiritual character and authority. This spiritual character, thus legitimately conferred upon them, originating, as I have shown you, in the consecration of the four Prelates at Westminster in 1661, completely qualifies those upon whom it is conferred for the spiritual superintendence of those who belong to the communion of their Church. To this Communion, it appears to me, that all Protestant Episcopalians, residing in Scotland, are bound, by their profession as Episcopalians, to belong; for otherwise, neither they, nor the clergy who officiate in their chapels, will find it easy to say of what Church they are really members. While they reside in Scotland they neither are nor can be, strictly speaking, members of the Church of England. The Bishops of the Church of England have no authority in Scotland, and never lay claim to such authority. On the contrary, they invariably acknowledge the *spiritual* authority of the Scottish Bishops within the boundaries of their own Church, whenever circumstances call upon them to do so. I will give you instances of this, which consist with my own experience.

" When the question of the union of the English ordained clergy and their congregations with the Scottish Episcopal Church was much agitated some years ago, I had frequent occasion to know the opinion of many of the English Bishops upon the subject; and all to whom I had access uniformly recommended the measure as the *duty* of the clergy and their people; and two of them (one of whom had unquestionably

* Remains of Bishop Sandford, vol ii. Appendix, No II

no superior in learning on the Bench) declared to me, without hesitation, that they considered the Episcopal clergy and their congregations who continued independent of the Scottish Bishops to be guilty of schism.

"Again, it is the custom in the Church of England, as in every other Episcopal Church, that when a candidate for holy orders, or for institution to a benefice, presents his letters-testimonial to the Bishop from whom he is to receive ordination or institution, if the clergy who have signed the testimonial do not belong to the diocese of that Bishop, their signatures must be ratified by the subscription of their own Diocesan before it can be received. Since I have been a Bishop, it has happened to me to be called upon several times to *countersign* the signatures of my clergy to testimonials presented to the Bishops of London and Durham; and but very lately I had occasion to do the same in the case of a testimonial for holy orders, which was presented to the Archbishop of York, but which his Grace refused to receive when first laid before him, because my signature was not added to it. I mention these things merely to show you that the Bishops in England consider the Scottish Bishops as fully competent to the exercise of the spiritual authority of their order in their respective dioceses; and, moreover, that they consider the Episcopal Church in Scotland as in full communion, in spiritual matters, with the United Church of England and Ireland.

"The Episcopal Church in Scotland is, we hope, a pure branch of the Catholic or Universal Church of Jesus Christ; and her Bishops, regularly consecrated to their sacred office, are thus duly authorised to exercise their spiritual powers within the jurisdiction belonging to them. This authority they do not cease humbly to assert; and you see that those whose learning and station in the Church of England well qualify them to appreciate the validity of the claim, acknowledge it upon all occasions. At the same time the Scottish Bishops lay no claim to the *temporal* distinctions which belong to a *political* Episcopacy, that is, to a Church connected with the State, as is the United Church of England and Ireland. We have no title of ' Lord,' as if we were Peers of Parliament, although we assert our claim to be addressed as ' Right Reverend'—a designation which prejudice or ignorance may withhold, but which belongs to us as Bishops, without any reference to political establishment. Our Church is completely *tolerated*. and while we continue to exercise our privileges as such inoffensively, it is a strange prejudice indeed which will hesitate to give the designation of *Bishops* to those who hold, through a regular succession, an office which is necessary to the existence of an Episcopal Church. I have sometimes heard it said, and heard it with no little surprise, ' that there are no Bishops in Scotland :'—But there are Bishops in Scotland (the late venerable Bishop Horne used to say, ' as good Bishops as himself,' as regularly consecrated to their office), although those Bishops pretend to that authority only which appertains to their *spiritual office* ; that authority which was exercised by the rulers of the Christian Church in the primitive ages of her history, before ' the kingdoms of this world had become the kingdom of God and his Christ.'

" The exercise of the spiritual authority thus vested in us can be offensive to no one. It is impossible almost to imagine a case in which it should be so. We are ' ordained for men in things pertaining to God,' and the discharge of our office is confined ' to these things.' We claim no temporal authority, no temporal distinctions ; we interfere with no temporal rights of the congregations who adhere to our communion Our appeal is to the conscience of our people, and to their sense of the blessings and comforts they derive from the regularity and integrity of the sacred offices of the Church. From the clergy we require no more than the canonical submission which was ever paid to the governors of the Church in the best and purest ages of its history. From the laity we seek no more than that reverence and regard which no well principled member of our Communion will hesitate to render ; and no such persons will deny the importance of Episcopal superintendence to the regular administration of " the word of God, and the sacraments of his Church.' "*

The example of Dr Sandford in Edinburgh was followed by the Reverend Archibald Alison, LL.B.,† Prebendary of Sarum ; the Rev. Robert Morehead, D.D , then of Leith, afterwards for many years Mr

---

* Remains of Bishop Sandford, vol ii p 332–338.

† The distinguished author of " Essays on Taste," " Sermons on the Seasons," &c one of the most eminent men of his day, then one of the clergymen of the Cowgate Chapel, and afterwards, at the removal of the congregation in 1819, of St Paul's Chapel, York Place Mr Alison died full of years and honour in 1839. He was the father of Archibald Alison, Esq , the distinguished historian of the French Revolution, and of William Pulteney Alison, Esq , M D , Professor of the Practice of Physic in the University of Edinburgh

Alison's colleague in St Paul's Chapel ;* and by other clergy in the city. The only congregation in the Scottish metropolis who had remained in a state of separation was that of St George's Chapel, York Place. This congregation was added to the Church on the appointment of the Rev. Richard Q. Shannon, A.B., of Trinity College, Dublin, as incumbent †

Among the laity who zealously promoted the union of the clergy of English and Scottish ordination, thus consolidating proper diocesan jurisdiction in the Church, Sir William Forbes of Pitsligo, Bart., must not be omitted. To this truly distinguished and excellent gentleman— the descendant and representative of one of the most ancient families in Aberdeenshire—much of the present prosperous and extended sphere of the Scottish Episcopal Church may in a great measure be ascribed; and it is appropriately observed, that " it is the chief glory of that Church to have formed the principles and trained the virtues of one of the most perfect specimens of the Christian character which Great Britain has ever produced." In the language of the Rev. Mr Alison, there was no person of the age " who so fully united in himself the same assemblage of the most estimable qualities of our nature ; the same firmness of piety, with the same tenderness of charity ; the same ardour of public spirit, with the same disdain of individual interest ; the same activity in business, with the same generosity in its conduct ; the same independence towards the powerful, with the same generous humanity towards the lowly ; the same dignity in public life, with the same gentleness in private society." By descent, if it may be so expressed, and by conviction, ardently attached to the Scottish Episcopal Church, while he evinced the utmost charity to those of other religious communions,‡ no

* This excellent and much respected clergyman, also well known for his eloquent published Sermons and other works, resigned St Paul's Chapel in 1832, at his appointment to the rectory of Easington in Yorkshire, and was succeeded by the Right Rev C H. Terrot, consecrated Bishop of Edinburgh in 1841.

† Mr Shannon resigned St George's Chapel in 1841, when nominated one of the Prebendaries of St Patrick's Cathedral, Dublin, by Archbishop Whately of Dublin, and was succeeded by the Rev. T G. S. Suther, A.B.

‡ The acts of munificence and public spirit which Sir William Forbes rendered to his country and to society are too numerous to be here noticed, and properly belong to the department of biography. But to illustrate the allusion in the text, it may be stated, that after 1783, the year he laid out the village of New Pitsligo, and rendered every assistance to the feuars by lending them money, and often allowing them to go rent free, he not only built an Episcopal chapel, with a dwelling-house for the

one ever laboured more assiduously to promote its prosperity. He attended Baron Smith's Chapel in Blackfriars' Wynd, of which he was one of the Vestry, with the esteemed Sir Adolphus Oughton, then Commander-in-Chief in Scotland. In 1771, when it was resolved to join this congregation with two others in the Old Town of Edinburgh, and erect a commodious edifice for them all, the labour of the undertaking, as in many other cases, devolved on Sir William Forbes, and by his personal exertions the Cowgate Chapel was built—for many years one of the most popular places of worship in the Scottish metropolis. It may be curious to those familiar with the present state of Edinburgh to know, that when the new chapel was projected for the accommodation of the three congregations, it was proposed to build it at the end of the North Bridge, near where the Theatre-Royal now stands, but after mature deliberation this was relinquished, as it was *" not thought possible that the projected New Town would come to any thing."* Sir William Forbes took the principal lead in the affairs of the Cowgate Chapel, and when a vacancy occurred in the incumbency in 1808, he was chiefly instrumental in bringing to it the Rev. Archibald Alison, whom he had known from his infancy, and who was then officiating at a remote rectory in Shropshire. It is hardly necessary to add, that under the influence of that distinguished clergyman the congregation rapidly increased, until at length they were enabled by their own exertions, and by the indefatigable efforts of Sir William's second son, the Hon. John Hay Forbes Lord Medwyn, a Judge and a Lord Commissioner of Justiciary in Scotland, to erect the beautiful and capacious Gothic edifice of St Paul's, York Place, in 1818. At that very period Sir William's eldest son and successor in the Baronetcy, Sir William Forbes, Bart., effected by similar exertions the erection of the not less beautiful Gothic edifice of St John the Evangelist's Chapel, Prince's Street. Thus, by the influence of two members of the distinguished family of Pitsligo, Sir William Forbes and his second son Lord Medwyn, was a large and influential portion of the

clergyman, but he also erected and endowed a Presbyterian chapel-of-ease in connection with the Establishment, with a manse for the minister, and a schoolhouse, in which the Society for the Propagation of Christian Knowledge placed a schoolmaster The present Episcopal chapel at New Pitsligo is an elegant little Gothic edifice, erected in 1836 by Sir John Stuart Forbes, Bart., the grandson of Sir William, from a design by Mr John Henderson, architect, Edinburgh flock of the Scottish Episcopal Church raised from their humble localities in Blackfriars' Wynd, and other alleys in the Old Town, first to the Cowgate Chapel, and next to York Place; and, in conjunction with St John's Chapel, the congregations were accommodated in two edifices, the ornaments of the city, raised at the expense of above L.30,000. But as it respects the union of the English clergy with the Scottish Episcopal Church, from which the above details are a digression, Sir William Forbes was most earnest in his endeavours to accomplish it, and he had much correspondence on the subject with Archbishop Moore the English Primate, Bishop Porteus of London, Sir William Scott, afterwards Lord Stowell (brother of Lord Chancellor Eldon), and many other persons of influence, both clerical and lay, connected with the Church of England, as well as with Bishop Abernethy Drummond, Bishop Skinner, and others in Scotland. He succeeded in a great degree during his own lifetime in effecting the object he had at heart; and his death, in 1806, in the sixty-seventh year of his age, prevented this great and good man from witnessing other events equally gratifying, if his valuable life had been spared some years longer.

Only two attempts were made to disturb the prosperity of the Church occasioned by the union. The one was by the Rev. Alexander Grant, D.D., who styled himself " Minister of the English Episcopal Congregation in Dundee," in a pamphlet which he wrote against the union, entitled, " An Apology for continuing in the Communion of the Church of England." Dr Grant transmitted a copy of his pamphlet to the Archbishops and Bishops of the Church of England, but he received only one reply, and this was from Bishop Horsley, then of St Asaph, which silenced him in that quarter, though he continued all his life in a state of separation. " It has long been my opinion," says Bishop Horsley to Dr Grant, " and very well known to be my opinion, that the laity in Scotland, if they understand the genuine principles of Episcopacy which they profess, ought, in the present state of things, to resort to the ministry of their indigenous pastors; and the clergymen of English or Irish ordination, without uniting with the Scottish Bishops, are, in my judgment, doing nothing better than keeping alive a schism. I find nothing in your tract to alter my mind on these points "

The other opposition was of a more serious nature, as it caused a litigation in the Supreme Court of Scotland. The Rev. Charles Cordiner of Banff, who had been ordained deacon by Bishop Newton of Bristol in 1769, and presbyter in 1770 by Bishop Trail of Down and Connor (strange to say *in the town of Arbroath,* though nothing remarkable when that Prelate's ecclesiastical rise is considered), adhered to the Church in 1792, and the Rev. John Skinner, the son of Bishop Skinner, and author of the "Annals of Scottish Episcopacy," at that time pastor of the other chapel, became Mr Cordiner's colleague in St Andrew's Chapel, which accommodated both congregations. Mr Cordiner died two years afterwards; and whatever dissatisfaction may have existed among a few of the united congregations at the time, it appears to have been trivial till the year 1805, when a gentleman named Cumming, an officer of the Royal Marines then residing in Banff, raised an action in the Court of Session. The case was ably argued in favour of the defenders by Robert Dundas, Esq of Arniston, afterwards Lord Chief Baron of the Scottish Exchequer, and was decided against Captain Cumming the pursuer. As this action is not reported in the printed series of cases before the Court of Session, nothing is known of the arguments advanced by the pursuer, except what is contained in a statement drawn up by the defenders,* and laid before Bishop Horsley of St Asaph and other friends of the Church in England, requesting their assistance in the expenses they had incurred of L.200, though they were successful in the Court. Captain Cumming, it appears from that document, contended, that " the coalition of the two chapels had been productive of an abandonment of the principles in support of which the English chapel had been erected," and he farther adduced several erroneous and unfounded doctrinal objections, which were incompetent to be entertained by a Court of Law. Bishop Horsley, notwithstanding a severe family bereavement at the time, sympathized with the united congregation of St Andrew's Chapel, and collected in subscriptions L.189, 10s., in addition to L.61, 15s., remitted by the Bishops of London, Durham, Winchester, Worcester, Oxford, Bangor, Salisbury, Gloucester, and St David's, "through other hands," says his Lordship to Bishop Skinner, " before my application, which was retarded by the dismal circumstances of my family." The sum collected in all amounted to L.294, 5s., of which the expenses of process and in-

* Inserted in " Annals of Scottish Episcopacy," p 376, 379.

cidents were L.270, 17s., leaving a balance of L.23, 8s ; and thus, by the generous exertions of Bishop Horsley, which were cordially met by all the English Bishops, and the Archbishops of Armagh and Dublin, the united congregation at Banff were relieved from their difficulties, and they expressed their gratitude to his Lordship in a neat address transmitted by Bishop Skinner.

The Diocese of Edinburgh being then vacant, and the ecclesiastical union happily effected, Bishop Skinner, as Primus, issued his mandate to the clergy at the end of 1805, empowering them to elect a Bishop. The day of election was fixed by the Dean [Dr Gleig] for the 15th of January 1806, and Dr Sandford was unanimously chosen their Diocesan. The interest which Sir William Forbes took in this important matter is sufficiently intimated by a letter to Bishop Skinner, after the election was declared to have fallen on Dr Sandford, to the great satisfaction of all connected with the Church. The consecration was held at Dundee on Sexagesima Sunday, the 9th of February 1806, by Bishops Skinner, Watson, and Jolly, in Bishop Strachan's chapel. The sermon was preached by Bishop Sandford's successor in the episcopate, Dr Walker, and was published at the request of the Bishops present. At the conclusion of the solemn service, Bishop Skinner delivered an eloquent and affecting address to Bishop Sandford, which is printed in the valuable collection of documents, the "Annals of Scottish Episcopacy." The elevation of Bishop Sandford elicited expressions of satisfaction from several influential friends of the Church in England, whose letters on the subject are inserted in that work. The following observations, in reference to the consecration of an English presbyter on this occasion, are appropriately expressed:—" The effects of Bishop Sandford's episcopate were immediate, and they have been progressive. The present state of the branch of the Church over which he presided, contrasted with its condition when he accepted its charge, is perhaps the best criterion of his usefulness. Yet in England his appointment was regarded in some quarters with suspicion, and a Prelate of the English Bench [the Bishop of Bangor], to whom Dr Sandford was personally known, scrupled not to affirm that it was both uncanonical and inexpedient. The elevation of an English presbyter to an episcopate in Scotland it was thought would lead to questions of great difficulty and delicacy, and it was feared might also excite some jealousy in the National [Presbyterian] Establishment. These questions of difficulty, however, never occurred, and the uniform kindness with which Bishop Sandford was always regarded by the Presbyterian ministers of Edinburgh proved at once his own fitness for the station he filled, and their superiority to the sentiments of which they were suspected. He was convinced in his own mind of the propriety of his election; and in the correspondence in which he engaged on this subject, whilst he rendered the respect that was due to the station and ability of his opponent, he never compromised his own opinion, or relinquished his own right."*

Bishop Sandford held his first confirmation in the Cowgate Chapel, and it is thus described by Sir William Forbes in a letter to Bishop Skinner, dated April 5, 1806:—" I must say, I never was present at a more solemn, a more agreeable, or a more impressive service. It could not but be very edifying to every seriously disposed person to see our chapel, which is the largest in this country, filled with a numerous congregation of the upper ranks of life, and upwards of a hundred young persons confirmed, who not only comported themselves with the utmost decorum, but seemed, as well as many of their parents, to be very much affected with the ceremony, and who, I hope, shall be the better for it to the end of their lives   Three of my own young people were of the number, the older part of my family having been confirmed by the Bishop of Man, when he passed through Edinburgh a good many years ago. But hereafter, thank God, we shall have no need of foreign aid."

The exertions of Sir William Forbes, in behalf of the Church at this period were manifested in a more tangible manner. He well knew the poverty and depression of the clergy, especially those in the rural districts. His son-in-law, the late esteemed Colin Mackenzie, Esq. of Portmore, in Peebles-shire, prepared a plan for establishing a fund in aid of the Bishops and such of the clergy as required pecuniary assistance to increase their scanty stipends. Sir William Forbes zealously approved of the scheme, and drew up a memoir on the state of the Church, which was circulated in 1806, and produced most beneficial results. He subscribed L.400, and his example and influence were of essential importance   This " Memoir" was " respectfully submitted to the consideration of the nobility and gentry of the Episcopal Church in

---

* Remains of Bishop Sandford, vol. i. p 50, 51.

Scotland."* The subscription was of a strictly private nature, and no application was ever thought of being made to Government. The Committee in London, to further the object of the Scottish Episcopal Fund, originally consisted of Sir James Allan Park, Chairman, the Rev. Gerard Andrews, Dean of Canterbury, the Rev. Dr Gaskin, the Rev. Robert Hodgson, Rector of St George's, Hanover Square, William Stevens, Esq., John Bowdler, Esq , and Sir John Richardson. Three of those gentlemen belonged to the Committee for procuring the repeal of the penal statutes. Mr Stevens was the first English subscriber of the sum of L.100. The support of this Fund was among the last acts of Sir William Forbes connected with the Church. He closed his valuable life, lamented by all who knew him, and by his countrymen at large, on the 28th of June 1806, supported in his last illness by the hopes and consolations of religion, during the lingering illness which terminated his career of beneficence His friend, Mr Stevens, survived him only till February 1807. In the year 1806 also died the illustrious Bishop Horsley, another devoted friend of the Scottish Episcopal Church, who took a heartfelt interest in its affairs, and for several years had exerted himself to promote its welfare.

In 1807 the Rev. John Skinner of Longside, the revered father of Bishop Skinner, was also removed by death. Some particulars are already stated of this distinguished, learned, and truly upright presbyter. He had been for upwards of sixty-four years pastor of the congregation at Longside, in Aberdeenshire, and his residence was the small cottage at Linshart in the vicinity. It is previously noticed that he bore his full share of the severities inflicted on the Episcopal clergy after the suppression of the Enterprise of 1745, and his chapel was one of those burnt by the soldiers of the Duke of Cumberland. Although no partizan of the Stuart Family, he was committed to prison by the Government for having officiated to more than four persons. In 1799 Mr Skinner sustained a heavy loss in the death of Mrs Skinner, who had been his affectionate partner for fifty-eight years. He recorded his grief at that severe bereavement, and the attachment which he cherished to her memory and her many virtues, in some beautiful and affecting Latin verses, expressive of the desolation which

* Inserted in Appendix, No. VI of " Annals of Scottish Episcopacy," p. 555-560.

had overtaken him by her death. In 1807 Bishop Skinner was also bereaved in a similar manner, and it was now resolved that the venerable pastor of Longside should spend the remainder of his days with his son the Primus in Aberdeen On the 4th of June 1807 he bade farewell to his primitive cottage at Linshart, and when he arrived at Aberdeen he had the satisfaction of meeting his grandson, the late Rev. John Skinner of Forfar, and others of his descendants, in unison with his own wish " to see once more his children's grandchildren, and peace upon Israel." The sorrow evinced by his flock at Longside at their final separation may be easily conceived After his arrival at Aberdeen he was for ten days in his usual health, taking a lively interest in ordinary conversation, and often relating stories and anecdotes of men and things connected with a past generation. On the twelfth day after his arrival, however, he became ill when at dinner, and almost immediately expired, in the eighty-sixth year of his age. This venerable pastor was interred in the churchyard of Longside, where his congregation erected a monument to his memory, and an elegant marble tablet records his talents, acquirements, and virtues. Mr Skinner's first publication was a pamphlet, in 1746, entitled, " A Preservative against Presbytery," to animate the minds of his flock, who thought they saw in the severities inflicted by the Government on the Episco pal clergy the total extirpation of the succession. In 1757 he published in London a learned " Dissertation on Job's Prophecy," which received the high approbation of Bishop Sherlock ; and in 1767 he vindicated, in a pamphlet, the Scottish Episcopal Church from the aspersions of the Rev. Norman Sievewright, minister of the " English" congregation at Brechin, which Dr Brown of Langton would have done well to have diligently perused before he quoted the same Mr Sievewright as an authority, in his " Letters" on what he calls " Puseyite Episcopacy," addressed to Dr Pusey of Oxford. Mr Skinner's varied and profound biblical and theological acquirements are farther evinced in his various works, collected in two volumes, and published by his family. He was one of the best Classical and Hebrew scholars of his age. In 1788 appeared his " Ecclesiastical History of Scotland," in two volumes—a work now extremely scarce—in a series of letters, in which he gives a luminous account of the affairs of the Episcopal Church from the Reformation, till its ministers consented, at the death of Prince Charles Edward, to acknowledge the reigning dynasty. This work is dedicated in elegant Latin—" Ad Filium et Episcopum"—to his son and Bishop, the Primus. The livelier graces of his genius are displayed in those delightful contributions to Scottish song which have procured for him a high place among the true poets of his native land. His memory, his learning, and his many virtues, will long be cherished by the members of the Church which his name and descendants have adorned.

In 1808 died the Right Rev. Bishop Watson, in the forty-seventh year of his age. He was removed in 1791 from the charge of the congregation in Banff to the chapel at the village of Laurencekirk, on the nomination of Francis Garden, Esq., a Judge in the Supreme Court of Scotland by the title of Lord Gardenstone. This patriotic gentleman, though a Presbyterian, built and endowed the Episcopal chapel in the village, which, previous to 1762, when he purchased the estate of Johnstone, consisted only of a few houses, but subsequently by his Lordship's exertions extended so rapidly, that before his death, in 1793, it had attained a degree of importance and prosperity which far exceeded his most sanguine expectations. Lord Gardenstone endowed the Episcopal chapel of his village with L.40 per annum, forty bolls of oatmeal, a parsonage-house, garden, and three acres of the best land in the vicinity. Bishop Watson was the first incumbent, but small as his income was, he had to encounter about the time of his death an action in the Court of Session, to ascertain whether Lord Gardenstone's deed of endowment was so technically and legally correct, as to constitute the stipend and other emoluments of the Episcopal incumbent a permanent burden on the estate of Johnstone in the county of Kincardine. This action was rendered necessary, because the new proprietor to whom Lord Gardenstone's heir sold the lands, of which the village of Laurencekirk forms a part, refused to pay the stipend and other endowments after his Lordship's decease, unless Bishop Watson granted receipts so expressed that the payments were in no way to be considered as precluding the proprietor of the said lands of Johnstone from challenging the rights of the Episcopal incumbents. The Court found, though the decision was not given till after Bishop Watson's death, that Lord Gardenstone's deed of endowment was valid, and could not be set aside. " Although cut off in the prime of life," says the Rev. John Skinner, " yet did Bishop Watson's death proceed from as complete prostration of strength, and as much from bodily imbecility, as if he had reached that period of human life when all is labour and sorrow. The Bishop was a native of Banffshire, and, like most of his contemporaries of the diocese of Aberdeen, had been trained to the ministry of the Scottish Episcopal Church by the venerable pastor of Longside, the father of his friend and patron Bishop Skinner. His classical and theological attainments did honour to his master, and showed that he himself was a diligent and successful student. Though raised to the episcopate in earlier life than usual, this excellent man's deportment was marked by something so decorous in society, and by a mien, a voice, and manner so attractive in the immediate discharge of his sacred office, as to command the respect of all who knew him, or who witnessed the performance of his duties; and as he lived universally esteemed, he died universally regretted "

The death of Bishop Watson rendered vacant the diocese of Dunkeld, and the clergy, having duly received their mandate, met at the village of Alyth to elect his successor. Two presbyters were nominated, the Rev Dr Gleig of Stirling, and the Rev. Patrick Torry of Peterhead. Dr Gleig recommended the clergy to make the election unanimous in favour of the latter, which was accordingly done, and approved by the Episcopal College. Bishop Torry was consecrated at Aberdeen on the 12th of October 1808, by Bishops Skinner, Macfarlane, and Jolly.

The advanced age of Bishop Strachan induced the clergy of the diocese of Brechin to apply to Bishop Skinner for a mandate to elect a coadjutor and successor. This was granted, and the presbyters met at Montrose on the 27th of September 1808, when they unanimously elected the Rev. Dr Gleig of Stirling. After some correspondence between Bishop Skinner and Dr Gleig respecting the Scottish Communion Office, the latter was consecrated in St Andrew's Chapel, Aberdeen, on the 30th of October 1808, by Bishops Skinner, Jolly, and Torry. The sermon on this occasion was preached by the Rev. Heneage Horsley, M.A., son of the distinguished Bishop Horsley, and afterwards published at the request of the Episcopal College.

Bishop Strachan died in 1810, and Bishop Abernethy Drummond on the previous year, each nearly ninety years of age. They were both consecrated on the same day in 1787, the one as coadjutor to the other, but Bishop Abernethy Drummond was soon afterwards elected by the presbyters of Edinburgh, in which city was his pastoral charge, to be their diocesan We have seen that he resigned Edinburgh in favour of

Dr Sandford in 1805, when he superintended the affairs of the diocese of Glasgow, the pastoral connection with the clergy of which he retained to his death. It is said that Bishop Abernethy Drummond paid his respects to Prince Charles Edward in Holyroodhouse, which was subsequently to him the source of much annoyance and danger. He wrote numerous small tracts, and zealously embarked in theological controversies both with Protestants and Roman Catholics, among the former having an occasional feud with the late Sir Henry Moncreiff, Bart., a distinguished minister of the Presbyterian Establishment in Edinburgh; and among the latter with the late Bishop Hay, who had left the Scottish Episcopal Church for that of Rome, and who was in consequence often reminded of his apostacy by his antagonist It is said of Bishop Abernethy Drummond, that " his intemperate manner defeated in most cases the benevolence of his intentions, and only irritated those whom he had wished to convince."* The Bishop, who was connected with the family of Abernethy of Saltoun in Banffshire, and was the son of John Abernethy, Esq. of Corskie, assumed the surname of Drummond when he married Barbara, only daughter and heiress of William Drummond, Esq. of Hawthornden, the lineal descendant of the celebrated Poet. This interesting mansion, the " Classic Hawthornden," as it is termed by Sir Walter Scott, on the romantic banks of the North Esk, upwards of seven miles from Edinburgh, is still the property of the Bishop's collateral relatives. His sister married Robert Forbes, Esq. of Corse, a gentleman who represented an ancient and distinguished family in the county of Aberdeen † Their son John Forbes, Esq , R.N., married Mary, daughter of Dr Ogilvie, heiress, by special settlement, of Mrs Abernethy Drummond her cousin, and assumed the sirname of Drummond. He was created a Baronet of Great Britain in 1828, with remainder to the husband of his only surviving child, who married Francis Walker, Esq. of Dalry, near Edinburgh, connected with the Noble families of Lauderdale and Tweeddale in the Peerage of Scotland, who succeeded to the Baronetcy as Sir Francis Walker Drummond at the decease of his father-in-law in 1829.

* Bishop Russell's Appendix to Keith's Catalogue of the Scottish Bishops, p. 545.
† The names of Patrick Forbes, consecrated Bishop of Aberdeen in 1618, the great ornament of the Scottish Church in his time, and of his son, the Rev. John Forbes, D.D., Professor of Divinity in King's College, Aberdeen, will always be held in veneration by those who appreciate profound theological learning.

CHAPTER XXII.

SYNOD OF ABERDEEN IN 1811—THE CANONS FOR THE DISCIPLINE OF THE SCOTTISH EPISCOPAL CHURCH RATIFIED—DEATH AND CHARACTER OF BISHOP SKINNER OF ABERDEEN.

AFTER the repeal of the Penal Laws the Bishops and clergy of the Scottish Episcopal Church embraced every opportunity of presenting congratulatory and other addresses to the Throne, and in 1809 they were conspicuous among those who evinced their loyalty when his Majesty George III. entered on the fiftieth year of his reign Their address on this occasion was transmitted to the Earl of Liverpool, at the time Secretary of State for the Home Department, but presented by his Lordship's successor, the Right Hon. Richard Ryder, second son of the first Lord Harrowby, and brother of the Right Rev. Henry Ryder, D D., Lord Bishop of Lichfield and Coventry. The "jubilee year" of the sovereign was also duly observed by the Bishops and clergy, in obedience to an order issued by the Privy Council on the 27th of September, and public prayers and thanksgivings were offered for the Divine protection vouchsafed to his Majesty during his long, arduous, and auspicious reign. This is said to have been the first order issued by the Privy Council, which has since been duly followed, of distinguishing the Bishops and clergy from the Scottish Dissenters, in directing prayers and thanksgivings on public occasions

In 1810 no event of any general interest occurred in the history of the Church. Various minor affairs induced Bishop Skinner and his brethren of the Episcopal College to summon the Synod held at Aberdeen in 1811 ; in which the Code of Canons for the regulation of the

Church was solemnly ratified. The necessity of convening this Synod is thus stated by Bishop Skinner in a letter to Bishop Sandford, dated February 22, 1811 :—" At an early period of the reign of Charles I. an attempt was made to give the Church of Scotland a set of Canons and Constitutions, similar to those which had been drawn up and sanctioned in the preceding reign for the Church of England. But that feeble attempt, as well as the introduction of a Liturgy, was completely frustrated by the disastrous fate of Charles, and even the restoration of his son did not much mend the matter, as, during the whole of his reign and the short period of his brother's, the attention of the Government seems to have been wholly taken up with making provision for the outward peace of the kingdom, rather than for the internal order and unity of the Church. At last the Revolution gave a final blow to the legal established Episcopacy of Scotland, and for several years after that era our Bishops had enough to do in keeping up a pure episcopal succession, till it should be seen what, in the course of Providence, might be farther effected towards the preservation, though not of an established, yet of a purely primitive Church in this part of the United Kingdom. For this purpose a few Canons were drawn up and sanctioned in 1743, which, though very well calculated to answer the purposes for which they were intended, are yet far from exhibiting any thing like a complete code of ecclesiastical discipline even for our small society. The English Canons are in general inapplicable to our situation, and of the whole, one hundred and forty-one in number, there are not above four or five that could even with some alterations be adopted and enforced among us. It is surely time, therefore, now that we are fully tolerated, but without the smallest prospect of ever being more than tolerated, that we should turn our attention to the means which Providence has put in our power of making the best of our situation, and rendering it as conducive as we possibly can, to the great and good design for which our Church has been so happily preserved—so signally supported—even the glory of its Almighty Protector, and the comfort and edification of his faithful people."

The suggestion of Bishop Skinner was readily sanctioned by his right reverend colleagues, and after it was decided that the Synod should consist of a certain number of delegates from the dioceses instead of the whole body of the clergy, it was summoned to meet on the 19th of June. On that day all the Bishops assembled at Aberdeen, with the Deans of

Edinburgh, Aberdeen, Brechin, and Dunkeld, those of Ross and Moray being absent by indisposition. The delegates from the respective dioceses were the Rev. Archibald Alison for Edinburgh, the Rev. John Cruickshank of Turriff for Aberdeen, the Rev. Heneage Horsley of Dundee for Brechin, and the Rev. John Skinner of Forfar for Dunkeld. The Synod was duly constituted by Bishop Skinner as Primus, and the presbyters, consisting of the Deans and Delegates, withdrew to their chamber, where they prepared the following minute :—" At Aberdeen, this 19th day of June 1811 years, the Deans and representatives of the several dioceses of the Episcopal Church in Scotland having met in a separate chamber by the authority of the Right Reverend the Bishops of the said Church, did then and there unanimously elect the Very Reverend James Walker, Dean of the Diocese of Edinburgh,* as their prolocutor, and the Rev. William Skinner of Aberdeen, as their clerk.† Before the Deans and representatives retired to their separate chamber, they heard the Primus deliberately read the introduction or preamble, proposed for the Code of Ecclesiastical Laws, to be determined upon and enacted in the present Synod of the Scottish Episcopal Church, of the general tenor of which they instruct their prolocutor to state to the chamber of Bishops that they do unanimously approve." The Synod continued two days, and the Code of Canons was framed which is more particularly noticed in the sequel, and which are now binding on all the clergy, as revised and ratified by the Synod of Laurencekirk in 1838, and those of Edinburgh in 1829 and 1838. The Canons refer of course to the discipline and government of the Church, and are framed to preserve order and regularity in a communion unconnected with the State as it respects temporal endowments. As a proof of the strict adherence maintained towards the doctrines and ritual of the Church of England, the Sixteenth Canon expressly prohibits any alterations or insertions in the Morning and Evening Service of the Liturgy, and no deviation from the *ipsissima verba* is allowed. The Fifteenth Canon, however, which, according to the Rev. Mr Skinner of Forfar, was proposed by the Rev. Archibald Alison of Edinburgh and the Rev. Heneage Horsley of Dundee, sets forth, that although permission is granted " to retain the use

* Afterwards the successor of Dr Sandford as Bishop of Edinburgh, and of Bishop Gleig as Primus.
† The successor of his distinguished father as Bishop of Aberdeen

of the English Communion Office in all congregations where the said Office hath been previously in use, the Scottish Office is considered as the authorised service of the Episcopal Church in the administration of the Lord's Supper," and is " to be used in all consecrations of Bishops," every Bishop, when consecrated, "giving his full assent to it, as being sound in itself, and of primary authority in Scotland," and binding himself "not to permit its being laid aside, where now used, but by authority of the College of Bishops."*

After the business of the Synod was completed, a circular was addressed by Bishop Skinner to all the Archbishops and Bishops of the United Church of England and Ireland, enclosing a copy of the Canons. Most of the Bishops acknowledged Bishop Skinner's circular in the kindest and most fraternal manner, especially those of Salisbury, Peterborough, Carlisle, Sodor and Man, Cork and Ross, Leighlin and Ferns, and Cloyne. Dr Bennet, the last mentioned Prelate, after thanking Bishop Skinner and the other Bishops for the copy of the Canons, adds—" I have always highly esteemed the Christian piety and honourable independence of the Episcopal Church in Scotland, and earnestly pray that, under the guidance of her excellent Prelates, she may continue that purity of doctrine for which she has been so long and so deservedly celebrated." The services of Bishop Skinner at the Synod of Aberdeen is thus expressed in a letter from Bishop Walker to the Rev. John Skinner of Forfar :—" I need not remind you of the very important Synod held at Aberdeen in 1811, of which you were a member. I recollect that period with serious satisfaction, and I know that your father's conduct on that occasion made a deep impression on those clergy who previously knew him very partially, and only by hearsay. His kind and easy hospitality as our landlord, the ability and accuracy with which he prepared the matter of our deliberations, his impartial conduct as president of our assembly, and the readiness with which he yielded those points which we from the South thought most necessary for general conciliation, stand strongly in my recollection, and are certainly worthy of special consideration in the estimate of your father's character." It is apparent to every one who investigates the history of Scottish Episcopacy, that the Church is under the deepest obligations

* Annals of Scottish Episcopacy, p. 516, 517.

to Bishop Skinner. His persevering exertions, patient assiduity, and zealous superintendence of its affairs, are conspicuous throughout his whole important episcopate, and his name must ever be honoured with respect and veneration.

At and after this period the Church was annually increasing in numbers. Several new congregations were formed, and elegant edifices erected for divine service in the large towns by the exertions of the laity, aided by subscriptions and donations from distinguished and benevolent friends in England. These chapels present a striking contrast to the obscure and uncomfortable structures in which many of the congregations had assembled after the prosecutions of 1745.

In 1814, the Rev. Martin J. Routh, D D., the learned and venerable President of Magdalen College, Oxford, published and dedicated to the Scottish Bishops and clergy his " Reliquiæ Sacræ, sive Auctorum fere jam perditorum Secundi Tertiique Sæculi Fragmenta quæ supersunt: accedunt Epistolæ Synodicæ et Canonicæ Nicæno Concilia Antiquiores."*—" Nor does the learned author," says Mr Skinner of Forfar, " omit his reasons for singling out the Bishops and clergy of the Scottish Episcopal Church, personally unknown to him, as the objects of such veneration and regard. To the inscription, and in Latin of the most classical purity, an address is annexed, in which he tells them that 'enjoying, as they do enjoy, the praise of maintaining the manner of Christian antiquity joined to the Catholic faith and to the discipline of the Apostles,' he, the author, did on this account present them with ' *aurea hæc Primorum Sæculorum scripta,*' literally, *these golden productions of the First Ages* ;—that, ' though fragments merely, and picked up from a general shipwreck, the memorials only of what the Church was in her then depressed and humble state, he yet considers them the more fit to be presented to those whose lot it is to be placed even in less prosperous circumstances than was the Primitive Church itself ;'—that, ' though he laments to see the Scottish Bishops and clergy deprived of civil establishment, secular dignities and honours, this deprivation in his opinion affords not subject of regret equal to that which afflicts the

* The dedication of this interesting collection is—" Patribus in Christo admodum Reverendis, Virisque Optimis et Venerabilibus Episcopis et Presbyteris Ecclesiæ Scoticæ Episcopalis, Doctis, Piis, Orthodoxis, Martinus Josephus Routh Paternitati Dignationique eorum D.D.D."

mind versed in Christian antiquity, when it beholds a people of such renown as the people of Scotland, and withal so justly famed for the repect which they show to religion, torn from their pristine Hierarchy, and placed in a state of schism from Episcopal communion ;'— that still ' it is to himself matter of joy unspeakable to have it in his power to congratulate his Episcopal brethren in Scotland on possessing the privilege, which of right belongs to all mankind, of exercising their ministry in peace ; which privilege, as it can never be violated but by acts of heinous atrocity, he trusts, now that our country has emerged from the agitating waves of civil discord, will be rendered to the Scottish Episcopalians both stable and permanent ;'—and that ' he remembers well with what patriotic fidelity and devotion they conducted themselves in the hour of trial, never allowing their tempers to be ruffled by reason of the neglect cast upon their humble petitions for relief from penal statutes, or by reason of the very precarious footing on which they were at one time permitted to minister in holy things.' "

Nothing of importance occurred in the history of the Church till 1816, the year in which died the excellent Primus, Bishop Skinner. This deprivation was a very severe loss to the Church. The public life of this unwearied and indefatigable man is completely associated with the Communion over which he long worthily and honourably presided, and he had the satisfaction, under Divine Providence, of conducting the affairs of the Church to the peace and prosperity in which they were at his lamented death. He presided at a period when both the clergy and laity were subjected to various penalties and political disabilities, which, though not enforced by the Government when he was invested with the episcopate, were still in the statute-book. These tended to keep many congregations whose clergy were of English or Irish ordination in a state of schismatical separation, and who, as they considered, could not, consistently with the oaths they had taken at their ordination, submit to the jurisdiction of the Scottish Bishops. Bishop Skinner had the happiness of seeing two great measures accomplished in which he had been most actively engaged—the repeal of the Penal Laws, and the subsequent union of most of the English with the indigenous clergy. The other great services he rendered to the Church by his theological works are previously noticed.

Bishop Skinner was the second son of the venerable pastor of Longside, and was born on the 17th May 1744. He was educated at Marischal College, Aberdeen, and was early admitted into holy orders by Bishop Gerard of that Diocese. His first charge, as already mentioned, was that of Ellon, a village and parish in the county on the Ythan seventeen miles distant from Aberdeen and Peterhead. The pastoral charge of Ellon then consisted of two congregations, one in the village, and the other about sixteen miles distant, to both of which he officiated regularly several years during Sundays in summer. The emoluments he received from his united charge generally varied to from L 25 to L.30 per annum! For eleven years he discharged the pastoral duties of Ellon, till 1775, when he was removed to Aberdeen by the unanimous invitation of Bishop Kilgour and the people as successor to the Rev. William Smith. When Bishop Skinner was first removed to Aberdeen his congregation was small, but additional accommodation was soon required. After the repeal of the Penal Laws another chapel was erected by subscription in 1795. In this structure the Bishop officiated twenty years, until finding it too limited for the congregation, " the public-spirited members of his flock," says Mr Skinner, " urged him not many months before his death to set about erecting, in the spacious street which forms the north entry to the city of Aberdeen, a truly magnificent structure, capable of containing no fewer than 1100 persons, and fitted up in a manner more appropriate and church-like than any edifice of the kind north of the Forth " Bishop Skinner, however, was not spared to see the completion of this fine edifice. He had been overtaken by severe illness in 1814, from which he so far recovered as to be able to resume his labours, and he terminated his honourable career on the 13th of July 1816, in the seventy-second year of his age. " So short," says Mr Skinner, " was his confinement at last, that the very forenoon on which he died he was in his dining-room, and on Friday, the day preceding, at prayers in the chapel." At this period his former flock at Ellon were united in a commodious chapel, which he intended to have opened personally on St James' Day, the 25th of July. The sermon which he had prepared for that occasion was found in his desk, and was preached, with a few additions, suitable to the loss which the Church at large sustained, by the Rev. Nathaniel Grieve the incumbent. The death of Bishop Skinner was more particularly lamented by his friends and fellow-citizens of all ranks and persuasions in Aberdeen, where he had been long personally esteemed. We are told that "hundreds, besides the large company who were specially invited, followed his body to the grave. And although apparently a rude rabble had seated themselves on the walls of the Mausoleum, a burying-place in the Spital church-yard of Old Aberdeen, near to which his mortal remains are deposited, yet when the officiating clergyman commenced the funeral service not a breath was heard—not a head but was instantly uncovered; and while tears were seen to flow apace, not a trace of disrespect marked the conduct of the most ragged spectator of the scene." The funeral sermon was preached on the following Sunday by the proximus resident Bishop, the Right Rev. Dr Patrick Torry of Peterhead. A full length marble statue, by Flaxman, of Bishop Skinner in his episcopal robes, is placed in St Andrew's Chapel, at the west end under the organ, as a mark of the estimation in which he was held by those who knew him and appreciated his labours.

The local historian of Aberdeen supplies us with some information respecting the state of the Episcopal Church in that city during Bishop Skinner's episcopate The house which the Bishop fitted up as a chapel in 1776 was in Long Acre, which was demolished in 1795, and a more commodious edifice erected on its site, dedicated to St Andrew, at the expense of the congregation. The present St Andrew's Chapel in King Street was completed in 1817, and consecrated on the 27th of July. It is in the Gothic style of architecture, 90 feet long by 65 feet broad, the front towards the street of polished freestone brought from Leith. The architectural ornaments, such as mouldings, leaves, foliage, and towers, are very beautiful, and the top of the gable, between the large towers, is finished with a balustrade of Gothic figures, in the centre of which is St Andrew's Cross. This splendid edifice altogether cost nearly L.8000. On Christmas Day, 1817, during the celebration of divine service, the Chapel narrowly escaped destruction by overheating the flues of the stove, and considerable damage was done to the interior before the fire was extinguished by the exertions of the congregation and citizens.*

St John's Chapel in Golden Square, on the north side of Union Street, is a neat edifice, erected about 1806, having a small spire on

* Kennedy's Annals of Aberdeen, vol ii. p 180, 181

the north end. The congregation are said to be the representatives of that formerly under the pastoral care of Bishop Gerard.

St Paul's Chapel, on the west side of the Gallowgate, is externally a plain edifice, described as "inconvenient and insufficient," capable of containing 1000 persons. On the north side is an aisle, and galleries are round the whole building, supported by Tuscan columns of wood, over which are placed Ionic columns, in the centre of which is a cupola about nine feet in diameter. This congregation has been in existence since the time of the Revolution. The Chapel was erected by voluntary subscription in 1722, and two clergymen appointed to officiate in it as colleagues. The congregation of St Paul's was unconnected with the Scottish Episcopal Church till 1840, when the union was happily effected under the auspices of the Bishop of Aberdeen and the gentlemen officially connected with the Chapel.

As it respects the state of the Church in Aberdeen at and after the Revolution, Mr Kennedy says, in his "Annals" of that city—"Although Prelacy had been abolished in 1689, yet, as we formerly had occasion to observe, the ministers of St Nicholas' church continued to administer the sacred ordinances of religion according to the forms and ceremonies of the Episcopal Church, until the year 1694, when they were dispossessed of their charges under the authority of a Committee of the General Assembly.—From the time of the separation from the church of Aberdeen, as established after the Revolution, there were generally two [Episcopal] meeting-houses in the town, one of which was for many years under the pastoral charge of Bishop Gerard —The other of these meeting-houses, which was situated in the Guestrow, had been for a long period under the pastoral charge of Mr William Smith, who was also a descendant of the original ministers of the Episcopal Church." This gentleman, we have seen, was succeeded in the incumbency by Bishop Skinner.

CHAPTER XXIII.

CONSECRATION OF THE REV. WILLIAM SKINNER—BISHOP GLEIG ELECTED PRIMUS—CONSECRATION OF DR LOW—VISIT OF GEORGE IV. TO SCOTLAND IN 1822—CONSECRATION OF BISHOP LUSCOMBE—SYNODS OF LAURENCEKIRK IN 1828, AND OF EDINBURGH IN 1829—DEATH OF BISHOP SANDFORD—CONSECRATION OF BISHOP WALKER—STATE OF THE CHURCH.

AT the death of Bishop Skinner, his second son, the Rev. William Skinner, ordained deacon in 1802, and priest in 1803, by Bishop Horsley, was unanimously elected his father's successor in the episcopate by the presbyters of the diocese, and was consecrated at Stirling, on the 27th of October 1816, by Bishops Gleig, Jolly, Sandford, and Torry. Bishop Gleig was elected Primus of the Episcopal College, and this distinction was justly conferred on one of the most distinguished theologians and metaphysicians of his day in Scotland, whose high reputation shed a lustre over the Church by his several learned works, well known in England.

The venerable Bishop Macfarlane, of Ross and Argyll, died at a very advanced age at Inverness in 1819. From the peculiar nature of the districts included within the limits of the united diocese, comprehending the wildest and most sequestered parts of the Western Highlands, it was of importance that the successor of Bishop Macfarlane should be possessed of no common zeal and ardour in the discharge of his duties. The presbyters elected the Right Rev. David Low, LL.D., of Pittenweem, in Fifeshire, as their Diocesan, who was consecrated at Stirling on the 14th of November 1819, by Bishops Gleig, Jolly, and Torry. The consecration sermon was preached by Bishop Walker, then a presbyter of the diocese of Edinburgh, and was afterwards published. The wisdom of the choice of the presbyters of Ross and Argyll was soon made apparent by Bishop Low, who greatly increased the number of clergy, and congregations, instituted schools, and appointed proper teachers. Bishop Low may also be regarded as the founder of the Gaelic Episcopal Society, now incorporated with the Scottish Episcopal Church Society, as more particularly noticed in the sequel.

No event of any consequence occurs after the consecration of Bishop Low till 1822, when George IV. visited his ancient kingdom of Scotland, and the temporary brilliancy of a royal court was witnessed within the deserted walls of Holyrood. The Scottish Bishops and clergy were not behind in expressing the loyal congratulations to their Sovereign. An address was prepared, which was admired for its eloquence, moderation, and historical allusions, and was only attacked in one solitary instance, which, considering the quarter whence the hostile criticism emanated, excited no surprise.* The journalist had the boldness to insinuate that the Scottish Bishops and clergy cherished some ambitious design of endeavouring to re-establish the Church, as if the loyal expressions in an address to the throne on that occasion could have possibly achieved that event, although the King had that very day assured the deputation from the General Assembly of the Presbyterian Establishment that he would " maintain inviolate those rights and privileges to which the Church of Scotland is entitled by the most solemn compacts." The address of the Bishops and clergy was farther pronounced to be *sycophantish*; but of this they had no reason to complain, when it is remembered that the same authority declared the address of the General Assembly *servile* and *blasphemous*. The deputation from the Scottish Episcopal Church consisted of Bishops Gleig, Jolly, Sandford, Torry, Skinner, and Low; and the Rev. Archibald Alison, and the Rev. Dr Morehead, both of St Paul's Chapel, Edinburgh, the Rev. James Walker (afterwards Bishop) of St Peter's Chapel, Edinburgh, the Rev. Dr Michael Russell (afterwards Bishop) of Leith, the Rev. Heneage Horsley, of St Paul's Chapel, Dundee, and the Rev. Alexander Cruickshank of Muthill They were graciously

* This was THE SCOTSMAN newspaper, published in Edinburgh—a print of great ability, the political principles of which are well known, and the advocate of what is called " Voluntaryism" in ecclesiastical matters.

received by his Majesty in the royal closet—an honour exclusively conferred on them, and the address was read by the Rev. Heneage Horsley. Previous to 1842, exactly twenty years afterwards, when Queen Victoria and Prince Albert visited Scotland, the one half of that deputation had left the scene of their earthly ministrations. "The fathers, where are they? and the prophets, do they live for ever?"

In 1825 occurred the consecration of the Right Rev. Matthew Henry Luscombe, LL.D. Cambridge, as a Missionary Bishop to the Continent of Europe, which occasioned no little controversy and even acrimony, especially in England. Dr Luscombe, in the course of his pastoral duties as chaplain to the British Embassy at Paris, having perceived the great laxity among the members of the Church of England, occasioned in a considerable degree by the want of episcopal superintendence, came to England to consult his friends about this painful state of affairs. By law the Bishop of London has diocesan authority over all British chaplains and factories on the Continent, but this jurisdiction did not in the least correct the deficiencies which Dr Luscombe stated to exist. It was plain that the Bishop of London could not regularly hold confirmations or ordinations in France; and in that kingdom in particular were many English families, and the descendants of such, not to mention French Protestants, who adhered to the communion of the Church of England. These facts being duly and seriously considered, Dr Luscombe came to Scotland, and after an ample correspondence with the Bishops was consecrated at Stirling, on Sunday the 22d of March 1825, by Bishops Gleig, Sandford, Skinner, and Low. The Rev. Walter Farquhar Hook, D.D., the distinguished and learned Vicar of Leeds, preached the consecration sermon, which was published, with an introduction and notes, and dedicated to the Scottish Bishops. The controversy which this consecration caused appears to have been finally adjusted by the Bishop of London constituting Bishop Luscombe his commissary on the Continent, with the superintendence of the chaplaincies and factories, and authority to report to his Lordship at stated periods.

In 1828 Bishop Gleig, as Primus, summoned an Ecclesiastical Synod to meet at Laurencekirk during the summer of that year, to revise and consolidate the Canons of the Synod of Aberdeen. Bishops Gleig,

Torry, Sandford, and Skinner, attended on the appointed day, with the delegates of the clergy chosen from the different dioceses, but Bishop Jolly of Moray and Bishop Low of Ross and Argyll either refused or hesitated to concur, on account of some peculiar difficulties on the subject. The Synod nevertheless assembled and revised the Canons, which were ordered to be printed and circulated among the clergy, and the Primus communicated the proceedings to the Archbishop of Canterbury. Some important matters, however, were overlooked in the business of this Synod, which, added to the objections of Bishop Jolly and Bishop Low, caused Bishop Gleig to convene another Synod at Edinburgh in July 1829, when all the members of the Episcopal College and the delegates of the dioceses attended, and finished the revisal of the Canons for the internal regulations and discipline of the Church

In the beginning of 1830 the Right Reverend Bishop Sandford died at Edinburgh in the sixty-fourth year of his age, and twenty-fourth of his episcopate The death of this excellent and pious Bishop was universally lamented in the Scottish metropolis by men of all persuasions, who evinced their respect to his memory by their voluntary attendance at the last solemn offices of religion in St John's Chapel, in the eastern part of the cemetery of which he was interred. The congregation of St John's testified their regard for him as their pastor, by erecting an elegant marble monument within that fine edifice at the east end of the aisle, on the north side of the reading-desk and communion-table, and an appropriate inscription on the tablet records his many virtues and the manner in which he discharged his duties. The worthy Bishop was in delicate health several years before his death. His last moments were peaceful and affecting, and he died, as he lived, in the "sure and certain hope of a blessed immortality." Shortly previous to his dissolution, the only words he was heard to utter audibly were—"For Christ's sake." We are told by the author of his Memoir that "twice he raised his arm to its utmost extent, and pointed with his finger to the heavens. His last words were a request that his family would pray for him, and his son-in-law continued to pronounce appropriate texts of Scripture until he fell asleep. At eleven o'clock at night, without a struggle, he resigned his breath. A slight flutter, a gentle sigh, and his happy spirit had returned to God. His wife and children gathered round him, and as they looked on the expression which the parting soul had left as the impress of its bliss, they felt more resigned, and retired, praising God."* It is stated in another part of the same sketch, that "he had often indulged an idea of resigning his Episcopal charge, and spending his declining years in the society of his several children. But it was otherwise appointed, and he retained until the last his connection with a Church with which he had been so long and so honourably associated." Bishop Sandford was happy in his surviving children. His son, the late Sir Daniel K. Sandford, who received the honour of knighthood from William IV., and was returned Member of Parliament for Paisley in 1834, was Professor of Greek in the University of Glasgow, and died in the prime of life, lamented by all, in 1837. Another son, Erskine Douglas Sandford, Esq. Advocate, a distinguished member of the Scottish Bar, was appointed Sheriff or Steward of Kirkcudbrightshire in 1841. The Bishop's youngest son, the Rev. John Sandford, M.A., was presented to the vicarage of Chillingham, by Bishop Van Mildert of Durham, in 1827, and has since held other preferments in the Church of England, of which he is a worthy and esteemed clergyman.

The successor of Bishop Sandford was the Rev. James Walker, D.D., who had resigned his share of the pastoral charge of St Peter's Chapel in Edinburgh in 1829, when his colleague became the sole incumbent, that he might altogether devote himself to his duties as Professor of Divinity. Never was there an election which gave greater satisfaction than that of Bishop Walker, and it was only doubtful if the delicate state of his health might not induce him to refuse. Fortunately, however, Bishop Walker accepted the election, and he was consecrated at Stirling on Sunday, the 7th of March 1830, by Bishops Gleig, Jolly, Skinner, and Low. The consecration sermon was preached by Bishop Russell, and was afterwards published, entitled—"The Historical Evidence for the Apostolical Institution of Episcopacy," several editions of which have been printed. Bishop Walker entered upon the duties of the episcopate by visiting officially all the congregations in Edinburgh, those of Leith, Portobello, Musselburgh, Haddington, Kelso, Dumfries, Glasgow, Paisley, Greenock, and in the county of Fife, which,

* Memoir in Remains of Bishop Sandford, vol. i. p. 75. In this Memoir the character of the Bishop is admirably delineated.

with the exception of Pittenweem, then formed part of the extensive united diocese of Edinburgh, Fife, and Glasgow. On those occasions he held confirmations in most of the provincial congregations, and a primary visitation of the clergy in the several districts

A retrospective view of the state of the Scottish Episcopal Church will form an appropriate conclusion to the present division of the narrative. Its prosperity after the consecration of Bishop Sandford is evinced from the fact, that during his episcopate the number of clergy increased from seven to twenty-five, five of whom, formerly independent, submitted themselves to his jurisdiction, and seven were appointed to new congregations licensed for the first time by him The splendid Gothic edifices of St Paul's and St John's Chapels in Edinburgh are already mentioned as having been chiefly erected through the influence and exertions of Lord Medwyn and his brother Sir William Forbes It is also stated that the congregation of the former removed from the Cowgate Chapel in 1818. The congregation of St John's removed in 1818 from Charlotte Chapel, a small plain building at the west end of Rose Street, near Charlotte Square, now occupied as a Baptist meeting-house, in which Bishop Sandford officiated for twenty years, after he left the temporary place of worship in the upper storey of a tenement in West Register Street. In 1821 St James' Chapel, Broughton Place, was opened under the incumbency of the Rev. Edward Craig, who in consequence resigned the pastoral charge of St Paul's, Carrubber's Close. The most recent Episcopal Chapel erected in Edinburgh must be merely noticed prospectively in point of date. This is Trinity Chapel, Dean Bridge, a beautiful Gothic edifice, from a design by John Henderson, Esq. architect, Edinburgh, and erected in 1838 during the episcopate of Bishop Walker, who consecrated the funeral vaults beneath, and also the terraced cemetery overhanging the deep and romantic ravine of the Water of Leith, crossed by the Dean Bridge.

In the pleasant sea-bathing village of Portobello, three miles from Edinburgh, the Rev. Thomas Langhorne, incumbent of the Episcopal Chapel of Musselburgh, was induced by the urgent request of several individuals to commence the erection of St John's Chapel in Brighton Street in 1825, which was duly consecrated by Bishop Sandford in 1826. When the walls of this edifice were almost erected, St Mark's Chapel was commenced by a private individual. As it was evident that the size and population of Portobello could not support two congregations, local contentions subsequently arose, and considerable loss was incurred by the projector of St John's Chapel. Meanwhile St Mark's Chapel was completed—a large and elegant edifice, more than sufficient for the accommodation of the Episcopal inhabitants of the place. St John's Chapel afterwards passed through several hands as property, and was eventually sold to the Roman Catholics, whose attempt to collect a congregation in it completely failed. St Mark's Chapel is now the only Episcopal chapel in Portobello.

In the city of Glasgow, the only places of worship connected with the Episcopal Church for many years were St Andrew's Chapel near the Green, under the pastoral charge of the Very Rev. William Routledge; and a temporary hall for another small congregation. In 1820 St Mary's Chapel, a large and elegant Gothic edifice, was erected in the new part of the city, in Renfield Street. The others subsequently built are Christ Church, in the eastern suburb called the Calton, chiefly by the private munificence and zealous activity of the Rev. David Aitchison, M.A., who, in 1842, became the pastor of a new congregation at Lochgilphead, and was appointed, in 1842, by the Right Rev. Bishop Low, Archdeacon of Argyll and the Isles; and St Jude's Chapel, Blythswood Square, of which the Rev. Robert Montgomery, M.A., the celebrated author of the "Messiah," the "Omnipresence of the Deity," and other popular poetical works, was the first incumbent.

In Paisley, Trinity Chapel owes its erection to the indefatigable exertions of the incumbent, the Rev. W. M. Wade, and was opened in 1833 St John's Chapel in Greenock is a large and spacious Gothic edifice, built a few years earlier; and that of Ayr was opened about 1837. Proceeding to Dumfries, the Episcopal chapel in that fine town is an elegant modern structure. Thence, in a different direction, the neat chapel of Peebles accommodates the congregation there first formed about 1828.

The chapels in Fife are few in number. The congregation of St Peter's Chapel, Kirkaldy, was formed chiefly by the exertions of Bishop Walker. In Cupar-Fife an Episcopal congregation has always existed since the Revolution. The present chapel, dedicated to St James, is a fine edifice, having a kind of Grecian exterior to correspond with the plan of the street, and a Gothic interior. This chapel owes its erection to the indefatigable efforts of the late Colonel Spens of Craigsanquhar. The chapel in St Andrews, a beautiful little Gothic building in the form of a cross, accommodates the congregation who formerly met in an upper room of a tenement in that venerable seat of the Primacy of Scotland. The chapel at Pittenweem is neat and plain, built during the incumbency of Bishop Low, whose flock previously met in an apartment of a house. Alloa and Dunfermline are subsequently mentioned.

In the various towns and villages north of the Tay, and in the Highland counties, several new Episcopal chapels have been erected, others have been repaired and enlarged, and in some places they are provided in the meantime with such temporary accommodation as they can procure in their respective localities The chapel of Muthill in Perthshire, near Drummond Castle, may be particularly noticed as a fine specimen of Gothic architecture, and judiciously arranged in the interior.

Such is a limited sketch of the progress of the Church for some years previous to the consecration of Bishop Walker in 1830. It will thus be seen that Scottish Episcopacy, notwithstanding the many obstacles, the bigotry, and, in not a few cases, the enmity with which it had to contend, has steadily maintained its ground by an increase of members. In the above enumeration very few of the older chapels and congregations are mentioned, as these for the most part have been long in existence. More recent additions are subsequently added, in continuation of this retrospective view of the state of the Church, towards the close of the present volume.

CHAPTER XXIV.

THE CONSTITUTION OF THE SCOTTISH EPISCOPAL CHURCH STATED BY BISHOP GLEIG AS SETTLED BY THE SYNODS OF 1828 AND 1829—THE GAELIC EPISCOPAL SOCIETY—CONSECRATION OF BISHOPS RUSSELL AND MOIR—DEATH OF BISHOP JOLLY—BISHOP WALKER ELECTED PRIMUS—THE SCOTTISH EPISCOPAL CHURCH SOCIETY INSTITUTED—THE FIRST ANNUAL MEETING—PASTORAL ADDRESS BY THE BISHOPS IN 1839—ACT OF PARLIAMENT, IN 1840, IN FAVOUR OF THE BISHOPS AND CLERGY—DEATHS OF BISHOPS GLEIG AND WALKER—CONSECRATION OF BISHOP TERROT.

IN a Communion such as the Scottish Episcopal Church, undisturbed by controversial disputations, and still less excited by popular contentions, few events of general interest occur to engage public attention. The Bishops hold their ordinations when necessity requires, and their annual and occasional confirmations of the young in the respective congregations within the dioceses; they deliver charges to the clergy at their triennial visitations, and the usual Diocesan Synods are held every year, in which the Deans preside in absence of the Bishops; but beyond these duties, and the exercise of the ordinary pastoral office by the clergy, which requires no description, the aspect of affairs undergoes little change, except that which results from deaths and other casualties. As an ecclesiastical body the Scottish Bishops and clergy never interfere in public matters, either political or civil, beyond transmitting loyal addresses of congratulation or condolence to the sovereign, and strictly confine themselves to the discharge of their ministerial duties.

The internal government of the Church is described in a Charge delivered to the clergy of the diocesan district of Brechin in August 1829, by the Right Rev. Bishop Gleig, entitled—" The Constitution of the Scottish Episcopal Church concisely stated."—" By the present constitution," says the Bishop, " as settled by the two last Synods of Laurencekirk and Edinburgh, a consistory or diocesan meeting of the Bishop and clergy must be annually holden in each diocese or district, at such a time and place as the Bishop, or the Dean empowered by him, shall appoint; and the clergy being assembled, and the consistory constituted by prayer, the Bishop, or in his absence the Dean, or, should both be necessarily absent, the senior presbyter present, must call upon every incumbent to lodge with the diocesan clerk his yearly report of the congregation under his charge, the number of baptisms, marriages, and deaths; the number of communicants at the several festivals and other communions, and the names of the persons baptized, married, and dead, with the dates at which these events took place; all which shall be duly entered in the minute-book of each diocese. After which the clergy shall deliberate among themselves whether any change in the mode of discipline or form of public worship might not be advantageously introduced into the district, and the result of their deliberations shall be transmitted to the Bishop, if not present, to be approved or rejected by him If the proposal of the presbyters obtain his approbation, it shall then, but not till then, be recorded on the minute-book as one of the local rules of the district or diocese."

This extract elucidates the manner in which the affairs of every diocese are now conducted As it respects General Synods, the Bishops, in conformity to the custom of the Primitive Church, form one chamber, and the Deans and Delegates, or presbyters, from every diocese, are the second chamber, of which the Professor of Divinity, if a presbyter, is *ex officio* a member. No layman is permitted to act as a representative, or allowed to take any part in the deliberations of either general or diocesan Synods, these being strictly ecclesiastical meetings. Bishop Gleig proceeds to state, that " no change in the general modes of administrating the discipline of the Church at large can be introduced but by the authority of a General Synod;" and that " there is now no occasion for the frequency of General Synods, as was the case in the Primitive Church, when, according to the 30th of the Apostolical Canons, a Synod of Bishops was enjoined to be held twice every year."—" When a General Synod shall be canonically convoked, for any specified purpose, the Bishop who shall neglect to attend, without sending to his Primus a sufficient apology for his absence, shall incur such a censure by his colleagues as to the majority of them his conduct may appear to deserve; and when any member of the second chamber, whether Dean or delegate, shall be absent, without sending a sufficient apology to the Primus, he shall, if a Dean, be deprived of his office, and, if a delegate, be declared inadmissible into any future Synod. It is not, however, in General Synods only that it is the duty of Bishops to meet when summoned canonically by the Primus; they must meet synodically when called on to hear particular appeals from the judgment of any particular diocesan; and the Bishop who, without a very satisfactory apology, shall absent himself from the discharge of this painful part of his duty, shall incur at least as heavy a censure as for absenting himself without cause from a General Synod. But though *appeals*, when regularly lodged with the Primus or clerk, must be heard, no *accusation* shall be received against a Bishop, or a Bishop-elect, unless proceeding from and supported by the testimony of credible persons, who are regular communicants in the Scottish Episcopal Church; nor shall the testimony of a single such witness be considered as sufficient to substantiate the charge, for the Scripture saith that ' in the mouth of two or three witnesses shall every word be established.' But if a Bishop, or Bishop-elect, shall be so accused, his supposed offence, whether in doctrine or in morals, shall be distinctly stated to him, and time given him to prepare for his defence, when he is cited by the Primus (or, should the Primus be the Bishop accused, by the next senior Bishop), to appear and plead; and if he do not obey the summons, he shall be cited a second time, in the name and by the authority of the Episcopal College; and if he be then guilty of contempt for not appearing, let the College pronounce such a sentence against him as they think equitable, that he may not be a gainer by declining justice."

It is to be observed that this sketch of the constitution and discipline of the Church, as delineated by Bishop Gleig, has altogether a reference to its position in Scotland as a non-established communion, entirely unconnected with the State. The duties of the Bishops in ecclesiastical and episcopal matters are similar to those of England. They are generally incumbents of congregations, wherein they officiate as the regular pastors, having an assistant, colleague, or curate, as may happen; but in their dioceses they appear as the spiritual governors of their clergy and people. The functions of the ordinary clergy are precisely the same as those of the Church of England. The Liturgy is used in divine service, subscription to the Thirty-Nine Articles is imperative, and the clerical vestments are similar.

In 1837, the Gaelic Episcopal Society was instituted for the benefit of the members of the Church in the Northern and Highland districts, chiefly, as already mentioned, through the exertions of Bishop Low. The Bishop had previously for some years supported a few schools in the united diocese of Ross and Argyll partly at his own expense, assisted by subscriptions from his own immediate friends, and by an occasional collection in his congregation As this Society has merged into the Scottish Episcopal Church Society, and is not now in existence, it may be here stated that the object of it was to organize schools in the Highlands under Gaelic teachers, and also to educate students for holy orders who were capable of officiating in the Gaelic language His Grace George fifth and last Duke of Gordon, who died in 1836, accepted the office of patron, Bishop Walker of Edinburgh was constituted President, and the other Bishops, with sundry noblemen and gentlemen, were the Vice-Presidents. The income of the Society for the first year amounted to L.514. An auxiliary was formed in London, among the patrons of which were the Bishops of London, Durham, Ely, Lichfield and Coventry, Lincoln, Chester, Oxford, Nova Scotia, Quebec, Lord Kenyon, and Lord Bexley.

In 1835 a sympathizing address on the distressed state of the Irish clergy was transmitted from the Scottish Episcopal Church to the Archbishop of Armagh, which was promptly acknowledged. Collections were also held in several congregations. The Presbyterian ministers of the Synod of Aberdeen liberally sent a similar address and subscriptions to the Irish Primate, which his Grace duly honoured by a reply. During the political contentions of those years nothing occurred in the Church to disturb its internal peace, or to retard its progressive prosperity. In 1837 the increasing ill health of Bishop Walker, not from the infirmities of age, but from long continued bodily debility, and the precarious state of Bishop Gleig, then at a very advanced period of life, rendered additions necessary to the Episcopal College. By the consent of Bishop Walker the diocesan district of Fife was disjoined from Edinburgh, and annexed to the jurisdiction of the Right Rev. Dr Torry, Bishop of the united diocese of Dunkeld and Dunblane; Glasgow was constituted a separate diocesan district, which it had not been since the death of Bishop Abernethy Drummond, and the Very Rev. Dr Michael Russell of Leith, Dean of the formerly united diocese of Edinburgh, Fife, and Glasgow, was elected by the presbyters their Bishop. About the same time a coadjutor and successor to Bishop Gleig in the diocese of Brechin was imperative, and the presbyters, having received their mandate, elected the Rev. David Moir, M.A., presbyter in the city of Brechin. At the time of the election of Bishop Moir as coadjutor of Brechin, Bishop Gleig also resigned the office of Primus of the Episcopal College, to which Bishop Walker was subsequently nominated by his brethren.

The choice of the presbyters of Glasgow and Brechin gave the utmost satisfaction to all the members of the Church. The learning and reputation of Dr Russell in the literary world are well known, and Dr Moir had been long a justly respected presbyter in the Diocese of Brechin. The consecration of Bishops Russell and Moir was held on Sunday, the 8th of October 1837, in St John the Evangelist's Chapel, Edinburgh, by Bishops Walker, Skinner, and Low, in presence of a crowded congregation, who were deeply impressed with the solemn ceremonial. The consecration sermon was preached by the Rev. E. B. Ramsay, M.A., incumbent of the Chapel, and was afterwards published. It well deserves to be ranked high among the several eloquent sermons which Mr Ramsay has on particular occasions given to the public. This sermon is entitled—" The Church considered as the Pillar and Ground of the Truth," and contains many admirable elucidations of the scriptural, apostolical, and primitive argument for Episcopacy. The following passages are selected from Mr Ramsay's statement of the peculiar manner in which the Reformed Episcopal Church is "distinguished from the two great divisions of the Christian world, that is to say, we are to meet the Romanist on the one side, and the anti-Episcopal on the other."

" With the Romish Church the grounds of our disagreement are sufficiently obvious, and the principles on which we contend are clearly established. We maintain the absolute necessity of the Reformation; that, from the manifold corruptions of the Church in the sixteenth century, it was an imperative duty upon men to examine into the causes of the great evils which had grown up, that they might return to the simplicity of gospel truth, and adopt the Bible as the only rule of faith, and as containing all things necessary for salvation. The supremacy of the Scriptures in all matters of doctrine required to be asserted and upheld; the Church to be purified from numerous practices and opinions which *they* distinctly and decidedly condemned.

" This is a principle of difference sufficiently explicit and intelligible; nor do we shrink from the argument with Romanists on the ground of church authority, ecclesiastical antiquity, and primitive testimony. We admit fully the reverence due to these; and we admit that they are essential elements towards the attainment of truth, nor do we fear the results which are deducible from them. Whoever gives up the respect for antiquity, and abjures any deference for the opinions of the early Church, resigns most important ground to the Romanist, giving him, for the time, the semblance of a triumph; for these can neither be safely nor consistently abandoned in the controversy. The Romish churchman can only be refuted by the Catholic churchman; and, therefore, the divines of our Church meet the Romanists on this ground, and contend against them on their own principles: And they have proved, as clearly as any moral and historical argument can prove, that the Romish Church has erred, not because she has taken Catholic antiquity for a guide, but because she has *not* taken it; that she is wrong, not in her adherence to ancient and uniform tradition, but in her *departure* from it, that the Romish Church has been led into such errors as the Papal supremacy, the worship of images, transubstantiation, and many others, from substituting the inventions and devices of the seventh and eighth centuries for the Catholic opinions of the second and third. *We* value the unity of the Church as much as they can, but we cannot maintain unity and fellowship at the expense of doctrine; and we assert that our reformers were in everything borne out by the principles of ecclesiastical polity which they professed; and that their motto, ' Hear the Church,' was in fact the only real ground on which it was possible that sound and consistent opinions could be established; therefore, they were fully justified in seeking again for the old paths, in returning to the uncorrupted doctrine of a Scripture rule of faith, and to the purer ritual of primitive times"

Mr Ramsay thus forcibly illustrates the second proposition :—" Such is the state of the argument regarding the first question—namely, the identity of our own Church with the primitive and apostolical community ; such are the grounds upon which are formed our polity, our doctrines, and our ceremonies ; but this is not an ultimate question, nor is it an inquiry in which we should rest satisfied, for it is not merely as Episcopalians, nor as theologians merely, and still less as controversialists, that we should be desirous of establishing the accordance of our communion with the Church of the Apostles ; but that we may be assured of our connection with the Church of Christ so as to partake of its promises, and to share in its privileges. Now, it is here that many of the theological errors of our day have their rise and origin. Men's minds are but little affected with the consideration, that the blessings of the new covenant are communicated through a society incorporated by the Saviour for specific purposes, governed by distinct orders of ministers, endowed with certain privileges, and invested with specific immunities. To the indifference and ignorance which are so prevalent on this subject we trace much of the sectarian spirit and sectarian practices of our times—much that is vague and imperfectly understood of the Christian privileges and blessings. Considerations connected with the Church of Christ, as a *body*, frequently amount to little or nothing ; the prevailing fashion of our day is to seek edification in the preaching and exertions of *individuals*, and to look to the clergy far more *as* individuals, than in their official capacity as the appointed ministers of Christ. It is on this account that we are desirous of drawing your attention to the very remarkable description of the Church in the text, as ' the pillar and ground of the truth'—a description which implies, that in the economy of salvation far more is assigned to the Church as a society than persons in general are now disposed to believe ; which implies that in the communion of the Church are to be found the elements and principles of all Christian truth, the means and opportunity of being wise unto salvation."

The preacher then proceeds to notice " the advantages of thus looking to the Church in its *corporate* capacity, as the selected depositary of the Redeemer's love and blessings," some of which he enumerates as in the following extract :—

" We find, in numerous passages of the New Testament, a distinct appropriation of the arrangements of the Church referred to for such specific ends and purposes. Christians are reminded of their being gathered together out of the world, and to be separated in a society, having neither worldly views nor worldly objects; and thus are they to enjoy a heavenly communion with Christ as Head and Lord of the Church, which he purchased with his own blood. These are advantages far beyond the ministrations of any individual, however able or however eloquent; whilst, at the same time, his official authority, when rightly considered, adds a weight and dignity to his ministrations as an ambassador for Christ, altogether independent of personal influence. Blessed be God, the efficacy of the sacraments, and the advantages of a Christian ministry, are not made to depend upon the personal abilities or zeal of individuals, but are vested in a corporate society over which the Holy Spirit exercises a continual superintendence, and against which the gates of hell shall not prevail! Thus have we a most substantial pledge for the *permanency* of our Church privileges, that our faith should not stand in the wisdom of man, but in the power of God. Men may err, and the best have erred. The wise and the good pass away, and their personal influence and superintendence are lost to the world; but the society which Christ purchased with his blood remains a witness and a depositary of his goodness until he come again. Amid the darkness, the errors, and the wickedness of the world, there will always be a ' Church of the living God' to stand as ' the pillar and ground of the truth '"

On the 29th of December 1837, died at Fraserburgh the venerated Bishop Jolly of Moray, in the eighty-third year of his age, and forty-second of his episcopate. Though he departed at a good old age, when life could scarcely be expected to be much longer prolonged, yet his piety, his virtues, and his learning, had endeared him in the Church, and his death was universally and sincerely regretted. The Bishop had been many years pastor of the congregation of Fraserburgh. The following delineation of his character, which appeared in a local print* of well known respectability, is from one who knew well how to appreciate this truly venerable man, and is worthy of being preserved in this narrative. "It is impossible," says the writer, "in a notice such as this, to pay an adequate tribute to the memory of this most amiable and revered individual;

* The " Aberdeen Journal," of 29th January 1838

nor, indeed, would it be easy to do justice to his character. It might not be difficult to form an estimate of his attainments as a divine, but no one, perhaps, is qualified to enter fully into the higher excellencies of his character as a Christian, who has not in some measure realized the spirit which had grown up in him to a degree of saintly virtue, seldom equalled and never surpassed. The reputation of Bishop Jolly for profound and varied learning, extended far beyond the limits of the Church of which he was so distinguished an ornament. The most eminent divines of the Church of England sought his correspondence, and presented their works to him, as one well qualified, by his familiarity with the higher departments of theological erudition, to form a just estimate of their merits. His theology was that of the Church Catholic, not cast in the narrow or distorted mould of modern systems, but drawn from the pure sources of divine truth in the Holy Scriptures, and the writings of the Primitive Fathers and succeeding Doctors, who have handed down to us 'the faith once delivered to the saints.' Had he been called upon to make a public declaration of his faith, he would probably have adopted the dying words of his admired Bishop Ken, whom he greatly resembled in the spirit and practice of 'divine love'—' As for my religion, I die in the Holy Catholic and Apostolic Faith professed by the whole Church before the disunion of the East and West; more particularly, I die in the communion of the Church of England as it stands distinguished from all Papal and Puritan innovations, and as it adheres to the doctrine of the Cross.' The Bishop had devoted a long life to the studies of his profession; the whole range of theology was open to him, but the Scriptures in their original languages, and the writings of the Fathers, were his familiar food—these he had thoroughly digested. The result is partly exhibited in his valuable work on the Eucharist, published in 1831, of which one of the most learned divines of the age remarked, that 'it reminded him so forcibly of the writings of the ancient Fathers, that he could often have imagined that they were still speaking.' The retiring modesty of the Bishop's character rendered him averse to appear before the public as an author; but on the few occasions when he was induced to break through that reserve, what he gave to the world bears the impress of sound judgment, ripe erudition, and deep and earnest piety. In 1826, he published a 'Friendly Address to the Episcopalians of Scotland on Baptismal Regeneration,' briefly tracing the authority and uniformity of the Church doctrine on that important subject. In the department of practical divinity he published, in 1828, ' Observations on the several Sunday Services throughout the Year'—a most admirable and useful manual, which no devout Christian can peruse without having his understanding informed, and his piety elevated. He was a living example of the intrinsic beauty and attractiveness of religion, as it may be developed through the Church system. It might, perhaps, be easy to find a divine as deeply learned, but seldom can the name of one be recorded who so thoroughly imbibed and exemplified the spirit of the blessed saints, whose works and history were the subjects of his study. The last book which the venerable Bishop had in his hand the evening before his death was the treatise of Christopher Sutton, ' Disce Mori—Learn to Die ' It was an art which the good man had been learning all his life long, and he had so learned it, that the 'last enemy' had no terrors for him. He remarked to a friend a few days previous to his decease, that he was waiting his call, not impatiently, yet longing for it: it did not, therefore, come suddenly. Death was to him but the removal of the veil which divided him from a world in which he had for years ' habitually dwelt in heart and mind.' On Thursday, 5th July, the remains of the Bishop were deposited, according to his own desire, in the grave of his brother, in the church-yard of Turriff, in presence of a numerous assemblage of the clergy, and of the people of his late flock at Fraserburgh, as well as of the Episcopal congregation at Turriff, of which he had at one time been pastor. The services were read by the Right Rev. Bishop Skinner, assisted by the Rev. James Walker of Huntly, Dean of Moray." An elegant monument is erected to Bishop Jolly's memory within the chapel at Fraserburgh, the appropriate inscription on which it is said was written by Lord Medwyn.

At the death of Bishop Jolly the diocese of Moray was annexed to the united diocese of Ross and Argyll, and placed under the episcopal jurisdiction of Bishop Low, conjoined as the united dioceses of Moray, Ross, and Argyll The valuable theological library of Bishop Jolly, which long before his death he had made over to the Church, only reserving the use of it during his lifetime, was removed to Edinburgh, and is under the immediate superintendence of the Professor of Divinity.

On the 22d of August 1838, a General Synod was held at Edinburgh of the Bishops, Deans, and Delegates of the several dioceses, to enact and ratify a Canon "for establishing and maintaining a Society in aid of the Church." This was the foundation of the Scottish Episcopal Church Society, and the special Canon constituting it is the 40th in the Code of Canons. To no one is the Society more indebted than to the Rev. E. B. Ramsay, the Secretary, who from the commencement devoted his talents, influence, and services, to promote its interests with the most unwearied and unabated ardour. The Thirty-Fourth Canon of that Synod also renders it imperative on the Bishops to hold an Episcopal Synod annually at such time and place as the majority of them shall appoint. In the meantime the Bishops, as Trustees of the Pantonian and other funds, meet in Edinburgh every year on the first Wednesday of September. In each successive year matters of difficulty may be thus referred to the Bishops in Synod assembled for their consideration and counsel, and matters of discipline can at the same time be presented, by appeal or otherwise, as the Canons direct, to be then duly considered and determined, in conformity with the canon law, constitution, and uniform practice of the Church.

The Fortieth Canon, enacted by the Ecclesiastical Synod of Edinburgh, is to the following effect:—"Whereas in the Primitive Church, and by apostolic order, collections were made for the poorer brethren, and for the propagation of the gospel, it is hereby decreed that a similar practice shall be observed in the Scottish Episcopal Church. Nor ought the poverty of the Church, or of any portion of it, to be pleaded as an objection, seeing that the divine commendation is given equally to those who, from their poverty, give a little with cheerfulness, and to those who give largely of their abundance. For this purpose, a Society, called the SCOTTISH EPISCOPAL CHURCH SOCIETY, shall be formed, the objects of which shall be, 1*st*, To provide a fund for aged or infirm clergymen, or salaries for their assistants, and general aid for congregations struggling with pecuniary difficulties. 2*d*, To assist candidates for the ministry in completing their theological studies. 3*d*, To provide Episcopal schoolmasters, books, and tracts for the poor. 4*th*, To assist in the formation or enlargement of diocesan libraries. To promote these important purposes, a certain day shall be fixed upon annually by every Diocesan Synod, when a collection shall be made in every chapel throughout the diocese, and the nature and object of the Society in reference to the existing wants of the Church, shall be explained to the people."

The design of this Society—an association of the utmost importance in the peculiar circumstances of the Church, and the want of which was long severely felt, is forcibly expressed in one of the first printed circulars addressed to the subscribers in 1838, and signed by the Rev. E. B. Ramsay.

"This Society having been lately constituted in Edinburgh at a public meeting, the Right Rev. the Primus in the chair, the General Committee are desirous of laying before the friends of the Church a short statement of some of the causes which have led to its formation, and of the objects which it is intended to accomplish.

"Those who judge of Episcopacy in Scotland from what they observe in the large towns, will form a most incorrect estimate of its condition in some of the country districts. In fact, the Scottish Episcopal Church has in different parts, for many years, been suffering under the pressure of extreme poverty. It is proposed that, by the next general meeting of the Society, a more particular *detail* of the extent and circumstances of this poverty shall be laid before the public. Suffice it at present to state, that there are many Episcopalian congregations utterly unable, without aid, to contribute for their clergymen *the bare means of subsistence;* and some more permanent and efficient funds are now especially and imperatively called for in cases where the clergymen, either from sickness or old age, are unequal to the duties. In such instances an assistant is required, and for this arrangement many most respectable congregations are scarcely able to make a decent provision; some find it quite impossible. In the northern counties, where Episcopalians are numerous, the people are extremely poor, and of late years have experienced such difficulties in procuring the necessaries of life, that they cannot be supposed to have much to spare for ecclesiastical purposes This poverty is the more to be deplored, inasmuch as it has been found that so many excellent and highly respectable young men have been studying for the ministry, as to give a promise of a *rising* generation of useful, intelligent, devoted labourers in the Lord's vineyard. Their means for education, for procuring books, and for subsisting, before being placed in charges, are sadly limited, and their ultimate prospects sufficiently discouraging. In many parts of the country, also, the poor Episcopalian families have little means of educating their children according to the principles of their own faith, and hence the difficulty of providing Schoolmasters, of furnishing Bibles, Prayer-Books (Gaelic and English), Books for Education, Tracts, &c. has been severely felt by the clergy of those districts. From these and other similar considerations, the friends of the Church have frequently turned their attention to supplying some remedy for these deficiencies. The Scottish Episcopal Fund was raised in 1806 for the benefit of the Church, and a short extract from a report of its Trustees in 1830 will show how little it has effected, and how much is left to be done ; and it should be remembered also that this Fund is, by its constitution as well as means, precluded from giving aid in such cases as retired clergymen, students in divinity, repairs of chapels, schools, books, &c.

" ' It was a matter of deep concern to many of the laymen of the Scottish Episcopal Communion, to see their Bishops and pastors unable to support that decent rank in society, to which they were so justly entitled by their piety and learning, and which was so necessary to give weight to their ministrations. With a view to provide some permanent remedy for this great evil, several individuals formed themselves into a body in the year 1806, and exerted themselves to procure subscriptions both in England and Scotland for the purpose of establishing a fund, the interest of which, together with annual subscriptions, should be applied to make such moderate additions to the incomes of the Bishops, and of the most necessitous of the clergy, as might, in some degree, relieve them from the extreme pecuniary distress to which they had so long submitted, without murmur or complaint.

" ' At present there are many of the Episcopal clergy in Scotland whose situation certainly demands some permanent assistance, but whose claims, however necessitous, the Trustees have been obliged, from want of funds, to reject altogether; and hitherto they have not been able, in any instance, even of the most urgent necessity, to raise their annual allowances to any inferior clergyman higher than the pittance of L.15.'

" In 1832 the Gaelic Episcopal Society was instituted for the purpose of supplying some of these necessities, but its operation was too limited, and it has now merged into the Scottish Episcopal Church Society—

an association which has been constituted under the sanction and authority of the whole Church, and which, it is earnestly hoped, will meet with the support and sympathy of every congregation, and every individual throughout the Church. There has somehow been an unaccountable apathy in members of our Church, generally speaking, toward its poverty and privations. In our community are found some of the wealthiest congregations in the country, and at the same time some of the poorest provisions for the clergy. It is the object of this Society, therefore, to unite *all* our congregations under Episcopal sanction and authority, in a benevolent association of Christians and of Churchmen; the objects shall be entirely ecclesiastical; and were *each individual* of the Church to make an offering from the means with which God has blessed him, and such an one as he might make *cheerfully* and without *inconvenience*, many of the evils now felt in different portions of the Church would be removed; and by relief from their pressure, it is humbly hoped that, under the Divine blessing, an increased efficiency would be imparted to the ministrations of the clergy."

The first Patron and Vice-Patrons of the Society may be here enumerated. Patron—His Grace Walter Duke of Buccleuch and Queensberry, K.G. Vice-Patrons—His Grace James Henry Robert Duke of Roxburghe, K.T , the Most Hon. John William Robert Marquis of Lothian,[*] the Right Hon. William George Earl of Erroll, the Right Hon. George Sholto Earl of Morton, the Right Hon. David Earl of Airlie, the Right Hon. Archibald John Earl of Rosebery, the Right Hon. James Andrew John Viscount Strathallan, the Right Hon. James Oconchar Lord Forbes. The first President was the Right Rev Bishop Walker, Primus of the Episcopal College; and the Vice-Presidents in the following order:—Right Rev. Bishop Torry, of Dunkeld, Dunblane, and Fife, Right Rev. Bishop Skinner, of Aberdeen, Right Rev. Bishop Low, of Moray, Ross, and Argyll, Right Rev. Bishop Russell, of Glasgow, Right Rev. Bishop Moir, of Brechin, Right Hon. Lord William Douglas, Hon. Lord Medwyn, Hon. Walter Forbes, Master of Forbes, Sir John Stuart Forbes, of Pitsligo Bart., Sir John Hope, Bart of Craighall, Sir James Ramsay, Bart. of Bamff, Sir James M. Riddell, Bart., of Ardnamurchan, Adam Duff, Esq., Sheriff of Edin-

---

[*] This Nobleman died in the prime of life in England in 1841.

burgh,* Colonel Fraser of Castle Fraser, Alexander Falconar, Esq., of Falcon Hall, near Edinburgh, W. E. Gladstone, Esq., M.P.† The General Committee, with power to form Sub-Committees, comprising the Episcopal Clergy of Scotland and all Sub-Committees, and a specified number of gentlemen, chiefly resident in Edinburgh.

The first public meeting of the Society was held in the Hopetoun Rooms, Queen Street, Edinburgh, on the 4th of December 1838, the Right Rev. Bishop Walker in the chair. It may be noticed that this was the last meeting of any kind which the Primus attended, and the last time he was out of his own residence before his death. Three Resolutions, proposed and unanimously adopted, were respectively moved and seconded by the Right Rev. Bishop Low and the Right Hon. the Earl of Morton, the Right Rev. Bishop Russell and George Forbes, Esq., the Very Rev. C. H. Terrot and Hercules Robertson, Esq , Advocate ‡ This Meeting, however, was only preliminary or preparatory, but, as it is officially stated, " considering how much was to be arranged and settled, it could not well be otherwise ;" and " it was desirable that the Society should be constituted without loss of time, in order that Diocesan Associations might be formed in due course, that they might deliberate upon the plans proposed, and thus the constitution of the Society be finally adjusted after full communication from every portion of the Church."

The stated Annual Meeting of the General Committee was held in the Hopetoun Rooms, Edinburgh, on the 4th of September 1839, the Right Rev. Bishop Skinner in the Chair. Bishops Low, Russell, Moir, Lord William Douglas, Alexander Falconar, Esq., of Falcon Hall, lay delegates from St Paul's and St John's, Edinburgh, the congregations at Leith, Portobello, Haddington, Kelso, and Alloa, a number of the clergy and laity, were present. The returns from the several dioceses were laid before the meeting, from which it appeared that the subscriptions, donations, annual contributions, collections, and congregational offerings, including L.710 from the Treasurer of the Gaelic Episcopal

* The worthy and much respected Sheriff Duff died in 1840
† Appointed Vice-President of the Board of Trade and Master of the Mint in 1841, and the author of the valuable work, " The Church in its Relation to the State," one vol. 8vo. 1840.
‡ Appointed Sheriff of Renfrewshire in 1842.

Society, amounted to very nearly L.4265, and making allowances for expenses, the sum of L.4000 was available to the purposes of the Society. The meeting then resolved to remit the appropriation of money for this year to a Sub-Committee, consisting of the Right Rev Bishops Skinner, Low, Russell, Moir, &c., with instructions to distribute a sum not exceeding L.1200, and of this to apply a sum not less than L 600, nor greater than L.700, *in aid of clerical incomes ;* the remainder of the L.1200 for other objects of the Society. The Sub-Committee met in the Episcopal Library, Hill Street, Edinburgh, on the following day, and grants were sanctioned amounting to L.1236.

The first stated Annual Meeting of the Society was held in the Hopetoun Rooms on the 4th of December 1839, the Right Rev. Bishop Low in the chair, supported by Bishop Russell, the Earl of Morton, Viscount Milton, Lord Berriedale, Archdeacon Williams, Hon and Rev. J. Sandilands, Sir William Scott, Bart. of Ancrum, General Sir George Leith, Bart., Sir Charles Bell, K H., Colonel Blanshard, C.B., Captain Hunter, H.E.I.C.S., and numbers of the clergy and influential laity. The Right Rev. Bishop Low, after constituting the meeting by the prayers appointed in the regulations, thus briefly addressed the meeting :—" You are all acquainted with the objects of the Society whose interests we have met to forward, and I have only to bear my humble testimony that in my diocese it has been the means of gladdening many sequestered glens and the lonely islands of the Scottish sea. The Secretary will now lay before you the first Annual Report of the Society, and I am satisfied that it will prove to you a source of high gratification. I feel it necessary to restrict myself to a very few words, in consequence of the very important business which is to come before you."

The Report was then read by the Rev. E. B. Ramsay, the Secretary, and as it is a document of considerable importance, containing a complete and luminous statement of the formation, object, and operations of the Society, it is considered proper to incorporate it with the present work.

" On presenting the First General Report of the Scottish Episcopal Church Society, the Committee are desirous of placing before the Subscribers and the Church at large an account of the progress which has been made in following out the benevolent purposes originally contemplated in its formation, and at the same time of explaining the principles on which it is proposed to act in its future proceedings. In order to make their statement in as compendious a form as the circumstances may admit of, they arrange the materials of this Report under three separate heads: 1. To exhibit the objects of the Society. 2. Its constitution; and, 3 The progress which it has made.

"1. The objects of the Society have been already sufficiently defined by the 40th Canon, under which it is constituted. They are thus described in the Canon itself:—'1st, To provide a fund for aged or infirm clergymen, or salaries for their assistants, and general aid for congregations struggling with pecuniary difficulties; 2dly, To assist candidates for the ministry in completing their theological studies; 3dly, To provide Episcopal schoolmasters with books and tracts for the poor; 4thly, To assist in the formation or enlargement of diocesan libraries.' The operation of this Society, therefore, may be considered as an attempt to supply our Church with some of the advantages which have been secured to the Church of England by its various endowments, and by its active religious associations,—by Queen Anne's Bounty, the Societies for Promoting Christian Knowledge, for Church Building, for Education of the Children of the Poor, for providing additional Curates in large and poor Parishes, and by the associates of the late Dr Bray for providing libraries for the clergy, &c. In a Church unestablished and unendowed, a society like this is the only means we have for supplying the numerous deficiencies under which we labour, and an appeal is now made for its support, under the full confidence that ultimately these desired ends and objects will be attained.

"The Committee, however, are far from considering all the objects of the Society as equally important, or as requiring an equal share of the funds. Perhaps the order in which they stand in the Canon marks their comparative importance; at any rate, they consider the objects in the first clause of the Canon as those most urgently demanding attention; and they refer particularly to the 5th Regulation of the Society, *explanatory* of that clause, which is, that 'the principal object, to be included 'under general aid for congregations struggling with pecuniary difficulties,' shall be, to assist them in furnishing the incumbent with such an income as may be, in the opinion of the Committee of the Society, sufficient for his support.' They would rejoice in the Society attaining such success as might enable them to rescue the

Church from the depressing effects of that poverty which now exists in some portions of it,—a poverty which no one can have witnessed without perceiving the many evils which it produces, and the many impediments which it often throws in the way of ministerial usefulness. By the statistical returns appended to this Report, it will be seen that of thirty-two incumbencies described, not one has reached L.80 yearly; that many are under L.40; and that in several the incomes strictly derived from the congregations have been *merely nominal*; that they have besides various local difficulties to contend with, and expenses to incur, which they are little able to bear, from the necessity of travelling great distances in visiting their scattered flocks, and of attending Diocesan Synods, and such other assemblies of their brethren, at which the Bishop, in consequence of some unexpected emergency, may require their presence. Besides these, there are upwards of ten incumbencies of which the stipends vary from L.80 to about L.100; but where the incomes are by no means permanent or secure, and where great difficulties are frequently experienced in providing for the necessary expenditure, and in keeping up the decent performance of divine service. Returns from the northern districts of the Church, where the Society's schools have been established, represent the poverty of the Episcopalian families as extreme—that many are unable to pay even the penny a-week required for the school-fees, and yet are exceedingly desirous of education for their children. One very painful consequence of this poverty must be apparent—the utter incapacity of providing, in addition, a salary for an assistant when the incumbent is compelled, by age, sickness, or infirmity, to discontinue the whole or part of the duty. It has been the chief object of the Committee this year to assist those among the clergy who have been lowest in the scale of income. They have appropriated about L.700 to that purpose, distributed among thirty-two incumbents, to bring up their incomes to L.80 each, and have aided Congregations in procuring *assistants* to the extent of L.125.

"2. The second object contemplated by the Canon is, ' To assist candidates for the ministry in completing their theological studies.' With reference to future proceedings in this department, the Committee are desirous of correcting a possible misapprehension which may arise on this head of expenditure. They have no intention of turning any portion of the funds of the Society towards general educational purposes, nor would they, by undue encouragement, induce a greater number of young men to enter the ministry than are ever likely to be provided for in it. But as they cannot avoid the conclusion that facilities for right professional training and sound theological knowledge bear directly upon ministerial efficiency, they are desirous that the Society should contribute something towards that important end. These two principles they would always keep in view, viz., 1st, To give no aid except to students *bona fide* of theology; and, 2dly, To take such security as they may deem proper, under the circumstances, that should the student change his purpose the money expended by the Society shall be repaid. The children and relatives of Scottish Episcopal clergymen themselves may often be disposed to look to the ministry of their own Church as their profession. This is a class of students especially likely to need assistance, and at the same time possessing a strong claim upon our sympathies. By the 6th Canon of our Church, in ordinary cases—' All candidates for the ministry are required to produce a certificate of their having attended at least one course of the lectures of the Pantonian Professor of Theology, and of our Professor of Ecclesiastical History in Edinburgh' Now, as both these Professors are to be attended in Edinburgh, journeys from the country, and residence in the capital for the session, may in many cases involve expenses which are inconvenient. Some assistance, therefore, at that period may be of the utmost consequence, and by awarding it according to the recommendation of the Professor, his authority and influence with the students may be preserved and strengthened. It might be of much service also in the same cause, were the Society to endow bursaries or scholarships as a reward of diligence, good conduct, and proficiency in study, to be awarded to those who shall be approved in these points by the Professors. The Committee have this year granted L.55 to theological students.

"3. The third object stated in the Canon, viz., ' The support of schools for the education of the children of the poor,' although an object intimately connected with the inculcation of sound, moral, and religious principles, cannot, however, under present circumstances, be fully carried out, nor is it the intention of the Committee to attempt an universal system of education, purely episcopal, for the poor of their communion. There are cases, however, in the Highland districts especially, where the supply of schoolmasters is so scanty, and the schools so distant and difficult of access, as to render education itself one of the greatest boons that can be conferred. Upon this feeling, the ' Gaelic Episcopal Society' for some years supported three schools; one at Highfield, one at Balachelish, and one at Arpafeelie, by returns from which it appears that there is an average attendance of 300 children. These returns, attested by the clergymen, bear witness to the benefits conferred by the schools upon the congregations to which they are attached. Keeping in view the same principles, the Committee of this Society, to which the funds of the Gaelic Episcopal Society devolved, have resolved to maintain these schools, and have added to them some others, especially four in the city of Glasgow, it having been the decided opinion of the clergy there, that nothing, under divine aid, would be more likely to benefit the families of the poor Episcopalians generally than attention to the early religious training of the children.* The annual expenditure of the Society for schools would thus be about L.130.

"Under this division of objects contemplated by the Canon are included 'books and tracts for the poor;' and on this point the Committee have come to the resolution of issuing only Bibles, Testaments,

---

* At the public meeting held in Glasgow, April 10, 1839, for the formation of a Diocesan Association of this Society, the circumstances of spiritual destitution among the poor Episcopalians of that City were dwelt upon with much force by Mr Sheriff Alison and the Rev. Robert Montgomery. The following is an extract from the report of that Meeting:—

"According to a moderate estimate, upwards of 300 families from Airdrie, Monkland, Lanark, and other places in our own neighbourhood, apply annually to St Andrew's Chapel for the solemn services of the Church. Now, allowing five individuals to each family, here are 1500 souls totally destitute of clerical guidance, and virtually deprived of the blessing of public worship. Regarding Glasgow, according to Dr Cleland's Statistics for 1831, there were, of Episcopalians in the city, 3022; Barony Parish, 4450, Gorbals, 1079· total, 8551. The increase in seven years may be safely estimated at 1449, making the present total 10,000. Of these a large proportion are miserably poor, without the means, and, what is worse, without the inclination, of supplying themselves with spiritual instruction In Anderston there are at least 500 souls attached to the Episcopal Communion. Of these only fifty-four individuals are in the habit of attending any church, a large number of whom assign the want of clothing as the reason why they absent themselves. It has also been ascertained that many poor Protestant Episcopalian children have been attending a Roman Catholic school some time ago established in that burgh"

Prayer-Books, English or Gaelic, the Homilies, and such spelling-books or mere primers as the Committee shall unanimously approve. The Society have to acknowledge with deep gratitude a prompt and liberal reply to the Secretary's application to the venerable SOCIETY FOR PROMOTING CHRISTIAN KNOWLEDGE, by a grant of L.100 worth of Bibles, Testaments, and Prayer-Books, some of which are of the *largest* size of print, and are thus calculated to form desirable presents for the aged poor.

" 4. The last object referred to in the Canon, the formation and enlargement of diocesan libraries, may certainly be considered as the least urgent want, and will therefore be held as subordinate to the others; at the same time the Committee cannot but consider this as a strictly ecclesiastical object, and as intimately connected with the efficiency of the Church in general. With incomes so limited as those of many of our clergy, it must be a matter of great difficulty, if not sometimes impossible, to procure such books as, in a professional point of view, may be considered essential. Let it be remembered that in the present times, when the principles of Church polity and the doctrines of religion are so frequently discussed, theological books are the more required, and, at the same time, from the greatly increased demand, have risen in price. On these grounds it may be considered a subject for much congratulation that the foundation of a valuable theological library *has been* laid, and that such a possession is secured to the Church in perpetuity. The books, which were the property of the late venerable Bishop Jolly, are now deposited in a suitable house, No. 8, Hill Street, Edinburgh. The preservation and increase of this collection, as a library for general reference in theological studies, form a subject of great interest to the Scottish Episcopal Church at large, and especially on account of the students attending the Pantonian lectures.

" II. On the Constitution of the Society the Committee are desirous of making a few observations. Religious associations, with their machinery of public meetings, committees, reports, &c., although, comparatively speaking, novelties in the Christian Church, may in the present state of society be considered as indispensable elements of all great, useful, and benevolent undertakings. It cannot, however, be questioned that occasionally these associations may in their operation somewhat interfere with the full exercise of Episcopal discipline, and the due course of ecclesiastical order. Without adverting to the practice or the principles of any other Societies, the Committee would simply notice that the Scottish Episcopal Church Society possesses this excellency, and so far as is known this *peculiarity* in its constitution. It forms a part of the Canon law of the Church itself,* and whilst it calls for the aid and cooperation of the Laity as office-bearers, delegates, and members of Committee, still it is in all points strictly under the control of Episcopal jurisdiction. It may be considered as THE CHURCH acting through a Society, or the Church itself resolved into a Committee. From such a constitution, combining as it does the active operations of a society, with the strictest observance of the Church's authority, many advantages may be anticipated. A community of feeling between the clergy and the laity, in promoting the general objects of the Society, will extend itself beyond the limits of their own immediate congregations to the Church at large ; the Clergy will have, with their Bishops and among themselves, an additional bond of union, and additional opportunities of communication. All of us may thus exercise that common sympathy which as churchmen we should feel for the less affluent members, and endeavour to realise the beautiful picture of church unity drawn by the great Apostle, 1 Cor. xii. 25, 26, 'That there should be no schism in the body ; but that the members should have the same care one for another. And whether one member suffer, all the members suffer with it ; or one member be honoured, all the members rejoice with it.'

"III. The last subject on which the Committee have to report is the progress which has been made in fixing the rules and regulations of the Society, in organizing district committees and associations, and in raising the funds necessary for the purposes and objects contemplated. The Society was instituted Dec 4, 1838, at a public meeting of Episcopalians, called by advertisement, and held in the Hopetoun Rooms. The Primus, as President of the meeting, in the Chair :—

"'The meeting, which was held in the large hall, was one of the most numerous and respectable we ever remember to have witnessed.

"'The proceedings were opened by prayer, after which the Right Rev. Bishop Walker, Primus, rose and said—The object of the meeting, for

* " Canon XL of the Code of Canons of the Episcopal Church in Scotland "

which they were now assembled, was to establish the 'Scottish Episcopal Church Society,' as provided for in the 40th Canon of the Episcopal Church. The first object of this Society will be to provide for its poor and decayed clergymen, or salaries to their assistants, and general aid for congregations struggling with pecuniary difficulties—to assist candidates for the ministry in completing their theological studies—to provide Episcopal schoolmasters, books and tracts for the poor—and, lastly, to assist in the formation or enlargement of diocesan libraries. Now, the meeting was aware that these desirable objects were not to be obtained in their position without a direct appeal being made to their benevolence for voluntary contributions. It was true these claims and others were frequent, but they were indispensably necessary, and they had high scriptural authority for enforcing them, since it is found in the law of Moses, ' that the poor shall never cease out of the land,' and as recorded in Matthew, 25th chapter. And if it was the case that the poor were to be provided for, who, he would ask, had a greater claim on their sympathies, than those men who have devoted their whole time in the service of God ? The meeting were aware that their Church was not an established Church now—they were an unendowed Church—a mere tolerated Church—they were a Voluntary Church, and as a Voluntary Church they now confidently appealed to the Christian benevolence of their people in behalf of their poorer brethren ; but he must say, that though he belonged to a Voluntary Church, he was sure he spoke the sentiments of his brethren now present, when he disclaimed, in the strongest possible manner, any communion of feeling with those persons calling themselves Voluntaries, who were constantly pouring forth fierce attacks upon the Established Church, and were sowing political divisions and animosities throughout the community. With such Voluntaries the Episcopal Church had no community of feeling—the Episcopalians have no feelings of hostility towards the Established Church. In conclusion, he was quite sure that when their case was fully made known to the meeting, it would be speedily answered, and as the poor of the land were a part of God's family, he therefore made the present appeal, confident that it would not be in vain.'*

" The Rules and Regulations, as they now stand, were finally agreed

* From the Edinburgh Courant of December 5, 1838.

upon at the meeting of General Committee, held in Edinburgh, September 4, 1839, when a Sub-Committee was appointed to make a distribution of funds for the first year.

" In reporting upon the pecuniary resources of the Society, and printing the list of donations and subscriptions for the first year, the Committee have upon the whole a pleasing and satisfactory duty to perform. The *donations* this year, including six of L.100 each, have amounted to about L.1900 ; the *annual subscriptions* to about L.500. In some instances they have certainly not met with encouragement equal to their expectations The Committee would attribute this to the circumstance of the objects of the Society not being yet sufficiently known. They have good hope that as these become better understood, the Society will meet with a corresponding support from *all* the members of the Church.

" By the 40th Canon it is enacted that ' a certain day shall be fixed upon annually, by every Diocesan Synod, when a collection shall be made in every chapel throughout the Diocese, and the nature and object of the Society, in reference to the existing wants of the Church, shall be explained to the people '

" The advantage of this arrangement is, that *every one* has an opportunity of contributing towards the objects of the Society. The result of those congregational offerings for the first year has been exceedingly gratifying. They have produced in all about L 1000. But the Committee are desirous of pressing on the attention of churchmen, that the usefulness and success of the Society must depend upon the regularity and permanency of its annual income. This will be derived from interest of stock, annual subscriptions, and chiefly from congregational offerings. Should these fall away to any extent, the result must be a failure of the whole scheme, and the disappointment of those who have looked to the Society for relief and assistance ; on the other hand, were the means at the disposal of the Committee to be enlarged, it is impossible to estimate the extent of benefit which might be conferred upon the Church.

" The Committee have received very gratifying encouragement from Prelates of the Church of England. The claims made upon them for ecclesiastical and benevolent objects within their own Dioceses are numerous ; notwithstanding which, the Archbishop of Canterbury has become a subscriber of L.20 annually, the Bishop of London of L.10 annually, the Bishops of Winchester and Chester of three guineas annually, and the Bishop of Lincoln is a donor of L.10, as he had previously been to the Gaelic Episcopal Society. Some liberal donations and subscriptions have been received from laymen of the Church of England, and an earnest of assistance from the Universities, in an annual contribution of L.10 from the Master and Fellows of Magdalene College, Oxford.

"Such, then, is a plain statement of the objects, constitution, and progress of the Scottish Episcopal Church Society The plan is still an experiment, and it remains to be proved whether the Society will be enabled to produce those beneficial results which are anticipated from its operation. When great and unusual exertions are made by every denomination of Christians in the land to strengthen and extend the sphere of their own usefulness, it seems but a reasonable expectation that the Scottish Episcopal Church should receive the aid of all who love the cause of primitive truth and order, toward removing some of the difficulties and privations under which many of her ministers have long suffered, and suffered with patience. In proof that this Society is *required*, and rightly demands regular and cheerful contributions from all the members of the Church, the Committee confidently appeal to the statement of incomes on which the clergy have to support a becoming and respectable appearance in the world, and to educate their families. It is fondly hoped that for them better days are approaching. The Society has commenced under favourable auspices, and the contributions raised in the first year of its formation are, it is believed, a guarantee for a regular and efficient support for the time to come.

"This is, strictly speaking, a *Home Church Society*, intended to supply deficiencies, and to correct evils which have been long felt, but too long neglected. When it is said that the specific claims of our own Church have hitherto been overlooked, in the general career of Christian benevolence, no invidious comparison is intended. The home and the foreign labours are equally Christian duties, and thus, while all our Members are called upon to unite in aiding a Society of which the express object is the benefit and prosperity of the Church at home, congregations are left to follow out their own views, or the suggestions of their respective pastors, for regulating and directing their encouragement and pecuniary contributions towards foreign missions. Every believer is unquestionably called upon to contribute of his abundance towards strengthening the hands of those who, under the sanction and direction of the Church, are preaching to the heathen 'the unsearchable riches of Christ.' But no less imperatively is every Christian called upon to aid and co-operate in a plan which has for its object the efficiency of *his own* Church, struggling with poverty which a very little exertion from each would relieve, and more especially when called upon to do so according to a method approved by her Bishops, and required by her Canons. The words of the blessed Redeemer to the Jews (Luke xi. 42) are well calculated to impress upon our minds our Christian duty and obligation in this particular—' These things ought ye to have done, and not leave the others undone.'"

The principal speakers at this first meeting of the Society were, James Strange, Esq., who moved the adoption of the Report; the Rev. Daniel Bagot, of St James' Chapel, Edinburgh; the Rev. Robert Montgomery, of St Jude's, Glasgow; the Right Rev. Bishop Terrot, of St Paul's Chapel, Edinburgh, then Dean of the Diocese; Adam Urquhart, Esq., Advocate; and the Right Rev. Bishop Russell. Mr Urquhart, in moving the third resolution, said, " That as a layman he had great pleasure in moving this resolution, because it reminded them all of their obligations to fulfil those duties which had been so eloquently and so ably enforced by his reverend friends. Respecting that duty he had only to say, that it had not escaped the notice of the friends of the Church before the formation of this Society—that thirty years ago, this duty had been well considered by certain pious and holy men, who now rested from their labours He trusted that he was not presumptuous in thus speaking of such men as Lord Dunsinnan, as Mr Justice Park, as Mr Bowdler, as Sir William Forbes, the father of his excellent friend Mr George Forbes, now on the platform. Those men, seeing with grief the necessities under which ministers of the Church were labouring, formed a Society, the objects of which were in some respects similar to the present one. That Society was the Scottish Episcopal Fund, which still existed, and had been found to co-operate very effectually with this Society." Mr Urquhart then said, " That there were two objections which he had heard urged respecting this Society in connection with that Fund The first was, What was the need of the Society when the Fund was in existence? The second was, Why continue the Fund, now that the Society had commenced? To the first of these objections he answered, that of the four objects proposed by the Society, the Fund only partially embraced one; and that was the providing of an increase of stipend for ministers in destitute districts; and what was most important to notice, *it could give no relief except to clergymen actually officiating*, and was thus precluded from promoting one most essential object of the new Society, viz. providing for the subsistence of Clergymen who have been compelled, by age or infirmity, to retire from the discharge of duty. Besides this, it could take no account whatever of the other objects of this Society, viz. assisting students in theology, providing Episcopal teachers for poor children, and forming diocesan libraries for the clergy. Then, with regard to the other objection, Why was not the support of the fund discontinued when the Society commenced? he answered, because the Society had altogether left out of view the principal object contemplated by the Fund, namely, to make some provision for the College of Bishops. No Episcopalian would deny that this was an object of vast importance, yet it was omitted by the Society; and all that the Trustees of the Fund could raise for them, he blushed to mention it, was sixty guineas per annum. He could well understand, however, how this important object had been left out of the views of the Society. It was formed under the sanction of a Canon of the Church; that Canon must have been framed by the very reverend fathers the Bishops; and they, with their accustomed disinterestedness, had overlooked their own claims and their own rights in their anxiety to administer to the relief of the suffering clergy. He had only to mention, that the two Societies did not injure each other; on the contrary, the more the Society flourished, the more would the fund be able to fulfil its principal object; for the Society would then take the relief of the clergy into its own hands, and leave the Trustees of the Fund free to give a more becoming allowance to the College of Bishops."

In the Episcopal Synod, composed of the Bishops, at the usual annual meeting held at Edinburgh in September 1839, a Pastoral Letter to all the members of the Church was prepared, ordered to be printed, and read to all the congregations by the officiating clergy after the forenoon service on a certain Sunday, as appointed by the Bishops in their respective dioceses. This Pastoral Letter bears internal evidence to have been the composition of Bishop Walker, and is written in his usual energetic and zealous manner.

In 1840, a very important act affecting the Scottish Episcopal Church was passed by Parliament, and received the Royal Assent on the 23d of July, by which the communion with the Church of England is rendered more intimate. It is entitled, "An Act to make certain Provisions and Regulations in respect to the exercise within England and Ireland, of their office by the Bishops and Clergy of the Protestant Episcopal Church in Scotland, and also to extend such provisions and regulations to the Bishops and Clergy of the Protestant Episcopal Church in the United States of America; and also to make further Regulations for the Bishop and Clergy other than those of the United Church of England and Ireland." By the act repealing the Penal Laws in 1792, the clergy of Scottish ordination were prohibited from officiating in England, but this act 4 Victoria in 1840 completely recognizes the Scottish Episcopal Church *as a Church*, draws her closely into connection with the Church of England, and sanctions the diocesan authority of the Bishops. The act contains seven clauses, and the benefits of it extend to the Bishops and clergy of the Church in the United States 1. The Bishop of any diocese in England or Ireland is empowered, on the application of a Scottish Bishop, or of any clergyman of the Scottish Episcopal Church ordained by a Scottish Bishop, to grant under his hand permission to such a clergyman to perform divine service, preach, and administer the sacraments, for any one or two Sundays, the days and places of worship to be stated in the permission. 2. Permission is not to be granted unless on production by the party of letters recommendatory, dated within six months before, under hand and seal, if he be a Bishop, from two Bishops, and if he be a priest, from a Bishop within his district, and also a testimonial, dated, signed, &c by the like parties, to the effect that the applicant is a person of honest life and godly conversation, professing the doctrines of the Church of England and Ireland. 3. This provision is extended to the clergy of the United States 4. Certain penalties are incurred by the clergy of England and Ireland who allow persons to officiate otherwise than in terms of the preceding clauses. 5. A Scottish clergyman violating the regulation forfeits L.50 to Queen Anne's Bounty, recoverable

in the Court of Session. 6. No one who has been ordained by a Protestant Bishop *not* of the Church of England or Ireland, and is, after the date of the act, ordained by a Bishop of England or Ireland, can officiate in England or Ireland except as above. 7. Appointments in contravention are void. The Bill was read a first time on Thursday the 18th of June, when it was presented by the Archbishop of Canterbury, and a second time on the 22d of June. On the 25th of that month it was again brought before the House of Lords, on the motion of the Archbishop of Canterbury to go into committee. On that occasion his Grace said—" In order to show to your Lordships the grounds upon which the Bill is considered desirable by the members of the Scottish Episcopal Church, I shall read to your Lordships an extract from the Register of the Episcopal College of that Church. It is thus:—
' The proposed modification of the statute of 1792 would prove beneficial to Scottish Episcopal ministers, inasmuch as it would remove a ground of misapprehension, from which inferences are drawn very much to their disadvantage. From their not being allowed to officiate in England, it is concluded by the great body of their countrymen, and suspected, it may be, by some of their own persuasion, that there must be a defect in their clerical authority—that their orders are not valid—that they are not clergymen in the proper sense.' I wish also, my Lords, to call your Lordships' attention to the following extracts from a letter addressed to me by a Scottish Bishop, for the purpose of showing that the Bill is satisfactory to himself and his brethren. He says—
' My Lord Archbishop—Permit me to offer my sincere acknowledgments for the great kindness you have shown to the Scottish Episcopal Church, by bringing forward the Bill which your Grace recently laid on the table of the House of Lords.—Our object was rather to establish the important principle of Catholicity among Protestant Episcopal Churches, than to gratify any vain or aspiring feeling in reference to our personal importance, in being permitted to appear in the established churches of the South. We, therefore, consider the permission as sufficiently ample. Two Sundays, with the power of renewing the permission, will meet with all the occasions of any clergyman from Scotland Our interesting duties keep us at home; and we have reason to thank God that our labours, joined to our peaceable habits, our sound doctrines, and our admirable Liturgy, are not in vain. The boon about to be conferred

on us will add to our strength, while it will increase our respectability; for it will remove a cloud which seemed to darken the countenance of our mother Church, and will place us in a position more advantageous than we have enjoyed since the years 1715 and 1745, when attachment to a falling cause brought on our fathers the ban of an angry law.' Your Lordships will perceive from these opinions that this Bill is highly approved of where approval is most to be desired; and I therefore anticipate that it will meet with your Lordships' concurrence." On the 26th of June some amendments were reported, and the bill ordered to be engrossed; and, on the 29th, it was read a third time, and sent to the Commons. On the 10th of July it was returned from the Commons, agreed to, with amendments, and those of the Commons considered and approved. On the 23d of July it received the Royal Assent.

In 1840 died the venerable Bishop Gleig at his residence in Stirling, on the 9th of March, in the eighty-seventh year of his age. He was ordained in 1773, and was in the thirty-second year of his episcopate. For some years previous to his decease Bishop Gleig had been compelled by the infirmities of age to retire from active life, and the termination of his course may be described as an event which had for a considerable time been almost daily expected. Dr Gleig was one of the most eminent men of his day, and as a scholar, a theologian, a metaphysician, and a critic, his name stood for more than sixty years among the most distinguished of his contemporaries in England and Scotland. He was the author of numerous treatises on morals, metaphysics, and theology, which at the time of publication acquired great celebrity, and his edition of Stackhouse's " History of the Bible" is itself a monument of his extensive reading, profound research, and just discrimination of historical and theological details. Bishop Gleig's name is farther identified with the literature of his country by his connection with the " Encyclopædia Britannica," of the third edition of which he was the editor, completed in 1797, in eighteen volumes, and of some of the most elaborate articles in which he was the author. Among these may be mentioned the History of Ethics, forming part of Moral Philosophy and Theology. "In this edition," says Mr Macvey Napier, " it [the Encyclopædia Britannica] rose greatly above its former level, and that in fields of speculation and research which lie far out of the ordinary paths of inquiry. In proof of this it is only necessary to mention its admirable treatise on General or Philosophical Grammar; its copious survey of Metaphysics by the late Right Reverend Dr Gleig; its profound articles on Mythology, Mysteries, and Philology, by the late Dr Doig;* and its elaborate view of the Philosophy of Induction by the late Professor Robison.† The powers thus displayed in speculative philosophy and ancient erudition were, however, more than equalled by the other contributions of the last mentioned writer in the wide field of physical science. Though his accession did not take place till the edition had advanced to the thirteenth volume, the number and value of these contributions were such as strongly to attract the attention of the scientific world, and the very high place which they then took they still in a great measure maintain in its estimation. Shortly before, the work had been committed, owing to the death of the editor, Mr Macfarquhar, to the direction of Dr Gleig, and to this occurrence Professor Robison's accession, and its important consequences, would seem to be owing."‡ In private life Bishop Gleig was kind, generous, of unbounded hospitality; and his mind, until age prevailed in a great measure over his faculties, was singularly vigorous during a long life of activity, zeal, and ardour. His son, the Rev. G. R. Gleig, M.A., author of "The Subaltern," &c., and Chaplain of Chelsea Hospital, is too well known in the various departments of literature to require any encomium.

A year had not elapsed after the death of Bishop Gleig, when he was followed to the grave by the Right Rev. Dr Walker, Bishop of Edinburgh, Primus of the Church, and Professor of Divinity. This lamented event occurred at his residence in Edinburgh on the 5th of March 1841, in the seventy-first year of his age. The following notice of Bishop Walker appeared shortly after his death,§ and is so eloquently expressed that no apology is necessary for transferring it to these pages:—" This distinguished person has been long respected, not less on account of his public station than for the influence of his character as a private individual. Having passed through the regular course of a Scottish College

* Dr Doig was master of the Grammar School of Stirling, and was the intimate friend of Bishop Gleig.

† Professor Robison, of the University of Edinburgh, was another distinguished friend of Bishop Gleig.

‡ Preface to edition of the Encyclopædia Britannica, completed in 1842, p. xvi.

§ Edinburgh Evening Courant, Saturday, March 12, 1841.

[Aberdeen], he entered the University of Cambridge [St John's College] as a freshman, where, after residing the usual number of terms, he took the several degrees in Arts   Upon his return to his native country in 1793 he devoted himself to literature, as sub-editor of the Encyclopædia Britannica, the third edition of which was then passing through the press under the auspices of Bishop Gleig. While in this employment he contributed many valuable articles to that national work, and also exercised, in the frequent absence of his friend, a general superintendence over the whole publication. At this period, too, he gave to the world several tracts and discourses, but without his name, considering himself too young to be justified in inviting public attention to his opinions in an avowed discussion on controverted subjects. Being induced towards the close of the century to go abroad as tutor to a young Baronet [Sir John Hope, Bart. of Craighall], he spent two or three years on the Continent, where, as he enjoyed the society of some of the most distinguished men in Germany, he made himself acquainted with the principles of their philosophy, more especially of those transcendental speculations which at that epoch occupied the minds of metaphysical inquirers. The article on the system of Kant, inserted in the Supplement to the Encyclopædia, was the fruit of his researches while resident at Weimar. But as his heart was chiefly attached to the profession he had chosen, he had no sooner attained the order of priesthood, than he settled in Edinburgh as minister of St Peter's Chapel—a charge which he held till ill health compelled him to relinquish its more active duties. On the death of Bishop Sandford, in January 1839, he was unanimously elected his successor as superintendent of the Episcopal congregations in the district of Edinburgh; and on the resignation of Bishop Gleig he was chosen by his brethren to be their head or president under the ancient title of Primus. In discharging the duties thus devolved upon him, added to those of Divinity Professor, he found full employment for his time; and, though impeded in his exertions by an increasing infirmity of body, he bent the whole vigour of his mind, which mercifully continued unimpaired till the last hour, to the discharge of the weighty obligations connected with his office. But amidst all his avocations his favourite pursuit was theology, in which he had read much, and systematized his knowledge with great success. Hence his conversation was always found exceedingly instructive, and strangers more especially, who knew not his habits of close study, were surprised at the richness of the professional learning which flowed from his lips. On such occasions, too, it might be perceived that, to a considerable ardour of temperament derived from nature, he joined the utmost placidity of manner, the effect of a sincere benevolence, and of an extensive intercourse with good society; and it may be confidently asserted that, though resolute in maintaining his own principles, both political and religious, he never cherished an angry feeling even against those who differed with him the most widely. To the scenes of domestic life, and the duties of personal piety, belong a sacredness with which a stranger ought not to intermeddle. In these respects Bishop Walker taught by example as well as by precept; and those who knew him best will ever have the highest opinion of his character, and particularly of that rare consistency between profession and practice which showed that the former had its seat in the heart. He was beloved by his friends, highly respected by the clergy under his inspection, and venerated by the whole body of the Church over which he presided." Bishop Walker published, in 1829, a valuable volume, entitled "Sermons on Various Subjects and Occasions," and subsequently a few Charges to his clergy. He was interred in the burying-ground of St John's Episcopal Chapel, on the south side of the edifice, where a tombstone marks his grave, and an elegant marble monument is erected to his memory by subscription within the Chapel, on the north wall, near that of Bishop Sandford.

The death of Bishop Walker caused a vacancy in the diocese of Edinburgh, and the presbyters, having received their mandate for an election, unanimously chose the Very Rev. Charles Hughes Terrot, D.D., formerly Fellow of Trinity College, Cambridge, for several years Bishop Walker's colleague in St Peter's Chapel, to be his successor. Bishop Terrot was consecrated in St Andrew's Chapel, Aberdeen, on Wednesday, the 2d of June 1841, by Bishops Skinner, Torry, Low, Russell, and Moir. The consecration sermon was preached by the Hon. and Rev. Grantham Yorke, one of the ministers of St Paul's Chapel, Edinburgh, and was afterwards published. After the consecration the Bishops met to choose a Primus of the Episcopal College, when the Right Rev. Bishop Skinner of Aberdeen was unanimously elected to preside over the Church, and the Right Rev. Bishop Terrot was appointed interim Professor of Divinity. On the high reputation of

Bishop Terrot it would be superfluous to dilate. Distinguished as a scholar, biblical critic, and theologian of the first order, the choice of the presbyters of Edinburgh could not have fallen on one more eminently qualified to be the successor of Bishop Walker. As it respects Bishop Skinner, his election as Primus auspiciously commenced with the union of St Paul's congregation in Aberdeen to the Church, and the schism of "independent chapels" is now happily extinct in that district.

In 1842, the members of the Episcopal College in Scotland consisted of the following Bishops, the dates of whose consecrations are prefixed :

1816. Right Rev. WILLIAM SKINNER, D D , Bishop of ABERDEEN and PRIMUS.
1808. Right Rev. PATRICK TORRY, D D , Bishop of DUNKELD, DUNBLANE, and FIFE.
1819. Right Rev. DAVID LOW, LL.D., Bishop of MORAY, Ross, and ARGYLL.
1837. Right Rev. MICHAEL RUSSELL, D D C L , Bishop of GLASGOW.
1837. Right Rev. DAVID MOIR, D D , Bishop of BRECHIN.
1841. Right Rev. CHARLES H. TERROT, D D , Bishop of EDINBURGH.

In September 1842, when Her Majesty Queen Victoria and His Royal Highness Prince Albert visited Scotland, the Bishops transmitted the usual loyal addresses to their sovereign and her illustrious consort, which were graciously received. These addresses were universally admired for the appropriateness of the phraseology and the simplicity of expression. In the one to her Majesty, the boon conferred on the Church by the Act of 1840 was duly acknowledged, and sectarian or political criticism was silent on this occasion. The Church, however, did not escape a furious attack from a well known party in the Presbyterian Establishment. In conformity with the will of the Sovereign, who wished to pass her first Sunday in Scotland in the strictest privacy, expressly declared on most undoubted authority from the time when the Royal Visit was first contemplated, weeks before it was known to the public, the Rev. E. B. Ramsay, of St John's Chapel, of whose congregation the Noble Family of Buccleuch are members, performed divine service, and preached before the Queen in Dalkeith Palace. This was construed by the newspapers belonging to that party as an insult to the Establishment, and they could see nothing else but an attempt to replace the Episcopal Church as the legal and national Church. The bitterness and hatred they evinced in their opinions on the subject are rarely displayed in honourable controversy, and probably they felt more poignant by their knowledge of the fact that all these attacks would fall utterly harmless. As the event was sufficiently discussed by the press at the time, it is unnecessary to dwell upon it in the present work, or to enter into the controversy which it originated. The harsh names, the furious tirades, and the gross misrepresentations with which the Church was assailed, simply because the most eminent and eloquent of her presbyters, a clergyman of the Church of England, conducted the devotions of his Sovereign, sufficiently indicate the enmity which is cherished towards the Scottish Episcopal Church within the Presbyterian Establishment, and at once proclaim to the clergy and laity who are their inveterate and relentless foes. Prejudices may be understood and even forgiven, religious principles, however erroneous or mistaken, may be defended with a zeal and honesty such as may cause the respect of those opposed to them, and the high ground of controversy on important points of doctrine and church government may be maintained without party bitterness and personal attack; but mean, unfair, and false misrepresentations, wilful and deliberate perversions of facts, unfounded jealousies, and angry invectives, will be considered by every Christian mind as displaying a feeling which cannot be mistaken, and which seizes every opportunity to calumniate. Such has been the conduct evinced towards the Scottish Episcopal Church by the majority of the Presbyterian Establishment for some time; and the Bishops, clergy, and laity, have been, and are, assailed by every species of obloquy and reproach by men who seem utterly to disregard the ordinary courtesies of life, and who, if they had the power, would actually carry on a war of extermination against all who are not of their party.

But if such opposition and malevolence is daily displayed in Scotland towards the Church, what shall we say of those clergy of the Church of England who make common cause with her inveterate enemies? It is indeed consolatory to know that these are comparatively few, unimportant, and uninfluential; yet there are such, of whom the Rev. J. Jordan is a specimen, whose letter to the editor of a well known London print* was enthusiastically copied into all the Presbyterian newspapers, and who seemed to be labouring under the hallucination, which evidently pervaded some of the Irish journalists, that the people of Scotland were for weeks talking of nothing else than Queen Victoria's

* The RECORD, the organ of a certain section in the Church of England.

religious observances at Dalkeith Palace. "According to the judgment of the Bishop of London," writes Mr Jordan, dated Enstone, Oxon., "the Episcopal Church in Scotland is schismatical. He says—'When people of the same communion separate themselves from the Church of that country, not differing from it in fundamentals, no such plea can be advanced; they may not be chargeable with *heresy*, but I do not understand how they can escape the guilt of schism.'"—"The Kirk of Scotland," continues Mr Jordan, "is in that kingdom the Church of the community. The Episcopal Church there separates itself from the Church of the community, not differing from it in fundamentals, and consequently the Episcopal Church is, according to the Bishop of London, chargeable with the guilt of schism. This schismatical Church was one preferred by her Majesty's advisers to minister before her in Scotland."

The Bishop of London will probably be not a little surprised at this extraordinary exposition of his sentiments on schism, but the best answer to it, as it respects his Lordship, is, that on the 25th of September 1842, his Lordship preached in St Paul's Episcopal Chapel, Edinburgh, and officiated along with Bishop Terrot in the communion office; and that, on the afternoon of that day, his Lordship also preached in St John's Episcopal Chapel, and the Rev. E B. Ramsay officiated at the evening service. On the 26th, the following day, Mr Jordan's letter appeared in the London print referred to. These facts may enlighten such clergymen as Mr Jordan in their inferences from the Bishop of London's opinions on schism. If Mr Jordan is correct in his notions of the "Church of the community," from which we are not to separate without incurring the guilt of schism, if it does not differ from us in fundamentals—it follows that in France, Italy, Spain, and Portugal, we should become Romanists, for most assuredly the Roman Catholic Church agrees with us in *fundamentals*; and it is almost unnecessary to observe, that if we reject *all* which Romanists believe, we must completely reject Christianity. As to the "Kirk of Scotland" being the "Church of the community," that can only be admitted to a certain extent, for not much more than a third of the whole population of Scotland are its members. Mr Jordan's observation applies admirably to the great bodies of Presbyterian Dissenters in Scotland, of whose existence he does not seem to be aware. It may be farther stated, in conclusion, that however much the Scottish Episcopal Church may agree with the Presbyterian Establishment on some important doctrines, which are held in common by all Christians, that Church does differ with it on what Scottish Episcopalians, as is the case with the Church of England, consider most essential *fundamentals*—of such vital importance as to involve the entire constitution of the Church Catholic, as a spiritual kingdom, in opposition on the one hand to the pretensions of Romanism, and, on the other, to the unauthorized polity of any modern body of religionists, notwithstanding their temporal endowments, their high-sounding claims, and their alleged scriptural warrant for their system. When the Episcopal Church was re-established in Scotland by the act of 1662, the reason solemnly assigned by the Parliament was, that they found it to be " the Church government most agreeable to the Word of God, most convenient and effectual for the preservation of truth, order, and unity, and most suitable to monarchy, and the peace and quiet of the State."* The two latter may be matters of opinion, but most assuredly every conscientious member of the Episcopal Church takes his deliberate vantage ground on the former. The act of 1689 did not appeal to such high authority. It referred solely to human passions, prejudices, and political events, and it accordingly declares that the Presbyterian polity was established " in this kingdom " for no other reason than that it is " most agreeable to the inclinations of the people!"

* Acta Parl. Scot. vol. vii p. 372.

CHAPTER XXV.

STATE OF THE SCOTTISH EPISCOPAL CHURCH—ANDERSON'S MORTIFICATION—PANTONIAN FUND—FRIENDLY SOCIETY—EPISCOPAL FUND—EPISCOPAL CHURCH SOCIETY—THE SNELL EXHIBITIONS—TRINITY COLLEGE

In reviewing the state of the Scottish Episcopal Church from 1831 to the end of 1842, it is peculiarly satisfactory to record the steady progress of the congregations; and this is a subject which demands some attention, because the enemies and vilifiers of the Church are constantly endeavouring to show that, as an ecclesiastical communion, it is limited in point of numbers. Nearly twenty congregations have been added to the Church in the various dioceses from 1831 to 1842, and though some of these are small, yet their increase is annually perceptible, and affords a well founded hope that every succeeding year will add both to the numbers of each congregation, and also include several others. It must be remembered, that, with the exception of the cities and large towns, the members of the Church are scattered over the whole of Scotland, and many of the congregations in the villages and rural districts are composed of individuals who reside a considerable distance from their respective places of worship. Some of the clergy have also the pastoral care of more than one congregation, and extend their ministrations to villages and districts in their neighbourhoods where Episcopalians are located, though they have no chapel for their accommodation.

To commence with the Diocese of EDINBURGH, it is true that only two congregations have been added to the Church, between 1831 and 1841. —those of Trinity Chapel, in the city of Edinburgh, and of Alloa, the neat chapel in the latter town erected in 1837, and Trinity Chapel in 1838. But it must be observed that the Diocese of Edinburgh is limited since the disjunction of Glasgow and of Fife, the greater number of the congregations being within the city of Edinburgh,* and the only provincial chapels those of Portobello, Musselburgh, Haddington, Stirling, and Alloa. In the present divisions of the dioceses or districts, the boundaries of the former Established Dioceses are carefully recognised, and that of Edinburgh was not very extensive at the foundation and erection of the See by Charles I. in 1633. In one town, however, in which no Episcopal clergyman has been settled, and no congregation has existed for nearly a century, a strong desire is manifested by numbers for regular Episcopal ministrations. At the Annual Meeting of the Scottish Episcopal Church Society in 1840, the Right Hon. W. E. Gladstone, Esq. M.P., stated, towards the conclusion of his eloquent and interesting address—"A highly respected clergyman has placed in my hands, since I entered this meeting, a petition signed by one hundred and twenty persons resident in and about Dalkeith. They are persons who never have enjoyed the blessing of our worship and ministry among them. They are persons who have not in the public eye been known as an Episcopal body. They are persons of humble, or of the humblest station. They are persons not moved through the influence or solicitations of the great, the wealthy, or the noble, but by a warm attachment to the Episcopal Communion, and they are moving the great, the wealthy, and the noble, to aid them in giving effect to that attachment. Their petition is addressed to the Duke of Buccleuch, the Marquis of Lothian, the Earl of Stair, Lord Viscount Melville, Mr Ker of Woodburn, Mr Wardlaw Ramsay of Whitehill, Mr Burn Callander of Prestonhall, &c., and it sets forth that—' We, the undersigned inhabitants of the town and neighbourhood of Dalkeith, being *bona fide* members of the Episcopal Catholic Church, have for a long time lamented that, unless at considerable inconvenience, we enjoy no opportunity of worshipping God according to that form and ritual to which we are sincerely and conscientiously attached. In order to remove this disadvantage, we therefore most respectfully appeal to you, soliciting your sanction, concurrence, and assistance, in the building of an Episcopal Chapel, and the establishment of an Episcopal congregation in the town or vicinity of Dalkeith ; and we beg to inclose a copy of resolutions passed at a meeting of Episcopalians in reference to this subject. That you will be pleased to take

* The congregation at Leith is included in the Diocese of Glasgow during the episcopate and incumbency of Bishop Russell.

this matter into your serious consideration, that you would confer on the subject, and render your co-operation and assistance in whatever way may appear to you the most desirable and effectual, is the humble prayer of, my Lords and Gentlemen, your most obedient, humble servants.' Signed by one hundred and six Episcopalians, to whom more have since been added."

The Diocese of GLASGOW next claims our attention, and considering the state in which it was about 1820, as appears from the list in the Edinburgh Almanac, a very great accession has been made to the Church. Before 1817, there were only three congregations in the whole of the ancient archiepiscopal district, viz : St Andrew's Chapel, of which the Very Rev. William Routledge, the Dean, has been long the incumbent, and a small congregation in a rented hall, both in the city of Glasgow, and the congregation of Dumfries. In 1817 the large congregation at Paisley was formed under the ministrations of the Rev. W. M. Wade, who encountered numerous discouraging obstacles before he was enabled to place it in its present state of stability, in the neat and commodious Gothic Chapel erected under his inspection. For some years after that period the only other chapel in the whole district was that of Kelso, which was in separation from the Church. Since 1821 the large and elegant St Mary's Episcopal Chapel in Renfield Street, Christ Church in the suburb of the Calton, and St Jude's Episcopal Chapel in Blythswood Square, all in Glasgow, have been erected; and congregations formed at Greenock, Helensburgh, Ayr, Annan, and Peebles. The congregation at Hamilton was constituted under the ministrations of the Rev. Alexander Henderson, M.A., in 1842; in that year the chapel at Coatbridge, near Airdrie, was advancing to completion; the formation of a congregation at Jedburgh was in progress, and also one at Dunbarton, in addition to which encouraging openings in other quarters were anticipated.

The Diocese of BRECHIN acquired an extension in the fishing village of Katerline, a village consisting entirely of fishermen and their families, who have regularly belonged to the communion of the Church, and who formed part of the congregation of Drumlithie, seven miles distant. Bishop Moir's statement of the circumstances of the fishing community of Katerline, read at the Annual Meeting of the Scottish Episcopal Church Society by Erskine Douglas Sandford, Esq., Advocate, in 1841, is interesting, and is applicable to various others similarly situated.—" The late incumbent seeing the great hardship and disadvantages they laboured under in being at so great a distance from their place of worship, and that efforts were being made to draw them away from the Church, agreed at their earnest requests to perform divine service on Sunday afternoon at Katerline, in a house belonging to the Coast Guard, which they had fitted up for the purpose, having, through Lord Arbuthnott's recommendation, obtained permission to do so —The case of a number of the members of our Church, almost deprived, by the circumstances of their situation, of the benefits of public worship and pastoral attention, strongly claimed my sympathy and consideration ; and, after much thought on the subject, it is my humble opinion, that the only way of preserving these people in the Communion of the Church is by settling a clergyman among them. This they have earnestly requested me to endeavour to accomplish. Their number is considerable, being by the last return one hundred and thirty souls, of whom fifty are communicants. They are chiefly fishermen, and persons of sober and industrious habits. Without any assistance they have fitted up in a decent manner a place for the celebration of divine service, and they would undertake to raise among themselves L.30 annually for the support of a clergyman. Being at a great distance from the parochial school, they have been obliged to employ a young man to teach their children, and they have represented to me, that it would be of great advantage to them, and might help to provide for a clergyman's maintenance, if a person could be found to act both as pastor and schoolmaster. I flatter myself that an application to the Church Society would not be rejected ; for it is not asked for the uncertain purpose of drawing together a congregation from other denominations of Christians, but to provide the benefits of Christian communion to a considerable number of respectable though poor persons, who are warmly attached to the Episcopal Church, and whose forefathers adhered to it under all the vicissitudes through which it has passed in this country. I may add, that Katerline being a good fishing station, there is reason to believe that the population will increase." Among the other local matters connected with the Diocese of Brechin may be mentioned the enlargement of the chapel at Arbroath, rendered necessary by the increase of the congregation under the pastoral care of the Rev. William Henderson, M.A., and the auspicious progress of the union with the Church of the large and important congregation of St Peter's Chapel in Montrose.

In the Diocese of ABERDEEN the vigilant care of the Right Rev. Bishop Skinner has added one congregation to the Church at Inverury, where a neat chapel is erected, which was consecrated by the Primus in 1842. The congregation of Fraserburgh reverted to the Diocese at the death of Bishop Jolly, and that of Peterhead at the resignation of the incumbency by Bishop Torry. The union of St Paul's congregation in Aberdeen with the Church is previously noticed.

In the United Diocese of DUNKELD, DUNBLANE, and FIFE, one congregation has been added at Dunfermline, and the chapel consecrated by Bishop Russell, acting for Bishop Torry, in October 1842. In various parts of this United Diocese appearances are favourable to the spread of the Church, and doubtless, when circumstances are matured, will be duly encouraged. In 1842 a congregation was formed in the ancient episcopal city of Dunblane.

In the United Diocese of MORAY, ROSS, and ARGYLL, great accessions have been made by the unwearied exertions of the Right Rev. Bishop Low. At Aberchirder and Forres, in the ancient Diocese of Moray, congregations have been formed in addition to those in other places during Bishop Jolly's episcopate. In 1837 Bishop Low founded the congregation at Carroy, in the Island of Skye, at which a neat chapel is erected.- At Stornoway in the Island of Lewis a congregation was formed about the same period; the Rev. Samuel Hood constituted the congregation at Rothesay in the Island of Bute; in 1842 the Rev. David Aitchison, M.A., undertook the pastoral care of one newly formed at Lochgilphead in Argyllshire; and another is in progress at Oban in the same county. All the above, it is to be observed, are additional congregations to those who had been some time in existence, and most of whom have been constituted during Bishop Low's episcopate; for it is a remarkable fact, that when the Bishop succeeded Bishop Macfarlane in the United Diocese of Ross and Argyll in 1819, the number of presbyters was scarcely one-third of those who formed the clergy of the United Diocese previous to the annexation of Moray.

The preceding statistics respecting the increase of the Church are not mere vague assertions, but may be ascertained by any one who consults the lists of the clergy duly authenticated in the Edinburgh Almanac, and compares these documents since 1820, or even 1830. Still the opponents of the Church continually exclaim that it is a small and limited communion in proportion to a population of nearly three millions in Scotland, and they appeal to this fact, or rather their representations of it, as a proof that Episcopacy is obnoxious to the great mass of the Scottish people. It is admitted that the Scottish Episcopal Church is comparatively a small communion, and it would indeed be wonderful if it were otherwise, considering the difficulties, prejudices, and discouragements with which it has had and still has to contend. They even scruple not to assert that the Church does not number a larger population than 25,000 throughout Scotland, rabidly seizing a very erroneous and unfounded statement to that effect which appeared in the Times newspaper in 1842. In the peculiar circumstances and position of the Church, it is perhaps impossible to obtain any thing like a correct statement of the numbers within the pale of its communion, or of those who profess to belong to it, although unfortunately they neglect its services, of whom, as in other religious societies, there are too many, or reside at such distances in districts which render their attendance almost impossible. In the city of Glasgow and suburbs alone the Episcopalians were estimated by Dr Cleland, at the census of 1831, at 8551, and as it is not likely that they have decreased, they may be considered in 1842 to have amounted to 10,000. "Of these," as was observed by the Rev. Robert Montgomery of St Jude's, Glasgow, in his speech at the First Annual Meeting of the Church Society in 1839, "a large proportion are miserably poor, without the means, and what is worse, without the inclination, of supplying themselves with spiritual instruction. In Anderston there are at least 500 souls attached to the Episcopal Communion. Of these only fifty-four individuals are in the habit of attending any church, and a large number assign the want of clothing as the reason why they absent themselves." The following passage from the same eloquent appeal is sufficiently explanatory of the state of the Church, and illustrates the melancholy condition under which the poorer Episcopalians are labouring along the West coast. "In the town of Greenock, for instance, owing to the establishment of various manufactures, there has of late years been a great influx of Episcopalians. These consist chiefly of hatters from Lancaster—manufacturers of earthenware from the potteries—glass-blowers from Newcastle—chain-cable-makers from Liverpool, besides a large number of Irish Protestants, and many sugar-boilers from Germany, members of the Lutheran Church. The number of these individuals may be safely stated at 800, the great majority of whom are in the very humblest walks of life, and totally without the means of spiritual instruction and superintendence. They reject Presbyterian baptism and communion, and although there is an Episcopal chapel in Greenock, the congregation is chiefly composed of the wealthier classes. Along the whole coast, and in the Northern and Western Highlands, including Argyllshire, are many poor Episcopalians (the exact number of which is still unascertained), who are totally without the means of supplying themselves with spiritual instruction. It is true, many of the leading proprietors in these districts belong to the Episcopal Church, but they are too far separate from each other to render the establishment of places of worship a practicable measure."

Among the upper classes in Scotland the Church has ever numbered many of it members. It is well ascertained, and has not been denied, that three-fourths of the landed proprietors of Scotland are Episcopalians. The Peerage of Scotland in 1842 consisted of eight Dukes, four Marquises, forty-two Earls, six Viscounts, and twenty-three Barons:—in all eighty-four members, including one Baroness, yet of these noblemen probably not above twelve are Presbyterians.* Of the Peers and Peeresses of the United Kingdom of Great Britain and Ireland connected with Scotland, and for the most part possessing extensive estates in the various counties, who, in 1842, were in number twenty-seven,† only three, or at most four, are considered to be Presbyterians, viz., the Earl of Camperdown, the Earl of Minto, Lord Campbell, and Lord Dunfermline. Probably Lords Abercromby and Panmure may be added, yet even these six noblemen when in England conform to the Church of England. In fact, with probably the exception of the Duke of Argyll, the Marquis of Breadalbane, and Lord Belhaven, the most of the above mentioned noblemen may be designated *Establishment men*, who conform on either side of the Tweed to what

---

* Only two Scottish Peers are Roman Catholics, viz., the Earls of Newburgh and Traquair. The former appears to have no property in Scotland. The religious opinions of a few others are not well known, but they do not own themselves to be Presbyterians.

† One of these, Lord Lovat, is a Roman Catholic.

they consider the law of the land. A very large proportion of the Baronets of Scotland, and of the Baronets of Great Britain connected with Scotland, are known to be members of the Episcopal Church, and not a few of the others are also merely *Establishment men*, who deem it their duty to support that of Scotland and the Church of England simply for the sake of example and propriety.

These facts are mentioned not in the spirit of boasting exultation or of pride, because those noblemen and gentlemen who are avowed members of the Church have often been severely attacked, even by Presbyterians, for allowing its clergy in the rural districts so long to continue in a condition of poverty which is scarcely known even among the common dissenting sects. This charge is unfortunately too true, but the liberal donations which many of them have given to the Scottish Episcopal Church Society have to a certain extent obviated what was undoubtedly at least a matter of surprise. Yet, since the Presbyterian opponents of the Church often dwell on their imaginary correct information respecting its statistics as it regards the number of members, how does it happen that their system is so little appreciated by their own countrymen in England? What may be the number of Scotsmen domiciled in England it is probably impossible to determine, but without referring to Liverpool, Manchester, and other large towns, it was long since calculated that London alone contained upwards of 100,000 Scotsmen and their descendants, which must be admitted to be a very moderate computation. Now, supposing that the majority of these Scotsmen were or professed to be Presbyterians when they went to England, is it possible that the great mass of them have become irreligious? The city of Edinburgh and Leith, by the census of 1841, contained a population of only 163,726, without including children in charitable institutions, persons in hospitals, asylums, and the Military in the Castle, who may comprise about 1200 or 1300 more. In that city and Leith, with such a population, which is by no means increasing, there are eight Episcopal congregations attended by persons of all ranks, four at least of which are large, viz., St Paul's, St John's, St James's, and Trinity Chapel. In the city of London, with its 100,000 Scotsmen, there are only *six places of worship* in connection with the Scottish Presbyterian Establishment, which, it is well known, are very indifferently attended, and not containing accommodation, if all were filled, for 5000 persons; but as probably not above the half of that number constantly or even occasionally attend, here is a complete proof of the all but complete desertion from or renunciation of Presbyterianism in London. It would be absurd to conclude that, supposing two-thirds of the 100,000 Scotsmen in the British metropolis had been originally Presbyterians, they must all be living without religious instruction of any kind, except the 2500 or 3000 who continue to resort to the six meeting-houses called the "Scotch churches." It appears that the Seceders in London have four meeting-houses, so that allowing them 2000 persons, which is much more than the collective average, here are not 5000 persons who adhere to or support the system in which they had been educated. The truth is, that though much indifference to and neglect of religion prevails among the Scotch in London, particularly the operatives, thousands have conformed to the Church of England. Of this fact many examples could be given.

Nor is this desertion of the Presbyterian banner solely confined to London. The large, important, and populous town and sea-port of Liverpool has only four Scottish meeting-houses, and in contrast to this the city of Aberdeen, with probably not a fourth or fifth part of the population, has three Episcopal Chapels, two of them very large congregations. Manchester has only two meeting-houses; and Glasgow, the Scottish Manchester, has four Episcopal Chapels. Newcastle, nearer the Border, has three meeting-houses, but it may be questionable whether their congregations are so flourishing as the large, influential, and important congregation of St Paul's Chapel, Dundee. With the two meeting-houses in Berwick-upon-Tweed may be contrasted the Episcopal congregations at Arbroath, Montrose, or Inverness. In short, it appears from the Edinburgh Almanac for 1842, that in a country containing a population of 16,000,000, the "Synod of the Presbyterian Church in England in connection with the Church of Scotland," contains only *forty-four congregations*, served by as many ministers, while the Scottish Episcopal Church has between *ninety and one hundred congregations*, some of them doubtless small, but many of them very large, in a country which does not contain a population of 3,000,000!

It appears that in 1842 there were in addition twenty-five congregations throughout Northumberland, in "communion" with the Scottish Establishment, though apparently not within the jurisdiction of the "Synod;" but this very little affects the preceding statistical facts, considering the utter disproportion of the population of the two countries; and, besides, numbers of these twenty-five Northumberland congregations are well known to be very small, and struggling with pecuniary difficulties. The Seceders had also between forty and fifty congregations in England, but as that large body of Scottish Presbyterian Dissenters have no connection with the Establishment, their English congregations, small as many of them are in point of adherents, cannot be taken into account. The reader will thus perceive that there is no great cause of triumph on the part of the opponents of the Scottish Episcopal Church, which, unlike their system in England, is annually increasing in numbers and respectability. It is needless to allude to those who style themselves peculiarly *English Presbyterians,* who have lapsed into miserable Socinianism.

Thus far, then, as it respects the state of the Scottish Episcopal Church, and the "contendings" of its enemies respecting the numbers of its members and congregations. A thorough investigation of the religious statistics of Scotland would be both curious and important, and would probably astonish those who are continually declaiming about the hereditary dislike which the Scottish people generally are alleged to cherish towards the Episcopal Church. That such long existed, and that such exists to a very considerable extent, studiously fomented by parties to preserve their influence and domination, is not denied, but succeeding generations are viewing matters in a different light, and a spirit of inquiry is abroad which all the misrepresentations, calumnies, and bold perversions of facts circulated against that Church cannot prevent. If even Wodrow in his day laments the incipient leanings of the people to what he calls a "moderate Episcopacy without ceremonies," and records with regret their "growing attachment to the English Service," such feelings are now more widely diffused; and there are many thousands in Scotland, who, though they continue members of the Presbyterian Establishment, unhesitatingly admit that they admire the ritual and service of the Church.* It is easy to form theories, and set forth

* Many incidental occurrences prove this statement, which may be verified by what is often mentioned in private society. When, for instance, the Lord Bishop of London preached in St Paul's and St John's Episcopal Chapels in Edinburgh, on Sunday, the 25th of September 1842, a part of the year in which most of the members of the Church, of the upper classes, in the Scottish metropolis, are at their country quarters, the crowded congregations were to a great extent composed of respectable Presbyterians.

dogmatical assertions. The sentiments uttered by the Right Hon. W. E Gladstone, in his speech at the annual meeting of the Scottish Episcopal Church in 1840, are neither visionary nor unfounded. On that occasion the Right Rev. Bishop Low presided, and Mr Gladstone thus proceeded :—" Now, Right Rev. Sir, when we contemplate the aspect of this Church, we shall see that the work before us is indeed a great work. And yet I trust from day to day new wants will be revealed in different parts of the country ; for I am convinced that as new wants are revealed, new energies will be put forth for their supply, and with the operations of the Society will be multiplied the blessings that have attended them. I am one of those who can find many consolations under our present circumstances. It is difficult for mortal man to anticipate the course of events. Yet I cannot but cherish the belief that this Church has an important mission confided to her. I cannot venture to conjecture what her destiny for the next half century may be. Yet I feel that it will be as distinct from the destiny of the last half century, as that was from the destiny of the preceding half century of legal suspicion and prescription. It is true, circumstances are greatly altered. It is true that we stand in the position of a Church receiving no aid from the State. It is true we have not the advantage of those temporal means which we once possessed. But with those temporal means have we not got rid of many evils ? There was a time, in the reign of Charles II., when Episcopacy was presented to the people of Scotland, but presented in connection with an arbitrary system of civil government, which was calculated justly to offend the minds of men, and to throw discredit on pure religion. Is it no advantage to have escaped from that unfortunate association ? We have also escaped from a class of prejudices which at a later time prevailed, and with respect to which I must say, that though we may in some sense condemn them, yet we cannot wonder that they existed— those prejudices, I mean, which prevailed when Episcopacy was considered synonymous with disaffection to the established settlement of the succession to the throne. We are free from those disadvantages, and we now stand on grounds precisely ecclesiastical and spiritual—on grounds from which, I trust, Right Reverend Sir, you and your brethren will never be moved. It is true, that in being removed from the position of an establishment we have not gained all those facilities for the warfare of the moment which some other systems may possess. There are some means of popularity which others reputed Dissenters from the National Establishment may employ, but which the ministers of this Church have never called, and never can call, to their aid. They cannot accommodate themselves to the prejudices, the self-will, the self-love of their flocks. They cannot flatter the lust of power which lies so deep in the human heart. They cannot say, 'You are judges of our doctrine; we stand here, that you may do what you desire with us.' On the contrary, they must hold out the idea of the Church to their flocks as something superior to us and to themselves—as something independent of the will of man—as an historical institution delivered down through countless ages from the very period and from the very hand of Christ himself. And if they cannot appeal to this self-love, which is a great power in the hands of some for procuring temporary popularity and success for an institution, far less can they resort to other weapons of a much more questionable character. There is another kind of warfare which is now waged both keenly and rudely against religious establishments. They cannot join with those who term themselves the friends of the Voluntary principle in this warfare. On the contrary, I feel convinced that not only no strength of preference for the Episcopal constitution, but that no sense, however strong, of the exclusiveness of the duty which in a religious view we owe it, will tempt us to lend a hand to aid in the establishment of a principle which must terminate in social atheism. And this sentiment I state where I now stand with the same fearlessness of contradiction, as I would, if it were possible, in an assembly of our Presbyterian brethren, so convinced am I that we feel as one man with regard to this principle. These, Right Reverend Sir, are considerations on which I have thought it right for me to touch, feeling myself precluded, by the terms of the resolution committed to me, from entering into topics arising out of the operations of the Society. I have considered some of those particulars in which the Episcopal Church of Scotland has apparently sustained great loss from the withdrawal of temporal advantages, though, as I believe, it has gained along with that loss what more than counterbalances it. But there are other advantages which are greater than merely negative advantages. I cannot but highly value those blessings of religious peace which distinguish this Church, that harmony and union which have brought us here in regular ecclesiastical order, in presence and with the sanction of our spiritual governors, to unite heart and hand, without any distinction of sentiment or purpose, in a cause which is so intimately connected with the prosperity of the Church. I am confident of a continuance of that order and spiritual harmony and peace, because it does not rest on any thing contingent or peculiar to one season rather than another—because it is founded on what is both original and fundamental in our Church polity. And shall we believe that other fruits than these will ever be reaped where men shall accept of the treasure which God hath given them, instead of substituting devices of their own? In the present day it is impossible not to feel that we ought to be moved to the most profound thankfulness, when we behold the distraction which is at present pervading the land, and rending the national establishment of religion. If I allude to those divisions at all, I do so from no disposition to exult in their existence. Far be it from me. On the contrary, in alluding to them I would say that it is far easier to point out the evils connected with their existence than to blame the agents on this side or that. I am not one of those who believe that ambition or vanity on one side, or inertness or torpor on the opposite side, are the causes of those distractions. On the contrary, I believe that the roots lie far deeper; and we who are free from them are bound to express our gratitude to God that we are placed within a sphere which they seem never to disturb. It is said, indeed, by some that Episcopacy is a plant that can take no root in Scotland. *So far as I have looked into the history of Scotland, I must say that I am not convinced of the truth of that statement. Let me see Episcopacy tried on its own merits, and then I will abide by the issue.* But when Episcopacy was mixed up with civil or secondary considerations, it did not stand on its own merits. It is well known that among the rich and noble of the land a large proportion are adherents of our Church; but it is supposed that there is something in Episcopacy peculiarly repugnant to the common people. But the nature of the people of Scotland is human nature; and the nature of Episcopacy is, if our belief be sound, according to the nature of that scheme which God has ordained to redeem human nature. And let us not be told that it will not take root in the soil of this land, if it be indeed a plant which God hath planted. We are not left in this matter to consider mere general probabilities, or to rely upon such anticipations as faith might suggest, but the evidence we would entertain is that afforded by a number of cheering indications. Enough has already transpired, since the foundation of this Society, to render it impossible for any man to venture upon saying at this moment to what extent Episcopacy is cherished in the hearts of Scotsmen." At that meeting Sir John M'Niel thus eloquently concluded his powerful address:—" Remember the unequal struggle your fathers long maintained, that they might transmit to you as an inheritance the place in the Church which you are now met to aid in entailing on your children. I wish I could call to mind the eloquent and impressive terms in which I and many of you lately heard allusion made to the struggles which our Church has survived. We were told how, in poverty and neglect, without ambition to excite, without fame to reward them, that scattered remnant of a Christian flock endured all hardships and all privations for conscience-sake, and endured unto the end. And now that better days have come—that persecution has ceased and contumely has passed away—that the sun of prosperity has shone upon some, and the bitterness of contention is forgotten by all, how small are the sacrifices we are called upon to make compared with those which were cheerfully made by the men to whom, under Providence, we owe the preservation of the Scottish Episcopal Church? Living under the reign of a beneficent Sovereign, under a Government as careful of the rights of the people as of the prerogatives of the Crown, and under impartial laws equally administered for the protection of all, we have no hardships—no privations to endure—no scorn to encounter—no persecution to dread. Respected but not feared—unaided but unopposed—we are left at full liberty to repair what has been preserved to us of the sacred edifice in which we have found shelter. To this the Society is pledged by its acts, and I have too much confidence in you to doubt that the pledge will be amply redeemed."

The Institutions peculiarly connected with the Scottish Episcopal Church are, though few, of considerable importance. To several of the congregations belong small bequests and endowments, known in Scotland by the quaint name of "*mortifications,*" left or granted by pious individuals. These are generally added to the stipends of the officiating incumbents. The most prominent of such bequests is "Anderson's Mortification," consisting of one by a gentleman of that name in

Aberdeen, the legal interest of which was ordered by the testator to be divided into four equal portions, and each assigned to one of the clergy of the Scottish Episcopal Church officiating in the four University cities of Aberdeen, Edinburgh, Glasgow, and St Andrews. It is said that the sum thus annually paid amounts to L.10.*

The *Pantonian Fund* is designated from Dr Panton, who left certain property to the Church for the benefit of the poorer clergy. It is vested in Trustees, who arrange the distribution of the proceeds. Connected with this Fund is the *Pantonian Professorship of Divinity*, founded and endowed by the same benevolent individual. The Professor has the control of the now large and valuable library for the use of the clergy and theological students, placed in commodious premises in Hill Street, Edinburgh. The sum required for the purchase of the house fitted up as the library was collected by subscriptions and donations, among which those of the late Bishop Walker, the late Rev. Alexander Cruickshank of Muthill, and of Bishop Low, were munificent, each having subscribed L.100. This library contains the collection, chiefly theological, of Bishop Jolly A suitable lecture-room is fitted up for the Professors of Divinity and Church History, the latter of whom holds the Lectureship on the Madras Sytem of education, founded and endowed by the late Rev. Andrew Bell, LL.B., Prebendary of Westminster. It may be here mentioned that the Bishop of Edinburgh is, *ex officio*, one of the three Patrons of the Madras College, St Andrews, the princely bequest and endowment of Dr Bell. The others are the Lord Justice-Clerk and the Sheriff of the county of Fife. The Bishop of Aberdeen is partly patron of a Bursary in Marischal College, founded by Alexander Scott of Craibstone, who " mortified " the interest of L 500 for four years to the son of " any poor clergyman of the Scottish Episcopal Communion, who is meant to be brought up and educated for the ministry of that Church ;" and, failing an applicant of that description, " then to any other young man in needy circumstances who intends to be brought up for the ministry of that Church." This gentleman also mortified a similar sum as a bursary for the son of any poor minister of the Presbyterian Establishment; failing whom, to one whose father was

* Evidence of the Rev. C J Lyon, M.A., before the Commissioners of Religious Instruction in Scotland, Sixth Report, 1839, p 505.

or is a resident in Huntly; failing whom, to one who belongs to the district included within the limits of the Presbytery of Strathbogie. The Bishop of Aberdeen presents to the one, as already mentioned, and the Presbytery of Strathbogie to the other.*

Among the various schools connected with the Church in the several dioceses is the *Episcopal Free School*, attached to St James' Chapel, Edinburgh, endowed by the bequest of Colonel Scott of L 2000, for the purpose of " educating boys and girls according to the principles of the Scottish Episcopal Church," the interest of which constitutes the salary of the teacher. The children, upwards of one hundred in number, regularly attend divine service in the chapel, and are under the superintendence of the incumbent.

Of a more general and comprehensive nature is the *Scottish Episcopal Friendly Society*, already noticed as instituted in 1793, in consequence of the Act of the Legislature for the encouragement of Friendly Societies. The objects of this Society are previously stated. The business is transacted at Aberdeen, in which city the annual meeting is held to audit the accounts, and a general meeting every third year, when all the members are expected to be present, under penalty of a fine unless the excuse is valid. The President must always be the Bishop of Aberdeen, the other Bishops who are members being Vice-Presidents according to seniority of consecration, the Primus taking precedence. The contributions enjoined to be paid annually by members is the small sum of L.2 for fifteen years, after which no farther one is required. The articles and regulations of the Society were revised at the triennial meeting in 1828, when it was enjoined that all those clergymen of Scottish ordination serving cures in the Church must enter within three years after their ordination as deacons or priests, the obligation on the part of deacons being optional till advanced to the priesthood, otherwise they cannot afterwards be admitted. All clergymen of English and Irish ordination must enter within three years after induction, failing which they are excluded. The non-payment of the annual contributions and fines for three years forfeits all the privileges and benefits of the Society. By the care and assiduity of the office-bearers, the original stock, consisting of the balance of the money subscribed to defray

* Second Report of the University Commissioners, 1830, vol. xxix. p 19, 20.

the expenses of the repeal of the Penal Laws, increased by legacies and donations from benevolent individuals, has greatly increased, and the Society has continued to flourish beyond the anticipations of its most sanguine projectors. A part of the funds is vested in Government stock, but the greater portion is lodged in the Bank of England under the Friendly Society Act. The participants of the Society are the widows and children of the members, though a provision is also made for the assistance of indigent clergymen whenever the annuities to widows amount to L.30 per annum. The annuities to widows are raised L.5 for every sum of L.500 the Society increases available for all its purposes. The surviving children of a member who is a widower receive a balance of ten years' annuity; and, if no will is left, that sum is divided equally among them. A widow forfeits her annuity if she marries a person who is not a member of the Society.

The objects of the *Scottish Episcopal Fund*, instituted in 1806, are more varied and extensive. It is already stated that it originated with some zealous laymen of rank and influence in Edinburgh and elsewhere, one of the most active of whom was Sir William Forbes, Bart. The reasons for the institution of this Fund, as stated in a Memorial drawn up by Sir William Forbes, and addressed to the Episcopal nobility and gentry, evinced an attachment to the Church worthy of admiration. It was to establish a fund, by appeals to the friends of the Church in Great Britain and Ireland, which would tend to lessen the expenses of the Bishops when visiting their Dioceses, and afford some pecuniary assistance to the more necessitous of the inferior clergy. "As all income arising from the State," says Sir James Allen Park, in his Memoir of the excellent William Stevens, Esq., "was cut down at the Revolution, these reverend persons, bishops, as well as priests, had nothing to rely on but the emoluments arising from their congregations, which were often so limited in number; and in such narrow circumstances, that the stipends of many of these pious and exemplary men did not exceed the wages of a day labourer. It could not, therefore, but be a matter of regret to every well disposed Christian—indeed to every feeling heart—to see those who had a liberal education, and who filled the distinguishing station, whatever the worldling may think, of ambassadors of their blessed Master, with such pitiful incomes." A committee was appointed in London, consisting of well known and tried friends of the

Church, and in England the Fund was munificently supported. The illustrious Bishop Horsley recommended it in a sermon replete with his powerful reasoning. Many of the Bishops and clergy, the laity of various ranks and professions, the Universities, particularly Oxford, and individuals in private life, came forward liberally in support of an institution so Christian in its purposes. By their exertions, the sums collected from 1806 to 1810 amounted to L.12,077—which sufficiently evinced the sympathy manifested towards a branch of the Church Catholic which had experienced so many vicissitudes and privations. More than the sum of L.1600 was subscribed by the Bishops of the Church of England, and, exclusive of the contributions of the various Colleges in Oxford, the University gave L.300. The late Bishop Heber, then a private clergyman, and the late Archdeacon Daubeny, contributed together L.700. Mrs Sheppard of Arnport, a benevolent lady well known in the Church of England, transmitted the munificent sum of L.1000. The Bishops of Dromore, Ferns, Killaloe, and Clogher, each subscribed L.50, and Trinity College, Dublin, L.250. More recently, the Archbishop of Canterbury, two years after his removal from the See of London to the Primacy in 1828, sent L.200. The Fund is vested in a permanent committee of nine Trustees, who are laymen, with the power of filling up vacancies, and are subject in the management to certain rules specified in the deed, which were approved by the contributors, who elect the Trustees, with whom the Bishops are associated. These rules can only be altered by a general meeting of the contributors, and of the heirs-male of such as are deceased. This general meeting is held on the second Monday of February once in twenty years. The principal sum vested in the Trustees has been considerably increased by donations and subscriptions since 1810, and now amounts to upwards of L.20,000. The greater part of this sum was allotted to the purchase of the estate of Collielaw in Berwickshire, from which, however, the returns have not been very productive, and the rest is lent on sufficient securities, though liable to the unavoidable fluctuations of interest. It appears from a statement circulated by the general meeting held in 1830, that the annual revenue is altogether L.750; and that from this sum the Trustees were enabled to distribute, during the previous twelve or fourteen years, from L.60 to L.70 annually to each of the Bishops, with additions, in term of the trust-deed, to the Primus of the Episcopal College, and to the Bishop of Edinburgh; and salaries of from L.10 to L.15 to about twenty-two of the inferior clergy.

The foundation of the *Scottish Episcopal Church Society* in 1838 is already noticed, and the proceedings of the first Annual Meeting narrated. The Rules and Regulations of this important institution are printed in all the Annual Reports circulated among the subscribers. In the Report presented to the second Annual Meeting in 1840, at which the Right Rev. Bishop Low presided, the following statement appears:—
"It is gratifying to the Committee to be able to report an increasing interest and friendly feeling in England towards the Society. In addition to the English Prelates who had given it their countenance, viz. the Archbishop of Canterbury, the Bishops of London, Winchester, Chester, Lincoln, and of Nova Scotia, the Bishop of Durham has become a liberal subscriber. The Very Rev. Dr Goodenough, Dean of Wells, and the Hon. and Very Rev. Dr Howard, Dean of Lichfield, have contributed to the Society, and have accompanied their donations with kindly expressions of regard and interest. A grant of some valuable theological books has been made by the trustees of the late Dr Bray for the Diocese of Ross and Argyll. These are intended to form the nucleus of a Diocesan Library, and have been conveniently deposited for that purpose. A most gratifying mark of sympathy has been received through the Rev. Mr Aitkinson, Rector of Gateshead Fell, in a sum of L 20, subscribed by himself and neighbouring clergy, as a testimony of their good will and kindly feeling towards our impoverished Church A similar testimony has been received from the Rev. Mr Dalton of Wolverhampton, namely, a grant of L.10, from funds raised in his district for *Church and Missionary* purposes. Nor can the Committee omit this opportunity of making their acknowledgment for the munificent contribution of a member of their own Church. John Guthrie, Esq. of Guthrie, has paid over this year L.400, in addition to the L.100 which he contributed last year. The Society has this year received three legacies, namely, L.100 from the late Mrs Colonel Farquharson, L.18 from the late Mrs Grant, and L.10 from the late Miss Smith."

The Report of the third Annual Meeting in 1841, at which Bishop Low presided, contains some interesting information which shows the operations of the Society:—"The Committee consider that the best proof which can be offered is the statement that upwards of L.1600 have been expended this year in promoting the objects of the Society. Of this sum L.774 have been paid towards raising the incomes of thirty-two incumbents to L.80, whilst L.315, paid over to the Episcopal Fund, have enabled the Trustees to extend the scale of *their* grants among the smaller incumbencies of the Church; L.157, 14s. 9d., have been paid to twelve schools; L.100 for allowances to retired incumbents; L.280 for repairs and erections in nine particular cases, where there was a difficulty in raising the necessary funds; L.20 for Bibles, Prayer-Books, and Testaments. Whilst the income has been expended for these objects, the donations received during the year have been added to the capital stock of the Society, the dividends on which go to increase the annual disposable fund for distribution. It is with peculiar pleasure that the Committee refer to the formation of a most respectable and efficient Auxiliary Committee in London, for which the Rev. Mr Bowdler of Sydenham, and the Rev. Mr Mackenzie of St James', Bermondsey, Surrey, have kindly agreed to act as Secretaries; and the Committee are desirous of expressing, in the strongest terms, their grateful sense of the interest evinced towards our Church by the venerable Society for the Propagation of the Gospel in Foreign Parts, who have permitted the London Committee the use of a room in their house, 79, Pall-Mall, for quarterly meetings, and as a depôt for receiving contributions and their communications. The names of two Prelates of the Church of England have been added to those already on the list of subscribers, viz. His Grace the Archbishop of York and the Lord Bishop of Hereford. An Auxiliary Association has been formed at Bridgnorth, under the patronage of the Archdeacon and neighbouring clergy, for which the Rev. Mr Dear and Rev. Mr King kindly act as Secretary and Treasurer. An addition has been received this year to the Offerings recorded in last Report from the neighbourhood of Gateshead. By the kind exertions of some friends in India, the claims of the Society have been brought before churchmen both at Bombay and Madras. A handsome remittance has been sent from each of these Presidencies, towards which the Bishops were contributors." The Bishop of Madras accompanied his donation of 200 rupees with a note expressive of his Lordship's kind feeling towards the Church. A munificent donation of L.100 was presented to the Society by the Archbishop of Armagh. It is farther stated, that—" In the present prospects of our Church claims upon our benevolence are more likely to increase than diminish, as several new congregations are about to be formed, and under very interesting circumstances. Although in the cities and large towns in Scotland, Episcopalians are enabled to keep up their churches and supply incomes for the clergy, yet in retired parts of the country there are congregations deeply attached to the apostolic order of the Church, and to its ordinances and services, who must be either wholly or in part dependant upon their more wealthy brethren for the possession and continuance of these spiritual blessings. Such congregations are especially incapable of meeting *extraordinary* demands, such as the necessary repairs of old chapels, and the erection of new ones, where those at present occupied have become insufficient or insecure. The Committee particularly regret the limited sum at their command for meeting applications of *this* kind: L.280 afforded a most inadequate assistance to the many cases which were laid before them."

Eloquent addresses were delivered at the Annual Meeting of 1841, by the Earl of Rosebery, Sir James Ramsay of Bamff, Bart., the Rev. Norman Johnstone of Kirkaldy, Erskine Douglas Sandford, Esq. Advocate, Bishop Terrot, and the Rev. Henry Mackenzie, of St James', Bermondsey, Surrey. Bishop Terrot said—" When I consider, Right Reverend Sir, what *has* been the success of our Society, I feel that it would be foolish, I might almost say sinful, to doubt of its future extension and stability. When we commenced, as our hopes were low, so our views were comparatively narrow, and we thought of little more than securing the continuance of existing congregations, by supplying the means of clerical maintenance, where from poverty congregations were unable to support their pastor. This great point we have secured. But we now are forced to look to the formation of new congregations. I am not referring to any attempts to proselytize the members of other communities, but the calls that are made upon us to provide the means of grace for the poor members of our own communion from England and the North of Ireland, who in the vicissitudes of trade crowd into the manufacturing districts of Scotland. Especially in the Diocese of my Right Rev. Brother the Bishop of Glasgow, such cases abound. The poor Episcopalians know of our Society, and wishes, that might otherwise have been extinguished in their breasts, are now openly and hope fully expressed, and we are urgently invited to come and help them. The full extent of these new demands upon our funds we do not yet know, but we know that they are great and increasing. And we rejoice in them, not because they betoken the increase of *our* sect of the Episcopal Church of Scotland, but of the Catholic Church of Christ—of that great instrument which God has appointed for the salvation of sinners, and to whose custody and administration all the means of grace have been committed. And if, as members and ministers of that one true Church, we are bound to preach the gospel to every creature, we cannot surely, without great guilt, shut our ears to the applications of those who, though by baptism and early education members of the body of Christ, are now as sheep without a shepherd, and in danger of learning to live without God in the world. Were it not for these new claims, had we nothing to do but to keep up our existing poor congregations, as we at first contemplated, I should rely with confidence on the liberality of the wealthier portions of our Scottish Church. But when I consider how wide a field is opening before us I should have feared, but for the belief that there is help for us in England. To that help we ought not to be too hasty in recurring. The home and foreign exertions of the Church of England at the present time are on a magnificent scale, and she seems determined not only to do the work of her own day, but to compensate for the deficiencies of the two former centuries, during which no adequate effort had been made to render the means of civil and religious education, of church accommodation, and of ministerial superintendence, commensurate with the rapid increase of the English population at home, and of the British Empire abroad. Knowing, then, the various pressing claims on the English public for schools, churches, additional curates, missionary presbyters, and Colonial Bishops, we ought not, I think, except in urgent cases, to press our wants upon them. We have not done so; but in brotherly confidence we have informed them of our position and prospects, and the result has been liberal and rapidly increasing assistance. On a late visit to England I found that our Communion was an object of deep interest and sympathy to many who had no natural connection with Scotland; and though I never, directly or indirectly, solicited subscriptions, I returned with considerable contributions to our Church Society, which had spontaneously been offered for my acceptance. While we thankfully receive and rely on the continuance of this aid, it is right we should consider whether we may not do more for ourselves than we have yet done. On the same journey I had the pleasure of meeting with a very able and zealous pastor of the Catholic Church in the United States of America, Dr Doane, Bishop of New Jersey ; and, as was natural, our conversation turned much on the state of the several portions of the body of Christ with which we were personally connected. Of course I spoke of our Church Society, and of the machinery by which its funds were raised. He informed me that, when he took charge of the Diocese of New Jersey, he found that their Canonical Societies, for they have several, were supported like ours by annual subscriptions and church collections. He altered this, and calling upon the members of the Church individually, he ascertained what sum each was able and willing to contribute weekly with the probability of continuance. The sums so engaged for were deposited in a plate at the church on the first Sunday of every month, and, I think, afterwards presented on the altar as an offering to God for the service of his Church. The result was, that from the very first the sum thus collected more than doubled what had previously been obtained by the more ordinary practice. I do not mention this as a plan to be adopted by us ; but I do consider it as worthy of being mentioned, and of being kept in mind. For the supply, then, of all that was originally contemplated by our Society, I look with perfect confidence to the liberality of our own native Scottish Episcopalians, who, I believe, are daily learning more and more to recognise and to practise the duty of administering to the spiritual wants of those who are of the household of faith. For the means of cultivating the larger field that is opening before us, I rely with equal confidence upon the liberality of our English friends, whose assistance I have found to increase exactly in proportion as the knowledge of the real position of the Scottish portion of the Church is disseminated among them. I am happy to see among us a tried friend from England, Mr Mackenzie, Secretary to our London Committee, and I have to request that he will favour us with communicating to the meeting any information he may think fit respecting the movement that has already been made in London on our behalf. But while we thus anticipate future aid, it is most becoming we should acknowledge with gratitude the favours we have already received, and I have accordingly much pleasure in seconding the motion."

At Bishop Terrot's request Mr Mackenzie rose and said—" Right Reverend Sir—Though I should have been most unwilling to intrude myself on the notice of this meeting, yet I feel that it is incumbent upon me to obey the call made upon me by the Right Rev. the Bishop of the Diocese; and I must express also my sense of the high privilege to be identified personally with such a meeting as this, where faithful members of Christ's holy Church are banded together to promote the glory of their common Lord. At the same time, I must regret that this duty has not fallen upon my reverend colleague Mr Bowdler, 'an elder and a better soldier' in his Master's cause, who would have traced out more ably the slender assistance that we in England have been enabled to afford to the Scottish Episcopal Church Society. It is, I believe, Sir, well known to this meeting, that a Branch Association of the Gaelic Episcopal Society existed for several years in England. When, however, that Society was merged into the Scottish Episcopal Church Society, the London Committee also transferred their services to the new Society then constituted. Some difficulties, however, stood in the way of the active operation of the London Committee, until the commencement of the current year, when we were enabled to extend that Committee considerably, and place the performance of its duties on a regular though still limited footing. As the names of the Committee will be printed with the Report of this year's proceedings about to be circulated, I need not detain this meeting by reading them; but when I mention the names of Gladstone, Hope, and Wilberforce, I doubt not this will be accepted as a guarantee for the soundness and efficiency of the Committee in general. We are indebted to the kindness of the Committee of the Society for the Propagation of the Gospel in Foreign Parts, for the use of their house to hold the quarterly meetings of our London Committee, when we assemble for conducting the business, which we find gradually increasing upon our hands. And here, Sir, perhaps I may be allowed to say, that we have not had recourse to personal pleading, or to a begging system in England, in order to strengthen the hands of the Church in Scotland. Whatever your brethren of England have been enabled to do towards your assistance they have done voluntarily, as they became acquainted with the facts of your case—not grudgingly, nor of necessity, but as cheerful givers—esteeming it a privilege to have such a means of expressing their Christian sympathy with a pure and holy branch of Christ's universal Church. Among various parts of England with which communications have been opened, I ought perhaps specially to name Oxford, Cambridge, Eton, and Bridgenorth, at which latter place a considerable Local Association has been formed in aid of the funds of the Parent Society. And now, Sir, having given a slight outline of our doings in the South, perhaps I may be permitted to take up the tone of the Right Rev. Prelate who preceded me, and offer a few remarks on the Catholic character of this Society, as connected with the present state and prospects of the Reformed Church at large. It seems to be proved by experience, that the scrutinizing spirit of the age leads the mass of people to look too much to detail, and neglect to regard the aspect of the whole, as a whole. I speak this abstractedly, as true of almost any given subject. Now, Sir, I conceive it to be one of the great merits of the Scottish Episcopal Church, that she has not fallen into this error. She is not acting through the instrumentality of this Society, simply in a selfish view, but as endeavouring to fulfil her responsibilities alike towards her Lord and her children, as a part of one great system—as an integral portion of that one universal and apostolic Church, which the Head of the Church ordained to be the evangelizer of the nation!"

Such is an abstract of the proceedings of the Scottish Episcopal Church Society, as reported at the second and third Annual Meetings. The benefits which have been already conferred on the Church are every year more and more perceptible. If the present writer may be allowed a suggestion, it might be of some importance to impart to the Society's operations a kind of *home missionary* or *church extension aspect*, embracing the opportunity of constituting a congregation in every town and village of the country where members of the Church are to be found.

The SNELL EXHIBITIONS at Baliol College, Oxford, might be rendered of essential consequence to the Scottish Episcopal Church, if conferred according to the bequest of the founder. As the history of these important Exhibitions is very imperfectly known, and as they have been for many years given, by some influence or other, to persons whom the founder unquestionably never intended to enjoy them, an account of them will not be unacceptable to the reader.

It has been asserted in several local works that Mr Snell founded his Exhibitions after the Revolution of 1688, when the Church was deprived of its temporalities One writer gravely states, that "in the year 1688 Mr John Snell, with a view to support Episcopacy in Scotland, devised to trustees a considerable estate near Leamington, in Warwickshire, for educating Scottish students at Baliol College, Oxford."* This is utterly erroneous as it respects the date. Mr Snell executed his Will in 1679, when the Episcopal Church was the Established Church of Scotland, and when there was not the least probability of its ejection from the temporalities. This is proved from the " Copy made from the Extract of Mr Snell's Will, from the Registry of the Prerogative Court of Canterbury," printed in the Appendix to the Report of the Commissioners appointed by his Majesty George IV., and re-appointed by his Majesty William IV., for visiting the Universities of Scotland.† At the time, too, when Mr Snell made his munificent bequest the University of Glasgow was Episcopal, the professors were of necessity members of that Church, and the Chancellor was the Archbishop of the diocese.

The following extracts from Mr Snell's Will sufficiently set forth the objects of the founder, of whose personal history nothing is known:—
" In the name of God, Amen. I, John Snell, of Uffeton, in the county of Warwick, being in health of body, and of perfect memory and understanding, God be praised for the same, and for all other his great mercies bestowed upon me, yet, considering my mortality, and the certainty of my death, but the uncertainty of the time thereof, and being minded to settle and dispose of that estate wherewith it hath pleased my most gracious and bountiful God to bless me in this world, do make and ordain this my last will and testament, as followeth." He bequeaths to his wife, Johanna Snell, an annuity of L.100 sterling, to be paid out of the manor and lands of Uffeton ; the sum of L.100 to be paid her within one month after his death, and his dwelling-house in the Savoy, and the use of all his " household stuff, plate, and jewels therein, during her widowhood." Mr Snell next bequeaths to his daughter, Dorothy Snell,

* Cleland's Annals of Glasgow, vol. ii. p. 103. New Statistical Account of Scotland—Lanarkshire.

† Presented to both Houses of Parliament, and printed in 1837, vol. ii. of Reports of Commissioners, and vol. xxxvi. of Parliamentary Returns.

the sum of L.2000, to be paid when she completed her eighteenth year, or day of marriage, if she married with the consent of his executors, or the survivors or survivor of them; but in case she married without such consent, he orders that legacy to become void, and he gives her only L 500, to be paid within six months after her marriage, and an annuity of L.100 for life; and the sum of L.60 per annum is allowed to his wife for the "support and education, maintenance, diet, and apparel," of his daughter, whom he orders to reside with her mother till she is eighteen years of age. After sundry small legacies to his own nephews named Stewart, and his wife's nephew and niece named Mason; to his executors L.10 each, to purchase mournings; to his sister, Silvester Cooper, L 5, to " buy her a ring; and to every one of her children who shall be living at the time of his death, twenty shillings a piece, to buy them rings;" to the poor of the parish of Uffeton, L.10; to the poor of the parish of St Clement-Danes, and of St Mary's-le-Savoy, in Westminster, L.5 to each parish, and L 50 for the repair of the church of Uffeton, Mr Snell thus orders his bequest:—" And my farther will and mind is, and I do hereby desire, direct, and appoint, that after all my debts, legacies, annuities, and rents, charges hereby devised and appointed, and my funeral charges shall be all discharged, satisfied, and paid, or otherwise sufficiently secured to be paid, the said Johanna Snell, William Bridgeman, Benjamin Cooper, William Hopkins, and Thomas Newcombe,* and the survivors or survivor of them, and the heirs, executors, and administrators of the survivor of them, shall convey and settle all the rest and residue of my estate, which shall then remain in their hands, upon five or more persons, to be named Trustees for that purpose, and upon their heirs, such as the Vice-Chancellor of the said University of Oxford, the Provost of Queen's College, the Master of Baliol College, and the President of St John's College, in the same University, for the time being, or any three of them, shall nominate and appoint, upon trust, that the profits and product thereof may be employed and disposed of for the maintenance and education, in some College or Hall in that University to be appointed by the said Vice-

* Those personal friends of Mr Snell are described in his Will as " William Bridgeman, of St Martin's-in the-Fields, Esq, Benjamin Cooper, Register of the University of Oxford, William Hopkins of Oxford aforesaid, gentleman, and Thomas Newcombe, citizen and stationer of London."

Chancellor, Provost, Master, and President, for the time being, or any three of them, and in such proportions, and with such allowances, and in such manner as they, or any three of them, shall elect, think fit, and appoint, such and so many scholars, *born and educated in Scotland,* who shall each of them have spent *three years, or two at the least, at the College of Glasgow in that Kingdom, or one year there, and two at the least in some other College in that Kingdom,* as they, the said Vice-Chancellor, or Provost, Master, and President, for the time being, or any three of them, shall think fit, *not exceeding the number of twelve, nor being under the number of five,* at any one time, unless the revenue and profits of my estate, for the purposes foresaid hereby devised, by the discreet and prudent management of my Executors and Trustees, shall increase to such a condition as may bear an allowance competent to maintain a greater number. And my farther mind and will is, *that every such scholar and scholars,* upon each of their admission to such College or Hall as aforesaid, shall be *bound and obliged,* by such security as the said Vice-Chancellor, Provost, Master, and President, for the time being, or any three of them, shall think fit, to some person or persons, to be by them, or any three of them, thereunto appointed, that the said *scholar or scholars shall respectively forfeit and pay to that College or Hall* whereof or wherein he or they shall be respectively admitted, *the sum of L.500 a-piece if he shall not enter into holy orders,* and if he or they shall, *at any time after his or their entering and admission, take or accept of any spiritual promotion, benefice, or other preferment whatsoever, within the Kingdom of England or Dominion of Wales,* it being my will and desire that every scholar so to be admitted *shall return into Scotland,* and there to be advanced as his or their capacity and parts shall deserve, *but in no case to come back into England, nor to go into any other place, but only into the Kingdom of Scotland,* for his or their preferment. And my will also is, that none of the scholars to be elected and admitted as aforesaid, shall take any benefit of this my bequest above the space of ten years, or eleven at the most; for after that time they are, and it is my express will and desire that they shall and may be, *removed into Scotland, as aforesaid.* And it is my farther will and meaning, and I do hereby appoint, that when any one or more of the said scholars shall be removed or die, that the said Vice-Chancellor, Provost, Master, and President, for the time being, and the Governor or

Principal, for the time being, of such College or Hall whereof such scholar or scholars so removed, or dead, shall be a member or members, or any three of them, shall, from time to time, for ever, as often as occasion shall be, have power to elect and admit one or more other scholar or scholars, born and educated as aforesaid, to succeed in the room and stead of such scholar or scholars so removed or dead. And my farther will and mind is, that all such scholars as shall from time [to time] be elected and admitted, shall before their admittance be recommended by the Principal of the said College of Glasgow, the Professor of Divinity, the Regent, and other the chief officers of the said College for the time being, or three of them at the least, whereof the Principal for the time being to be one, by their letters-recommendatory under their College Seal; and also that every such scholar, so as aforesaid to be elected, shall come as a probationer to such College or Hall whereunto he shall be appointed as aforesaid, and shall there continue at his own charges for six months at the least, to give evidence of his behaviour, learning, and abilities, before he shall be admitted to receive any benefit of this my desire and will; after those six months are expired, he shall be allowed and admitted, or disallowed, according to the discretion of the persons before appointed, for that purpose, or any three or more of them; and to every such scholar I do allow and appoint twenty pounds a-year after that time, to be paid him half-yearly at the least; but if my estate will bear a greater allowance than what is herein expressed, I desire the scholars may have the benefit of it, and to be paid by half-yearly payments at Midsummer and Christmas." The other details are merely directions about the management of the estate, and the document is concluded in the usual manner:—" In witness whereof to this my last will and testament, contained in six sheets of paper, all of my own handwriting, I have set my hand and seal at the bottom of every sheet; and I do declare this to be my last will and testament, this nine-and-twentieth day of December, in the nine-and-twentieth year of the reign of our sovereign Lord Charles the Second, by the grace of God, of England, Scotland, France, and Ireland, King, Defender of the Faith, &c. Anno Domini 1677.—(Signed) JOHN SNELL. Signed, sealed, and published, to be the last will and testament of the said John Snell, the day and year above written, in the presence of us, Richard Taylor, Thos. Fowle, Fra. Cane, Robert Fenwick. Republished and declared to be the last will and testament of me, the said John Snell, the sixth of August 1679, and all the interlineations and alterations are made by my own hand; and all this is done in the presence of Ric. Lydall, Tho. Mundy, John Mundy, Tho. Snell, Thomas Adams." Then follows the proof of Mr Snell's Will in the Prerogative Court of the Archbishop of Canterbury :—" Probatum fuit testamentum suprascriptum apud London, coram venerabili et egregio viro Domino Leolino Jenkins, milite, Legum Doctore, Curiæ Prærogativæ Cantuariensis Magistro Custode, sive Commissario legitimo constituto, 13° die mensis Septembris, anno Domini 1679, juramentis Johannæ Snell relictæ, Gulielmi Bridgeman, armigeri, Benjamini Cooper, Gulielmi Hopkins, et Thomæ Newcombe, executorum, &c. quibus, &c. debere, &c. vigore commissionis jurat, viz. dictis Johanna Snell, Gulielmo Bridgeman, et Thoma Newcombe, coram venerabili viro Henrico Fauconberge, Legum Doctore Surrogato dicti Commissarii nec non prefatis Benjamino Cooper et Gulielmo Hopkins vigore Commissionis jurat. Sic subscribitur, Wm. Legard, Pet. M'Evoy, Dlen. Stevens, Deputy-Registers.—Ed. A. Yuille."

The Professors of Glasgow College, thus constituted nominators to the Snell Exhibitions, are not all entitled to vote. The right to exercise the presentations is limited to the Principal, and the Professors of Logic and Rhetoric, Moral Philosophy, Natural Philosophy, Greek, Divinity, Humanity, Mathematics, Oriental Languages, Physic, Civil Law, and Law of Scotland, Anatomy, Ecclesiastical History, and Astronomy—fourteen in number, who, in the phraseology of the University of Glasgow, are designated exclusively the *College Professors*, having the entire control of the revenue and property of the College, and exercising the patronage. There are ten Exhibitioners, who hold their presentations for ten years, but vacating by marriage, or obtaining preferment above the value of the Exhibitions. It is farther stated in the Parliamentary Report—" The income of Mr Snell's charity established in Baliol College, Oxford, in 1693, for natives of Scotland, *attached by education and principles to the doctrine and discipline* of the Church of England, arises from the rent of a manor and estate at Uffton in the county of Warwick. This property was let in 1809, upon a lease of twenty-one years, at an annual rent of L.1500, out of which the following payments were by order of the Court of Chancery appointed to be made, viz.—To ten Exhibitioners, at L.133, 6s. 8d. per annum each, L 1333, 6s. 8d.; the Master of Baliol, for gubernation money, L.31, 15s.; the College, L.63, 10s.; ditto, for an entertainment of the meeting of the Trustees to audit the accounts, L.11, 2s. 2d.; the steward, or receiver of the rents, L 33, 6s. 8d.; the surplus-fund, for expenses in visiting and inspecting the estates, and if not so applied, to be vested in the public funds, in the name of the accountant-general for the benefit of the estates, L 26, 19s 6d.—in all, L.1500." The whole estate is managed by the Master and Fellows of Baliol College, regulated by the Court of Chancery. If the Principal and *College Professors*, as they are called, in the University of Glasgow, or three of them at the least, fail to nominate any eligible person by letters recommendatory under their College Seal, the right falls for that time, *jure devoluto*, to the Master and Fellows of Baliol, to "nominate and elect any person born within the Kingdom of Scotland, and also provided the person so nominated has such qualifications as are required by the said will and decree, viz—1. That he be a native of the Kingdom of Scotland [which the Master of Baliol requires to be proved by an extract of the parish register of baptisms]. 2 Such as hath been educated in one of the Universities of Scotland, and hath spent *three, or two years at the least*, in the College of Glasgow, or one year there, and three, or two at the least, in some other College in that Kingdom. 3 Such as hath not taken any degree in any one of the said Universities, but is an undergraduate, and, with respect to his age, of learning and disposition towardly and hopeful. 4. *Such whose education and principles shall lead him to the promoting of the doctrine and discipline established in the Church of England*, being that *which was chiefly intended by the testator's benefaction* 5. Such person judged thus qualified, and thought fit to be nominated to the Master and Fellows of Baliol for their approbation and admission, must bring with him the testimony of the nomination by the Principal and Professors of Glasgow College, under the common seal of their said College. 6. It is enjoined by the said will and decree, that every scholar to be thus nominated and approved is to continue for the space of six months by way of probation; that is to say, as he shall give evidence of his behaviour, learning, and abilities, he is to be admitted or rejected at the expiration of six months."

It is already stated that though the Exhibitions were not established in Baliol College till 1693, Mr Snell's Will was executed when the Episcopal Church was the Established Church of Scotland, in 1677, eleven years before the Revolution, and farther declared by him to be his last will and testament in 1679. No human being could then have anticipated the Revolution, or the ejection of the Episcopal Church as the national establishment. The express object of the bequest for " natives of Scotland, attached by education and principles to the doctrine and discipline of the Church of England," being that which, according to the explicit declaration of the Master and Fellows of Baliol, as one of the essential qualifications, was " *chiefly intended by the testator's benefaction.*" Connected with this there are other conditions solemnly set forth in the founder's Will, viz. that the Exhibitioners shall enter into holy orders in that Church, and never " take or accept of any spiritual promotion, benefice, or other preferment whatsoever, within the Kingdom of England or Dominion of Wales," but shall return to Scotland for their preferment, and " in no case come back into England, nor go into any other place," under the penalty of forfeiting *five hundred pounds sterling* to the Master and Fellows of Baliol College. In short, the great purpose of Mr Snell, in founding these Exhibitions, and ordering those appointed to them to enter into holy orders and return to Scotland, was, as a local writer observes, to assist in preserving a regular Episcopal ministry in Scotland in all time coming, that the Church of England in that Kingdom " might never be without a witness."

Now, instead of the founder's wishes being carried into effect, and the Snell Exhibitioners of right compelled to enter into holy orders and return to Scotland, to devote themselves and their energies to the service of the Episcopal Church, under the penalty of *five hundred pounds sterling*, it is notorious that the very reverse of all this is the case, and that persons are nominated to and obtain these Exhibitions whose " education and principles" are not only altogether opposed to the " promoting of the doctrine and discipline established in the Church of England," but are not, and never were, members of that Church, or of the Scottish Episcopal Church. It is clear that these benefactions were strictly limited to the members of that Church, or to those who conformed sincerely and conscientiously to the Church of England; yet it is an extraordinary fact, that they have for the most part been held by Presbyterians, who qualified themselves by an attendance of three years at the University of Glasgow. It is true they would make an appearance of adherence to the Church of England after their admission into Baliol College, and would of necessity sign the Thirty-Nine Articles; but it is also true that they have returned to Scotland after graduating at Oxford, and openly professed themselves Presbyterians, even while they were enjoying the emoluments of the Exhibitions during the ten years they are tenable. The case of Sir James W. Moncreiff, Bart., who became a member of the Scottish Bar in 1799, and took his seat as a Judge in the Court of Session by the title of Lord Moncreiff in 1829, is one of the numerous examples of this class. His Lordship's father was Sir Henry Moncreiff, Bart., a very distinguished minister of the Presbyterian Establishment; and this fact is merely mentioned to show that his Lordship never had any connection with the Episcopal Church. Yet here is a gentleman who enjoyed the benefits of Mr Snell's munificent benefaction, and instead of entering into holy orders, as he ought to have done, and returning to Scotland to advance the cause of Episcopacy, betakes himself to the more lucrative profession of the Bar, and continued, as is well known in Scotland, a prominent leader for many years in the General Assembly, in which he introduced and carried the famous Veto Act, in the opinion of many members of the Presbyterian Establishment the origin of all their subsequent troubles, contentions, and numerous expensive litigations. It is undeniable, therefore, that Lord Moncreiff incurred the penalty of L.500 to the Master and Fellows of Baliol, which he ought to have paid. But if Lord Moncreiff's conscience was thus so pliable, what shall we say of his son, Mr Henry Moncreiff, also a Baliol Exhibitioner, who took the degree of Bachelor of Arts at Oxford, and who, instead of returning to Scotland in holy orders, came back as he went, and was actually *inducted Established Presbyterian Minister of East Kilbride in the county of Lanark in* 1836? This is a most flagrant case of dereliction of principle, and probably the most noted on record connected with the Baliol Exhibitioners, not one of whom, to whatever professions they betook themselves, ever at least became Presbyterian ministers, and thus grossly perverted and misapplied the benefaction of Mr Snell, whose sole object was to encourage " natives of Scotland " to promote the " doctrine and discipline established in the Church of England " in Scotland. Every one of them who did not enter into holy orders and comply with the terms of Mr Snell's Will incurred the penalty of L.500 to the Master and Fellows of Baliol. This Mr Henry Moncreiff has done; but he also notoriously and most ungenerously contrived to reap the benefits of a bequest never intended by the testator for such as he, and he evinced his gratitude to the founder by becoming a parochial minister of the Presbyterian Establishment—an Establishment collectively noted for its enmity to the Episcopal Church. The want of conscientious feeling is here so undeniable, that it is time the Master and Fellows of Baliol College should insist on the Exhibitioners strictly fulfilling Mr Snell's will and express desire, or demand the penalty of L.500. If such an appropriation of a Presbyterian bequest had been made by Episcopalians, loud would have been the denunciations in Presbyteries, Synods, and General Assemblies, and every effort would have been very properly made to apply the benefaction to the parties for whom it was specially intended by the founder. If Mr Snell's Will was enforced as it ought to be by the Master and Fellows of Baliol College, they would confer a vast obligation on the Scottish Episcopal Church; and this they could easily do without in the least interfering with the right of nomination vested in the Principal and Professors of the University of Glasgow, who have no connection with the right of admission to the benefits of the Snell Exhibitions. Every one who holds them should be made deliberately to promise that he will enter into holy orders after he graduates, *and return to Scotland;* or, if he should subsequently betake himself from inclination to any other profession whatever, he should be made to pay the penalty of L.500. It is lamentable to convert what was piously intended for religious and ecclesiastical purposes into an object of temporal and secular advancement, in any other profession than that specified by the founder. It appears, from the Second Report of the Glasgow University Commissioners, that in the list of the names of the ten gentlemen who enjoyed the Snell Exhibitions from 1827-8 to 1836-7, only three of them entered into holy orders, viz. the Rev. G. M. Drummond, B.A., who officiated some years as minister of St Mark's Episcopal Chapel in Portobello, the Rev. Archibald Crawford Tait, M.A., appointed in 1842 Head Master of Rugby School, vacant by the decease of Dr Arnold, and the Rev. James Connel.

In the Answers from the University of Glasgow to the University Commissioners, printed in the Second Report of 1839, occur the following statements :—" The College have further to regret, that in the former Report too much weight was given to certain complaints respecting the selection of Exhibitioners to Baliol College on Mr Snell's foundation. If the College have to court inquiry on one subject more than another, it is in the exercise of this branch of their patronage. Their selection is invariably made in strict conformity to the conditions prescribed by the foundation, and repeated in every notification of a vacancy transmitted from Baliol College. That all their appointments should be equally successful is not to be expected, but the records of Oxford will show that their Exhibitioners have obtained a share of University honours far beyond the proportion of their average number. The wish ascribed to the students (and to the expression of which they have been most industriously stirred up), that the Exhibitions should be publicly competed for can be entertained only in ignorance. Distinguished scholarship is an essential, but not the sole qualification to be regarded in making such appointments. It is necessary that those who go to Oxford should possess *manners and habits* suited to that seminary; that they should have a fair prospect of benefiting by the education they receive there ; and that they should possess the means of expending, in addition to the amount of the Exhibition, a sum more than double the average expenditure of a student at Glasgow. To invite in such circumstances a competition, by which scarcely an individual could profit, would be an absurd and insulting mockery. On this charge the Professors desire to be judged not by vague surmise, or a reference to failures, invidiously selected, and forming exceptions to the general character of their Exhibitioners, but by the broad fact, that of no class of students has a larger proportion risen to the highest professional and literary eminence than of those who have gone from Glasgow to Oxford." While the general principles here maintained may be admitted to the fullest extent, and while it is undeniable that some of the Snell Exhibitioners have secured for themselves a distinguished reputation, the Professors ought to respect one of the most important qualifications for eligibility, which they appear in the great proportion of cases to have utterly disregarded. They allege to the Commissioners that " their selection is invariably made in strict conformity to the conditions prescribed by the foundation, and repeated in every notification of a vacancy transmitted from Baliol College." Now, it is seen that the fourth condition of eligibility, as set forth in every such notification by the Master and Fellows of Baliol, is, that the individual nominated shall be one " whose education and principles shall lead him to the promoting of the doctrine and discipline established in the Church of England, being that which was *chiefly intended by the founder.*" It is clear that Presbyterians, who never intend to conform to the Church of England, have not the slightest claim, and no right whatever to enjoy Mr Snell's benefaction ; and it is undeniable that the Glasgow Professors have paid little or no attention to this very important qualification. From the list of Exhibitioners, too, it appears that not a few of them were the sons of Professors, and of persons connected with the city of Glasgow and neighbourhood, who have never risen to any " high and professional and literary eminence ;" and the only son of an Episcopal clergyman who was nominated to the Exhibition for many years, was Mr Samuel Horsley, son of the Very Rev. Heneage Horsley, M.A , Dundee, and grandson of the illustrious Bishop Horsley, appointed in 1828-9. These are the facts of the whole matter, and the causes of complaint are that the founder's express injunctions are not fulfilled, and that these Exhibitions are made available for and are appropriated to private and secular purposes. No one can ever allege, after perusing the extracts from Mr Snell's Will already given, that the benevolent testator had no objections though his Exhibitioners became Judges in the Scottish Supreme Courts, continued members and elders of the Presbyterian Establishment, betook themselves to the English or Scottish Bar, or became Presbyterian ministers. The Church of England never attempted to seize Lady Hewley's charity, about which there has been a vast litigation in the Court of Chancery; and the Scottish Presbyterians have no right to monopolize any, or enjoy even one, of the Snell Exhibitions, if they do not intend in after life to comply with the conditions of the founder.

In 1841 was projected TRINITY EPISCOPAL COLLEGE, and no sooner was this academical institution announced than an excitement was evinced by a certain predominating section of the Presbyterian Establishment almost unprecedented. They either misunderstood or purposely misrepresented the objects of the College ; for though it was repeatedly stated that no other doctrines were to be taught than those of the Church of England, as set forth in the Thirty-Nine Articles,

Homilies, and ritual of that Church, very different views were taken. Names with which the Church has no connection, and applied by its enemies to designate certain alleged opinions said to be maintained by some divines in England, were applied with extraordinary virulence, and an alarm was manifested as great as if the erection of Trinity College was to overthrow the Presbyterian Establishment. The bigoted folly of all this controversy on one side, for the Scottish Episcopal Church disdained to take the least notice of it, was as undeniable, as it was partial, unjust, and persecuting in spirit. The distinguished clergy and laity, presumed to be the chief promoters of Trinity College, were also assailed by the most rancorous phraseology in particular newspapers, the gross ignorance displayed by the writers in which respecting the foundation of the College was as astonishing as their credulity in believing every rumour without inquiring into its authenticity.

The well informed and prudent members of the Presbyterian Establishment were not infected by this spirit of prejudice and bigotry. They saw neither cause for alarm in the institution of the projected College, nor any unreasonableness on the part of its promoters. Most of the Presbyterian Dissenters have their own "Divinity Halls," as they are called, for the theological training and instruction of those who intend to become preachers in their respective religious communities, and yet they were never denounced for setting up rival institutions, in which, moreover, the voluntary principles, subversive of all Church Establishments, are diligently inculcated. Their students withdraw from the Scottish Universities after the attendance of four years, during which they apply themselves to their literary course, and place themselves under the teachers appointed by the body to whose principles they are attached. Thus, the Seceders have a regular Divinity Hall, and six Professors, attendance on whose course includes a period of six years. The Relief Synod, another class of Presbyterian Dissenters, have two Professors of Theology; the "Reformed Presbyterian Church," or Cameronians, one; the "Associate Synod of Original Seceders," two; and the Independents, or "Congregational Union of Scotland," have two in their Academy in Glasgow. Even the Roman Catholics have their College of St Mary at Blairs, near Aberdeen, under a President, three Professors, and a Procurator, for the education of candidates for the priesthood, and yet no fierce denunciations were ever levelled at them for maintaining such an institution. When they exhibited themselves in a much bolder manner, and opened the Convent of St Margaret's near Burntsfield Links, Edinburgh, with grand ceremonial in 1836, no pamphlets or newspaper attacks were made on the part of the Presbyterian Establishment respecting the first convent erected in Scotland for the reception of nuns since the Reformation. All was allowed to pass unnoticed; even a pontifical mass excites no enmity from them; and they seem to have resolved no longer to offer the Romanists any molestation. The Scottish Episcopal Church has as good a right to assume the theological superintendence of its clergy as any of the sects now mentioned; yet it appears, that they may do what they please with impunity, while the Church cannot take the slightest step to promote its own interests, in a country in which its Bishops and clergy are recognised as such by law, without undergoing the ordeal of abuse. There is something excessively mean in all this which is too palpable to be mistaken, and reflects little credit on the zealots by whom this conduct is exhibited. The English Dissenters have their theological academies, to the institution of which the Church of England never made the slightest opposition. To make the inconsistency of the enemies of the Church in the Presbyterian Establishment more apparent, at the very time they were assailing Trinity College as an innovation of their alleged rights, they evinced no such scruples in England—a country where they are a mere fraction of the people, and were actually encouraging the formation of a kind of Presbyterian "College," for the same object as that of Trinity College in the Scottish Episcopal Church.

But the truth is, that for several years the *nucleus* of a College had existed in the Church. The Pantonian Professorship of Theology was the first instituted, and subsequently the Church History Professorship, conjoined with the Bell Lecture. As it respects candidates for holy orders, it is generally required in present circumstances that they shall have attended one or other of the Scottish Universities, and complete the usual course of four years, a regular attendance at which qualifies the student for his degree in Arts. They then withdraw from the University, and attend the lectures of the Pantonian Professor of Divinity and the Professor of Church History. It hence appears that the Scottish Episcopal students have no connection with the theological prolections communicated in the Universities. Thus far does the Church follow the Canon set forth by Royal Authority in 1635, when established by law, entitled—" Of Presbyters and Deacons, their nomination, ordination, and functions;" and the Fifth Canon of the Synod of Laurencekirk, 1828, in quoting the Canon of 1635 enjoins, that though "in the present state of this Church it may be found expedient, in some particular instances, to dispense with the observance of part of what is there ordained," nevertheless, every candidate for holy orders, who has not received a regular academical education, shall be examined as to his literary qualifications by two or more presbyters appointed by the Bishop who is to ordain him. He must also show that he is sufficiently acquainted with the Four Gospels and the Acts of the Apostles in the original Greek, give an account of his faith in Latin, and deliver a discourse in English on any text of Scripture which the examinators shall prescribe, and answer any questions on theology and ecclesiastical history which they may deem necessary.

When these facts are considered, the institution of a College in the Scottish Episcopal Church was an event likely to take place sooner or later, and the opposition to it on the part of a certain section of the Presbyterian Establishment is astonishing, more especially when it must have been well known that all such display of enmity would be utterly impotent. In addition to the above statements, it must be recollected that the system of education pursued in the Philosophy Classes of the Scottish Universities is notoriously defective, and has been long the subject of very serious objections. Even in the elementary departments to which the students first resort, such as the Latin, Greek, and Mathematics, there is too much abstract lecturing, and too little practical instruction by proper and thorough examinations communicated. As to the discipline it is a complete mockery, and any student may do what he pleases if he attends with tolerable regularity during the hours appointed for the meeting of his classes, is peaceable and decorous in his behaviour, and performs the exercises prescribed. This occupies from two to four hours during the day, after which he may go anywhere, or do and say what he pleases, as he is under no farther restraint, and he must prepare himself in the best manner he can. The whole system, in short, abounds with marked inconveniences, which have been often felt, and as often pointed out, to effect an alteration. It was natural, therefore, that the Scottish Episcopal Church, yearly increasing in numbers, should assert its right, enjoyed by the Dissenters and the Roman Catholics, to have its own College, in which the literary and theological education of many who are to be its future clergy will be conducted in a manner efficient and satisfactory to those entrusted with the responsibilities of its control. As to the charge originated by the Presbyterians, that certain alleged religious and doctrinal opinions, which have attracted great attention in England, would be taught exclusively in Trinity College, it is almost unworthy of notice. This clamour consisted of mere surmises, circulated for obvious purposes, especially to generate suspicion and alarm in the minds of those who might otherwise be disposed to come forward liberally with their subscriptions to promote the work. The most unfounded and erroneous motives were imputed to the projectors, and though these were occasionally denied, yet they were studiously unnoticed by the enemies of the Church, who were not scrupulous even to draw on their inventive faculties to excite the prejudices of the public. As it was it completely failed, and the members and friends of the Church both in Scotland and England evinced by their liberality that party bigotry and sectarian virulence had poured forth their abuse in vain.

As the proceedings connected with the institution of Trinity College will hereafter be interesting in the history of the Scottish Episcopal Church, any of the public documents connected with it are of importance, though these, whatever the private correspondence may have been, are neither numerous nor of great length. The "Proposals" for founding the College first demand attention. These were finally arranged at the annual meeting of the Bishops, and of the Committee of the Scottish Episcopal Church Society, on the 2d of September 1841, when the Synodal Letter of the Bishops was sanctioned and signed. The first announcement appeared in Edinburgh on the 13th of December 1841.* The Synodal Letter is addressed "to all faithful members of the REFORMED CATHOLIC CHURCH"—a designation which gave offence to several persons connected with the Scottish Episcopal Church, and it still farther served to incite the Presbyterians to renew their misrepresentations. But while the opposition of the latter was to be expected under any circumstances, it might have occurred to the former that the title REFORMED CATHOLIC CHURCH was not inappropriate, because the Scottish Episcopal Church

* In the "NORTH BRITISH ADVERTISER."

is a part of the Church Catholic or Universal throughout the world, and the Synodal Letter of the Bishops was not intended to be confined exclusively to Scotland, but is addressed to all members of the same Church Catholic whom it might reach, in whatever country or quarter of the globe. The following is the first intimation of the projected College, with the Synodal Letter, and " Proposals for the foundation of an Academical Institution in connection with the Scottish Episcopal Church," which has been the object of most extraordinary virulence on the part of a large section of the Established Presbyterians.

"The Committee have very great satisfaction in bringing before the notice of the members of the Episcopal Communion in Scotland the scheme for the establishment of TRINITY COLLEGE, of which the general features are delineated in the accompanying ' Proposals.'

"The Committee are fully persuaded that the want which it is now proposed to supply has been long felt, especially by those who desire to undertake the duties of the holy ministry ; and while they regard, with feelings of the warmest sympathy and most affectionate interest, the efforts which are now making to ameliorate the temporal condition of their clerical brethren, they are convinced that the establishment of the proposed College is eminently calculated not to impede but to further that good work.

"The Committee desire to take the present opportunity of saying that their object is perfectly plain and straightforward. They utterly disclaim any peculiar or party views ; they have no purpose beyond that which is plainly set forth in the printed statement ; they have received the sanction of, and are acting in concert with, their Bishops ; and they have the utmost gratification in stating, that, having submitted their proposals to the Archbishops of Canterbury, York, and Armagh, they have been favoured with the approbation and encouragement of these Prelates. The Committee believe, that, taken in connection with the Synodal Letter of the Scottish Bishops, the names of these venerated Prelates will afford the best guarantee that the individuals who now come forward, earnestly entreating, on behalf of TRINITY COLLEGE, the support of all who take an interest in the Episcopal Church of Scotland, have no object in view but that of promoting her best and dearest interests.

"SYNODAL LETTER to all Faithful Members of the Reformed Catholic Church, the BISHOPS IN SCOTLAND, greeting. Grace be with you, mercy and peace from God the Father, and our Lord Jesus Christ.

"WHEREAS certain lay members of the Church, moved by a pious desire to promote the glory of God, and the welfare of the flock over which He hath made us overseers, have represented unto us that our Church, having been long depressed, hath suffered the total loss of temporal endowments; and that hence great difficulty hath been found in maintaining the decent administration of God's Word and Sacraments, more especially in so far as the same depends upon the due education of candidates for holy orders; that the sense of this deficiency hath been frequently declared by various pious but inadequate bequests for this purpose, and more recently by the Church herself in the Canon XL., and that the same still exists in almost undiminished magnitude:

"AND WHEREAS they have represented unto us their desire, under God's blessing, to attempt a remedy for this want; and, in pursuance of such design, have proposed to us the foundation of a school and theological seminary, to be devoted to the training, under collegiate discipline, of candidates for holy orders, and at the same time of such other persons as may desire the benefit of a liberal, in conjunction with a religious education:

"AND WHEREAS they have represented unto us, that sufficient pecuniary support hath been secured to warrant their perseverance in the design, and that they are now desirous, under our sanction, to make a public appeal to the members of the Church in its behalf:

"Now WE, the Bishops of the Reformed Catholic Church in Scotland in Synod assembled, desire to express our warmest gratitude to those with whom this proposal hath originated, and above all, to God, who hath put it into their hearts to attempt the supply of wants, the reality and urgency of which we have long painfully experienced; and having maturely considered the said design, We do hereby formally approve the same, and recommend it to you, our brethren in Christ, as a fitting object for your prayers and alms.

"WE have farther, for the promotion of this good work, requested certain discreet persons to act in Committee, and, in concert with ourselves, to prepare a scheme for its execution, to be submitted to the members of the Church.

"In thus endeavouring to awaken your zeal and charity in behalf of that portion of the Church committed to our charge, We deem it fitting to state, solemnly and explicitly, that We are moved by no feelings of rivalry towards any religious community, but by a desire to supply the wants of our own Communion, and thereby to fulfil a duty implied in the first principles of the Christian Church.

"Brethren, the Grace of our Lord Jesus Christ be with your spirits. Amen.

"W. SKINNER, D.D , Bishop of ABERDEEN and PRIMUS.
PATRICK TORRY, D.D., Bishop of DUNKELD, DUNBLANE, and FIFE.
DAVID LOW, LL.D., Bishop of MORAY, ROSS, and ARGYLL.
MICHAEL RUSSELL, LL.D., Bishop of GLASGOW.
DAVID MOIR, D D., Bishop of BRECHIN.
C. H. TERROT, D.D., Bishop of EDINBURGH.

"*Edinburgh, 2d September* 1841."

"The Institution mentioned in the accompanying Synodal Letter is designed to embrace objects not attainable in any public foundation hitherto established in Scotland, viz. the combination of general education with domestic discipline and systematic religious superintendence.

"It is proposed to found, in a central part of Scotland north of the Frith of Forth, and removed from the immediate vicinity of any large town, a College, to be called the COLLEGE OF THE HOLY AND UNDIVIDED TRINITY, which may receive and board a large number, say ultimately from 150 to 200, of youths from eight to eighteen years of age ; and also afford a sound clerical education to young men destined for holy orders, of whom a considerable number, in addition to those required in Scotland, may be usefully employed in supplying the demands which are now made for clergymen in the British Colonies.

"It is intended that the Institution shall provide Exhibitions, or Bursaries, to be conferred principally on boys likely to become divinity students.

"It is anticipated that, by the means proposed, parents would be enabled to secure all the advantages of a liberal and scientific education at a very moderate rate, varying probably from L.50 to L.80 per annum, according to the age of the scholar. They would also escape the great evil of separating specifically religious from general education;

and would feel that on leaving home their children would continue to enjoy some of its best blessings.

"Such an Institution must, of course, be placed under a clergyman of very high character and attainments, together with assistants, who will thoroughly comprehend the design, and imbue all the details with a religious spirit. It is also contemplated to provide instruction in Classical Literature, Mathematics, and those branches of Mental and Natural Philosophy usually comprehended in academical courses.

"The Scottish Bishops have now, by their Synodal Letter, authoritatively declared their approval of the principle of the scheme, and their desire that aid should be solicited for its support through the instrumentality of a Committee.

"It is obvious that, in order to carry the object into effect, a very considerable sum will be required.

"The purposes to which the Funds will be devoted comprise the providing a Chapel, with Halls and other suitable buildings, the salaries of a Warden, Professors, and Teachers, and the foundation of Bursaries.

"It is calculated that the lowest amount of capital which would justify the commencement of the Institution is L 20,000; and as soon as that sum is raised, a meeting of the subscribers, as afterwards specified, will be called, to confer with the Bishops on the permanent constitution of the College.

"A sum of nearly L.7000 has been already privately contributed, and it is proposed to raise the remainder by a general subscription under the following conditions :—

"(1.) That all contributions of L.50 and upwards are to be payable either at once, or (at the option of the Donor) in five equal instalments; the first to be due when the Committee shall declare that L.15,000 have been subscribed, the others at successive intervals of six months.

"(2.) That all payments whatever are to be returned, unless the subscription, including the price received for nominations, shall reach L.20,000.

"(3.) All donations of L.100 and upwards are to entitle the donor, being a member of the Scottish Episcopal Church, or of the United Church of England and Ireland, to a voice, in conjunction with the

Bishops and the members of Committee, in the settling of the permanent constitution of the establishment at the meeting to be held for that purpose.

"(4.) Perpetual rights of nomination to the College shall be purchasable as follows —One for one hundred guineas, two for two hundred, three for five, and five for a thousand. Nominated pupils to be received with a deduction of ten per cent. from the current rate of annual payment for board and education."

On the 29th of January 1842 a second advertisement appeared, in which many munificent subscriptions were announced. Among these were Her Majesty the Queen Dowager, L 100. His Grace the Archbishop of Canterbury, L.100; his Grace the Archbishop of York, L 100; his Grace the Archbishop of Armagh, L 105; the Lord Bishop of London, L.100, the Lord Bishops of Bangor, St David's, Gloucester and Bristol, and the Lord Bishops of Elphin, Kilmore, and Ardagh, L.50 each; the Lord Bishop of Salisbury, L.25; the Lord Bishop of Calcutta, L.10; the Right Rev. Bishop Skinner, a right of nomination, L 105; Bishops Low, Russell, and Terrot, L.50 each; Bishop Moir, L.20; the Society for Promoting Christian Knowledge, L.1000; the Duke of Buccleuch, L.1000; the late Marquis of Lothian, L.1000; Lord Douglas, L.500; Robert Wardlaw Ramsay, Esq. of Whitehill, L.500; John Gladstone, Esq of Fasque, L.800, and two rights of nomination, L 210; the Right Hon. W. E. Gladstone, M. P., L.210; Mrs W. E. Gladstone, L.500; Thomas Gladstone, Esq., a right of nomination, L.105; J. W. Gladstone, Esq., a right of nomination, L.105; R Gladstone, Esq, a right of nomination, L.105; Rev. Lord Henry Kerr, a right of nomination, L 105; James R. Hope, Esq, theological books, value L.400; Anonymous, L 300; Anonymous, L.100; Edward Badeley, Esq., L.100; J. W. Colville, Esq., L.105; Rev J. C. Robertson, Boxley, L.100; Sir J. S. Richardson, Bart. of Pitfour, a right of nomination, L.105; John Cay, Esq., a right of nomination, L.105; Neil Malcolm, Esq., of Poltalloch, L.100; Sir Gilbert Stirling, Bart, L 105; Alexander Falconar, Esq. of Falcon-Hall, a right of nomination, L.105; James R. Mackenzie, Esq younger of Scatwell, a right of nomination, L.105; Major Maclaren, Portobello, L.100; Sir Patrick Murray Threipland, Bart., L.105; the Earl of Home, L.100; Dr Anderson's Trustees, Aberdeen, L 200 ; Albert Cay, Esq , a right of nomination, L.105 ; the Earl of Dunmore, a right of nomination, L.105 ; C. A. Moir, Esq. of Leckie, a right of nomination, L.105 ; John Stirling, Esq. of Kippendavie, a right of nomination, L.105 ; Rev. C. J. Lyon, St Andrews, a right of nomination, L.105 ; W. Hay, Esq of Dunse Castle, a right of nomination, L.105 ; A. Campbell, Esq. of Blythswood, a right of nomination, L.105 ; Alexander M'Neill, Esq , Advocate, a right of nomination, L.105 ; Alexander Oswald, Esq., Auchincruive House, L.100 ; Lord Kenyon, L 105 ; John Stuart, Esq., Queen's Counsel, L.105 ; James Stirling, Esq. of Garden, L.100 ; Jesse Watts Russell, Esq. of Ham Hall, Staffordshire, L.500 ; Principal and Fellows of Jesus College, Oxford, a right of nomination, L.105 ; Anonymous, from London Committee, L.100 ; Anonymous, L.1000 ; Sir James Ramsay, Bart. of Bamff, a right of nomination, L.105 , William Forbes, Esq. of Callendar, M.P., L 105 ; W. Warring Hay, Esq. of Blackburn, F. M. Gillanders, Esq Liverpool, D. Robertson, Esq. Bedford Square, London, Miss Johanna Robertson, of Carleton Gardens, London, Rev George May, Upper Harley Street, London, Sir Archibald Edmonstone, Bart of Duntreath, Miss May of Clifton Hall, Bristol, a right of nomination, each L 105 ; Miss Boswall of Blackadder, L.110 ; John Guthrie, Esq. of Guthrie, L.100 ; the Trustees of the late Countess Dowager of Rosse's Fund, an exhibition for a divinity student, L.30 per annum ; Sir John Stuart Forbes, Bart. of Pitsligo and Fettercairn, L.52, 10s. ; Archibald Campbell, Esq. of Auchindarroch, a right of nomination, L 105 ; Robert Hay, Esq. of Linplum, a right of nomination, L.105 ; William H. Macdonald, Esq of St Martin's, a right of nomination, L.105 ; John Anstruther Thomson, Esq. of Charlton, a right of nomination, L.105 ; John Grant, Esq. of Kilgraston, a right of nomination, L.105 ; Rev. Dr Pusey, Canon of Christ Church, Oxford, a right of nomination, L.105 ; Magdalen College, Oxford, L.100 ; Robert Clerk Rattray, Esq. of Craighall, a right of nomination, L.105 ; J. D. Morries Stirling, Esq L.105 ; A. J. B. Hope, Esq , L.100.

The subscribers of from L.50 to L.10 and under are numerous, and include many distinguished clerical and lay members of the Church in England and Scotland. According to another announcement on the 29th of July 1842,* the subscriptions amounted to L.18,000, and, including the anticipated remittances from India, it may be stated that

* In the " EDINBURGH ADVERTISER" newspaper.

in December that year, within twelve months after the first advertisement, the sums collected for Trinity Episcopal College exceeded L.21,000.

Among the several sites which rumour assigned to the College, it being deemed prudent by the Committee not to erect it near the University seats of St Andrews, Aberdeen, Glasgow, and Edinburgh, the town of Perth was generally supposed to be the place, and certainly the " Fair City" has many central and local advantages. This alarmed sundry members of that Established Presbytery; and accordingly Mr. Andrew Gray, minister of the West Church, Perth, brought the projected College before the notice of the said Presbytery on the 12th of March 1842, in a long, incoherent, and rambling address, mentioned in the outset of the present volume, entitled, " Oxford Tractarianism, the Scottish Episcopal College, and the Scottish Episcopal Church." The occasion of this " Speech," which, it was stated at the time, was heard with great impatience and indifference by several of the members, was to " overture," in the Presbyterian phraseology, the ensuing General Assembly in May, in the following manner:—" Whereas," said Mr Gray, in his document proposed for the adoption of the Presbytery, " pretensions of a very exclusive and intolerant character, pointing against the Established Church of Scotland, and such other churches of Christ as are not constituted according to what is usually denominated the Episcopal form of church government, and amounting to a denial that the said churches are churches of Christ at all, are put forward with extraordinary activity and zeal at the present day by many members and office-bearers of the Episcopal churches: Whereas great efforts appear to be making by persons who have wealth and influence at their command, for the propagation of the principles on which these offensive pretensions are founded; and whereas the Presbytery of Perth seem specially called on to look to this matter, in consequence of the reported intention to erect a College within their bounds where the principles referred to will be taught: It is therefore humbly overtured to the next General Assembly to adopt such measures, as to their wisdom shall seem meet, for providing the members of this Church with information suited to existing circumstances on the subject of her scriptural constitution and authority, and particularly for having all students in theology thoroughly trained in those principles of ecclesiastical order and government which fortify and vindicate the cause of Presbyterianism against the overbearing and unworthy assumptions of its adversaries."

This " overture," in which nothing is peculiarly objectionable, considering the quarter from which it emanated, and the opinions of its supporters, was carried by a considerable majority, notwithstanding many sensible and judicious remarks made by those who opposed its adoption. It was sent to the General Assembly, but it must have been expunged from the business which came before that body, as it was never even noticed, and has never since been mentioned. Probably the leaders had prudence enough to see that any endeavour on their part to oppose the erection of Trinity College in any parish in Scotland would be a mere *brutum fulmen*, and treated as a ludicrous and impotent attempt at a power which the Presbyterian Establishment could not wield, and, fortunately for the Episcopal Church, it never will possess.

Mr Gray's " Speech " consists of quotations, with comments, from the celebrated Oxford Tracts, the British Critic, the Rev. William Palmer's " Treatise on the Church of Christ ;" certain proceedings of the Society for Promoting Christian Knowledge, as he finds these reported in the " Record " newspaper : Scottish periodical controversies on the projected College ; his notions of the " doctrinal views of Scottish Episcopalians;" the " Exclusive Dogma," as he calls the Apostolical Succession; and passages from " Tracts for all Places and all Times," published at Edinburgh in 1840 by some members of the Episcopal Church. He produced " Documentary Proof that the Scottish Episcopal Church *unchurch* non-episcopal Denominations," by numerous passages, as he selects them, from the following writings of the eighteenth century :—1. " A Friendly Letter, &c. touching Presbytery, in which is plainly and fairly made appear how justly the *horrid sin of Schism*, and sundry other gross errors, are chargeable upon the Presbyterians of Scotland, by a Suffering Member of the Afflicted Church in Scotland. Edinburgh, 1726." 2. " The Nature and Constitution of the Christian Church," published in 1750, " of which I find," says Mr Gray, " that the late Bishop Jolly had a high opinion." 3. " An Essay on the Festival of Christmas, by a Presbyter of the Suffering Church of Scotland," 1753. These are succeeded by some extracts from Bishop Abernethy Drummond's Preface to the " Abridgement of the Rev.

Charles Daubeny's Guide to the Church, by a worthy Scots Episcopal Clergyman," by passages from the " Abridgement ;" from Bishop John Skinner's " Primitive Truth and Order Vindicated," and from his two Catechisms ; from Bishops Sandford and Gleig, in their edition of " A Brief Explanation of the Church Catechism, by the Rev. Basil Woodd," and published, with a Prefatory Letter to the clergy of their Dioceses, in 1824 ; from Bishop Innes' Catechism ; from Bishop Jolly's Catechism, and his tract entitled " Some Plain Instructions concerning the Nature and Constitution of the Christian Church, the Divine Appointment of its Governors and Pastors, and the Nature and Guilt of Schism " The Twenty-Second Canon of the Scottish Episcopal Church on Baptism, from the Code of Canons of 1828, is next cited, followed by passages from the acknowledged writings of the Rev. Patrick Cheyne of Aberdeen, the Rev. J. B. Pratt of Cruden, the Rev. Heneage Horsley of Dundee ; A Presbyter's Sermon, preached at an ordination held by Bishop Low at Pittenweem, Fife, on the 4th of April 1838, entitled, " The Tradition of the Christian Fathers, the Standard Interpretation of Holy Scripture ;" and Bishop Russell's discourse at Bishop Walker's consecration in 1830—" The Historical Evidence for the Apostolical Institution of Episcopacy," carefully stating that Bishop Russell is " the author of the *History of the Church in Scotland.*" Next are cited " A Plea for Primitive Episcopacy," by the Rev. W. C. A. Maclaurin, M.A , Elgin ; the Rev. David Aitchison's little work, published in 1841 —" The Truth with Boldness ;" and the Right Hon. W. E. Gladstone's celebrated volume—" The State in its Relations with the Church." Mr Gray concludes the whole with sundry observations, to the effect that " the Scottish Episcopal Church stands alone in its bigotry ; no, not quite alone ; the Church of Rome keeps it in countenance"—although he knows not " that even she will go so far as to hold that the people of Scotland are not baptized." He says—" We [the Presbyterians] have never maintained that the baptism of Episcopalians is null, or that Episcopalian ministers are not validly ordained." He then quotes " the enlightened and truly scriptural views contained in our Confession of Faith, chapter twenty-five," and adds—" Let it no more be said that Scottish Episcopalians do but say of us what we say of them. It is directly opposed to the fact. We unchurch them not, but they unchurch us. We deny not their baptism, but they deny ours.

We acknowledge the validity of their ordination, but they condemn us as usurpers of the priesthood, and class us with Korah, Dathan, and Abiram."

Much could be said on these statements, inferences, and conclusions, but as this narrative is not controversial it would be out of place. Whether Mr Gray has quoted fairly his authorities, or has taken merely garbled and isolated passages, the present writer cannot say, as the works cited are not in his possession, but in the spirit of charity it may be conceded that he has done so in an honourable manner. By what authority, then, did he take upon himself to give titles to his extracts, as if these titles were the *ipsissima verba* of the passages he selects? Thus, Bishop Jolly is introduced as alleging that " forgiveness of sins is confined to the Episcopal Communion"—that, " in order to be Christians, we must be Episcopalians"—that " the only way to have communion with Christ is to receive Episcopacy"—and that " the people of Scotland are not baptized " The Rev. J. B. Pratt is brought forward as maintaining, that " if a man were to leave the Episcopal Church he would turn his back on the Redeemer;" the Rev. Heneage Horsley, that— " the promise of eternal salvation and the covenant of God pertain to Episcopalians;" the Rev. W. C. A. Maclaurin, that there is " no hardness of heart in denying the name of churches to Presbyterian congregations;" the Rev. David Aitchison, that " Episcopacy is the spouse of Christ and Bride of the Lamb"—that the present religious position of Scotland is unwholesome and wicked—that " John Knox made ' desolate' a ' smiling' land," and an alleged " lament" by Mr Aitchison " over the Reformation," is prominently selected ; and that the compilers of the " Tracts for all Places and all Times," of whom the present writer was one, maintain that " all the covenant promises are made to Episcopalians," and " saving faith necessarily implies obedience to Prelacy." Yet these are the titles which Mr Gray thought proper to affix to the passages he selected and printed in his " Speech"—and this every candid mind will pronounce most unfair and reprehensible. Mr Gray's ignorance of the state of the Scottish Episcopal Church is evident from a sentence he quotes from the biographical notice of Bishop Jolly, by the Rev. Patrick Cheyne of Aberdeen, prefixed to the well known " Address to the Episcopalians of Scotland on Baptismal Regeneration." Mr Cheyne observes, that at the time of Bishop Jolly's ordination "the clergy of Scotland had to struggle with manifold privations, and were exposed to no inconsiderable danger in the exercise of their functions." Mr Gray thus comments—" The 'clergy of Scotland' is the name he gives to thirty or forty individuals who at that time formed the office-bearers of the Episcopal Church." Now, even previous to the period of Bishop Jolly's ordination, there were thirty or forty presbyters in the Diocese of Edinburgh alone.

The array of Episcopal artillery brought forward in the Established Presbytery of Perth was very wisely not encountered by the General Assembly, and though the whole was printed for the edification of the citizens of Perth in particular, it failed to have the effect which the since famous author of the "Speech" anticipated. He was indeed comforted by a complimentary article on the subject in the "Presbyterian Review," probably written by a Mr Campbell, a preacher in Manchester, the reputed author of several attacks on the Scottish Episcopal Church in that periodical; but some of the denizens of the "Fair City" and neighbourhood had the hardihood to come forward liberally in support of the so much dreaded Trinity College. Thus we find in the list of subscribers already cited—Sir John Stuart Richardson, Bart., of Pitfour, a right of nomination, L 105; John Grant, Esq., of Kilgraston, a right of nomination, L 105; Robert Clerk Rattray, Esq., of Craighall, a right of nomination, L 105; B. L., Perth, L.45; E. M., Perth, L.45; John Fitzmaurice Scott, Esq., of Seggieden, L.20; William H. Macdonald, Esq, of St Martin's, a right of nomination, L.105; Sir Patrick Murray Threipland, Bart, of Fingask, L.105, Lady Murray Threipland, L.15; Misses Murray Threipland, L.10; J. Stuart, Esq., Marshall Place, Perth, L.10; W H. Hunter, Esq., Banker, Perth, L.5; William Ross, Esq, Perth, L 5; Mr James Lawrence, slater, King Street, Perth, L.5, 5s.; Anonymous, Perth, L.1; and several others, not to mention some munificent subscriptions in various parts of the county. And, as if to crown the whole, the Town Council, by the casting vote of the Lord Provost, voted L.500, or an equivalent in value, if Trinity College was erected near the city.

Such is the history of Trinity College during the first year of its projection, and it may in future years be considered of some importance in the annals of its foundation. The only other attempt to interfere with it, though not in a hostile manner, was in the Town Council of Edinburgh in 1842, when Sir William Drysdale of Pitteuchar, the Treasurer of the city, succeeded in his eccentric motion to obtain a Committee to correspond with the projectors,* and attempt to incorporate the whole, distinctly under Episcopal superintendence, with the University of Edinburgh, lest its foundation should injure that institution, of which the Town Council are the principal Patrons. As the proposition was well meant and respectfully expressed, a friendly answer was returned, to the effect that such a proposal could not be entertained for various reasons. This reply, written by William Pitt Dundas, Esq., the Treasurer, finally extinguished a scheme on the part of Sir William Drysdale which many of the members of Town Council declared at the time would never be entertained for a moment.

Thus far have we followed the history of the Scottish Episcopal Church through all its difficulties, hardships, vicissitudes, and discouragements. We see that its succession was preserved by men, many of whom were indeed humble as it respects personal influence or temporal advantages, but entitled to veneration on account of their conscientious principles, their conviction of the vast importance of the deposit which had been entrusted to them, and their steady, resolute, and devoted perseverance in their course. One generation succeeded another, and the episcopate always derived new vigour by the addition of some younger and zealous presbyter, until the Church emerged from its depression, and the Noble, the rich, and the powerful, as well as the artizan, the peasant, and those of humble degree, worship at its altars, and are comforted and edified by its public and private services of religion, expressed, as its members believe and maintain, by a time-hallowed ritual in the "beauty of holiness." What Divine Providence may have in store for this branch of the Church Catholic futurity alone will disclose, and it would be presumptuous even to conjecture. Certain it is that the depression of the Scottish Episcopal Church can never be worse than that which it endured for upwards of a century, whatever political changes and convulsions may happen by the passions and prejudices of misguided

* The original projectors, according to Mr Gray, on the authority of the PERTHSHIRE CONSTITUTIONAL, of 27th October 1841, a newspaper which fought valiantly to have Trinity College erected in Perth, are "the Right Hon. W. E. Gladstone, Mr Hope, and the Rev. E. B. Ramsay, of St John's Chapel, Edinburgh."

men; while, on the other hand, there is every reason to anticipate that propitious years are approaching, which will enable the members of the Church, of every order, rank, and profession, still more vigorously, faithfully, and zealously, to rally round the standard of apostolical unity, true religion, and sound learning, that they may be protected equally against the errors of the Romanists and the uncertain and dangerous courses of sectarianism It would indeed have cherished and animated the humble pastors in the episcopate of the eighteenth century, if amid their privations they could have foreseen the formation of societies for the relief of their suffering Church; such an Act of the Legislature as that passed in 1840, connecting it more closely in spiritual communion with the Church of England; and, above all, the rich and the powerful in England and Scotland munificently contributing towards the foundation of a College for the education of many of the future clergy. They rest from their labours, some of them in graves unnoticed and unknown, and they are constantly succeeded by others, who in turn are gathered to their fathers. This is the lot of the Church on earth, the succession ever changing, yet still the same; but as no member of the Scottish Episcopal Church need be ashamed of its past history, even during its eventful century after the Revolution, when a mistaken attachment to an unfortunate dynasty rendered many liable to the charge of political disaffection, so, in reference to the then succession of Bishops, we see a steadiness of principle manifested in all their proceedings, the wisdom of which is completely developed by subsequent circumstances of comparative prosperity. Of each of those humble pastors in the Scottish episcopate it may truly be said, in the eloquent apostrophe of Tacitus to his father in-law Agricola—" Placide quiescas, nosque, domum tuam, ab infirmo desiderio, et muliebribus lamentis, ad contemplationem virtutum tuarum voces, quas neque lugeri, neque plangi, fas est: admiratione te potius, temporalibus laudibus, et, si natura suppeditet, militum decoremus. Is verus honos, ea conjunctissimi cujusque pietas."

To promote the future prosperity of the Scottish Episcopal Church, much depends, humanly speaking, on the zealous co-operation of the laity of its communion, and much on the liberal sympathies of the Church of England. As it respects the former, it is pleasing to record that this is already manifested to a great extent, much of their former apathy has disappeared, and a disposition is evinced of devoted and enlightened attachment to those principles which the Church has ever maintained. It is only justice to state that no appeal, properly authorised, has ever been made to the Church of England in vain, and the venerable Society for Promoting Christian Knowledge can never be forgotten by the Scottish Episcopal Church.

"Our attachment to our own doctrines," says Bishop Russell,* "has never rendered us intolerant towards others whose tenets are different, who either have not taken the trouble to examine into our system, or who are disposed to undervalue it because it has not the authority of a legal establishment. On all occasions we have maintained our peculiarities without any wish to infringe on the Christian liberty of others, or allowing the remotest grudge to harbour in our minds. Did we not differ from the Presbyterian church in some very essential points, we should have no apology for dissenting from her pale, nor be able to acquit ourselves of the blame of a needless and disgraceful schism. But let us maintain our differences in the spirit of Christian affection and esteem, and live, as we have hitherto lived, on terms of friendship with the members of the national communion, joining with them in promoting all objects of benevolence, and all schemes of public utility. Should any of them, in an unguarded moment, attack our principles, or, as is sometimes done, ascribe to us principles which we do not really hold, let us protect ourselves with reason and calmness; never imitating the injustice we condemn, nor falling into the intemperance which they themselves at a cooler hour must heartily regret.

"If the Episcopal Church in Scotland enjoys no protection from the State, farther than is implied in a liberal toleration, neither is she in any degree impeded in the exercise of her discipline, or restricted in her spiritual prerogative, by the pressure of laws emanating from a secular source. In these respects she enjoys all the freedom which belonged to the Primitive Christians, before any of the kingdoms of the world professed to belong to the kingdom of the Redeemer. Following in her laws those principles which she believes to have regulated the government of Christian communities in the purest times, and adopting in her administration the maxims which appear to have guided the

* Charge delivered to the Episcopal Clergy of the City and District of Glasgow, May 4, 1842, p 20, 24.

ministers of Christ, before ambition could awaken in their breasts those less sacred motives which adhere to worldly things.

" The form of Episcopacy which exists among us is that which has been properly described as moderate, and for the attainment of which a great effort was made about two centuries ago. The legislative power is vested alike in the Bishops and clergy, the consent of each being held indispensable to the enactment of our Canons. The administration of our laws, too, is entrusted to both orders, as represented in the Synods annually held, the Diocesan and the Episcopal The rights and influence of the presbyter are as carefully guarded as those of the Bishop ; and the union of the two, acting either separately or together, gives a beauty and a strength to our system which will never be impaired so long as we have confidence in one another—so long as we remember that it is our duty and our interest to be of one mind in the things pertaining to God, and to seek that unity and forbearance which the blessed Redeemer so strongly recommended to his immediate disciples. Our strength and security rest entirely on principle, warmed and enlightened by confidence and mutual affection ; and the history of the Church in these Northern parts will show how effectual such means are to resist the heaviest pressure of external circumstances, the weight of persecution, the frown of power, the alienation of the great, and the contempt of those whose opinions are formed by a regard to mere outward appearance. Principle cannot be destroyed, and it will never die. You may depress a man to the lowest depth of poverty, you may tear his flesh on the rack, and give his body to be burned, but you cannot reach the inward part where is lodged the covenant which he has made with his God and with his own soul. He fears not them which kill the body, and after that have no more that they can do ; and hence the last breath of the expiring martyr rises to heaven, and becomes a flame which will either enlighten or consume.—No Church was ever more tried by adversity than that to which we belong, and by a species of adversity, too, which sooner exhausts the principle of endurance than a direct persecution pointed against the life. When men are dragged forth to scaffolds, and held up as a spectacle to a sympathizing and admiring multitude, a power of reaction is created in the soul, which laughs to scorn the weapons of such a warfare, and at the same time forges other weapons which will in due season avenge their cause, and bring back their captivity like rivers in the south. The iron which entered into the soul of the poor Episcopalian during the evil days when penal laws hung over his head, was not taken from the burning fiery furnace; it was rather like that cold and sharp instrument which pierced the heart of the young Hebrew when he lay in the prison of Egypt, suffering at once from forgetfulness, groundless suspicion, and contempt. But the pains and penalties denounced against the Scottish churchmen made no change on their principles nor on their determination to adhere to them; and hence, when the hour of sorrow had passed away, they were found unaltered as to their creed, their solemn ritual, and their apostolical constitution. In this issue we cannot fail to perceive the value of a fixed and intelligible principle. Other communions, differently constituted, if they ceased to be held together by the bond of a legal establishment, would fall asunder; they would separate into numerous sects, and in a short time lose all the characteristics which now distinguish them. The fate of the Puritans in England illustrates what I am now attempting to unfold—the difference between a system founded on a well-defined principle, acknowledged by all and held indispensable by all—and a system which rests merely on local opinion, is supported by a few leaders who succeed in impressing their sentiments on the passing age, and which, having such an origin, cannot be expected to continue long in one stay.

"In the circumstances which distinguish the position of our body, our principles, while they are clear and distinct, are most easily reduced to practice; and as our views and motives are the same, so, generally speaking, are our feelings and conduct. With us there can be no such distinction as High-churchman and Low-churchman—a distinction perhaps that has no appreciable meaning any where, but which here must be positively absurd. Were we not churchmen, we ought not to be professional members of the Communion to which we belong; and I see not how we can be either more or less.

"Being such as we are, and hence necessarily, in point of ritual and ecclesiastical constitution, different from the church by law established in Scotland, we have certain duties to perform and sentiments to cherish in regard to our Presbyterian brethren. In return for the toleration which we enjoy and the countenance bestowed upon us by the Government of the Empire, we owe to the Establishment the respect and support which are due to an institution which is sanctioned by the legislature, and by the consent of a large body of the people. Upon this principle the Episcopalians have ever been found to act; and though no other class of dissenters in this country would profit so much as they would, by the withdrawal from the established church of her endowments and honours, yet they have uniformly appeared on the side of her friends; refusing to participate in the designs of those who wish to limit her influence and her means of usefulness. In truth, the principles, I might almost say the prejudices, of the Scottish Episcopalian are all pointed towards the maintenance of order, subordination, and the supremacy of legitimate power; and, therefore, though he may be called to suffer loss, or to endure privations, for the support of national institutions, he is in general found to persevere in his endeavours to uphold what the law of the land has sanctioned. He is a Conservative, not in the narrow acceptation of party nomenclature, but in that broader and more comprehensive sense which embraces national welfare, and the permanent advantage of the whole community."

APPENDIX.

APPENDIX.

No. I.

STATISTICS OF THE SCOTTISH EPISCOPAL CHURCH.
1836, 1837, 1838, AND 1839.

THE following statistical details of the state of the Scottish Episcopal Church, the congregations, chapels, number of sittings in each, stipends of the incumbents, and other matters, are taken from the Nine Reports of the Commissioners appointed by Parliament to inquire into the state of Religious Instruction in Scotland, whose First Report was ordered by the House of Commons to be printed in 1837. Some of the more minute details, such as seat rents, the number of communicants, and average attendance at public worship, are omitted, because these are fluctuating, or at least in many instances variable. The statements were all furnished by the incumbents themselves, and are here given in their own language, as they answered the queries transmitted to them by the Commissioners, or according to their personal declarations when examined.

I.—DIOCESE OF ABERDEEN.

ABERDEEN.—1. ST ANDREW'S CHAPEL. The congregation has existed since the Revolution of 1688, and the present elegant Gothic edifice, opened for public worship in 1817, at an expense of nearly L.8000, is vested in Trustees, and applied solely to congregational purposes. There are very few poor, strictly speaking, belonging to the congregation, but a great proportion of it belong to what may be termed the working classes, in which number are included tradesmen and shopkeepers. Total sittings, 1100; supposed to be connected with the congregation, nearly 1400. The annual stipend of the senior minister is variable, according to the funds of the Chapel; that of the junior minister is fixed, and amounts to L.120, derived from seat rents and collections. The civil affairs are conducted by a body of managers, appointed for life, and a Treasurer. Public worship is performed in the Chapel twice every Sunday, also on every Wednesday and Saturday throughout the year, and on the Fasts and Festivals of the Church of England, besides the day before and after communion, amounting in all to 167, besides Sunday services. The members of the congregation are so widely scattered, that it is impossible for the ministers to extend week day superintendence to the whole of them. There is a Sunday school connected with the congregation in the Flour-Mill Brae, attended by from 140 to 150, and open to all denominations. It is supported principally from a bequest.*

2. St John's Chapel was established in 1812. The chapel was built by subscription, and a loan from the Scottish Episcopal Friendly Society, whose property it afterwards became. The Society sold it, and took an obligation from the purchaser to keep it up as a place of Episcopal worship. The present proprietor gives it for the use of the congregation rent free. Total sittings, 386; the stipend is from L.120 to L.130, arising from seat rents and collections, and is dependant on the clear revenue, the balance of which, after defraying the ordinary expenses, is paid to the minister. Divine service is performed in the chapel 162 times in the year, including the two services every Sunday, besides occasional services. A Sunday school is connected with the congregation.†

3. St Paul's Chapel, according to the evidence of the Rev. John Brown, is "a very inconvenient, badly aired, ill situated, and insufficient, though church-like building. It belongs to the managers and constituent members, and is applied to none but congregational purposes. The chapel was erected in 1722 at an expense of L.1000. It has been enlarged at

---

* Evidence of the Rev. William Browning.
† Evidence of the Rev. Patrick Cheyne, M. A.

various times, and every spot turned to account. It is said to be perhaps the richest in Scotland, being possessed of a chapel, house, and ground, valued at L.2400, without any debt, besides a sum of L.5425." Total sittings, 900 The amount of stipend is L.213, derived from endowments, by bequests, and otherwise, and seat rents. The managers are eleven gentlemen elected for life by the congregation, in terms of the deed of constitution. "There are between 3000 and 4000 persons, not including children, in this and the neighbouring parishes, claiming the ministrations of the minister of St Paul's Chapel. The great bulk of the congregation reside in the city of Aberdeen. The rest are very much scattered over the country, some as far off as twenty or thirty miles, and some attend the Chapel pretty regularly from a distance of seven miles." - Divine service is performed twice every Sunday, and on the Fasts and Festivals, and other days appointed by the Church The Chapel is called a collegiate charge, but hitherto, at least during Mr Brown's ministry, it was not so *

ARRADOUL.—The congregation assembles in the village of Arradoul, parish of Rathven, Banffshire, in an old chapel which is applied to no other purposes. Total sittings, 210, and the whole number of souls connected with the chapel is 300, a few of whom reside in the adjoining parishes of Deskford and Bellie. The income of the minister is derived from the interest of a sum of L.150, bequeathed for the benefit of the Episcopal clergyman at Arradoul, being L.5, 14s., half of the produce of a small piece of ground mortified for the purpose, being L 9, and whatever is derived from seat rents and collections. The minister has a house. Public worship is performed in the chapel twice every Sunday.†

BANFF —The congregation in the royal burgh of Banff has existed since the Revolution The present chapel is a substantially built edifice erected in 1833-4, at the cost of about L.1000, by voluntary subscriptions; and is not applied to any other purpose. Total sittings, 356. A number of the congregation reside in Gamrie parish, and a few in those of King-Edward, Alvah, and Boyndie. The stipend is from

---

* Evidence of the Rev John Brown, M.A.
† Evidence of the Rev. John Moir, M A

L.110 to L.115, but variable, derived from seat rents and collections, and from some individuals contributing certain sums in addition to their pew rents by way of gratuity. The minister enjoys the interest of L.200 bequeathed for behoof of the incumbent of the chapel, under control of the Bishop of the Diocese. Public worship is performed twice every Sunday, and once on all the holidays appointed by the Church of England.*

CRUDEN.—This congregation is not reported.

CUMINESTONE.—The small congregation in the village of Cuminestone was formed about 1791. Some idea may be formed of the primitive state of the Church in this quarter, from the fact that the congregation, five-sixths of whom are of the poor and working classes, assembled in a small thatched building erected in 1792, the cost of which was only L.30. Total sittings, about 100. In 1836 the stipend was rated at L.53, of which the sum of L.25 was contributed by the congregation. Public worship is performed in the chapel twice every Sunday, and nine times in the course of the year on week days.†

ELLON.—The congregation has existed in this village and parish since 1688. The chapel, which is only applied to the purposes of the congregation, was erected in 1815 at the expense of L.600, and is held by the clergyman on a lease of 99 years at a rent of L.2, 10s. per annum, with half an acre of ground. Total sittings, 262. The stipend is from L.70 to L.80, derived from seat rents, collections, and the Episcopal Society. Upwards of a hundred persons belonging to the congregation reside in different parishes adjoining. Public worship is performed twice every Sunday during summer, once during the rest of the year, and upon ten week days.‡

FORGUE.—It is not known when the congregation was formed in this parish. The present chapel is a comfortable stone and slated building erected in 1795; it belongs to the congregation, and is used only for public worship. Total sittings, 230. Several members reside in the adjoining parishes of Inverkeithney, Huntly, Marnoch, and Drumblade. The

* Evidence of the Rev. Alexander Bruce, M A.
† Evidence of the Rev. John Taylor, M A
‡ Evidence of the Rev. Nathaniel Grieve, M A.

incumbent has a house and glebe, but the emolument is not stated, and is described as variable. Public worship is performed in the chapel as frequently as required by the Rubric.*

FRASERBURGH.—The Episcopal congregation has existed in this town and parish since the Reformation, and this was long the scene of the ministrations of the venerable Bishop Jolly. The chapel was erected in 1793, at the cost of L.325, and has since been enlarged and improved. It is the property of the congregation, and is solely used for Divine service. The total number of sittings before it was enlarged and altered was 288. Between 200 and 300 members are of the poor and working classes. The seat rents and collections are applied towards the support of the incumbent, the amount of which, it is stated, cannot be accurately ascertained. Public worship is performed in the chapel twice every Sunday, and once on all the inferior holidays. A Sunday school meeting in the Town Hall is attached to the congregation, and a regular course of religious instruction is held every Sunday after the evening service. Between 200 and 300 persons belong to the congregation who reside in the parishes of Rathen, Tyrie, Aberdour, and Pitsligo †

INVERURY.—This congregation was formed since the Report of the Commissioners was printed, and the chapel was consecrated in 1842.

LONGSIDE.—The congregation has existed in this parish since the Revolution, and this was for upwards of half a century the scene of the ministrations of the Rev. John Skinner. The congregation assembles in a chapel erected in 1800 at the cost of L.429, defrayed by a subscription among the members, on the property of James Bruce, Esq. of Innerquhomry and Longside, and is held, with a fourth of an acre attached, on a lease of fifty-seven years from January 1801. Total sittings, 551. The seat rents are solely appropriated to the clergyman's income, and the collections, after a deduction of L.6, 12s. paid to the beadle and clerk, are distributed among the poor. Public worship is performed in the chapel on the morning and evening of each Sunday from May to September, and once throughout the rest of the year, besides eighteen services on different week days. Communicants from 400 to 440. The number of persons under the charge of the minister is

---

* Return by the Rev. Andrew Ritchie.
† Evidence of the Rev. Charles Pressley, M.A.

from 600 to 700, with about 90 from the parishes of St Fergus, Deer, Peterhead, and Lonmay. About four-fifths of the whole are comprehended under the denomination of agricultural labourers, operatives, handicraftsmen, and others of like condition *

LONMAY.—The Episcopal congregation was established in the parish of Lonmay soon after the Revolution. The chapel was erected by the congregation in 1797 at the cost of about L.230, and is solely used for religious purposes. Total sittings, 342. The seat rents and collections are applied towards paying the minister, and were stated in 1836 to amount to L.50, more or less. Public worship is performed in the chapel every Sunday, and on the Festivals of the Church The number of persons, old and young, in the parish of Lonmay connected with the congregation, is about 200 ; and 300, old and young, who reside in the neighbouring parishes of Rathen, Crimond, Strichen, and St Fergus †

MEIKLEFOLLA.—This congregation in the village of Meiklefolla, parish of Fyvie, is principally drawn from the other parishes, and was stated by the Presbyterian incumbent of the parish to be 188. No farther information was given.

MONYMUSK —This congregation is not reported.

NEW PITSLIGO —This congregation was formed in the parish between 1800 and 1805. The present chapel was built in 1835 at the cost of L.400, by Sir John Stuart Forbes, Bart., whose property it is, and is applied solely to religious purposes. Total sittings in the chapel, 160, the whole of which are the property of Sir John Stuart Forbes, Bart., by whom they are let, and a few are set apart for the poor. The stipend is L 60 per annum, paid by Sir J. S. Forbes, with a house and glebe, the latter worth about L.13, 10s. Public worship is performed every Sunday morning throughout the year, and on the principal Fasts and Festivals Communicants, 120, who, with the exception of two families, are all of the poor and working classes. A number of persons belonging to the congregation reside in the adjacent parishes of King-Edward, Aberdour, Tyrie, Strichen, and New Deer ‡

OLD DEER —The congregation has existed in this parish since the

---

* Evidence of the Very Rev. John Cumming.
† Evidence of the Rev George Hagar.
‡ Evidence of the Rev. William Laurie

Revolution, and assembles in a chapel erected in 1776, used solely for the celebration of Divine worship. Total sittings, 500. The seat rents are applied to make up the minister's salary, and the ordinary collections to the poor members of the congregation. The stipend is L.82, including L.2 per annum, left by a pious individual, with a house, but no glebe. Divine service is performed twice every Sunday from the Festival of Whitsunday to the end of August, and once on the remaining Sundays, and on twenty-two week days throughout the year. Between fifty and one hundred members reside in the adjacent parishes of Longside, Lonmay, New Deer, Strichen, and Methlic. With the exception of a few families, chiefly landed proprietors, they are all of the poor and working classes.*

OLD MELDRUM.—The congregation is supposed to have existed in this parish since the Revolution, and assembles in a small chapel erected at the cost of L.200 in 1813, which is used solely for the celebration of Divine service. Total sittings, 170. The seat rents and collections are applied towards the support of the minister, who has a house and about an acre of ground, for the latter of which a feu-duty of L.2 per annum is paid. Public worship is performed twice in the chapel fully one half of the year, and once during the remainder, with usually eight week day services throughout the year. Upwards of fifty members reside in neighbouring parishes, most of whom are of the poor and working classes.†

PETERHEAD.—This congregation was established in the Parliamentary burgh and parish of Peterhead in 1689, and assembles in a chapel in the town which belongs to the members, who erected it by voluntary subscription in 1814, at the cost of about L.3000. The property is vested in the treasurer for the time being, who is appointed by a body of fifteen managers, elected annually by the subscribers Total number of sittings, 763; connected with the congregation, old and young, 1172; communicants, about 700; poor and working classes two thirds of the whole. The stipend is L.150, permanently secured, and derived from the seat rents and ordinary collections. Public worship is performed

* Evidence of the Rev. Arthur Ranken, M A.
† Evidence of the Rev. William Robertson, M.A.

twice every Sunday, and on the Fasts and Festivals of the Church. A Sunday school is connected with the chapel.*

PORTSOY.—The congregation in this town and parish was originally formed in the neighbouring parish of Fordyce previous to the Revolution, and assembles in a chapel erected in 1797, and used solely for the celebration of Divine service. Total sittings, 120. The seat rents and collections are applied towards the support of the incumbent, and amount to L.40, but he has neither house nor glebe assigned. Public worship is performed twice every Sunday throughout the year, and on all the Fasts and Festivals of the Church. The poor and working classes constitute two fifths of the congregation.†

TURRIFF.—This congregation is not reported.

WOODHEAD.—The congregation in this village, in the parish of Fyvie, has existed since the Revolution. The chapel was built in 1795, and enlarged in 1821, and is used solely for the celebration of Divine service. Total sittings, 180; communicants, 160; connected with the congregation, about 200 The members are chiefly composed of small farmers. The stipend is not stated. Public worship is performed twice every Sunday during summer, and once in winter, besides Holidays and Festivals.‡

II.—UNITED DIOCESE OF DUNKELD, DUNBLANE, AND FIFE.

ST ANDREWS.—The congregation has existed ever since Episcopacy was the established religion in Scotland. The present chapel was finished in 1825 at a cost of about L.1500; total number of sittings, 170. It belongs to the minister, vestry, and congregation for the time being, and is applicable to no other than sacred purposes. Minister's stipend, L.90, besides L.10 from the Andersonian Episcopal Fund in Aberdeen.

* Return of the Right Rev Dr Torry, and evidence of Mr George Mudie, Treasurer.
† Evidence of the Rev. Alexander Cooper, M.A
‡ Evidence of the Rev. David Wilson, M. A.

Permanent so long as the chapel revenues admit. Public worship performed twice every Sunday, besides prayers on Holidays.*

CUPAR-FIFE.—Established in 1688. The present place of worship was finished in 1820, and cost about L.3000; sittings, 122. It is vested in trustees for the Scottish Episcopal Church and the congregation, and is not applied to other than congregational purposes. Minister's stipend, L.100 per annum, besides the interest of L.450, bequeathed by the Rev. Dr Bell; permanent so long as the revenues of the chapel admit. Public worship is performed twice every Sunday.†

KIRKALDY.—Established about 1813, under the spiritual jurisdiction of the Scottish Bishops. The place of worship called St Peter's Chapel was built in 1813 by subscription, under the chartered provision of the congregation, at a cost originally of L.600; about L.200 have been laid out upon it since; number of sittings, 122. The property is vested in the minister and managers for the time being, the latter chosen from year to year. It is used only for public worship. The minister's stipend consists of what remains in the general funds after defraying all expenses. Public worship is performed on Sundays, and on the Fasts and Festivals of the Episcopal Church of Scotland.‡ In 1842 the congregation had so much increased under the pastoral care of the Rev. Norman Johnston, A B., that subscriptions were commenced for a new chapel, the present edifice being too small, and very inconveniently situated.

DUNFERMLINE.—This congregation was not formed when the Commissioners were pursuing their inquiries. The chapel was finished and consecrated in 1842.

PITTENWEEM.—This congregation is included in the United Dioceses' of Moray, Ross, and Argyll, during the episcopate of the Right Rev. Bishop Low. It is not reported.

BLAIR-ATHOLL.—Established shortly after the Revolution. The congregation assembles for public worship in a chapel which was built about 1797, at Kilmaveonaig; cost not ascertained. No person has any right over the church but the clergyman for the time being. It is applied to no other purpose. Number of sittings about 200. The stipend is L.80, chiefly derived from the Scottish Episcopal Church Society.

* Evidence of C. J. Lyon, M.A.
† Evidence of the Rev. G. G. Milne, M.A.
‡ Evidence of Mr Thomas Millar, Treasurer.

Divine service performed twice every Sunday, Christmas Day, Good Friday, and Ascension Day, and once at least six other days throughout the year *

[PERTH.—The chapel belongs to a number of gentlemen in the district, and is applied to no other purposes than those of the congregation. Number of sittings not stated, but probably upwards of 300. The minister's stipend is L.180; public worship is performed twice on Sundays, besides on Festivals] †

COUPAR-ANGUS —The congregation was established in 1824, and assembles for public worship in the upper flat of a house fitted up as a chapel, and applied to no other purpose, belonging to a private individual, and the rent paid by some of the members. The sittings are 60 : Annual emolument of the minister, L.45. Public worship is performed once every Sunday. The minister also officiates at two other chapels in the adjoining parishes of Meigle and Alyth.‡

BLAIRGOWRIE.—The chapel was erected in this village and parish in 1842, by the Rev. John Marshall

KIRRIEMUIR.—This congregation is stated to have existed since 1561, and assembles for public worship in the chapel, built in 1795, the private property of Mr Lyell of Kinnordy. It is used for no other purposes. Total sittings, 800. The annual emolument is from L.60 to L.70, derived from the voluntary subscriptions of a few families, a very few seat rents, and Sunday collections. It is described as very variable, and not permanent, depending greatly upon regular attendance and residence in the country. Public worship is performed twice every Sunday, and once a-day on the other Festivals and Fasts appointed by the Episcopal Church. Members of congregation reside in the parishes of Cortachy, Airlie, Kingoldrum, Kinnettles, Oathland, and Tannadyce.§

FORFAR.—The congregation has existed in the parish and town of Forfar from time immemorial, and assembles in a chapel erected in 1824, at the expense of about L.1000, used solely for public worship. The chapel is officially vested in the Bishop of the Diocese of Dunkeld and his successors. Total sittings, 350. The annual stipend is L.130,

---

* Evidence of the Rev W. C A. M'Laurin, M.A.
† Evidence of John M'Whannell, Esq. Treasurer. The Episcopal congregation at Perth was not in communion with the Church in 1842
‡ Evidence of the Very Rev. John Torry, M A.
§ Evidence of the Rev. John Buchan.

derived from seat rents, Sunday collections, and the private subscriptions of individual members. Public worship is performed in the chapel twice every Sunday, on every Friday during Lent, and on the usual Fasts and Festivals of the Church. From 50 to 100 persons reside in other parishes.*

MUTHILL.—This congregation is not reported by the Commissioners.

STRATHTAY.—Not reported by the Commissioners.

DUNKELD.—No information.

DUNBLANE.—The congregation was formed in 1842, and public worship was performed on Sunday, the 30th of October, by the Rev. B. F. Couch, M.A. of St Peter's College, Cambridge.

III.—UNITED DIOCESE OF MORAY, ROSS, AND ARGYLL.

ABERCHIRDER.—The congregation in this village, in the parish of Marnoch, was formed about 1817, and assembles in a chapel built by the late proprietor of the estate of Auchintoul, the use of which is given gratuitously. Total sittings, 100; almost the whole of the members are of the poor and working classes. Public worship was only performed in the chapel on each alternate Sunday till 1836, when a stated clergyman was appointed.

FORRES.—Not reported by the Commissioners in 1836.

FOCHABERS.—This congregation is not reported by the Commissioners.

HUNTLY.—This congregation has existed in the town and parish of Huntly since the Revolution, and long assembled in a small slated chapel, applied to no other purpose than that of Divine worship, erected on the Gordon estate by subscription in 1770. The chapel is calculated to contain from 130 to 140. The seat rents and collections are applied to the support of the minister, whose other emoluments are derived from the dividends of three sums of L.500, L.200, and L.100, invested in the three per cent. stock, in the name of certain Trustees. The greater part of the congregation are of the working classes, and of those possessing small farms.†

* Evidence of the Rev. John Skinner, M.A.
† Evidence of the Rev. James Walker.

KEITH.—The congregation in this parish assembles in a small chapel erected by the Rev. John Murdoch, the incumbent, in 1807, at the expense of about L.200, and is only used for Divine worship. Number of sittings, 150, all occupied by the poor and working classes. The minister states, that though under no obligation to do so, he intends to make over the chapel, with the house and garden attached to it, to his successor without compensation, the congregation being too poor to redeem it. The sums drawn for sittings, though there are no regular seat rents, and collections, belong to the minister. Public worship is performed in the chapel as frequently as the Rubrics of the Church require, or as circumstances will permit.*

INVERNESS.—The congregation has existed in the town of Inverness since the Revolution. The former chapel was built in 1801, at the cost of L.1000, but an elegant and commodious one was erected after 1836, containing 600 sittings. The annual emolument is L.180, derived from seat rents, collections, offertories, and fees for occasional offices, such as marriages, baptisms, and funeral services. Public worship is performed twice every Sunday, and on all the Fasts and Festivals of the Church. The minister does not extend his exertions beyond his own congregation, except when occasionally called upon to officiate to the Troops at Fort-George, twelve miles distant. Members of the congregation reside in the parishes of Kirkhill, Daviot, Moy, Croy, and Nairn.†

ROTHESAY, in the Island of Bute.—The congregation was not formed till after 1838, by the Rev. Samuel Hood.

LOCHGILPHEAD.—This congregation was formed in 1842.

APPIN.—The congregation in this sequestered district of Argyllshire has existed since the Revolution. According to a census taken in 1831, the total number of persons amounted to 1439, and, with the exception of a few gentlemen's families, all are of the poor and working classes. The new chapel at Balachelish, erected in 1842, can accommodate 800 persons. It is near the valuable slate quarries belonging to Charles Stewart, Esq. The chapel is used solely for the celebration of Divine service. In the Fourth Report of the Commissioners, printed in 1836, it is stated that the annual sum raised by seat rents was L.31, and that all the emoluments amounted to L.67. Service was then performed

* Evidence of the Rev. John Murdoch, M A.
† Evidence of the Very Rev. Charles Fyvie, M.A

every alternate Sunday at Balachelish and Portnacroish, and in one or other of the chapels on the Holidays of the Church. An occasional Sunday service was given in Duror and Glencrerin for the benefit of such old people as could not attend the chapels; but the number who availed themselves of it could not be accurately ascertained. When the number attending was larger than the chapels could accommodate, Divine service was performed in the open air.*

PORTNACROISH —This congregation has now a stated pastor. The affairs, by the feu-charter granted at the time of the erection of the chapel, are managed by the Trustees, and their heirs and successors, so long as they shall continue members of the Episcopal Church. The chapel cost about L.200, and has sittings for 120 persons. The annual sum raised by seat rents was L.14, and the average collections only L.1 annually.†

CARROY.—The congregation at this locality in the Island of Skye was formed by the exertions of the Right Rev. Bishop Low, and the Rev. William Greig, M.A. was the first incumbent. Bishop Low thus writes of the state of the Church in Skye to the Society for Promoting Christian Knowledge, as it appears in the Annual Report for 1837— " You will be pleased to learn that our primitive Apostolic Communion in Scotland is gradually extending itself. Within the last twelve months I have had the good fortune to establish a new Episcopal congregation in a very remote part of my Diocese, the Isle of Skye, but at present the congregation is totally destitute of a place of worship, and the poor Islanders can contribute nothing towards the building. I am not forgetful of, and do now thankfully acknowledge, the Society's repeated munificence to my Diocese on former occasions." The Board, at the request of the Bishop, agreed to grant L.25 towards building the chapel in the Island of Skye.

STORNOWAY.—The congregation in the remote sea-port town of Stornoway, in the Lewis, was formed about 1837, and a neat chapel is now erected.

FORT-WILLIAM.—The congregation at Fort-William, in Kilmalie parish, Inverness-shire, was formed soon after the Revolution. The present chapel is a well built edifice, erected in 1817 by voluntary sub-

* Evidence of the Rev. Paul MacColl.   † Ibid.

scription, and cost from L.500 to L.600. It is the property of the congregation, for whom it is held by six trustees, two of whom are always the Bishop of the Diocese and the incumbent. The chapel is applied to no other purpose. Total sittings, 250. The stipend is now increased by the Scottish Episcopal Church Society to L.80 per annum. Divine service is performed twice every Sunday, in the forenoon in English, and in the afternoon in Gaelic. The incumbent has, since 1828, superintended the scattered members of the Church in the remote and mountainous districts of Morven, Sunart, and Moydart.*

DINGWALL and STRATHNAIRN.—Not reported by the Commissioners

ARPAFEELIE and FORTROSE.—Not reported by the Commissioners.

HIGHFIELD.—This congregation is not reported by the Commissioners.

IV —DIOCESE OF BRECHIN.

BRECHIN —The congregation has existed in the city of Brechin ever since the non-establishment of Episcopacy in Scotland. The chapel is held in trust by certain members of the congregation, and is applied to no other purposes. Total sittings, 300. The annual emolument of the minister is L.100, derived from seat rents and collections, permanently secured by a written obligation by the managers or vestrymen. Public worship is performed twice every Sunday, and on the Holidays of the Church † Several members of the congregation reside in the adjoining parishes of Menmuir, Strickathrow, Marykirk, Caraldstone, Farnwell, Marytown, Edzel, and Fettercairn.

DUNDEE.—The congregation has been established in this town since the Revolution. The present St Paul's Chapel was erected in 1812, at the expense of L 3686, of which the sum of L.2366 was defrayed by contributions and by the sale of the old chapel. In 1829 the congregation was joined by the one known by the designation of the " English Episcopal congregation." Total sittings, 504. Since 1835, the number of communicants and of persons in the habit of attending has increased, in consequence of another small Episcopal congregation having

---

* Evidence of the Rev Alexander M'Lennan
† Evidence of the Right Rev. Bishop Moir, D D

been united to St Paul's. The stipend is L.200 per annum, derived from the general revenue. Public worship is performed in the Chapel twice every Sunday, and on the Fasts and Festivals of the Church, once on the Saints' Days, and on every Wednesday and Friday during Lent.*

ARBROATH.—The congregation has existed since the Revolution. The chapel belongs to the congregation, and is used only for the purposes of public worship; sittings, 390. The stipend is L.112 per annum, with L.10 arising from a mortification, and the interest of L.220 in lieu of a manse. Public worship is performed twice every Sunday, and on the Holidays of the Church.†

MONTROSE —The one congregation has no record of the date of its formation. The house which the members, who, with the exception of a few genteel families, are operatives, occupy, was not originally built for a chapel, and is rented from a society of Masons. It is applied to no other purposes than as a place of worship. Total number of sittings, 170. No annual amount of the emoluments is stated, because, being derived from precarious sources, it varies considerably. Public worship is performed twice every Sunday, and occasionally on week days on the Festivals of the Church.‡

[The congregation of St Peter's Chapel, Montrose, was first established after the Revolution. The present Chapel was erected in 1724, and is used solely for the purposes of Divine service. The cost is not ascertained, and the building belongs in a great measure to the descendants of the original founders or proprietors. Total sittings, about 800. The annual stipend is L.186, derived partly from the interest of money bequeathed to the funds of the Chapel, and partly from the congregation, secured by a written promise. In lieu of a house the minister enjoys the interest of a legacy of L.600 for the erection of a house for the incumbent. Public worship is performed in the Chapel twice every Sunday, and on the Holidays of the Church. Several members of the congregation reside in the parishes of Farnwell, Dun, St Cyrus, and Logie-Pert.]§

* Evidence of the Very Rev. Heneage Horsley, M A.
† Evidence of the Rev. William Henderson, M.A
‡ Evidence of the Rev. Patrick Cushnie, M.A.
§ Evidence of the Rev. John Dodgson.

LAURENCEKIRK.—The congregation was established in 1793, when the chapel was built, at the expense of about L.1000, by public subscription. It belongs to the clergyman and congregation, and is applied to no other purposes than the celebration of Divine service. Total number of sittings, 205. The stipend is about L 100 per annum, including the parsonage-house and glebe. It partly consists of L.40 in money, and forty bolls of oatmeal, secured on the estate of Johnstone by deed of Lord Gardenstone. Public worship is performed twice every Sunday, and on the Festivals of the Church. Members of the congregation reside in the parishes of Fettercairn, Fordoun, Arbuthnot, Bervie, Benholme, St Cyrus, Garvock, and Marykirk.*

MUCHALLS —The congregation in this fishing village, in the parish of Fetteresso, Kincardineshire, was formed soon after the Revolution. With few exceptions the members are all poor people, and the greater part of them fishermen and their families. The congregation assembles in a chapel belonging to the members, and applied solely to the purposes of Divine worship, built in 1831 at the expense of L.300, which is stated to be considerably below its value. Total sittings, 176. The annual emolument of the minister is now L.80, of which the congregation contribute L.26, as seat-rents and ordinary collections. The incumbent has a house and about half an acre of ground, the former built by subscription among the members. Public worship is performed twice every Sunday during four months in summer, and once during the rest of the year, and sometimes on week days, such as Ash-Wednesday, Good Friday, &c.†

KATERLINE.—The congregation in the fishing village of Katerline in Kinneff parish, Kincardineshire, was long connected with that of Drumlithie, but a resident pastor was appointed in 1842.

DRUMLITHIE.—The congregation in this village, in the parish of Glenbervie, assemble in a neat chapel dedicated to St John. Divine service is performed twice every Sunday, and on the Fasts and Festivals of the Church. The statistics of this congregation are not reported by the Commissioners.

STONEHAVEN.—Not reported by the Commissioners

* Evidence of the Rev. W. M. Goalen
† Evidence of the Rev James Smith

V.—DIOCESE OF GLASGOW.

LEITH.—The congregation of St James' Episcopal Chapel has existed at least since the reign of Queen Anne, and a Nonjuring congregation of an earlier date merged into it shortly after 1802. The Chapel in Constitution Street was built in 1805 at the expense of about L.1600, and belongs to the congregation, who are represented by twelve of their number as managers. The chapel is not applied to any other purpose than the celebration of Divine service Total sittings, 380, and the whole of those who attend are resident in nearly equal numbers in the parishes of South and North Leith. They consist of the mercantile classes, including a few shopkeepers, with the exception of some individuals of the poor and working classes. The seat-rents and proceeds of the ordinary collections are applied to the general purposes of the Chapel, including the minister's salary, the organist's, feu-duty, and the expense of repairs, and occasionally to the relief of the poor. The total amount of emolument enjoyed by the clergyman is L.200.*

GLASGOW.—1. ST ANDREW'S EPISCOPAL CHAPEL, near the Green, was established in 1750, and was united to the Scottish Episcopal Church in 1806. The congregation assembles in a substantial stone edifice, surrounded by a cemetery, built in 1750 at the cost of about L 2000, repaired in 1813 at the expense of L.400, and again in 1834 for L.200. Total sittings, 630. Upwards of 200 are of the poor and working classes, consisting of weavers, petty shopkeepers, and dealers in old clothes, and the whole congregation is scattered throughout the city and neighbourhood. The seat-rents, ordinary collections, and produce of mortifications, are applied to the payment of the minister's salary, clerk, organist, beadles, pew-opener, and interest of debt, The extraordinary collections are applied to their special purposes. The poor for whom the collections are made are aged infirm people belonging to the congregation. The minister had a stipend of L.200 per annum previous to 1836, of which the sum of L.100 was a fixed salary. Divine service is performed twice every Sunday, on the Fasts and Festivals of the Church, on Wednesdays and Fridays during Lent, and every day on

* Evidence of the Right Rev. Dr Russell, and of Mr Gunn, Treasurer.

Passion Week. The minister stated that there were in the city of Glasgow and Gorbals about 10,000 Episcopalians, of whom he calculated about 4000 were chiefly Irish weavers and labourers, altogether destitute of church accommodation and the means of religious instruction in connection with their own Church.*

St Mary's Episcopal Chapel accommodates the congregation existing in Glasgow since the Revolution. The Chapel was finished in 1825, at the expense altogether of L.6324, and belongs to the contributors. The number of sittings is about 930. By the constitution of the chapel the one half of the whole seat-rents and ordinary collections go to the minister in name of stipend, and the other half are applied to the ordinary expenses of the congregation. The sacramental collections are devoted entirely to the benefit of the poor, and the extraordinary collections to their special purposes The stipend for 1835-6 was L 273, and though the annual amount varies, the principal is permanent, and is secured by deed of constitution. There is besides a sum of L 200 vested in trust in the Scottish Episcopal Friendly Society, the interest of which goes to the clergyman, and also a bequest of L.100 to the clergyman and managers for the education of children of the congregation. Public worship is performed twice every Sunday, and on the Fasts and Festivals of the Church; also a monthly lecture previous to the Lord's Supper, and a weekly lecture during Lent. Catechetical instruction is afforded to the young members of the congregation for about nine months in the year, and there is a Sunday School for the children of the poor. The minister considers the week-day superintendence of his own congregation to be more than he can accomplish to his satisfaction, and that it must be very inadequate when the whole duties are devolved upon one clergyman.†

The congregation of Christ Church, in the suburb of the Calton or Mile-End, was formed by the exertions of the Rev. David Aitchison, M.A. in 1835. There were then two places of worship, one in Main Street, Bridgeton, and the other in Claythorn Street, each seated for about 300. The following account of the congregation before the erection of Christ Church, to which the Society for Promoting Christian

---

* Evidence of the Very Rev. William Routledge.
† Evidence of the Rev. George Almond

Knowledge voted L.100, is from a letter of Bishop Walker, an extract of which is given in the Annual Report for 1837 :—" After my visitation held at Glasgow on the 31st of August [1836], I went with my family to Dunoon on the Clyde, having arranged to visit Mr Aitchison's interesting congregation, and to administer the sacrament of the Lord's Supper there on Sunday the 2d of October. This, notwithstanding the state of the weather, I happily accomplished. I first saw the school, on which Mr Aitchison's exertions have evidently not been lost, and a most interesting sight it was. A congregation of poor and decent people was assembled, and the room crowded. I never was so much moved as when I heard those poor people raise their morning hymn. The whole service, though in a wretched place, was admirable. Fifty persons, old and young, all poorly but all decently dressed, communicated with every mark of decency and true devotion." The present edifice of Christ Church was partly erected by subscription, but chiefly by the munificence of Mr Aitchison. It is seated for about 1000 persons, and the whole cost, including two school-rooms, and nearly three-fourths of an acre of burying-ground, was upwards of L.2000. Almost all are of the poor and working classes, and a great proportion are hand-loom weavers. Many are Irish emigrants, and a very few are Highlanders. Public worship is performed twice every Sunday, and the minister superintends a Sunday School of boys and girls. Mr Aitchison calculated that there were still 7000 Episcopalians in Glasgow and the suburbs, consisting chiefly of Irish emigrants, without any place of worship.*

St Jude's Episcopal Chapel, near Blythswood Square, was erected, and the congregation formed, subsequently to the Second Report of the Commissioners printed in 1837. This congregation is chiefly composed of the upper classes. The chapel is a large oblong Grecian edifice.

Airdrie.—In the village of Coatbridge, near the populous town of Airdrie, eleven miles from Glasgow on the Edinburgh road, the erection of the chapel was in progress in 1842.

Hamilton.—This congregation was formed in 1842, and a hall fitted up as a temporary place of worship until the erection of a proper chapel.

Paisley.—The Episcopal congregation in Paisley was established in

* Evidence of the Rev. David Aitchison, M A.

1817, and assemble for public worship in Trinity Chapel, erected in 1833, at the cost of L.1200. The building is held by Trustees for the congregation, and is only used for Divine service and religious instruction. Total sittings, 310. The Episcopalians in the town and neighbourhood are estimated at nearly 2000, all, with the exception of from fifteen to twenty families, of the poor and working classes. The clear stipend of the minister in 1838 was stated to be L.56, without house or glebe, or any provision in lieu. Public worship is performed three times every Sunday, twice on Christmas Day, and once on New Year's Day, Ash-Wednesday, and Good Friday. The minister states, that " he gives instruction regularly in a Sunday school, and to the children and young people of his charge on Thursday evenings. He has attempted to establish missions in Johnstone and Barrhead, but failed for want of funds. He does not extend his exertions as a minister beyond his own congregation, except when an English or Irish Regiment is stationed in Paisley Barracks, in which case he acts as chaplain.*

GREENOCK.—The congregation in this important sea-port was formed in 1824, when the present elegant Gothic chapel was erected, which is vested in Trustees, consecrated, and applied solely for the celebration of Divine service. Total number of sittings, 400. The stipend is L.125, permanently secured by the constitution of the chapel, which makes it a preferable claim to debts, &c. Public worship is performed twice on Sundays, and on the Festivals of the Church. A Sunday and day school is connected with the congregation, and the teacher's salary is defrayed by subscription †

HELENSBURGH.—This congregation was formed after 1838.

AYR.—The congregation was established in 1832, and now assembles in a neat chapel erected in 1837 by subscription, appropriated solely for the celebration of Divine service. The seat-rents are applied to the support of the minister, whose emoluments are estimated at about L 100. There are two services on Sundays, Christmas, and Good Friday, but on the first Sunday of each month, when the minister goes to Maybole, there is only one service in the chapel.‡ In the Report of

* Evidence of the Rev. W. M Wade, and of Mr Samuel Southwell.
† Evidence of the Rev. Richard Martin, A.B., and of Mr Roger Aytoun, Chairman of the Trustees.
‡ Evidence of the Rev W. S. Wilson, M.A.

the Society for Promoting Christian Knowledge for 1837 is the following account of the formation of the congregation at Ayr :—" The Board took into their consideration a letter from the Rev. W. S. Wilson of Ayr, respecting the Episcopal congregation recently formed in that place under his pastoral charge. He stated that some families and individuals, residing in the neighbourhood of Ayr, had in 1832 procured the use of a small chapel, and with the sanction of Bishop Walker formed themselves into a congregation in communion with the Episcopal Church of Scotland. Since that time, the congregation having greatly increased, a suitable building was required in lieu of the chapel, which then was the upper floor of a building originally designed for a granary. The number of Episcopalians in Ayr and the immediate vicinity exceeds 400 souls, and there are many others in the towns and villages around whom Mr Wilson periodically visits as their minister. The great majority of the congregation are poor Irish, unable to contribute much towards this object, but anxious to do what they can. The sum required would probably be about L.700. Bishop Walker, who had himself made a donation towards this object, recommended Mr Wilson's application, and said that if a new and suitable chapel could, be obtained, the congregation would no doubt be respectable; that many persons came over from Maybole, a distance of nine miles from Ayr; and that Mr Wilson periodically visits the people at Maybole, who pay with gratitude the expense of his journeys to see them. The Board granted L 100 towards the erection of a chapel."

MAYBOLE.—The Episcopal clergyman at Ayr goes to Maybole once a month, for the purpose of performing Divine service to the members of the Church resident in that neighbourhood. It is stated that "the preaching in this parish is a mere temporary arrangement until something farther can be done to afford the means of public worship to the Episcopalians here."*

ANNAN.—This congregation was formed since 1838.

DUMFRIES.—The congregation appears to have been established in this town in 1762, and assembles in a chapel erected in 1817 at the cost of L.2200, the property of the congregation, and solely used for the celebration of Divine service. Total sittings, 300. The members are,

* Evidence of the Rev. W. S. Wilson, M. A.

with few exceptions, of the upper classes, and extend over the county of Dumfries and Galloway. The stipend averages L.250 per annum, but is variable, and is derived from seat-rents, collections, offertories, fees paid at the celebration of baptisms and marriages, and at funerals, and the interest of L.300 bequeathed as a legacy to the chapel. Public worship is performed twice every Sunday, and on week days, during the Festivals of Christmas and Easter, &c.*

KELSO.—The congregation in this town is supposed to have existed since 1689, and was regularly formed in 1757. The chapel, which was built by subscription in 1763, with a vestry and small burying-ground, is the property of the congregation, and is used solely as a place of worship. Total number of sittings, 218. Few or none of the attenders and communicants belong to the poor and working classes, and some members reside in the adjoining parishes of Ednam, Roxburgh, Nenthorn, and Eckford. The emoluments of the minister are fluctuating, and depend on the amount of the funds. Public worship is performed twice every Sunday, and on the Fasts and Festivals of the Church.†

PEEBLES.—This congregation is not reported by the Commissioners. In the Annual Report of the Society for Promoting Christian Knowledge for 1837 it is stated—" James Burnett, Esq. of Barns, near Peebles, forwarded a petition for and from the Society, in behalf of St Peter's Episcopal chapel in Peebles. The petition, signed by Mr Burnett, by appointment of the managers of the fund for the erection of this chapel, stated that such a building was greatly needed, the Episcopal chapel which is nearest to it being more than twenty miles distant, and the want of accommodation being daily more felt. The Right Rev. Bishop Walker having informed the Society that the institution of the chapel owed much to the exertions of Mr Burnett, and merited favourable attention, it was agreed to grant L.50."

VI.—DIOCESE OF EDINBURGH.

1.—ST PAUL'S CHAPEL, YORK PLACE.—This congregation, which was founded in the earlier part of the eighteenth century, removed from the

---

* Evidence of the Rev. C. M. Babington, M.A.
† Evidence of the Rev. William Kell, B.D.

Cowgate Chapel to the present edifice in 1818, which is devoted exclusively to the celebration of Divine service. The erection cost L.13,533, chiefly raised by subscription. Number of sittings, 1012. This congregation is composed of families residing indiscriminately in all the parishes in Edinburgh. The revenues of the chapel are applied to the payment of salaries, including those of the two ministers, interest on debt, repairs, charities, and other charges. The ordinary collections are applied in part to the general purposes of the chapel, and part is given in charity. A small sum is entrusted to the ministers for that purpose, which they may dispose of as they think right, without being limited to members of the congregation; besides this, a few pensions are given by the Trustees. Public worship is performed by the ministers in the chapel about 133 times in the course of the year, including the Fasts, Festivals, and Holidays of the Church. The ministers are able to extend their week-day ministrations to the whole of their congregation. The children are catechized every Sunday after the morning service, and instructed in the elements of religious knowledge.*

2. St George's Chapel, York Place.—This edifice was erected in 1794 at the cost of L.3000, and belongs to a body of shareholders who subscribed L 25 each; and the remainder of the sum necessary for the erection was borrowed by twelve gentlemen who act as the Vestry, and manage the affairs of the chapel. Total number of sittings, 642 No accurate information was obtained in regard to the average attendance at each celebration of public worship, or the total number of persons in the habit of attending the Chapel. Many of the unlet sittings are generally occupied. Many persons belonging to the Episcopal Church, resident in Edinburgh for longer or shorter periods, will not incur the expense of taking sittings in a chapel, and some of them resort to St George's. Out of the ordinary collections relief is afforded to deserving applicants, whether belonging to the congregation or not, given in annuities Some of the annuitants are paupers, and may derive aid from parochial funds. It is stated in the Appendix to the First Report by the Commissioners, that the emoluments of the clergyman are from L.280 to L.290, of which L.250 was the salary then afforded by the funds of the Chapel. The remainder consists of surplice fees, which

* Evidence of the Right Rev. Dr Terrot, Rev. John Sinclair, M.A., and Mr William Marshall, Treasurer.

vary much in amount. Public worship is celebrated twice every Sunday, twice on the chief Festivals of the Church, twice a-week during Lent, and once on certain Saints' Days.*

3. St John's Chapel, Prince's Street.—This edifice was built in 1817, and was occupied by the congregation of Charlotte Chapel. The cost of the building was L.16,013, including the organ, communion plate, and L.512 expended in repairing damage caused by a storm. The Chapel was built under an arrangement with the Magistrates of Edinburgh and the proprietors of Prince's Street, and, being in a conspicuous situation, was made more ornamental, and consequently more expensive than would have been deemed requisite under other circumstances. The funds were raised by subscriptions and donations, and some of the former were afterwards converted into donations. It is now held in 257 shares of L.20 each, making L 5140, upon which is paid an yearly dividend of three per cent. Total number of sittings, 821; connected with the congregation, about 900; and probably one-fifth of the communicants are of the poor or working classes. A clear sum of L.1266, after payment of incumbrances and expenses, has been derived from the sale of the burying-ground purchased from the Town of Edinburgh by certain members of the Vestry, and in 1829 conveyed to the proprietors of the Chapel. This sum has been applied to the reduction of the debt, which at Martinmas 1835 was L 6596, but in the subsequent four years reduced to L.1561 The annual stipend of the minister is L 550, out of which he pays his assistant. It arises from seat-rents and collections Public worship is performed twice every Sunday, and on the Fasts and Festivals of the Church.†

4. Trinity Chapel, Dean Bridge.—This Chapel was not erected, and the congregation was not formed, when the Commissioners returned their Reports. The edifice, a beautiful Gothic design by John Henderson, Esq. Architect, Edinburgh, contains sittings for about 800 persons.

5. St James' Chapel.—This Chapel, in Broughton Place, was erected in 1821, when the congregation was formed. The expense of the building was about L.4000, raised by voluntary contributions. It is the property of the congregation, and is not applied to any other purposes.

* Evidence of the Rev. R. Q Shannon, B.A., and James Stewart, Esq W S, Treasurer.

† Evidence of the Very Rev. E. B. Ramsay, M.A, and of Mr Rollo, Treasurer.

Total sittings, 850. The seat-rents are applied to the general expenses of the congregation, and the ordinary collections are given partly to the poor. The stipend is L.500, and occasional fees. Public worship is performed twice every Sunday, and on the usual Fasts and Festivals of the Church, and catechetical instruction is given on Saturdays and Sundays.*

St Paul's Chapel, Carrubber's Close.—This congregation is generally supposed to have been first formed at the Revolution, and assembles in an edifice fitted up at the time which was originally a wareroom. The upper floor is said to have been occupied by one of the ejected Bishops, and was purchased by the congregation in 1741. The other portions of the building were acquired in 1786, and converted to its present form and use. The Trustees in whom it was vested conveyed it in 1820 to the Trustees of the Scottish Episcopal Fund, who have since been recognized as the proprietors. The congregation has a constitution approved by the Trustees of that Fund, acknowledging the right to occupy the chapel during pleasure at a moderate rent, which is not exacted. The seat-rents are applied to the payment of the minister's stipend, and of the salaries of the organist, clerk, and beadle, with the expense of repairs and insurance. Number of sittings, 360. The salary of the clergyman is variable, and is not secured in any way. Public worship is performed twice every Sunday, and on Ash-Wednesday, Good Friday, and other days appointed to be observed.†

St Peter's Chapel, Roxburgh Place.—This Chapel consists of the first and second storeys of a house, and was originally constructed at the expense of a clergyman, who soon after let it at a rent of L.105. In 1806 it was sold by him to a private individual, who, after many additions, divided the price, L.1575, into fifteen shares of L 105 each, only six of which were sold, and the other nine remain with the proprietor. No lease of the Chapel is guaranteed to the congregation, whose right to occupy it is not permanent; but by deed it is set apart exclusively for the Episcopal Church, and it is provided that the congregation must be in communion with the Church, and under the jurisdiction of the Bishop

* Evidence of the Rev. Daniel Bagot, B.D., and of Mr Smith Ferguson, Treasurer.

† Evidence of the Rev D. T. K. Drummond, B.A , and of Mr Alexander Bruce, Assistant Treasurer.

of the Diocese. Very few poor attend the Chapel, the communicants being chiefly of the richer class. Number of sittings, 420. The revenues are applied to defray the minister's stipend, communion elements, and other expenses, and towards defraying the debts of the Chapel (L.246), and on the fifteen shares into which the price is divided. Part of the revenue is applied to public charities beyond the bounds of the congregation. It appears from Mr Skinner's Return, that in the year 1834-5 the minister had received, under the head stipend, L.78, 15s., and had in addition drawn the whole amount of the collections and offertories for the same year. The clergyman performs Divine service twice every Sunday, and on the Festivals and other days held sacred by the Church. He instructs the younger part of his congregation between services on Sundays.*

PORTOBELLO.—The congregation was first formed in this place in 1825, by the Rev Thomas Langhorne of Musselburgh, who erected St John's Chapel in Brighton Street. When this Chapel, which was duly consecrated by Bishop Sandford in 1826, was nearly completed, St Mark's Chapel was begun by an individual resident in Portobello, and though the congregation now assembles in it, the Chapel is private property, and as such a rent is annually paid. Total sittings, 440. The stipend, as stated in the Appendix to the First Report of the Commissioners printed in 1837, was then L.80, fixed for a time, and secured by the lessees. The seat-rents, offertories, and ordinary collections, are applied to the payment of the minister, of interest, and other expenses. Divine service is performed twice every Sunday, and on the Fasts and Festivals of the Church.† The cemetery surrounding St Mark's Chapel was the cause of an action in the Scottish Supreme Court in January 1832, when it was decided that a body of Dissenters cannot be prevented by the Kirk-Session or Heritors of the parish from establishing a place of sepulture of their own. The case is thus reported as it was brought before the Court:—" Colonel Hallyburton and certain other individuals, having taken a feu in the village of Portobello, which is situated in the parish of Duddingston, and erected thereon a chapel in connection with the Scottish Episcopal Communion, proposed to convert the ground surrounding it into a cemetery for the use of the congre-

* Evidence of the Rev. J. W. Ferguson, M A., and of J. R. Skinner, Esq W S
† Evidence of the Rev. G. M. Drummond, B.A.

gation, and those persons who might acquire burying places within it, and with this view they had it duly consecrated according to the ritual of the Episcopal Church. An attempt was immediately made by a neighbour to interdict them, on the ground that the churchyard would constitute a nuisance, and pending proceedings which ensued, the Kirk-Session of the parish for themselves, and taking burden on them for the Heritors, raised an action against Hallyburton and others, concluding to have it declared that they, or the Heritors, had the exclusive right of managing the parish churchyard and letting out mortcloths to hire, and that no other parties were entitled to establish within the parish a place of common sepulture, and to have Hallyburton and others interdicted from keeping up their cemetery. In support of this action they maintained that the Heritors, who were bound to provide sufficient burying-ground for the parish, or the Kirk-Session acting for them, had the exclusive privilege of keeping up a place of common sepulture for the parish, and of making profit by disposing of and selling parts thereof to individuals; and that the Kirk-Session had also the exclusive right of levying mortcloth and other funeral dues, the collection of which would be materially impeded if parties were allowed to bury elsewhere than in the proper churchyard. In defence it was pleaded, that as the defenders had never interfered with the management of the proper churchyard, or the right to let out mortcloths, the conclusions as to these matters were improperly directed against them;—that as to the other conclusions, there was no authority whatever for maintaining an exclusive right on the part of the Heritors or Kirk-Session to keep up a place of sepulture; —that any dues for the use of mortcloths would be equally well levied, if the Kirk-Session were entitled to them, whether the interment took place in the churchyard, or another burying place;—that all the other dues were for services performed, and went to the persons who performed them, and not to the poor or to the Session; and that it was contrary to law to make a profit by selling to private individuals parts of the churchyard, which (except the Heritors' private burying-grounds) was appropriated to the common use of the inhabitants; but that at any rate the Kirk-Session or Heritors could never prevent the establishment of other places of sepulture in order to increase their dues or profits; and further, that the burial of the dead in consecrated ground being in the view of the Episcopal Church part of their religious ritual, it was contrary to the Toleration Act to interfere with it, so as to compel the members of that Communion to bury their dead in unconsecrated ground. The Lord Ordinary [Lord Mackenzie] sustained the defences, and assoilzied. The Kirk-Session reclaimed, but the Court, without calling on the defenders' counsel to answer, adhered."*

MUSSELBURGH.—The congregation in this town, in the parish of Inveresk, has existed since 1688, and assembles in a chapel erected about 1800 at the cost of L 600, raised by private donations. It belongs to the congregation, and is applied to no other than religious purposes. Total sittings, 200. The minister's stipend is about L.80, but variable, and derived from the seat-rents, which, with the collections, are applied to defray the necessary expenses of the congregation. Public worship is performed twice every Sunday, and on the usual Fasts and Festivals.†

HADDINGTON.—The Episcopal congregation in this town is supposed to have existed since the Reformation. The chapel was built about 1770 on ground which was a gift from the Earl of Wemyss, is vested in Trustees, and is applied solely to the celebration of Divine service. Total number of sittings, 279. The congregation consists chiefly of the higher classes in the county, and the average attendance varies greatly, being dependent upon their residence or non-residence. The number in the habit of attending cannot be stated, as some of the congregation are not always in the county, and some attend only at the Festivals of the Church. The stipend is L.110, with a house and garden worth L.25 per annum. Public worship is performed twice every Sunday, and on Festivals.‡

STIRLING.—The congregation has existed since the establishment of Presbyterianism. The chapel belongs to the congregation; being held by Trustees, and is used only for religious purposes. It was erected about 1797, and cost nearly L.600. Total number of sittings, 200. Minister's stipend, about L.150. Public worship is performed every Sunday, besides on Fasts and Festivals. The minister officiates as

* Cases decided in the Court of Session, vol. x. p. 196, 197.
† Evidence of the Rev. Thomas Langhorne
‡ Evidence of the Rev James Traill, M A.

chaplain to the troops in Stirling Castle.* In 1842, the erection of a new and more commodious chapel was projected.

ALLOA.—The place of worship was closed for about fifteen years, and re-opened in June 1837. It contained 80 sittings, and was the property of the congregation. Since 1837, the present neat Gothic edifice was erected. It is applied solely to religious purposes. The minister's stipend is L.80. Public worship is performed twice every Sunday, and also on Festivals days observed by the Church.†

The Commissioners state respecting Edinburgh—" In computing the rates [or seat-rents] of the Dissenters, we necessarily leave out some sects which do not admit of seat-rents, whose sittings, however, amount to upwards of 4000 ; and we have distinguished from the others the Episcopalians, who, being generally of the wealthier classes, differ materially in that respect from the Dissenters." The neglect of public worship in the Scottish metropolis is thus described :—" If we were to assume, and the assumption does not seem unreasonable, that the number of persons in the habit of attending in those churches of the Establishment where the number has not been given, exceeds the average attendance in the same proportion as in those churches of the Establishment where both numbers have been returned ; and to follow the same rule in regard to the Dissenting congregations, excluding the Episcopalians and Roman Catholics, the number in the habit of attending would in the one case amount to about 35,877, and in the other to about 31,675. By applying the same calculation to the Episcopal congregations, the number of persons in the habit of attending therein would amount to about 3703 ; and adding the number of 3000 in the habit of attending the Roman Catholic chapels, 450 at the Unitarian chapel, and 90 for the Hebrews, there would appear to be about 74,795 persons in the habit of attending public worship out of a population in Edinburgh and Leith of 162,292. It would appear, therefore, as was indeed universally admitted in the Evidence, that there is a large number of persons capable of attending, who habitually absent themselves from public worship. The number cannot be less than from 40,000 to 50,000, according to the age at which children may be supposed capable of attending church. It need scarcely be remarked, that all these persons

* Evidence of the Rev. Robert Henderson, M.A.
† Evidence of the Rev. John Hunter.

are not chargeable with the same degree of neglect of public worship, as a part of them may attend occasionally. This neglect of public worship appears by the Evidence to be almost entirely confined to the poorer classes, and chiefly to the very lowest. Various causes are assigned for its prevalence ; but the principal reason, and that of which all parties concur in admitting the force, is the indifference of the people themselves. This appears to spring from various causes. Some are in extreme poverty, so occupied in obtaining the means of subsistence, and so absorbed in their own sufferings, that they have no thoughts to bestow on other subjects —A large portion, again, are sunk in habits of debauchery, which render them quite insensible to every feeling either of religion or morality."

In reference to Glasgow, the Commissioners observe :—" We cannot make any precise statement of the number of persons within the united district who may be considered to be in the habit of attending public worship. The tables which we have exhibited would show the number to be about 81,013, but as in the majority of cases we have stated the number of persons in the habit of attending no higher than the average of attendance, that number is probably considerably under the actual amount. If we were to assume, and the assumption does not seem unreasonable, that the number of persons in the habit of attending in those churches of the Establishment, where the number has not been given, exceeds the average attendance in the same proportion, as those churches of the Establishment where both numbers have been returned ; and to follow the same rule in regard to the Dissenting congregations, excluding the Episcopalians and Roman Catholics, the number in the habit of attending would, in the one case, amount to about 33,569, and in the other to about 38,547 ; and adding the number 1500 in the habit of attending at the Episcopal chapels, 12,500 for the Roman Catholics (although a proportion of these must reside beyond the united districts), 23 for the Society of Friends, and 40 for the Hebrews, there would appear to be about 86,179 persons in the habit of attending, out of a population of 213,810." This is the census of 1831. " With regard to the causes of this neglect of public worship, we deem it sufficient, on the present occasion, to state that the views upon this subject which were laid before us coincided generally with the evidence upon the same point which we received in Edinburgh."

No. II.

STATE OF THE EPISCOPAL CHURCH IN 1708.

IN the Library of the Faculty of Advocates at Edinburgh is preserved a MS. list, entitled, " An Account of the Names of the Ministers and Parishes within the several Synods and Presbyteries of Scotland at and since the late Revolution 1689, who have either been deprived by the State, or deposed by the [Presbyterian] Church, or voluntarily deserted, or turned out by the people, or yet continue to preach in their churches. The names marked X are Episcopal, the rest are Presbyterian " It is already stated that during the Establishment of the Episcopal Church before the Revolution the Dioceses comprised the Provincial Synods and Presbyteries as at present, with the exception of those Presbyteries which have since been erected The number of Provincial Synods was then fourteen.

The MS. now quoted appears to have been written about 1708. It commences with the Synod of Merse and Teviotdale, and the following Episcopal clergy contrived to preach in their [parish] churches by the connivance of the Government up to 1707 :

1. Synod of MERSE and TEVIOTDALE—Presbyterian ministers, 61 ; Episcopal clergy, 3 ; vacant parishes, 7.
2. Synod of LOTHIAN and TWEEDDALE—Presbyterian ministers, 105 ; Episcopal, 3 ; vacant, 9.
3. Synod of DUMFRIES—Presbyterian ministers, 52 ; Episcopal, 0 ; vacant, 1.
4. Synod of GALLOWAY—Presbyterian ministers, 34 ; Episcopal, 0 ; vacant, 1.
5. Synod of GLASGOW and AYR—Presbyterian ministers, 115 ; Episcopal, 0 ; vacant, 11.
6. Synod of ARGYLL—Presbyterian ministers, 41 ; Episcopal, 3 ; vacant, 5.
7. Synod of PERTH and STIRLING—Presbyterian ministers, 63 ; Episcopal, 12 ; vacant, 5.

8. Synod of FIFE—Presbyterian ministers, 64 ; Episcopal, 4; vacant, 5.
9. Synod of ANGUS and MEARNS—Presbyterian ministers, 50 ; Episcopal, 21 ; vacant, 14.
10 Synod of ABERDEEN—Presbyterian ministers, 57 ; Episcopal, 38 ; vacant, 9.
11. Synod of MORAY—Presbyterian ministers, 26 ; Episcopal, 19 ; vacant, 13
12. Synod of ROSS—Presbyterian ministers, 8 ; Episcopal, 14 ; vacant, 8.
13 Synod of CAITHNESS—Presbyterian ministers, 13 ; Episcopal, 5 ; vacant, 3.
14. Synod of ORKNEY and ZETLAND—Presbyterian ministers, 28 ; Episcopal, 0 ; vacant, 1.

The writer gives a kind of double list By the preceding it appears that 112 Episcopal clergymen were in possession of their parishes, in defiance of the Presbyterian Establishment, up to 1707 ; but in the other list he makes the number 116 ; and he thus exhibits the state of the parishes in Scotland. In April 1707, there are

Presbyterian Ministers,	719
" Intruders" (Episcopal clergy),	116
" Intruders" (Episcopal) into vacant parishes,	97
	932
In April 1708 there are Presbyterian ministers,	720
Episcopal clergy, including " intruders,"	133
Vacancies, besides " intruders,"	79
	932

By "intruders" is, of course, indicated those Episcopal clergy who were kept in possession of the parishes by the attachment of the people, and to whom the authorities of the new Establishment were obliged to allow possession for life.

No. III.

CONTEMPORARY SKETCH OF THE STATE OF THE SCOTTISH EPISCOPAL CHURCH FROM 1715 TO 1746—ANECDOTES—THE USAGES.

[THE following account of the controversy caused by the "Usages" is from a manuscript volume in the Advocates' Library, Edinburgh, entitled " Some short Memoirs of the Affairs of the Episcopal Church of Scotland since the Death of Queen Anne ;" which at one time belonged to the celebrated Lord Hailes, and has his autograph, David Dalrymple, Hailes, 1786. Who the author was is not stated, but it appears sufficiently evident that he was a determined opponent of the "Usages," and a supporter of the "College Party."]

In the end of Queen Anne's reign the Episcopals in Scotland promised to themselves great things by the change of the Ministry, insomuch that a great many meeting-houses were set up in town and country, and their enemies caressed them on all hands, by which means the ministers went in very boldly in the prosecution of the several duties of their function, and none or but very few set themselves in opposition to their proceedings. And thus they continued till the sudden death of that Queen, and the accession of King George the First to the throne, which very much disappointed all their hopes, and put a great damp on their spirits.

However, they went on without any prosecution or disturbance, for ought I remember, till the fatal year 1715, when there happened a very great insurrection of the noblemen, gentlemen, and commons of this kingdom, to assert the rights and interests of K— J—— the Eighth. In which the Episcopal clergy could not be wanting, considering their principles, and the many grievous hardships and sufferings they lay under since the Revolution. And a great many of the Presbyterian teachers, having abandoned their churches and their respective charges, they of the other [Episcopal] persuasion thought themselves obliged (though perhaps unadvisedly) to take possession of them; which upon the ruin of that noble undertaking, proved their ruin also. Some of them had not only prayed expressly for the King * in the churches, read all his declarations, and several instructions which were given them; but addressed him formally by a set speech in their gowns, which was afterwards printed, and strange observations made upon it. And though there were but few in comparison to the rest involved in these things, yet this drew a general persecution upon the whole Church, so that nothing was to be found in several places but driving the Episcopal clergy from their meeting-houses.

Those who were immediately concerned thought it proper to withdraw and hide themselves in some secure place, which they did till the Indemnity came out a long time after Yet some of them being searched for and taken, were led about with a great deal of contempt, till they were lodged in my Lord Winton's house† in the Canongate, which was then made a prison, and there they remained till they either made their escape, or were relieved some other way.

The ministers of Edinburgh were then taken notice of, and being summoned before the Lords of Justiciary, were fined L.20 sterling, which obliged them to take shelter in the Abbey,‡ and employ others to officiate in their several meeting-houses for a considerable time after.

The storm fell upon other parts of the kingdom, and so the Earl of Moray § having qualified to the Government for reasons best known to himself, not being any way engaged in the late insurrection, his chaplain must either pray *nominatim* [for George I.] or leave that family, the latter of which he rather chose readily to do.

The minister of Fortrose in the county of Ross had laid aside the exercise of his function, having so many enemies round about him, who constantly threatened to harass or imprison him. He that continued to officiate in a neighbouring congregation, about a mile from that town,

---

* The author, who was a zealous adherent of the exiled Family, means the Chevalier St George, whom the Jacobites always mentioned as "King."

† This mansion, which is now removed, stood on the north side of the Canongate, nearly opposite Queensberry House George fifth Earl of Winton was attainted in 1716, for being concerned in the Enterprise of 1715.

‡ The Abbey or Sanctuary of the Palace of Holyrood is here indicated.

§ This Nobleman was Charles fifth Earl of Moray, who succeeded in 1700, and died in 1735.

was one morning taken out of his bed, and carried to the prison of Dingwall, where he remained three months not in a fire room, so that had the day been never so cold or rainy he could not have the convenience of a fire. And even after, when he was set at liberty by the soldier who had some compassion on him, he was arraigned before my Lord Justice-Clerk,* then on his northern circuit, and could not get free without very hard terms. That clergyman afterwards perished going by boat to some part of the Highlands where he was to officiate, which, though it happened some years after, I could not omit here, in order to finish his story.

The two ministers were banished from Inverness. One of them, it seems, was so much regarded by his enemies that he was watched whether he would come near the town, and the other took sanctuary in a gentleman's family, and after various tossings chose to go and be his chaplain.

But the most unmanly as well as barbarous action happened with respect to a clergyman in Elgin of Moray; for, dreading no harm, the commanding officer there (I am sorry I do not remember his name, that I might transmit him infamous to posterity) ordered his sergeant to cudgel him, which he did so unmercifully, that though he lived some years after, these blows stuck to him, and I am persuaded contributed to his untimely death in the very flower of his age, which happened in the town of Linlithgow, very much regretted by all who knew him.

The end of the year 1717 passed with the prosecution of several of the Aberdeenshire clergy, who were summoned before the Lords of Justiciary at Edinburgh; but what was the final issue of the pleadings, on all hands, which were solemnly managed in the Parliament House† before a vast crowd, I do not so well remember. The government being sufficiently glutted with these prosecutions, the Church had some rest till 1719. Then K—g J——s thought fit to make another push for his interest, so that some noblemen and gentlemen, and some Spanish soldiers, landed in the Highlands, and had not Providence been pleased to disappoint the projects laid down, they might have shaken the W—g

---

* This Judge was the Hon James Erskine of Grange, brother of the Earl of Mar, whose infamous conduct to his wife is previously noticed.

† The Parliament House, Edinburgh, is here intended, in which the Judges of the Supreme Court of Scotland hear pleadings.

P——r; but they being defeated at Glenshiel, this put an end to that undertaking at that time.

This raised a fresh trouble upon the Church, so that the ministers of Edinburgh were convened before the magistrates of that city, and their meeting-houses were ordered to be shut up for six months, which accordingly was done, their doors being padlocked: and so strict the ruling powers were, that a minister, happening accidentally to be at Inverness, and thinking himself obliged privately to say prayers and preach in a room, a note was sent to him that he was in danger of being apprehended by the commanding officer there, so that upon Sunday night he was advised to leave his lodgings and retire to another.

Thus stood matters at the death of Dr Alexander Rose, Bishop of Edinburgh, the only surviving one of those before the Revolution, which opens a new scene of troubles and difficulties; for hitherto the Church was harassed by enemies from without, but then began they to breed in her own bosom.

It will be here necessary to trace some things which were done long before, but could not so conveniently be taken in till now.

The Bishop of Edinburgh's great care was to preserve such a succession as might serve the exigencies of the Church, that when it pleased God to restore that primitive apostolical order to the Church of Scotland, they should not be obliged to have recourse to any foreign Church, either for the consecration of their Bishops, or for the ordination of their several ministers, and in the meantime to ordain all such as should offer themselves, being duly qualified, for both congregations and families. And so the Bishops of Scotland, when there were but few of them remaining, consecrated Mr Fullarton, Mr Sage, Mr Falconar, and Mr Christie, and the two dying before Dr Rose, Bishop of Edinburgh, to wit, Mr Sage and Mr Christie, they consecrated Mr Millar and Mr Irvine.

All this was privately done, for Dr Rose managing all the affairs of the Church, and applications from all places being made to him only, it was not so necessary that these consecrations should be publicly known.

But his death happening the 19th day of March 1720, it was then needful that the clergy of the kingdom should know their several

Bishops, to whom they might apply in their respective counties. Accordingly, a few days after the Presbyters of Edinburgh were convened, and those Bishops who were then in town showed their several diplomas [or letters of consecration], but at the same time said they could do nothing with respect to the choice of a successor to the Bishop of Edinburgh, till Mr Fullarton, the senior Bishop, was come to town, whom they expected in a few days, having dispatched an express to him, and when he came the Presbyters should be acquainted, and would be told also of all the means necessary to be followed. So in some little time, when Mr Fullarton had arrived, the presbyters were ordered to meet to make choice of one of the College of Bishops, as it came then to be called, to be Bishop of Edinburgh, which they then thus understood, whatever stir has been made about that matter since.

All the ministers in and about Edinburgh did meet in one of the meeting-houses there, which being the largest meeting of them I believe since the Revolution, I think it not amiss here to set down the names of the most of them.

Mr Wm. Abercrombie, *Moderator*.
Mr Andrew Lumsden, *Clerk*.
Mr Patrick Trant, by proxy.
Mr Andrew Cant, by proxy.
Mr James Henry.
Mr Robert Wright,
Mr David Rankine, by proxy.
Mr David Laurie.
Mr George Johnston.
Mr Patrick Middleton.
Mr David Freebairn.
Mr James Walker.
Mr Henry Walker.
Mr Alexander Sutherland, senior.
Mr Alexander Sutherland, junior.
Mr Thomas Auchinleck.
Mr David Spence.
Mr Robert Skene.
Mr Robert Cheyne.

Mr William Gillan.
Mr William Cockburn.
Mr William Wylie.
Mr George Erskine.
Mr Thomas Carstairs.
Mr John Robertson.
Mr Alexander Mackenzie.
Mr Alexander Campbell.
Mr James Watson.
Mr Patrick Hume.
Mr Robert Keith.
Mr Robert Calder.
Mr Daniel Taylor.
Mr James Inglis.
Mr William Elphinstone.
Mr Gideon Guthrie.
Mr Alexander Guthrie.
Mr Robert Bowers.
Mr John Maclauchlan.

Mr Patrick Littlejohn.   Mr Adam Peacock.
Mr Daniel Robertson   Mr Patrick White.
Mr Robert Colt.   Mr Thomas Moubray.
Mr Henry Foulis.   Mr Patrick Lyon.
Mr Duncan Murchieson.   Mr Thomas Wilkie.

Some of the ministers met together in a house the night before the meeting, where it was moved that since the Bishops of Scotland were pleased to appoint the presbyters to choose their Bishop, it was but mannerly to refer back again the choice to themselves, and so the most part of them were for the reference. Accordingly, the Bishops pitched upon Mr Fullarton for the Diocese of Edinburgh as the Senior, which he accepted as from the College, as an authentic deed under his and the rest of their hands, I am told still extant, manifests and declares.

The late Bishop of Edinburgh, Dr Rose, taking the whole care of the Church upon himself, except in very important matters where he thought it proper to consult with his colleagues, found it not necessary to make the consecrations public, which was the reason, as is said above, why the presbyters were desirous to know who were Bishops of this Church, and when they were known, were all owned as such, and submitted to, without the least notion then of that which they afterwards started, concerning Utopian Bishops, or Bishops at large, who had no concern with this Church, as some have since very confidently as well as strangely asserted.

But though these Bishops had not any great share in the government of the Church before, they thought fit by common consent to have particular districts, over which they might preside, and have an immediate inspection. So Mr Fullarton had Edinburgh, Mr Millar the Merse [Berwickshire], Mr Irvine the old Diocese of Dunblane, and part of Perthshire, Mr Falconar had Fife, Angus [Forfarshire], and the Mearns [Kincardineshire],* Mr Freebairn had Annandale.† Mr Cant was so infirm, that, as I believe he desired none, so none was allotted him, being yet repute by all as much a Bishop of this Church as any of

---

* Most of these counties of Forfar and Kincardine, anciently Angus and Mearns, are in the present Diocese of Brechin.

† A district of Dumfries-shire in the Archbishopric of Glasgow.

the rest. Thus I think they continued without any disturbance or molestation, all the presbyters in the several districts submitting to them, till the arrival of Mr Gadderar in this kingdom in the summer of 1722.

I should have told above, that besides these mentioned Bishops, there were two consecrated in England—Mr Archibald Campbell, uncle to the Duke of Argyll, and the just named Mr Gadderar, who was a minister in Scotland before the Revolution, but then resided in England. These two were consecrated Bishops of this Church, and were always esteemed such, though none of them at that time lived in Scotland.

There were certain persons in our own neighbouring nation who endeavoured to revive, sometime before this, some ancient Usages or customs, which obtained in the Primitive Church, such as mixing water with the wine in the Holy Eucharist, prayers for the dead,* and chrism in baptism and confirmation;† and to such a length they went, that they must strike out the Decalogue out of the Liturgy, for the Fourth Commandment, which was Jewish, and in place of it use that summary of the Moral Law delivered by our Lord—" Thou shalt love the Lord thy God with all thy heart, with all thy soul, with all thy mind, and with all thy strength, and thy neighbour as thyself."‡

All these things spread so in England, among the Nonjuring clergy there, and were so tossed even among ourselves, a considerable party of them appearing against such things, that there were a great many pamphlets written on the one side and on the other; which made the matter be much farther known than I believe the first revivers intended, and brought their enemies more into their secrets than otherwise; and perhaps made them set themselves more to crush and overthrow them, than without this would have been done.

While these things were agitating in England, several letters were sent to Dr Rose, then Bishop of Edinburgh, to have his concurrence with respect to these Usages, and so to bring over the rest of the clergy

---

* If by the words *prayers for the dead* the writer means the Roman Catholic practice, he is completely mistaken. All that was maintained in this Usage was the duty of commemorating the faithful departed in the administration of the Holy Eucharist.

† In these assertions he errs most egregiously.

‡ This, if correct at all, must only refer to the practice of a few individuals, for it nowhere appears that such an alteration or substitution was at any time prevalent, or sanctioned by authority.

of Scotland to favour such things; but he was too wise a man, and had the affairs of the Church too much at heart, to consent to any such thing.

When they found that their several negotiations by letter succeeded not, they sent hither one Mr Peck, a clergyman of their number, to try not only to persuade the Bishop with respect to these things in debate, but to bring over, if he could, some of the inferior clergy to his way. He prevailed with none, for ought I could learn, but one Mr Cockburn,* in whose meeting-house he frequently officiated, and being sent away with a full answer to all they required.

I was told it was a great many months before that answer was notified to the [Nonjuring] clergy of England, being for a long time industriously kept up, that they might not know the judgment of the Church of [in] Scotland, which might perhaps have stumbled them in their particular way of thinking

But that Bishop [Dr Rose] being dead, as I hinted above, Dr Gadderar was sent down under the pretence of being chaplain to the Viscount of Arbuthnot.† While he was in town [Edinburgh], he did visit and was visited by the several Bishops who resided in Edinburgh; and though they seriously conferred on matters which regarded the peace and unity of the Church, they could bring him to no terms; he would not so much as communicate with them.

The Presbyters of Aberdeen had, it seems, met together, and chose Mr Campbell, then in England, for their Bishop. He could not, or was not inclined to come to Scotland, and so he devolved his right which he had to Aberdeen over to Mr Gadderar, he designing to come and reside near them.

When the other Bishops and he communed together, he said he had accepted the See of Aberdeen as by deputation from Mr Campbell, so would own none of them in it, and, therefore, without any more, away he posts to my Lord Arbuthnot's family, and in some time after visits the clergy of Aberdeen, who accepted him for their Bishop without any regard to the rest. And he, favouring mightily the Usages, brought over a great many of the clergy to these, so that an open rupture threatened

---

* Probably the Rev William Cockburn, enumerated in the preceding list of the presbyters residing in and near Edinburgh

† This Nobleman must have been John fifth Viscount, who died in 1756.

the Church, and all seemed to go to ruin and confusion by the several different methods which some in the North very violently pursued. Upon which the Bishops of Scotland thought it proper to bestir themselves in a matter of so great consequence, and, therefore, they wrote frequently to Mr Gadderar, but without any satisfactory returns. He wished they might delay matters of that nature, and not inquire narrowly into his conduct with respect to the management of his diocese, and I believe as little did he promise to meddle with them.

But since they justly thought that the government of the Church resided in them, and that they were to allow nothing to be introduced into it which might tend to its disadvantage, those shifts did not please them. However, Mr Gadderar still went on, and gained proselytes every day to his new opinions. He made his circuits in great pomp and parade,* with a numerous retinue of the clergy still attending him, and those of the bounds where he came appointed to wait on him, which they did, and no doubt received his commands. And so forward was he in those matters, that he will not content himself with the See of Aberdeen only, but he must needs travel into Moray; so he came as far as Elgin, confirmed all the children in the way, and exercised all the rest of the parts of the Episcopal function and jurisdiction. And now those who adhered to him called more loudly to introduce all things they thought fit into the public worship of God; nay, it was said actually practised these Usages, as they spoke for them in all conversations, thus to bring over the laity also to their particular way of thinking, and make them favour what they intended to do.

All this still more alarmed the plurality of the Bishops, who saw plainly what dismal effects and consequences must ensue upon these things when some followed one way, some another. They would at last become a prey to their enemies, who wanted nothing but to gain by their divisions. Upon this the clergy of Edinburgh were summoned, and all the Bishops in town were present, where they resolved that a presbyter should be sent to Mr Gadderar with all the necessary instructions, and if he would not at all go in to necessary measures for preserving and governing the Church of [in] Scotland, in conjunction with

* These "circuits" are noticed by Wodrow in the extract from his Analecta, inserted in the present volume (p. 249), but he takes no notice of the alleged "pomp and parade" of Bishop Gadderar.

the rest of his colleagues, they intended, much against their inclination, to proceed to the utmost sentence against him ; and this no doubt was accordingly notified to him, and he persuaded to take advice not to run into such courses, as certainly he would repent, when it was far better to do it in time

In the meantime, the Bishops thought it proper to guard all the presbyters of the kingdom as much as they were able against everything that might tend to endanger the interest of that Church which they were so much bound to preserve. Accordingly, they drew up a Formula, as it was called, by which every presbyter was bound to subscribe that he would use no innovations on the worship of God, particularly by mixing water into the wine in the Holy Eucharist, prayers for the dead, and such like, which, for the peace of the Church, they obliged themselves to stand up against, and only make use of the English or Scottish Liturgy, either of which was freely granted to all as their several inclinations led them, because this was insisted on by some, and at the same time was represented as not at all breaking the unity and order of the Episcopal Church *

So they began with the clergy of Edinburgh to subscribe this Formula, all of whom did it excepting one or two, who were told that if they did it not they must give over their charges, they [the Bishops] being positively resolved that none who officiated in Edinburgh should remain there while they refused any such thing ; and so I was told they frankly went in as well as the rest.

The Aberdeenshire clergy laughed at any such thing, exclaiming that it was not in their power thus to bind up the consciences of presbyters, there being no full convocation of the whole Church to enact things of so great moment as they thought them, and far less when they did not own their authority at all However, it was sent to the several parts of

---

* The " Formula " was as follows —" Edinburgh, April 1724 —Considering the present danger of the Church, and that her peace and unity are like to be broken by the endeavours of some to introduce certain Usages, such as the mixture of water with wine in the celebration of the Holy Eucharist, prayers for the dead, and some others, I, A B , do faithfully declare and promise, that, for preserving the peace and unity of the Church, which to all good men ought to be very dear and precious, I shall not make any innovation in the doctrine and worship of this Church, as now received among us, by introducing or practising any of the said Usages "

the kingdom where there were any presbyters, and some appearing against it, the gentlemen in whose houses they resided would not so well bear their disregard to the authority of those who they justly thought as a College had power to order the affairs of the Church. And when they proceeded farther to insist upon introducing these Usages into the worship of God, they told them plainly they would admit no such things, and if they were resolved on these they must seek out other places for themselves.

So Mr R——t J——n left Logie-Almond's family,* Mr A——w G—d my Lord Nairne's,† and Mr A——s Balgowan's ;‡ and, which was very strange, they all went off without letters-demissory from their Bishop, and yet were received in other places, which shows what dismal confusion there was then in the Church, and how far it might go if not prevented. In several other places of the kingdom the Formula was well enough received ; and they whose minds were not yet prejudiced or biassed by those Usages cordially went into it.

But the care and vigilance of the governors of the Church [the College of Bishops] did not rest here ; considering what influence the gentlemen might have, and how necessary, therefore, it was to bring them to just and worthy sentiments in these matters,§ they directed a circular letter to all in the kingdom, in which the clergy were movingly put in mind of their duty, and at the same time the laics were addressed ; and so I have set it down at large, the copy of which is as followeth :—

" Unto the Episcopal Church of Scotland, as well Clergy as Laity, the plurality of the College of Bishops who have the inspection and superintendence of the said Church, send greeting :—The peace and unity of

---

* Drummond of Logie-Almond in Perthshire

† Murray, Lord Nairne, a Peerage created in 1681, and afterwards merged into a younger branch of the Ducal House of Atholl. The family seat was Stanley House in the parish of Auchtergaven, Perthshire, an old mansion, built at different times, delightfully situated amid magnificent scenery on the banks of the Tay near the village of Stanley. Both the mansion and thriving village derive their name from Lady Amelia Stanley, daughter of James Earl of Derby, who married the first Marquis of Atholl.

‡ Graham of Balgowan, in Perthshire, a family represented by the gallant Lord Lynedoch.

§ It is here to be observed, that long before and after this period many of the principal nobility and gentry of Scotland retained Episcopal clergymen in their families as private chaplains, and in some cases as preceptors to their children.

this National Church is a matter of so great importance to us, and to all who wish well to religion, that we cannot think without horror and the utmost detestation of allowing anything to be brought forward into the doctrine or worship of this Church that tends in the least to separate or divide us. Which was the reason why we refused to give our consent to some of our brethren their practising in the public worship some Usages, such as the mixing of water with the wine in the celebration of the Holy Eucharist, praying for the dead, and some others, which the godly and learned divines, pious confessors, and holy martyrs, who compiled the Liturgy which now we use, thought fit and expedient upon the review thereof to keep out and lay aside, none of the divines at that time expressing any dissatisfaction thereat, or murmuring against the want of these Usages: and seeing the unreasonable reviving and pressing of these Usages by an incompetent authority have broken and divided our brethren in England, and cannot miss to have the same fatal effect if they are in the same unwarrantable manner introduced among us: Wherefore these are earnestly to exhort and obtest, in the bowels of Jesus Christ, all of you, our dear friends, carefully to shun these fatal rocks whereon others have been shipwrecked before you And for this purpose we judge it meet to lay before you, our reverend brethren of the clergy, for refreshing of your memories, that at your ordination, conform to the Ordinal, you promised solemnly to maintain and set forward, as much as lies in you, quietness, peace, and love, among all Christian people, and especially among them that are or shall be committed to your charge: to which promise your reviving of these Usages at this unseasonable time is not reconcileable.

"You also farther promised in that same Ordinal by which you were ordained, to give faithful diligence always to minister the doctrine and sacraments as the Lord hath commanded, and as this Church and realm have received the same.

"Now the Church and Realm mentioned in the said Ordinal did and do still minister the doctrine and sacraments without these Usages, in the same manner as we do at present. And if you will keep faithfully that religious promise which you made to God and his Church on so solemn an occasion, then ye will forbear the mixture and the foresaid Usages, and the incurring our just and necessary censure.

"So great was our condescending care, that it induced us to indulge our scrupulous brethren in the use of the Communion Office as in our Scottish Liturgy, hoping thereby to prevent all further disturbance. But seeing neither this, nor their own express passing from the absolute and indispensable necessity of these said Usages, can restrain them from such measures as do plainly tend to rend and destroy this afflicted Church, we have found it necessary to issue out this our loving remonstrance and injunction.

" Finally, brethren, farewell. Be perfect, be of good comfort, be of one mind. Live in peace, and the God of peace shall be with you.

"(*Sic subscribitur*)—JOHN, *Bishop of Edinburgh* ; AR. MILLAR, *Bishop* ; WILL. IRVINE, *Bishop* ; AND. CANT, *Bishop* ; DAV. FREEBAIRN, *Bishop* Given at Edinburgh, February the 12th, 1723."

Mr Gadderar, finding that matters thus run high against him, and that he must either satisfy the rest of the Bishops or else stand by himself, and so make a grievous rupture in the Church, upon mature deliberation thought it more advisable to submit himself, and so he came to Edinburgh, and was fully pleased to enter into terms of agreement with them, which were accordingly drawn up, and were called the CONCORDATE, by which he promised not to disturb the peace of the Church by any public use of these Usages, and accepted the Bishopric of Aberdeen, not as by deputation from Mr Campbell, in England, nor merely by the election of the presbyters, but from the College of Bishops appointing him to inspect the affairs thereof, by which he was to act in concert with them in public concerns. And thus stood matters till some time after the College of Bishops were to consecrate one Mr Norrie, minister in Dundee, [when] Mr.Rattray of Craighall, of whom frequent mention will be made hereafter, made a formal protestation against it, which went so far as to be printed, but there being very few copies of it, I never yet could see one.

Now it was that Bishops of districts, or provincial Bishops, and Bishops at large, who have no places assigned to them particularly, made so great a noise, which was only whispered before, but now loudly spoke. However, they went on to consecrate Mr Norrie, and great interest was made that Mr Rattray should be so too ; but having embarked with Mr Gadderar, it was not thought proper. Mr Norrie died some time after, but the dispute did not die with him, for there being some persons named by the K— to be consecrated, particularly Mr Rose, brother to the late Bishop of Edinburgh, Mr Ouchterlonie, and Mr Gillan, the presbyters of Edinburgh made a terrible outcry against the last for reasons not worth mentioning, but which made him decline the promotion out of great modesty for some time.

Mr Fullarton, Bishop of Edinburgh, having retired a little to his country seat in the West, desired that in his absence those Bishops who were in Edinburgh would be pleased to consecrate the three named by the K—g. Mr Gillan, as I said, declined it for that time; but the other two, to wit, Mr Rose and Mr Ouchterlonie, were accordingly consecrated. A very little after accounts came of the Bishop of Edinburgh's death in April 1727, and then the presbyters of Edinburgh convened, and some of them hastily chose Bishop Millar for Bishop of Edinburgh; others of them thought that election too predisputal and irregular, and so dissented, which some of the Bishops thought too. However, some time after, the Bishops meeting in Edinburgh, matters might have been made up among them, but unhappily Bishop Millar had struck in with the Usage Party, as it was called, and so would not own the College of Bishops, nor exercise any authority as by their permission or consent.

Mr Gadderar, looking on this as a favourable juncture wherein to have Mr Rattray consecrated, which was attempted in vain before, plied Bishop Millar so close, and persuaded Mr Cant to join in with them, that he was instantly consecrated. Mr Gadderar and Mr Rattray buoyed up Mr Millar so with a metropolitical power, of which he was too fond, and was indeed a great weakness in him, that he could deny those persons nothing who fed him up with that weak fancy to which the others would never assent, as having all a joint right and interest in the government of the Church. Now things came to an open rupture. Mr Millar would not so much as meet with those Bishops who were on the other side of the question, to wit, against his high metropolitical power;* and he, together with the rest of his faction, to strengthen themselves, assumed into the episcopate one Mr Dunbar, a minister in the North, and Mr Keith,† a minister in Edinburgh

The others, considering these things to give great weight to their

* This "high metropolitical power," mentioned by the writer with such bitterness, seems to have been the office of Primus

† The distinguished author of the History of Scotland during Queen Mary's reign, and of the Catalogue of the Scottish Bishops.

consultations and authority, consecrated Mr David Ranken and Mr John Gillan, the latter of whom, as I said, should have been consecrated before, but was not till the 11th of June, St Barnabas' Day, being Sunday, 1727. The others standing much on districts, Mr Dunbar was chosen Bishop of Moray; and Mr Millar being old and failed, Mr Keith was chosen *in coadjutorem nostrum*, in order to cover all their designs.

And thus the unhappy division broke out fully, six against six—Mr Millar, Mr Gadderar, Mr Rattray, Mr Dunbar, Mr Keith, and Mr Cant, on the one part, the last of whom, though he was very much *ab agendo*, being far advanced in years, and very little advised by them, yet was by other arts still looked on as one of them. Mr Duncan, Mr Freebairn, Mr Rose, Mr Ouchterlonie, Mr Ranken, and Mr Gillan, on the other; and frequent messages were sent from the one side to the other, and terms proposed, those from the Provincial Bishops, as they called themselves, were thus—"Terms laid down by the Bishop of Edinburgh and his comprovincial or diocesan Bishops, and proposed by them to their brethren the Bishops at large, in order to the establishing the peace of the Church.

"I. Seeing there can be no order or unity preserved in any national or provincial Church without a metropolitan, that all do own Bishop Millar for Bishop of Edinburgh, and that as vicar-general the metropolitical powers are lodged in him.

"II. Seeing all assemblies of Bishops are intended principally for deliberating upon and regulating the affairs of the flock of Christ, respectively committed to them, it is evident none can have a decisive vote but such Bishops as have a *portio gregis* entrusted to them.

"III. The Bishop of Edinburgh and his other comprovincial Bishops are willing to maintain good correspondence with such Bishops as have no *portio gregis* committed to them, but are only Bishops at large, to call them to their meetings, and ask their advice on weighty matters, and if any of them shall hereafter have particular charges, *i. e.* Dioceses or Districts committed to them by a regular election from a competent number of Presbyters, confirmed by the comprovincial Bishops, they will then come to have a right to a decisive vote in affairs relating to the general benefit of the Church."

These were not at all satisfying, and, therefore, after all methods had proved ineffectual, the Bishops on the opposite side having summoned Bishop Millar to compear before them, and he refusing, they suspended him from all exercise of his episcopal function, and ordered this to be notified to him and the clergy, which was accordingly done. However, he, not in the least regarding this, went on in his usual way to ordain presbyters,* and to hold several meetings, till he was taken away by death, which happened in October that year, 1727.

Some time after his death, the presbyters met together to choose a Bishop of Edinburgh, and they pitched upon one Mr Andrew Lumsden, an old and discreet presbyter, who all thought would have put an end to the troubles of the Church, but he striking in with the Usage Bishops, as they were then called, and receiving his consecration from them, left matters in the same unhappy state they were before. He would not, he said, disclaim his right and title to a metropolitical power, though he was frequently urged to this, because it might prejudice his successor, but he would not employ it even when given him, which the other Bishops did not think fit to consent to.

While matters stood thus the Right Rev. Mr David Ranken died in November 1728, a person of indefatigable labour and diligence in promoting the peace and concord of the Church, which being very much defeated by the restless spirit of some, troubled him exceedingly, and the gravel increasing on him at last cut him off.

All the Bishops at length reflecting how fatally dangerous to the Church their divisions were, resolved to meet together, and put an end to them, which they happily did in December 1731—all mutually embracing each other, owning all the consecrations as good and valid, and promising to do what in them lay to preserve and promote the unity and peace of the Church. And considering it might contribute to this, to put what marks of regard they could upon Bishop Freebairn, they constituted him their Primus or Preses, to convocate them together upon the necessary affairs of the Church. But this was so displeasing to Bishop Lumsden, that he seldom after attended any of their meetings, or regarded their authority, doing every thing as he thought proper, without advising them, which they took so ill that they were resolved to

---

* The writer adds—" I do not remember he ordained any but one presbyter, who is since dead."

meet, to expostulate the affair with him, and to advise that they should take joint measures for the government of the Church.

But it happened that the very day before their meeting, which was the 20th day of June 1733, Bishop Lumsden died, and so Providence prevented any misunderstanding which might have risen among them. This year proved fatal to the Episcopal Church in the death of many eminent of her Bishops; for in January died Mr Duncan at Glasgow; in March, Mr Gadderar at Aberdeen; and in April, Mr Rose at Cupar [Fife]; and the 19th day of June, Bishop Lumsden at Edinburgh. Upon the 28th of that month, Bishop Freebairn was unanimously chosen Bishop of Edinburgh, and on the same day his election confirmed by the rest of the Bishops, being then in the place; and Mr Dunbar was chosen Bishop of Aberdeen with the approbation also of all his colleagues.

There was one Mr Maben, a deacon, who being arraigned before Bishop Lumsden for an irregular marriage, was suspended before the thing was fully proved. The Bishops, upon application to them, found this a bad precedent, and therefore ordered that Bishop Freebairn, a month after his coming to the See of Edinburgh, should take off this sentence till the fact libelled should be proven, and then to proceed against him as he pleased. The presbyters who supported their plea against Mr Maben thought this bore hard on them; and, on the other hand, the two Bishops in town, Messrs Gillan and Keith, were for maintaining the authority of the Bishops. However, the presbyters came to have the better of it, for they so dealt with Bishop Freebairn, that he not only continued the sentence, but fixed it with all solemnity; by which means a little misunderstanding happened between the Bishops in Edinburgh and Bishop Freebairn, who so represented things to the rest of the Bishops, that when Bishop Freebairn as Primus called a meeting of the Bishops at Edinburgh [on] the 3d day of July 1734, they all unanimously declined it except Bishop Ouchterlonie. All the rest, to wit, Bishops Rattray, Dunbar, Gillan, and Keith, gave in a formal declinature subscribed by each, upon the receipt of which Bishop Freebairn wrote a letter full of disagreeable expressions, and which showed too much an angry resentment, copies of which he caused deliver to the four Bishops, who dissented from his proceedings, and two of them, Bishops Rattray and Dunbar, returned answers to convince him how unreasonable he was, but they were not at all satisfying; however, after some replies matters were laid asleep.

I cannot here omit to remember the piety of a certain considerable lady in England, who, considering the distresses that the Episcopal clergy of Scotland lay under, did very charitably bequeath to them in legacy L.400 sterling, L.10 to every Bishop, the rest to be divided equally among the presbyters, which was accordingly done in December 1734, and by this means a list of all the presbyters in the kingdom being necessary, it was found that there were only about *a hundred and thirty—a smaller number than was at first supposed.*

The beginning of the year 1735 appeared in the death of the Right Rev. Mr John Gillan, who died the 3d day of January. He was a person of great learning, an admirable preacher, and much concerned for the differences of the Church; and it was thought that the slanders and detractions of some contributed not a little to hasten his end. The meeting-house in which he preached was so considerable, that the gentlemen invited Bishop Rattray to officiate among them, which some thought a step to his having the See of Edinburgh, upon the demise of Bishop Freebairn, but he declined, so the gentlemen chose a discreet young gentleman, Mr William Harper in Leith, who accepted it, and appeared there March 9th.

As the year before Bishop Freebairn indited a meeting of the Bishops, so this year another, he said, at their own desire, to wit, of the rest of the Bishops, on the 18th of June. They would not meet, unless he promised to consecrate Mr White, minister of Cupar in Fife, who was to preside over the district of Dunblane, in place of Bishop Gillan deceased. For the Presbyters had made application to all the Bishops to provide them with one, which Bishop Freebairn took amiss, because they did not first make application to him, and to him only as Primus, and therefore would not so readily concur in the consecration. But Bishops Rattray, Dunbar, and Keith, proceeded without him or Bishop Ouchterlonie, and so, on the 24th of June 1735, consecrated Mr White, which still contributed to make the breach wider, so that nothing now appeared among them but remonstrances, or admonitions and protestations from Bishops Freebairn and Ouchterlonie on one side, which were answered by Bishops Rattray, Dunbar, and Keith, on the other.

About the beginning of the year 1738 a fresh dispute arose between

Bishop Freebairn and Bishop Keith, concerning the ordination of one Mr Spens.* He was designed for the meeting-house at the Wemyss [in Fife], and, therefore, that district belonging to Bishop Keith, he ought to have passed trials before the Presbyters of Fife; but I know not now he applied to Bishop Freebairn, who appointed them accordingly before some presbyters of Edinburgh, and did put him in deacon's orders.† This was resented by Bishop Keith, who therefore would give him no allowance to preach at the Wemyss. Mr Spens, however, submitted, and that [affair] was over.

In April or May that year Bishop Rattray came to Edinburgh, and dealt with the Bishops there to have a meeting of all called, which was indited for the 11th of July; but when they met there was a proxy, one Mr Robert Lyon, minister at Crail, from Bishop Dunbar, who could not himself come,‡ which neither Bishops Freebairn nor Ouchterlonie would allow, and so would by no means constitute the meeting; upon which Bishops Rattray, Keith, and the proxy, removed to a meeting-house in the town, and constituted themselves into a meeting without the others, and then received Bishop White, and did what they pleased, as yet unknown to us. Endeavours were still used to bring the Bishops to an accommodation of the points in debate before them, but all to little purpose. And thus stood matters when it pleased God to call away by death Bishop David Freebairn, the 24th of December 1739, in the 83d or 84th year of his age, leaving the Church in too much

---

* This gentleman was the Rev. Nathaniel Spens, of the family of Spens of Craigsanquhar, near Cupar-Fife. He was afterwards Episcopal clergyman at Pittenweem in the same county. The old edifice, a kind of castellated building, in an apartment in which the Episcopal congregation at Wemyss assembled, is still standing in ruins on the shore of the Frith of Forth, near the stately mansion of Wemyss Castle, then the seat of the Earls of Wemyss, who were the supporters of the congregation, which has long become extinct.

† This was a most uncanonical procedure on the part of Bishop Freebairn, who had no right to interfere in Bishop Keith's diocesan district, without his express concurrence. It appears from the above details that much personal animosity existed among the Scottish Bishops about this period.

‡ The fact of Mr Lyon, a presbyter from Crail, appearing as a proxy for Bishop Dunbar, in a meeting of the Bishops, if what is above stated is correct, is most extraordinary, as is also the subsequent conduct of Bishops Rattray and White, in adjourning to a "meeting-house," and allowing Mr Lyon to sit.

trouble and confusion; for though he was a man that might understand the interests of it, yet he was too easily biassed by every counsel and advice given him. The presbyters met a few days after his death, and having chosen Mr William Harper to preside, did notify the vacancy of the See to the Bishops, and begged an order for choosing their Bishop as soon as their convenience could allow. But none coming in the month of April 1740, they thought proper to make an humble remonstrance to them again, but all in vain, for since they found the presbyters would not chime in with some measures they projected, therefore they would allow no meeting.

As Mr Dunbar was old and infirm, to strengthen themselves they proposed to the presbyters of Aberdeen to accept Mr Andrew Gerard, as coadjutor to their Bishop, who should succeed upon his demise; but the presbyters following the pattern they themselves [the Bishops] had set, would do nothing without an election, and giving no grounds to think they would choose Mr Gerard, the matter for that time was dropped. But the Bishops consecrated one Mr Falconer, in September 1741, as coadjutor to Bishop Keith in Orkney and Caithness, and other places he could not visit.

In May 1742 Bishop Ouchterlonie died at Dundee. He was the last of those Bishops who appeared against any innovations in the then received worship of the Church. Soon after the Bishops gave a mandate to the presbyters of that district [the Diocese of Brechin] to choose a Bishop for themselves, who accordingly elected Mr Rait, a minister of another meeting-house in Dundee, who was consecrated at Edinburgh by Bishops Rattray, Keith, and White, in October 1742.

The presbyters of Edinburgh, considering their circumstances in being destitute of a Bishop to oversee them, met together [in] February 1743, and chose Bishop Rattray to take the temporary inspection of them till in a fuller meeting one might be elected. Accordingly, there was a letter written to him, and subscribed by most of the Edinburgh clergy. He returned an obliging answer; and, though he did not fully accept, said he would be with them as soon as he could; and about the end of April came, yet did not call the presbyters, till, as was said, there should be a meeting of the Bishops, which was indited the first week in June. But it pleased God to call hence Bishop Rattray; for, being taken ill on Monday, May 9, he died on the 12th, on Ascension Day, in the sixtieth year of his age, to the surprise and regret of many, being vigorous and strong.

In the meantime, there arose great heats at Dundee, about choosing a minister for that congregation which was formerly Bishop Ouchterlonie's. That congregation was always against any innovations in the Liturgy of the Church of England, and Mr Robertson their minister showing great inclination that way, and shuffling with them, they resolved to call one Mr Fyfe, which both Bishop Rait and Mr Robertson not at all allowing, they, however, brought him to town; and the Sunday after Mr Fyfe took possession of the pulpit, some time before Divine service ordinarily begun.*

In August 1743, the Bishops met for the consecration of Mr Alexander to the district of Dunkeld, in place of Bishop Rattray, and after this formed themselves into a Synod, where they enacted several Canons not very agreeable to the major part of the presbyters of Edinburgh, and where also Bishop Rait complained of the conduct of Mr Fyfe. Upon which two or three of the Bishops were desired to assist Bishop Rait in examining into that affair, and finding Mr Fyfe resolved to that congregation which had called him, they instantly depose him; but he, notwithstanding, went on in the exercise of his ministry.

The presbyters of Edinburgh, taking into their consideration the Canons made in the late Synod, gave in or sent to the Bishops a humble representation against them in January 1744,† showing not only that some of them were made without due reflection, but also that the Bishops without presbyters could make none such binding upon them. This alarmed the Bishops, and occasioned some papers upon both sides. And Mr Fyfe insisting that he was deposed for adhering to the English Liturgy, this made his interest be espoused by some of the Nonjuring Bishops of that Church, and more warmly by one Bishop Smith. He wrote earnestly to Bishop Keith, to be communicated to the rest, entreating, for sundry weighty reasons, that Mr Fyfe, upon his humbling himself, might be restored to the peace of the Church; but all being to no purpose, Bishop Smith by letters received him into communion. This mightily displeased the Bishops, complaining that he unduly meddled

---

* This very outrageous conduct on the part of Mr Fyfe indicates that the congregation was divided into two parties.   † See p. 270. of the present volume.

in what only concerned them ; and so they drew up a heavy declaration against his proceedings, which they sent to the presbyters of Scotland, to be subscribed by them, which a great many did ; but when laid before the presbyters of Edinburgh, they gave their reasons for declining to meddle in that affair, which they sent to Bishop Keith, and he rejoined.

In this situation were things when the Prince, King James' eldest son, landed in Scotland, about the end of July 1745, and having gathered some of the Highlanders, he marched first to Perth, and then towards Edinburgh, where he came the 17th of September ; and General Cope having landed from the North, the Prince went out to meet him on the 20th, and on St Matthew's Day gained a complete victory. Then returning to Edinburgh, he stayed to be joined by the rest of his forces, and in the beginning of November marched towards England. In a few days after he had Carlisle surrendered to him, and then went forard as far as to Derby, still hoping that a great many of the English would join him. But finding few or none of them would stir, and the army under the Duke of Cumberland before him, the Prince was obliged to make a retreat back again to Scotland, which he performed in so gallant a manner, that he lost very few of his men. This retreat he made about the end of December, and in order to favour this he left some at Carlisle to keep the Duke in play, while he marched to Annan, Dumfries, and so forward to Glasgow, where he stayed some days, and then made towards Stirling, which he intended to take. In the meantime the army gathered, and set forward to Falkirk, when the Prince thought proper to engage them, and defeated them on the 17th day of January 1746, that they retired in great precipitation, and would have been cut off, or made prisoners, had they been pursued. But the Prince's army, contenting themselves with the advantage they gained, returned to Stirling, which they battered strongly ; but Cumberland returning, and having gathered his forces, the Prince thought fit to pass the Forth in the beginning of February, and go northward, which he did the length of Inverness, took the fort there, and continued recruiting his army. Cumberland followed, came to Perth, and judging the Highland roads not passable by his horse, and fatiguing to his men, he marched by the coast to Aberdeen, where he stayed till the beginning of April ; and then setting forward, he met the Prince's army at Drummossie [Culloden], about two miles from Inverness, and there gained a full victory on the 16th day of April, after which ensued terrible plunderings, devastations, and slaughters all over the North, especially in the Highlands; and the Earls of Kilmarnock and Cromarty, and Lord Balmerino, being taken prisoners, they were arraigned and condemned by the Peers. Earl Cromarty was reprieved, and Kilmarnock and Balmerino were executed on Tower Hill the 18th day of August. Terrible murders ensued, and many suffered at London, Carlisle, and other places. In the meantime, the Prince wandered over the Highlands, frequently in danger of being surprised and taken; but at last he and a great number of his followers got safe to France, in the end of September or beginning of October 1746.

The meeting-houses of the Episcopal clergy continued undisturbed till Cumberland's going North; and then there were parties sent out, who burnt or demolished thirty or forty of these places of worship, burning the very Bibles and Prayer-Books; and after the battle of Drummossie the meeting-houses in Edinburgh were shut up, and by the act, refusing all, confined to four only.

[The summary of the Enterprise of 1745-6, which concludes the preceding sketch, is much more moderately expressed than might have been expected, considering the writer's political principles. The same MS. volume contains another document on that interminable subject the "Usages," which is said to have been written by Bishop Ranken, one of their most resolute opponents. It is entitled—"A Vindication of the Conduct, in a late affair, of those who stand up for the peace of this afflicted Church, so much disturbed by certain persons; together with a short Account of those woeful divisions which have happened among those of the Episcopal Communion in Scotland, and upon whom they are to be charged."]

"It is," says Bishop Ranken, "with inexpressible grief and sorrow of heart that we find ourselves obliged to appeal to all impartial and unprejudiced readers of this paper, with relation to our conduct in this affair. That we may set in the clearest light those woeful divisions which have happened in this poor distressed Church, we shall trace them up to their original and source.

"They of the Episcopal Communion in Scotland, both clergy and laity, enjoyed profound peace, unity, and concord, among themselves, until some unhappily began to propagate opinions concerning certain antiquated Usages, viz. the mixing of water with the wine in the holy sacrament of the Lord's Supper, prayers for the dead, the use of chrism to the sick, and to do all that was in their power to gain proselytes to have their opinions. And more especially till Bishop Gadderar came hither from England, he, having got himself, by what method we shall not inquire, made Bishop of the Diocese of Aberdeen, did forthwith use his utmost endeavours to introduce the mentioned Usages into that Diocese and elsewhere, with the assistance of others, as he and they had any influence, and that after a most schismatical manner, not only without a lawful convocation, which such an alteration in divine worship, though it had been innocent as to the rites themselves, undoubtedly required and called for, but also in plain opposition to the majority of the College of Bishops, who had not only declared against the use of the Usages themselves, but had also passed an act obliging the presbyters of this Church to subscribe the Formula, by which they were bound not to use the mentioned Usages.

"Bishop Gadderar, with his adherents, carried on their unwarrantable practices with so much eagerness and contention, that the rest of the Bishops, to prevent the scandal of an imminent rupture, made some concessions to him, with respect to the Diocese of Aberdeen allenarly, the said Bishops at the same time declaring they did not approve the use of any [of] the mentioned Usages, and particularly of the mixture, either publicly or privately, as is clear from the Concordate then agreed to; but this concession was so far from remedying the evil for which purpose it was designed, that by the conduct and management of Bishop Gadderar and his adherents, it contributed to the growth thereof.

"At length, shortly after the death of the Right Rev. Mr Fullarton, late Bishop of Edinburgh, whose easiness Bishop Gadderar and they of his party had lamentably abused, Bishop Gadderar and some others with him came to Edinburgh, with a view, as appeared by their actions afterwards, to give the finishing hand to their long projected work, by practising on and gaining over to their interest the Right Rev. Bishop Millar, the pretended successor to the vacant Diocese of Edinburgh. Now, of this and some material things of the late affair, we shall give a short account, referring those who need farther satisfaction therein to the full narrative thereof, in a paper which may be seen by such as inquire for it.*

"Now, how far Bishop Millar has been in the interest of those above named, and how he has put them in a capacity to promote their designs, will appear—First, by considering that, notwithstanding the Bishops were advertised even by himself to meet at Edinburgh the 8th day of June last, about the important and weighty affairs of the Church, yet he, upon the very Lord's Day immediately preceding the said 8th of June, with the assistance of Bishop Gadderar and Bishop Cant, upon whom they had imposed, and entirely without the knowledge of the Bishops, though the major part of the College, he and they stole away the consecration of Dr Rattray of Craighall, whom they, the injured Bishops, would have embraced with open arms, and to whose consecration they would have cheerfully consented, even notwithstanding his former deep concern in the matter of the Usages, if he would have given them just and full satisfaction that he would do so no more —Second, What we charge Bishop Millar with appears the more evident, because that after he had so far gratified the desires and answered the designs of his new friends, he took not a very courteous farewell of his former brethren, by pretending to adjourn their meeting on the 8th of June, some days before it, to the 22d of that month. By this he and his associates concluded that the injured Bishops would be forced to leave the town, and that his and their irregular deed would be concealed, and to escape that censure it deserved, and then they might go on with the rest of their projects undisturbed.—Third, He hath farther strengthened the patrons and abettors of those rites and practices, to which the Church of [in] Scotland hath been a stranger since the Reformation, by consecrating Mr William Dunbar—a zealous promoter of them.

"Bishop Millar did fully manifes thow entirely he was in the interest of Bishop Gadderar, Dr Rattray, and Mr Dunbar, for when he understood that the injured Bishops continued still in town [Edinburgh], employed about the affairs of the Church, then he most imperiously, though having no authority to do so, adjourned them *sine die*, that is,

---

* The preceding sketch seems to be here indicated, of which probably Bishop Ranken was also the writer.

not to meet till it be his pleasure to call them together, as is to be seen in a letter under his hand.

"After all this, we may justly put the question to the Right Rev. Bishop Millar, to whom we wish sincerely well, what moved him to neglect and forsake so many of his colleagues, and so plainly to contradict his own former sentiments and practices? Was it, as he boasts, to procure peace to this distressed Church, by uniting to her the persons so often named upon just and reasonable terms, such as may be owned before the world? Why, then, did he conceal from us so good a design, and not allow us the pleasure of being witnesses and approvers of the agreement, which, if such as it ought to have been, would have yielded us the greatest satisfaction? And why, even after the complaints we made of his very irregular proceedings, if they whom he had lately consecrated had, by their subscriptions under their hands, given full and satisfying security with relation to the Usages, did he not show it to us?

"Since we think that Bishop Millar cannot justify his conduct, by the questions stated after this manner, then we shall put it another way.

"Did he neglect and forsake so many of his colleagues, and plainly contradict his own former sentiments and practices, because he was jealous that these his colleagues would not confirm his uncanonical and irregular election to the Diocese of Edinburgh? This reason is very insufficient—1. Because he ought to have had patience, until he did meet with them, and knew their mind. 2. He had put in execution the surprising measure he had taken in the consecration of Dr Rattray, before his said colleagues came to town, or knew any thing about it. 3. His injured colleagues being moved by an ardent desire of peace, were willing, and that by the consent of their presbyters who had withdrawn from their brethren, when they proceeded most uncanonically to elect a Bishop for the Diocese of Edinburgh—his colleagues, I say, were willing to pass over the irregularity of his election, and to consent that he should have the inspection and government of the Diocese of Edinburgh, and that he should be constant Preses in their meetings, and be empowered to call them together, when the exigencies of the Church required it, with these conditions—1. That he should not pretend to an exorbitant power and jurisdiction, and [not] to govern this Church without the consent and joint authority of his colleagues. 2. That he would give full assurance to them that he would discourage and oppose the use of those

Usages, which have so much disturbed the peace of this distressed Church, and that likewise his new associates should forbear and discourage the use of them. 3. That it should be enacted, that for the time to come presbyters should not meet to elect a Bishop to any vacant district without the knowledge and allowance of the College; and that he who accepted of an election so irregularly made should be deposed. Yea, farther, the greatest part of the College were so desirous of peace that they were willing to ratify the uncanonical consecration of Dr Rattray, providing he would give them just and full satisfaction with relation to the Usages. And upon the knowledge of Mr Dunbar's consecration, they for peace sake were also ready to confirm his consecration upon the terms mentioned, with relation to Dr Rattray.

"These most condescending and reasonable overtures of peace were again and again, both by letters and conferences, offered to Bishop Millar, and urged with the greatest earnestness; and he was desired to communicate the same to those to whom he had now joined himself; but it was labour in vain, for his new friends, as they were not willing to give just and proper satisfaction in the matter of the Usages, so they offered him, upon pretence of his being Bishop of Edinburgh, a high, paramount, and metropolitical power, and called him the centre of unity, and what not. And as by this method they first got him into their interest, so they designed to keep him in it. But they had by it a farther view, namely, that upon his death some of themselves, or some other in their interest, might succeed him, and so lay claim to that exorbitant power.

"Here, then, lies, so far as concerns Bishop Millar's particular, his aversion to peace upon the terms offered by his injured colleagues—that, though after all the wrongs done to the Church, and then by his unaccountable conduct, they were willing to consent to his being Bishop of Edinburgh, as is already related; yet they were not inclined to grant him that exorbitant power so eagerly contended for on pretence thereof.

"Now, how much they are to be justified in this, they may safely appeal to all impartial judges, yea, even to himself; for, 1. He knows that the Bishops of this Church had unanimously agreed, that in her present circumstances she should be governed by a College of Bishops of equal authority and power. 2. He knows that in prosecution of this agreement, Bishop Fullarton, though regularly elected to the Diocese of Edinburgh, and confirmed therein by the consent of all the other Bishops, was nevertheless obliged to renounce all pretensions to a metropolitical power, and to govern this Church with the consent and joint authority of his colleagues; and Bishop Millar may remember that none of the Bishops was more forward than he in demanding this of Bishop Fullarton. 3. Bishop Millar knows well, that when Bishop Fullarton was reckoned to have made any encroachments contrary to his engagement, he exclaimed bitterly against it, which can be proved by many ear witnesses of unquestionable credit, and by a remonstrance under his own hand. 4. It is not to be thought strange that the injured Bishops, the greater part of the College, were not forward to invest Bishop Millar with an excess of power, when they considered that though he was not truly Bishop of Edinburgh, yet, upon an unjust claim to it, he had done so many injurious and unjustifiable things. Lastly, It justly created in them an aversion to gratify Bishop Millar in this matter when they reflected that Bishop Gadderar, and they of his way, do so zealously contend that this exorbitant power belongs to Bishop Millar, and have, with so warm a concern, advised him obstinately to claim and own it; for as by this they have already prevailed with him to accomplish many of their designs, so by it they hope to confirm him in their interest, and to use him as an instrument for advancing their projects.

" To come to a conclusion of this melancholy story, Bishop Millar had so unaccountably and obstinately rejected all the reasonable overtures of peace, which were made to him and his new friends by the injured Bishops, the major part of the College, then they, with those they had lately assumed into their own order, found themselves obliged in conscience, and from a conviction of the duty they owed to God and this distressed Church, to cite Bishop Millar to appear before them, and answer to a libel to be exhibited against him, concerning the many unwarrantable, uncanonical, and dangerous facts, he of late hath been guilty of; then, after he had contumaciously refused to compear, as can be instructed by a letter under his own hand, and after he had been thrice called to compear, and not compearing, the libel against him was read, and all the facts therein contained were found clearly proven. And then the Bishops in the College assembled did, with great grief of heart, pronounce the sentence against him, whereby they suspended him from the exercise of any part of the episcopal office within this Church, until he submit himself, and give satisfaction to them, and accept of the reasonable offers made him by them for preserving the peace and unity of this Church. And they appointed this their sentence to be intimated to him, and to the presbyters of the Diocese of Edinburgh, that none might pretend ignorance; which was accordingly done.

"This is a true and short account of what is mentioned at the head of this paper, from which all who consider it without prejudice will clearly see to whom the beginning and progress of our woful divisions are to be ascribed, and who are to be blamed for the continuance of them; and that the injured Bishops, and those they have lately consecrated, stand clear of the schism which is now commenced. Thus we hope that all impartial judges in this matter will absolve us from any accession to the mentioned divisions; and we most earnestly beseech all of the Episcopal communion to put up their ardent prayers to Almighty God, that of his great mercy he may pity the sad state of this Church, heal her divisions, and bestow on all her members the spirit of charity, unity, and concord; and that he may grant to us all, of both sides, most serious repentance for our unprofitableness under the Gospel, for which in his righteous judgment he has thought it fit to give way to our being chastised with this great calamity; and may God give unto all those who have contributed to the disquiet of this Church a sight and sense of their error, and may they return to a better mind; and then we with the greatest joy shall embrace them as brethren."

[The result of this denunciation of Bishop Millar in particular, and of the disputes about the Usages, is given in the preceding narrative. The ideas which the College Party formed of the Bishop grasping at what the writer calls "metropolitical power" were completely fallacious. They were so wedded to their system of governing the Church by a College of Bishops, that they could see nothing in Diocesan Episcopacy but ecclesiastical innovation. The statements now given intimate the personal animosities which existed between the College and Diocesan Parties, which usually evaporated in mutual recriminations of unjust election to their dioceses, uncanonical practices, and such like, until the dispute was happily adjusted, and the College Party yielded the discussion. The interest which the laity took in the strife about the government of the Church and the Usages does not appear. It is probable that they generally thought these to be matters with which they had no right to interfere.]

No. IV.

THE CODE OF CANONS OF THE EPISCOPAL CHURCH IN SCOTLAND,

AS REVISED, AMENDED, AND ENACTED, BY AN ECCLESIASTICAL SYNOD, HELD FOR THAT PURPOSE, AT EDINBURGH, ON THE 29TH DAY OF AUGUST, AND CONTINUED BY ADJOURNMENT TILL THE 6TH OF SEPTEMBER, INCLUSIVE, 1838.

RELIGION, implying the obligation which we lie under to the service of God, must be of divine institution; because God alone can tell how He will be worshipped and served by his creatures. Having revealed his will for this purpose, He has also from the beginning constituted and set apart certain persons to act as his more immediate servants or officers, and in that official relation to assist mankind in the performance of their religious duties. That this was the case under the Patriarchal and Mosaic institutions, is evident from the history of both contained in the Old Testament; and that the case is the same under the dispensation of the Gospel, is no less manifest from the account which the New Testament gives of the establishment of the Christian Church. It is there recorded for our instruction, that our blessed Saviour, the author and finisher of our faith, and the head over all things to His Church, when he had " called his disciples unto him, chose twelve of them ;" whom He was pleased to distinguish by the title of " Apostles," or persons *sent* with a particular commission to preach the Gospel; and with power to work miracles for evincing the authority with which they were vested. The appointment afterwards of other seventy disciples appears to have been of a temporary nature, to prepare for their Lord's reception in " every city or place" which He was to bless with His presence. After His resurrection from the dead, He enlarged the commission given to His apostles, extending the object of it to the conversion of " all nations," making them His disciples, and bringing them under His tuition and discipline, by baptizing them after the form and order of His appointment. Hence it is evident, that as long as there are nations or people upon earth to be thus converted, disciplined, and baptized, so long must there be persons duly authorised for that purpose; and whose authority can flow down in no other channel than that which leads up to the only source from which it can be derived—the command issued by Him to whom all power was given, both in heaven and on earth; and who, after declaring himself invested with this universal sovereignty, immediately added, as a consequence of it, this extensive commission to his Apostles—" Go ye, *therefore,* make disciples to me of all nations, baptizing them in the name of the Father, and of the Son, and of the Holy Ghost; and teaching them to observe all things whatsoever I have commanded you: and, lo' I am with you always"—in the act of handing down this commission—" even unto the end of the world."—This is the fundamental charter, by which the Church of Christ holds its continuance in the world, and will do so as long as the world itself continues. The preservation of its spiritual powers, in the way of Episcopal succession, has ever marked the " continuance" of Christians after the example of the early converts, " in the Apostles' doctrine and fellowship;" and from the constant attention shown to this ecclesiastical arrangement in the apostolic age, we may justly infer, that it was then considered as one of those things which our Lord's Apostles were commanded to teach the nations to " observe," to watch over and preserve, in its pure and original form. Such is the form, in which has been regularly handed down the ecclesiastical authority of the Episcopal Church in Scotland; a Church in itself completely constituted and organized, in respect of spiritual power and sacred ministrations by its own Bishops, Priests, and Deacons. In this character, being in full communion with the United Church of England and Ireland, and adopting as the standard of her faith the Thirty-Nine Articles of Religion, as received in that Church, she claims the authority which, according to the thirty-fourth of those Articles, belongs to " every particular or national Church, to ordain, change, or abolish ceremonies or rites of the Church ordained only by man's authority, so that all things be done to edifying."

The *doctrine* of the Church, as founded on the authority of the Scripture, being fixed and immutable, ought to be uniformly received and adhered to, at all times and in all places. The same is to be said of its *government*, in all those essential parts of its constitution which were prescribed by its adorable HEAD. But in the *discipline*, which may be adopted for furthering the purposes of ecclesiastical government, regulating the solemnities of public worship, as to time, place, and form, and restraining and rectifying the evils occasioned by human depravity, this character of immutability is not to be looked for. The discipline of the Church is to be determined by Christian wisdom, prudence, and charity; and when any particular Church has drawn up a body of Canons for its own use, regard has always been had to its peculiar situation at the time when its discipline was thus regulated. In one country, a pure apostolic Church is found to be legally established, amply endowed, and closely incorporated with the State; while in another, forming a part of the same empire, it is only tolerated by the State; and as to all matters of spiritual concern, derives no support from the civil government.

Such is precisely the difference of situation between the established Church of England and Ireland, and the unestablished, the merely tolerated Episcopal Church in Scotland. In things of a purely ecclesiastical nature, embracing the doctrine and government of the Church, the faith peculiar to Christianity, and the mode of transmitting an apostolic Episcopacy—in these respects the Reformed Episcopal Church is the same in every part of the British empire. That system of religious faith and ecclesiastical order by which it is distinguished in every district of England and Ireland, is also its mark of distinction to the remotest corner of Scotland; and although in this country it is wholly unconnected with the State in the exercise of its spiritual authority, yet does it still depend, under God, on the civil power for peace and protection, in the enjoyment of all its rights and privileges, as a society purely spiritual, and constituted for the purpose of affording the means of grace and salvation to the members of Christ's mystical body.

Viewing it in this light, the clergy of the Episcopal Church in Scotland declare, in the most sincere and unequivocal manner, that the ecclesiastical commission handed down to them has no relation to such secular powers and privileges as are peculiar to a national establishment; nor does it in the least interfere with the rights of the temporal state, or the jurisdiction of the supreme civil magistrate. On the contrary, the clergy of this church, of every rank and order, feel no hesitation in asserting and maintaining that the King's Majesty, to whom they sincerely promise to bear true allegiance, is the only " supreme governor within his dominions, whose prerogative it is to rule all estates and degrees committed to his charge by God; and to restrain, with the civil sword, the stubborn and evil-doers of every denomination, clergymen as well as laymen. They further declare, that no foreign prince, person, prelate, state, or potentate, hath, or ought to have, any jurisdiction, power, superiority, pre-eminence, or authority, ecclesiastical or spiritual, within this realm; and they do, from their hearts, abhor, detest, and abjure, as impious and heretical, that damnable doctrine and position, that princes excommunicated or deprived by the Pope, or any authority of the See of Rome, may be deposed or murdered by their subjects, or any other whatsoever."

Such are the solemn acknowledgments of the King's Sovereignty required from candidates for holy orders in the United Church of England and Ireland A similar obligation, as extended to all ecclesiastical persons, was enforced in a Code of Canons intended for the Established Church of Scotland in the reign of Charles the First. But the attempt to introduce a proper system of discipline, conjoined to the uniform use of a Liturgy, was completely frustrated by the events of that disastrous period; and the troublesome state of affairs, in the two succeeding reigns, was equally unfavourable to the establishment of order and unity in the Church. The Revolution in 1688 set aside the legally established Episcopacy of Scotland; and for several years after the shock which our Church received by the termination of that national struggle, the Bishops had enough to do in keeping up a pure Episcopal succession, till it should be seen what, in the course of Providence, might be further effected towards the preservation, though not of an established, yet of a purely primitive Episcopal Church, in this part of the kingdom. For this purpose, a few Canons were drawn up, and sanctioned by the Bishops, in the year 1743, which, though very well calculated to answer the purposes intended by them, while the Church was under legal restraint and threatened with persecution, have yet left room for considerable enlargement, and require to have embodied with them, or added to them, several regulations suited to the now happily tolerated and protected state of the Episcopal Church in this country.

In accomplishing this good work, some aid might be expected from the Canons appointed for the Church of England in the year 1603, for the Church of Ireland in 1634, and for the Church of Scotland in 1636. For the purpose of collecting from these, and other sources, a System of Ecclesiastical Discipline proper for the Church under their Episcopal charge, the Protestant Bishops in Scotland came to the resolution of holding a General Ecclesiastical Synod ; and being duly convocated by the Primus, did accordingly meet at Aberdeen, on Wednesday the 19th day of June in the year of our Lord 1811, together with the Deans of their several dioceses, and a representative of the clergy from each diocese containing more than four presbyters, when a Code of Canons for preserving and regulating order and discipline in the Protestant Episcopal Church in Scotland was adopted and sanctioned. A second General Synod met at Laurencekirk, in the county of Kincardine, on Wednesday the 18th day of June 1828, when the Canons of 1811 were revised and altered. A third was held in Edinburgh on Wednesday 17th of June 1829, when some enactments in the sixteenth Canon of 1828 were repealed. A very general desire being expressed throughout the Church, especially in the year 1837, that a further revision of the whole Code should be made, another General Synod was in consequence duly summoned, and met accordingly in Edinburgh on Wednesday the 29th August 1838, and being then and there duly and solemnly constituted with prayer, after full deliberation and discussion during several successive days, the Synod so assembled and constituted did, and hereby do, ADOPT and SANCTION the following revised and amended Code of Canons, and declare them to be in future the stated rules and regulations for preserving order and discipline in the said Church in Scotland. In testimony whereof, WE, the members of the said Synod, have hereunto annexed our names and designations in the register-book of the Episcopal College, and we have, moreover, entrusted to a committee in Edinburgh the duty of causing the revised and amended Canons now approved and sanctioned to be faithfully inserted in the foresaid register, and together with this introduction, to be carefully printed.for the general use of the Church. For these purposes, an authentic copy, verified by the Primus, the clerk of the Episcopal College, and by the prolocutor of the second chamber, in the presence of the Synod, has been given to the Committee, which they are required to preserve when

APPENDIX. 551

these purposes are attained, along with the register-book aforesaid; committing the custody thereof to the clerk of the Episcopal College, whose duty it is to preserve the said register, and the general records of the Church.

CANON I.

For preserving the Episcopal Succession.

The Episcopal Church in Scotland, as a branch of the Holy Catholic and Apostolic Church of Christ, inviolably retaining in the sacred ministry the three orders of Bishops, Priests, and Deacons, as of divine institution, requires, according to the apostolic Canon, that a Bishop be ordained by two or three Bishops; not fewer than three in all ordinary cases; and Priests and Deacons by one Bishop; the right of ordination belonging to the order of Bishops only. And it is hereby decreed, that no person shall be consecrated a Bishop of the Episcopal Church in Scotland before he hath completed the thirtieth year of his age; nor without the consent and approbation of the majority of the Bishops; and that if any Bishop or any Bishops, not being a majority, shall presume without such consent to consecrate any person to that office, all the parties concerned shall be held schismatics.

CANON II.

Regulating the Election and Office of the Primus.

Before the distinction of Archbishop was introduced into Scotland, one of the Bishops had a precedency under the title of *Primus Scotorum Episcopus*; and the Episcopal College having for a century past adopted the old form, it is hereby decreed that the Bishops shall, without respect either to seniority of consecration or precedency of diocese, choose a Primus, by a majority of voices, who shall have no other privilege among the Bishops but the right of convocating and presiding; and that expressly under the following restrictions :—1st, That he shall be obliged to notify to the other Bishops the reasons of his calling a meeting, as well as the time and place for holding it; and if the majority shall dissent, as judging either the reasons insufficient, or the time or place improper, the proposal of such meeting shall be either wholly set aside, or the time or place altered, as shall seem to them most expedient. 2dly, That if the Primus shall at any time refuse to call a meeting when desired by a majority of the other Bishops to do so for some specified purpose, or if he shall refuse to consecrate or sanction the consecration of a priest, canonically elected to a vacant diocese, when that election shall have been confirmed by a majority of the Bishops, they shall, in such cases, have authority to meet and act without him. 3dly, That the Primus thus chosen by the majority is to continue in that office only during their pleasure. That the Church may suffer as little inconvenience as possible, by the death or resignation of the Primus, the senior Bishop shall instantly succeed to his powers, until a majority of the Bishops shall appoint one to the office by a formal deed of election.

CANON III.

For providing vacant Dioceses with duly elected Bishops, and regulating the Conduct of the Presbyters in such Dioceses.

Every Bishop is hereby required to appoint one of the presbyters of his diocese to act under him as Dean, who, in the absence of the Bishop, shall preside in all diocesan Synods, and the Dean thus canonically appointed shall, upon the demise or translation of any Bishop, notify the same to the Primus, who, being empowered by his colleagues, shall thereupon issue a mandate to the presbyters of the vacant diocese, requiring them to proceed to the election of a successor. Should they make choice of a person already invested with the Episcopal character, the Bishop so elected shall have no jurisdiction over that diocese, unless his election be ratified by the majority of the Episcopal College transferring to him, by a formal deed, the superintendence of the diocese. But if the presbyters of the vacant diocese shall elect a presbyter to be their future diocesan, of whose fitness for that office the Bishops shall declare they have sufficient reason not to be satisfied, in that case the presbyters shall be required to proceed to a new election.

During the vacancy of any diocese, if any case relating to discipline shall occur for which there is no particular provision made by the Canons of this Church, the presbyters shall have recourse to the Primus, who, with the advice and consent of his colleagues, shall determine the same, and who shall also provide for the performance of any Episcopal offices that may be required among them.

All elections of Bishops shall be notified to the Primus, according to the form prescribed.

CANON IV.

For the Appointment of Coadjutor-Bishops.

It shall be lawful for a Bishop, whose age or infirmities require it, of which the majority of the College of Bishops shall be the judges, to have a coadjutor or assistant, provided the said Bishop consent that the election of such coadjutor by the clergy of the diocese shall be free, uninfluenced, and unbiassed, and provided the person so elected shall succeed on the death or resignation of the diocesan. Such assistant-bishop, during the life of his principal, shall be entitled to attend episcopal and general synods of the Church, to give his opinion and advice on any matter under consideration, but to have no vote except in the absence of the Diocesan Bishop.

CANON V.

Respecting the Jurisdiction of the Bishops in a Particular Case.

If it shall happen that a Bishop has his Chapel and residence within the diocese of another Bishop, a practice to be justified only by the circumstances of this Church, then shall his congregation, as well as any presbyter or deacon that may be employed as his assistant, be exempted from the jurisdiction of the Bishop in whose Diocese they are locally situated, the latter being required to signify, by a subscribed deed, his consent to this arrangement. But such assistant shall have no vote in either diocese. But whereas the residence of a Bishop within the diocese appears to be expedient for the good of the Church, it is hereby decreed that every Bishop hereafter collated to the charge of a diocese shall reside within the bounds of the same, wherever that is found practicable.

CANON VI.

Enjoining the Studies and Qualifications of Candidates for Holy Orders.

In the Canons intended for the Church of Scotland, and sanctioned by royal authority in the year 1635, the second chapter, entitled, " *Of Presbyters and Deacons, their Nomination, Ordination, Function, and Charge,*" is thus very properly introduced : " Forasmuch as the weight of the ministerial calling doth require such a measure of sufficiency as human weakness can attain unto, and is often discredited by the ignorance, insufficiency, and scandalous conversation of many who undertake the same ; it is ordained, that no person hereafter shall be admitted to that holy function who hath not been bred in some University or College, and hath taken some degree there, and who shall verify the same by the subscriptions and seals of the University or College where he received the degree of learning." In conformity with the spirit of this extract, it is hereby decreed that no person be received as a candidate for holy orders in this Church who shall not have first gone through a regular academical course in some University or College. It is, moreover, expressly ordered, that no person shall be admitted into the holy order of Deacons in this Church, until he shall have been properly examined as to his literature by two or more presbyters appointed for that purpose by the Bishop who is to ordain him, and whom, as his examiners, he must satisfy of his being sufficiently acquainted with the whole of the New Testament in the original Greek, and at whose bidding he must compose a short treatise in Latin on some article of faith, as also a discourse in English on any text of Scripture which they shall prescribe ; and answer such questions connected with theology and ecclesiastical history as they shall think proper to put to him ; and before his admission to examination, the Bishop must, by sufficient letters testimonial, and by an attestation, that the form usually called *Si Quis* has been publicly read, be satisfied of his good life and conversation, as well as his good learning. It is also required that he produce a certificate of his having attended at least one course of the lectures of the Pantonian Professor of Theology, and of our Professor of Ecclesiastical History in Edinburgh ; unless peculiar circumstances in his case may have rendered such attendance impracticable, of which the ordainin

Bishop is to be the sole judge. And no one shall be promoted to the order of Priest until he shall have passed a still more full and complete satisfaction.

CANON VII.

Respecting the Age, the Prudence, the Place or Charge of Persons to be Ordained ; and in what Case Letters Dimissory are necessary.

No Bishop of this Church shall, in ordinary cases, admit any person to the office of deacon, until he shall have attained the age of twenty-three years ; and in no case to the order of priests, until he shall have attained the full age of twenty-four ; and in both cases a *bona fide* title shall be required : But whereas the necessities of this Church, in some cases, may render it inconvenient to defer ordination till the person to be ordained hath fully attained what hath been usually called the canonical age ; therefore, in any such case, a Bishop may admit a candidate to the order of deacons if duly recommended when he hath completed his twenty-first year ; and after serving in that capacity, he may be promoted to the order of the priesthood, if the Bishop be satisfied, that, during his service as a deacon, he hath conducted himself in a prudent and becoming manner ; hath attained the full canonical age of twenty-four ; and *hath also a particular place or charge assigned to him, wherein he may use or exercise his function ;* without which relation to a particular place or congregation, no person shall be advanced to the order of priesthood in this Church ; neither shall any of the Bishops admit any person into holy orders whose title is not within his own diocese, unless he shall bring letters dimissory from the Bishop of the diocese wherein his charge is placed.

CANON VIII.

Appointing the Solemn Performance of the Office of Ordination, and the Form to be used in Making, Ordaining, and Consecrating, Bishops, Priests, and Deacons.

The welfare of the Church being most intimately connected with the ordination and function of the clergy, the ancient Fathers, led by the example of the holy Apostles, appointed prayers and fasts to be used for imploring the Divine blessing and direction in setting apart for their solemn office those who were "ordained for men in things pertaining to God" The Episcopal Church in Scotland, therefore, sincerely venerating the appointment of the Ember Weeks, hereby requires that all her ordinations shall be performed at those seasons, unless, for reasons of necessity, the Bishop shall appoint another time; and also that all her ordinations be performed with public prayer, and imposition of hands, and (as hath been the practice of the Church ever since the Restoration of King Charles II.) according to the "form and manner of making, ordaining, and consecrating, of Bishops, Priests, and Deacons," used in the united Church of England and Ireland, adopting only a few necessary verbal alterations, such as saying "this Church," instead of "this realm," or "this Church of England."

CANON IX.

Requiring from Persons to be Ordained Subscription to the Thirty-Nine Articles of Religion, and certain Oaths to be taken by them.

Whereas by the act of the thirty-second of George III., entitled, "An Act for granting relief to pastors, ministers, and lay persons of the Episcopal Communion in Scotland," it is enacted, that every such pastor or minister shall subscribe a declaration of his assent to the Thirty-Nine Articles of the Church of England: Therefore, no person shall hereafter be received into the ministry of the Episcopal Church in Scotland until he hath first subscribed, willingly and *ex animo*, to the book of articles of religion, agreed upon by the Archbishops and Bishops of both provinces of the realm of England, and the whole clergy thereof, in the convocation holden at London in the year of our Lord one thousand five hundred and sixty-two, and hath acknowledged all and every the articles therein contained, being in number thirty-nine, besides the ratification, to be agreeable to the Word of God. And, forasmuch as the Bishops of this Church have no authority to administer the oaths which are required by law, at the ordinations of deacons and priests, every Bishop shall, at the ordination of any candidate for the ministry, obtain the presence of a magistrate at the time of ordination, for the purpose of administering the oaths at the regular period of the service; but if this cannot be done, he is to require from such candidate a certificate from the magistrate before whom he shall have taken the said oaths; and together with these oaths, every person at his ordination shall promise to render due obedience to the Canons of this Church, and to show in all things an earnest desire to promote the peace, unity, and order of that part of the flock of Christ in which he shall be authorised to exercise his ministry.

CANON X.

Appointing the Conditions, and Mode of Institution to a Pastoral Charge.

Whereas it has never been the practice of this Church, nor the wish of her Bishops, to interfere, directly or indirectly, with the funds or temporalities of her congregations; it is, therefore, fully acknowledged, that the right of presentation to any chapel, vacant within her pale, is vested in those who are appointed to manage its affairs, whether known by the title of trustees, church-wardens, vestry-men, managers, proprietors, or directors, and who, in virtue of their office, procure the means of the ministers' support; yet, to preserve the ancient and regular discipline of an Episcopal Community, it is hereby enacted, that no presbyter shall take upon himself the pastoral charge of any congregation to which he may be presented, before the deed of presentation be duly accepted by the Bishop: And no Bishop shall institute to a pastoral charge in his diocese any clergyman, without requiring him to produce letters of orders from some Bishop of this Church, or of one of the Churches enumerated in Canon XV., together with the proper testimonials required for institution, countersigned by the Bishop of the diocese. Likewise, it is required that he shall present a certificate, that he has gone through a regular course of education in some College or University, as is required of our own native students by Canon VI. And if the candidate for institution shall have come from any one of these Churches, and have resided in Scotland for any length of time, he must present not only the proper testimonials from his mother church, but likewise a similar testimonial from two or more Episcopal clergymen, to whom he has been known during the period of his residence in Scotland, as well as a solemn promise of obedience to the Canons of this Church, as enjoined by Canon IX., in which case no Bishop shall refuse to grant institution to a person so presented. But if no election shall be made within six calendar months after a vacancy hath taken place, the right of nomination of a pastor shall then elapse to the Bishop of the diocese, whose appointment shall be binding on all the members of the congregation.

CANON XI.

Requiring Presbyters to make Personal Residence in the place where their Pastoral Charge lies, and not to be Absent but for a limited time.

In Chapter III. of the Scottish Canons above mentioned, entitled, "Of Residence and Preaching," it is justly observed, that "the many inconveniences which result from the non-residence of ministers, require that some provision be made thereanent:" Therefore, it is hereby decreed, that every Presbyter having a pastoral charge in this Church shall reside in some place of easy and convenient access to the members of his congregation, and shall not at any time leave or absent himself from his charge (unless for some very urgent cause), without providing a substitute, in terms of Canon XV., and also obtaining the permission of the Bishop.

CANON XII

Requiring Soberness of Conversation and Decency of Apparel in Ecclesiastical Persons, as well as a proper attention to the Good Order of their Families.

In the Canons of the United Church of England and Ireland, as well as in those intended for the Church of Scotland, it is expressly ordered, that "no ecclesiastical persons shall at any time, other than for their honest necessities, resort to any taverns or alehouses, neither shall they give themselves to any base or servile labour; or to drinking or riot, spending their time idly by day or by night, playing at dice, cards, or tables, or any other unlawful games unbecoming their sacred function; but at all times convenient they shall hear or read somewhat of the Holy Scriptures, or shall occupy themselves with some other honest study or exercise, always doing the things which appertain to honesty, and endeavouring to profit the Church of God." To the spirit of what is here enjoined, the clergy of this Church are therefore required carefully to attend. And they shall use such a decent form of apparel as becomes their sacred character; avoiding every appearance of fashionable levity, either in dress or demeanour, that is inconsistent with the gravity of their profession, or which might deprive it of that respect which is due to it. For the same reason, the ancient Canons of the Church did strictly prohibit "the admitting of any to the office of a Bishop, Presbyter, or Deacon, who had not brought their families to be Christians," whereby all ecclesiastical persons are taught the necessity of looking well to the order and good government of their households, and of training up their families in such a religious course as may show to others an encouraging pattern of piety and virtue. All which must be duly observed under pain of the censures of the Church, to be inflicted according to the quality of the offence.

CANON XIII.

Pointing out the Proper Clerical Studies.

A studious life being of great consequence to the right discharge of the duties of the clerical office, it is hereby earnestly recommended that the clergy of this Church apply themselves diligently to the study of the Holy Scriptures in the original languages, and the writings of the fathers of the apostolic and two next succeeding ages, and that the younger clergy, in particular, be attentive and diligent in the course of study prescribed to them, so that they may be able to answer such questions as the leading books in that course may suggest, and which the Bishop at his visitation may think proper to put to them, as well as that they may be able in their sermons, and otherwise, to instruct the people under their charge in the truly Catholic principles of that pure and primitive Church.

CANON XIV.

Requiring the Clergy of this Church to continue in their Sacred Profession.

As every clergyman of this Church, as well as of the United Church of England and Ireland, at the time of his receiving authority to execute the office of a Deacon, declares himself to be "inwardly moved by the Holy Ghost to take upon himself this office and ministration, to serve God for the promotion of his glory, and the edifying of his people;" therefore, in order that he may be warned of the danger of dissembling with the Spirit of Truth, it is hereby declared, that if any person exercising his ministry in this Church shall afterwards give up the exercise of his ministerial functions, and betake himself wholly to any worldly business, he shall be incapable of ever resuming the exercise of any ministerial office in the Church, the sacred service of which he hath thus shamefully abandoned.

CANON XV.

Concerning the Admission of Strangers to Officiate in this Church.

The Episcopal Church in Scotland recognises as in full communion with herself the United Church of England and Ireland, the colonial branches of the same, and the Protestant Episcopal Church in the United States of America; and it is hereby decreed, that none but clergymen canonically ordained by the Bishops of the Scottish Episcopal Church, or of the above-mentioned Churches, or episcopally ordained clergymen, conforming to the doctrine and discipline of the said Churches, shall be permitted to officiate in sacred things, either permanently or occasionally, to any congregation in this Church. And, moreover, it is decreed, that no clergyman shall henceforth be permitted to officiate in this Church, unless his principles and clerical character be known to the clergyman by whom he is to be employed, to be correct and consistent with the doctrine and discipline of the Scottish Episcopal Church; and if he be personally unknown, unless he produce from the Bishop of the diocese whence he comes, or from some other clergyman known to be worthy of all credit, a letter of recommendation; and no clergyman shall officiate in this Church beyond the period of one month without the licence of the Bishop.

CANON XVI.

The Names of Stranger Preachers to be Noted in a Book.

That the Ordinary may be able to ascertain the nature of the doctrine taught in every chapel of his Diocese, the pastor of each congregation shall see that the names of all the preachers who come to his chapel

APPENDIX. 561

from any other place be noted in a book which he shall keep in his Vestry for that purpose, wherein every preacher shall inscribe his name, the day when he preached, the title of the Bishop by whom he was ordained, and the date of his ordination.

CANON XVII.

Respecting the due Administration of the Sacrament of Baptism.

As the Sacrament of Baptism is to be considered a public act, it ought, unless unavoidable circumstances prevent it, to be administered in a place of public worship. Parents, therefore, ought to be admonished of the propriety of bringing their children to be baptized to the place where they usually assemble for Divine service; and either of becoming sponsors themselves, or of procuring Godfathers or Godmothers, who shall always be communicants, that the Church may be certified that all who are admitted within her pale will be brought up in the knowledge and practice of Christianity. But as uniformity in the administration of this Sacrament is as desirable as in the other services of the Church, the privacy of the administration shall be no reason for any departure from the form prescribed for public use, to which the minister shall always strictly adhere, except in cases of extreme danger, where the form of private Baptism shall be used as directed by the Rubric. And whereas, from the unhappy multiplicity of religious sects in this country, cases frequently occur in which persons, from conscientious motives, express a desire to separate themselves from such sects, and to unite themselves to the Episcopal Communion, it becomes a matter of serious importance to furnish a rule to the clergy, by which they may be directed in such cases. It is therefore enacted, that in all instances where the applicants shall express a doubt of the validity of the Baptism which they have received from the minister of the sect to which they formerly belonged, the clergyman of the Scottish Episcopal Church to whom the application is made, shall baptize the person in the form of words prescribed in the Book of Common Prayer by the Church of England in cases of doubt—" IF THOU ART NOT ALREADY BAPTIZED, N., I baptize thee in the name of the Father, and of the Son, and of the Holy Ghost. Amen."

And whereas the Episcopal Clergy are frequently called upon to baptize infants whose parents are not members of the Church, it is hereby enacted, that the clergy of this Church shall not administer the Sacrament of Baptism, except to children for whom proper sponsors are provided.

CANON XVIII.

Requiring a regular Course of Catechising in all Congregations.

The Christian Church having ever maintained the necessity of early and sound instruction in the first principles of her holy Faith, it is therefore hereby enacted, that constant attention be shown to this important duty; for which purpose, the season of Lent, and other convenient time on Sundays or Holidays, shall be set apart for examining and instructing the young members of every congregation in the Catechism contained in the Book of Common Prayer; but no Catechism shall be used in the further instruction of the young but such as is approved and sanctioned by the Bishop of the diocese. And the clergy shall earnestly exhort and admonish their people respecting the great usefulness of this mode of instruction, and point out to parents and others who may have the charge of young persons, the necessity of bringing them regularly to be catechised.

CANON XIX.

Appointing Confirmation to be administered in every Diocese once in three years, and the care to be taken that due Preparation be made for that solemn Service.

Whereas it has been a sacred and solemn appointment in the Christian Church, continued from the times of the Apostles, that all Bishops should in their several dioceses regularly administer the holy ordinance of Confirmation by imposition of hands upon persons who have been baptized and duly instructed in the principles of Christ's religion. Therefore, it is hereby enacted, that every Bishop of this Church shall visit his diocese, if he be able to do it, once in three years, and administer this sacred ordinance in every congregation within the same; and if unable to visit his diocese personally, he shall obtain one of his colleagues to do so in his stead. And every pastor or minister, on receiving information from the Bishop of the time of his triennial visitation, shall use his best endeavours to prepare for Confirmation those whom he is to present to the Bishop to be confirmed; giving him a list of their names, and being ready to answer any questions he may put respecting their age and qualifications.

CANON XX.

Requiring due Intimation and Preparation to be made for the Holy Communion.

In every congregation of this Church, the holy Sacrament of the Lord's Supper shall be administered, so often and at such times, as that every member of the congregation, come to a proper time of life, may communicate at least three times in the year, whereof the feast of Easter, or of Pentecost, or of Christmas, shall be one. Due warning shall be publicly given to the congregation during Divine service on the Sunday before each holy Communion, that the people may the better prepare themselves for the participation of that venerable Sacrament. For this purpose, every clergyman shall pay attention to the spirit and design of the Rubrics prefixed to the order for the administration of the Lord's Supper in the Book of Common Prayer; and shall be diligent in enforcing the duties there prescribed on all those who are committed to his pastoral charge, instructing them carefully in the nature and design of that holy Sacrament, and warning them of the danger of receiving the same unworthily. And because strangers, or those who have but lately joined his congregation with the intention of remaining therein, cannot always be so well known to him as to enable him to judge whether they be meet to be partakers of those holy mysteries, such persons, if required by him, shall produce from the clergyman to whose congregation they formerly belonged, or in case of a vacancy, from some respectable member of this Church, an attestation that they are regular communicants in the Episcopal Church.

CANON XXI.

Respecting the Communion Service as the most Solemn Part of Christian Worship.

Whereas it is acknowleged by the twentieth and thirty-fourth of the

Thirty-Nine Articles, that " not only the Church in general, but every particular or national Church, hath authority to ordain, change, and abolish ceremonies or rites of the Church ordained only by man's authority, so that all things be done to edifying;" the Episcopal Church in Scotland, availing herself of this inherent right, hath long adopted, and very generally used, a form for the celebration of the Holy Communion, known by the name of the *Scotch Communion Office*, which form hath been justly considered, and is hereby considered, as the authorised service of the Episcopal Church in the administration of that sacrament. And as, in order to promote an union among all those who profess to be of the Episcopal persuasion in Scotland, permission was formerly granted by the Bishops to retain the use of the English Office in all congregations where the said Office had been previously in use, the same permission is now ratified and confirmed: And it is also enacted, that in the use of either the Scotch or English Office no amalgamation, alteration, or interpolation whatever, shall take place, nor shall any substitution of the one for the other be admitted, unless it be approved by the Bishop. From respect, however, for the authority which originally sanctioned the Scotch Liturgy, and for other sufficient reasons, it is hereby enacted, that the Scotch Communion Office continue to be held of primary authority in this Church, and that it shall be used not only in all consecrations of Bishops, but also at the opening of all General Synods.

CANON XXII.

Respecting the Solemnization of Matrimony.

The law of the land having required the publication of banns before marriage, no clergyman of this Church shall take upon him to solemnize matrimony without having previously received a sufficient attestation that the law in this respect hath been duly complied with. He shall not join persons in matrimony who are within the forbidden degrees, nor under the age of twenty-one years, unless with the consent of their parents or guardians. In the solemnization of matrimony, such prayers only shall be used as are contained in the form prescribed in the Book of Common Prayer.

CANON XXIII.

Respecting the Visitation of the Sick, and the Burial of the Dead.

As in all the days of their spiritual warfare, from their baptism to their burial, Christians have provided for them the benefit of assistance from the ministry of the clergy, so ought they more especially to apply for the spiritual aid in the time of sickness, when their need of such assistance is more urgent. Therefore, it is hereby enacted, that when any presbyter or clergyman of this Church is called to visit any sick member of his congregation, he shall not neglect to perform this duty; but repairing to the sick person's house, shall be there ready to administer all suitable comfort and instruction, either according to the order for the visitation of the sick as appointed in the Book of Common Prayer, or in any other way as he shall think most needful and convenient; and take the advice or direction of his own Bishop in any case which may particularly call for it. When the prayers of the congregation are desired in behalf of any sick member of it, the clergyman is at liberty to use the Collect appointed for the Communion of the Sick, inserting after the words " visited with Thine hand," the words " for whom our prayers are now desired;" or any other of the prayers in the " Order for the Visitation of the Sick," as the case may require. And he shall also be ready to do the last duty when he shall be called upon to read the " Order for the Burial of the Dead," which he shall use as prescribed in the Book of Common Prayer, as far as circumstances will permit that order to be observed by the clergy of this Church.

CANON XXIV.

Registers to be kept by every Clergyman.

It is decreed that every clergyman of this Church shall keep a correct register of baptisms, marriages, and burials, catechumens, and communicants at the several festivals and other celebrations; which, if required, he shall produce to the Bishop at the time of his visitation, and also take care that such register may be given to the person who succeeds him in his pastoral charge.

CANON XXV.

Against exacting Money for Performance of Occasional Duties.

It is decreed, that no minister in this Church shall make, or permit the officers of his Chapel to make, any charge of money for the administration or registration of baptism, marriage, or any other ecclesiastical service, under pain of ecclesiastical censure, and of suspension, if he persist against the reproof of his Ordinary. But it is to be understood that no minister is hereby precluded from accepting a gratuity spontaneously offered.

CANON XXVI.

Enjoining a Reverent Observance of the Lord's Day.

It is required of every member of this Church to hallow the Lord's day and keep it holy; which duty will be best fulfilled by "not doing on that day our own ways, nor finding our own pleasure, nor speaking our own words;" but by a regular and devout attendance in the sanctuary to learn God's ways, to find His pleasure, to be taught His word, and to join in the petitions, confessions, and thanksgivings of the Church; always bearing in mind, that, at the appointed and stated hours of public worship, no one can absent himself from the congregation without crime; unless his absence be caused by illness, or some other equally urgent occasion, or necessity of life; or that he be engaged in a work of charity and mercy.

CANON XXVII.

Regulating the Times, and Public Assemblies for Divine Service, on other Days besides Sundays.

Whereas in the Episcopal Church in Scotland, and in conformity with the practice of the Church universal, besides the Lord's Day, certain solemn days, especially the anniversaries of our Saviour's birth, crucifixion, and ascension, have been always observed for the public worship of God: It is hereby decreed, that the clergy do reverently and devoutly attend to these sacred solemnities, and to the regular celebration of Divine service in their several congregations; that the people, being accustomed to see every thing, according to the Apostle's rule, " done decently and in order," may be ready and well disposed to bear their part in that form of worship which is so well calculated to impress on their minds a just sense of that which they are taught to believe as an article of their Creed—" THE COMMUNION OF SAINTS."

CANON XXVIII.

On the Uniformity to be observed in Public Worship.

As in all the ordinary parts of Divine service it is necessary to fix, by authority, the precise form, from which no Bishop, Presbyter, or Deacon, shall be at liberty to depart, by his own alterations or insertions, lest such liberty should produce consequences destructive of " decency and order," it is hereby enacted, that, in the performance of morning and evening service, the words and rubrical directions of the English Liturgy shall be strictly adhered to : And it is further decreed, that, if any clergyman shall officiate or preach in any place publicly without using the Liturgy at all, he shall, for the first offence, be admonished by his Bishop, and, if he persevere in this uncanonical practice, shall be suspended, until, after due contrition, he be restored to the exercise of his clerical functions. In publicly reading prayers and administering the sacraments, the surplice shall be used as the proper sacerdotal vestment.

CANON XXIX.

Enjoining all due Reverence and Attention in time of Divine Service.

It is hereby decreed, that all proper care be taken of the places of public worship in this Church, and every endeavour used to have them decent and commodious, kept thoroughly clean and in good repair, and that they be used only for sacred and religious purposes. In the time of Divine service the most devout attention shall be given by the people to what is read, preached, or ministered. And, that they may glorify God in body as well as in spirit, agreeably to what an Apostle enjoins, they shall humbly kneel when the general confession, the Litany, and other prayers, are read, *making the appointed responses with an audible voice, in a grave and serious manner;* and shall reverently stand up at the repetition of the creed, and at the reading or singing of the psalms, hymns, or anthems, bowing devoutly at the name of Jesus in the creed; and, when the minister mentions the Gospel for the day, the people, rising up, shall devoutly say or sing (where the custom hath so been), "Glory be to Thee, O God." And, in like manner, when the minister declares the holy Gospel to be ended, they shall answer, "Thanks be to Thee, O Lord, for this thy glorious Gospel." During the time of Divine service no person shall depart out of the place of worship without some urgent and reasonable cause.

CANON XXX

Respecting National Fasts and Thanksgivings.

All national fasts and thanksgivings enjoined by the civil authority shall in this Church be religiously observed; and every Bishop shall give directions to his clergy what form of prayer they are to use on such particular occasions.

CANON XXXI.

For appointing Diocesan Synods, and regulating the Business of the same.

A diocesan synod shall be holden annually in every diocese of the Church, at such time and place as the Ordinary, or as the Dean empowered by him, shall appoint, and shall consist of the Bishop, the Dean, and such clergymen as have been instituted to their charges; and shall be attended by all the clergy of the diocese, unless hindered by some sufficient cause, whereof notice shall be given to the diocesan. And if no such notice be given, the absentee shall be subjected to the censure and reprimand of his Ordinary. Previously to the sitting of the synod, Divine service shall be performed, and a sermon preached by one of the clergy in rotation. After which, the synod being duly constituted by the Ordinary, or in his absence by the Dean, every incumbent shall lay before the meeting a report of the state of the congregation under his charge, containing the number of souls and communicants in it, of baptisms, marriages, and deaths, of persons catechised and confirmed, of communicants at the several festivals and other communions, and a list of the stranger clergymen who have preached in this chapel within the year, and such other particulars as the Bishop shall prescribe: All which reports shall be entered by the clerk in the diocesan minute-book. Every diocesan synod may also suggest rules for the regulation of ecclesiastical affairs, which, if approved by the Bishop, and not inconsistent with the constitution and Canons of the Church, shall have the force of laws within the diocese.

CANON XXXII.

Appointing General Synods, and regulating the Business of the same.

Every general synod shall consist of two chambers; the first composed of the Bishops alone: the second of the deans, the Pantonian Professor of Theology, *ex officio*, and the representatives or delegates of the clergy; one such delegate being chosen by and from the incumbents of each diocese. The second chamber shall elect a preses or prolocutor, who shall at all times have free admission to the first chamber, when communication is on either side required.

Canons or rules for the order and discipline of the Church shall be made and enacted by a general synod only; and no law or Canon shall be enacted, abrogated, or altered, but by the consent and with the approbation of the majority of both chambers. If the chambers shall happen to be equally divided in their opinions on any question, the Primus in the upper-house, and the prolocutor in the lower, shall have the casting vote.

And whereas the assembling of a General Synod can only be necessary when important business occurs in the Church, it is hereby decreed, that the times for holding such Synods shall be left to the determination of a numerical majority of the Bishops. When any Bishop is disabled from being personally present at a General Synod, through infirmity or pressing inconvenience (to be duly notified to the Primus, and by him to the other Bishops), he may propose to the Synod, in writing, any measure which he shall judge expedient, or express his opinion concerning any question or matter to be brought before the Synod, which opinion shall be entitled to due consideration and respect, but shall not be held as his canonical vote.

When a General Synod shall be convoked, or an Episcopal Synod called, for any specified purpose, the Bishop who shall neglect to attend either of these meetings, without sending to the Primus a sufficient excuse for his absence, arising either from bad health, the infirmities of old age, or some very important business which absolutely demands his presence elsewhere, shall incur such a censure by his colleagues in office as to the majority of them his conduct may appear to deserve.

And any Member of the other Chamber, whether Dean, or Delegate, or Professor, who, without sending a similar excuse either to the Primus or to his own Diocesan, shall neglect to attend a General Synod to which he has been regularly summoned, shall, if a Dean, be deprived of his office, and if a Delegate, be declared inadmissible to any future Synod.

CANON XXXIII.

On the Legislative Power of General Synods.

A General Synod of the Church, duly and regularly summoned, has the undoubted power to alter, amend, and abrogate the Canons in force, and to make new Canons; and the said alterations, amendments, abrogations, and new Canons, being in conformity with the recognised constitution and acknowledged practice of this Church, shall not only oblige the minority in the said Synod, but all the absent members of the Church.

CANON XXXIV.

Appointing Episcopal Synods.

It is hereby decreed, that an Episcopal Synod shall be holden every year, at such time and place as the majority of the Bishops shall appoint, and that no such Synod shall be deemed canonical unless three Bishops at the least be present. Episcopal Synods shall receive appeals from either clergy or laity against the sentence of their own immediate ecclesiastical superior.

CANON XXXV.

Prescribing the Conditions of Appeal.

In any differences which may arise between a Pastor and members of his flock, which cannot be amicably settled, the matter in dispute must be carried in the first instance before the Ordinary: And if either party think themselves aggrieved by his decision, then the case may be appealed by letter or petition to a Synod of Bishops. But no such case can be carried before an Episcopal Synod until the Ordinary's decision be first had thereon: And no appeal against his decision shall be admissible, unless the contending parties solemnly promise to hold the sentence of a majority of the Bishops present final and conclusive; such regulation being conformable not only to the Canons of the Universal Church, but also to the principle laid down by our Saviour himself: "If he neglect to hear the Church, let him be unto thee as an Heathen man and a Publican."

And moreover, it is further provided by this statute, that if any dispute arise between a Deacon and his Bishop, or a Presbyter and his Bishop (the congregation in which the Deacon or Presbyter officiates in no way participating therein), it shall be lawful for the said Deacon or Presbyter to appeal to the Episcopal College, under the condition already specified, viz., that the appellant give a solemn promise to receive the sentence of a majority of Bishops canonically assembled as final and conclusive.

In all cases of appeal, the appellant or appellants may be heard personally in his or their own defence, but not by counsel.

CANON XXXVI.

Respecting Accusations against Bishops, Presbyters, and Deacons.

No accusation shall be received against a Deacon, or Presbyter, or Bishop, unless proceeding from and supported by the testimony of credible persons, who are regular communicants in the Scottish Episcopal Church: Nor shall the testimony of a single witness be considered as sufficient to establish the charge, for the Scripture saith, "In the mouth of two or three witnesses shall every word be established." But if a Bishop be accused, and the accusation, proceeding from three or more respectable persons, lay or clerical members of the Scottish Episcopal Church, be lodged before the Primus, or in case of the Primus being accused, before the next senior Bishop, he shall be cited to appear and plead, and if he do not obey the summons, he shall be cited a second time in the name and by the authority of the Episcopal College; and if he be then guilty of contempt in not appearing, let the College pronounce against him such sentence as they think fit, that he may not be a gainer by declining justice

It is further provided by this Canon, that if, without any formal accusation, a Bishop shall have reason to believe that any one of his clergy is faulty in any matter; if the matter be of small importance, and not implying any grave delinquency in doctrine, discipline, or morals, the Bishop shall deal privately with the erring brother, and admonish him of his error; but if such remonstrance be neglected, or if the fault be of a grave or scandalous nature, then the Bishop shall, after due notice of the charge, stated in precise terms to the parties concerned, summon them before himself sitting in Diocesan Synod, and shall appoint the Dean, or, if necessary, some other presbyter, to state the charge, and bring forward the evidence; and having fully heard both the accuser and the accused, and all the evidence that either can produce, he shall, after having received the opinion of each member of the synod, proceed to pronounce sentence; and if the accused shall appeal against the sentence of his Bishop to the College of Bishops, as is by the preceding Canon declared to be lawful, the College shall, as speedily as possible, and at latest within six months, examine and decide upon the appeal.

CANON XXXVII.

Prohibiting the Clergy of one Diocese from interfering with the Concerns of another.

It is hereby decreed, that the Clergy of one Diocese must not interfere in the concerns of another, nor take any direction for their official conduct but from their own Ordinary; it being always understood that they shall retain the right of appealing from any sentence of their own Bishop, by which they may think themselves aggrieved, to the Primus and other comprovincial Bishops in Synod canonically assembled.

CANON XXXVIII.

Providing for the Clergy and Laity of this Church being furnished with an accurate View of its State and Condition from time to time.

Whereas, under Providence, no measure seems better adapted to promote the welfare and stability of this Church, or to perpetuate harmony and concord among its members, than that they should be accurately informed as to its actual state and condition, it is hereby ordained,

APPENDIX. 573

with a view of attaining this desirable object, that the Bishops, when assembled in the annual Episcopal Synod, shall, if they deem it necessary, issue a pastoral letter, containing an account of all the circumstances and occurrences, adverse as well as prosperous, which they think it may be for the benefit of the Church to be generally known; and the pastoral letter agreed upon by the Bishops shall be printed, and a sufficient number of copies sent to each Ordinary to supply the charges under his jurisdiction, who shall require the incumbent of every charge to read the pastoral letter to his congregation during the time of Divine service, on the first Lord's Day after he receives it that may be most convenient.

CANON XXXIX.

Appointing the Mode of admitting new Congregations into the Church.

Should any number of Episcopalians, living in any town or village in Scotland where there is an Episcopal Chapel already in existence, entertain a desire to be formed into a congregation in communion with this Church, it is hereby decreed that the following mode of procedure be adopted:—

1*st,* A meeting of the *bona fide* Episcopalians, or of persons desirous of becoming such, who wish to form such congregation, shall be held agreeably to a public advertisement; at which meeting, when duly constituted, a resolution expressive of their intentions, together with the reasons that render it necessary that such new congregation should be formed, shall be formally drawn up, and signed by all the applicants, to be transmitted to the Bishop of the diocese within which the town or village is situated.

2*dly,* The Bishop, upon receiving such notification, shall, after consulting the presbyters of his diocese, communicate to the applicants his determination. Should he follow the advice given him by a majority of his presbyters, his determination shall be final; but if he shall decide against the majority, the applicants, or any party or parties, who may consider themselves aggrieved by the decision, may appeal to the College of Bishops, and shall have the right to appear before them by a delegate, to state the grounds of their appeal.

3dly, Should the Bishop, with the advice already mentioned, find it expedient to sanction the formation of the proposed congregation, the congregation thus formed and acknowledged shall then proceed to elect a minister, according to Canon X., and present him to the Bishop, agreeably to the form prescribed But previously to his institution, they shall lay before the Bishop the articles or constitution of the proposed chapel, a copy of which, when approved by him, shall be preserved among the documents and papers of the diocese.

The Bishops shall urge the vestries in their respective dioceses to insert in the constitution of all existing chapels a clause enforcing the discipline of the Scottish Episcopal Church.

CANON XL.

For Establishing and Maintaining a Society in Aid of the Church.

Whereas, in the Primitive Church, and by apostolic order, collections were made for the poorer brethren, and for the propagation of the Gospel, it is hereby decreed, that a similar practice shall be observed in the Scottish Episcopal Church. Nor ought the poverty of the Church, nor of any portion of it, to be pleaded as an objection, seeing that the Divine commendation is given equally to those who, from their poverty, give a little with cheerfulness, and to those who give largely of their abundance. For this purpose, a society, called " The Scottish Episcopal Church Society," shall be formed ; the objects of which shall be, 1*st,* To provide a fund for aged or infirm Clergymen, or salaries for their assistants, and general aid for congregations struggling with pecuniary difficulties ; 2*dly,* To assist candidates for the ministry in completing their theological studies ; 3*dly,* To provide Episcopal schoolmasters, books, and tracts, for the poor ; 4*thly,* To assist in the formation or enlargement of diocesan libraries. To promote these important purposes, a certain day shall be fixed upon annually by every Diocesan Synod, when a collection shall be made in every Chapel throughout the Diocese, and the nature and object of the Society, in reference to the existing wants of the Church, shall be explained to the people.

CANON XLI.

Declaring what Censure or Spiritual Penalty is to be incurred by a Breach of these Canons.

If it shall be ascertained, by clear and sufficient evidence, that any Bishop of this Church hath neglected any of the duties, or acted contrary to any of the regulations prescribed to him by this Code of Canons, he shall be censured or dealt with by the other Bishops as they may reasonably judge that his neglect or transgression requires. And, in all cases of complaint, whether they regard Bishop, Presbyter, or Deacon, the sentence of the Bishops, that is, of the whole, or of the majority of their number, shall be final and conclusive.

All laws must have an obligatory sanction ; and, in respect of these Canons or Rules, the LOVE OF CHRIST will point to that sanction, and will produce a ready observance of whatever the authority which He hath given to His Church shall duly and regularly enjoin, for the honour and glory of His name.

But as in all societies, ecclesiastical as well as civil, there will always be some individuals whose conduct is not so much guided as it ought to be by the love of Christ, and, as it is chiefly for the direction of such persons that Canons and Laws are enacted, it is hereby decreed, that, if any Clergyman, whether Bishop, Presbyter, or Deacon, shall disobey any of the above Canons, he shall, after the first and second admonition by his proper judge, be rejected, and publicly declared to be no longer a Clergyman of the Episcopal Church in Scotland. But afterwards, on giving sufficient evidence of a sincere repentance, he may be restored to his former station by the sentence of a majority of the Bishops.

[The CANONS of the Church are here inserted at the urgent request of several distinguished clergymen in England, who wish to possess them in a more substantial form than as a pamphlet.]

No. V.

SUCCESSION OF THE SCOTTISH EPISCOPAL CHURCH

FROM THE RESTORATION OF KING CHARLES II. TO THE CONSECRATION OF THE RIGHT REV. DR TERROT IN 1841.

[FROM " AN APOLOGY FOR THE DOCTRINE OF THE APOSTOLICAL SUCCESSION. BY THE HON. AND REV. A. P. PERCIVAL, B.C.L., CHAPLAIN IN ORDINARY TO THE QUEEN." SECOND EDITION, 1841]

THE valuable little work, from which the following table of the succession of the Scottish Bishops is taken, contains in a condensed form the whole argument for the Scriptural and Apostolical institution of the Episcopal government of the Church Catholic, in opposition particularly to Presbyterianism and Congregationalism. As there may be some readers of the present volume who have not seen Mr Percival's work—of which, if such be the case, they would do well to possess themselves—the insertion of the Table of Contents will give some notion of the subjects discussed by the eminent and learned author. The INTRODUCTION comprises the following important points :—
" The authority of God necessary for the validity of the acts of the Christian ministry—Question as to the mode of conveying this authority—Belief of the English Church, and of the Church Catholic and Primitive—Presbyterian Scheme—Origin of it—Congregationalist or Independent Scheme—Proposed comparison of testimony, scriptural and ecclesiastical, in behalf of the three schemes respectively." The Hon. and Rev. author then developes the plan of his treatise in eight Chapters :—" I. *Congregationalism.* Scriptural passages and precedents resembling the Congregationalist system examined, and shown to be either condemnatory of it or irrelevant.—Micah—Dathan and Abiram—Jeroboam—The sons of Sceva—Apollos—The man casting out Devils—Matt. xviii. 20—The transactions at Antioch—2 Tim. iv. 3—The Seven Deacons. II. *Congregationalism.* Ecclesiastical precedents for the Congregational scheme, *None.* III. *Presbyterianism.* Scriptural

passages and precedents resembling the Presbyterian system examined, and shown to be either condemnatory of it, or irrelevant—Korah—2 Cor. x. xi. xiii.—Acts xx.—Diotrephes—The followers of Korah—False Apostles—Indiscriminate application of titles in Scripture—Our Lord called an Apostle, a Bishop, a Deacon—The Apostles called Presbyters and Deacons—Their office a Bishopric—Consideration and reputation of the Presbyterian argument on Phil. i. 2—Acts xx.—The Epistles to Timothy—Especially 1 Tim. iv. 14. IV. *Presbyterianism.* Ecclesiastical precedents appealed to by the Presbyterians—Corinth—Alexandria—Iona—In all these the very contrary established—Waldenses doubtful—The expressions of individual writers how to be understood. V. *Presbyterianism.* This scheme suicidal, even if the theory could be admitted. VI. *Episcopacy.* This system unassailable, even if the evidence of Divine Institution should fail—Antecedent objections to it considered—Uncharitableness—Exclusiveness—Popishness—Judaism—Matt. xxiii.; Mark x.; Luke xxii.—Protestant Reformers—Historical evidence—Corruption of the channel—Non-importance. VII. Ecclesiastical testimony in support of Episcopacy—Universal consent of the Christian world for 1500 years—Clement of Rome—Ignatius—Irenæus—Clement of Alexandria—Tertullian—Origen—Cyprian—Firmilian—Clarus a Muscula—Anti-Nicene Code—Catholic Code. VIII. *Episcopacy.* Scriptural testimony in support of Episcopacy—Churches of Asia Minor—Churches of Crete and Ephesus—All the Churches during the Apostles' lives—The whole Church during our Lord's abode on earth—Our Lord's addresses to the Apostles—Corroborative incidental passages—Appeal to the Presbyterians."

Mr Perceval has inserted several valuable details in his Appendix, not the least interesting of which are the Episcopal Tables, prepared with great accuracy, labour, and research. These are entitled—" Episcopal descent of the present Archbishop of Canterbury traced in full for four Cuccessions—Episcopal descent of the present Archbishop of Canterbury from Archbishop Warham traced in a single line—Consecrations among the English Nonjurors—Episcopal Succession in Scotland—Episcopal Succession in America—Succession of Bishops in the Irish Church." As it is with the Episcopal Succession in Scotland that this narrative is connected, the following are Mr Perceval's remarks introductory to his Table.

578   APPENDIX.

" The ancient line of Scottish Bishops, by whom the greater part of Saxon England had been evangelized, who had supplied our Northern Dioceses with many Bishops, and furnished many worthies for the Christian rolls, came to an end in the person of James Beaton, Archbishop of Glasgow, who died April 24, 1603.

" Seven years afterwards the Christians in Scotland received a fresh succession of Bishops from England, when John Spottiswood, Andrew Lamb, and Gavin Hamilton, were consecrated respectively Bishops of Glasgow, Brechin, and Galloway. The mandate for the consecration, directed to the Bishops of London, Ely, Rochester, and Worcester, is in Archbishop Bancroft's Register, at Lambeth, f. 175. But the record of the consecration itself I have not been able to find. In Bishop Keith's Catalogue of Scottish Bishops it is stated to have taken place in the Chapel at London House, Oct. 21, 1610.

" This succession came likewise to an end, as concerns Scotland, in the person of Thomas Sydserff, who died Bishop of Orkney in 1663, though it was transmitted to Ireland by John Lesly, Bishop of the Isles, who was translated to Raphoe in 1633, and to Clogher in 1660; and who in that year and 1663 assisted at the consecration of thirteen Bishops; one of whom (Fuller, Bishop of Limerick) brought it back again to England, when he was removed to Lincoln, and assisted at our consecrations, But previously to Sydserff's death another consecration of Bishops for the Church in Scotland had been obtained from England. For on Dec. 15, 1661, as appears by Archbishop Juxon's Register at Lambeth, f. 237, James Sharp, Andrew Fairfoull, Robert Leighton, and James Hamilton, were consecrated respectively to the Sees of St Andrews, Glasgow, Dunblane, and Galloway."

[It may be here observed, that every attempt to discover the Diocesan Records and Registers from 1662 to 1688 has hitherto failed, and it is impossible to ascertain the Bishops who assisted at the consecrations of their brethren. There may probably be some documents in the General Register House, Edinburgh; for the proceedings at every Consecration, and the Bishops present, must have been reported to the Scottish Privy Council, and by them to the Sovereign in England. The present writer has ventured some additions to Mr Perceval's Table, as it respects the filling up of the Dioceses after the Revolution In other respects the note at the end of the list of the Succession is correct.]

APPENDIX. 579

No.	Name of Bishop.	Name of See.	Date of Consecration.	Names of Consecrators.
1	James Sharp.	St Andrews.		Gilbert *London*.
2	Andrew Fairfull.	Glasgow.	Dec. 15, 1661.	George *Worcester*.
3	Robert Leighton, translated to Glasgow, 1671.	Dunblane.		Richard *Carlisle*. Hugh *Llandaff*.
4	James Hamilton.	Galloway.		
5	George Hallyburton.	Dunkeld.		
6	Murdoch Mackenzie.	Moray.		James *St Andrews*, 1.
7	David Strachan.	Brechin.	May 7, 1662.	Andrew *Glasgow*, 2.
8	John Paterson.	Ross.		James *Galloway*, 4.
9	David Fletcher.	Argyle.		
10	Robert Wallace.	The Isles.		
11	George Wishart.	Edinburgh.		
12	David Mitchel.	Aberdeen.	June 1, 1662.	
13	Patrick Forbes.	Caithness.		
14	Alexander Burnet, translated to Glasgow, 1664; to St Andrews, 1679.	Aberdeen.	1663.	
15	Patrick Scougall.	Aberdeen.	Easter, 1664.	
16	Andrew Honyman.	Orkney.	1664.	
17	Henry Guthrie.	Dunkeld.	1664–5.	
18	William Scroggie.	Argyll.	1666.	
19	Alexander Young, translated to Ross, March 29, 1679.	Edinburgh.	1671.	
20	James Ramsay, translated to Ross, 1684.	Dunblane.	1673.	
21	John Paterson, translated to Edinburgh, 1679; to Glasgow, 1687.	Galloway.	1674.	Robert *Glasgow*, 3. Alex. *Edinburgh*, 19. (The other Bishop is not mentioned.)

APPENDIX.

No.	Name of Bishop.	Name of See.	Date of Consecration.	Names of Consecrators.
22	Arthur Ross, translated to Galloway, 1679; to Glasgow, 1679; to St Andrews, 1684.	Argyll.	April 28, 1675.	Robert *Glasgow*, 3. Alex. *Edinburgh*, 19. (The other Bishop is not mentioned.)
23	Robert Laurie.	Brechin.	1676.	{
24	William Lindsay.	Dunkeld.	May 7, 1677.	{
25	James Aitkins, translated to Galloway, 1680.	Moray.	1677.	{
26	Andrew Wood, translated to Caithness, 1680.	The Isles.	1678.	{
27	George Hallyburton, translated to Aberdeen, 1682.	Brechin.	1678.	{
28	Andrew Bruce, translated to Orkney, 1688.	Dunkeld.	1679.	{
29	Colin Falconar, translated to Moray, 1680.	Argyll.	Sept. 5, 1679.	{
30	Hector Maclean.	Argyll.	1680.	{
31	Archibald Graham.	The Isles.	1680.	{
32	Robert Douglas, translated to Dunblane, 1684.	Brechin.	1682.	{
33	Alexander Cairncross, translated to Glasgow, same year; to Raphoe, 1693.	Brechin.	1684.	{

APPENDIX. 581

No.	Name of Bishop.	Name of See.	Date of Consecration.	Names of Consecrators.
34	James Drummond.	Brechin.	Dec. 25, 1684.	
35	Alexander Rose, translated to Edinburgh, 1687.	Moray.	1686.	
36	John Hamilton.	Dunkeld.	Oct. 19, 1686.	
37	William Hay.	Moray.	1688.	
38	John Gordon.	Galloway.	Sept. 4, 1688.	

The Bishops in Scotland were now deprived of their Temporalities.

No.	Name of Bishop.	Name of See.	Date of Consecration.	Names of Consecrators.
39 40	John Fullarton. John Sage.		Jan. 25, 1705.	John *Glasgow*, 21. Alexander *Edinburgh*, 35. Robert *Dunblane*, 32.
41 42	John Falconar. Henry Christie.		April 28, 1709.	Alexander *Edinburgh*, 35. Robert *Dunblane*, 32. John Sage, 40.
43	Archibald Campbell.		Aug. 24, 1711.	Alexander *Edinburgh*, 35. Robert *Dunblane*, 32. John Falconar, 41.
44	James Gadderar.	Aberdeen.	Feb. 24, 1712.	George Hickes. John Falconar, 41. Archibald Campbell, 43.
	Jeremiah Collier. Nathaniel Spinckes. Samuel Hawes.	For the English Nonjurors.	June 3, 1713.	George Hickes. Archibald Campbell, 43. James Gadderar, 44.
45 46	Arthur Millar. William Irvine.	Edinburgh.	Oct 22, 1718.	Alexander *Edinburgh*, 35. John Fullarton, 39. John Falconar, 41.

No.	Name of Bishop.	Name of See.	Date of Consecration.	Names of Consecrators.
47 48	David Freebairn. Andrew Cant.	Edinburgh.	Oct. 17, 1722.	John Fullarton, 39. Arthur Millar, 45. William Irvine, 46.
49 50	Alexander Duncan. Robert Norrie.	Glasgow.	1724.	John Fullarton, 39. William Irvine, 46. Arthur Millar, 45.
	Henry Doughty.	For the English Nonjurors.	Mar. 30, 1725.	John Fullarton, 39. Arthur Millar, 45. William Irvine, 46. David Freebairn, 47.
51 52	John Ouchterlonie. James Rose.	Brechin. Glasgow.	Nov. 29, 1726.	David Freebairn, 47. Alexander Duncan, 49. Andrew Cant, 48.
53	Thomas Rattray.	Dunkeld.	June 4, 1727.	James Gadderar, 44. Alexander Duncan, 49. Andrew Cant, 48.
54 55	John Gillan. David Rankine.	Fife. Glasgow.	June 11, 1727.	David Freebairn, 47. Alexander Duncan, 49. James Rose, 52. John Ouchterlonie, 51.
56 57	William Dunbar. Robert Keith.	Moray. Caithness.	June 18, 1727.	James Gadderar, 44. Arthur Millar, 45. Thomas Rattray, 53.
58	Andrew Lumsden.	Edinburgh.	Nov. 2, 1727.	Andrew Cant, 48. Thomas Rattray, 53. Robert Keith, 57.
59	Robert White.	Dunblane.	June 24, 1735.	Thomas Rattray, 53. Robert Keith, 57. William Dunbar, 56.
60	William Falconar.	Caithness.	Sept. 10, 1741.	Thomas Rattray, 53. Robert Keith, 57. Robert White, 59.
61	James Rait.	Brechin.	Oct. 4, 1742.	Thomas Rattray, 53. Robert White, 59. Robert Keith, 57.
62	John Alexander.	Dunkeld.	Aug. 9, 1743.	Robert Keith, 57. Robert White, 59. William Falconar, 60. James Rait, 61.

APPENDIX.

No.	Name of Bishop.	Name of See.	Date of Consecration.	Names of Consecrators.
63	Andrew Gerard.	Aberdeen.	July 17, 1747.	Robert White, 59. William Falconar, 60. James Rait, 61. John Alexander, 62.
64	Henry Edgar.	Fife.	Nov. 1, 1759.	Robert White, 59. William Falconar, 60. James Rait, 61. John Alexander, 62.
65	Robert Forbes.	Ross and Caithness.	June 24, 1762.	William Falconar, 60. John Alexander, 62. Andrew Gerard, 63.
66	Robert Kilgour.	Aberdeen.	Sept. 21, 1768.	William Falconar, 60. James Rait, 61. John Alexander, 62.
67	Charles Rose.	Dunblane.	Aug. 24, 1774.	William Falconar, 60. James Rait, 61. Robert Forbes, 65.
68	Arthur Petrie.	Moray.	June 27, 1777.	William Falconar, 60. James Rait, 61. Robert Kilgour, 66. Charles Rose, 67.
69	George Innes.	Brechin.	Aug. 13, 1778.	William Falconar, 60. Charles Rose, 67. Arthur Petrie, 68.
70	John Skinner.	Aberdeen.	Sept. 25, 1782.	Robert Kilgour, 66. Charles Rose, 67. Arthur Petrie, 68.
	Samuel Seabury.	Connecticut.	Nov. 14, 1784.	Robert Kilgour, 66. Arthur Petrie, 68. John Skinner, 70.
71	Andrew Macfarlane.	Moray.	March 7, 1787.	Robert Kilgour, 66. Arthur Petrie, 68. John Skinner, 70.
72	William Abernethy Drummond.	Brechin.	Sept. 26, 1787.	John Skinner, 70. Robert Kilgour, 66. Andrew Macfarlane, 71.
73	John Strachan.			
74	Jonathan Watson.	Dunkeld.	Sept. 20, 1792.	John Skinner, 70. Andrew Macfarlane, 71. William A. Drummond, 72. John Strachan, 73.

APPENDIX.

No.	Name of Bishop.	Name of See.	Date of Consecration.	Names of Consecrators.
75	Alexander Jolly.	Moray.	June 24, 1796.	William A. Drummond, 72. Andrew Macfarlane, 71. John Strachan, 73.
76	Daniel Sandford.	Edinburgh.	Feb. 9, 1806.	John Skinner, 70. Jonathan Watson, 74. Alexander Jolly, 75.
77	Patrick Torry.	Dunkeld.	Oct. 12, 1808.	John Skinner, 70. Andrew Macfarlane, 71. Alexander Jolly, 75.
78	George Gleig.	Brechin.	Oct. 30, 1808.	John Skinner, 70. Alexander Jolly, 75. Patrick Torry, 77.
79	William Skinner.	Aberdeen.	Oct. 27, 1816.	George Gleig, 78. Alexander Jolly, 75. Daniel Sandford, 76. Patrick Torry, 77.
80	David Low.	Ross and Argyll.	Nov. 14, 1819.	George Gleig, 78. Alexander Jolly, 75. Patrick Torry, 77.
	M. H. Luscombe.	*To go abroad.*	Mar. 20, 1825.	George Gleig, 78. Daniel Sandford, 76. David Low, 80.
81	James Walker.	Edinburgh.	Mar. 7, 1830.	George Gleig, 78. Alexander Jolly, 75. William Skinner, 79. David Low, 80.
82 83	David Moir. Michael Russell.	Brechin. Glasgow.	Oct. 8, 1837.	James Walker, 81. William Skinner, 79. David Low, 80.
84	Charles H. Terrot.	Edinburgh.	June 2, 1841.	William Skinner, 79. Patrick Torry, 77. David Low, 80. David Moir, 82. Michael Russell, 83.

The Bishops in this list who have no Sees following their names were consecrated either as members of the Episcopal College, or as coadjutors to other Bishops.

"It is with regret that I find myself unable to give more particulars of the Consecrations in Scotland between 1662 and 1688. A collection of Ecclesiastical Records belonging to the Church of Scotland, which had been deposited by Bishop Campbell (43) in the Library of Sion College, London, was burnt in the fire which destroyed the Houses of Parliament, where it had been taken for some purpose of inquiry. These records (I am informed) related to the Archbishopric of Glasgow, and would probably have furnished information of the consecrations in that Archbishopric. It is possible that the Registers of St Andrews may be still in existence, though it is not at present known where."

The present writer has made some additions to the above list, such as the consecration of Bishop Terrot in 1841, and two of the consecrators of two Bishops in 1674. It is to be farther observed, that though after the Revolution the College Party could not be considered Diocesan Bishops, yet Mr Perceval omits to mention the Dioceses to which several of the coadjutor Bishops were elected. Mr Perceval observes that the Scottish Episcopal Succession was transmitted to Ireland "by John Lesly, Bishop of the Isles, who was translated to Raphoe in 1633, and to Clogher in 1660." A preceding Bishop of the Isles, however, was translated to Raphoe, whom Bishop Leslie succeeded. This was Andrew Knox, nominated Bishop of the Isles and Abbot of Iona in 1606, and translated to Raphoe in 1622, where he died in 1632. The Episcopal Succession was also subsequently transmitted to Ireland in the person of Dr Alexander Cairncross, Archbishop of Glasgow, most irregularly and unconstitutionally deprived of his See by James II. in 1687, and appointed to the See of Raphoe by William III. in 1693, in which he continued till his death in 1701.

As the political principles of the Scottish Bishops after the Revolution identified them considerably with the English Nonjurors, we find several of the former intimately connected with the affairs of the latter. The English Prelates deprived at the Revolution for refusing to transfer their allegiance to William and Mary were, as is well known, Archbishop Sancroft of Canterbury, Bishops Lloyd of Norwich, Turner of Ely, Frampton of Gloucester, Ker of Bath and Wells, White of Peterborough, Thomas of Worcester, Cartwright of Chester, and Luke of Chichester; but Bishops Thomas, Cartwright, and Luke, died before

the act of deprivation was passed. Apparently relying upon the canonical validity of one of the last acts of Archbishop Sancroft's life, signing a deputation of his powers as metropolitan to Dr Lloyd, the deprived Bishop of Norwich, that Prelate, assisted by the deprived Bishops of Ely and Peterborough, consecrated George Hickes as Suffragan of Thetford, and Thomas Wagstaffe as Suffragan of Ipswich. "Under what plea," says Mr Perceval, "consecrations performed in the Province of Canterbury, without consultation or approval of the Bishops of the Province, whose legitimate institution was never called in question, and without the approval of the now existing metropolitan, can be regarded otherwise than as irregular and schismatical, I am at a loss to conceive. It should seem that the deprived Bishops themselves had misgivings on the subject, for they made no attempt to repeat the step, and it was not till after a lapse of twenty years, during which all the deprived Bishops and Wagstaffe had died off, that Hickes determined to keep up a succession of Bishops for the Nonjurors; for which purpose he applied to the Bishops in Scotland, two of whom, paying more regard apparently to their political attachments than to the Canons of the Church, agreed to meddle with the affairs of a Province in which they had no voice, and, together with Hickes, consecrated Collier, Spinckes, and Hawes." The Scottish Bishops here mentioned were Bishops Campbell and Gadderar, who then resided in England, but it must be recollected that, in accordance with their political principles, they in common with the English Nonjurors held peculiar views of the then position of the Church of England There can be no doubt, however, of the correctness of Mr Perceval's statement. Without offering any opinion as to whether Hickes, Collier, and their brethren, were canonically consecrated, or are to be held as Bishops in the proper sense, it is explicitly declared in the 36th of the Apostolical Canons, which are of such antiquity as to be ascribed to the Apostolic Age, and were certainly framed not later than the end of the second or beginning of the third century—" Let not a Bishop presume to ordain in cities or villages not subject to him. And if he be convicted of doing so, without consent of those to whom such places belong, let him and those whom he has ordained be deposed."*
In the 22d Canon of the Synod of Antioch it is set forth—" Let not

---

* Beveridge's Pandect, i 24

a Bishop go into another city or district, not pertaining to him, to ordain any one, unless with the consent of the proper Bishop of the district. If any one dare to do so, let the ordination be invalid, and himself be punished by the Synod."* Bishops Hickes, Campbell, and Gadderar, consecrated Collier, Hawes, and Spinckes, on the 24th of March 1713. The learning of those Nonjuring Bishops, especially Collier and Spinckes, is well known by their works. On the 25th of January 1715, those Bishops, assisted by Bishops Campbell and Gadderar, consecrated Mr Henry Gandy and Mr Thomas Brett; and on the 25th of November 1722 we find Bishop Campbell assisting Bishops Collier and Brett, in consecrating Mr John Griffin. "Before this time," says Mr Perceval, "another division had arisen among the hapless Nonjurors, in consequence of Brett, Collier, and the Scottish Bishop Campbell, who had settled himself in England, insisting upon making alterations in the Liturgy (particularly requiring water to be mixed with the wine in the Eucharist), to which Hawes, Spinckes, Gandy, Taylor, and Bedford, would not consent; accordingly a separation of communion took place. After the death of Hawes, of Taylor, and of Bedford, Spinckes and Gandy, being desirous of a succession in their line, applied to the Bishops in Scotland, and they (again, as it seems to me, unmindful of their duty) consecrated Mr Henry Doughty for their friends in England." The date of this consecration was March 30, 1725, and the Scottish consecrators are stated to have been Bishops Fullarton, Millar, Irvine, and Freebairn. Bishop Campbell appears as assisting with Bishops Brett and Griffin at the consecration of Mr Thomas Brett, jun., on the 9th of April 1727. This line of the Nonjurors became defunct at the death of Bishop Gordon in 1779, who was consecrated on the 11th of July 1741, by Bishops Brett, sen., Smith, and Mawman.

There was another line of Nonjurors, distinctly separated from the above, and never recognised, because the consecrations were performed by single Bishops. We find Bishop Campbell intimately connected with this line. In 1733 he consecrated Mr Roger Laurence, the author of "Lay Baptism Invalid," who was the first of this new line, and in that year he and Mr Laurence consecrated Mr Thomas Deacon. The successors were Messrs P. J. Brown, Kenrick Price, William Cart-

* Beveridge's Pandect, i 450.

wright, Thomas Garnet, and Charles Boothe. Mr Boothe died in Ireland in 1805, which terminated this line of the English Nonjurors, the notices of all of whom, says Mr Perceval, " painful and melancholy as they are, as records of the errors of high-minded and honourable men, will not be without their use if they shall assist in convincing any person of the wretchedness of schism." Such was the extinction of the Nonjurors, with whom after the death of Bishop Campbell the Scottish Episcopal Church had little intercourse, and we find Bishop Keith seriously expostulating with one of them for unnecessary interference in Scottish Episcopal affairs. This was Bishop George Smith, consecrated on the 26th of December 1728, by Henry Gandy, John Blackburn, and Richard Rawlinson, the sixth, eleventh, and fourteenth line of Bishops of that line.

It seems that Messrs Welton and Talbot, two of the early Nonjuring Bishops, whose consecration, however, was never recognized by the rest of their brethren, because it was done by only one individual, Ralph Taylor, without their approval, went to North America, and performed episcopal duties. Welton located himself at Philadelphia, but by the complaint of the Bishop of London to Government he retired to Portugal, where he died in 1726. Talbot submitted by taking the oaths. Dr Samuel Seabury was therefore the first Bishop of the Church in the United States. As related in the present history, he was consecrated in 1784 by Bishops Kilgour, Petrie, and Skinner. In 1787 Bishops White and Provoost were consecrated for the American Church by the Archbishops of Canterbury and York, and the Bishops of Peterborough and of Bath and Wells. In 1790 Bishop Madison of Virginia was consecrated by the Archbishop of Canterbury and the Bishops of London and Rochester. The first consecration in the United States was that of Bishop Claggett for the Diocese of Maryland, at which Bishop Seabury of Connecticut assisted, with Bishop Provoost of New York, Bishop White of Pennsylvania, and Bishop Madison of Maryland, thus amalgamating the Scottish and English consecrations, from which the succession in the American Church is derived.

Preparing for Publication, in one large volume 8vo, uniform with the present Work, price 15s.

HISTORY

OF THE

EPISCOPAL CHURCH OF SCOTLAND,

WHEN ESTABLISHED BY LAW,

FROM THE

REFORMATION TO THE REVOLUTION.

BY

JOHN PARKER LAWSON, M.A.

‌‌* It is respectfully requested that those Subscribers to the present Work who are disposed to promote the publication of the above Volume, will transmit their names to MESSRS GALLIE & BAYLEY, 69, GEORGE STREET, EDINBURGH, either direct, or by their respective Booksellers. This, and the present Volume, will form a complete and authentic History of the Episcopal Church of Scotland from the Reformation, including the exciting Reigns of James I., Charles I., and Charles II., the whole derived from valuable MSS. and other documents. Many curious and interesting details will be given of the TRUE ecclesiastical state of Scotland in the Seventeenth Century, not hitherto published. The Author confidently relies on the patronage of the Members and Friends of the Church to enable him to venture on the publication of the Volume now announced, that it may appear in December 1843.

GALLIE & BAYLEY beg respectfully to inform Members of the EPISCOPAL CHURCH, that they will always find at their Premises a Select and Extensive Stock of approved THEOLOGICAL WORKS, BOOK OF COMMON PRAYER, CHURCH SERVICE, &c., in every VARIETY of BINDING; and being themselves in constant personal attendance, Strangers and others honouring them with a visit may rely on the most assiduous attention.

69, GEORGE STREET,
Edinburgh, December 1842.

COLUMBIA UNIVERSITY LIBRARY

This book is due on the date indicated below, or at the expiration of a definite period after the date of borrowing, as provided by the rules of the Library or by special arrangement with the Librarian in charge.

DATE BORROWED	DATE DUE	DATE BORROWED	DATE DUE

BRITTLE DO NOT
PHOTOCOPY

937.41   L 44
Lawson, J.P
Scottish Episcopal Ch

937.41   L44

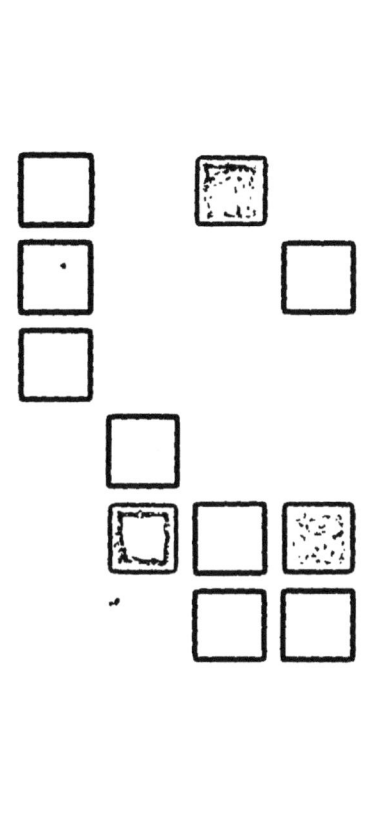

Lightning Source UK Ltd.
Milton Keynes UK
UKHW052205190522
403195UK00014B/1086